Feminist Legal Theory
Volume II

Feminist Legal Theory Volume II

Positioning Feminist Theory within the Law

Edited by

Frances E. Olsen

University of California at Los Angeles
School of Law

NEW YORK UNIVERSITY PRESS
Washington Square, New York

New York University Press
Washington Square
New York, N.Y. 10003

Printed in Great Britain

ISBN 0-8147-6184-4 (2 Vol set)
 0-8147-6186-0 (Vol II)

To
Katya Komisaruk
and

Petra Bläss

Contents

PART III   TOWARDS A POSITIVE PROGRAMME?

Acknowledgements

The editor and publishers wish to thank the following for permission to use copyright material.

Academic Press Limited for the essays: Judy Fudge (1989), 'The Effect of Entrenching a Bill of Rights upon Political Discourse: Feminist Demands and Sexual Violence in Canada', *International Journal of the Sociology of Law*, **17**, pp. 445–63; Joanne Conaghan (1986), 'The Invisibility of Women in Labour Law: Gender-neutrality in Model-building', *International Journal of the Sociology of Law*, **14**, pp. 377–92.

The American Society of International Law for the essay: Hilary Charlesworth, Christine Chinkin and Shelley Wright (1991), 'Feminist Approaches to International Law', *The American Journal of International Law*, **85**, pp. 613–45. © The American Society of International Law.

Cornell Law Review and Fred B. Rothman & Company for the essay: Lucie E. White (1992), 'Seeking "...The Faces of Otherness...": A Response to Professors Sarat, Felstiner, and Cahn', *Cornell Law Review*, **77**, pp. 1499–511. © copyright 1992 by Cornell University. All Rights Reserved.

Karen Engle (1992), 'Female Subjects of Public International Law: Human Rights and the Exotic Other Female', *New England Law Review*, **26**, pp. 1509–26. Copyright © Karen Engle.

Mary Joe Frug (1992), 'Rescuing Impossibility Doctrine: A Postmodern Feminist Analysis of Contract Law', *University of Pennsylvania Law Review*, **140**, pp. 1029–47. © copyright 1992, Gerald E. Frug. Reprinted by permission of University of Pennsylvania Law Review and Fred B. Rothman & Company.

Harvard Law Review for the essay: Vicki Schultz (1992), 'Telling Stories About Women and Work', in Mary Joe Frug (ed.), *Women and the Law*, pp. 284–97. Published by Foundation Press 1992. Also in *Harvard Law Review*, **103**. Copyright © 1990 by The Harvard Law Review Association. Frances E. Olsen (1983), 'The Family and the Market: A Study of Ideology and Legal Reform', *Harvard Law Review*, **96**, pp. 1560–78. Copyright © 1983 by The Harvard Law Review Association.

Journal of Legal Education for the essays: Martha Minow (1988), 'Feminist Reason: Getting It and Losing It', *Journal of Legal Education*, **38**, pp. 47–60; Deborah L. Rhode (1988), 'The "Woman's Point of View"', *Journal of Legal Education*, **38**, pp. 39–46.

Journal of Social Philosophy for the essay: Karen Elizabeth Davis (1990), 'I Love Myself When I am Laughing: A New Paradigm for Sex', *Journal of Social Philosophy*, **21**, pp. 5–24.

Michigan Law Review for the essay: Frances Olsen (1986), 'From False Paternalism to False Equality: Judicial Assaults on Feminist Community, Illinois 1869–1895', *Michigan Law Review*, **84**, pp. 1518–41.

New York Law School for the essay: Martha Albertson Fineman (1992), 'Legal Stories, Change, and Incentives – Reinforcing the Law of the Father', *New York Law School Law Review*, **37**, pp. 227–49. Copyright © Martha Albertson Fineman.

Elizabeth M. Schneider (1986), 'Describing and Changing: Women's Self-Defense Work and the Problem of Expert Testimony on Battering', *Women's Rights Law Reporter*, **9**, pp. 195–222. © copyright Elizabeth M. Schneider.

Southern California Law Review for the essay: Martha R. Mahoney (1992), 'Exit: Power and the Idea of Leaving in Love, Work, and the Confirmation Hearings', *Southern California Law Review*, **65**, pp. 1283–319.

Stanford Law Review and Fred B. Rothman & Company for the essay: Olga Popov (Hartwell) (1991), 'Towards a Theory of Underclass Review', *Stanford Law Review*, **43**, pp. 1095–132. © 1991 by the Board of Trustees of the Leland Stanford Junior University.

Texas Law Review for the essay: Linda R. Hirshman (1992), 'The Book of "A"', *Texas Law Review*, **70**, pp. 971–1012. Copyright 1992 by the Texas Law Review Association.

The University of Chicago Press for the essay: Patricia J. Williams (1988), 'On Being the Object of Property', *Signs: Journal of Women in Culture and Society*, **14**, pp. 5–24.

University of Michigan Law School for the essay: Frances E. Olsen (1985), 'The Myth of State Intervention in the Family', *University of Michigan Journal of Law Reform*, **18**, pp. 835–64.

K.C. Worden (1985), 'Overshooting the Target: A Feminist Deconstruction of Legal Education', *The American University Law Review*, **34**, pp. 1141–56. © copyright K.C. Worden.

The Yale Journal of Law and Feminism for the essay: Ruth Colker (1991), 'Marriage', *Yale Journal of Law and Feminism*, **3**, pp. 321–6.

The Yale Law Journal Company and Fred B. Rothman & Company for the essays: Jennifer K. Brown (1993), 'The Nineteenth Amendment and Women's Equality', *The Yale Law Journal*, **102**, pp. 2175–204; Drucilla Cornell (1991), 'Sexual Difference, the Feminine, and Equivalency: A Critique of MacKinnon's *Toward a Feminist Theory of the State*', *The Yale Law Journal*, **100**, pp. 2247–75.

Introduction

This second volume of a two-volume set is intended to stand alone. The first volume introduced the field of feminist legal theory, presented important foundational essays and recent debates within the field, and concluded with identifying some of the new directions which scholars are exploring. This second volume, in three sections, is directed more to the teaching of law and to positioning feminist legal theory within law in general. Part I focuses on some of the major issues involved in teaching feminist legal theory as a separate course. The middle section examines a number of feminist issues that are likely to arise in other law courses. Part III indicates the kinds of major or sweeping changes in law and society which could result from the influence of feminist theory sometime in the future.

It has not always been easy to get feminist articles published, and still remains difficult in a number of countries. Since 1983, however, when the *Harvard Law Review* and the *Yale Law Journal* each published their first feminist article,[1] virtually every US law journal has followed suit, as have a gradually increasing number of journals elsewhere. While this proliferation of interest has been excellent for the development of the field, the fact that feminist articles appear in such a wide variety of journals, some quite obscure, has made access to a large collection of law journals indispensable. The essays in this volume have been drawn from 20 different journals. The chapters are unedited and double-paginated to facilitate citation to the original source.[2] The collection includes ideas with which I do not necessarily agree. To provide maximum variety, I have favoured short contributions.

Part I includes four essays which directly or indirectly address the issue of teaching feminist legal theory in law schools. K.C. Worden's paper was written while she was still at university and presents her personal view of studying feminist legal theory in a jurisprudence class. While illustrating the effectiveness of personal narrative, she also presents important criticisms of legal education from the perspective of a perceptive student. Mary O'Brien and Sheila McIntyre next focus on the more abstract ideas of two deceased male theorists – Karl Marx and Antonio Gramsci. Arguing that feminist insights suggest revisions in these theories, they use their amended notion of Gramsci's hegemony concept to propose that women's presence in law school is inherently counter-hegemonic or subversive to male dominance. Feminist legal theory can be similarly counter-hegemonic with respect to the legal curriculum.

Martha Minow's piece, which is a shorter version of her much-cited Foreword to Volume 101 of the *Harvard Law Review*,[3] suggests the importance of feminist critiques to contexts beyond gender, such as religion, race, physical handicap, sexual preference and age. Women as a group are more able than men as a group to appreciate that their own perspective is not universally true or simply 'the way the world is'. Minow argues that no transcendent perspective exists upon which everyone can agree; thus she emphasizes the importance of coming to understand and appreciate multiple perspectives. In Chapter 4, Deborah Rhode suggests some of the complexities of trying to discuss the 'woman's point of view' and warns against any naive use of a feminist or feminine perspective. Integrating feminist ideas into the legal curriculum will require more than an 'add-woman-and-stir' approach.

Part II presents essays that suggest the range of feminist analyses and their importance to many other aspects of law. In addressing ten different fields, I have used one essay each for five of the areas (constitutional law, contracts, jurisprudence, legal practice and property). These present challenges to their respective fields and, in most cases, describe or cite other relevant feminist critiques. I have included two or three essays where topics have been extensively examined by feminists – such as labour law and family law – and also where the feminist influence, though relatively recent, appears to be having dramatic effects, as in international law.[4] Finally, I twice use a contrapuntal approach. Chapter 7 considers the use of criminal law to protect women from violence, whereas Chapter 8 addresses the deployment of criminal law against women when they try to protect themselves. Chapter 19 uses legal history to develop an interesting constitutional law point, while Chapter 18 adopts legal history to develop a critique of the same treatment-different treatment debate (also discussed in Volume I, Part III) and of the loose feminist condemnation of 'paternalism'.

Part III concludes this volume with three different views concerning the way forward. Most feminist legal writing focuses on what is wrong with the treatment of women; however important and necessary critique is, some students and scholars become discouraged as they focus on the pervasiveness of the subordination of women and become depressed by the negativity of critique. These final three essays have struck many people as more cheerful and encouraging. 'The Family and the Market, Part III', tries to open discussion about what it might mean to break out of the dichotomy between family and market; it presents a positive view about ending the antithesis between male and female – what is sometimes called 'androgyny'. In the context of an interesting, if to me ultimately unpersuasive, critique of Catharine MacKinnon's *Toward a Feminist Theory of the State*, Drucilla Cornell presents an argument in favour of women's sexual difference and a positive appreciation of feminine sexuality. Using concepts of metaphor and building on the work of the French philosopher Luce Irigaray,[5] Cornell urges an expansive positive programme that would re-figure and embrace femininity and sexual difference. In Chapter 24, Karen Davis briefly reviews the debate between so-called 'anti-sex' and 'pro-sex' feminists which has played so important a role in legal debates over sexual harassment, date rape, prostitution and pornography. Davis challenges the idea that sexual desire is like hunger and proposes a new metaphor for sexuality. She likens coerced sexuality to aggressive, uninvited tickling, and consensual sexual intercourse at its best to shared and enjoyable tickling, which, however pleasant, lacks the rich inter-subjectivity possible in laughter. In a positive view of sexuality quite different from Cornell's, Davis invites us to imagine a sexuality that is as full and varied, as nuanced and meaningful, as the broad range of laughter in which human beings engage.

Notes

1 See Frances Olsen (1983), 'The Family and the Market: A Study of Ideology and Legal Reform', *Harvard Law Review*, **96**, 1497; Ann E. Freedman (1983), 'Sex Equality, Sex Differences, and the Supreme Court', *Yale Law Journal*, **92**, 913.
2 There are two exceptions – essays whose original versions were too long for inclusion in these volumes. For Chapter 15 in Volume I and Chapter 16 in Volume II, I have used edited versions that appeared in Mary Joe Frug (1992), *Women and Law*, Foundation Press. In these two cases, the double pagination is to the Frug book, which provides the alternative citation.

3　Martha Minow (1987), 'The Supreme Court, October 1986 Term, Foreword – Justice engendered', *Harvard Law Review*, **101**, 10.

4　For example, the status and education of women have begun to be recognized as pivotal to the issue of international population control. The World Population Conference in September 1994 focused major attention on the relationship between women's advancement and 'development'. Similarly, the World Bank recently concluded that the most important investment an underdeveloped country can make is in women's education.

5　Luce Irigaray is one of the best known of the 'New French Feminists', a group of writers drawing heavily on post-structuralist theory. See, for example, Elaine Marks and Isabelle de Courtivron (eds) (1981), *New French Feminisms*. For a criticism of the 'feminism' of the group, see Claire Dutchen (1986), *Feminism in France: From May '68 to Mitterrand*.

Part I
Teaching Feminist Legal Theory

[1]

OVERSHOOTING THE TARGET: A FEMINIST DECONSTRUCTION OF LEGAL EDUCATION

K.C. Worden*

Introduction

In Mankiewicz's [film] *Julius Caesar*, all the characters are wearing fringes.[1] Some have them curly, some tufted, some oily. . . . What then is associated with these insistent fringes? Quite simply the label of Roman-ness. . . . Everyone is reassured, installed in the quiet certainty of a universe without duplicity, where Romans are Romans thanks to the most legible of signs: hair on the forehead. [But,] a Frenchman, to whose eyes American faces still have something exotic, finds comical the combination of the morphologies of these gangster-sheriffs with the little Roman fringe: it rather looks like an excellent music-hall gag. This is because for the French, the sign in this case overshoots the target and discredits itself by letting its aim appear clearly.

R. Barthes[2]

Barthes' observations about "signs overshooting the target" fascinates me. The notion that the signs that inform social experience lose their power of persuasion when exposed as artifice rather than natural presents a potentially powerful political strategy. This Article attempts to pursue that strategy within the realm of feminist critical legal theory.

My concern is the effect of legal education on women. My approach, adopted from Barthes, is to "track down, in the decorative display of 'what-goes-without-saying' the ideological abuse which in my view is hidden there."[3] With "Roman fringes in France" in

---

* J.D. expected, 1986, Washington College of Law, The American University.

1. "Fringes" is an English expression for bangs.

2. R. Barthes, Mythologies 26 (1972).

3. *Id.* at 1. The author wishes to express her appreciation to the following authors, who were very influential to her Article: J. Boyle, *The Politics of Reason*, 133 U. Pa. L. Rev. 685 (1985); J. Boyle, Critical Legal Studies: A Young Person's Guide (1984) (unpublished); M. Foucault Power/Knowledge (1980); Gabel, *Reification in Legal Reasoning*, in The Politics of

mind, the objective of this piece is to expose, and thereby discredit, several ways in which the "what-goes-without-saying" of legal education contributes to the subjugation of the "female voice" in law. The first question, however, is what is the "female" voice?

I. THE VOICES[4]

> Heinz's wife is going to die unless he can get her a drug which he cannot afford to buy. Should he steal the drug? Jake immediately responds that Heinz should steal it. He construes the moral dilemma "sort of like a math problem with humans." To Jake, it is perfectly clear that in this equation, life takes priority over property. "For one thing, a human life is worth more than money, and if the druggist only makes $1,000, he is still going to live, but if Heinz doesn't steal the drug, his wife is going to die." Amy cannot respond so categorically; to her it is not an either/or situation. "Well, I don't think so. I think there might be other ways besides stealing it, like if he could borrow the money or make a loan or something, but he really shouldn't steal the drug—but his wife shouldn't die either. . . . If he stole the drug, he might save his wife; but then if he did, he might have to go to jail, and then his wife might get sicker again, and he couldn't get more of the drug, and it might not be good. So, they should really just talk it out and find some other way to make the money. . . . If Heinz and the druggist had talked it out long enough, they could reach something besides stealing."[5]

Amy and Jake are two eleven year-old participants in a study on adolescent moral development. According to traditional development theories,[6] Amy's responses are a full stage lower in maturity

---

LAW: A PROGRESSIVE CRITIQUE 294 (D. Kairys ed. 1982); Gordon, *New Developments in Legal Theory*, in THE POLITICS OF LAW: A PROGRESSIVE CRITIQUE 281 (D. Kairys ed. 1982); Greer, *Antonio Gramsci and 'Legal Hegemony,'* in THE POLITICS OF LAW: A PROGRESSIVE CRITIQUE 304 (D. Kairys ed. 1982); Griffin, *The Way of All Ideology*, in FEMINIST THEORY: A CRITIQUE OF IDEOLOGY (1982); Kennedy, *Legal Education as Training for Hierarchy*, in THE POLITICS OF LAW: A PROGRESSIVE CRITIQUE 40 (1982); D. Kennedy, LEGAL EDUCATION AS TRAINING FOR HIERARCHY: A POLEMIC AGAINST THE SYSTEM (1983); Peller, *The Metaphysics of American Legal Thought*, (forthcoming in CALIF. L. REV.); Peller, *Cultural Terrorism and the Faculty Cocktail Party*, 2 LIZARD 3 (1984); Scholes, *Uncoding Mama: The Female Body as Text*, in SEMIOTICS AND INTERPRETATION 127 (1982); Lorde, *Uses of Erotic: The Erotic of Power*, in SISTER OUTSIDER (1984); F. Olsen, The Sex of Law (1985) (unpublished manuscript).

4. The following discussion is based on C. GILLIGAN, IN A DIFFERENT VOICE: PSYCHOLOGICAL THEORY AND WOMEN'S DEVELOPMENT 24-63 (1982).

5. *Id.* at 26-30.

6. This refers primarily to Lawrence Kohlberg's theory of the six stages in the development of moral judgment. These stages are derived from an empirical study of 84 boys whose development Kohlberg has followed for over 20 years. The higher stages reflect a conception of maturity based on individualism and a morality of human rights where relationships are subordinated to rules (stage 4) and rules to universal principles of justice (stages 5 and 6). C. GILLIGAN, *supra* note 4, at 18. More generally, it refers to the theories of Freud, Piaget,

than Jake's. Her answers seem evasive and unsure; she appears incapable of thinking systematically about abstract concepts or of ordering her values according to priority. Her reliance on relationship and communication are interpreted as reflecting her dependency, vulnerability, and cognitive immaturity.

In *In a Different Voice,* Carol Gilligan challenges the analysis of these traditional development theories and their failure to recognize the differences between "male" and "female" modes of thought, expression, and reason. Amy's failure to score as well as Jake, argues Gilligan, stems not from her intellectual puerility, but from the fact that her "female" response was judged according to "male" standards. By suggesting that there are two different modes of thought, Gilligan is able to explore the standards and structures embodied in the divergent ways that men and women perceive and act in the world around them. To depict those two modes, Gilligan develops the "female voice"-"male voice" metonymy.[7]

"Male voice" rationality is the traditional notion of logical thought with which we are all familiar but not necessarily comfortable. This rationality values reason over passion, objectivity over subjectivity, and scientific clarity over interdependent relativity.[8] It reasons by deduction and linear logic and perceives and conceives social reality as a set of hierarchically ordered rules, equations, and normative truths. It resolves conflict by abstraction, detachment, and formulas of objective certainty. Jake's responses epitomize "male voice" reasoning.

The "female voice," Gilligan's research suggests, perceives and conceives social reality in terms of weblike, interconnected, and intersubjective[9] dynamics. Holding this web of relationships together is a morality based on the values of continuity, communication, and interdependence. This morality values relationship over right, subjectivity over objectivity, and care over conquest. Moral dilemma is context-bound and entails personal choice rather than equational

---

Kramer, Erikson, Lever, and Mead as discussed by Gilligan in the chapter of her book entitled "Woman's Place in Man's Life Cycle." *Id.* at 5-23.

7. C. Gilligan, *supra* note 4, at 24-35. For a further discussion of metonymy in the legal context, see Harris, *Metonymy as Manipulative Mode,* 34 Am. U. L. Rev. — (1985).

8. *Id.* at 26-38.

9. "Intersubjective" is a concept that originated with Jürgan Habermaus, and refers to the existential interrelations between subjective beings and experience. It also portrays reality as a phenomenon of shared subjective experiences rather than as objective structures. *See generally* J. Habermas, Theory and Practice, (J. Viertel trans. 1973). *Cf.* Boyle, *The Politics of Reason: Critical Legal Theory and Local Social Thought,* 133 U. Pa. L. Rev. 685, 762-64 (1985) (noting that tension between structuralism and subjectivism may show formative process of theoretical development).

abstraction. "Female voice" reasoning is inseparable from the contextual web of relationships within which it operates.

Amy's focus on working things out with the druggist reflects sophisticated female voice comprehension and not male voice inadequacy. Gilligan elaborates:

> [Amy's] world is a world of relationships and psychological truths where an awareness of the connection between people gives rise to a recognition of responsibility for one another, a perception of the need for response. Seen in this light, her understanding of morality as arising from the recognition of relationship, her belief in communication as the mode of conflict resolution, and her conviction that the solution to the dilemma will follow from its compelling representation seem far from naive or cognitively immature. Instead, Amy's judgments contain the insights central to an ethic of care, just as Jake's judgments reflect the logic of the justice approach. Her incipient awareness of the "method of truth," the central tenet of nonviolent conflict resolution, and her belief in the restorative activity of care, lead her to see the actors in the dilemma arrayed not as opponents in a contest of rights but as members of a network of relationships on whose continuation they all depend.[10]

I like and use the "female voice" metonymy because for me it works: it seems to help explain some troubling existential quandaries in a way that energizes rather than anesthetizes. The idea that "male voice" rationality is not *the only* form of legitimate thought is really liberating; it encourages one to strive for ideological freedom, self-understanding, and social change. It is an adrenalin rush that wakes one up from the stupor of accepting the status quo without question or recognition of the choices involved.

I do not accept that these "voices" are mutually exclusive or essentially gender specific. Rather, I associate the "male voice" with the "dominant" mode, and the "female voice" with all those "other" forms of cogitation and expression that are repressed or invalidated by the tyranny of dominant ideologies. I think most people have both "male" and "female" voices within them, in varying degrees and combinations. But I also recognize, as Gilligan's research suggests, that empirically the "male voice" tends to predominate in men as does the "female voice" in women.[11] The

---

10. C. GILLIGAN, *supra* note 4, at 30.

11. Obviously, there is tension here as to whether the "female voice" is characterized by gender or by theme. I am schizophrenic on this point. I cannot accept the idea that there is an essence to gender that dictates fundamental modes of thought and perception because I reject the existence of essences altogether. And yet, there is no doubt in my mind that Gilligan's depiction of the different "voices" captures some very real and very apparent

injustice is that society has historically chosen to recognize only the "male voice." This has resulted in the subjugation, silencing, and misunderstanding of the "female voice" in both men and women. This ideological prejudice is acutely evident in law and legal education. As noted by Sheila McIntyre, "[g]oing to law school is learning to speak male as a second language, and learning it fluently."[12] It is this process of denial and subordination of the "female voice" in the "what-goes-without-saying" of the law school experience that the following stories portray.

II. PARAPHRASING WITH PREJUDICE

I'm sitting in jurisprudence class. The discussion is becoming more and more animated. Jeannie, a woman who rarely talks, suddenly joins the discussion and begins a long and complex narrative. Her narrative is intensely personal. It touches on her past, her struggle for independence, her religious training, her relationship with her father and husband, and her difficulties being a "law student." It is through this intricate, intersubjective structure that she perceives and relates to the jurisprudential discussion raging around her:

> I don't know, I feel like the figures and structures of authority in my life (the church, my dad, my husband, and now "the law" and professors . . .) are always forcing me into these little boxes of how I must think and act . . . . I always conform, 'cuz [sic] who am I to question their authority . . . but, I feel so trapped and dishonest . . . Why do they always get to define the boxes? . . . Why boxes at all? . . . It makes me feel so emotionally disconnected from who I am and what my own values are. . . . Like today in crim. law, the way we discussed that rape case infuriated me, but I couldn't say anything because we were trapped in some technical doctrinal box that I couldn't even relate to . . . .

Suddenly feeling the sting of critical incomprehension from her classmates, she abruptly concludes with an anxious giggle, a mur-

---

differences between men and women. I mediate my schizophrenia by believing that this tension can be attributed to the forces of socialization. As Gilligan points out, "[c]learly these differences arise in a social context where factors of social status and power combine with reproductive biology to shape the experience of males and females and the relations between the sexes." *Id.* at 2.

Attempting to resolve and circumscribe the nature and origin of the "female voice," however, is something I specifically do not want to do. My interest and use of the "voices" abstraction is limited to its potential as a tool for deconstructing the traditional monolithic depiction of reason. It is, however, only a disposable tool. Once the "male voice" monopoly on rational thought is broken up and the full spectrum of "voices" and different forms of thought are legitimated, the male/female dichotomy will be moot (in this context).

12. Address by Sheila McIntyre, 8th Annual Conference on Critical Legal Studies, Georgetown University Law Center, Washington, D.C. (Mar. 16-18, 1984).

mur about being unsure of whether she made sense to anyone, and
an apology for not being able to better articulate her point.

Fred immediately jumps in to "save" her. "Yeah," he begins in
supportive agreement, "what Jeannie is saying is . . .," and he proceeds to rephrase Jeannie's entire argument in terms of descriptive
and prescriptive linguistics:

> . . . like in prescriptive linguistics, the grammatical rules pre-
> exist the text. So, in a sense, the text has to 'conform' to the
> structure, rather than vice versa. Classical legal thought is the
> same way. It's as though there are these boxes called legal rules
> that are just 'out there,' and 'the law' gets pushed around until it
> fits into one of those boxes. That is how the variables in these
> equations are factored out, or presupposed. . . .

Fred re-presents Jeannie's point in depersonalized abstraction,
structures it in terms of rules, and relates it to jurisprudence by way
of parallel linear logic. Fred sits back, confident in the superior clarity of his reformulation, feeling satisfied that he successfully "translated" Jeannie's meandering narrative into a valid, substantive
argument.

The tragedy of this story is the lesson learned by Jeannie. That is,
unless you think and speak "their" language, you have inferior capabilities. If you try to speak your own language, you won't be understood (unless "translated") and will feel stupid and embarrassed for
having spoken up. Moreover, if you are "lucky" enough to be translated, it is more likely than not that the rich texture of your comment will be distorted or lost in the translation.

This scenario is not unusual. I see it happening in all my law
school classes. Personalized commentary is constantly rephrased,
paraphrased, and re-presented in terms of decontextualized abstraction. The implicit (and sometimes explicit) message is not only that
"male voice" reasoning is a superior form of expression and understanding, but that anything else is not even communicative. This
message is simply wrong. Personally, I found Jeannie's narrative
web of intersubjective description and relationships far more insightful and thought provoking than Fred's arithmetic formula.
(And yes, I did say so to the class.) Furthermore, I often find "logical" analysis and discourse meaningless until it has been woven into
the complex and amorphous plexus of personal significance.[13]

The rephrasing or translation of ideas from one conceptual mode

---

13. This does not mean, however, that all personal and contextual commentary is always
relevant and good. Rather, its relevance must be judged according to "female voice" standards as well as "male voice" standards.

to another need not be a bad thing. In fact, an ideal classroom setting would be one in which both modes are represented, compared, and considered equally valid. But this is not the case. "Male voice" expression is designated the only legitimate form of rational legal thought. The "translation" process goes in only one direction, and it does so with prejudice. Paraphrasing with prejudice subjugates the "female voice."

III. Double Bold

In *Emmanuels, Gilberts, Legal Lines* and the other "bibles" of legal education, double bold printing indicates key concepts—the "law" boiled down to four or five word epitaphs. (Why else would it be called "black letter"?) The implicit lesson is that, no matter how intricate, complex, or contextually bound a case or theory may appear, it can always be reformulated into a generic logical statement of ten words or less. Double bolding epitomizes the notion that male voice rationality is the only form of reasoning considered appropriate for legal analysis. As Fran Olsen notes, " 'Justice' may be depicted as a woman, but law is male, not female. Law is supposed to be rational, objective, abstract, and principled, like men; it is not supposed to be irrational, subjective, contextualized or personalized, like women.[14]

The effects of this prejudice permeate the spectrum of physical and metaphysical jurisprudential experiences. It is expressed in the requirement of reasoning by deduction and the notion of stare decisis. It also appears in the way that legal opinions do not discuss the political, moral, social or economic context of a case, and the way casebooks usually omit the few facts a decision may once have included. The depersonalized writing style of legal scholarship, the glorified hierarchy of law firms and law review, the required emotional detachment from one's clients and cases, the dismissal of "female voice" analysis as "*just* emotional" (hence irrational, hence invalid), and double-bolding are all signs of the "male voice" depotism of law. In fact, the entire adversarial system itself is a classically "male voice" approach to dispute resolution. This bias is so familiar to us, and so pervades legal experience, that it seems almost silly even to be describing it.

Let me emphasize, however, that I use these examples to expose

---

14. F. Olsen, The Sex of Law, 4 (1985) (unpublished manuscript). This quote reflects but one of the three feminist critiques of law discussed in the article. It is not Fran Olsen's personal viewpoint. Fran Olsen agrees that law is often ideologically oppressive to women but disagrees that it is essentially "male." *Id.* at 19-26.

ways in which the subjugation of the "female voice" perpetuates a *reification*[15] of the law as male, and not to suggest, or in any way intimate, that the law is naturally or necessarily male. Given that Realism and Critical Legal Theory have demonstrated that the law has no fundamental, immutable essence, but is a belief system created and perpetuated by human activity, it cannot possibly be either essentially male or female.

Subjugation of the "female voice" in law seems to me a result of the fact that it has been predominantly men who have created and perpetuated the belief clusters which form "the legal system." But with the increasing numbers of women in law, and the growing cognizance of other "voices," I see no reason why the "female voice" should remain unspoken and/or unheard throughout jurisprudential experience. It seems to me that recognition and legitimation of this ethic of care, connection, and contextuality could only enliven and improve our present system.

IV. MOOT COURT AND BOW TIES

I decided to participate in moot court despite my better judgment. I felt compelled to take advantage of the opportunity for practical experience even though I had no intention of becoming a litigator. It was something everyone told me I should do because it would be good for me—like taking foul tasting medicine when you're sick. So I played along and played diligently. I spent hours studying the briefs, preparing notecards, memorizing cases, and practicing in front of the mirror. I put on my little pumps, nylons, and straight grey skirt. I adopted the I-can-act-as-though-legal-rules make-sense-and-are-not-hopelessly-indeterminate mode. I argued the case in the best "male voice" I could muster.

In my performance evaluation, however, the chief justice ("Mr. Moot Court") focused not only on the substance and delivery of my legal argument, but on my failure to wear a suit. The absence of a jacket, he said, made me look unprofessional and detracted from the content of my presentation. He admitted that my opponent was not wearing a jacket either. But, her blouse had a soft bow which tied at

---

15. Reification is the "thingification" of ideas and the creation of ideological constructs within which subjective experience is objectified (and then "frozen"). *See generally* Gabel, *Reification in Legal Reasoning,* in 3 RESEARCH IN LAW AND SOCIOLOGY 25 (S. Spitzer ed. 1980) (describing reification as abstracting a concept from a concrete milieu and then mistaking the abstraction for the concrete); Gordon, *New Developments in Legal Theory,* in THE POLITICS OF LAW: A PROGRESSIVE CRITIQUE (D. Kairys ed. 1982) (discussing, in part, how the "law" constitutes a reified structure that people have externalized and allowed to rule their lives); K. MARX, *Economic and Philosophic Manuscripts of 1844,* in THE MARX-ENGELS READER 52 (R. Tucker ed. 1972) (describing how objects come to rule the producers instead of being ruled by them).

the neck. That bow, he informed me, made her lack of a jacket less offensive.

This experience blew me away. I could not believe that success in moot court depended on total conformance to a fossilized standard of appearance and conduct. Somehow, within that standard, one's neckline is a crucial feature of legitimacy! Scoop neck, v-neck, ruffles and clinging sweaters, are all unacceptable: they are too feminine, and hence, "unprofessional." On the other hand, men's neckties are too masculine, too severe, and, therefore, equally taboo. The best bet seems to be a large (but not too large) soft bow (feminine) tied at the neck (masculine) which calls as little attention as possible to the chest beneath it. The implicit patriarchal message is that prospective female attorneys must silence their "female voice," but should not try or expect to be like men either. The message is a variation of the self/other conflict:[16] "Be like us, but not totally; join our game, play by our rules . . . but not on our team, and not on their team." It is a catch-22.

Moot court promotes this catch-22. Even worse, it encourages students to put their classmates "through the ringer" and to reproduce the worst hierarchical and patriarchal aspects of the legal system under the pretext of preparation for the "real world." Moot court reifies a particular vision of "the real world" and prepares us to act within that reification. Consequently, when we do go out into the "real world," we *will* recreate and live that vision, because that is what we have been trained to do. The inherent circularity in this process is devastating. By disregarding all forms of thought and conduct external to the original reification, we perpetuate, legitimate, and "close" ourselves within a rigid ideological construct of the status quo that denies possibilities for change.

It need not be this way. There is a choice. Moot court need not indoctrinate us into the worst of the legal profession. Floppy bow ties need not be the sole destiny for women in the law. Like "Roman fringes in France," when floppy bow tie mores are exposed as "signs overshooting the target," they can lose their power of indoctrination and become catalysts of demystification and liberation.

---

16. The self/other conflict refers to the tension arising from our desire for freedom conflicting with our desire to form relationships with others. Kennedy, *The Structure of Blackstone's Commentaries*, 28 BUFFALO L. REV. 205, 213 (1979) (arguing that self/other conflict is fundamental contradiction of society). *But see* Gabel and Kennedy, *Roll Over Beethoven*, 36 STAN. L. REV. 1 (1984) (recanting fundamental contradiction).

V. EXPERIENCING "OTHERNESS"

Looking back on the feminism classes of my Modern Legal Theory course, which we attempted to conduct exclusively in the "female voice," it seems that our most valuable discussions concerned the experience of "otherness." Of particular significance were the men's avowals of their feelings of surprise, frustration, anger, and reticence when talking in or about the "female voice." Ralph felt attacked and misunderstood. He thought that every time he spoke his words were twisted and misinterpreted as patronizing or defensive. Bob announced, with a nervous chuckle, that when he read Gilligan, his thought processes exactly paralleled Jake's. He wasn't sure if that was good or bad, or what it meant. Todd's reading of Gilligan also revealed to him his typically "male voice" reactions. In the middle of reading, he pulled out a calculator and checked Gilligan's statistical authority. As he was punching in numbers, he realized what a classically "male" thing he was doing; but he did not stop because that was the way he related to what she was saying. Jim was offended and upset by the assumption that all men were cold, rational, and egotistical, and that all women were caring, contextualized, and passionate. The assumption that men were not or could not be emotional and contextual, he asserted, was painfully wrong.[17] Jesse felt that by "turning the tables" and denigrating "male voice" qualities we were merely re-creating the existing hierarchical relationship in reverse order.[18] Peter remained silent throughout most of the discussion, but the pained expression on his face revealed his malaise. When he finally spoke, he tried to explain how distressingly adrift he felt. He was uncomfortable and dissatisfied with the discussion. He stumbled, but could not pinpoint exactly why. He could not even understand his frustration enough to express it. "I just need something familiar to grab onto . . .," he said, unconsciously reaching out with his hand. "I feel so groundless, like I'm being condemned for something I didn't do, and can't convince anybody of my innocence . . . I want to say more, but I just feel so tangled. . . ."

These are experiences of "otherness." This is what it feels like to be judged and excluded by a standard which one may not hold or understand. This is what it feels like to sit in a law school class,

---

17. Several women responded that no one ever asserted men were *never* contextual and sensitive.

18. This attack was immediately countered by the students leading the discussion. Reversing the existing hierarchical relationship, they asserted, was *not at all* their goal. Their objective was to legitimate the "female voice" so that it could *begin* to emerge and coexist with "male voice" authority and thereby expunge the hierarchical relationship between them.

knowing you are a reasonably intelligent person, but unable to follow the professor's reasoning because your mind just does not work that way. These are the feelings of insecurity that accompany constantly being misunderstood. This is what women face in law school all the time.[19]

The men's experience of "otherness" during those feminist discussions and their willingness to share them with us so honestly, made those classes enormously enlightening for all concerned. For most of the men, it was the first time they had ever experienced not being part of the privileged group. Some said it was the first time they understood or *felt* what it might be like to be the "other." For the women, it reassuringly revealed that our feelings of reticence and frustration often are directly attributable to being "other" in a society of patriarchal oppression. For all of us, the fact that we did conduct two weeks of classes in an "other voice", despite its failures, demonstrated that "male voice" closure[20] *is* socially created, and *can* be dispelled by subjective choice and effort.

VI. THE ENEMA

I can think of no better example of the effects of internalized "male voice" tyranny than the intellectual and emotional traumas I have experienced while writing this paper. Aware of the possibility of publication, I viewed this effort as an opportunity to prove my academic capabilities to myself and colleagues. My conception of scholastic excellence, however, penetrates to the depths of my self-conflict. One side of me strives to challenge "male voice" domination, to legitimate "other" forms of legal discourse, to avoid the universal and essentialist undertones of large scale theory, and more personally, to free, grow comfortable with, and learn to respect my own "female voice." My other side, however, still equates intellectual prowess and legitimacy with "male voice" attributes.

This conflict blatantly embodied itself in the difference between

---

19. This is a blatant example of my schitzophrenia about whether the "female voice" is characterized by gender or by theme. Although I recognized it, I have not yet resolved it.

I must emphasize here that "otherness" is by no means an exclusively female problem. In the wonderful world of legal thought, factors of class, race, religion, and national origin are repeatedly denied, marginalized, and subordinated to the dominant ideologies of the white, upper class, male. I am writing about the "otherness" associated with being a woman because as a white upper middle class woman, that is the "otherness" with which I am most familiar. All forms, however, of systemic bias and oppression are offensive and must be challenged.

20. Closure is the process by which the ideological entrenchment of certain norms closes out or denies alternative possibilities. Closure is an inevitable result of reification. *See supra* note 15 (discussing reification). By representing all forms of thought and conduct external to a reified norm, closure dictates resignation to the status quo under the guise of objective fact rather than subjective choice.

the first and final drafts of this paper. Draft one began with twelve pages of decontextualized, definitional discourse about reification, closure, hegemony, phenomenology, existentialism, and other big word fancy concepts to extoll "female voice" ideology. I realized the ironic absurdity of trying to legitimate the "female voice" through a "male voice," but could not escape the feeling that that was the only way I *could* do it. Having internalized dominant standards for so many years, I was unsure if, or how, I could write otherwise; I had somehow convinced myself that the "male voice" was actually more natural for me! I, therefore, continued arduously writing in abstraction with citations to famous dead Europeans, Critical Legal Studies articles, and feminist theorists after every eighth word or so. (Somehow thousands of citations signify an analysis that is an authoritative equation of deductions from influential precursors [i.e., the gold "male voice" seal of approval] rather than a lack of originality or intellectual creativity.)

Twelve pages later, however, I realized that I was actually moving backwards, not forwards. So, with the encouragement of a friend, I discarded that draft. In his words, those pages were like an enema: something I had to endure to rid myself of the reified, ideological shit blocked up inside me. The expurgation was truly liberating. Despite the influence that "male voice" standards still exert over me, dumping that first draft brought me closer to resolving my inner conflict.[21] It was also an incredible adrenaline rush. Writing in a style that conforms to the way one thinks about, and relates to the surrounding world is extremely rewarding (despite the fact that my inner "male voice" still feels very anxious about the style and quality of this final product).

This Article may be but another enema. Fine; it is better than the last. My point is simply that "male voice" tyranny runs very deep. Even when doing feminist critical theory it is often difficult to break free from years and years of internalized socialization.

VII. JUDICIAL EFFICIENCY

Someone just challenged the professor. The class is looking relatively bored, but I am excited because I hear in it the "female voice." I think the professor is somewhat sympathetic because he decides to take the bait and run with it for awhile. The challenge concerns a judge's failure to recognize and probe the contextual realities inherent in the legal issue being decided.

---

21. This does not mean that I consider all my "male voice" characteristics worthless. All I am trying to do is learn to hear, speak, understand, and respect my "other voices" too.

The student keeps pushing: "But the case makes no sense unless you also recognize the defendant's relationship with her father, her economic status, her feelings of guilt towards her children, and the political and racial climate of that town."

Professor: "You think all of that is *relevant?*"

"Yea, I do."

"Huh. Well, O.K. Assuming it is relevant, how are you going to prove all that?"

"I don't know. Uh . . . I'm sure you could get some kind of evidence, testimony from friends, neighbors, the local paper . . . some . . . ."

"You're going to end up," cuts in the professor sarcastically, "having trials within trials . . . all to set up a contextual foundation. Litigation could go on for years before you even *got* to the merits of the legal issues. The courts are clogged up enough as it is. Can you imagine what it would be like under your system? The realities of judicial administration and the need for at least a minimum standard of efficiency simply make your proposal untenable."

This is a false necessity. Its underlying premise is that discussions regarding abstracted legal principles are less digressive from the "meat" of a case than are inquiries into its factual setting. This presupposition is another manifestation of the "male voice" prejudice that we must begin to challenge. There is no "essential" reason why the court cannot manage to recognize the contexual web within which a case takes place. My god, the court can put a price on the value of mental distress or the loss of one's body parts, but can't manage to evaluate or consider the moral, political, and social fibers of legal issues?! Be serious.

This judicial efficiency argument closes out contexuality by presupposing the superiority of abstraction. It is the perfectly circular argument; it assumes its conclusions and concludes its assumptions. How can one break free? It may sound obvious, but this type of sophistry can only be broken by actually being broken. It is feasible, but I see no magic swords which will make it effortless. I believe that it requires a continual chipping away at the process of mystification and circularity. It involves heightened mutual vulnerability and risk taking. For me, it means a personal commitment to questioning the "what-goes-without-saying." It is not a one-shot deal. It is a life-long project that continually pushes for social change and ideological freedom. For me it is the pursuit of these goals that renders the existential experience of living, and consequently practicing law, meaningful and rewarding.

VIII. ANDY ROONEY LOOKS AT LAW SCHOOL: "HAVE YOU EVER NOTICED . . . AND WONDERED WHY?"

* That when class discussion becomes too controversial or strays too far into politics, morals, or emotions, that professors love to rephrase student comments in a way that distorts their meaning and neutralizes their controversial impact.

* That professors and students, depending on their level of self-perceived "groovyness":

  -always use the pronoun "he";

  -always use the pronoun "he" to refer to judges, lawyers, experts, and "reasonable men", but use "she" to refer to auto collision defendants, the emotionally unstable and the like;

  -question one's use of the pronoun "she" ("how do you know it's a woman?") but never question the parallel use of "he";

  -make a conscious effort to use "she" regularly, but then assume that this habit licenses them to treat women "as always" because they are "hip and non-sexist."

* That men interrupt three or four times more frequently than women.

* That some men assume they can improve the legitimacy of a woman's comment merely by repeating it with the resonating authority of a baritone pitch.

* That women are the ones who tend to focus on, and question professors about, the facts of the case.

* That men more frequently rely on scientific, statistical, and abstract legal authority.

* That men tend to ask questions in abstract hypotheticals, whereas women tend to do so in terms of personal experience.

* That on the rare occasions when moral, political, or emotional opinions are expressed and explored in class discussion, all pens and pencils go down . . . and that after a few minutes someone (usually, but by no means always, a male) demands that the class get back "on point" (and then all pens resume the ready position and students start listening "for real" again).

* That the law school environment gradually forces many female professors to abandon their "female voice" teaching styles for excessively "male voice" methods, often more "male" than those of most male professors, in order to maintain their legitimacy and status.

* That intense emotional responses generally are dismissed or diffused without even being considered (usually a snide smirk or sarcastic comment will shatter emotional comments and escape unchallenged).

* That generally men have less trouble than women compartmentalizing priorities and obligations, in legal analysis as in personal matters.

These kinds of "Roman fringes" are out there everywhere. Just take a look. You may be surprised by what you discover in the decorative display of the "what-goes-without-saying" of legal education. You may be surprised just how exciting, empowering, and liberating deconstructing can be.

IX. IT'S NOT IMPOSSIBLE

The kinds of changes I envision in legal education are not impossible or hopelessly utopian. I just sat through a large class of ninety-five students conducted by four men in ties that was a wonderful "female voice" discussion. The class was ethics; the topic was "Issues in Criminal Practice." The men were two clinicians, a prosecutor, and a defense lawyer. The class was structured as a dialogue. On each issue presented, the men went back and forth commenting on their personal perspectives, opinions, interpretations of the Code of Professional Responsibility, and practical experiences. By exchanging ideas and thoughts, they wove a contextual web that simultaneously rendered the topic comprehensible, meaningful, and real, while encouraging recognition of the elements of subjectivity and personal choice. The lack of a linearly developed presentation, the divergence of opinion, the grounding of legal interpretation in personal relationships, and the acknowledgment of the reticular connections between law and politics, morals, and economics, were all additions to, rather than detractions from, the legal legitimacy and educational effectiveness of their presentation.

Wouldn't it be nice if similar attempts to enrich the educational process were made in other classes as well? Despite the fact that Ethics is one of those continually "marginalized" classes, it is a facile and unsubstantiated conclusion that such a format would be inappropriate for any course other than Ethics. Ethics is no more inherently indeterminate, personal, or political than other legal fields. That there is precedent for almost any position adopted in any area of law negates the fiction that judges and law professors are bound by objective legal rules. If rules are indeterminate and there are no external, objective restraints on judgment, then all decisions must be based on subjective personal, moral, and political choice. Thus, as with this ethics class, recognizing the value of a "female voice" perspective in torts, contracts, business associations and other law school courses would enrich legal education. If it was possible in ethics, it is possible in other classes too. Someone need only make that choice.

CONCLUSION

There are many grounds on which one could choose to discount the ideas presented in this article. For example, I can be accused of further perpetuation of "female" stereotypes, or triviality and failure to recognize power relationships, or utopian idealism in believing that thinking about the world differently will change it, or insignificance for lack of universality, or "safe" self-proclaiming ivory tower radicalism, etc.

I consider and struggle with many of these critiques frequently. In the end, however, I reject them because they always seem to be used to justify passivity and conclusions such as "[t]he capitalist economic state, or the impotency of utopian theory, or and the fundamental human condition . . . is such that immediate challenges to the injustices of daily life are futile," (hence meaningless; hence unnecessary; hence passive acquiescence to the status quo appears inevitable). I do not want to trap myself in that kind of closure no matter how cynical or radical it purports to be.

Actively striving for personal and social freedom makes life exciting. I find unveiling the "what-goes-without-saying" a useful and energizing means towards that end. I cannot be sure that thinking about the world differently will change it, but I can be sure that apathy will doom me to an existence of perpetual submission. Unquestioning acceptance of the immutability of a "male voice" monopoly on legal thought and practice would be such an existence. Who knows what we may discover in ourselves and others if we learn to break free of the myriad, repressive, ideological constructs we have iternalized and justified for so many years. Of course there are risks. Who knows whether we will inadvertently box ourselves into new and equally stifling ideologies in our attempts to break free from old ones? I don't. But I do find using fear of the unknown to justify inaction against known and present forms of oppression pathetic and offensive.

[2]

Vol. 2   1986   69

Patriarchal Hegemony and Legal Education

Les auteures examinent les contributions de Karl Marx et Antonio Gramsci à notre compréhension de la (re)production des rapports de classes et critiquent les lacunes des théories découlant des ouvrages des deux hommes pour étudier et évaluer l'importance politique des dimensions particulièrement patriarcales du droit et de l'enseignement du droit. En faisant l'analyse féministe de la théorie de l'hégémonie, Mary O'Brien et Sheila McIntyre veulent montrer comment l'enseignement traditionnel du droit inculque les valeurs et renforce les intérêts du capitalisme patriarcal chez les praticiens de la profession juridique et comment ce processus a des conséquences diverses choquantes sur les étudiants de sexe tant féminin que masculin. Elles soutiennent que même si les étudiantes subissent des pressions considérables pour assimiler les valeurs patriarcales institutionnalisées et légitimées par la profession et par les facultés de droit, leur conscience spécifiquement féminine de femmes au sein d'une culture si expressément mâle les amène à se dresser contre cette hégémonie. Les auteures insistent particulièrement sur la disjonction de la conscience reproductive des hommes et des femmes — a première abstraite et incertaine, la seconde matérielle et spécifique — la qualifiant d'écart que les lois patriarcales tentent de combler en ce qui concerne la famille et la séparation de ce qui est public et ce qui est privé. Elles soutiennent que la (re)production de l'hégémonie et la résistance à l'hégémonie attribuables à cet écart et que la présence des femmes en droit bouleversent le consensus dont dépend l'hégémonie mâle.

The authors review the contributions of Karl Marx and Antonio Gramsci to our understanding of the (re)production of class relations, and criticize the inadequacies of theories derived from both men in addressing and evaluating the political significance of the specifically patriarchal dimensions of law and legal education. By bringing feminist analysis to hegemony theory, Mary O'Brien and Sheila McIntyre seek to show how traditional legal education instills the values and reinforces the interests of patriarchal capitalism in legal practitioners, and how this process has disparate consequences to female and male students. They argue that even while women students experience substantial pressure to assimilate the patriarchal values institutionalized and legitimized in and by law and law schools, women's specifically female consciousness in so male a culture has counter-hegemonic impact. They focus in particular on the disjunction between male and female reproductive consciousness — the former abstract and uncertain, the latter material and specific — as a gap sought to be bridged by patriarchal laws concerning the family and the separation of public and private. They argue that it is within such gaps that (re)production of and resistance to hegemony take place and that women's location in the legal profession is subverting the consensus on which male hegemony depends.

I

It is easy to be cynical about law. The historical reality of codes and courts, of "going to law," of incarceration and punishment, of the separation of powers, of constitution and crime is complex enough: to try to unify these with abstract conceptions of justice tempts one to abandon analysis and description in favour of rhetoric. Cynicism arises within this dialectic of law and justice, but we shall argue that it is also within this gap that the socio-political processes of legitimation of law operate. The relationship of law and justice may be implicit, explicit, or ideological, but the socio-political processes which seek to define consent to systems of law are real enough.

The nature of these legitimation processes, the social activities through which a particular legal system and jurisprudential philosophy become confirmed as right and just, are not generally studied in law schools. Modern law claims its socio-political legitimacy on the grounds of the rational consent of the governed. Like their counterparts in medicine, lawyers tend to feel that they have long transcended their historical origins in shamanism, elitism, superstition, and violently defended privilege. Perhaps, after all, Moses really did learn something on that mountain; perhaps Zeus' castration of his father actually did guarantee a more orderly and thoughtful legitimacy for the exercise of power; it may be that Clytemnestra's banishment to the underworld left more room for Athenia's rational justice; perhaps Magna Carta transcended the particular interests of a gang of thugs. In any case, speculation on myths of the origins of justice is not generally considered to be a very useful exercise for lawyers or laity. Legal folk wisdom is fraught with messy fairy tales which the historical processes of codification and legislation are considered to have dealt with. The resulting common sense view of law is that it is a little like work: one may not like it, but it is a necessary condition of political stability and cultural durability.

On this view, those who argue the partiality of the law — that it favours the rich or that it is not for women,[1] for example — fail to understand that law

---

1. See, e.g., P. Beirne and R. Quinney, editors, *Marxism and Law* (New York: John Wiley & Sons, 1982) for a class analysis of law. See Susan Boyd and Elizabeth Sheehey, "Canadian Feminist Perspectives on Law," in this volume, and for primarily United States sources, Mary Joe Frug and Fran Olsen, "Bibliography of Feminist Legal Scholarship," 1986, unpublished. Copy available with *Canadian Journal of Women and the Law.*

stands between citizens and the arbitrary terror of lawlessness on the one hand and the unfettered authoritarianism of the state on the other. Aristotle made the key statement of this position: "Law is order and good law is good order."[2] This juxtaposition of law-in-general with specific legal systems, of course, does not foreclose argument on what is good law: legal reform has been central to revolutionary strategies for a long time. In any case, in an age when folk wisdom has long yielded to the rigours of scientific analysis, critical dissatisfactions with the relation of law to justice tend to pass from the rusting swords of populist agitation to the rational halls of academe. We live in an age in which the spaces between reality and concept have been resolutely filled in by objective, logical, and preferably quantified information.

Consensual politics of the modern kind embody a crucial popular consent to law in general, a more tentative consent to particular forms of law, and no consensus at all on the meaning of justice. Consensus is stabilizing but not monolithic, even in totalitarian states. The purpose of this paper is to raise the question whether lay discontents and academic critique cannot be conjoined in a radical strategy for the mediation of the contradiction between law and justice. The impetus for such an effort is two-fold: contemporary efforts to develop a specifically feminist politics in which legal reformism is distrusted as a bourgeois blind alley[3] and a certain discontent with radical critiques of law from marxist perspectives.[4]

Feminists ask whether the undoubted fact that the law reflects the interests of the ruling classes in both practice and theory should be allowed to obscure the fact that it also reflects the interests of patriarchal control of cultural truths and women's lives. This is clearly a crucial theoretical and strategic question. Our themes therefore are the adequacy of left critique -- most specifically that conducted under the rubric of hegemony theory — to transcend the sexism of marxist theory in general, and to do this in a critical discussion of legal education. Hegemony theory is concerned with the (re)production of culture and ideology,[5] and in this process education is regarded as a powerfully

2. Aristotle. *Politics.* V.11.4
3. See literature in sources at note 1, *supra.* especially: Catharine A. MacKinnon. "Feminism, Marxism, Method, and the State: An Agenda for Theory," *Signs* 7 (1982): 515 [hereafter referred to as *Signs I*] and "Feminism, Marxism, Method, and the State: Toward a Feminist Jurisprudence." *Signs* 8 (1983): 635 [hereafter referred to as *Signs II*]; Diane Polan, "Toward a Theory of Law and Patriarchy," in *The Politics of Law,* David Kairys, editor, (New York: Pantheon, 1982); Fran Olsen, "Statutory Rape: A Feminist Critique of Rights Analysis," *Texas L. Rev.* 63 (1984):387; Ann Scales, "The Emergence of Feminist Jurisprudence: An Essay," *Yale L.J.* 95 (1986):1373; and Kathleen A. Lahey, *Equality and Specificity in Feminist Thought* (Toronto: Charter of Rights Educational Fund, 1983).
4. See, e.g., P. Beirne and R. Quinney, eds., *Marxism and Law* (New York: John Wiley & Sons, 1982). Much of the scholarship, particularly by men, located under the loose umbrella of the Critical Legal Studies movement has neo-marxist roots or retains a primary focus on class analysis. See Duncan Kennedy and Karl Klare, "A Bibliography of Critical Legal Studies." *Yale L.J.* 94 (1984):461; David Kairys, ed. *The Politics of Law: A Progressive Critique* (New York: Pantheon, 1982); and *Critical Law Studies Symposium. Stan. L. Rev.* 36 (1984):1.
5. The debt of cultural (re)production to Antonio Gramsci will be discussed later. The contemporary interest in England and the United States is generally agreed to have originated in the work of Raymond Williams, *The Long Revolution,* (London: Chatto & Windus, 1961); *Marxism and Literature* (Oxford: Oxford University Press, 1977), chapter 2. Note: in this paper *reproduction* is rendered as (re)production except when it relates to physical species reproduction. This is an attempt to restore some specificity to female reproductive processes (while retaining the flavour of cultural production as containing an element of reproduction)

conservative but very active cultural institution within which knowledge comes to be socially legitimated. Such knowledge, of course, includes ambiguous consent to constitutional and juridical legitimacy.

II

Simplistic marxism — which is not necessarily the intellectual practice of unsophisticated people — is inclined to dismiss jurisprudential dilemmas on the grounds that a successful dissolution of class divisions will produce that long-sought "good" law, for forms of law arise from modes of production. Classless production will presumably create equitable law. Karl Marx himself was not especially interested in law except as a historical adjunct to class transformation and subsequent power formations. "After the restoration of the Stuarts," he wrote, "the landed proprietors carried, by legal means, an act of usurpation effected everywhere on the Continent without legal formality...."[6] This was of course the abolition of feudal tenure. The law is legitimate, is the conclusion, when it demonstrably serves the interests of the ruling class: and this is most clearly visible when a new ruling class appears. Contemporary marxists have to do more, however, than demonstrate the class bias of law; they also have to explain why the proletariat have failed to rise up and destroy the economic relations which are the ground of oppressive law.

Certainly, the hierarchical structure of legal systems does reflect class divisions. Judges are generally drawn from the bourgeoisie, and lawyers as well as law professors are either middle class or upwardly mobile.[7] Only a few lawyers and occasional legislators in liberal democracies become dissident intellectuals who self-consciously adopt proletarian struggles as their own.[8] The proletarian in legal process is the cop, the lowly, lawful essence of false consciousness.

The problem for marxist social science, however, does not lie in the storied hierarchies of legal structure; instead, it lies in the misty valleys which not only separate theory from practice, but also appear to separate class struggle from the reality of a consensual politics which has successfully blunted proletarian revolutionary consciousness. This may, of course, be the very same chasm which intrudes between the fact of law and the concept of justice. In any case, what is missing in this vacuous middle is an account of the actual social relations and activities in which consent is developed and solidified: neo-marxists have thus turned increasingly to the examination of the processes of cultural and

---

at the same time that we differentiate production (material subsistence processes) from (re) production (cultural and ideological processes).

6. Karl Marx, *Capital*, Vol. I (New York: Vintage Books, 1977), 883. The final chapters of volume I detail, with relentless contempt, the setting in place of political and legal institutions which capitalists need. *Ibid.*, 896-904.

7. See, John Hagan, Marie Huxter, and Patricia Parker, "Class Structure and Legal Practice: Inequality and Mobility Among Toronto Lawyers," paper presented at the Seventh Biennial Conference of the National Association of Women and the Law, 1987, published in the conference Programme.

8. Karl Marx's slightly defensive canonization of intellectuals as potential proletarians is to be found in "The Manifesto of the Communist Party," in *Marx and Engels: Selected Works, Vol. I* (Moscow: Progress Publishers, 1969), 98-137.

ideological (re)production.[9]

The whole notion of consent has been an important part of liberal democratic ideology and practice, a consent sustained by effective strategies of permitting but controlling dissent. The development of party politics has played a crucial role in this process. It is easy to dismiss the consenting polity as the materialization of false consciousness, but it is more important to uncover the ways in which liberal democracies actually produce and reproduce consent to prevailing power structures. This involves a perception of the relation between the modern state and the ruling class which can provide some understanding of the relative stability of capitalist societies and of public toleration and, indeed, overt support for the exploitive practices and fancy ideological footwork of state institutions.

The theoretical comprehension of the hegemony which the consensual state exercises over dissenting forces is not easily deducible from Karl Marx's gnomic pronouncements on the state, which was relatively under-developed in his own time.[10] The state does indeed act as executive for the desires and interests of the ruling class, but the contemporary state is much more than a mere committee. Even the more recent notion of the bourgeois state as a superstructure rising upon the substructure of modes of production, which is the vulgar interpretation of marxist social theory,[11] cannot give a complete nor convincing account of how capitalist states actually function. Nor can it deal with the problem of the participation of the working class in the perpetuation of the liberal state.

The substructure/superstructure model is simply too crude and too abstract, to say nothing of the intrinsic impoverishment of materialist dialectics that are involved in the marxian structural-functional model of society. It was this inadequacy that led the Italian marxist Antonio Gramsci to spend his twenty years in a fascist prison attempting to give a dialectical account of the development of the totalitarian state. In doing this, he had begun to develop a more dynamic perception of social structure. It is not systematic: Benito Mussolini's jails were scarcely intellectual cloisters, and it says much for Antonio Gramsci's intellectual vitality and strength of character that he persisted in his labours under brutal conditions.[12] His major contribution to the

9. For a collection of somewhat loosely related work in this field, see Roger Dale et al., editor, *Education and the State. Vol. 2: Politics, Patriarchy and Practice* (Barcombe: Palmer Press, 1981).
10. Karl Marx's most famous statement of the state as executive committee of the ruling class is in *The Manifesto*, but the notion of the state as instrument of class interests permeates much of his work.
11. Freidrich Engels is often blamed for this positivist tendency in marxism, especially in *Anti-Duhring* (W. Emile Burns, International Publishers, 1939). The comtemporary brand of reductionist marxism ("correspondence theory") is represented in the sociology of education. See, for example, Samuel Bowles and Herbert Gintis, *Schooling in Capitalist America* (New York: Basic Books, 1971). For a feminist discussion of the difficulties of abstract theories of the state, see Mary O'Brien, *The Tyranny of the Abstract: Structure, State and Patriarchy* (The Maurice Manel Memorial Lecture, Atkinson College, York University, 1983), and Catharine A. MacKinnon, *Signs I*, note 3, *supra*.
12. Not all of Antonio Gramsci's work is available in translation. The major English sources are A. Hoare and S.N. Smith, editor and translator, *Selections From the Prison Notebooks* (London: Lawrence and Wishart, 1971), and L. Lawner, translator, *Letters from Prison* (London: Jonathan Cape, 1975). There is as yet no systematic English edition of Antonio Gramsci's writing on education or family.

historical development of Karl Marx's analysis of capitalism came from his experience of early totalitarianism, and the historical appeal to the Italian proletariat of the conservatism of the church and later of fascism. He had been an active trade unionist and socialist journalist, and an independent scholar who had studied and criticized the idealism of both Georg Hegel and his Italian interpreter. Benedetto Croce.[13] The major refinement of the dialectical materialist model which Antonio Gramsci developed was his analysis of false consciousness as a socially generated praxis, the production of a continuous social process of (re)producing and deploying bourgeois ideology.

Antonio Gramsci understood clearly that a substructural/superstructural model was neither adequate nor sufficiently sophisticated. Contradiction is, after all, mediated by praxis, and the inert juxtaposition of substructure and superstructure leaves no space in the middle for theory and practice to develop in real class struggle. The confusion of dichotomy and dialectic, variously referred to as reductionism or correspondence theory, is endemic on the left. Antonio Gramsci introduced as a middle term a socio-ideological realm of mediation-by-praxis which he called "civil society," a nomenclature borrowed from the Enlightenment. Civil society was the space between the mode of production and the forces of control by violence in which popular consent could be organized and ideology and culture (re)produced — not by force, but by bourgeois class praxis. He was thus engaging the actual social and political processes of bourgeois states in which culture is (re)produced, knowledge is certified, and law and order is sustained. The consensual state is able to keep its "armour of coercion" under cover,[14] and totalitarianism was doomed in his view because it could not do this: it continually resorted to overt violence. By keeping the means of violence in wrapped reserve, ruling classes are able to present particular interests as general interests.

In terms of our present theme, it might be said that the consensual state has as a condition of its success the need to present itself as a *just* state, as well as to objectify the principle of justice in a visible legal system. Legal practice, equality before the law, legal knowledge, codified law, democratic legislative practice, and limited popular participation through party systems are the concrete conditions which can do this. Ideology is not simple fraud nor a triumph for propaganda: it is a complex social production in which class power is clothed in the seemly robes of democratic consent in ways that are experienced intangibly.

Antonio Gramsci considered that the most important institutions of civil society were the school and the family. He (or his translators)[15] have been much more concerned with the former than the latter, a tendency continued by contemporary hegemony theorists. The predictable result is that there is no examination of patriarchal hegemony, no recognition of the particular oppression of women by men of all classes. Consequently, the function of law in the private realm, for example, or the ideological significance of early childhood

13.   For an accessible account of Antonio Gramsci's life and major theoretical propositions, see Carl Boggs. *Gramsci's Marxism* (London: Pluto Press, 1976).
14.   Hoare and Smith. *Prison Notebooks*, note 12. *supra*, 263.
15.   Boggs, *Gramsci's Marxism*, note 13, *supra*.

socialization, are not analysed as instruments of ideological (re)production, and women's specific oppression is lost in the one-way maze of class struggle. Civil society for Antonio Gramsci is really the arena of localized political struggle. Thus the separation of the culturally (re)productive public/private nexus from the repressive state emerges not as a contradiction, but as a slightly more adequate structuralism.

The familiar feminist concern with the dialectic of public and private is an advance on Antonio Gramsci's work, for feminists understand the separation of public and private to be the ground and locus of gender struggle. Such a view permits an analysis of the relations of capitalism *and* of patriarchy in the cultural (re)production of patriarchal capitalism and indeed, of most known modes of production. Democracy, of course, is supposed to diffuse class struggle by the protection of "rights," and has recently turned a little anxiously to the issue of women's rights, especially now that feminist struggles evince signs of extending political activism beyond acceptable questions of equality and rights. Hegemony theorists, like marxists in general, regard equality and rights as ideological symbols. Male critical legal scholars, for example, have drawn attention to the "circular nature" of rights discourse, which takes for granted a separation of passive civil society and active state.[16] However, they have failed to notice that "passive civil society" is precisely where women live.

Struggles on issues of rights keep people busy. The petty bourgeoisie regard all rights (except property rights) with suspicion, as do many proletarians who have felt the caress of relative affluence. People deficient in rights tend to believe that this particular absence is the cause of their general oppression and deprivation. Trade unions and other organizations fight hard for legal protection and for legislative entrenchment of rights, and feminists have also turned to law and justice as redress for ancient wrongs.[17] This is not strategically naive. Legal struggles for rights are progressive in a dialectical way: they may achieve some concrete improvements at the same time that they demonstrate experientially the partiality of law, its costs and delays, its mystified procedures and occasional flares of sheer brutality: all of these contribute to debate and equivocacy about the strained quality of justice. As Antonio Gramsci understood clearly, hegemonic activity constantly creates counter-hegemony.[18] Nonetheless, rights struggles do tend to conceal the hegemonic function of law in conserving class rule and enforcing social order.

16. See, for example, Duncan Kennedy, "Legal Education as Training for Hierarchy," in *The Politics of Law*, ed. David Kairys (New York: Pantheon, 1983), 48-49; and Duncan Kennedy's later qualification of this critique: Peter Gabel and Duncan Kennedy, "Roll Over Beethoven," *Stanford Law Review* 36 (1984): 1, 26-44. Janet Rifkin notes the way in which legally recognized rights generate other, often contradictory rights: the right to abortion for teenagers, for example, has come into legal conflict with parents' rights. See Janet Rifkin, "Toward a Theory of Law and Patriarchy," *Harvard Women's Law Journal* 3 (1980):83.

17. The struggle for enfranchisement, for example: see Catherine Cleverdon, *The Woman Suffrage Movement in Canada* (Toronto: University of Toronto Press, 1950), and more recent mobilization by women to improve equality guarantees in the *Canadian Charter of Rights and Freedoms*; see Penney Kome, *The Taking of Twenty-Eight* (Toronto: Women's Press, 1983). For a feminist critique of a liberal rights approach to women's equality guarantees under the *Charter*, see Sheila McIntyre, "The Charter: Driving Women to Abstraction," *Broadside* 6 (1985) No. 5: 8-9.

18. Hoare and Smith, *Prison Notebooks*, note 12, *supra*, at 323 24, 419-25.

Law is the price to be paid for access to justice, a reification perfectly in tune with the exchange mechanism of commodity production. Widely apprehended as the last fence against something worse than what we have, law achieves reluctant respect — which is enough to procure general consent to the legitimacy of the state. In this sense, law is a powerful instrument of ideological control and consent to ruling class authority.

The cultural persistence of perceptions of law as a system of rights-and-justice rather than as a hegemonic force with ultimate access to violent means is the theme of much marxist legal critique. Neo-marxist legal theories tend to view law as a social structure which channels, institutionalizes and purports to resolve social conflict by resort to formalized, "objective" rules and "legal" reasoning articulated within an authoritarian forum — all of which is said to deliver rights-and-justice impartially but which also codifies, restores and entrenches the apparent necessity and legitimacy of the inegalitarian status quo.[19] Transformation of law for many leftist theorists requires mobilization by radical lawyers to challenge legal "authority" (that is, precedent, reasoning and professional hierarchies),[20] much as the "new" sociologists of education advocate mobilization of teachers to challenge the hegemony of "legitimate" knowledge.[21] The radical lawyer must also "delegitimate" state control of the law, just as radical teachers are exhorted to delegitimate state control of curriculum. The problem is not perceived in terms of access to justice as such, but as an ideological and cultural definition of justice which embodies the will of the ruling classes executed through the activity of the state apparatus which they control. What is urged is a radical re-definition of justice and law by populist forces guided by a true consciousness of the alienating realities of systems of law.

III

Hegemony theory permits a more adequate understanding of the (re)production of the social relations and ideology of capitalism, but it is radically problematic because it fails to address patriarchal hegemony. Feminists are now developing critiques of the gender blindness of the sociology of education,[22] and it is important that legal critiques which claim to be progressive also be subject to feminist scrutiny. The omission of women is not accidental, trivial, nor irrelevant. The law has been a masculine redoubt for centuries. When one speaks of law to feminists, the odds are that they will speak fairly quickly of rape, which has become a political touchstone for feminist

19. See. e.g., David Kairys. "Introduction" and "Legal Reasoning," in *The Politics of Law*, David Kairys, ed. (New York: Pantheon, 1983); Peter Gabel, "Reification in Legal Reasoning," *Research in Law and Sociology*, ed. Stephen Spitzer, Vol. 3 (Greenwich: JAI Press, 1980), 25; and Karl Klare. "Judicial Deradicalization of the Wagner Act and the Origins of Modern Legal Consciousness," *Minnesota Law Review* 62 (1978) 265.

20. See, e.g., Peter Gabel and Paul Harris, "Building Power and Breaking Images: Critical Legal Theory and The Practice of Law," *Review of Law and Social Change* 11 (1982-83): 369.

21. Michael Apple, *Ideology and Curriculum* (London, Boston: Routledge and Kegan Paul, 1979), 120-22.

22. Angela McRobbie, "Settling Accounts with Subculture," *Screen Education* 34 (Spring 1980): 37-49; Mary O'Brien, *The Commatization of Women: Patriarchal Hegemony in the Sociology of Education* (paper presented to the British Sociological Association, 1982).

perception of law, just as the fate of the witches is a historical touchstone. Recently, the relation between jurisprudence and enforcement, between legislator, judge, and policeman, has had difficulty in concealing its bias as a patriarchal as well as a class strategy. Abortion and wife abuse have become issues in the public dialogue on and practical administration of justice: abortion shows the system enforcing bad law while wife abuse shows it failing to enforce good ones. This is the stuff of which counter-hegemony is made.

The concern of hegemony theory with education as a major instrument of ideological reproduction is reflected in the work of some marxist scholars, but the specifically patriarchal modes of oppression to which women law students are subjected are not a matter of wide concern.[23] Problems in legal education are generally considered to be sex-blind or subject to the process which may be called "commatization."[24] There is an excellent example of this class comma sex comma race comma kind of elision in Robert Condlin's discussion of legal pedagogy.[25] Robert Condlin presents diological data on classroom interactions. He is careful to use gender-neutral nouns (persons) but English pronouns inevitably defeat him, so that women students become "he's." One of his tapes involves a student who, Robert Condlin tells us in a footnote, had role, status, power, ability, sex, knowledge, experience, values, beliefs, objectives, and needs different from those of the instructor. This array of commatized characteristics implies that all these attributes are equally significant, even though he is sensitive to the complexity of their interaction.

Robert Condlin's first concern is the possibility of ambiguity in dialogue. Marxist education critics, on the other hand, are primarily concerned with the relationship of pedagogy and curriculum to class hegemony. In neither case is the dialectic of "sex" as biological datum and "gender" as social construction observed, far less analyzed. Yet the sex/gender system[26] has its material grounds in reproductive necessity, just as class is grounded in productive necessity: both gender and class are historical formations grounded in material necessity. They are a different order of phenomena than socio-cultural variables of an abstract, pseudo-scientific kind. Marxists might claim that all of the listed characteristics are reducible "in the last instance" to class.[27] This is simply untrue of biological sex, but also of gender, which is materially grounded in the necessity of reproductive rather than productive labour. Class formulations also

---

23. Feminist legal scholars, however, are beginning to analyze the systemic (rather than individually perpetrated) nature of patriarchal oppression and male dominance within legal education. See, e.g., K.C. Worden, "Overshooting the Target: A Feminist Deconstruction of Legal Education." *The American University Law Review* 34 (1985): 1141; Sheila McIntyre, "The Maleness of Law and Its Impact on Women Students," unpublished, available from the author; and Christine Boyle, "Teaching Law as if Women Really Mattered or What About the Washrooms?" in this volume.

24. O'Brien, *Commatization*, note 22, *supra.*

25. Robert J. Condlin, "Socrates' New Clothes: Substituting Persuasion for Learning in Clinical Practice Instruction." *Maryland Law Review* 40 (1981): 223-83.

26. Sandra Harding, "Why has the Sex/Gender System Become Visible Only Now?" in *Discovering Reality*, ed. Sandra Harding and Marilyn Hintikka (New York: D. Reidel Publishing, 1983).

27. The "last instance" formulation of class causality is that of Louis Althusser. For a critique, see E.P. Thomson, *The Poverty of Theory and Other Essays* (New York, London: Monthly Review Press, 1978). 86-114.

make it difficult to *think* the integration of sex and gender which many feminists believe patriarchy has systematically dismantled. Commatization buries women in a plethora of abstract "characteristics" and "concrete" variables which obscure the oppression of women by men *of all classes* — and, it may be added, in all classrooms.

Critiques of legal education are not of course the prerogative of the left: Robert Condlin relies on a range of theories of social construction in his appeal for socratic persuasion rather than didacticism in clinical instruction. A recent study of legal education under the aegis of the Social Sciences and Humanities Research Council of Canada, for example, deploys a number of research methodologies and finds that, among other things, law schools have "too narrow a focus of intellectual activities" and suggests that "scholarly activity of the kind which has been consistently undervalued by the legal community, and even by legal academics, is essential ...."[28] Further, there is no evidence that legal pedagogues are excited about feminist and marxist interest in educational process in law schools; if this work is perceived at all, it is regarded as marginal or discreditable.[29]

Law school is neither a simple means to an end nor a discrete stage of professional training. The continuity of education and practice in, for example, experience of institutional hierarchy, dependency on and deference to superiors, and a particular definition of knowledge all repeat themselves indefinitely in legal lives. Legal education does not merely provide intellectual tools and rules of procedure, just as it does not simply "reflect" the structure of a mode of production. It is a living social process which reproduces in a majority of students prescribed patterns of thought, conduct, and socio-political allegiances essential to both capitalist and patriarchal hegemony. It procures consent and creates dissent by combining a living matrix of pedagogical technique, classroom mores, institutional rules, and prescribed faculty/student relations with a "traditional" curriculum to constitute an effective hegemonic practice. Added to these social relations is the historical bulk of precedent and prescription, of theory and practice, of sheer *legitimacy* — all of which is culturally powerful and ideologically persuasive. It is not without emotional clout either. Students are not overtly forced into conformity; they are shown that conformity is an objective, rational course of action. Added to this is the implicit promise of the material rewards for the social class whose values are explicated, a class to which many students already belong and others look forward to joining.

Organizational structures are also hegemonic instruments which may be administered in a discriminatory way.[30] Affirmative action is perceived as

---

28. *Law and Learning/Le droit et le savoir. Report on a Study of Legal Education and Research* (Ottawa: SSHRC, 1983).
29. See Sheila McIntyre, "'Gender Bias Within the Law School': The Memo and Its Impact," forthcoming in *CJWL* 2:2.
30. David White and Terry Roth, "The Law School Admission Test and the Continuing Minority Status of Women in Law Schools," *Harvard Women's Law Journal* 2 (1979):103. Note that women have higher undergraduate grade point averages but lower LSATs which, depending on the weight each of them are given in a particular admissions formula, could screen them out.

inimical to elite formation, and is predictably unpopular in law schools.[31] Of course, the principle of hierarchy is used to grade law schools themselves, and top-ranked schools develop particularly rigid organizational controls. Elite formation has other strategies: admission policies; the restriction of numbers, currently a matter of much concern;[32] the near-absence of provision for part-time legal studies, the justification of extravagant fees; a rigid distinction between professionals and laity; restrictions on advertising to obscure the commercial nature of law-as-big-business. All of these are practical instruments of control of the social structure of the profession. Assembling a proficient case for the drama of professional practice is the organizational pole; classroom interaction is the social pole. Curriculum mediates these macro/micro processes. To describe this process as ideological (re)production is useful, but deficient to the extent that it fails to notice that the interests of male supremacy are as important as class hegemony.

Classroom interaction is governed by an authoritative pedagogy, and is inhospitable to student criticism or innovative ideas. Classroom topics are circumscribed by the "objective" necessity to prepare for the all-or-nothing finals as the entry ticket to the job market. Rewards for conformity, and punishment of attempts to question the range, utility, or legitimacy of current doctrine are seen as not only proper but considerate and practical ways of keeping students on course. Emphasis on structural similarities between classroom and courtroom, between school success and other success (defined as practice with a large, prestigious metropolitan law firm), persuades students both ideologically and pragmatically to prefer the *status quo*. Further, power relations within hierarchical structures become the norm of legal practice, hence the importance of deference. For the student, disobedience of professorial fiat carries with it at least the threat of violation of one's self-respect, the mockery of one's peers, poor or withheld letters of reference, inferior grades, and poor job prospects in an increasingly competitive market. Such practices, at whatever level of intensity they develop in individual instances, are institutional practices in the (re)production of the facticity and ideology of an elite profession: access to the study of law is in no sense access to justice.

It is precisely this type of non-violent coercion by ruling class interests that Antonio Gramsci explicated in his theory of civil society: control is worked out in everyday social relations. The curriculum which mediates organizational structure and classroom interaction presents the class and gender ideology which the curriculum embodies as objective, rational knowledge, and presents as packaged facts a problematic theory of knowledge and a defence of liberal assumptions.

This process is not unique to law schools: it is central to all pedagogy in societies of all political stripe. This is not necessarily reprehensible, for culture

---

31. There has been increasing activism by women and visible minority students and faculty challenging law school administrators' failure to implement effective affirmative action hiring practices in American and Canadian law schools. See, for instance, *Harvard Law Record* 76 (1983):1,7 and 83 (1986):5,1; "Open Letter to Our Colleagues," August 1986 (on file with *Canadian Journal of Women and the Law*); and "Recruitment of Feminists Curbs Academic Freedom," Queen's University *Journal*, January 30, 1987, 11.
32. Letters to the editor. *Law Society of Upper Canada Gazette* 15 (1981) 123:446.

does indeed have the task of passing on moral values, certified knowledge, and approved social praxis. The crucial questions are which values, whose knowledge, and whether students are able to develop a critical faculty. Perhaps the most damaging forms of education are the ones which claim not only to be "value free," but which fetishize objectivity as such. Fetishization is ideological process: Karl Marx described it in terms of commodity exchange, where the actual social relations of production are obscured in the exchange of things.[33] It is therefore essential to pay attention to curricular content and theories of knowledge if we want to posit legal education as a specific instance of ideological training, for curriculum may obscure the actual social relations which constitute malfeasance, crime, legislative acts, and elusive justice itself.

IV

Legal education as vehicle of (re)producing patriarchal and capitalist hegemony relies extensively on a fabric of dichotomies which both obscure and reinforce the gap between law and justice. Bourgeois thought prefers to posit dichotomy rather than contradiction: we have already noted Antonio Gramsci's concern with the gap in the middle of abstractly formulated dichotomies, and we have raised this question as an epistemological puzzle and structural gap in the relation of law and justice. Dichotomizing is a long-standing strategy of analysis in the western tradition: the belief that power is the sole healer of dichotomies can hardly be said to have disappeared from political or intellectual practice.[34]

Legal education carries on the tradition of dichotomizing: over against a holistic perception of a natural legal order stands the concretely social organization of learning which entrenches in students' minds a number of dichotomies of considerable significance.[35] At the approved pole are rules, reasoning, modes of discourse and course offerings which fit the interests of the dominant culture. Approval is signalled and (re)produced by characterizing such rules and reasoning as "objective", "neutral" and "rational"; such discourse as "rational" and "dispassionate" and such course offerings as "doctrinal" rather than "political", "hard" rather than "soft". These institutional marks of approval are conjoined with character attributes for the successful lawyer: rational, detached, capable of hard-hitting argument and partisan by function (a "hired gun"), not by personal principle. The personal aspect of the process of legal education is neglected in hegemony theory, which is committed to marxist notions of social class, and banishes personality to the webs of false consciousness and the idealist traps of bourgeois psycho-sciences.

---

33. Marx, *Capital*, 163-77.
34. "There must necessarily be a union of the naturally ruling element with the element which is naturally rules, for the preservation of both." Aristotle, *Politics*, 1252, 15-69. Aristotle regarded the relation of man and woman as the paradigm case.
35. The ways in which epistemological and pedagogical dichotomization are used in legal training to legitimize the class bias of law and of lawyers are enumerated in considerable detail by Duncan Kennedy in note 16, supra. Our analysis borrows significantly from his. Kennedy, however, virtually never remarks on the gender load of law's dichotomies or of the process and content of legal education or of the relationship of these dichotomies and their impact on the reproduction of male domination.

Vol. 2   *1986*   81

The legal mind, however, is not allowed to slip into the subjective mode; for idealized epistemologies of objectivity, rationality, and value neutrality are both pedagogical principles and practical virtues.

That which is not fact is fancy or, in the lugubrious vocabulary of scientism, it is subjectivity, emotion, irrationality, or evaluative ideology. These constitute the negatively classified pole, encompassing the unorthodox, the non-traditional, and the innovative, whether applied to critical reasoning, study choices, or career ambitions. Non-mainstream study, views and practice are thus marginalized: they are unprofessional, unserious, Other. Their marginality is underlined by reference to the ultimate dichotomy: law vs. politics. Rules and reasoning in the interest of the dominant classes constitute "Law"; observation that "Law" is drafted, interpreted and administrated by the dominant in their interests is "politics". Law students must learn the rules so that as lawyers they may apply them; students who wish to learn *about* the rules and to pass (subjective) judgment on them are in the wrong faculty.

Pedagogically, this favours a rather attenuated teaching technique. Duncan Kennedy notes that in traditional teaching of doctrine, eighty percent of the rules tend to be introduced as "one or two sentence, tag-like, formulaic justification."[36] This suggests that such rules are inherently rational and necessary, and need nothing more than statements of their obviousness. Another ten percent of these rules are labelled "historic anomalies" and dismissed or marginalized as such; and the remaining ten percent are packaged as "the future cutting edge of the law" which students are invited to discuss in an unstructured way. The overall impression, Kennedy notes, is "powerfully legitimating. It doesn't say all the rules are right. Just eighty percent."[37] The textbooks and the professor suggest that it all hangs together so coherently that taking classroom time to question either the formula justification or the values assumed by the rule and the teacher to be self evidently meritorious would be a misuse of instructional resources. Thus students arriving in law school, highly motivated to learn doctrine but innocent of any perception of what it is, are subjected to an ideological immersion which they have no critical tools to evaluate. It is reasonable for them to conclude that what the law is and what it ought to be have been happily wed by the benign and immensely intelligent accoucheurs of legal history.

The dichotomous mode of reasoning which characterizes the teaching of legal doctrine is not, of course, peculiar to law: it embodies western man's dualist perceptions of knowing in general. Objective/subjective; rational/emotional; factual/opinionated; impartial/partisan: all these are the staples and evaluative dichotomies of hegemonic discourse. In the legal community, they not only distinguish the mainstream agenda from the "para legal" by relegating non-traditional academic and professional pursuits to the mushy, subjective realm of policy, but further stigmatize legal unorthodoxy with qualities androcentric culture devalues as feminine. Rendering non-mainstream students and student interests effeminate is powerfully delegitimizing in as pervasively

36. Duncan Kennedy, *The Political Significance of the Structure of the Law School Curriculum* (Lecture given as Lansdowne Visitor, University of Victoria, B.C., Feb. 1980), 21–22.
37. Ibid., 22.

male an institution as law; but this vehicle of invalidation is not gender-neutral. Women are doubly marginalized, doubly pressured to assimilate the discourse, stances and academic focus consistent with the interests of the dominant. For even if women aspire to the mainstream model, they are always reminded by the ideology buried in law's dichotomies, that to be female in law is to be associated with the non-legal.

Hegemonic rationality also prevails within the curriculum, where objective/subjective, rational/emotional, doctrinal/policy-oriented dichotomies prevail. The "core" program — the heart and indeed the muscle of the matter — embraces property, contracts, torts, criminal, wills, trusts, and commercial law: the anatomy of the body capitalist written in statute and precedent. "Perspective" courses are second tier and ancillary, the "civil society" courses, if we may borrow once more from Antonio Gramsci, bodies of law which mediate between capitalist and state power and the "ungrounded" academic courses which represent the private interests of individuals: tax law, family law, labour law. It is common practice to use phallic imagery to describe the difference between these sets: the first is "hard" law and both perspective and "civil society" law is "soft." We shall examine this imagery in a moment. Meanwhile, we must note that the division of courses is practical as well as evaluative: the hard group are bread and butter courses, looming large in bar admission examinations, in work prospects, and in curriculum credit ratings. Perspective courses are less prestigious, perhaps because they can provide students with a critical standpoint: policy analysis implies that students can think about law as well as learn it and stresses the relation of law to political process. "Civil society" courses such as Women and Law, environmental law, Native rights, social theory, legal history, and civil liberties disproportionately attract (and console) non-mainstream students, but there is no doubt that an A in commercial law trumps an A in women's studies.

The pedagogical processes which dichotomize and evaluate "hard" and "soft" courses cannot sustain a credible claim to logical consistency. To say that environmental law is more policy oriented than property law is simply wrong: it is at best an ideological assertion whose internal logic is derived from the "rationality" of the capitalist mode of production for which the good and the rational is any process which maximizes profit. Such processes require policy decisions, including those which consider the practicality of propping up less competitive corporations with taxpayers' money. Should a student dissent from this mode of reasoning, she or he will be considered irrational, emotional, and subjective, those regrettable characteristics of "soft" thinking. Hard thinking is rational and neutral, of course. This is the stuff of ideological training, the suspension of practical consciousness, the learning to "think like a lawyer." It is enforced in institutional structure, in curriculum content, and classroom interaction.[38]

---

38. Pedagogical abuse takes many forms. A student observes that the rule under discussion is "unfair". The professor observes that his four-year-old daughter make remarks like that. Moral: intuitive or common-sense judgments are immature and girlish. A student claims that criminal law is not a largely neutral web of rules protecting values of universal application but a partisan political scheme partially enforced to entrench the interests of the dominant class.

The effects of prevailing forms of pedagogy are damaging to disaffected students, who are forced into a number of counter educational survival tactics: assimilation, minimal attendance and non-participation in class, instrumental course and term paper selection, self-censorship on exams and painful rationalization of conformity. These options gradually destroy the motivation and self-esteem of non-mainstream students; they also virtually eliminate the possibility of counter-hegemonic struggle from within the law school.[39] Silent dissent functions the same as silent assent. Which is not to say there is a complete absence of student dissent; but professors are accorded the right to use their local classroom power in ridicule, insult, and grading. Not all of them do this, but — like the instruments of violent coercion which the state keeps in the attic with the War Measures Act — faculty authoritarianism, utilized or not, is acceptable at the institutional level. Yet too heavy a hand may initiate counter-hegemonic rumblings, student refusal to participate in the manufacture of consent may force them to look behind local power to the coercive institutional reality it is designed to conceal.[40] Classroom relations in general are power relations, and the adversarial ethos penetrates educational practice.[41]

V

The ideological nature of legal education and the role of institutional hierarchies in the socialization of lawyers tend to obscure three other critical insights: the abuse of power in class systematically channels student attention away from critical scrutiny of the role of law in institutionalizing inequality; legal training and process have a disparate impact on male and female students; and the (re)production of hierarchy effected by legal education serves patriarchy no less than it serves capitalism.

Work on the particular significance of these procedures for women in law school is just beginning. The theoretical understanding of patriarchy is an essential part of this. In economic/class terms, women and men are not

---

race and sex. Professor (smirking): "It's so endearing to have a few idealists in class." Moral: radical analyses are unrealistic and utopian. A student asks how commercial contract principles can be reconciled with domestic contract rules. Professor (looking at watch): "That's an interesting line of thought. Perhaps we can pursue it after class." Moral: lecture time is for facts, rules, the prescribed curriculum; personal/political questions waste other students' time. When all else fails, professors may pre-empt critical discussion and analysis by magisterially pronouncing that the topic raised by a student will not be on the 100% final exam. Finis.

39. See Sheila McIntyre, "The Maleness of Law and Its Impact on Women Students," unpublished paper on file with *The Canadian Journal of Women and the Law*.
40. Gramsci, *Prison Notebooks*, 323-24, 419-425.
41. The dialectic of hegemony is logically dependent on hostility: abstract contradiction is concrete social conflict. Consensus among either set of protagonists will encounter coercion of those who threaten the majority or the most powerful. Procedurally, however, it is necessary to preserve some substance to myths or benign pluralism which are ideologically functional. See Massima Salvadori, "Gramsci and the PCI: Two Conceptions of Hegemony," in *Gramsci and Marxist Theory*, ed. Chantal Mouffe, trans. Hal Sutcliffe (London, Boston, Henley: Routledge and Kegan Paul, 1979), 237-58; see also Henry Giroux, "Hegemony Resistance and the Paradox of Educational Reform," *Interchange* 12 (1981) 2 3: 3-26. For an analysis of the institutionalized hierarchy, power politics and adversarialism modelled in the law school classroom, see Toni Pickard, "Experience as Teacher: Discovering the Politics of Law Teaching," *University of Toronto Law Journal* 33 (1983): 279.

necessarily discriminated against differentially, but there is clearly discrimination related specifically to gender.[42] In addition to the distinction between sex and gender which feminists have made, however, a further distinction must be made between "feminine" and "feminist," for the first is a patriarchal construct and the second is its historically developing antithesis. If one assumed, simplistically, that women students fall along a continuum stretched between counter-hegemonic activists and ambivalent women who are sufficiently unorthodox to pursue a "male" career but are otherwise socially conventional, there is no "scientific" way to judge the degree of conformity or numerical distribution along the line. The popular press has recently taken to discussing the "feminization" of the law: it is perhaps more a question of the masculinization of women, not only in a vulgar sense of deportment, but in terms of the transformation of the "soft" characteristics "natural" to women to conformity with the "hard" high status characteristics of man and his works.[43]

Law schools are historically male preserves.[44] There are still disproportionately few women on law school faculties, and those women who are granted full-time continuing appointments, because they are held to unreflectively male standards of teaching, research and collegiality, experience relentless pressure to assimilate and endorse these standards. Although assimilation does not *per se* promise collegial acceptance and respect, refusal to adopt male standards guarantees professional discreditation.

Man has been and is the norm, not only in the minds of the seventeenth century grammarians who embedded he-ness in language, but in notions of the rights of "man," the nine "man" bench, and the ubiquitous "ordinary reasonable man" who is the both the litmus of legal rationality[45] and the constituent base of "community standards". Published instructional legal

---

42. As well, economic/class discrimination and sex discrimination may compound each other. It is not merely that women are economically disadvantaged by discrimination in employment opportunity, pay and promotion; it is that their disadvantage also makes them more vulnerable to male abuse within the workplace, notably in the form of sexual harassment. See Catharine MacKinnon, *Sexual Harassment of Working Women: A Case of Sex Discrimination* (New Haven, London: Yale University Press, 1979), 9-23.

43. For a sampling of recent scholarship exploring the ways legal training and practice alter women and the ways women alter legal practice, see: Ava Baron, "Feminization of the Legal Profession — Progress or Proletarianization?: A Review of *Women in Law*" ALSA *Forum* 7 (1983): 330, James Foster, "Antigones in the Bar: Women Lawyers as Reluctant Adversaries," *Legal Studies Forum* 10 (1986): 287; Carrie Menkel-Meadow, "Portia in a Different Voice: Speculations on a Woman's Lawyering Process," *Berkeley Women's Law Journal* 1 (1985): 39; and Faith Seidenberg, "The Bifurcated Woman: Problems of Women Lawyers in the Courtroom," *Canadian Journal of Women and the Law* 1 (1985): 219.

44. See Mary Jane Mossman, *Portia's Progress: Women as Lawyers: Reflections on the Past and Future* (Law Society of Upper Canada Continuing Legal Education Program, May 1986). For United States data, see Cynthia Fuchs Epstein, *Women in Law* (New York, Doubleday, 1983); and Elyce Zenoff and Kathryn Lorio, "What We Know, What We Think We Know, and What We Don't Know About Women Law Professors," *Arizona Law Review* 25 (1983): 869.

45. There is a growing body of feminist legal writing critical of applying the ordinary reasonable man standard, whether explicit or implicit, to women victims or defendants/accuseds. See, for instance, Dolores Donovan and Stephanie Wildman, "Is the Reasonable Man Obsolete? A Critical Perspective on Self Defence and Provocation," *Loyola Law Review* 14 (1981): 435; MacKinnon, *Signs I and Signs II*; Catharine A. MacKinnnon, "Women Who Kill" (book review), *Stanford Law Review* 34 (1982): 410; and Phyllis Crocker, "The Meaning of Equality for Women Who Kill," *Harvard Women's Law Journal* 8 (1985): 121.

materials no less than informal classroom discussions not uncommonly describe lawyers, judges, shareholders, fiduciaries and mortgagors as men while referring to women — if at all — primarily within the categories of victim, the narrowly limited range of deviant exception to the rule, or of minor character personifying/sex stereotypes.[46] Course content routinely excludes coverage of legal history and contemporary laws of central significance to women's inequality — for instance, the marital rape exemption and domestic violence in criminal law, or sexual harassment and occupational segregation in employment law -- while male professors continue to overuse and abuse rape hypotheticals to manufacture classroom controversy or to test dontrinal mastery in graded assignments. The value structures and assumptions underlying community standards codified in law which are alleged to be common to all "mankind," are packaged, accepted and strung together as if self-evidently objective and/or rational according to reasoning which women, not blessed by a "natural" perception of the laws of masculine logic, must learn. Women's sense of deficiency in these areas may be shared by instructors, setting the scene for self-fulfilling prophecy. The heavy irony is that "weak" women, disadvantaged by "soft" characteristics, not only have to work through the tough curriculum, but learn a whole new *persona* which, embodying as it does "mastery" of legal "objectivity," logic, and masculine adversarial norms, constitutes a complete curriculum in its own right.

The experience of women in law school is generally related to that of women in higher education and indeed at all levels of education, but it also has a particular significance.[47] Law is a vital instrument in the hegemony of male supremacy, for it legitimates the patriarchal form of family, male control of women's bodies and the separation of public and private life.[48] Hegemony theory helps us to understand the cultural forms of ideological production and social structure, but it does not help us to answer certain questions. For example, why are women entering law school *now*? This is a historical question, and Karl Marx's perception of historical dialectic does not help us here. Women entering law school are but one aspect of the wider historical development of feminism.

Feminism can of course be understood as a logical progression of liberalism, a further step in the pursuit of equality. In some ways it may be, but the current wave of feminism has a significant radical component, women who consider that the practical and philosophical aspects of liberal radicalism faded in the aftermath of the bourgeois revolutions and are now congealed in the past. There can be little doubt that many women entering law are inspired by liberal theories of equality, but even so, the evidence suggests that even these women will tend to choose "soft" law in school and in practice.[49] If hegemony theory is extended to include patriarchal hegemony, we can make some sense of this, for

46. See Mary Joe Frug, "Re-Reading Contracts: A Feminist Analysis of a Contracts Casebook," *American University Law Review* 34 (1985): 1065.
47. Michael Apple, "Work, Gender and Teaching," *Curriculum Praxis: Occasional Paper No. 22* (Edmonton, University of Alberta) discusses the education of women educators.
48. Frances Olsen, "The Family and the Market: A Study of Ideology and Legal Reform," *Harvard Law Review* 96 (1983): 1497.
49. Epstein, *Women in Law*, 96-129, 197-206; Zenoff and Lorio, "What We Know," 878-881.

Antonio Gramsci's model of the mediating space of civil society permits a certain freedom from the restrictions of mechanical economism in favour of wider cultural dialectic.

One could argue that the appearance of women in previously forbidden activities is simply the kind of state response to electoral pressure which democratic parties obviously understand to be essential to their survival. Yet the democratic state sets boundaries as to how far and how fast women's struggles may go, and these boundaries are policed by the law.[50] The difficulties and "soft" choices of women in law school can therefore be understood as the fruits of the contradictions between liberal equality theory and liberal family practice, between women in public and women in private, but this is an insight before which liberal and marxist analysis both stop short.

Women's professional choices might also be attributed to the patriarchal socialization process, which has taught them social roles which preclude self-confidence, adversarial posturing, the skill of masking emotion, and a set of optimistic economic and career expectations.[51] These are boys' characteristics: boys are socialized as team players, but liberal individualism ensures that the swagger of the advocate comes easily to them. Women's individualism is held to be muted by the needs of motherhood which condemn them to unselfishness, which is not high on the list of desirable bourgeois characteristics. John Seeley and his co-authors, for example, in their well-known study of the socialization practices of the Canadian middle classes, found that the most profound contradiction in such practice was related to values: mother taught boys to be good, while father taught them how to succeed in business.[52] The two, of course, are incompatible. Both parents prepared daughters for a short career and a suitable marriage.

All of these views offer an analysis of the stereotyping nature of the socialization of girls. The possibility that women make choices from a perspective which is specifically female, grounded in women's existential experience and ethical consciousness, is not considered. Women, the social sciences tell us, do not make choices; they obey the will of men. This is obviously how it looks from the standpoint of men, who want to believe that they are able to force women into certain positions and then despise them for being there, for they are positions which are defined as lesser, inconsequential, "soft."

---

50. It is a bitter irony to women who place any faith in the potential of law to advance women's equality that the belated advent of formal equality guarantees, whether in the form of judicial creation of an "intermediate standard" for sex equality cases under the Fourteenth Amendment of the U.S. Constitution or in the form of human rights legislation and constitutional equality rights, has resulted in a host of successful challenges by men to legal benefits previously enjoyed by women only due to rigid interpretive formalism by judges who interpret legal guarantees as proof women are *de facto* equal to men. Equality law has gotten men alimony, custody of children, access to women-only schools; equality law may lose women pregnancy leave and pregnancy-related benefits, non-invasive rape evidence rules, statutory rape law, post-separation support and their children. See, e.g., Kathleen A. Lahey, *Feminist Jurisprudence: Coming or Going?* (Chicago: NAWL Conference, 1986).

51. E.R. Robert and M.F. Winter, "Sex-Role and Success in Law School," *Journal of Legal Education* 29 (1978): 449.

52. John R. Seeley et al., *Crestwood Heights* (Toronto: University of Toronto Press, 1956), 382-94.

VI

Clearly, we need some kind of perspective which can mediate the dialectic of gender and class experience with less partiality. This has not yet been attempted seriously by hegemony theorists. Indeed, the possibility that the material ground of gender (or of any other social process) lies outside the realm of necessity, defined by Karl Marx as the necessity to produce subsistence, is not seriously considered by his followers. This is why the problem of reductionism constantly recurs in marxism: in predicating the relation of the historical world and the natural world as a dialectical one and in rooting the mediation of that contradiction in human activity, Karl Marx scores his major achievement, which is the development of a conception of history which does not drift off into the realm of idealism. He attempts to unify human thought and action in historical process, a process which itself develops momentum from the dynamic of contradiction.[53]

The empirical contradiction which arises from the dialectic of productive necessity is, of course, class struggle. In capitalism, this takes the form of individual ownership and social labour. Antonio Gramsci attempts a theoretical refinement which permits understanding of the power of capitalism to control class struggle by fostering hegemony of a partial interpretation of cultural truth which obscures class struggle, identifying the particular interests of the bourgeoisie as the general 'truth' of the capitalist state. This it does by sophisticated management of "acceptable" knowledge and "certified" truth which is carried from generation to generation not only in the workplace, where "man"[54] is alienated from his labour, but in the institutions of "civil society" — mainly family and school. The development of false consciousness is in effect pedagogy conjoined with economic alienation to justify ruling class hegemony; it involves a general consent to an ideological view of the world. Such ideologies of consent arise in the everyday social relations in which political actions and opinions develop, in which children are raised, in which knowledge becomes definitive, in which strikes are called and settled, in which poems are written, in which law and order are maintained. This is the realm of civil society, in which people are not mere pawns to vast historical forces, but participate actively and with pragmatic rationality in social life and cultural reproduction, in productive labour, and in species reproduction.

What is particularly original in Antonio Gramsci's thought is his perception that social transformation can arise in this realm of civil society which stands between the coercive state and the economic substructure.[55] While he certainly believes that such historical activity can be subsumed under the

53. A dialectical contradiction is always that of universal and particular; see, for example, Karl Marx's famous analysis of the production of value, which arises in analysis of the relation of a particular commodity to a generalized commodity production. Marx, *Capital*, I. This is where he turns Georg Hegel upside down, for hegelian analysis would seek after the *idea* of commodity.

54. Antonio Gramsci rejects notions of "man-in-general," not because they are sexist but because they are abstract-idealist. Man is a social product, his subjectivity grounded in the "subjectivity of a social group." Antonio Gramsci, "Material, Storico e la filoso fia di Benedetto Croce," 191, quoted by Leonard Paggi, "Gramsci's General Theory of Marxism," in Mouffe, *Gramsci and Marxist Theory*, 123.

55. The distinction is between state coercion or "direct domination" and "the function of

general category of class struggle, he refuses to accept direct determination by the mode of production as the only condition of social change. Civil society is the realm of *needs* rather than the fundamental *necessity* embodied in production: it is therefore the private realm, where personal needs are traditionally met. Needs are real and deeply felt, but their social expression is shaped by rather than directly emergent from the economic realm. Among these needs is education, which is especially important for both hegemonic and counter-hegemonic activities. Also among them is the species reproduction process which Antonio Gramsci names but does not analyse.

Antonio Gramsci's omission of any sense of patriarchal hegemony from his analysis cannot be cured by simply putting women back in, any more than an increase in the number of women judges and lawyers will necessarily transform legal structures. The man in the Clapham omnibus does not change his perception of common sense simply because his wife sits speechlessly beside him. Still, the notion that the private realm is a source of transformative politics is provocative. Attempts to develop a materialist analysis of the private realm merely in terms of women's domestic labour are deeply problematic: they raise the question of women's double work load, but they evade the issue of male control of women's productive and reproductive labour and female sexuality.[56] In the understanding of most marxists, biological reproduction is "immaterial" in the philosophical sense, a sort of pre-historical phenomenon. There is a curious hysteria in male insistence that birth is immaterial on the grounds that it is historically ungrounded, of nature and not of culture.

To understand birth process as a material ground of human history we need to examine reproduction from the standpoint of women, a sense which demystifies the contradictions inherent in both reproduction and production.[57] This is to make the heretical claim that in a recognizable sense, women are materially different from men because their relation to reproduction is a relation of specifically female experience and knowledge. The birth of a child is labour, a mediative mode of labour which unifies the birth of each individual with the continuity of the species. It is not, as patriarchs believe, a philosophically irrelevant, ahistorical, and intellectually unchallenging event. It is on such an ideological basis that the fact that reproductive process is fundamentally and integratively social is ignored. We could, with a suitable environment, produce our personal survival all by ourselves, but we could not reproduce the species. The central contradiction of marxism is that it posits the productivity by which individuals survive as the universal dynamic of history, yet it reduces the universal reproduction of the species to brute biology. This accounts for the troublesome disappearance of individuals in marxist thought. Having a baby, according to patriarchal perceptions in general, is an act without significance, a non-transcendence of that biological world which patriarchy perceives as mindless enemy.

'hegemony' which the dominant group exercises throughout society." Gramsci, *Prison Notebooks*, 12.

56. See, for example, Bonnie Fox, editor, *Hidden in the Household* (Toronto: Women's Press, 1980); and MacKinnon, *Signs I* and *II*.

57. Mary O'Brien has constructed such an analysis. See Mary O'Brien, *The Politics of Reproduction* (London, Boston, Henley: Routledge and Kegan Paul, 1981).

Maternity is actually, of course, praxis — the unification of reproductive labour and reproductive consciousness — and thus an active mediation between individual and species, between culture and nature. Reproductive consciousness, however, is not rendered dialectically in terms of class struggle but in terms of gender struggle. Female reproductive consciousness is an integrative consciousness, linking the generations in continuity over time and linking people as equal values created by reproductive labour. It is a material and historical consciousness. Paternal consciousness, on the other hand, is abstract consciousness, essentially ideal. It is based on concept rather than on experience and on the particular mode of reasoning which relates cause and effect. It is also alienated consciousness, for the nature of men's participation in reproduction is problematic. The historical objectification of male reproductive consciousness is the separation of public and private life. The historical discovery of paternity, of which we know nothing, is nonetheless a discovery of the causal connection between sexuality and the birth process which is also for men an alienation from the act of birth.

Paternity is radical uncertainty, and the efforts to mediate this contradiction are writ boldly in the history of mankind. The premier mediation is clearly the family and forms of marriage which legitimate the appropriation of women's reproductive labour, embedded in women's children. Patriarchal society is imbued by the need for men to affirm continuity over time and species integration in historical praxis, of which the privatization of women and the appropriation of women and their children are vital parts, as is the transfer of continuity to political symbols such as the state itself. At the same time, the creation of the private realm is a limitation of men's freedom, which the public realm must be organized to reinstate, at least for selected men. The organization of consent is never without violence, but just as the state keeps its weapons sheathed as long as culture and ideology can be reproduced by legitimate means, so patriarchy hides its violence in the private realm. Patriarchy is publicly and privately violent, but the legitimation of these forms requires a different legal approach. In any case, if civil society is to become the locus of dissent and social transformation, this must entail struggles to revolutionize the social relations of reproduction as well as those of production. It must also involve a direct challenge to male consent to private and public violence.

VII

An understanding of law is extremely important in trying to work out the theoretical and political implications of a dialectical understanding of social relations. There are contradictions between production and reproduction as well as within these spheres. Consensus and social stability demand that both a particular mode of production and a particular organization of reproduction are generally accepted as right, good, and proper; in older times, one would have said that they must be in harmony with the essence of man. Feminist analyses reveal that the "essence of man" includes the exclusion of women from the public realm and control of women's reproductive function. This has persisted for a long time; the biological realities of reproduction have not changed radically since men discovered the problematics of paternity. They are changing now as technological innovation radically transforms birth process: whether this means more control or a new kind of mystification is still unclear. What is clear is that such a transformation is a world-historical event, and feminism itself is the expression of this radical transformation in dogmas of biological determinism, male supremacy, liberal equality, and the historical potency of class struggle.

In terms of the law itself, there is a clear inability to deal with these developments at the practical level. On the experiential level, neither consensual legitimacy nor creative legislation is developing to keep pace with issues related to contraception, technological reproduction, reproductive contracts, nor the development of appreciation for women's productive and reproductive labour. The increase in the number of females entering law school will not change this, for law school is an organized hegemonic institution in terms of political and familial conservatism. Further, the strategy of defining knowledge in the interests of an individual class and a universal gender requires an entirely new kind of theory and practice. What is developing is a social struggle to create consent to new perceptions of law in, for example, reproductive control. Law schools cannot stand forever aloof from these issues, and men in general will not be able to treat patriarchy as "objectively natural" rather than as hegemonically reproduced.

The understanding that law as an institution which mediates the separation between economic production and political authority is more useful than objective epistomologies of "positive" law, but neither ultimately helps us to understand why certain bodies of law are "hard" and others "soft." If we understand law as also mediating the dialectic of public and private life, this evaluative distinction begins to make sense, but still only from the standpoint of patriarchy, which values public over private life. We have noted the idealist core of male reproductive consciousness, and suggested that paternity is essentially an idea, a product of mind. Yet that does not tell us why the transfer of idea to practice has achieved such enduring consent to the concept of patriarchy. Our critique of law allows us to bring the idea of paternity into the world, for we discover that father is also a legal fiction, logically necessary for the historically constituted right for a man to claim legitimately the fruit of a particular woman's womb as his own — even in the absence of objective certainty. Knowledge of paternity is "hard" knowledge precisely because it is alienated from experience and has to be reconstituted culturally and symbolically, just as hard sciences translate concrete nature to abstract symbolization in the effort to control the natural world. Such activities are ideological representations of absence, the absence of certainty, the gap between "man" and nature. Thus paternity, a radical uncertainty, is constructed in the public realm, the realm of the certification of knowledge, as a social truth which legitimates the control of women's maternal certainty. The private realm is *privation and deprivation*. Separated from the public realm of rights, the private realm is the paradigm model of hegemonic depoliticization.

The failure to understand that the separation of public and private is not arbitrary but a testament to human ingenuity in dealing with the material anomolies of paternity is no doubt due to the remoteness of the historical discovery of paternity and the immediacy of the interests of patriarchal hegemony. If we look at the development of law and the difficulties that women experience personally and conceptually in accepting uncritically its propositions and in fulfilling the role of deference to authority and precedent, we find the claim to objectivity is problematic. If, however, we look at law as the cultural institution charged with the ideological and cultural reproduction of the separation of public and private, then it makes more sense. It makes sense, for example, of the hard and soft evaluative principle. (The phallic aspect we can leave to psychologists and semioticians.) Structurally, the characterization of hard and soft law emerges in legislation, law practice, and law school curriculum, and it is both representation and evaluation of public and private concerns.

One of the ironies of capitalist vocabulary is the insistence that capitalism embodies "private" enterprise. This is the "hard," public definition of private, related to the notions of "hard" cash and the proprietorship involved. Economics are the heart of productive hegemony: the recently developed school of law and economics is predictably fashionable and influential, for the economic realm is in trouble and the law is there to help. Hard stuff is factual, therefore one learns it: it is objectively there, and consent to its thereness is logical. The "soft" is epitomised by family law. Many women feel that they "choose" family law, seeing it as the area in which they can help women, and indeed they can and do. The analytical question, though, is whether they choose or whether they are systematically streamed in this direction: we must put this in the context of theories that women "choose not to work" — i.e., become wives and mothers — or that girls "choose" secretarial courses rather than science and math in schools. In other words, in making specialization choices, women may be making hegemonically constituted ideological rather than rational choices, which all adds up to further evidence of their "softness": "Lawyers come closer to the professional ideal if they avoid cases that demand extra-legal services... matrimonial and family law, legal aid work, custody work... women lawyers serve these needs well."[58] Family law practitioners have the same low status as prevails in medical hierarchies, though as the numbers of women in family law increase, it is likely that some kind of technical rank similar to that of nurses will be introduced to deal with them: family law practice is not especially lucrative.

Nonetheless, the simplistic notion that making choices in curriculum and practice is simply a matter of socialization in male supremacy and male values is not too useful. The relation of public and private is a dialectical relation, a locus of struggle. The notions of hard and soft are shorthand for this struggle, which encompasses the historical development of gender relations, the epistemological and theoretical positions embraced by patriarchy, and also, we would argue, considerations emanating from the dialectical nature of biological reproduction. This is a struggle between men and women for rights to children, for certainty, for the mediation of alienation. Above all, it is a struggle about freedom. The alienation of men from birth produces a double freedom: freedom

---

58. Cynthia Epstein, *Women in Law* (New York: Anchor Press, 1983), 110, 101, 146, 266.

from reproductive labour and freedom to claim or not to claim the child. Over against this, it forces men into social relations with other men to organize the cultural management and ideological defences of ungrounded patriarchy. Marriage is simply the most efficient historical structure to achieve these ends, but it is again a problematic one: in cancelling alienation it negates the double freedom of paternity, for fathers must enter in some sense the "soft" realm of the private with its absence of freedom.

This dilemma is recognized in law. Such activities as rape, prostitution, and pornographic trading among other things compensate men for the loss of freedom which the family entails.[59] The law therefore has problems saying whether laws related to these are public or private, hard or soft.[60] It has no such reservations in placing domestic contracts or family law, which impact on home and marriage in an immediate way. So while all law which deals with reproductive considerations is soft in terms of prestige and rewards, a distinction must be made between private and interstitial law. Both are concerned with women's related sexuality and progenitive power, but men tend to separate these in an ideological and hegemonic reflection of their own reproductive experience. Birth is a private realm event, but the "birth certificate" *naming* the child as the father's is a legal document. Males and females are, of course, both sexual creatures, yet different laws and cultural representations have developed for sexual expression/repression, particularly the madonna/whore dichotomy. Further, sexuality has been thoroughly commoditized and marketed as a liberatory package which is the modern opium of the people. Dehumanized sexuality may well be the nodal point at which the alienation inherent in production and reproduction meet, and there is nothing in legal history — realist or reconstructionist — which permits the interaction of soft and hard law demanded by such an ahuman conjuncture. This is the basis of confusions about pornography, which makes explicit the public legitimation of women's "permissible" sex in patriarchal society. At the same time, reproductive process (private) is colliding with technology (public) in the development of modes of control of conception. These are the historical bases of contemporary feminist concern to re-think and revolutionize the social relations of reproduction.

Feminism has, in this context, redefined revolution. Long thought of as a political, public activity defined by violence, revolution in feminist practice is developing as the first revolution to be initiated in the private realm, a revolution which specifically rejects violence — making it "soft," of course. But softness is also a *critical* deportment towards hardness, which may be why soft

---

59. Such "compensation," of course, does not constitute full explanation. When sexual domination and abuse of women have become eroticized, these activities also enhance male power individually and collectively and supply sexual satisfaction. See MacKinnon, *Signs II*.

60. Criminal laws prohibiting rape, physical assault and obscenity, for instance, are "public" law. However, the formal, "public law" codified marital rape exemption or the informal public policies curbing enforcement of the law are rationalized in the name of "private" (male) rights. Abortion law also reveals the problematics of categorization. In Canada specific public law legalizes abortion under narrow legislated grounds, but the decision to provide the statutorily permissible resources for legal abortions remains a *private* matter for public hospital boards; in the United States, the "right" to an abortion is based on constitutionally protected (i.e. public) privacy rights.

courses incite more opposition in law school than would be necessary if softness merely meant weakness.

Soft law is law about women promulgated and evaluated by men. Women are perceived as part of the natural world — which like men they are — but as women's connection with that world is mediated by reproductive labour, they do not experience themselves as alienated. Men's struggle with nature is an endless battle with mindlessness, random fecundity, and unpredictability against which they seek to exert control. Softness is an elusive foe, and the struggle is hard. Soft fertile earth becomes hard as "real estate" (a different, harder reality) and animal species which trouble soft conservationists become hard commodities in cattle markets and tanneries. Softness is not soft, but counter-hegemonic: existing in the world, it challenges hardness, creating a critical standpoint and ethical consciousness which resist hardness and undermines capitalist and patriarchal values. This counter-hegemonic reality is not soft but subversive, and it is this aspect which is concealed in the hegemonic process of devaluation, which tries to fit the hard and the soft into a simplistically hierarchical ideological framework.

VIII

All structuralist theories of history and society are in some sense science fictions, which attempt to claim objectivity such as that embedded in the legal fiction of certified patriarchy. They are ideological representations which spring from very real dualisms: of mind and body, nature and culture, father and child. Experience of dualism, of alienation, Karl Marx insisted, was not natural but historical, and could be resolved by unifying thought and action in revolutionary practice. Yet his analysis of alienation is impoverished by his limited doctrine of human necessity, the need to work to produce subsistence. The gap between men and nature is grounded in reproductive process and has been mediated by a war against nature in a search for control. This is the "hardness" which "man-in-general" encounters as existential necessity, as a form of consciousness opposing and condemning the "softness" of the integrative consciousness embedded in women's (hard) experience of species continuity. This opposition of alienation and integration, of hardness and softness, has material grounds in generic experience. Just as the relation of "natural" worker with his corporeal labour to "legal" owner with his deed of incorporation is antagonistic, so the relation of natural mother and legal father with his certified paternity is antagonistic. These are complex relations gilded with legitimations and fecund of ideologies.

The social organization and hegemonic function of law demonstrate the tensions within and between productive and reproductive relations, for the absence of mediation of these "gaps" in necessity in favour of a strategy of power and coercion leaves interstices in experience and thought. Laws are developed to deal with these. Between productive labour and the economic law of the state (to say nothing of the imaginary 'laws' of the market place) — in this gap emerge environmental concerns, workers' compensation, consumer protection. Unregulated, these might threaten capital accumulation. But also in this space we find other threats to capital: maternity leave, equal opportunity, garnishees on wages for child support which expose the fragility of father fictions. These bodies of law in the interstices of hegemonic state/economy are soft. In the interstices of coercive state and consensual civil society we find the peace movement challenging the profits of the armaments industry and the morality of the state and progressive social forces challenging the legitimacy of violence in defence of private property in the practice of the police. We also find the laws pertaining to domestic violence, rape, pornography, which are concerned with men's violence against women.

It is these "interstitial" issues which make visible the fact that the "gaps" are not gaps at all, but the social spaces in which the cultural and ideological hegemony of ruling class and ruling sex is worked out and struggled over in social practice. These are also the spaces in which law is soft for reasons which have to do with the ideologically induced vulnerability of a legitimation process which runs counter to the lived experience of all workers, and doubly so for women, who are oppressed at work and at home, in production and reproduction. It is therefore at least doubtful that women's subject and career choices in law are triumphs of patriarchal socialization. They may well be integrated with the specifically female relation to the natural world from which men are naturally excluded, "making sense" in a way which does not conform to patriarchal paradigms.

Feminist politics insists on the integration of public and private, claiming that the personal is political whether or not it is "legal." If the interstitial bodies of law mediating violence and family can be said to be soft in any rational sense, it is in the sense that they are "softly" enforced.

The economic issues which cross both capitalist and patriarchal interests are particularly vulnerable to the charge of softness and subsequent ideological definition as unworkable and impractical. Equal opportunity is the obvious example, but the weapons issues, the acid test of the rationality of international law, is equally germane. The two are related dialectically to the family and the (re)production of individuals on the one hand and the reproduction of the species on the other.

The involvement of many women in soft law, both in education and practice, is ultimately both rational and counter-hegemonic, grounded in the current stage of development of contradictions in and between state/economy/public on the one hand and sex/gender/private on the other. The social construction of paternity as a legal fiction resting on an abstract idea is a vital cog in the legitimation of and consent to the social forms of public and private power relations: it is this construction which leads from the soft status of natural father to the hard reality of legitimate patriarch, the ideological link which transforms alienated man to the socially constructed male parent who fractures the objective integration of women and species continuity by forcibly alienating women from public life. Patriarchy is the creation and ideological reproduction of historical, cultural, legal, and epistemological relations which men have developed to deal with their dualist relation with nature, with continuity and with species. The father is a legal fiction because his objectivity rests on the fact that he is generally but not particularly necessary to species continuity, logically necessary only to the social construction of uncertain paternity as the "objectively" legitimate source of patriarchal power.

Vol. 2 *1986* 95

Patriarchy is vulnerable because it is an ideological construct, a soft core in the hard historical process of objectification, legitimation, and the enforcement of consent.

The conditions of transformation of patriarchal power are the ability of women to take control of their reproductive capacity, a process only now and only in an ambivalent way made possible by technological development. It is for these reasons that the separation of public and private is breaking down, and women are increasingly and unevenly refusing consent to patriarchal hegemony. To do this is not anarchic; it is not the destruction of knowledge, but the assertion of a distinct and integrative body of knowledge — women's knowledge — which is seeping from the porous walls of the privatized household into the gaps that patriarchal interpretations of human experience have never been able to fill. This new phase of gender struggle is sufficiently wide to permit many kinds of practice, turning patriarchal paradigms upside down. As far as legal education is concerned, one hopes that women will stick it out, however harsh the personal costs, for the exposure of the dialectic of hard and soft law and the importance of soft law for the historical development of justice cannot be exaggerated.

[3]

Feminist Reason: Getting It and Losing It

Martha Minow

As white women ignore their built-in privilege of whiteness and define [woman] in terms of their own experience alone, then women of Color become "other," the outsider whose experience and tradition is too "alien" to comprehend.
— Audre Lorde[1]

Judges and lawyers in the contemporary legal system in the United States, like managers in other systems of knowledge and control, treat their own points of reference as natural and necessary. Judges' preoccupation with neutrality, for example, especially notable in constitutional and statutory equality jurisprudence, upholds existing institutional arrangements while shielding them from open competition with alternatives. Thus, the Supreme Court recently sustained as "neutral" a state law denying unemployment benefits to a woman out of work due to pregnancy despite a federal statute forbidding discrimination on the basis of pregnancy in state grants of unemployment benefits. The Court reasoned that the state denied the woman benefits under a rule that also denies benefits to others who leave their jobs for reasons unrelated to the employer. The state's rule thus "incidentally disqualifies pregnant or formerly pregnant claimants as part of a larger group."[2]

Feminists have shown how such assertions of neutrality hide from view the use of a male norm for measuring claims of discrimination. Adopting such feminist critiques can deepen the meaning of equality under law. I advocate developing similar feminist critiques in contexts beyond gender, such as religion, ethnicity, race, handicap, sexual preference, socioeconomic class, and age.[3] Yet attempts to advance feminist analyses in new contexts come up against unstated assumptions about other traits—assumptions embedded in prevailing feminist arguments. In critiques of the "male" point of view and in celebrations of the "female," feminists run the

Martha Minow is Professor of Law, Harvard University. This article was prepared for the Annual Meeting of the American Political Science Association Conference, September 1987. An expanded version of the argument appears in The Supreme Court, October 1986 Term, Foreword—Justice Engendered, 101 Harv. L. Rev. 10 (1987).

1. Audre Lorde, Age, Race, Class, and Sex: Women Redefining Difference, *in* Sister Outsider 114, 117 (Trumansburg, N.Y., 1984).
2. Wimberly v. Labor and Indus. Relations Comm'n of Missouri, 107 S. Ct. 821, 825 (1987). This decision received far less attention than the Court's decision a week earlier upholding California's statutory requirement of unpaid pregnancy disability leaves with a qualified right to reinstatement. California Fed. Savings and Loan Ass'n v. Guerra, 107 S. Ct. 683 (1987), which I discuss *infra* text accompanying notes 43–48.
3. See Martha Minow, The Supreme Court 1986 Term—Foreword: Justice Engendered, 101 Harv. L. Rev. 10, 11–12 (1987).

risk of treating particular experiences as universal and ignoring differences of racial, class, religious, ethnic, national, and other situated experiences.

Thus, feminist analyses have often presumed that a white, middle-class, heterosexual, Christian, and able-bodied person is the norm behind "women's" experience. Anything else must be specified, pointed out. This set of assumptions recreates the problem feminists seek to address—the adoption of unstated reference points that hide from view a preferred position and shield it from challenge by other plausible alternatives. These assumptions also reveal the common tendency to treat differences as essential, rather than socially constructed, and to treat one's own perspective as truth, rather than as one of many possible points of view.

Feminism has contributed to the campaign that challenges the convergence between knowledge and power. Feminists question assertions of knowledge that owe their effectiveness to the power wielded by those making the assertions. Some feminists, however, assert as reality claims that hide the power of those doing the claiming. This essay thus pursues the perpetual critique initiated by feminist work while also searching, as feminists do, for practical justice, not just more theory.

I. Insights

Feminists have contributed incisive critiques of the unstated assumptions behind political theory, law, bureaucracy, science, and social science that presuppose the universality of a particular reference point or standpoint.[4] In field after field of human thought, feminist work exposes the dominance of conceptions of human nature that take men as the reference point and treat women as "other," "different," "deviant," or "exceptional."[5] Male psychology, feminist theorists argue, is the source in a male-dominated society of conceptions of rational thought that favor abstraction over particularity and mind over body. Similarly, the assumption of autonomous individualism behind American law, economic and political theory, and bureaucratic practices rests on a picture of public and independent man rather than private—and often dependent, or interconnected—woman.[6] The norms and the dynamics of the natural world—the way its biological, evolutionary, and even chemical and physical properties are explained— embody unstated male reference points.

---

4. See, e.g., Simone de Beauvoir, The Second Sex (New York, 1952); Carol Gilligan, In a Different Voice: Psychological Theory and Women's Development (Cambridge, Mass., 1982); Kathy E. Ferguson, The Feminist Case Against Bureaucracy (Philadelphia, 1984); Nancy C. M. Hartsock, Money, Sex, and Power: Toward a Feminist Historical Materialism (New York, 1983, 1985); Alison M. Jaggar, Feminist Politics and Human Nature (Totowa, N.J., 1983); Evelyn F. Keller, Reflections on Gender and Science (New Haven, 1985); Catharine MacKinnon, Feminism, Marxism, Method, and the State: An Agenda for Theory, 7 Signs 515 (1982), and Feminism, Marxism, Method, and the State: Toward Feminist Jurisprudence, 8 Signs 635 (1983); Jean Baker Miller, Toward a New Psychology of Women (Boston, 1976); Susan Moller Okin, Women in Western Political Thought (Princeton, N.J., 1979). I draw on these works in the following summary.
5. Or "baffling." See, e.g., Gilligan, *supra* note 4 (discussing Freud).
6. In addition to the sources cited *supra* note 4, see Frances Olsen, The Family and the Market, 96 Harv. L. Rev. 1497 (1983); Mary Joe Frug, Re-Reading Contracts: A Feminist Analysis of a Contracts Casebook, 34 Am. U. L. Rev. 1065 (1985).

Feminist work confronts the power of naming and challenges both the use of male measures and the assumption that women fail by them.[7] If, at times, feminists appear contradictory, arguing both for the right of women to be included and treated like men and for the right to have special treatment (which valorizes women's differences), feminists have an explanation. The inconsistency lies in a world and set of symbolic constructs that have simultaneously used men as the norm and denigrated any departure from the norm. Thus, feminism demands the dual strategy of challenging the assumptions that women are too different from the unstated male norm to enjoy male privileges and that women's differences actually justify denial of privileges or benefits.[8] For over a century now, feminists have claimed that distinctive aspects of women's experiences and perspectives offer resources for constructing more representative, more empathic, more creative, and, in general, better theories, laws, and social practices.[9]

II. New Claims, Old Risks

As many feminist theorists are beginning to recognize, our critique runs the great risk of creating a new standpoint that is equally in danger of projecting the experience of some as though it were universal.[10] By urging

7. A similar approach animates the development of labeling theory and challenges to stigmatizing labels. See Martha Minow, When Difference Has Its Home: Group Homes for the Mentally Retarded, Equal Protection, and Legal Treatment of Difference, 22 Harv. C.R.-C.L. L. Rev. 111 (1987) (discussing labeling theory and its use by law reformers).

8. Frances Olsen, The Sex of Law (unpublished manuscript); Martha Minow, Rights of One's Own (Book Review), 98 Harv. L. Rev. 1084 (1985) (reviewing Elisabeth Griffith, In Her Own Right: The Life of Elizabeth Cady Stanton (1984)) (showing how Stanton argued both that women are the same as men and that women are better than men). See also Jaggar, *supra* note 4, at 147 (the need to transform everything); Heather Wishik, To Question Everything: The Inquiries of Feminist Jurisprudence, 1 Berkeley Women's L. J. 64 (1985) (feminist inquiries have to cultivate paradox and question everything).

9. See Introduction, *in* Discovering Reality: Feminist Perspectives on Epistemology, Metaphysics, Methodology, and Philosophy of Science, ed. Sandra Harding & Merrill B. Hintikka, x (Boston, 1983); Gilligan, *supra* note 4; Keller, *supra* note 4; Miller, *supra* note 4; Mary Beard, The Legislative Influence of Unenfranchised Women, Annals, Nov. 1914, at 54, *reprinted in* Mary Ritter Beard: A Sourcebook, ed. Ann J. Lane 89 (New York, 1977); William Leach, True Love and Perfect Union: The Feminist Reform of Sex and Society (New York, 1980).

10. Audre Lorde puts it this way: "By and large within the women's movement today, white women focus upon their oppression as women and ignore differences of race, sexual preference, class and age. There is a pretense to a homogeneity of experience covered by the word [sisterhood] that does not in fact exist." Lorde, *supra* note 1, at 116. See also bell hooks, Ain't I a Woman: Black Women and Feminism 194–195 (Boston, 1981) (white females bring racism to feminism); Barbara Omolade, Black Women and Feminism, *in* The Future of Difference, ed. Hester Eisenstein & Alice Jardine, 247, 255 (New York, 1980) (black experience needed in feminism for black women to pursue dialogue with white feminists); Iris Marion Young, Social Movements, Difference and Social Policy, presented at Feminist Moral, Political and Legal Theory, 56 U. Cin. L. Rev. 535 (1987) (discussions of difference within women's movement mirror puzzles generated by assertion of difference in all oppressed social movements). Sandra Harding states her view of the problem: "[T]he feminist standpoint epistemologies appear committed to trying to tell the 'one true story' about ourselves and the world around us that the postmodernist epistemologies regard as a dangerous fiction." Sandra G. Harding, The Science Question in Feminism 195 (Ithaca, N.Y., 1986). See Gloria I. Joseph & Jill Lewis, Common Differences: Conflicts in Black and White Feminist perspectives (New York, 1982); Home Girls: A Black Feminist Anthology, ed. Barbara

the corrective of women's perspective, or even a feminist standpoint, feminists may jeopardize our challenge to simplifications, essentialism, and stereotypes.

Many feminists acknowledge that women fall into every category of race, religion, class, and ethnicity, and vary in sexual preference, handicapping conditions, and other sources of assigned difference.[11] Any claim to speak from women's point of view, or to use women as a reference point, threatens to obscure this multiplicity by representing a particular view as the view of all.[12] Some have expressly argued that sexism is more fundamental than racism.[13] This claim is disturbing because it suggests not just that feminists may fail to take account of other forms of oppression or domination beyond sexism[14] but that they may fail to take account of women's own experiences in all their variety.[15] Elizabeth V. Spelman persuasively argues that we ought to be "skeptical about any account of gender relations which fails to mention race and class or consider the possible effects of race and class differences on gender: for in a world in which there is racism and classicism, obscuring the workings of race and class are likely to involve—whether intentionally or not—obscuring the workings of racism and classism."[16] Focusing on the same danger, Nancy Fraser and Linda Nicholsen conclude that there is neither one "feminist method" nor one feminist epistemology, "since women's oppression is not homogenous in content, and since it is not determined by one root,

Smith (New York, 1983); With Wings: An Anthology of Literature By and About Women with Disabilities, ed. Marsha Saxton & Florence Howe (New York, 1987).

11. Other obvious differences among women include language, nationality, age, height, appearance. Consider also politics. See, e.g., Kristin Luker, Abortion and the Politics of Motherhood 127–46 (Berkeley, Calif., 1983) (comparing backgrounds and outlooks of prolife and prochoice activists).

12. This poses a special dilemma for feminism, which has celebrated "women's experience" as the touchstone for a new source of authority. If this authority speaks only for the individual, not for the group of women, how can it counter the predominant structures of societal authority? Barbara Johnson describes the dilemma that ensues in discussions of feminist pedagogy: "[I]t would be impossible to deny that female experience has been undervalidated. On the other hand, the moment one assumes one knows what female experience is, one runs the risk of creating another reductive appropriate—an appropriate that consists in the reduction of experiences as self-resistance." Barbara Johnson, A World of Difference 46 (Baltimore, 1987).

13. See Richard Wasserstrom, Racism, Sexism and Preferential Treatment: An Approach to the Topics, 24 UCLA L. Rev. 581, 581–615 (1977); Lawrence Thomas, Sexism and Racism, Some Conceptual Differences 90 Ethics 239 (1980).

14. Consider Elizabeth Cady Stanton's opposition to black male suffrage if white women could not have it. Elisabeth Griffith, In Her Own Right: The Life of Elizabeth Cady Stanton 123–43 (New York, 1984).

15. In his recent dissenting opinion, opposing the use of a voluntary affirmative action plan to assist the job chances for women and minority men, Justice Scalia maintains that such plans will injure the relatively powerless, who, like the white male plaintiff, are "predominantly unknown, unaffluent, unorganized," and "least likely to have profited from societal discrimination in the past." Johnson v. Transportation Agency, 55 U.S.L.W. 4379, 4396 (U.S. March 24, 1987) (Scalia, J. dissenting). Although he demonstrates his ability to identify with white ethnics like himself, Justice Scalia seems to forget that women too can be white ethnics. They, too, are unlikely to have benefited from societal discrimination in the past or from organized reform efforts in the present.

16. Elizabeth V. Spelman, Inessential Woman: Problems of Exclusion in Feminist Thought (Boston: Beacon Press, forthcoming) (chapter on Chodorow).

underlying cause."[17] Audre Lorde puts it powerfully: "Some problems we share as women, some we do not. You fear your children will grow up to join the patriarchy and testify against you, we fear our children will be dragged from a car and shot down the street, and you will turn your backs upon the reasons they are dying."[18]

III. Why Do We Make the Mistake We Identify in Others?

Such critiques of feminism are internal, voiced by feminists, admonishing feminists. In a sense, the method of consciousness-raising—personal reporting of experience in communal settings to explore what has not been said—enables a practice of self-criticism among feminists even about feminism itself.[19] Yet why, when it comes to our own arguments and activities, do feminists forget the very insights that animate feminist initiatives, insights about the power of unstated reference points and points of view, the privileged position of the status quo, and the pretense that a particular is the universal?

Perhaps our own insights elude us because of our attraction to simplifying categories, our own psychodynamic development, our unconscious attachment to stereotypes, and our participation in a culture in which contests over power include contests over what version of reality prevails.[20] We are afraid of being overwhelmed, which is what full acknowledgment of all people's differences may portend. Cognitively, we need simplifying categories, and the unifying category of "woman" helps to organize experience, even at the cost of denying some of it.[21] Ideas that defy neat

17. Nancy Fraser & Linda Nicholson, Social Criticism Without Philosophy: An Encounter Between Feminism and Postmodernism, forthcoming *in* The Institution of Philosophy: A Discipline in Crisis? ed. Avner Cohen & Marcelo Descal (Totowa, N.J., 1988). Fraser and Nicholson nonetheless conclude that feminism can continue to mean something: a commitment to actual diversity, and a complex, multilayered feminist solidarity. See also Harding, *supra* note 10, at 194 ("By giving up the goal of telling 'one true story,' we embrace instead the permanent partiality of feminist inquiry").

18. Lorde, *supra* note 1, at 119. And, "As a black lesbian feminist comfortable with the many different ingredients of my identity, and a woman committed to racial and sexual freedom from oppression, I find I am constantly being encouraged to pluck out some one aspect of myself and present this as the meaningful whole, eclipsing or denying the other parts of self. But this is a destructive and fragmenting way to live." *Id.*

19. See Elizabeth Schneider, The Dialectic of Rights and Politics: Perspectives from the Women's Movement, 61 N.Y.U. L. Rev. 589 (1986) (consciousness-raising as critical element of feminist legal practice as well as feminist legal theory). See also Gloria Steinem, Foreword, *in* Building Feminist Theory: Essays from Quest, xi, xii (New York, 1981) (heart of feminism is participation on your own behalf).

20. See Minow, *supra* note 3, in which I draw especially on work by William James, Felix Cohen, George Lakoff, Ludwig Wittgenstein, Nancy Chodorow, D. W. Winnicott, Ernest Becker, Charles Lawrence, Sanford Gilman, Erving Goffman, Stephen Jay Gould, Karl Mannheim, E. P. Thompson, Steven Lukes, and Barbara Christian.

21. George Lakoff suggests that this simplifying process works even in our development of unstated prototypes that give form to seemingly general linguistic categories. We discover the prototype when we use adjectives to modify the general category, adjectives that reveal the unstated norm. For example, the term "working mother" modifies the general category "mother," revealing that the general term carries an unstated assumption of the norm (a woman who cares for her children full time without pay); if the normal meaning is not intended, it must be explicitly modified. George Lakoff, Women, Fire, and Dangerous Things 80–81 (Chicago, 1987). The politicization of this very example, through arguments such as "every mother is a working mother," challenges

categories are difficult to hold on to, even though the idea itself is about the tyranny of categories.[22] We especially attach ourselves to such categories as male/female because of our own psychological development in a culture that has made gender matter, and our own early constructions of personal identity forged in relationship to parents who made gender matter.[23]

Feminist activities themselves also reveal relationships between knowledge and power. Feminists are no more free than others from the stereotypes in cultural thought.[24] White feminists may well carry unconscious stereotypes about people of color, and similar stereotypes may divide women of different religions, political persuasions, abilities and disabilities, and sexual preferences.[25] Some stereotypes may be an unconscious cultural inheritance, but they also may be clues to who has power to define agendas and priorities within feminist communities.[26] Ignoring differences among women may permit the relatively more privileged women to claim identification with all discrimination against women while also claiming special authority to speak for women unlike themselves.[27]

Finally, we share the version of reality that has for the most part prevailed in the entire culture. Not only does this instill conceptions of difference and stereotypic thinking, it also gives us internal scripts about how to argue, and indeed, how to know. The dominant culture has established certain criteria for theories, for legal arguments, for scientific proofs—for authoritative discourse. These established criteria are the

   the unstated prototype and also challenges its replacement by another unstated prototype. This essay, in a sense, seeks to challenge the unstated prototype behind feminism.

22. See Carn Kaplan, Deterritorializations: The Writing of Home and Exile in Western Feminist Discourse, Cultural Critique 187 (Spring 1987) (goal is to make a world of possibilities out of the experience of displacement). This point currently occupies debates among literary theorists who fear the routinization of deconstruction. See, e.g., Johnson, *supra* note 12.

23. This is the insight advanced by Nancy Chodorow's work. See Nancy Chodorow, The Reproduction of Mothering (Berkeley, Calif., 1978), and Mothering, Male Dominance, and Capitalism, *in* Capitalist Patriarchy and the Case for Socialist Feminism, ed. Zillah R. Eisenstein, 83 (New York, 1979). Chodorow underplays, however, the significance of early formation of racial, religious, and national identities, which are layered into the psychodynamic process of individuation with perhaps as much power as gender identities.

24. See Adrienne Rich, Blood, Bread, and Poetry 230 (New York, 1986); Elizabeth Spelman, Theories of Race & Gender: The Erasure of Black Women, 5 Quest 36, no. 4 (1982); Michael Omni & Howard Winant, By the Rivers of Babylon: Race in the United States: Part One, 13 The Socialist Rev. 31 (September-October 1983).

25. Majority and minority women may each have stereotypes of one another, but the majority's stereotypes of the minorities carry more power to implement the exclusion and control that stereotypes imply.

26. It may be a characteristic of white privilege to deny difference among women because admitting difference would mean overcoming stereotypes and giving up power, not through the mere tokenism of letting some women of color in but by actually giving up control over the definition of priorities. Audre Lorde attributes this phenomenon to white women's opportunities and temptations to share some of white men's power. Lorde, *supra* note 1, at 118. Emphasizing gender rather than other sources of difference and oppression may actually be a tool of social control.

27. "It is because white middle-class women have something at stake in not having their racial and class identity be made and kept visible that we may find it useful to raise some delicate questions about any theory of gender identity which reinforces the invisibility of race and class." Spelman, *supra* note 16 (on Chodorow); see also *id.* at ch. 4 (discussion of Simone de Beauvoir).

governing rules. If we want to be heard—indeed, if we want to make a difference in existing arenas of power—we must acknowledge and adapt to them, even though they confine what we have to say or implicate us in the patterns we claim to resist.[28]

IV. The Example of Pregnancy

The Supreme Court's treatment of issues concerning pregnancy and the workplace highlights the power of the unstated male norm in analyses of problems of difference. In 1975, the Court accepted an argument based on a male norm in striking down a Utah statute that disqualified a woman from receiving unemployment compensation for twelve weeks before the expected date of childbirth and for six weeks after childbirth, even if her reasons for leaving work were unrelated to the pregnancy.[29] Although the capacity to become pregnant is a difference between women and men, this fact does not justify treating women and men differently on matters unrelated to the pregnancy. That is, if men are used as the norm, any woman who can perform like a man should be treated like a man. A woman cannot be denied unemployment compensation for different reasons than a man would be.

What happens, though, to the woman's difference—the occasion of pregnancy? May the fact of this difference justify different treatment? What is equal treatment for the woman who is correctly identified, not stereotyped, and who differs from nonpregnant persons in ways that are relevant to the workplace? It was on this issue that the reliance on the male norm reached such a notorious result in the Supreme Court, twisting the meaning of sex discrimination to use male experience to measure discrimination against women. The Court considered, both as a statutory and a constitutional question, whether discrimination in health insurance plans on the basis of pregnancy amounted to discrimination on the basis of sex. In both instances, the Court answered negatively because pregnancy marks a division between the groups of pregnant and nonpregnant persons, and women fall in both categories.[30] Only from a point of view that treats pregnancy as a strange occasion, rather than a present, bodily potential, would its relationship to female experience be made so tenuous; and only from a vantage point that treats men as the norm would the exclusion of pregnancy from health insurance coverage seem unproblematic and free from forbidden gender discrimination.[31]

28. Forms of scholarship, such as law review articles, impose conventions of constraint, which some have begun to challenge—at the peril of being disregarded as irrelevant or unassimilable. See, e.g., Derrick Bell, The Supreme Court, 1984 Term, Foreward: The Civil Rights Chronicles, 99 Harv. L. Rev. 4 (1985); Duncan Kennedy & Peter Gabel, Roll Over Beethoven, 36 Stan. L. Rev. 1 (1984).

29. Turner v. Dep't of Employment Sec. of Utah, 423 U.S. 44 (1975) (decided on due process grounds).

30. Geduldig v. Aiello, 417 U.S. 484, 496–97 n.20 (1974) (equal protection); General Electric Co. v. Gilbert, 429 U.S. 125, 136–40 (1976) (Title VII).

31. Congress amended Title VII, in the Pregnancy Discrimination Act, to make clear that Congress intended to include within the span of illicit sex discrimination any discrimination on the basis of pregnancy. See 42 U.S.C. § 2000e(k) (1982).

With judicial decisions such as these, litigators working for women's rights have discovered that unless we fit our claims into existing doctrines, we are unlikely to be understood, much less to succeed.[32] Yet trying to fit women's experiences into categories forged with men in mind reinstates gender differences by treating the male standard as unproblematic. Feminist attacks on the problem face a double risk. Either we reinvest unstated male norms with legitimacy by trying to extend them to women, or we criticize those norms and posit a new, female norm that may be insensitive to the variety of women's experiences. A critique of the Supreme Court's decisions in *Geduldig* and *Gilbert*, for instance, runs the risk of positing a new essential female experience to counter the Court's conclusion that pregnancy is not sufficiently related to the female experience to count as a basis for sex discrimination. The Court was correct in noting that not all women at all times are pregnant. Indeed, some women will never become pregnant, and some who already have will never again. The medical, social, and psychological meanings of pregnancy vary by individual, and so do needs for medical and other treatment. Further, some women may argue that excluding health benefits for pregnancy is far less burdensome to them than denying them work leaves to care for a dependent parent, or restricting health benefits to the primary worker and spouse and excluding other intimate household members. Reformers approaching the issues of pregnancy and the workplace and seeking both litigation and legislation to establish women's right to pregnancy benefits and leaves may merely carve a new norm that produces new exclusions.

Political and legal reactions to past victories pose the real danger that legal decisions may grow worse for women and minority men. We are more likely than ever to attempt to frame conventional arguments that can succeed in the courts and legislatures, both of which enshrine convention. Arguments that women are just like men—and deserve to be treated like men—reappear when legal and political authorities reject arguments that mainstream institutions should be revamped to include women's experiences.

When formerly excluded groups such as women want to be recognized or represented in mainstream, established institutions, our own efforts at reform become most vulnerable to the version of reality that has in the past excluded us.[33] We risk becoming tokens, and taking our meanings and

32. Inventive lawyering remakes old categories to capture women's experience, as in the use of discrimination doctrine to recognize the harm of sexual harassment. See Catharine A. MacKinnon, Sexual Harassment of Working Women (New Haven, 1979).

33. Iris Marion Young calls this the risk of assimilation: "[T]he strategy of assimilation aims to bring formerly excluded groups into the mainstream. So assimilation always implies coming in the game after it is already begun, after the rules and standards have already been set, and having to prove oneself according to those rules and standards." Iris Marion Young, Social Movements, Difference and Social Policy, 56 U. Cin. L. Rev. 535 (1987). If self-identity depends on recognition by others with the power to accord recognition, the problem is pervasive. Avoiding participation in elite institutions does not afford escape from prevailing versions of reality that make assigned differences seem actual, inherited categories powerful, and assertions of essences necessary for authoritative knowledge. These are risks for those who want validation, any validation. A challenge, over the long haul, is to choose whose validation you want, for that may be as critical as choosing whom you want to become.

Feminist Reason 55

identities from those who have let us in.[34]

A similar problem arises in the production of knowledge. In established academic institutions, what has counted as theory meets criteria of coherence, value neutrality, and abstraction that themselves may embody the false universalism that feminists criticize. Yet to be counted by establishment institutions as theory, feminist approaches must resemble the objects of their attack.[35] This may be why Jane Flax notes that "We cannot re-vision the world with the tools we have been given."[36] We risk becoming embroiled in what we critique, entranced by what we would demystify.[37]

The problem is a familiar one—criticism's preoccupation with the subject of the criticism. When the subject of criticism is authoritativeness, the critic faces the special dilemma of how to claim authority while rejecting its usual forms of subduing and vanquishing others.[38] Feminists, no less than anyone else, and perhaps more than people who have felt at home in the prevailing conceptions of reality, want something to hang on to, some sense of the validity of our own perceptions and experience, some certainty—not more experiences of doubt.[39] Yet, each form of certainty

34. A similar problem may arise even when a "minority" group creates its own organization to speak and wield influence in established arenas. See Arif Dirlik, Culturalism as Hegemonic Ideology and Liberating Practice, 6 Cultural Critique 13, 48 (Spring 1987) ("To the extent that intellectuals of the Third World become part of [a Third World establishment], with its own language and its own organizationally defined goals, they too are alienated from the constituencies in whose name they speak . . . radical opposition to hegemony has been undercut by the incorporation of opposition into a new hegemonic structure of power").

35. See Jaggar, *supra* note 4, at 355–57; see Gilligan, *supra* note 4 (discussing empiricism).

36. Jane Flax, Mother-Daughter Relationships, *in* Eisenstein & Jardine, *supra* note 10, at 20, 38.

37. Giles B. Gunn, The Culture of Criticism and the Criticism of Culture 196 (New York, 1987) (advocating a postmodernism that "seeks to salvage the experience of otherness from the putative forms of its expression by submitting those forms to ever more searching scrutiny in the hope that, through the dislocations and deconstructions of inquiry itself one may discover their element of indecipherability, of incorrigibility, of alterity"). Note how unfortunately inaccessible this thought is—not much to hang on to, even in its attentiveness to the risks of most of what we hang on to.

38. See Josephine Donovan, Feminist Theory 180–81 (New York, 1985) (discussing Wittgenstein's critique in the Tractatus of a scientific and internally consistent world view that "prevents access to other kinds of knowledge, or of beings and reality that do not fit into the Newtonian world scheme." A critique of this view must embrace mystery, and "any sense of meaning must come not from subduing the world intellectually with abstract forms but from turning into that vast, marginal silence that exists beyond the scope of the Newtonian paradigm." This may seem frightening, like many features of modernism and postmodernism. See Jacques Barzun, A Stroll With William James 180–226 (New York, 1983) (discussing developments in science and culture in their struggle for order amid challenges to the old order); Edward A. Purcell, The Crisis of Democratic Theory 47–94 (Lexington, Ky., 1973) (discussing the impact of relativity and indeterminacy theory in physics on politics and law).

39. Compare Marge Piercy, Woman on the Edge of Time (New York, 1976) (women had to give up their one source of power—interuterine reproduction—in order to end hierarchical power) with Benjamin N. Cardozo, The Nature of the Judicial Process 166 (New Haven, 1921) ("I was much troubled in spirit, in my first years upon the bench, to find how trackless was the ocean on which I had embarked. I sought for certainty. I was oppressed and disheartened when I found that the quest for it was futile. I was trying to reach land, the solid land of fixed and settled rules, the paradise of a justice that would declare itself by tokens plainer and more commanding than its place and glimmering reflections in my own vacillating mind and conscience . . . As the years have gone by, and as I have reflected more and more upon the nature of the judicial process, I have

hazards a new arrogance, projecting oneself, one's own experience, or one's own kind as the model for all.[40]

Thus, feminists make the mistake we identify in others—the tendency to treat our own perspective as the single truth—because we share the cultural assumptions about what counts as knowledge, what prevails as a claim, and what kinds of intellectual order we need to make sense of the world. Like the systems of politics, law, and empiricism feminists criticize for enthroning an unstated male norm, feminist critiques tend to establish a new norm that also seeks to fix experience and deny its multiplicity.[41]

V. A Pointed Effort to See Points of View

No new principle or rule can solve the problem: challenging the hidden privileging of one perspective privileges another in its place. Instead we need a stance, one that helps us accept complexity but not passivity. As people who judge others and who face the judgments of others, we should challenge any ready assignment of "difference" that seems to allocate benefits or burdens as though the results were natural rather than chosen. This means doubting words and concepts that we take for granted, and looking to the consequences when we do use them. A useful strategy is to pay attention to competing perspectives on a given problem, and to challenge unstated points of view that hide their assumptions from open competition with others. In sum, we need to pay attention to what we give up as well as what we embrace.[42]

Rather than creating a new female norm for use in claiming equality, I suggest that we contest the ready association of sameness with equality and difference with inferiority. Similarly, we could take challenges to differential treatment as occasions to assess not difference but treatment, not individual and group traits but social arrangements that make those traits seem to matter.

Again, let us take pregnancy and the workplace as an example. Although tortured in its framework and controverted in its results, the Supreme Court's 1987 decision in *California Federal Savings and Loan Association v. Guerra*,[43] represents an effort to remake an apparent issue of neutrality toward gender differences in the workplace into an issue of neutrality toward gender differences in the conjunction between work and family. In so doing, the Court—and the legislatures whose enactments the Court construed—converted the difference question into a challenge to prevailing social arrangements that had made a gender difference significant. I will

become reconciled to the uncertainty, because I have grown to see it as inevitable. I have grown to see that the process in its highest reaches is not discovery, but creation . . .").
40. Cf. William James, What Makes A Life Significant, *in* On Some of Life's Ideals 49, 65 (New York, 1900) ("always the ancestral blindness returns and wraps us up").
41. In short, feminist work risks the danger of a new certainty, and the danger of certainty "is that it turns against the generous impulse to open oneself up to the other, and truly listen, to risk, the chance that we might be wrong." Drucilla Cornell, The Poststructuralist Challenge to the Ideal of Community, 8 Cardozo L. Rev. 989, 1018 (1987). Is there a different approach?
42. See Martha Nussbaum, The Fragility of Goodness 30–31 (Cambridge, England, 1986).
43. 107 S. Ct. 683 (1987).

explain and defend the Court's decision but also suggest alternative locutions to avoid the Court's contortions in the future.

Before the initiation of the *Cal. Fed.* lawsuit, Lillian Garland asserted protection under a state statute requiring employers to provide employees with an unpaid pregnancy disability leave of up to four months. The state commission had construed the state law to establish a qualified right to reinstatement in the job after the leave. While her case was pending with the state commission, Garland's employer, California Federal Savings and Loan Association, joined with others to seek a declaration from federal court that the state statute was inconsistent with and therefore preempted by Title VII's prohibition against discrimination on the basis of sex. The case thus put directly at issue the meaning of the Pregnancy Discrimination Act of 1978, the Congressional rejoinder to the Supreme Court's refusal to treat pregnancy discrimination as a violation of Title VII.[44] Triggering debates that fractured the Court and the women's rights community, the suit questioned whether the federal ban against discrimination on the basis of pregnancy allows treating pregnant workers like other workers, or instead allows special treatment. Thus framed, the problem treats men as the norm and presumes a workplace designed for men or for people who never become pregnant. Any effort to remake the workplace to accommodate pregnancy would be "special treatment" and would not be neutral with regard to the workplace. Yet a ban against such accommodation, focused on pregnancy, leaves in place the male norm that makes women and pregnancy seem "different."

The majority for the Court understood this and construed the statute to permit employers to remove barriers in the workplace that had disadvantaged pregnant people compared with others.[45] Most important, Justice Marshall's opinion for the Court shifted from the comparison between men and women in the workplace to a comparison of men and women in the conjunction of their workplace and family lives. "By 'taking pregnancy into account,' California's pregnancy disability leave statute allows women, as well as men, to have families without losing jobs."[46]

The majority's second rationale—that the state and federal laws are compatible because employers may comply with both by providing comparable reinstatement benefits to men and women following leaves for reasons such as pregnancy—uses women's experience as the benchmark.[47] The Court called for equal treatment of men and women and permitted the state's elected representatives to determine the minimum threshold level for such treatment. By allowing this legislative alteration of the employers'

---

44. 42 U.S.C. § 2000e(k) (1982). See discussion of Gilbert, *supra* text accompanying note 30.
45. See 107 S. Ct. at 694.
46. *Id.*
47. That this solution will impose costs on employers—costs that will undoubtedly be shifted to nonpregnant workers—should not be denied. But neither should this consequence be misunderstood: the costs of *failing* to accommodate pregnant workers—along with perhaps less calculable costs from underemploying women—are also borne by employers and shifted to individuals, partially adjusted by the social welfare system. To the extent that pregnant women have shouldered the costs of a workplace that has not accommodated them, the legislation requiring accommodation marks a decision not to create new costs but to spread existing costs more widely.

obligation to workers, the Court unmasked the employers' effort to rely on the federal law for what it was—an attempt to implant the male norm as the reference for workplace equality.[48] Although the task of asserting the permissible significance of gender-linked characteristics remains, the Court successfully resisted the role of reinstating social arrangements that had made gender difference at the workplace significant.

How can the *Cal. Fed.* decision be reconciled with the Court's decision in *Wimberly* one week later to permit a state to refuse benefits to a woman unemployed because of her pregnancy, despite a federal law banning discrimination because of pregnancy in unemployment benefits?[49] On one level, the cases are perfectly compatible. In both instances, the Court read federal antidiscrimination requirements to permit states legislative latitude to set minimum benefit levels at any chosen point, so long as pregnancy was not singled out as the basis for granting or withholding benefits.[50] On another level, however, the cases diverge significantly. Unlike *Cal. Fed.*, in which the Court used a guarantee against pregnancy discrimination to establish the pregnant person as the point of comparison, in *Wimberly* the Court superimposed a neutral nondiscrimination demand on a workplace world and a state statute that were modeled without pregnancy in mind.[51] The Court in *Wimberly* treated the federal equality statute as a neutrality requirement, although the baseline social arrangements are not neutral about the consequences of gender and/or class differences. But in *Cal. Fed.* the Court treated a federal equality statute as a requirement to eliminate obvious discrimination against women and to guard against new discriminations against men not by keeping women's lot small but by improving men's lot as well.

As if to demonstrate that the Court knows how to move beyond pretended neutrality to guard against discrimination even in the context of unemployment benefits involved in *Wimberly*, at just about the same time the Court required accommodation of an individual's religious beliefs in making unemployment benefits available. In *Hobbie v. Unemployment Appeals Commission v. Florida*,[52] the Court concluded that the Free Exercise Clause forbids denial of unemployment-compensation benefits to a woman discharged when she refused because of her sincerely-held religious beliefs to work certain scheduled hours.[53] The Court reached this conclusion despite

48. Thus, although my analysis focuses on tasks for Courts, it applies also to legislatures. For instance, in their efforts to remake social arrangements so that attributions of difference are disentangled from assignments of burdens and benefits, how much room should legislatures be given?

49. See *supra* note 2 and accompanying text.

50. This reading follows the second rationale in the *Cal. Fed.* majority opinion, which rejects the challenge to the state statute on the ground that employers could comply with the federal antidiscrimination requirement by providing comparable benefits to non-pregnant persons as well.

51. *Wimberly*, 107 S. Ct. 821, 825 (1987). "[I]f a State adopts a neutral rule that incidentally disqualifies pregnant or formerly pregnant claimants as part of a larger group, the neutral application of that rule cannot readily be characterized as a decision made 'solely on the basis of pregnancy.'"

52. 107 S. Ct. 1046 (1987).

53. The employer had argued that Hobbie's refusal to work during her religious Sabbath amounted to misconduct and rendered her ineligible for benefits under a statute

the even more explicit—and Constitutional—demand for neutrality in the context of religion. For the Court also concluded that the award of benefits under these circumstances—accommodating an individual's religious beliefs—does not violate the Establishment Clause.[54]

What the Court did in *Cal. Fed.* and in *Hobbie* was to pay attention to what is lost when power reinforces a version of reality that coincides with dominant social arrangements. The standard analysis would compare alternate perspectives to the unstated norm encased in the dominant social relations and then ask whether exclusion of the "different" perspectives contravenes a legal commitment to equality.[55] In these cases, in contrast, the Court took seriously versions of reality at odds with the structure of social arrangements: the perspectives of pregnant women and of religious individuals whose needs are not embedded in the rules of employers and the laws governing unemployment benefits. At the same time, the Court construed the federal obligations to permit state experimentation and judicial obligations to allow legislative initiative with an important limitation. Existing social arrangements are no more privileged or immune from challenge than any competing arrangement when confronting allegations of burdens based on a personal or group difference.

Discussing legal disputes in terms of how existing social arrangements appear in light of competing minority and majority perspectives would have the advantage of exposing initial answers to the same scrutiny. An explicit inquiry into these matters would help guard against the risk that new answers might reestablish a preference for one point of view disguised as the necessary and natural arrangement. The California employers may well face new claims that benefits comparable to the qualified reinstatement guarantee following pregnancy leave include a variety of reinstatement conditions not just for men but also for women facing short-term leave demands for reasons other than pregnancy.[56]

Feminist insights into the power of unstated norms demand just this perpetual reconsideration of the point of view buried within social arrangements and in critiques of them, the point of view that makes some

limiting compensation to persons who become "unemployed through no fault of their own." *Id.* at 1048. The Court rejected this attribution of fault to Hobbie and reasoned instead that the employer caused the conflict between work and belief by refusing to accommodate her religious practices.

54. *Id.* at 1049, 1051.
55. *Hobbie* involved the First Amendment's religious clauses and yet also presented a critical equality claim: Did this individual suffer unlawful discrimination, differential treatment, because of her religious beliefs? I believe that greater efforts to borrow across fields and reason by analogy would advance especially the jurisprudence of equality. Because different people are situated differently in relation to questions of difference and equality, they may perceive instances of discrimination in one context they would miss in another. "[N]either the whole of truth nor the whole of good is revealed to any single observer, although each observer gains a partial superiority of insight from the peculiar position in which he stands." William James, On a Certain Blindness in Human Beings, *in* James, *supra* note 40, at 3, 46. We could all learn, then, about the varieties of discrimination from the partial superiority of our own different sympathies.
56. See *supra* p. 54 for discussion of arguments for dependency leaves and for leaves that do not presuppose traditional nuclear family forms.

Feminist Legal Theory II

Journal of Legal Education

differences matter and others irrelevant.[57] Otherwise, outsiders who become insiders simply define new groups as "other."[58] Taking the point of view of people labeled "different" is one way to move beyond current difficulties in treating differences as real and consequential. Generating vivid details about points of view excluded from or marginalized by particular institutions is another. Seeking out and promoting participation by voices typically unheard are also crucial if equality jurisprudence is to mean more than enshrining the point of view of those sitting on the bench. The concerted and persistent search for excluded points of view and the acceptance of their challenges are equally critical to feminist theory and practice. Otherwise, feminists will join the ranks of reformers who have failed to do more than impose their own point of view.[59]

The more powerful we are, the less able we are to see how our own perspective and the current structure of our world coincide. That is just one of our privileges. Another is that we can put and hear questions without questioning ourselves. The more marginal we feel, the more likely we are to glimpse a contrast between other people's perceptions of reality and our own. Yet we still may slip into the world view of the more powerful because their view is more apt to be validated and because we often would like to be like them. It is hard to hang on to these insights because we prefer to have our perceptions validated; we need to feel acknowledged and confirmed. But when we fail to take the perspective of another, we deny just that acknowledgment and confirmation in return.

---

57. See Ann Scales, The Emergence of Feminist Jurisprudence: An Essay, 95 Yale L.J. 1373, 1378 (1986) ("So goes the process of objectification: the winner is he who makes his world seem necessary.").

58. See Holly Near & Adrian Torf, Unity, a song recorded on Speed of Light (Redwood Records, 1982) ("One man fights the KKK/ But he hates the queers/ One woman works for ecology/ It's equal rights she fears;/ Some folks know that war is hell/ But they put down the blind/ I think there must be a common ground/ But it's mighty hard to find.").

59. See Jaggar, *supra* note 4, at 386: "A representation of reality from the standpoint of women must draw on the variety of all women's experience. In order to do this, a way must be found in which all groups of women can participate in building theory"; Iris Marion Young, Impartiality and the Civic Public: Some Implications of Feminist Critiques of Moral and Political Theory, 5 Praxis International 381 (1986) (transcendent perspective is a myth; instead we must cultivate and search out multiple perspectives on public issues).

[4]

The "Woman's Point of View"

Deborah L. Rhode

For many women, the request for the "woman's point of view" provokes an ambivalent response. On one level, it is an improvement over all those circumstances and all those years in which no one thought to ask and no one was available to respond. On another level, the request, which often proceeds from feminist sympathies, risks perpetuating attitudes at odds with feminist commitments. What follows are a few cautionary remarks on the issue of perspective, on the implications of "woman's point of view" for legal, social, and feminist theory.

I.

One reason for ambivalence on the subject stems from its historical legacy. For most of American history, emphasis on women's distinctive perspective has worked against women's distinctive interests. An obvious example involves the legal profession's traditional response to female entrants. What is perhaps most striking about this response is the utter lack of self-consciousness with which exclusively male decision makers have coped with challenges to male exclusivity.

Although women occasionally acted as attorneys during the Colonial period, the formalization of entry standards during the post-Revolutionary period prevented further participation.[1] Despite the laxity of screening procedures during the Jacksonian era, females and felons remained two groups subject to categorical exclusions.[2] The reasons for resistance to women entrants varied, but what bears emphasis is the presumed difference in the sexes' capacity for legal work. In the view of many nineteenth-century jurists, the "Law of the Creator" decreed that women's nature was to nurture.[3] Divine inspiration revealed that domesticity was destiny; the "peculiar qualities of womanhood, its gentle graces, its quick sensibility, its tender susceptibility," were not qualities for "forensic strife".[4]

Deborah L. Rhode is Professor of Law and Director of the Institute for Research on Women and Gender, Stanford University. The author gratefully acknowledges the advice and encouragement of Barbara A. Babcock, Herma Hill Kay, Carrie Menkel-Meadow, Martha Minow, and Austin Sarat.

1. See Ada M. Bittenbender, Woman in Law, *in* Woman's Work in America, ed. Annie Nathan Meyer, 220–21 (New York, 1891); Sophie Drinker, Women Attorneys of Colonial Times, 56 Md. Hist. Soc. Bull. 461 (1961).
2. Deborah L. Rhode, Moral Character as a Professional Credential, 94 Yale L.J. 491 (1985). See sources cited *infra* note 5.
3. Bradwell v. State, 83 U.S. (16 Wall.) 130, 141–42 (1872) (Bradley, J., concurring).
4. *In re* Motion to Admit Goodell, 39 Wis. 232, 245 (1875). For other cases, see Albie Sachs & Joan Hoff Wilson, Sexism and the Law 4–66 (New York, 1978).

Long after women gained formal admission to the bar, many educators, employers, and bar associations continued to resist the "clack of . . . possible Portias."[5] The stated concerns were manifold, ranging from the risks of unchaperoned intellectual intercourse in libraries to the seemingly insurmountable difficulties of constructing separate lavatory facilities.[6] At least some of the resistance, however, rested on women's presumed intellectual incapacity and emotional instability. A prevailing assumption was that females were less adept at "thinking like a lawyer," whatever exactly that meant. Such attitudes were plainly apparent in hiring, promotion, and academic policies. Leading law schools, law firms, and law associations excluded women entirely or relegated them to subordinate roles. In many classrooms, the "female point of view" was welcome only on special "ladies' days" or on special issues (e.g., hypotheticals involving domestic skills or sexual relationships).[7] Employers similarly restricted women practitioners to specialties in which their nurturing qualities were thought particularly appropriate (e.g., family and estate work) and in which their status, financial compensation, and professional influence were likely to remain limited.[8] Minority women were doubly disadvantaged and significantly underrepresented at all professional levels.[9]

This is familiar history. However, as the companion pieces in this symposium and in other collections reflect, more subtle forms of bias remain. Although the last decade has witnessed substantial improvement in the demographic and cultural landscape of the profession, the rhetoric of gender equality does not yet match the reality of women's experience.

II.

Against this historical backdrop, contemporary discussions of the "woman's point of view" mark an important advance. The phrase has taken on new meanings that reflect broader changes in the landscape of the law and in other disciplines from which it draws. Feminist perspectives are helping to reshape not only legal doctrine and legal education but also their deeper intellectual foundations. Over the last two decades, the number of courses

---

5. Janette Barnes, Women and Entrance to the Legal Profession, 23 J. of Legal Educ. 276, 283 (1970) (quoting Irene L. Dulin, The Progress of Women in the Law, 4 J. Mo. Bar 163, 164 (1948)). See generally, Karen Berger Morello, The Invisible Bar: The Woman Lawyer in America 1638 to the Present (New York, 1986); Robert Stevens, Law School: Legal Education in America from the 1850s to the 1980s (Chapel Hill, N.C., 1983); Kathleen E. Lazarou, "Fettered Portias": Obstacles Facing Nineteenth-Century Women Lawyers, 64 Women Law. J. 21 (1978).

6. Lazarou, *supra* note 5; Cynthia Fuchs Epstein, Woman's Place 185 (Berkeley, Calif., 1970). See Stevens, *supra* note 5, at 82; Cynthia Fuchs Epstein, Women in Law 61, 66–67 (New York, 1981).

7. Epstein, Women in Law, *supra* note 6, at 65–67; Helene E. Schwartz, Lawyering 85 (New York, 1976).

8. See Epstein, Women in Law, *supra* note 6, at 101–111; James J. White, Women in the Law, 65 Mich. L. Rev. 1051, 1057 (1967); Deborah L. Rhode, Perspectives on Professional Women, 40 Stan. L. Rev. (1988) (forthcoming).

9. See generally Geraldine R. Segal, Blacks in the Law: Philadelphia and the Nation (Philadelphia, 1983); Julienne Malveaux, No Images: The Labor Market Status of Black Women (unpublished manuscript); Kellis E. Parker and Betty J. Stebman, Legal Education for Blacks, 407 Annals 144 (1973).

in women's studies has grown from a few hundred to well over 30,000, and related scholarship has increased at a comparable pace.[10] The result has been not only to increase knowledge about women's experience but also to challenge what counts as knowledge. Informed by other developments in critical social theory, feminist scholarship has drawn attention to the biases of traditional paradigms and to the way that data has been constructed, not simply collected. Together with other activists from the contemporary women's movement, feminist academics have helped to alter the categories and consequences of legal decision making. While much remains to be done, the increasing influence of "woman's point of view" has advanced our thinking about the premises and processes of the law. It should not in any sense detract from that achievement to raise certain concerns about its future direction. The concerns are not unique to law, but because they have not been aired as fully in legal arenas as in other contexts, a few general observations bear emphasis, first about "woman" and second about "point of view."

Over the last century, American feminists have centered theoretical and political attention on issues related to differences between men and women. Over the last decade, feminists have increasingly realized the importance of focusing also on differences among women. A crucial contribution of recent theory has been its emphasis on diversity of race, class, age, ethnicity, and sexual orientation.[11] Requests for "the woman's perspective" tend to obscure that diversity, and risk perpetuating a homogenized view of women's identity and a reductive analysis of women's interests. Such requests point up a central paradox for contemporary feminism. Much of the theoretical and political force of the feminist movement stems from its aspiration to identify values and perspectives that grow out of women's distinctive experience. Yet one of the critical lessons of that experience is its diversity, which demands attention to differences as well as commonalities.

Requests for a single and singular "point of view" raise related difficulties. To assume that feminism offers one theoretical stance is to miss a central point of recent feminist theory. Drawing on postmodernist analysis, contemporary feminists stress the inability of any single overarching framework, including a feminist one, to provide an adequate account of social experience. Theoretical approaches claiming such adequacy have often proved too broad and abstract to explain particular ideological, material, and historical relationships. Alternatively, such approaches have been too grounded in specifics to yield generalizable insights and illumine larger cultural patterns. These limitations have encouraged feminists not to renounce theory but rather to emphasize the need for theories—for multiple accounts from multiple disciplines at multiple levels that will avoid

10. Marilyn J. Boxer, For and About Women: The Theory and Practice of Women's Studies in the United States, 7 Signs 601 (1982).
11. See, e.g., Audre Lorde, Sister Outsider (Trumansburg, N.Y., 1984); Gloria I. Joseph & Jill Lewis, Common Differences: Conflicts in Black and White Feminist Perspectives (New York, 1981); Heidi Hartmann, The Unhappy Marriage of Marxism and Feminism: Towards a More Progressive Union, *in* Women and Revolution, ed. Lydia Sargent, 1 (Boston, 1981).

privileging any single methodological approach.[12]

Yet the importance of such diversity is too often obscured by the popularization of one strand of contemporary feminist research. This strand encompasses a range of methodologies and perspectives that do not coexist peacefully under any single label. For present purposes, however, it makes sense to borrow the generic term "relational feminism," which stresses the importance of relationships in explaining attributes historically linked with women. Theorists such as Nancy Chodorow, Dorothy Dinnerstein, Jean Bethke Elshtain, Carol Gilligan, Susan Griffin, Alice Rossi, and Sarah Ruddick all emphasize certain caretaking traits and values predominantly associated with women.[13] Despite the diversity among such scholars, their work is often presented as emblematic of the "woman's point of view."

The usefulness of relational feminism for legal analysis has been explored at length elsewhere and need not be rehearsed here. Most important, this body of work insists that values associated with women *be valued* and stresses the need for altering existing structures, not just assimilating women within them. It also provides theoretical foundations for legal reforms necessary to accommodate caretaking interests.[14] Yet the contributions of this scholarly framework have not come without cost, particularly given the unqualified way such perspectives have often emerged in contemporary legal and popular publications.

The problem stems partly from limitations in the theories themselves. An obvious example involves Carol Gilligan's *In a Different Voice*, which, of all relational work, has attracted the greatest following in legal circles. Drawing from psychological theory and empirical research on moral reasoning, Gilligan argues that women are more likely than men to use a "different voice," i.e., a voice unlike the one that prominent theorists have generally associated with the highest stage of ethical development. In Gilligan's terms, this different, predominantly female voice stresses concrete responsibilities and relationships rather than abstract principles of rights and justice. For purposes of legal analysis, her conclusion is that

---

12. See Jane Flax, Postmodernism and Gender Relations in Feminist Theory, 12 Signs 621 (1987); Sandra Harding, The Instability of the Analytic Categories of Feminist Theory, 11 Signs 645 (1986); Deborah L. Rhode, Gender and Jurisprudence: An Agenda for Research, 56 U. Cin. L. Rev. 521 (1987).

13. For discussion of the term "relational feminism," see Karen Offen, Defining Feminism; A Comparative Historical Perspective, 13 Signs (1988) (forthcoming). Prominent works emphasizing relationships include Nancy Chodorow, The Reproduction of Mothering: Psychoanalysis and the Sociology of Gender (Berkeley, Calif., 1978); Dorothy Dinnerstein, The Mermaid and the Minotaur (New York, 1976); Jean Bethke Elshtain, Feminism, Family, and Community, 29 Dissent 442 (1982); Susan Griffin, Woman and Nature: The Roaring Inside Her (New York, 1978); Carol Gilligan, In a Different Voice (Cambridge, Mass., 1982); Alice S. Rossi, A Biosocial Perspective on Parenting, Daedalus, Spring 1977, at 1; Sarah Ruddick, Maternal Thinking, 6 Feminist Stud. 342 (1980).

14. See, e.g., Kenneth L. Karst, Woman's Constitution, 1984 Duke L.J. 447; Herma Kay, Equality and Difference: The Case of Pregnancy, 1 Berkeley Women's L.J. 1 (1985); Sylvia Law, Rethinking Sex and the Constitution, 132 U. Pa. L. Rev. 955 (1984); Christine Littleton, Reconsidering Sexual Equality, 74 Calif. L. Rev. 1279 (1987); Carrie Menkel-Meadow, Portia in a Different Voice, 1 Berkeley Women's L.J. 39 (1985), Review, 1983 Am. B. Found. Res. J. 189 (reviewing Cynthia Fuchs Epstein, Women in Law (1981)), and remarks in Feminist Discourse, Moral Values, and the Law—A Conversation, 34 Buffalo L. Rev. 11 (1985) [hereinafter Feminist Discourse].

conventional approaches place excessive weight on rights rather than relationships.[15]

Like other relational work, Gilligan's makes important contributions. However, it also requires qualifications that are too often overlooked. In part, the difficulties are methodological, and stem from her work's inattention to differences in women's experiences across culture, class, race, ethnicity, and so forth. Related limitations involve the lack of focus on historical, social, and economic forces that mediate these experiences. Such limitations assume greater significance in light of a substantial body of other research that casts doubt on how different the different voice really is. For example, a review of some sixty recent empirical studies involving moral reasoning finds that most reveal no significant gender differences.[16] So too, much contemporary research on leadership styles and political values discloses less substantial variations between men and women than relational theory would suggest.[17]

In any event, the most critical issue is not empirical or methodological but normative. The extent to which women and men exhibit different values or reasoning styles is far less important than the consequences of stressing such differences in particular contexts. In assessing those consequences, a number of concerns require attention. On a theoretical level, an emphasis on difference risks oversimplifying and overclaiming. Males' association with abstract rationality and females' with interpersonal nurturing reflects longstanding dichotomies that have restricted opportunities for both sexes. The celebration of women's maternal instincts by some relational feminists bears striking resemblance to the assertions of antifeminists over the last several centuries. The claim that women's liberation does not lie in "formalistic" equality but in "the recognition of that specific thing in the feminine personality—the vocation of a woman to become a mother" reflects the phrasing of Pope Paul VI, but it could as readily be drawn from work of the New Right or the feminist left.[18]

These different constituencies do, of course, offer different explanations and draw different political conclusions from their points of common

15. Gilligan, *supra* note 13.
16. Catharine G. Greeno & Eleanor E. Maccoby, How Different Is the "Different Voice"? 11 Signs 310, 312 (1986). See also James C. Walker, In a Diffident Voice: Cryptoseparatist Analysis of Female Moral Development, 50 Soc. Res. 665 (1983); Lawrence Walker, Sex Differences in the Development of Moral Reasoning; A Critical Review, 55 Child Dev. 667 (1984); and Carol Stack, The Culture of Gender (unpublished manuscript, 1987).
17. See sources discussed in Linda D. Molm, Gender, Power and Legitimation: A Test of Three Theories, 91 Am. J. Soc. 1356 (1986); Barbara J. Florisha, The Inside and the Outsider: Women in Organizations, *in* Outsiders on the Inside: Women and Organizations, ed. Barbara L. Forisha & Barbara H. Goldman 22 (Englewood Cliffs, N.J., 1981); Rosabeth Moss Kanter, The Impact of Hierarchical Structures on the Work Behavior of Women and Men, *in* Women and Work: Problems and Perspectives, ed. Rachel Kahn-Hut, Arlene Kaplan Daniels & Richard Colvard, 234, 236–45 (New York, 1982). For discussion of voting behavior, see, e.g., Robert S. Erickson, Norman R. Luttbeg & Kent L. Tedin, American Public Opinion: Its Origins, Content and Impact 186–87 (New York, 1980); Jane S. Jaquette, Introduction, *in* Women in Politics, ed. Jane E. Jacquette, xiii–xxii (New York, 1974).
18. Pope Paul VI, *quoted in* Mary Daly, Beyond God the Father: Toward a Philosophy of Women's Liberation 3 (Boston, 1973).

emphasis. At least some relational feminists, however, including those with leftist backgrounds, advocate women's retention of primary caretaking roles or emphasize the physiological roots of caretaking capacities.[19] Yet much of this work obscures the extent to which ostensibly female characteristics are socially constructed and constrained. Sex-linked traits and values are profoundly affected by forces that are culturally contingent, not biologically determined. If women do sometimes speak in a different voice, it may be one that is more ascribed than intrinsic.

It is, moreover, a voice that speaks in more than one register. Missing from many relational accounts, particularly in popular and legal circles, is any attention to the dark side of difference, to the less benign aspects of women's caretaking roles and values. Mother-child relationships can involve physical abuse and psychological impairment as well as care and commitment. In addition, women's disproportionate family responsibilities may encourage forms of dependence, sex-role socialization, and parochialism that carry heavy costs.[20] Yet the tendency in too much relational work has been to ignore the downside of difference or assume that its negative aspects will vanish automatically as structures of subordination erode.

That tendency is understandable. Much of what is theoretically and politically empowering about relational feminism comes from its insistence on the positive attributes of women's experience. But that emphasis carries a price, one that escalates when rhetoric outruns experience. Certain strands of relationalism present the same risk of overclaiming that marred the suffrage campaign. Just as some late nineteenth- and early twentieth-century activists claimed that woman's involvement would purify politics, some contemporary theorists have assumed that her participation will of itself totally reshape the structure and substance of public decision making.[21] That assumption is problematic on several levels. It finesses the difficult question of how "woman's voice" will attain such influence. And it ignores the possibility that what will be reshaped is the voice rather than the context in which it is heard. An add-woman-and-stir approach does not of itself ensure transformation of the existing social order.

From a legal perspective, the simple dichotomies between rights and responsibilities that emerge in some relational feminist work present further difficulties. Rights can impose responsibilities and responsibilities can imply rights. Often the concepts serve identical ends; i.e., a right to freedom from intentional discrimination imposes a responsibility not to engage in it. The converse is also true, and privileging one form of discourse over the other is unlikely to reshape the foundations of American law. Our problems stem less from jurisprudential focus than from an absence of effective strategies for accommodating the needs of independence and interdependence.

19. Elshtain, *supra* note 13; Germaine Greer, Sex and Destiny: The Politics of Human Fertility (New York, 1984); Rossi, *supra* note 13.
20. See comments of Catharine A. MacKinnon in Feminist Discourse, *supra* note 14; Chodorow, *supra* note 13.
21. The History of Woman Suffrage, ed. Susan B. Anthony & Ida Husted Harper, 39 (Indianapolis, Ind., 1902).

III.

The "woman's point of view" can play an important role in developing such strategies, but not if it is equated with some single theoretical stance or perspective. In certain contexts the risks of such reductionism are especially acute. A common example involves circumstances in which females remain significantly underrepresented, and those in positions of power are more concerned about remedying the appearance than the fact of underrepresentation. In such settings, the request for a "woman's perspective" is best understood as a request for a woman. It just looks unseemly to leave half the race absent from committees, councils, conferences, boards, panels, etc. And it looks equally unseemly, and indeed ungrateful, for the chosen woman to decline, no matter how belated the invitation, how far removed from her interests or expertise, or how overcommitted her schedule. After all, such requests are clearly preferable to the traditional alternative. As Barbara Babcock once noted, when asked how she felt about being appointed an assistant attorney general because she was a woman: "It's better than not being appointed because I'm a woman." Those should not be the only alternatives.

Not all attempts to broaden representation fall into the "oh my God we've got to have a woman" category. Many requests stem from the well-meant desire for more inclusive perspectives. But in too many circumstances, the real desire is not for a female, let alone feminist, participant, but for an honorary male, for someone who is too acculturated, assimilated, or simply polite to draw attention to her gender or to the selection processes that make gender so apparent. The additional irony is that, in such contexts, it is women who end up feeling uncomfortable, rather than the men whose prior decisions have contributed to that discomfort. Under these circumstances, any response is on some level unsatisfying; token participation risks legitimating a selection process that is anything but legitimate, while exclusion risks perpetuating the patterns that perpetuate exclusivity.

Similar conflicts arise when the request is for a point of view, but the motive springs more from intellectual voyeurism than intellectual curiosity. A representative illustration is the academic who is well versed in political and jurisprudential theory but is unacquainted with feminist work and would like a five-minute summary over lunch. The subtle or not so subtle implication is that he has heard "you girls think differently," and he is interested in knowing a little about why. And a little is what he has in mind. Bibliographic suggestions will not suffice. A condensed version is what he is after, and again it is something of a no-win situation. A little knowledge is a dangerous thing, but the alternative is hardly better. To offer some reductive account that will be interpreted as *the* feminist perspective does violence to feminist premises. But it does not advance feminist politics to pass up opportunities to arouse curiosity. After all, sometimes one thing does lead to another.

A variation on this theme emerges when somewhat more knowledgeable colleagues become hell-bent on new footnote fodder. The problem comes if they are interested less in feminism than in feminist chic, i.e., in *the* latest intellectual fashions. The most obvious example involves individuals who want to keep up with what is being read by the "in crowd," not because they intend to read it but because they are intent on citing it. All too often the end product has a disturbingly *deus ex machina* flavor. Women's "different voice" arrives just in time to supply whatever dimensions the author finds important and undervalued in contemporary legal discourse. These dimensions could often just as easily be associated with humanism, socialism, or critical legal theory. The feminism comes largely in the footnotes, in the choice of citations. Instead of famous dead Europeans, these colleagues often want obscure living feminists, and the request for sources often comes attached with a request for a brief overview of the works suggested; e.g., one-sentence wrap-ups of the positions of Hélène Cixous, Luce Irigaray, and Julia Kristeva and their relevance for modern legal theory.[22] Usually this is all needed by yesterday. And frequently the request comes from colleagues who are most sympathetic in principle but least committed in practice to feminist premises. Once again. the situation is not lacking in irony, particularly when the scholarly emphasis on relational values emerges from an individual who often ignores them in collegial relations.

If these sketches have a familiar resonance, it is perhaps because few of us, least of all this author, are entirely free of such patterns in our own interactions with members of underrepresented groups. To break these patterns, we need to acknowledge the importance of "the woman's (or minority's) point of view" without homogenizing or essentializing its content. When a request comes for that perspective, we must offer a response, but not in the form the invitation assumes. The opportunity to provide a point of view is an opportunity to challenge the assumption that any single stance can adequately capture the diversity of our experiences and interests. Only by entering the debate about "women's views" can we challenge the terms on which it has traditionally proceeded.

---

22. If it is possible to escape with bibliographic suggestions, two options are New French Feminisms, ed. Elaine Marks & Isabelle de Courtivron (New York, 1980), and Toril Moi, Sexual/Textual Politics: Feminist Literary Theory (London, 1985).

Constitutional Law

Part II
Basic Law Courses
and
Feminist Legal Theory

[5]

Towards a Theory of Underclass Review

Olga Popov[*]

Traditional equal protection analysis accords heightened scrutiny to statutes that either discriminate on the basis of a suspect classification or burden the exercise of a fundamental right.[1] In *Democracy and Distrust*, Professor John Hart Ely gives content to these somewhat indeterminate phrases by formulating a "representation-reinforcing"[2] theory of equal protection review which regards the courts as a means of correcting malfunctions in the political process. According to Ely, a suspect class is a "discrete and insular minority" that is "barred from the pluralist's bazaar, and thus keeps finding itself on the wrong end of the legislature's classifications, for reasons that in some sense are discreditable."[3] In Ely's view, strict scrutiny of a state action that discriminates against such a group allows courts to smoke out unconstitutional motivations which may have materially influenced the legislature's decision.[4] Fundamental rights, according to Ely, include only those rights that directly affect an individual's ability to protect her interests in the political process, such as the right to vote and the right to travel, the latter of which allows her to move away from incompatible majorities to a place where her political voice is more likely to be heard.[5]

Ely's theory offers an elegant, rational system for resolving the tensions implicit in the countermajoritarian judicial review process.[6] It offers a guide

---

[*] Third-year student, Stanford Law School. I would like to thank Professor John Hart Ely for his generous encouragement and criticism, and Professors Barbara Fried and Mark Kelman for their helpful comments on an earlier draft.

1. San Antonio Indep. School Dist. v. Rodriguez, 411 U.S. 1, 17 (1973).

2. JOHN HART ELY, DEMOCRACY AND DISTRUST: A THEORY OF JUDICIAL REVIEW 87 (1980).

3. *Id.* at 152. Ely's suspect classification analysis in particular, and his participation-oriented theory of judicial review generally, are an elaboration of Justice Stone's famous "Footnote Four," in the *Carolene Products* case, which suggests that heightened judicial scrutiny might be appropriate where "legislation restricts those political processes which can ordinarily be expected to bring about repeal of undesirable legislation." Justice Stone added that

> prejudice against discrete and insular minorities may be a special condition, which tends seriously to curtail the operation of those political processes ordinarily to be relied upon to protect minorities, and which may call for a correspondingly more searching judicial inquiry.

United States v. Carolene Prods. Co., 304 U.S. 144, 152 n.4 (1938), *cited in* J.H. ELY, *supra* note 2, at 75-76. See *id.* at 75-77 and 151-53 for Ely's discussion of the relationship between his theory and the *Carolene Products* footnote.

4. J.H. ELY, *supra* note 2, at 138, 146.

5. *Id.* at 178-79.

6. Judicial review is countermajoritarian when a court invalidates a statute: "a body that is not elected or otherwise politically responsible in any significant way is telling the people's elected representatives that they cannot govern as they'd like." *Id.* at 4-5. According to Ely, this is "the central function, and it is at the same time the central problem, of judicial review." *Id.* at 4.

for interpretation which both responds to the underlying purpose of the Equal Protection Clause and imposes rational limits on judicial discretion. However, Ely's scheme leaves some significant gaps where it seems that the Equal Protection Clause ought to provide protection.

For example, Ely does not believe that laws which discriminate against women warrant heightened scrutiny. Women, he argues, are neither a "discrete and insular" group nor a minority, as they have extensive, close contact with men and constitute a majority of the voting population.[7] Therefore, he argues that there is no reason to conclude that women are unable to protect themselves through the political process and hence no reason to apply heightened judicial scrutiny to legislative action which disadvantages them. Ely recognizes that "there remains something that seems right in the claim that women have been operating at an unfair disadvantage in the political process, though it's tricky pinning down just what gives rise to that intuition."[8] He considers various arguments attempting to identify that disadvantage, but ultimately declines to accept them as "constitutionally relevant."[9]

Also, Ely does not regard procreative freedom as a fundamental right for equal protection purposes and therefore does not believe courts should apply heightened scrutiny to laws abridging a woman's right to an abortion.[10] It seems plausible to argue that forcing a woman to carry her pregnancy to full term interferes with her meaningful political participation,[11] and that guaranteeing a right to reproductive choice is therefore essential to ensuring such participation. That same argument, however, could be applied to a wide variety of other preconditions to effective political participation (e.g., adequate food, shelter, clothing) which Ely's model does not protect, probably because to do so would grant courts extremely broad discretion and involve them in projects they may not be qualified to undertake, such as determining

---

7. *Id.* at 164.

8. *Id.*

9. *Id.* at 165. Ely considers two major arguments that women operate at an unfair disadvantage in the political process. First, he acknowledges that because voters typically elect candidates rather than vote on single issues, the fact that women elect candidates who do not repeal gender-based legislation "may mean only that there are other issues about which they feel more strongly." However, he continues, to accept that as an argument that women are unfairly disadvantaged "changes the rules. Once we start to shift from a focus on whether something is blocking the opportunity to correct the stereotype reflected in the legislation, to one that attempts to explain why those who have that opportunity have chosen to pursue other goals instead, we begin to lose our way." *Id.* at 164-65. Second, he considers the possibility that "our society, including the women in it, has been so pervasively dominated by men that women quite understandably have accepted men's stereotypes, of women as well as on other subjects." *Id.* at 165. Although Ely concedes that this idea has some merit, he somewhat summarily dismisses it as inapplicable to "the situation of women in America in 1980." *Id.* at 165-66; *see* note 72 *infra*.

10. Ely has argued that the "super-protected right" identified by the Court in Roe v. Wade, 410 U.S. 113 (1973), "is not inferable from the language of the Constitution, the framers' thinking respecting the specific problem in issue, any general value derivable from the provisions they included, or the nation's governmental structure." John Hart Ely, *The Wages of Crying Wolf: A Comment on* Roe v. Wade, 82 YALE L.J. 920, 935-36 (1973); *see also* J.H. ELY, *supra* note 2, at 248 n.52 (asserting that *Roe* cannot be justified "in process terms").

11. *See* note 122 *infra* and accompanying text.

how much food and what kind of shelter would enable an individual to participate meaningfully in the political process.[12]

Still other laws that would be subject to strict scrutiny under Ely's model might nevertheless pass such scrutiny on the grounds that they further a compelling state interest. For example, although Ely does not consider the right to express oneself sexually to be a fundamental right,[13] he does classify homosexuals as a discrete and insular minority, and consequently he would subject laws against homosexual sodomy to strict scrutiny.[14] Yet, it is still possible that, under Ely's model, such laws would be upheld if a court considered the prevention of homosexual sodomy to be a legitimate and compelling state interest.

It seems to me that the Equal Protection Clause should do more than Ely says it should. Although it is hard to disagree with Ely's argument that women are not a discrete and insular minority when it comes to electoral politics, I share Ely's intuition that there is "something that seems right in

---

12. Others have argued, however, that Ely's theory, properly interpreted, mandates affirmative government provision of minimum welfare rights as preconditions to effective political participation. *See, e.g.,* Frank I. Michelman, *Welfare Rights in a Constitutional Democracy,* 1979 WASH. U.L.Q. 659. Michelman argues that "inequalities of resources and statuses, especially insofar as visibly correlated with salient group identification, almost certainly constitute a fundamental condition and cause of systematic bias in the functioning of majoritarian political institutions." *Id.* at 675. The "relationships between political efficacy and group socioeconomic status" underlie Michelman's argument for "identifying welfare rights as among those transtextual rights that ought to be judicially recognized as representation-reinforcing privileges or immunities, or as the negatives of representation-defeating inequalities, under Ely's quasi-interpretivist view of the fourteenth amendment." *Id.* at 675-76.

Michelman recognizes that broad application of his approach would leave the representation-reinforcement criterion "virtually boundless." *Id.* at 677. However, he believes that it is possible—and constitutionally required—for courts to identify a class of minimum welfare rights which constitute "the universal, rock-bottom prerequisites of effective participation in democratic representation," such as "life itself, health and vigor, presentable attire . . . [and] shelter not only from the elements but from the physical and psychological onslaughts of social debilitation." *Id.; see also* Paul Brest, *Further Beyond the Republican Revival: Toward Radical Republicanism,* 97 YALE L.J. 1623, 1626-27 (1988) (arguing that the "civic republican aims of participatory democracy are . . . undermined by economic inequality," which impairs the development of "the independence that civic republican theorists deem a prerequisite to civic virtue and produces political inequality"); Kenneth L. Karst, *The Supreme Court 1976 Term: Foreword: Equal Citizenship Under the Fourteenth Amendment,* 91 HARV. L. REV. 1, 4, 61 (1977) (suggesting that the "substantive core of the [fourteenth] amendment, and of the equal protection clause in particular, is a principle of equal citizenship" that, "when applied to inequalities of wealth, will produce results closely resembling the ones produced by Professor Michelman's 'minimum protection' theory"); Frank I. Michelman, *The Supreme Court 1968 Term: Foreword: On Protecting the Poor Through the Fourteenth Amendment,* 83 HARV. L. REV. 7 (1969); Laurence H. Tribe, *Unraveling* National League of Cities*: The New Federalism and Affirmative Rights to Essential Government Services,* 90 HARV. L. REV. 1065, 1065-66 (1977) (expressing conviction that "despite its difficulties, a doctrine will ultimately emerge that recognizes under the fifth and fourteenth amendments constitutional rights to decent levels of affirmative governmental protection in meeting the basic human needs of physical survival and security, health and housing, employment and education"). *But see,* Robert H. Bork, *The Impossibility of Finding Welfare Rights in the Constitution,* 1979 WASH. U.L.Q. 695; Ralph K. Winter, Jr., *Poverty, Economic Inequality, and the Equal Protection Clause,* 1972 SUP. CT. REV. 41, 100-02.

13. "Certain commentators would doubtless argue that . . . [a law criminalizing defined homosexual acts] violates some constitutionally unstated fundamental right. My opinion of that line of argument has been rendered clear." J.H. ELY, *supra* note 2, at 255 n.92.

14. *Id.* at 162-64.

the claim that women have been operating at an unfair disadvantage in the political process,"[15] and I am not convinced by his rebuttal of that proposition. Thus, I am left with the sense that at least some laws that disadvantage women should be subject to heightened judicial scrutiny. In addition, it seems that the Equal Protection Clause is the natural place to find both a constitutional basis for a woman's right to have an abortion and a prohibition against antisodomy laws.

I am fully convinced by Ely's rejection of natural law,[16] consensus,[17] or a "judge's own values"[18] as bases for equal protection review, and I do not expect my intuitive sense of "what the Equal Protection Clause should do," standing alone, to carry much weight with anyone who does not share my particular world view. I will argue instead that in order to give the Equal Protection Clause its full effect, Ely's model of equal protection review must be expanded to add a third test for heightened scrutiny, the "underclass" test, to supplement the traditional fundamental rights and suspect classification analyses. "Underclass review" is an elaboration, within the terms of Ely's representation-reinforcement theory, of Justice Blackmun's suggestion in his concurrence in *Plyler v. Doe*[19] that a statute which has the effect of creating a "discrete underclass" is inconsistent with the Equal Protection Clause and warrants heightened scrutiny even though no fundamental right or suspect classification is involved.[20] Underclass review is not a "sliding scale" theory,[21] nor is it a "quasi-fundamental rights/quasi-suspect classification" model.[22] It is distinct from both suspect classification and fundamental rights analysis, and it provides an independent basis for strict scrutiny.

Underclass review recognizes that there are harms the state can inflict upon a group that not only disadvantage the individual members of the group as compared with members of other social groups, but also will tend to subjugate the entire group, as a group, or entrench it in a subordinated position. In *Plyler*, Justice Blackmun recognized that education was not a

---

15. *Id.* at 164.

16. *Id.* at 48-54.

17. *Id.* at 63-69.

18. *Id.* at 44-48.

19. 457 U.S. 202 (1982).

20. *Id.* at 231-36 (Blackmun, J., concurring).

21. Justice Marshall has argued for a sliding scale, or "spectrum of standards," approach to equal protection review, whereby the degree of scrutiny appropriate in a given case would be determined by "the constitutional and societal importance of the interest adversely affected and the recognized invidiousness of the basis upon which the particular classification is drawn," rather than by rigid application of the narrowly defined fundamental rights or suspect classification tests. *See, e.g.,* San Antonio Indep. School Dist. v. Rodriguez, 411 U.S. 1, 99 (1972) (Marshall, J., dissenting); Dandridge v. Williams, 397 U.S. 471, 520-21 (1970) (Marshall, J., dissenting).

22. The Court has occasionally applied heightened scrutiny on the grounds that the interest at stake, though not fundamental, is extremely important, and the group affected, though not a suspect class, has some characteristics of a suspect class. *See, e.g., Plyler,* 457 U.S. at 223 (applying heightened scrutiny on the grounds that "more is involved in these cases than the abstract question whether . . . [the statute under review] discriminates against a suspect class, or whether education is a fundamental right . . . . [The statute] imposes a lifetime hardship on a discrete class of children not accountable for their disabling status.").

fundamental right of individuals;[23] instead, he concluded that strict scrutiny was required because denying education in the particular case under review would convert an identifiable *group* of people into an underclass. This view recognizes that state action can affect the development of the broad social order in addition to affecting individual members of society, and that there are certain types of social ordering, such as the construction of underclasses and the implementation of caste systems, that the Equal Protection Clause does not permit legislators to undertake.

Under my proposed theory, courts would subject to strict scrutiny[24] any law that creates or perpetuates an underclass in our society. A law creates or perpetuates an underclass when two conditions are satisfied. First, the law must substantially burden a discernible group in its efforts to attain equality with other groups in society. Second, there must be reason to believe that the political process that produced the law was distorted by the acceptance of exaggerated stereotypes about the disadvantaged group.[25]

From the start, it must be clear that underclass review is not another type of suspect classification analysis. Underclass analysis does not define ex ante who the underclasses in our society are; instead, courts must ask whether a statute has the effect of turning *any* group into an underclass, or of reinforcing the subordinated status of any group. Nor does underclass review attempt to define another set of fundamental rights. It does not define ex ante what kinds of legislative action have the effect of creating or perpetuating underclasses; instead, it is quite possible that there is legislative action which, if applied to one group, would create an underclass, but if applied to

---

23. *Id.* at 235 (Blackmun, J., concurring).

24. I assume throughout this note that a statute that satisfied the elements of the underclass test would be subjected to strict scrutiny, rather than the "intermediate" level of scrutiny occasionally applied by the Court. *See, e.g.,* Craig v. Boren, 429 U.S. 190 (1976) (intermediate scrutiny applied to a gender-based law disadvantaging men). Justice Blackmun, in his *Plyler* concurrence, left open the question of whether strict or intermediate review would be appropriate under his approach. Plyler v. Doe, 457 U.S. at 235 n.3 (Blackmun, J., concurring). I find it difficult to distinguish between these levels of review as a practical or theoretical matter and therefore have constructed my theory with only two possible levels of review in mind: the highly deferential "rational basis" standard, *see, e.g.,* Railway Express Agency v. New York, 336 U.S. 106 (1949), and a more probing level of review, which I term "strict scrutiny," or "heightened scrutiny." I use these latter terms interchangeably, and I do not intend them to carry any additional special significance. Furthermore, I do not intend for the "strict" level of review I propose to be fatal in fact.

25. Ely argues that a distortion of the political process has occurred when a legislature disadvantages a group based on "a generalization whose incidence of counterexample is significantly higher than the legislative authority appears to have thought it was." J.H. ELY, *supra* note 2, at 157. According to Ely, although this type of distortion differs from the process failure that occurs when a legislature disadvantages a group "essentially out of dislike," it nonetheless "implicates equal protection concerns in a related way."

> [T]o disadvantage—in the perceived service of some overriding social goal—a thousand persons that a more individualized (but more costly) test or procedure would exclude, under the impression that only five hundred fit that description, is to deny the five hundred to whose existence you are oblivious their right to equal concern and respect, by valuing their welfare at zero.

Id.; *see* text accompanying notes 45-48 *infra* (discussion of Ely's view of exaggerated stereotyping as political malfunction).

another, would have no such effect.[26] In addition, fundamental rights analysis focuses on the rights of individuals, while underclass review focuses on the relative status of social groups.[27]

By requiring a court to make a threshold judgment about the substantive effects of a statute or policy under review, the first element of the underclass test departs from Ely's process-oriented approach to equal protection. However, the second element of the underclass analysis ensures that the theory remains grounded in Ely's "representation-reinforcement" vision of judicial intervention, by limiting heightened judicial scrutiny to decisions which are the product of distortions in the political process.[28]

Underclass analysis does not eliminate discretion from the process of judicial review; the underclass test is not a theoretical machine, guaranteed to mass produce indisputably consistent results. Nonetheless, underclass analysis gives judges a set of viable and relevant standards that will enable them to fulfill the substantive goals of the Equal Protection Clause without going beyond their legitimate role as guardians of the political process.

In Part I of this note, I discuss Justice Blackmun's concurrence in *Plyler v. Doe*.[29] I suggest that Justice Blackmun's equal protection analysis could

---

26. *See* text accompanying note 69 *infra*.

27. A group-oriented approach to equal protection analysis of race- and gender-based discrimination has been proposed by Professor Ruth Colker. *See* Ruth Colker, *Anti-Subordination Above All: Sex, Race, and Equal Protection,* 61 N.Y.U. L. REV. 1003 (1986). Colker argues that "courts should analyze equal protection from an anti-subordination perspective," under which "it is inappropriate for certain groups in society to have subordinated status because of their lack of power in society as a whole." *Id.* at 1007. Colker proposes that any statute or policy that has a disparate impact on a particular race or sex should be subject to strict scrutiny, but that the state should be able to meet its burden of justification by showing that the statute or policy would "redress subordination." *Id.* at 1014-15. Underclass review is similar to Colker's theory in that it seeks to direct courts' attention to state involvement in broad social ordering. However, underclass review is potentially broader than Colker's theory because it addresses itself to groups classified in terms other than race or gender. On the other hand, underclass review is also potentially narrower than Colker's approach, in that it limits judicial intervention to situations where there is reason to believe the challenged state action is the product of a distorted cost-benefit analysis by the legislature.

An earlier group-oriented equal protection analysis was proposed by Professor Owen Fiss. *See* Owen M. Fiss, *Groups and the Equal Protection Clause,* 5 PHIL. & PUB. AFF. 107, 147-77 (1976). Under Fiss's approach, strict scrutiny would apply to "any state law or practice [that] aggravates (or perpetuates?) the subordinate position of a specialty disadvantaged group." *Id.* at 157. Fiss's view of the Equal Protection Clause as "a proscription against status-harm," *id.*, rests in part on an "ethical view against caste, one that would make it undesirable for any social group to occupy a position of subordination for any extended period of time," *id.* at 151. The first element of the underclass test is consistent with Fiss's ethical view against caste, as well as with his focus on the effect of state action on groups, rather than on individual members of groups. However, underclass analysis differs from Fiss's approach in two significant ways. First, his approach is a version of suspect classification analysis in that it requires an ex ante determination that the group affected by a statute is a "specially disadvantaged group" requiring extra protection. *Id.* at 154-55 (defining characteristics of such groups). Underclass analysis, on the other hand, protects *any* group whose access to equality with other groups is substantially burdened by state action. *See* Section II.C.2 *infra.* Second, underclass review explicitly limits judicial intervention to the correction of political malfunction. Fiss considers "circumscribed political power" to be one of the defining characteristics of specially disadvantaged groups, *see* Fiss, *supra,* at 155, but does not justify judicial intervention solely in process terms, *see id.* at 154 (discussing inadequacy of purely process approach).

28. *See* text accompanying notes 45-54 *infra* (elaborating the form and function of the second element of the underclass test).

29. 457 U.S. 203, 231-36 (Blackmun, J., concurring).

be extended to a broader range of situations, and that the scope of judicial review under this approach could be limited in accordance with Ely's representation-reinforcing model. In Part II, I define the scope of underclass review and discuss the ways in which it supplements the different types of judicial review advanced by Ely while nevertheless remaining anchored in Ely's representation-reinforcing theory of judicial intervention. In addition, I describe the function underclass review will serve and the gaps it will fill, particularly with regard to laws that disadvantage women. In Part III, I apply underclass review to a variety of test cases.

I. The Origins of Underclass Review

In *Plyler v. Doe*, the Supreme Court invalidated a Texas statute[30] which denied free public education to undocumented alien children. The majority, in an opinion by Justice Brennan, recognized that the affected group could not be treated as a suspect class, and that education could not be considered a fundamental right. Nevertheless, the majority subjected the statute to heightened scrutiny, on the grounds that the importance of the interest denied and the isolation and powerless status of the affected group warranted special judicial attention.[31] Thus, the majority's analysis combined fundamental rights analysis and suspect classification analysis to produce a hybrid approach, which extended the reach of the traditional forms of equal protection analysis.

Justice Blackmun joined the opinion of the court but wrote a separate concurrence suggesting an alternative rationale for the decision, based in part on an analogy to voting rights cases. Justice Blackmun reasoned that the right to vote is, "in equal protection terms, an extraordinary right" deserving special judicial protection, because "a citizen cannot hope to achieve any meaningful degree of individual political equality if granted an inferior right of participation in the political process."[32] "Those denied the vote," he followed, "are relegated, by state fiat, in a most basic way to second-class status."[33] To Justice Blackmun, the Texas statute under review in *Plyler* similarly relegated undocumented alien children to second-class status and was therefore inconsistent with the Equal Protection Clause:

> [T]he principle of the voting cases—the idea that state classifications bearing on certain interests pose the risk of allocating rights in a fashion inherently contrary to any notion of 'equality'—dictates the outcome here. . . . [T]he Texas scheme inevitably will create 'a subclass of illiterate persons' . . . [; thus making] the statutory scheme unconstitutional as well as unwise.[34]

By providing an education to some while denying it to others, Justice Blackmun continued, the state "immediately and inevitably creates class distinc-

---

30. *See* note 22 *supra.*
31. *Plyler,* 457 U.S. at 223-24.
32. *Id.* at 233 (Blackmun, J., concurring) (citations omitted).
33. *Id.* (Blackmun, J., concurring).
34. *Id.* at 234 (Blackmun, J., concurring).

tions of a type fundamentally inconsistent" with the purposes of the Equal Protection Clause.[35] Children who are denied an education are "placed at a permanent and insurmountable competitive disadvantage," because an

> uneducated child is denied even the opportunity to achieve. And when those children are members of an identifiable group, that group—through the State's action—will have been converted into a discrete underclass. Other benefits provided by the State, such as housing and public assistance, are of course important; to an individual in immediate need, they may be more desirable than the right to be educated. But classifications involving the complete denial of education are in a sense unique, for they strike at the heart of equal protection values by involving the State in the creation of permanent class distinctions. In a sense, then, denial of an education is the analogue of denial of the right to vote: the former relegates the individual to second-class social status; the latter places him at a permanent political disadvantage.[36]

Justice Blackmun did not argue that the Texas statute abridged a fundamental right. On the contrary, he recognized that unlike the right to vote, "it is undeniable that education is not a 'fundamental right' in the sense that it is constitutionally guaranteed."[37] Consequently, every conceivable denial of education would not warrant strict scrutiny. Instead, what made the Texas statute unconstitutional was that it converted "an identifiable group . . . into a discrete underclass."[38]

Justice Blackmun's conclusion that the statute in *Plyler* created "a discrete underclass" was based on two propositions. First, he recognized that the denial of education would place the children affected by it "at a permanent and insurmountable competitive disadvantage." Second, Justice Blackmun noted, the children were "members of an identifiable group."[39] These two propositions are reflected in the two elements of the underclass analysis that I propose.

The first element of the underclass test, which asks whether the statute under review substantially burdens a group in its efforts to attain equality with other groups, is a generalized form of Justice Blackmun's first proposition and will embrace a broader range of interests than the denial of education. It is unlikely that Justice Blackmun intended that his approach be extended in this manner, in view of his explicit statements that "classifications involving the complete denial of education are in a sense unique," and that denials of housing and public assistance would not pose the same constitutional problem.[40] However, Justice Blackmun's effort to distinguish among protected and unprotected interests may simply reflect the need to

---

35. *Id.* (Blackmun, J., concurring).
36. *Id.* (Blackmun, J., concurring) (citations omitted).
37. *Id.* at 235 (Blackmun, J., concurring).
38. *Id.* at 234 (Blackmun, J., concurring).
39. *Id.* (Blackmun, J., concurring).
40. *Id.* (Blackmun, J., concurring).

reconcile his analysis with previous Court decisions.[41] Furthermore, it is less coherent than his general approach.[42]

The second element of the underclass test asks whether there is reason to believe that the political process that produced the challenged statute was distorted by the acceptance of exaggerated stereotypes about the disadvantaged group. This is an elaboration of Justice Blackmun's second proposition—that the children in *Plyler* were members of an identifiable group—within the terms of Ely's representation-reinforcing model of equal protection analysis, and it provides a rational limit on judicial intervention.

II. The Form and Function of Underclass Review

A. *The Elements of Underclass Review*

Underclass review subjects to strict scrutiny any law that creates or perpetuates an underclass in our society. As noted above, a law creates or perpetuates an underclass when (1) the law substantially burdens a discernible group in its efforts to attain equality with other groups in society, and (2) there is reason to believe that the political process that produced the law was distorted by the acceptance of exaggerated stereotypes about the disadvantaged group. In this section, I lay out the contours of these two elements of the underclass test and demonstrate how underclass review fits into Ely's representation-reinforcing model.

The first element of the underclass test asks whether the challenged statute substantially burdens a discernible group in its efforts to attain equality with other groups in society. For purposes of this element, courts should measure the relative status of social groups in terms of their comparative access to two types of power: (1) institutional power, such as control of the courts, educational institutions, the military, and the government; and (2) economic power, namely the control of economic resources.[43] State action

---

41. *See, e.g.*, Dandridge v. Williams, 397 U.S. 471 (1970) (denial of welfare benefits not subject to heightened scrutiny).

42. In other words, it seems generally plausible to say that the Equal Protection Clause prohibits the state from creating underclasses, but it seems implausible to argue that while the denial of education places a child at a permanent competitive disadvantage, the denial of housing, food, or health care has no such effect. Michelman makes a parallel argument against Ely's limitation of fundamental rights to interests such as voting rights and proper districting, suggesting that education, health care, and shelter are at least as important to ensuring political participation. Michelman, *Welfare Rights in a Constitutional Democracy, supra* note 12.

43. This conception of the relative status of social groups is based in part on the chapter entitled "The Common Elements of Oppressions," in Suzanne Pharr, Homophobia: A Weapon of Sexism 53-64 (1988). Pharr sees the existence of a defined norm as one of the elements of oppression; economic power, institutional power, and violence or the threat of violence are used by the dominant group to reinforce the norm that group defines. The underclass test focuses on economic and institutional power, but not on violence, because the threat of violence underlies nearly every state action (as a means of enforcement) and consequently does not help to distinguish between legitimate and illegitimate state action for purposes of judicial review. Other elements of oppression that Pharr identifies include invisibility, stereotyping, blaming the victim, isolation, and internalized oppression. *See* Section II.B *infra* (discussing internalized oppression and the general tendency on the part of both dominant and oppressed groups to accept beliefs favoring the dominant groups' continuing control).

which inhibits a group's access to these forms of power substantially burdens that group's efforts to attain equality with other groups in society. State action which reinforces a particular group's political quiescence in the face of an existing inability to obtain access to these forms of power—by, for example, denying access to decisionmaking arenas, increasing the costs of political participation, or generating apathy by creating a sense of powerlessness—has a similar effect.[44]

The second element of the underclass test asks whether there is reason to believe that the political process which produced a challenged state action was distorted by the acceptance of exaggerated stereotypes about the disadvantaged group. An exaggerated stereotype is not one that is "false"; as Ely points out, "[s]tereotypes are not true or false (save only . . . in the unlikely event that *no* member of the class in question possesses the attributed characteristic), but rather are distinguished by their relative incidence of counterexample."[45] When a legislature disadvantages a group on the basis of "a generalization whose incidence of counterexample is significantly higher than the legislative authority appears to have thought it was," Ely argues, a distortion of the political process has occurred. Members of the disadvantaged group who do *not* fit the stereotype, and to whose existence the legislature is oblivious as a result of its underestimation of the stereotype's incidence of counterexample, have been denied their "right to equal concern and respect," by having their welfare valued at zero.[46] "No matter how many considerations may have entered into the cost-benefit balance," Ely continues, "a misapprehension regarding the incidence of counterexample . . . will have distorted the entire decision."[47] The problem, of course, is "how the Court should go about identifying such situations."[48]

For purposes of the second element of the underclass test, such a situation is deemed to arise whenever the first element of the test is met and there exist widely held stereotypes, logically related to the challenged state action, about the group disadvantaged by the action. Consider, for example, a statute which prohibits gays and lesbians from teaching in a state's public schools. Such a statute would satisfy the first element of the underclass test, because it impairs gays' and lesbians' access to an important institution in our society. To satisfy the second element of the test, a plaintiff challenging the statute could present evidence from historical texts, literature, opinion polls, and the mass media to demonstrate that many people in our society

---

44. *See generally* JOHN GAVENTA, POWER AND POWERLESSNESS: QUIESCENCE AND REBELLION IN AN APPALACHIAN VALLEY 3-32 (1980).

45. J.H. ELY, *supra* note 2, at 252 n.70 (emphasis in original).

46. *Id.* at 157. The Court has also recognized that legislation based on overgeneralization poses an equal protection problem. For example, the Court has suggested that the application of intermediate scrutiny to gender classifications is designed to ensure that the state action is "determined through reasoned analysis rather than through the mechanical application of traditional, often inaccurate assertions about the proper roles of men and women." Mississippi Univ. for Women v. Hogan, 458 U.S. 718, 726 (1982).

47. J.H. ELY, *supra* note 2, at 157.

48. *Id.*

believe that gays and lesbians are likely to molest small children.[49] One who accepted this stereotype could justify the exclusion of homosexuals from teaching jobs—in other words, the stereotype is logically related to the challenged state action. For purposes of the underclass analysis, this would be sufficient to show that there was reason to believe that the political process which produced the challenged statute was distorted by the acceptance of exaggerated stereotypes about gays and lesbians. I turn now to the chain of inferences that supports this conclusion.

To conclude that an exaggerated stereotype distorted the political process, a court would have to believe both that a legislature's decision was influenced by a stereotype, and that the legislature had misapprehended the stereotype's incidence of counterexample. It would be extremely difficult to determine whether the members of a legislature actually had a stereotype in mind when they passed a statute; such an inquiry would raise all the problems posed by any direct attempt to analyze legislative motivation.[50] However, if there exists a widely held stereotype in our society about the group disadvantaged by a challenged statute, and if common sense tells us that this stereotype could logically bear on the decision to pass the statute, then we can infer that the stereotype entered into the legislature's decision-making process.[51] Such an inference is justified even if the stereotype was never discussed, or if the legislators were not aware of the stereotype's exist-

---

49. I have left this standard vague deliberately. It would be very difficult to develop a precise rule for determining when a stereotype is sufficiently prevalent to cause concern, partly because stereotypes are often accepted on a subconscious level and are not acknowledged by those who believe them. *See* note 52 *infra*. The judge must use a "healthy dose of common sense," J.H. ELY, *supra* note 2, at 130 (discussing methods of identifying legislative intent), to determine whether the plaintiff's evidence reflects a stereotype which recurs in a variety of contexts and seems to be accepted on some level by a substantial number of people, or whether it represents aberrant opinions held only by a particular newspaper's editorial board. However, the vagueness of the analysis in this respect is counterbalanced by the further requirement that the stereotype be logically related to the state action under review in order to satisfy the second element of the underclass test. *See* note 51 *infra* and accompanying text.

50. *See* Palmer v. Thompson, 403 U.S. 217, 224 (1971), *cited in* J.H. ELY, *supra* note 2, at 137-38.

51. It is important to emphasize that the stereotypes relevant for purposes of the second element of the underclass test are those that are *logically related* to the particular state action under review. In other words, a stereotype is relevant only if it logically could have been used to justify, excuse, or trivialize any hardship imposed on members of the disadvantaged group as a result of the particular state action under review. Demonstrating the existence of generalized negative stereotypes about the group is not enough; only a stereotype specifically related to the challenged state action will satisfy the second element.

For example, suppose a state decided to charge tolls on state highways. Such an action is the equivalent of a regressive tax in that it imposes a greater economic burden on the poor than on the rich as a percentage of income. If the toll imposed a substantial economic burden on the poor (as it might, for example, if it imposed substantial additional commuting costs on poor workers), the first element of the underclass test might be satisfied. However, the second element of the test would not be met. While people generally accept a variety of negative stereotypes about the poor—for example, that they are lazy or ignorant—it is difficult to see how those stereotypes could have been used to justify, excuse, or trivialize the particular burden imposed by highway tolls. If generalized prejudice against a particular group were so severe that we could safely assume it would distort *any* political decision which disadvantaged them, the group would qualify as a "discrete and insular minority" subject to prejudice, and Ely's model of suspect classification analysis would require strict scrutiny. The underclass test does not rely on such a presumption and instead requires a showing that stereo-

ence, because the acceptance of cultural stereotypes often occurs on an unconscious level.[52]

Underclass analysis does not condemn *every* stereotype that might have crept into legislative decisionmaking; the point is to identify situations in which stereotypes are particularly likely to be exaggerated, resulting in a distortion of a legislature's cost-benefit balancing. Thus, it still remains to be shown that, under the circumstances identified by the second element of underclass analysis, a court would be justified in concluding that the legislature significantly misapprehended the incidence of counterexample to a stereotype which entered into its decisionmaking process. Ely argues that a stereotype is most likely to be exaggerated when "the generalization involved is one that serves the interests of the decisionmakers," either by justifying legislation that benefits them, or by confirming flattering views of groups to which they belong.[53] I would extend Ely's observation to argue that any stereotype that favors the interests of socially dominant groups is likely to be exaggerated, regardless of whether the groups constitute a majority of the legislature, or of the electorate. Furthermore, such a stereotype is likely to be exaggerated not only by the beneficiaries of unequal allocations of power, but also by the victims of such a system.[54]

At this point, the analysis circles back to the first element of the underclass test. When state action imposes a substantial burden on one group's efforts to attain equality in our society, it has the collateral effect of entrenching the power of other groups that already occupy relatively dominant positions. Thus, such state action serves the interests of dominant groups, and we have reason to suspect that any stereotypes that were likely to have been involved in the decision to take such action were also likely to have been exaggerated.

This completes the chain of inferences, and we can safely presume that the political process has been distorted whenever a statute meets the first element of the underclass test and there exists a widely held stereotype, logically related to the statute, about the group disadvantaged by the statute. We can infer that the stereotype likely played a role in the decision from the

---

types probably distorted the legislature's decisionmaking with regard to the particular statute under review, by insisting on a logical connection between the stereotype and the challenged decision.

52. Professor Charles Lawrence has argued that

the culture—including, for example, the media and an individual's parents, peers, and authority figures—transmits certain beliefs and preferences. Because these beliefs are so much a part of the culture, they are not experienced as conscious lessons. Instead, they seem part of the individual's rational ordering of her perceptions of the world. The individual is unaware, for example, that the ubiquitous presence of a cultural stereotype has influenced her perception that blacks are lazy or unintelligent. Because racism is so deeply ingrained in our culture, it is likely to be transmitted by tacit understandings: Even if a child is not told that blacks are inferior, he learns that lesson by observing the behavior of others. These tacit understandings, because they have never been articulated, are less likely to be experienced at a conscious level.

Charles R. Lawrence III, *The Id, the Ego, and Equal Protection: Reckoning with Unconscious Racism,* 39 STAN. L. REV. 317, 323 (1987).

53. J.H. ELY, *supra* note 2, at 158.

54. *See* Section II.B *infra.*

fact that the stereotype is widely held and that it is logically related to the challenged action. That the stereotype supported a decision favoring relatively dominant groups in our society allows us to infer that it was likely to have been exaggerated.

The state will have the opportunity to justify its action by demonstrating, for example, that the stereotype is sufficiently grounded in fact that the statute was necessary to further a compelling state interest. To return to the hypothetical statute prohibiting homosexuals from teaching in public schools, the state could attempt to prove that homosexuality is highly correlated with a propensity to molest children, and that there is no better way to protect students from sexual abuse than to exclude gays and lesbians from teaching in the schools. Because the state action meets both elements of the underclass test, however, such a justification would be strictly scrutinized.

The first element of the underclass test which asks whether the state action under review substantially burdens a particular group's efforts to attain equality with other groups, directly addresses a broad substantive goal of the Equal Protection Clause as interpreted by Justice Blackmun in *Plyler*: to prevent the state from involving itself in the "creation of permanent class distinctions."[55] The second element is also relevant to this substantive inquiry. Part of what makes a group an underclass is that its members are not treated with the same concern and respect accorded other members of society: Their desires are devalued, and their suffering is excused or ignored on the basis of exaggerated, commonly held negative or subordinating perceptions. Thus, by asking whether exaggerated stereotyping is likely to have influenced a legislature's decisionmaking, the second element identifies an important substantive aspect of underclass status.

Underclass review departs significantly from the process-oriented approach to equal protection analysis advanced by Professor Ely by involving courts in substantive inquiries concerning the distribution of institutional and economic power in our society. However, the second element of the underclass test ensures that underclass analysis remains grounded in Ely's representation-reinforcing theory of judicial intervention. As discussed above,[56] Ely believes that a distortion of the political process has occurred when exaggerated stereotypes have influenced the cost-benefit analysis underlying a legislative decision. By limiting judicial intervention to situations in which this type of political malfunction is likely to have occurred, underclass analysis remains consistent with Ely's representation-reinforcing vision of judicial review.

B. *Exaggerated Stereotypes and Internalized Oppression: A Brief Note*

In the previous section, I suggested that any stereotype that favors the interests of socially dominant groups is likely to be exaggerated, not only by the beneficiaries of current unequal allocations of power, but also by the

---

55. Plyler v. Doe, 457 U.S. 203, 234 (1982) (Blackmun, J., concurring).
56. *See* text accompanying notes 45-48 *supra*.

victims of such a system.[57] In this section, I present support for this assertion and define the extent to which it must be accepted in order for underclass analysis to fit within Ely's representation-reinforcing model of equal protection review.

Substantial evidence supports the proposition that people are generally disposed to accept beliefs that justify the dominance of relatively powerful social groups. Both the victims and the beneficiaries of the current status quo share this inclination. For example, Professor Cass Sunstein notes that

> the beliefs of both beneficiaries and victims of existing injustice are affected by dissonance-reducing strategies . . . . [T]he strategy of blaming the victim, or assuming that an injury or an inequality was deserved or inevitable, tends to permit nonvictims or members of advantaged groups to reduce dissonance by assuming that the world is just—a pervasive, insistent, and sometimes irrationally held belief . . . .
>
>   Victims also participate in dissonance-reducing strategies, including the lowering of self-esteem to accommodate both the fact of victimization and the belief that the world is essentially just.[58]

In addition to allowing people to believe that they live in a just world, the inclination to accept beliefs that justify the status quo may also be part of a broader adaptation of "preferences, beliefs, and desires" to current unjust social conditions.[59]

Because of their predisposition to accept beliefs which favor the status quo, both dominant and subordinated groups are predisposed to accept, and therefore prone to exaggerate, stereotypes that favor the interests of the relatively powerful. Gail Phetersen has argued that disempowered groups respond to oppression by developing a sense of "internalized oppression," which she defines as "the incorporation and acceptance by individuals within an oppressed group of the prejudices against them within the dominant society."[60] In a similar vein, John Gaventa has argued that the sense of

---

57. *See* text accompanying note 54 *supra.*

58. Cass R. Sunstein, *Preferences and Politics* 34-35 (1991) (unpublished manuscript on file with the *Stanford Law Review*) (citing JON ELSTER, SOUR GRAPES (1983); LEON FESTINGER, A THEORY OF COGNITIVE DISSONANCE (1957); MELVIN J. LERNER, THE BELIEF IN A JUST WORLD: A FUNDAMENTAL DELUSION (1980)).

59. Sunstein, *supra* note 58, at 34 n.34 (citing MARY WOLLSTONECRAFT, A VINDICATION OF THE RIGHTS OF WOMAN 43 (1975) (New York 1792)).

60. Gail Pheterson, *Alliances Between Women: Overcoming Internalized Oppression and Internalized Domination,* 12 SIGNS 146, 148 (1986). According to Pheterson, internalized oppression
> is likely to consist of self-hatred, self-concealment, fear of violence, and feelings of inferiority, resignation, isolation, powerlessness, and gratefulness for being allowed to survive. Internalized oppression is the mechanism within an oppressive system for perpetuating domination not only by external control but also by building subservience into the minds of the oppressed groups.

Id. Justice Marshall recognized this phenomenon, noting that "[s]ocial scientists agree that members of minority groups frequently respond to discrimination and prejudice by attempting to disassociate themselves from the group, even to the point of adopting the majority's negative attitudes towards the minority." Castaneda v. Partida, 430 U.S. 482, 503 (1977) (Marshall, J., concurring) (citing GORDON WILLARD ALLPORT, THE NATURE OF PREJUDICE 150-53 (1954); ARNOLD MARSHALL ROSE, THE NEGRO'S MORALE 85-96 (1949); GEORGE EATON SIMPSON & JOHN MILTON YINGER, RACIAL AND CULTURAL MINORITIES 192-95, 227, 295 (4th ed. 1972); Bruno Bettelheim,

powerlessness experienced by subordinated groups may lead to "a greater susceptibility to the internalization of the values, beliefs, or rules of the game of the powerful as a further adaptive response—i.e. as a means of escaping the subjective sense of powerlessness, if not its objective condition."[61] Pheterson maintains that members of dominant groups, on the other hand, develop a sense of "internalized domination," which moves them towards accepting negative views of subordinated groups, thereby affirming their own right to occupy a privileged position.[62]

Some have also argued that the preferences and desires of oppressed groups, as well as their self-perceptions, are distorted by the experience of disempowerment. For example, Sunstein notes that people are generally subject to an "endowment effect" which leads them to "place a higher value on rights or goods that they currently hold than they place on the same goods when in the hands of others."[63] Assuming that this observation is accurate, Sunstein argues, the initial assignment of entitlements in a society strongly affects people's preferences and desires: The "decision to grant an entitlement to one person frequently makes that person value that entitlement more than he would if the right had been allocated to someone else. (It also makes other people value it less than they otherwise would.)"[64] The implication of Sunstein's arguments is that relative disempowerment will lead people to undervalue the rights they do not possess, thereby distorting their preferences. It has also been argued that internalized oppression may affect people's associational preferences, thereby impairing effective coalition-building and leading them to act against their own group's interests.[65]

Both practical and philosophical problems arise from imputing "false consciousness" to disempowered groups.[66] For the purposes of justifying the chain of inferences by which a presumption of political malfunction is created in underclass review, however, it is not necessary to accept the view that the preferences and desires of disempowered groups have been distorted by their experience of oppression. It is necessary to accept only the more

---

Individual and Mass Behavior in Extreme Situations, 38 J. ABNORMAL & SOC. PSYCHOLOGY 417 (1943)); *see also* J.H. ELY, *supra* note 2, at 165-66 ("A sufficiently pervasive prejudice can block its own correction . . . by convincing even . . . [its victims] of its correctness.").

61. J. GAVENTA, *supra* note 44, at 17.

62. Pheterson, *supra* note 60, at 148.

63. Sunstein, *supra* note 58, at 6-8.

64. *Id.* at 6.

65. For example, Suzanne Pharr writes:
Sometimes the internalized oppression is acted out as *horizontal hostility.* If one has learned self-hatred because of one's membership in a "minority" group, then that disrespect and hatred can easily be extended to the entire group so that one does not see hope or promise for the whole. It is safer to express hostility toward other oppressed peoples than toward the oppressor. Hence, we see people destroying their own neighborhoods, displaying violence and crime toward their own people, or in groups showing distrust of their own kind while respecting the power of those who make up the norm. Sometimes the internalized oppression leads people to be reluctant to associate with others in their group. Instead, their identity is with those in power.
S. PHARR, *supra* note 43, at 61.

66. *See* Bruce Ackerman, *Beyond* Carolene Products, 98 HARV. L. REV. 713, 737 (1985).

limited proposition that subordinated groups as well as dominant groups are inclined to accept beliefs and therefore are prone to exaggerate stereotypes that favor the interests of the relatively powerful.

C. *Distinguishing Underclass Review from Ely's Bases for Strict Equal Protection Review*

As interpreted by Ely, the traditional models of equal protection review inadequately address certain situations in which the intersection of the right affected and the group disfavored creates a social order unacceptable to the goals of the Equal Protection Clause. Underclass review fills this gap while remaining within the representation-reinforcing terms of Ely's theory. Underclass review is not, however, a mere extension of the fundamental rights or suspect classification prongs of Ely's model. In this section, I demonstrate that underclass analysis is conceptually distinct from both prongs of Ely's approach to equal protection review.

1. *Fundamental Rights.*

Underclass review is not a substitute for expanding the reach of Ely's fundamental rights analysis.[67] Underclass analysis differs conceptually from fundamental rights analysis in two ways. First, fundamental rights analysis concerns the rights of individuals, while underclass analysis focuses on the effects of state action on groups in our society. Second, the group of rights considered fundamental can be defined abstractly and categorically, while the interests protected by underclass analysis can be defined only within the context of a particular state action under review.

Fundamental rights analysis takes an individualistic approach, which focuses on a category of rights that cannot be denied to any person without

---

67. As discussed above, Ely believes that fundamental rights review protects every person's basic right of access to the political marketplace, where she can bargain for her interests. *See* text accompanying note 5 *supra.* The group of rights recognized as fundamental by the Court is broader than the set of rights Ely would protect. *See, e.g.,* Zablocki v. Redhail, 434 U.S. 374 (1978) (heterosexual marriage); Roe v. Wade, 410 U.S. 113 (1973) (abortion); Griswold v. Connecticut, 381 U.S. 479 (1965) (privacy right to use contraceptives); Skinner v. Oklahoma, 316 U.S. 535 (1942) (procreation). Although I support the outcomes reached in all these cases, I agree with Ely that it is difficult to articulate a coherent rationale for including these interests within the "fundamental rights" branch of equal protection analysis, and I find it even more difficult in light of the Court's exclusion of other vital interests from constitutional protection. *See, e.g.,* San Antonio Indep. School Dist. v. Rodriguez, 411 U.S. 1, 37 (1972) (education not a fundamental right); Dandridge v. Williams, 397 U.S. 471, 485 (1970) (welfare not a fundamental right). Instead, I believe that the results reached in *Griswold* and *Roe* can be explained in terms of the underclass analysis I propose, *see* text accompanying notes 120-129 *infra* (abortion), and that the statute under review in *Skinner* could have been invalidated under the eighth amendment, as a cruel and unusual punishment. The statute at issue in *Zablocki* required men subject to a child support order to show that they had met their obligations, or that their children were otherwise provided for, before they could marry another time. As Justice Stewart argued in his concurrence, the statute, at least insofar as it applied to indigents, could have been invalidated under a rational basis standard. *Zablocki,* 434 U.S. at 391-92 (Stewart, J., concurring). For purposes of the remainder of this subsection, however, it is not necessary to distinguish between Ely's fundamental rights approach and the approach taken by the Court because the analyses are identical in structure if not in scope, in that both require a court to apply strict scrutiny to any state action abridging the exercise of a right deemed fundamental.

special justification by the state. Fundamental rights analysis does not concern itself directly with the effect such a denial might have on the *group* to which an individual belongs. For strict scrutiny to apply, it is sufficient as well as necessary to show that a fundamental right of the complaining individual has been abridged. Underclass review, on the other hand, focuses directly on how a particular legislative action affects a particular social group. While the interest at stake may not qualify as a fundamental interest, the effect of denying the interest may be to turn the affected group into an underclass. In such a case, strict scrutiny will be required under the underclass theory, even if no fundamental right of any *individual* has been impaired. Thus, Justice Blackmun, in his concurrence in *Plyler v. Doe*, explicitly recognized that education was not a fundamental right, but concluded that heightened scrutiny was required nonetheless, because of the effect of the particular denial of education under review in *Plyler* on the particular group burdened by it.[68] This broader, group-oriented perspective distinguishes underclass analysis from fundamental rights analysis.

A second distinction between underclass review and fundamental rights review is that fundamental rights are defined categorically, while interests protected under the underclass approach can only be defined within the context of a particular state action affecting a particular social group. Any individual, regardless of social group, may seek redress if denied a fundamental right. Underclass review, in contrast, does not ask whether the interest at stake is one of a set of previously defined, categorically protected interests; instead, it examines how the specific denial of that particular interest affected the particular burdened group. Thus, it is possible that the denial of a particular interest could warrant heightened scrutiny in one case, but that deference would be accorded to the denial of the same interest in a different context. For example, although the denial of education in *Plyler* was declared unconstitutional, one could imagine denials of education that would not warrant strict scrutiny under the underclass model.

Suppose a city enacts an ordinance denying school-age residents of an unincorporated area access to its public schools.[69] Suppose further that the relevant county government provides funding only to public schools in incorporated areas, and that the residents of the unincorporated area are free to incorporate by referendum. Finally, assume that, as a general matter, residents of both the incorporated and unincorporated areas are comfortably upper-middle class. The ordinance would not warrant strict scrutiny under an underclass analysis, because it does not satisfy the elements of the underclass test. First, the burden on the residents as a group is not substantial. The ordinance does not substantially impair their access to economic power. The residents of the unincorporated area have chosen to forego certain city services in exchange for lower taxes and lower home prices, but they could easily afford to move to an incorporated area without making undue sacri-

---

68. 457 U.S. at 234 (Blackmun, J., concurring).
69. *Cf.* Milliken v. Bradley, 418 U.S. 717 (1974).

fices. Furthermore, the ordinance does not burden their access to institutional power. By hypothesis, they can afford to send their children to private schools, or they can incorporate by referendum, thereby gaining access to the same county benefits distributed to incorporated areas. Because the second element of the underclass test is reached only if the first element is satisfied, the analysis would stop here and the ordinance would be upheld.

Underclass analysis might produce a different result, however, if the evidence demonstrates that the unincorporated area was a ghetto whose residents earned their living through low-paid domestic work or manual labor in the incorporated areas. Under such circumstances, the court might conclude that the denial of public schooling significantly burdened these residents in their access to economic and institutional power, thereby satisfying the first element of the underclass test. If additional evidence showed that residents of the incorporated area perceived residents of the unincorporated area as being ignorant or lazy, the second element would also be satisfied, and strict scrutiny would be required.

2. *Suspect Classifications.*

Underclass review also fundamentally differs from Ely's model of suspect classification analysis by not requiring a court to determine ex ante whether the affected group constitutes a suspect class. Ely's model requires heightened scrutiny of any state action which disadvantages members of discrete and insular minorities who are regularly short-changed in the political process as a result of prejudice.[70] Underclass review requires strict scrutiny whenever a statute creates or perpetuates an underclass, even where the group involved is one which ordinarily can be presumed to be able to protect its interests through the political process.

Like Ely's suspect classification analysis, underclass analysis attempts to identify situations in which a group has been disadvantaged as a result of a malfunctioning political process. The difference between the two approaches lies in the ways in which they create a presumption of political malfunction. Ely's suspect classification model presumes distortion whenever a statute discriminates against a discrete and insular minority subject to widespread hostility. In other words, the presumption of malfunction arises out of the identity of the disfavored group. On the other hand, underclass analysis

---

70. J.H. ELY, *supra* note 2, at 151-53. Ely's model of suspect classification analysis differs conceptually from the suspect classification approach applied by the Court. Ely's analysis focuses on the identity of the group burdened by a classification, while the Court's analysis has generally focused on the classification itself. *See, e.g.,* Craig v. Boren, 429 U.S. 190 (1976) (gender); Sugarman v. Dougall, 413 U.S. 634 (1973) (alienage); Loving v. Virginia, 388 U.S. 1 (1967) (race). For example, a race-based classification disadvantaging whites would not warrant heightened scrutiny in Ely's scheme because there is no reason to suspect that prejudice against whites would distort a predominantly white legislature's decisions. J.H. ELY, *supra* note 2, at 170-72. The Court, on the other hand, applies at least intermediate, if not strict, scrutiny to *any* race-based classification, regardless of the identity of the group the law burdens. *See, e.g.,* Regents of the Univ. of Cal. v. Bakke, 438 U.S. 265 (1978). For a comprehensive discussion of suspect classification analysis as it has been developed and applied by the Court, see GEOFFREY R. STONE, LOUIS M. SEIDMAN, CASS R. SUNSTEIN & MARK V. TUSHNET, CONSTITUTIONAL LAW 435-689 (1st ed. 1986).

presumes that when state action substantially burdens a group's access to equality with other groups, and existing stereotypes about the disfavored group relate logically to the challenged action, an exaggerated stereotype distorted the decisionmaking process.[71]

D.   *The Special Case of Women: An Example of the Need for Underclass Review*

The distinction between underclass analysis and suspect classification analysis is important in the case of women. According to Professor Ely, women cannot constitute a discrete and insular minority because they comprise a majority of the voters in the nation.[72] I agree with Ely that it is generally inappropriate for courts to intervene and provide women with extra protection from laws that disadvantage them but do not perpetuate their underclass status. After all, people generally know what is best for them, and courts can't be in the business of correcting everything that they believe is substantively unfair. However, where a statute disadvantages women in such a way as to create or perpetuate their status as an underclass, the fact that women constitute a majority does not—and ought not—rebut the presumption that exaggerated stereotyping distorted the political process.

It may be reasonable to say, as a general matter, that women can protect their interests in the political process, since they constitute a majority of the electorate. It is not reasonable, however, to say that women ought to protect themselves against the passage of a law that entrenches their status as a weak, impoverished, dependent underclass, where there is reason to believe that the cost-benefit analysis that produced the challenged statute involved a stereotype about women. Such a law favors the continuing dominance of men, and any stereotype about women involved in the law's enactment is likely to have been exaggerated, by women as well as by men.[73] In such circumstances, women's majority voting power cannot protect them adequately from the denial of equal concern and respect implicit in legislation based on overgeneralization and should not rebut the presumption that the challenged law was a product of political malfunction.

In this section, I examine in depth the way in which underclass review would protect women. First, I present an illustration of the way in which

---

71. *See* text accompanying notes 50-54 *supra.*

72. Ely does not accept the argument that internalized oppression justifies the treatment of women as a suspect class. Although he acknowledges the possibility that "until quite recently there persisted throughout America's female population . . . [an] acceptance of the prejudices of males, unventilated by more than token airing of their validity," Ely summarily concludes that it is no longer appropriate, in the case of women, to take such factors into consideration. "To apply all this to the situation of women in America in 1980, however, is to strain a metaphor past the breaking point." J.H. ELY, *supra* note 2, at 166-67. Therefore, Ely argues, "if women don't protect themselves from sex discrimination in the future, it won't be because they can't. It will rather be because for one reason or another—substantive disagreement or more likely the assignment of a low priority to the issue—they don't choose to." *Id.* at 169. My analysis departs from Ely's in that I believe it is possible to identify *some* situations in which it is fair to say women's self-perceptions have been distorted by their subordinated position in society.

73. *See* Section II.B *supra.*

exaggerated stereotyping might distort a political process so that a law extremely disadvantageous to women could be passed even where women are a voting majority. Second, I present an example of a law disadvantaging women which would be subject to strict scrutiny on the underclass theory. Finally, I give an example of a law disadvantaging women which underclass review would not subject to heightened scrutiny.

1. *Exaggerated stereotyping and political malfunction: an extreme example.*

Suppose that suttee had been practiced in the United States since the Pilgrims set foot on the continent: When a man died, tradition required his widow to throw herself on his funeral pyre, her life deemed over when her husband's life ended. Suppose that Congress codified this custom in a statute. Judging from data from countries in which suttee has been practiced, a significant number of widows would not go to the funeral pyre willingly, but rather would have to be beaten, dragged, drugged, and otherwise coerced into their ritual suicide. However, a significant number of widows would go compliantly to their deaths, having accepted the belief that their lives had no meaning now that their husbands were dead.[74] A woman's "voluntary"[75] choice to self-immolate in such circumstances is likely to reflect her acceptance of a variety of generalizations about women. For example, a woman might believe that she is by nature suited only to serving her husband and bearing his children and is incapable of worthwhile activity after her husband has died. She may also believe that a wife is her husband's property, which must be protected from "use" by another man. Her decision is also likely to be influenced by a variety of religious beliefs, to the effect that suttee represents a woman's final duty to her earthly lord and master, and that she will be rewarded in her next life for her sacrifice.[76]

---

74. *See generally* RAJENDRA KUMAR SAXENA, SOCIAL REFORMS: INFANTICIDE AND SATI 57-76 (1975) (discussing suttee (or "sati") in India). According to Saxena, there were

five species of Satis, namely, those who deliberately and with a cheerful countenance accepted the ordeal for their devotion to their departed husbands; those who were swayed by considerations of family traditions and customs and regarded the rite as a means for the aggrandizement of the reputation and social status of the family; those who could not bear the tortures of widowhood; others whose honour was at stake and craved for immortality and finally those who were actually dragged into the fire against their wishes.

Id. at 76.

75. It is questionable whether decisions made in such circumstances can accurately be described as "voluntary" in the sense of being products of free will. Sunstein has suggested that "[p]references might be regarded as nonautonomous insofar as they are reflexively adaptive to unjust background conditions." Sunstein, *supra* note 58, at 33 (footnote omitted).

76. Saxena describes the social and religious forces that contributed to the enforcement of the suttee practice as follows:

Hindu religion . . . holds widowhood as a sin lotted to [a widow] for her past doings. If a young wife possessed no individuality apart from her husband, a young widow had practically no existence . . . . The knowledge that they cannot unite themselves with a second husband without degradation from caste and family, accompanied with the life of hunger and scorn to which they would be subjected made their lot pitiable beyond comprehension . . . . [Widows were generally believed to bring] indelible stain on the family and possibly involve it in disgrace . . . . [Thus the relatives] impressed upon the widow the desirability

Now suppose that women are permitted to vote, and that they constitute 52 percent of the voting population. Suppose further that all laws disadvantaging women are stricken to relieve the newly enfranchised women of the burden of getting them repealed. Next, imagine that a man proposes to reinstate by law the suttee custom. Men are faced with a proposal solidly rooted in a tradition that ensures their dominance. The suttee tradition makes women dependent on men even for their right to live; it also controls and clarifies patriarchal ancestral lineage and prevents a man's "property" from being "used" by any other man. While some men may pause to consider whether the proposed law would be unfair to women, most see justification in the fact that women have been doing this for centuries and that suttee, although unfortunate, seems "natural" and "right." These men may consider how they would feel if they had to kill themselves when their wives died, but dismiss this as an entirely different matter: The tradition of suttee has itself taught them that men are far more valuable than women, so the situations do not seem comparable. In sum, a substantial number of men are likely to resolve their doubts in a manner distorted by the self-favoring implications of the other-disadvantaging law.[77] Suppose that, after all is said and done, 73 percent of the men—35 percent of the total voting population—vote to reenact the law.

Now let's turn to the women voters. This law clearly disadvantages them, so one might assume that all women would vote against it, thereby preventing its reenactment by a comfortable margin. This assumption, however, ignores the significant number of women who would have marched off placidly to the funeral pyre. There is little reason to think that their religious and social beliefs have changed overnight, simply because women now have the vote. These women are likely to continue to believe that suttee is "natural" and "right," that it preserves traditional family structures, that it ensures a good afterlife, and that it reflects an accurate assessment of the appropriate function of women in society. They may also believe that in order to protect their own souls, they must militate against allowing other women to commit the sin of living on after their husbands' death. Therefore, when the law comes for a vote, this portion of the female population—let's say 31 percent of the women, or 16 percent of the total voting population—votes for reenactment. Combined with the male vote for reenactment, these women secure passage of the suttee law by a margin of 51 percent to 49 percent.

This example suggests that ordinary forms of political access, such as majority voting power, may not protect marginalized groups from entrench-

---

of the rite . . . . These experiences, so desolate and crammed with misery and neglect made widow [sic] opt for the performance of the rite of Sati, for it would lead her from a position of sinner to one of beautification [sic]. People flocked, from far and wide, to receive [the widow's] dying blessings or imprecations, for she was supposed to be empowered with divine virtues and her last word would be carried out absolutely.
R.K. SAXENA, *supra* note 74, at 71-73.

77. This mode of thinking is analogous to Ely's description of legislative decisionmaking based on prejudice. *See* J.H. ELY, *supra* note 2, at 152-53.

ment at the bottom of the social order. In the suttee hypothetical, internalized oppression on the part of women and internalized domination on the part of men predispose *both* to exaggerate stereotypes about women so as to favor continuing male control.[78] Thus, when stereotypes about women—for example, that women are suited only to serve their husbands and to bear children—are likely to influence a decision to enforce male dominance by burdening women's efforts to attain equality, we can trust neither men nor women to estimate the incidence of counterexamples accurately. Underclass review identifies such situations and requires the state to offer heightened justification for its actions.

2. *Underclass review applied: a law disadvantaging women.*

Imagine that a state enacts a law requiring employers to ensure that female employees of childbearing age, defined as ages 16-50, are never exposed to unsafe levels of lead, on the grounds that such exposure can damage fetuses.[79] Suppose, however, that the statute does not apply to men. Consequently, employers can avoid the costs of cleaning the work environment by hiring only men. This statute satisfies both elements of underclass analysis; therefore, strict scrutiny applies.

The first element is met because the law imposes a substantial burden on women's access to economic power by making it more expensive for employers, particularly employers in certain industries, to hire women. The second element is satisfied because widely held stereotypes about women are logically related to the challenged statute. First, the law reflects the notion that only men belong in the workplace. Second, the statute reflects and reinforces the stereotype that children are primarily a woman's responsibility. The cost of lead damage to fetuses could be treated either as a cost of manufacturing, or as a cost of childbearing. By permitting employers to avoid the cost of cleaning the work environment, the statute implicitly treats the threat of lead damage as a cost of reproduction rather than as a cost of manufacturing. The statute shifts this cost of reproduction to women, by allowing employers to exclude them from the workplace, and thus it reflects the notion that children are "a woman's problem." Finally, the law covers every woman within a broad age range, even if she is infertile, lesbian, celibate, past menopause, or wholly uninterested in bearing children at this time in her life. Thus, the statute also rests upon the stereotype that women of childbearing age are likely to become pregnant, either because they "really" want to or because they are incapable of taking the necessary steps to prevent pregnancy.

Recall that underclass analysis does not require challengers to prove that exaggerated generalizations *motivated* the legislature to enact a challenged statute or provided a major justification for its decision. It is sufficient to

---

78. *See* Section II.B *supra*.

79. This hypothetical is based on the facts in International Union, UAW v. Johnson Controls, 59 U.S.L.W. 4209 (U.S. Mar. 20, 1991).

show that a widely held stereotype is *logically related* to the challenged statute, so that it can be presumed to have entered into the legislature's cost-
benefit analysis. If the stereotype was exaggerated, as we can presume from
the fact that the first element of the underclass test is satisfied,[80] the political
process was distorted and judicial intervention is required, "[n]o matter how
many [other] considerations may have entered into the cost-benefit
balance."[81]

This hypothetical case demonstrates the importance of underclass review
as a supplement to Ely's fundamental rights and suspect classification analyses. The hypothetical law at issue reinforces the subordinated social status
of women, thus perpetuating a social order inconsistent with the substantive
goals of the Equal Protection Clause identified by Justice Blackmun in his
Plyler concurrence.[82] Further, the law is the product of a political process
distorted by exaggerated stereotyping. However, it falls between the cracks
of Ely's model. Fundamental rights analysis is not appropriate, because
equal employment opportunity is not an essential aspect of an individual's
ability to participate in political decisionmaking and thus is not a fundamental right in Ely's view. Likewise, Ely's suspect classification analysis fails to
resolve the issue, because women are a voting majority and presumably can
protect their own interests through the political process.[83] Underclass review fills the gap.

3.   *Gender-discrimination not warranting strict scrutiny under
      underclass review.*

Underclass review is not appropriate for all state action that arguably
disadvantages women. If a statute fails to meet either element of the underclass test, strict scrutiny will not apply. Suppose a state sets the minimum
drinking age for men at 18 and for women at 20, perhaps in the belief that
women are more likely to be careless about birth control when intoxicated
and that the higher age requirement for women furthers the state's interest
in preventing teenage pregnancy. The law may reflect a variety of subordinating stereotypes about women. For example, it is logically related to the
notion that contraceptives are the "woman's problem," or that a woman
who becomes pregnant has only herself to blame. However, the law does not
satisfy the first element of the underclass test. Requiring women to wait two
years longer than men to drink alcohol may inconvenience them, but it does

---

80. *See* text accompanying note 54 & Section II.B *supra.*
81. J.H. ELY, *supra* note 2, at 157. It is important to remember that the underclass test does
not determine the ultimate validity of the statute; it merely determines the level of scrutiny required.
82. Plyler v. Doe, 457 U.S. 202, 231-36 (1982).
83. In addition, Ely might see this as a law that favors women, not one that disadvantages
them. Thus, even if gender classifications were questionable, the favorable treatment of women
would allay the initial suspicion generated by the statute. *See* J.H. ELY, *supra* note 2, at 253 n.75 (a
law drafting men but not women for military service would be constitutional because any suspicion
of the legislature's motivation is "allayed by the fact that in tangible terms the law is one whose
comparative disadvantaging of men is massive. A law exempting women from the possibility of
being ordered to pay alimony seems, if anything, even more clearly constitutional.").

not perpetuate their underclass status. The law does not burden their access to governmental, educational, or community institutions (institutional power); nor does it limit their earning capacity or perpetuate their lower economic status (economic power). Thus, strict scrutiny will not apply.

One could argue that underclass analysis should require strict scrutiny in this situation because the law burdens women in their efforts to attain equality simply by reinforcing the negative stereotypes it reflects.[84] However, such a weak interpretation of the first element would leave it with no independent meaning, reducing underclass review to a mere suspicion of legislation based on stereotypes. Such an analysis would lead everywhere and therefore nowhere, because generalizations based on stereotypes are, in the words of Professor Ely, "the inevitable stuff of legislation." Thus, if the underclass test "is to provide us with anything beyond a basis for begging questions, it has to be refined, so as to separate . . . the acceptable stereotypes from the unacceptable."[85]

A stereotype is fatal for purposes of underclass analysis only when it is logically related to a legislative decision that burdens a group in one of the ways identified by the first element of the test. Economic power and institutional power are directly determinative of the relative status of groups within our society. When a statute burdens a group's access to one or both of these forms of power or reinforces a group's political quiescence in the face of impaired access, it is clear that the statute obstructs the group's efforts to attain equality, thereby entrenching the power of relatively dominant groups. The fact that the interests of relatively dominant groups are favored by such a statute justifies judicial intervention by giving rise to the presumption that any stereotypes involved in its enactment were likely to have been exaggerated. On the other hand, where a statute simply reflects a stereotype, without directly affecting a group's access to an identifiable source of power, the conclusion that the statute favors dominant interests rests on shakier ground, because it requires judges to speculate about the stereotype's cultural impact.[86] For this reason, underclass review neither requires nor permits judges to engage in such an inquiry and limits heightened scrutiny to situations in which a directly identifiable loss of economic or institutional

---

84. Under Colker's antisubordination approach, for example, the reinforcement of subordinating stereotypes is sufficient to raise a prima facie case of unconstitutional discrimination. *See* Colker, *supra* note 27, at 1039-40. The Court has also suggested that the perpetuation of traditional gender role stereotypes poses an equal protection problem. *See, e.g.,* Mississippi Univ. for Women v. Hogan, 458 U.S. 718, 729 (1982) (excluding a male applicant from nursing school on gender grounds imposed a burden that was unconstitutional because it "perpetuate[d] the stereotyped view of nursing as an exclusively women's job").

85. J.H. ELY, *supra* note 2, at 156.

86. Generally, it is difficult to get people to agree as to whether a particular stereotype is subordinating, empowering, or simply descriptive. For example, I personally *do* think the hypothetical drinking age law burdens women by reinforcing the notion that men should not be held responsible for contraceptive use. Another woman, however, might see the same statute as empowering women by reinforcing a stereotype that holds them responsible for protecting themselves, rather than relying on their partners to prevent unwanted pregnancy.

power has occurred.[87]

III.   Applying Underclass Review

Thus far, I have sketched the broad outlines of underclass review. In this section, I develop the theory in more detail by applying it to three types of cases involving real and hypothetical state action: (1) state action that excludes a group from an activity, (2) state action that denies members of a certain group benefits granted to other groups, and (3) state action that criminalizes certain kinds of behavior. This discussion will involve some cases that may seem "easy," in that they clearly satisfy the elements of the underclass test, as well as some "harder" cases, in which the proper application of the test is not as clear.

A.   *Exclusions*

Suppose that a state passes a law denying women residents admission to the state university's professional schools. To support the law, the state argues that women are statistically more likely than men to abandon their professions in order to stay home and raise their children. Thus, the exclusionary policy enables the state to reserve its limited educational resources for those who are most likely to make the fullest use of them.

Education at a professional school is not a fundamental right, and women, according to Ely, are not a suspect class. Under the underclass test, however, this statute must be strictly scrutinized. The statute meets the first element of the underclass test by denying women a significant opportunity to improve their economic status. Moreover, the law affects the economic power of women as a class, and not merely the economic status of those individual women who want to attend professional school. First, more women will be available to work in jobs where a professional degree is not necessary, thereby driving up the supply of an entire class of female workers and depressing the wages for work that is open to them.[88] In addition, the law

---

87. It is theoretically possible that a few stereotypes are so debilitating that their mere reflection in a statute would satisfy the first element of the underclass test by reinforcing the disfavored group's political quiescence in the face of existing inequalities of economic or institutional power. For example, consider a statutory rape law forbidding sex with females, but not males, under a certain age. Such a law "treats women as sexual objects and inhibits their freedom, and . . . stereotypes women as passive victims whose virtue and chastity must be protected by the state." Frances Olsen, *Statutory Rape: A Feminist Critique of Rights Analysis,* 63 Tex. L. Rev. 387, 417 (1984) (footnote omitted). It is at least plausible that such stereotypes are so demeaning that their legitimation by statute reinforces women's political quiescence in the face of existing economic and institutional subordination. As a practical matter, however, it is difficult to imagine how such a case would be made.

88. Men, on the other hand, clearly benefit as a class by this exclusion. By limiting the competition from women, the statute entrenches male control of higher-paying jobs and allows men as a class to command higher wages for their work on opportunity cost grounds. That is, by increasing the rewards to men of obtaining a professional school education, the statute permits men in nonprofessional jobs to demand higher wages for staying in their current positions instead of attending professional school. In some situations, these men will be replaced by women, who cannot afford to hold out for a higher wage (because the alternatives open to them are not as appealing). However, this counterbalancing effect will be minimized by the fact that many nonprofessional jobs are as a

implicitly legitimates employer discrimination against women on the grounds that women are more likely to abandon their jobs for their home lives.

The statute also satisfies the second element of the underclass test, because a variety of widely held stereotypes about women are logically related to this exclusion. Many people believe that women are naturally better suited to work in the home, and that efforts to bring them into the professional world are likely to be wasted. Many also believe that men "need" their jobs more than women do and should therefore be given preference. Plenty of people, including plenty of women, already believe that women can (and should) find men to support them, or that most women who assert a desire to attend professional school and work actually want to find and marry rich husbands, and then stay home with the kids. Because both elements are satisfied, strict scrutiny is required by the underclass analysis.

A current example of an exclusionary policy is the refusal of the military to place women in combat positions.[89] This practice excludes women from one of the major areas of institutional power in our society, thereby satisfying the first element of the underclass test. Although they can serve in the military in other capacities, women can never be fully credible participants in decisionmaking about war.[90]

---

practical matter open almost exclusively to men and by the costs a firm incurs in replacing existing workers. *See* DOUGLAS L. LESLIE, CASES AND MATERIALS ON LABOR LAW: PROCESS AND POLICY 64 (2d ed. 1985) (costs to firm of exit by inframarginal employees).

89. *See* Rostker v. Goldberg, 453 U.S. 57, 76 (1981) ("The Army and the Marine Corps preclude the use of women in combat as a matter of established policy."); 10 U.S.C. § 6015 (1988) (Navy); *id.* § 8549 (Air Force). *Rostker* involved a challenge to a statute requiring men, but not women, to register for the draft. The Court rested its decision to uphold the statute partly on the grounds that women are ineligible for combat and therefore "are simply not similarly situated for purposes of . . . registration for a draft." *Rostker,* 453 U.S. at 78. The Court has yet to consider a challenge to the combat exclusion itself.

90.
> In war experience, perhaps more than in any other context except childbirth, there is a wide-spread conviction that before you can talk about it, *you had to be there.* Paradoxically, though men have never experienced childbirth, they have had the power to control it, largely in the abortion context and to an increasing extent with the advent of various reproductive technologies. But women do not and have never controlled war. And because we have not been there, whatever in the past we have had to say about war, or national security, or the survival of the planet, has by definition been illegitimate. Our commentary was sweet, but was ultimately the gushing of naive non-persons.

Ann Scales, *Militarism, Male Dominance and Law: Feminist Jurisprudence as Oxymoron?,* 12 HARV. WOMEN'S L.J. 25, 39 (1989) (emphasis in original) (footnotes omitted). Although male officers may rise to high levels within the military without actually having participated in combat, the fact that they could be called on to do so lends their decisions about military force a legitimacy that women's decisions do not have.

This exclusion from combat service may have very broad implications for the status of women in our society, even beyond the direct impairment of institutional power that satisfies the first element of the underclass test. Scales has argued that militarism itself rests upon "a radical distinction between the authority of men and women," in that a male soldier's ability to engage in warfare depends upon habits of objectifying other human beings which he has acquired as a male in a patriarchal society:

> The men at the front need to be expert at thingification before they can pull that trigger or push that button. Militarism requires of its participants an expertise in objectification. The privileged among us surely have learned to objectify, especially on the basis of class and

The exclusion also meets the second element of the underclass test because it is logically related to several widely held stereotypes about women. Women are perceived as unsuited to physical struggle. Their "natural" role, under another, related stereotype, is to stay home and take care of children while men protect them by doing battle in the outside world. It is possible that there are legitimate justifications for excluding women from combat; however, under an underclass analysis, those justifications would be subjected to strict scrutiny.

Another exclusion that would trigger strict scrutiny under underclass review is the military's exclusion of homosexuals from *any* military service.[91] This policy meets the first element of the underclass test because it excludes homosexuals as a group from a crucial area of institutional power. The second element is also implicated in that negative stereotypes about gays and lesbians are related to the decision to exclude them. It has been suggested, for example, that the promiscuity of gays and lesbians, and the hostility they inspire in heterosexuals, would cause discipline problems and harm military recruiting efforts.[92] Consequently, underclass analysis demands strict scrutiny.

A harder case is one that asks whether women, regardless of their sexual orientation, have standing to challenge the military's policy of excluding homosexuals on the grounds that it has been applied in such a way as to perpetuate the underclass status of women. Women in the military may have to submit to sexual harassment in order to keep their jobs, because to refuse the sexual advances of male soldiers is to risk accusations that they

---

race. And it is conceivable that a soldier could grow up with insufficient experience in those realms. The soldier must be able to thingify regardless of his own race or class. Genderization serves this purpose: almost all men in the United States have experience with that. If domination and submission were not so *usual,* not so embedded in our experiences of gender, the military would not be able to transform entire populations into The Other.

Id. at 43-44 (emphasis in original) (footnotes omitted). In this light, excluding women from full participation in military service can be seen as a means of preserving the separation, distinction, and hierarchy that make objectification possible. Thus, the exclusion of women from combat reinforces militarism, which, in turn, reinforces gender oppression and entrenches the dominance of males.

91. *See, e.g.,* Watkins v. United States Army, 875 F.2d 699, 713 & n.5 (9th Cir. 1989) (citing U.S. Army Regulation 635-200, ¶ 15-3 (requiring the discharge of all homosexuals regardless of merit); U.S. Army Regulation 601-280, ¶ 2-21 (barring homosexuals from reenlisting)), *cert. denied,* 111 S. Ct. 384 (1990). *But see id.* (Army estopped from barring soldier's reenlistment solely because of his acknowledged homosexuality where Army, with full awareness of his homosexuality, had allowed him to reenlist in the past).

92. *See, e.g.,* Beller v. Middendorf, 632 F.2d 788, 811 n.22 (9th Cir. 1980) (quoting affidavit from the Assistant Chief of Naval Personnel, submitted in connection with case arising out of discharge of three Navy officers pursuant to Navy's policy of excluding homosexuals), *cert. denied,* 452 U.S. 905 (1981).

It is interesting to note that prior to President Truman's racial integration of the armed forces by executive order in 1945, *see* MERLE MILLER, PLAIN SPEAKING: AN ORAL BIOGRAPHY OF HARRY S. TRUMAN 79 (1983), the military made similar arguments to support its separation of blacks and whites, *see, e.g., Watkins,* 875 F.2d at 729 (Norris, J., concurring) (noting that during World War II, the Army Chief of Staff and the Secretary of the Navy argued that because of racial tensions, racial separation was "necessary to maintain efficiency, discipline, and morale"); GILBERT WARE, WILLIAM HASTIE: GRACE UNDER PRESSURE 99, 134 (1984).

are lesbians.[93] The consequences of such accusations can be serious. The military's investigations and trials in such cases often are conducted with expediency rather than justice in mind[94] and may result in discharge from the military, and, in some cases, imprisonment.[95] In addition, the military's antihomosexuality policy makes it risky for women to build close support networks among themselves, as any close associations could raise suspicions that the participants are lesbians.[96]

Thus, the military's *implementation* of its antihomosexuality policy places a substantial burden on a woman's choice to serve in the military, thereby impairing women's access to institutional power and satisfying the first element of the underclass test.[97] The implementation of the policy satisfies the second element as well. When a woman is accused of being a lesbian because she refuses a man's sexual advances, a stereotype justifies this leap in logic: Women are "supposed" to be sexually available to men, and, if they choose not to be available, something is "wrong" with them.[98] Because both elements of the test are met, the military's policy of excluding homosexuals would be strictly scrutinized on the grounds that it has been implemented in such a way as to perpetuate the status of women as an underclass.

This last example raises two issues regarding the form and function of

---

93. *See, e.g.,* Lisa M. Keen, *Navy Discharges Female Sailor Who Denies That She Is a Lesbian,* Wash. Blade, Nov. 10, 1989, at 13, col. 2 (female sailor discharged after being labeled a lesbian by male sailors whose sexual advances she rejected). Of course, it is conceivable that a female sailor might make a similar accusation of homosexuality if a male sailor refused her advances. However, it seems unlikely that this would pose a significant risk to men in the military; in the civilian context, the overwhelming majority of sexual harassers are male, and it is likely that the same would be true in the military.

94. *See Marines Are Said to Suspend Alleged Lesbians,* N.Y. Times, Feb. 23, 1988, at A23, col. 1 (in connection with investigations of lesbianism among women at the Parris Island, S.C. boot camp, one woman said, "They've made up their minds. . . . Now they just need proof, and doesn't that throw all our rights out the window?"). *See generally* Victoria Slind-Flor, *Civilian Counsel Wary of Military Justice,* The Recorder, July 26, 1989, at 1, col. 2 ("military lawyers are hampered by the armed services' legal system, which, among other things, emphasizes expedience over quality").

95. *See, e.g., Court Overturns Conviction of Female Marine in Sex Case,* N.Y. Times, Feb. 19, 1990, at A10, col. 6 (discussing case of former marine corps corporal who served 226 days in the brig on charges of engaging in sex with another woman).

96. Close relationships among men may also be viewed with suspicion; however, women in the military may have a greater need to build networks in order to work together to improve their collective status in that institution.

97. One could also argue that the military's antigay policy, by reinforcing the heterosexist presumption that heterosexuality is "normal" and that any other sexual orientation is deviant, serves to reinforce a patriarchal social structure and therefore perpetuates the subordination of women to men. *See generally* Adrienne Rich, *Compulsory Heterosexuality and Lesbian Existence,* in THE SIGNS READER: WOMEN, GENDER, AND SCHOLARSHIP 141 (E. Abel & E. Abel eds. 1983). Rich also notes that " '[c]ompulsory heterosexuality' was named as one of the 'crimes against women' by the Brussels Tribunal on Crimes against Women in 1976." *Id.* at 161. However, as in the case of the hypothetical gender-based drinking law discussed at text accompanying notes 84-87 *supra,* it is difficult to link this stereotype directly to a denial of access to economic or institutional power to women; thus, it would not in itself be sufficient to satisfy the first element of the underclass test.

98. This stereotype need not have been involved in the initial decision to adopt the policy. The challenge in this case is to the *implementation* of the policy, rather than to the policy itself. Thus, a stereotype involved in the policy's implementation is sufficient to satisfy the second element of the underclass test.

underclass analysis. First, women are granted standing even though the antigay policy does not appear, on its face, to affect women directly as a group. To bring a challenge on the underclass theory, a plaintiff need only allege that the challenged state action creates or perpetuates the underclass status of a group of which she is a member. She may define the group as she pleases, though the requirements of the underclass test are likely to limit the range of plausible choices.[99] Second, because underclass analysis is broadly concerned with the *impact* of state action, the way in which a policy is implemented may be subject to challenge even where the policy on its face entails no adverse consequences to the complaining group. Thus, even though it is conceivable that the military's antigay policy could theoretically be implemented without directly impairing the ability of women to participate in the military, the facts regarding implementation justify a challenge.

All exclusions by socially dominant groups of other groups do not warrant strict scrutiny under underclass review. For example, a state college could have an all-male dormitory for entering freshmen without meeting the first element of the underclass test, as it would be difficult to show that the exclusion of women from that dorm substantially affected their access to economic or institutional power. However, underclass analysis might lead to a contrary result if the all-male dorm were specifically designated for male business school students in the top third of their class; the exclusion of female business school students from *this* dorm might substantially affect their ability to "network" with other successful students or to build contacts which would prove important in their future professional lives.[100]

B. *Denial of Benefits*

Consider a state-employee benefits plan that, like the plan upheld in *Geduldig v. Aiello*[101] denied unemployment benefits to female employees who had to leave work due to a pregnancy, but granted unemployment benefits if the absence was due to another disability. Underclass review would subject this plan to strict scrutiny. The possibility that a woman will be financially unprotected should she experience pregnancy-related disability substantially burdens her choice to work outside the home. As a result, women's access to economic power is impaired, and the first element of the underclass test is satisfied.

The statute also meets the second element of the underclass test. The denial of benefits is related to the stereotype of a male norm in the workplace, in that it reflects the notion that professional people do not—or should

---

99. In addition, the courts would have the power to consolidate actions brought by groups that stand in similar relation to a particular state action.

100. *Cf.* New York State Club Ass'n v. City of New York, 487 U.S. 1 (1988) (upholding municipal ordinance forbidding large private clubs from excluding women from membership).

101. 417 U.S. 484 (1974). In upholding the plan, the Court reasoned that differential treatment of "pregnant women" and "nonpregnant persons" did not constitute gender discrimination, because although the class of pregnant women was comprised only of women, the class of nonpregnant persons was comprised of both women and men. *Id.* at 496 n.20.

not—get pregnant. Like the hypothetical fetal protection law discussed above,[102] this statute shifts a joint cost of reproduction and industry onto women, reflecting the notion that children are primarily a woman's responsibility. The statute is also related to stereotypes and received ideas about the role of women in society: that women who get pregnant are (or should be) married, and that they have (or should have) someone else to support them, rendering unemployment benefits unnecessary. Finally, the statute reflects the belief that a woman's wages are not of primary importance to her family.

The imposition of a tax can be seen as the equivalent of a denial of benefits.[103] A flat percentage excise tax on gasoline is an example of a regressive tax, because it burdens the lower-middle class more heavily than the rich.[104] In some circumstances, such a tax might meet the first element of the underclass test, on the grounds that it impairs the relative access to economic power of members of the lower-middle class. For example, in relatively poor, sparsely populated rural areas in which people typically commute long distances to work, such a tax could substantially reduce low-income workers' access to economic resources. A similar situation might arise where low-income workers commute long distances to affluent areas in which they work but cannot afford to live. However, the tax does not satisfy the second element. Members of the lower-middle class are certainly subject to unfavorable stereotyping in our society, but it is difficult to think of any widely-held stereotype about them that would be logically related to the imposition of a gasoline tax. Thus, strict scrutiny would not be required.

A luxury tax, which burdens the rich more than the poor, also survives underclass review, but for the opposite reason. Such a tax clearly is related to stereotyped notions about the rich, to the effect that rich people squander huge sums of money on frivolities or excesses rather than sharing wealth with people who really need it. However, a luxury tax does not satisfy the first element, because the economic burden it places on the rich does not substantially impair their efforts to attain equality with other groups in our society. A similar analysis would apply to a steeply progressive income tax.

A reduction of benefits provided by the state presents a more difficult case. For example, suppose a state reduces Aid to Families with Dependent Children ("AFDC") benefits by 20 percent. The reduction arguably satisfies the first element of the underclass test, since it substantially reduces the economic power of AFDC recipients relative to other groups in society. In addition, many stereotypes could serve to justify the suffering of the affected group. For example, it is commonly believed that welfare recipients are lazy and therefore do not deserve state assistance; or that they spend all of their

---

102. *See* text accompanying notes 79-83 *supra.*

103. *See* Lionel S. Sobel, *First Amendment Standards for Government Subsidies of Artists and Cultural Expression: A Reply to Justices Scalia and Rehnquist,* 41 VAND. L. REV. 517, 522 (1988) (arguing that "there is . . . no difference between the denial of a subsidy and a tax").

104. To the extent that public transportation is unavailable as a cheaper alternative, demand for gasoline tends to be constant regardless of economic status. As a result, a flat tax on gasoline is regressive in that it probably takes a bigger bite as a percentage of the total income of lower-middle class drivers.

money on drugs, so the state is actually doing them a favor by reducing their income. Thus, both elements of the underclass test are satisfied and heightened scrutiny is required.

Such a result raises both practical and theoretical questions about the proper application of the underclass test. As a practical matter, a decision to reduce AFDC benefits probably would not survive strict scrutiny in most cases because a state could theoretically accomplish any general budget-cutting purpose by reducing expenditures in another area. From a public policy perspective, this outcome might be unfortunate, because it would discourage states from offering high levels of AFDC benefits at any time, to avoid being "locked in" to providing a high level of benefits in perpetuity.

However, as Ely notes, "if a theory is sound, we should live with the results."[105] Furthermore, the practical problems posed by this particular result are probably less severe than they initially might seem. First, there may be countervailing policy concerns that suggest that a state *should* be required to stand behind the current level of AFDC benefits it offers and to refrain from increasing benefits unless it expects to maintain them at the increased level in the future. For example, Sunstein's discussion of the "endowment effect" on people's preferences[106] suggests that AFDC recipients would be more adversely affected by a loss of benefits than by a failure to increase a lower initial endowment of benefits to the level they currently receive.[107] A second, related, point is that lawmakers probably already operate on the assumption that it is difficult as a political matter to reduce benefits once they have been granted, so the constraint imposed by the threat of strict scrutiny may have little additional effect on the tendency to "lowball" AFDC benefit levels. Finally, although strict scrutiny would be likely to invalidate a reduction of AFDC benefits in most cases, one can nonetheless imagine situations in which a state's justifications could survive such a test. For example, suppose a state had initially set AFDC benefits at a high level only to find that the population of eligible recipients was increasing rapidly as a result of immigration from other states and that, as a result, AFDC expenditures had greatly exceeded budgetary allocations. In such circumstances, a reduction in benefits could be justified as the only means of keeping the costs of the program reasonably close to original budget projections.[108] Or, for example, if the state believed it could provide more effectively for indigent children by shifting money from AFDC to other relevant

---

105. J.H. ELY, *supra* note 2, at 152.

106. *See* Sunstein, *supra* note 58, at 6-11.

107. *Id.*; *see also* Seth F. Kreimer, *Allocational Sanctions: The Problem of Negative Rights in a Positive State,* 132 U. PA. L. REV. 1293, 1359-63 (1984) (suggesting "history baseline" to judge state allocational decisions).

108. *But see* Shapiro v. Thompson, 394 U.S. 618 (1969). In *Shapiro,* the Court invalidated a one-year residence requirement for welfare recipients on the grounds that the disparate treatment of new and old residents impaired the fundamental right to travel and was not justified by the state's desire to "preserve the fiscal integrity of the state public assistance programs" by deterring additional indigent people from entering the jurisdiction. However, the problem in *Shapiro* was that the state sought to achieve its objectives via a classification that impaired a fundamental right. There was no suggestion in that case that the state's general objective of limiting welfare expenditures was

programs, such as state-provided day-care centers or state-funded school lunch plans, a corresponding reduction in AFDC benefits might survive heightened judicial review.

The application of the underclass test to the hypothetical AFDC reduction also raises a thorny theoretical problem, however. By treating the reduction as state action satisfying the first element of the underclass test and requiring the state to justify it, we implicitly treat the current level of benefits as a neutral "baseline" to which AFDC recipients have a presumptive entitlement. It would be equally plausible, as a theoretical matter, to argue that the state was under no initial obligation to provide *any* AFDC benefits, and that therefore the economic resources of AFDC recipients *absent* state intervention should be taken as the more appropriate baseline for assessing the first element of the underclass test. Under the latter view, the reduction in benefits would not involve the state in the affirmative creation of class distinctions, but rather would reflect a decision by the state to refrain from doing as much as it had done previously to remedy class distinctions that "naturally" exist.[109]

It is probably impossible to articulate a theoretically satisfying justification for the choice among baselines in any given case, or even to articulate an arbitrary but consistent rule to be applied to all cases. In most situations, the appropriate choice will seem intuitively apparent. Most would agree that the state has acted when it passes a fetal protection law, when it outlaws abortion, when it provides education to some but not to others, or when it provides unemployment benefits in connection with some disabilities but not others. In other cases, such as the hypothetical AFDC reduction, the choice will seem less clear, and ultimately will rest on considerations of public policy.

Any constitutional approach that distinguishes between state action and the state's failure to act will face this problem, however. For example, the Court confronted an implicit choice between baselines in *Maher v. Roe*,[110] in which it upheld a state regulation granting Medicaid benefits for childbirth, but denying such benefits for abortions that were not "medically necessary." The majority implicitly treated the resources available to poor women absent any state funding as a neutral baseline, reasoning that the state plan "imposed no restriction on access to abortions that was not already there" for a poor woman and therefore did not constitute a "burdensome interference" by the state into her freedom to decide whether to terminate her pregnancy.[111] On the other hand, Justice Brennan, in dissent, implicitly treated

---

unconstitutional, or that it could not have been achieved legitimately through an across-the-board reduction in benefits, as is contemplated in the hypothetical AFDC reduction in text.

    109. The Court has made this point on a number of occassions. *See, e.g.*, DeShaney v. Winnebago County Dep't. of Social Servs. 489 U.S. 189, 195 (1989) (the Due Process Clause "is phrased as a limitation on the State's power to act, not as a guarantee of certain minimal levels of safety and security"); Harris v. McRae, 448 U.S. 297, 316 (1980) ("although government may not place obstacles in the path of [the] exercise of [rights], it need not remove those not of its own creation").

    110. 432 U.S. 464 (1977).

    111. *Id.* at 474.

the state's funding of childbirth-related expenses as creating a different neutral baseline, from which the failure to fund abortions was a departure requiring heightened justification by the state.[112] Although there are policy arguments for favoring one approach or the other, there is no perfectly coherent *theoretical* rationale for choosing between the two: The decision must rest on a value judgment. Professor Ely's theory is equally vulnerable to attack in this context, as it also relies on an implicit reference state of a properly functioning political process that reflects inescapably value-laden choices.[113] Thus, in my inability to solve the "baseline problem" implicit in the first element of the underclass test, I can say only that I find myself in good company.

C. *Criminal Statutes*

Criminal laws impose obligations on all members of society. However, the obligations imposed by some criminal laws burden some groups more than others, such that underclass analysis would require strict scrutiny.

For example, laws prohibiting sodomy perpetuate the underclass status of gays and lesbians. Lesbians and gays are profoundly burdened by the mere existence of such laws, even beyond the extent to which compliance itself is a burden.[114] Antisodomy laws define gays and lesbians as deviant from the established norm of heterosexuality and drastically curtail their access to crucial forms of institutional power, regardless of whether they offend such statutes. Antisodomy laws serve to legitimate violence against lesbians

---

112. *Id.* at 488 (Brennan, J., dissenting) (by funding childbirth but not abortion, the state "has inhibited . . . [indigent women's] fundamental right to make that choice free from state interference").

113. In the words of Dean Paul Brest,
> The representation-reinforcing enterprise model is shot full of value choices, starting with the decision of just *how* representative our various systems of government ought to be and who ought to be included in the political community, and ending with (covert) choices about who is justifiably the object of prejudice and whether legislative goals are sufficiently important to warrant the burdens they impose on some members of society.

Paul Brest, *The Substance of Process*, 42 OHIO ST. L.J. 131, 140 (1981) (citations omitted). For related critiques of Ely's theory, see David Lyons, *Substance, Process, and Outcome in Constitutional Theory*, 72 CORNELL L. REV. 745 (1987); Laurence H. Tribe, *The Puzzling Persistence of Process-Based Constitutional Theories*, 89 YALE L.J. 1063, 1064, 1069-72 (1980); Mark Tushnet, *Darkness on the Edge of Town: The Contributions of John Hart Ely to Constitutional Theory*, 89 YALE L.J. 1037, 1045 (1980).

114. This discussion assumes that a person may identify himself or herself as gay or lesbian without breaking antisodomy laws. Such a person could have all her primary love relationships with members of her own gender, yet remain celibate. Also, only Missouri criminalizes manual/genital contact. MO. REV. STAT. § 10 (1988). Thus, in nearly all states, homosexuals who do not engage in oral/genital or anal/genital contact may be sexually active without violating the laws. *See generally* Janet E. Halley, *The Politics of the Closet: Towards Equal Protection for Gay, Lesbian, and Bisexual Identity*, 36 UCLA L. REV. 915, 947-56 (1989) (discussing the inadequacy of attempts to define homosexuality or homosexual activity for legal purposes and arguing that gay or lesbian identity cannot be described solely in terms of sexual acts).

Nonetheless for gays and lesbians in many states, complying with antisodomy laws imposes a significant burden on sexual expression. In itself, this would be insufficient to meet the first element of the underclass test, which focuses on access to institutional and economic power. However, as discussed below, the first element is clearly implicated by the collateral effects of the sodomy laws. *See* text accompanying notes 115-117 *infra*.

and gays.[115] And yet, a lesbian cannot go to court to complain of hate crimes directed against her because of her sexual identity without risking both prosecution under antisodomy laws and an intrusive and humiliating investigation into her private life. Any action she takes on her own behalf may also put her lovers or close friends at risk of investigation. She cannot use the legal system to fight against status-based discriminations in employment or housing. She cannot complain of police harassment. She cannot attempt to use the media to build political coalitions with other gays and lesbians without drawing attention to herself as a likely offender under the sodomy laws. This risk places a substantial cost on any active political participation and thus reinforces her group's quiescence in response to oppression.[116] Her access to economic power is also curtailed: Employment discrimination against lesbians or gays is easy to justify when a law comes close to criminalizing their status.[117]

Antisodomy laws also meet the second element of the underclass test. A wealth of speculative, hate-based stereotypes about gays and lesbians are available to justify antisodomy laws: For example, that homosexuality is antiChristian and antifamily, and that lesbians and gays are promiscuous pederasts. Accordingly, underclass review would subject antisodomy laws to strict scrutiny.

Under Ely's view of equal protection analysis, homosexuality would qualify as a suspect classification, and any statute disadvantaging gays and lesbians would warrant strict judicial scrutiny.[118] However, antisodomy laws would present a "difficult question" for Ely, because he believes that such laws are defensible as "a virtually perfect fit with a legitimate and substantial goal" of prohibiting an act to which the legislature has "a sincerely held moral objection."[119] Applying underclass analysis might lead to a different result once strict scrutiny is deemed to be required. A court applying underclass review would be forced to consider the far-reaching effects that a sodomy prohibition has on social ordering, and thus might be more critical of the "fit" between such a prohibition and the state interest. Furthermore, by focusing on the multitude of hate-based stereotypes underlying the pas-

---

115. "In the 25 states that still have sodomy laws, there is an increase in tolerance for violence against lesbians and gay men, whether it is police harassment or the lack of police protection when gay and lesbian people are assaulted." S. PHARR, *supra* note 43, at 56.

116. *See* J. GAVENTA, *supra* note 44, at 14 (citing the threat of sanctions as an example of a way to enforce quiescence on the part of an oppressed group).

117. By making heterosexuality a prerequisite of social legitimacy, antisodomy laws also reinforce the dominance of men over women. *See* note 97 *supra*. However, unless this dominance results in impaired access to the types of power relevant to underclass review, underclass analysis will not give women, as a group, standing to challenge such a statute.

118. J.H. ELY, *supra* note 2, at 163. The Supreme Court has not yet determined whether homosexuals are a suspect class, having ignored this possibility when it upheld the constitutionality of antisodomy laws in Bowers v. Hardwick, 478 U.S. 186 (1986).

119. J.H. ELY, *supra* note 2, at 255 n.92. Ely's argument that a sincerely held moral objection may satisfy the requirements of strict scrutiny is unconvincing. I doubt that Ely would allow antimiscegenation laws to be defended on the grounds that the legislature sincerely believed it was morally wrong for blacks and white to marry one another. For a critique of this aspect of Ely's argument, see Brest, *supra* note 113, at 135.

sage of such laws, a court might be more likely to challenge the legitimacy of the state interest itself.

Underclass review would also subject a state law prohibiting abortion to strict scrutiny on the grounds that it perpetuates the underclass status of women. Antiabortion laws clearly satisfy the first element of the underclass test. Such laws impair women's access to economic and institutional power and enforce their political quiescence, by imposing upon women a burden men do not have to bear.[120] Unwanted pregnancy can be costly, and the associated disability and health risks can impair a woman's access to economic power. Also, the burden of raising unwanted children falls disproportionately on their mothers, further damaging women's economic status. In addition, antiabortion laws "impair women's capacity for self-determination and their opportunity to plan their lives and choose their future,"[121] thereby interfering with women's abilities to develop and realize their professional ambitions. By making it more difficult for women to enter public life, antiabortion laws also burden women's access to institutional power. In particular, such laws interfere with women's effective participation in the political process, both by placing obstacles on their activity in the public sphere and by forcing women to direct their political efforts towards reproductive freedom instead of addressing the many other issues affecting women in our society.[122] Finally, by rendering women powerless over their bodies and

---

120. *See* Frances Olsen, *The Supreme Court, 1988 Term—Comment: Unraveling Compromise,* 103 HARV. L. REV. 105, 119 n.68 (1989) (citing Sylvia Law, *Rethinking Sex and the Constitution,* 132 U. PA. L. REV. 955, 1017 (1984)). Olsen continues her summary of Law's equality argument against abortion prohibitions as follows:

> Although nature, not the state, has determined that women and not men shall become pregnant, innumerable state actions either mitigate or exacerbate the physical burdens of pregnancy that women alone bear. . . . Social meaning and power also shape the experience of reproduction. Women's reproductive function does not make them unequal or oppressed; rather, the social demands placed upon them in connection with their reproductive functions oppress women. When state laws 'den[y] women access to abortion, both nature and the state impose upon women burdens of unwanted pregnancy that men do not bear.' "

Id.

121. *Id.*

122. Olsen notes that antiabortion laws "leav[e] . . . women involuntarily pregnant and unable to act in the world as freely as men do." *Id.* at 120. Thus, such laws make it more difficult for women than men to enter the public domain and to participate in political action. Furthermore, Olsen argues, the "antiabortion movement puts women into the position of having to fight for something they need rather than want," *id.* at 123, thereby undermining their ability to use the political process to improve the situation of women in society. "As an analogy," Olsen suggests,

> suppose some group believed that begging and sleeping out of doors or under bridges were immoral. The homeless and their supporters would find themselves having to fight for the right to sleep under bridges and beg in the streets. Instead of simply fighting to end homelessness, advocates would have to divert their attention to protecting the rights of people to live as homeless people.

Id. at 123-24. Similarly, the "abortion debate keeps women off-balance and less able to struggle against the unreasonable conditions that make unwanted pregnancy so common an occurrence." *Id.* at 124. It is interesting to note that the hypothetical analogy Olsen suggests is not as unthinkable as it might seem. *See* Young v. New York City Transit Auth., 903 F.2d 146 (2d Cir.) (reversing district court's invalidation of regulation prohibiting begging and panhandling in the New York City subway system), *cert. denied,* 111 S. Ct. 516 (1990).

their lives, antiabortion laws reinforce their political quiescence.[123]

Abortion prohibitions also clearly satisfy the second element of the underclass test because such laws are logically related to a variety of widely held stereotypes about women.[124] For example, antiabortion laws are related to the notion that childbearing is a woman's "natural" function. Also, by treating a fetus as morally equivalent to a child, antiabortion legislation "obscures the active role that mothers play in procreation and is yet another example of society's tendency to devalue the work that women do."[125] Such laws also depend on a comparative trivialization of women's interest in reproductive freedom; the Supreme Court has held that a child's needs do not take precedence over a man's right to marry,[126] but antiabortion activists argue that a fetus' needs must have priority over a woman's right to decide whether to become a mother. Furthermore, antiabortion laws denigrate the moral authority of women, reflecting a perception that woman are likely to have abortions out of whim or caprice.[127] Finally, although antiabortion laws inhibit the sexual activity of both sexes, by "inhibiting women more directly and severely than they do men, restrictions on abortion also reinforce the double standard of sexual morality, which divides women into two classes—'good' and 'bad'—and oppresses both of them."[128] Thus, both ele-

---

123. J. GAVENTA, *supra* note 44, at 15-20 (a sense of relative powerlessness reinforces the political quiescence of an oppressed group).

124. This is not to suggest that antiabortion laws are predominantly *motivated* by the stereotypes they reflect. On the contrary, most support for antiabortion legislation is probably motivated by sincere moral concern for the fetus. *But see* Law, *supra* note 120, at 1028, cited in Olsen, *supra* note 120, at 119 n.68 (speculating that "an affirmation of the value of a patriarchal society" may fuel efforts to criminalize abortion). As noted above, *see* text accompanying notes 47 & 80-81 *supra*, it is not necessary for purposes of the underclass test that a stereotype motivated or predominantly justified the challenged state action. For strict scrutiny to be required, it is sufficient that an exaggerated stereotype was likely to have affected the political process that produced the challenged decision, no matter how many other considerations were involved. *See* J.H. ELY, *supra* note 2, at 157. The state's justification for the challenged action will be considered after it has been determined whether strict scrutiny applies.

125. Olsen, *supra* note 120, at 120-21; *see also id.* at 121 n.71 ("Women create children from fertilized eggs; children do not just happen.").

126. *See* Zablocki v. Redhail, 434 U.S. 374 (1978) (invalidating a statute that required a father subject to a child support order to demonstrate that he had met his child support obligations before he could marry another time, on the grounds that the statute unjustifiably burdened the father's right to marry).

127. *See, e.g.*, Doe v. Bolton, 410 U.S. 179, 221 (1973) (White, J., dissenting) (characterizing the woman's choice to have an abortion as based on "convenience, whim, or caprice") (cited in Olsen, *supra* note 120, at 123 n.82). Scales has argued that it is

understandably unsettling to anti-choice activists and to the patriarchal world-view they espouse when women make the decision to abort. The abortion decision is too much like history-making: it is morally complex, it is often morally compromised, it is a matter of taking responsibility for difficult and sometimes unanticipated results. It is important for the right-wing to describe the abortion decision as capricious.

Scales, *supra* note 90, at 37.

128. Olsen, *supra* note 120, at 110. In a footnote, Olsen argues that the double standard denies sexual freedom to "good girls," while it legitimates the sexual exploitation of "bad girls." Men who exploit one class of women are considered suitable marriage partners for the other. By making a virtue of fending off men's advances, the double standard legitimates a significant degree of coercive male initiative in sex. The double standard stigmatizes and discourages female sexual experience, and especially female initiative in sex.

ments of the underclass test are met, and strict scrutiny is required.[129]

IV. CONCLUSION

In proposing an underclass theory of equal protection review, I have attempted to broaden Professor Ely's equal protection model while working within its general framework. Underclass analysis supplements the protection provided under Ely's model by directly addressing the substantive goals of the Equal Protection Clause as articulated by Justice Blackmun in *Plyler v. Doe*.[130] However, the underclass test limits judicial intervention to the "representation-reinforcing" role advanced by Ely, by requiring strict judicial scrutiny only in those cases where a malfunction of the political process can be presumed to have occurred.

While underclass review fills significant gaps left by Ely's model, there remain a number of theoretical and practical weaknesses in the approach I have proposed. First, by requiring courts to determine the degree to which a given state action impairs a particular group's access to economic and institutional power, underclass analysis invites judges to engage in indeterminate substantive inquiries. I can think of no way around this problem, but can only attempt to excuse it by pointing out that a similar problem arises under Ely's theory when a court must determine whether a particular group constitutes a discrete and insular minority subject to widespread hostility, or whether the state has articulated a "compelling" interest once it is determined that strict scrutiny applies.

A second problem lies in identifying the types of power which are relevant to determining whether certain state action creates or perpetuates underclass status. I am sure that there are scholars of subordination who would argue that impaired access to economic and institutional power, and enforcement of political quiescence, are not the most accurate ways of identifying underclass status. It is also likely that some will disagree as to the proper application of these factors to particular facts. I am sure that the factors I have identified could be refined through further research and study,

---

Id. at 110 n.24.

129. At first glance, it might seem that underclass analysis would require strict scrutiny of all criminal statutes because they seem to fit the basic requirements of the underclass test. For example, consider a statute prohibiting burglary. Burglars are denied access to economic and institutional power: They are jailed, and they cannot vote. Certainly, burglars are widely disliked, and stereotypes about them are logically related to the decision to enact this statute. Professor Ely confronts a similar problem in developing his suspect classification analysis, in that burglars seem to fit his definition of a discrete and insular minority subject to widespread hostility, so that statutes prohibiting burglary, which clearly disadvantage them, might have to be strictly scrutinized. *See* J.H. ELY, *supra* note 2, at 154. However, Ely notes that even under strict scrutiny, such laws

   plainly should survive. . . . There is so patently a substantial goal here, that of protecting our homes by penalizing those who break and enter them, and the fit between the goal and the classification is so close, that whatever suspicion such a classification might under other circumstances engender is allayed so immediately it doesn't even have time to register.

Id. (footnote omitted). *But see* Brest, *supra* note 113, at 134-37.

130. *See* text accompanying notes 30-42 *supra*.

but I believe they provide rough, viable, and approximately reliable indicators of state involvement in the creation of class distinctions.

A related problem arises in that the underclass test distinguishes between underclass status that is actively created or perpetuated by state action and class distinctions that exist absent any state intervention. This distinction between action and the failure to act is not a strong one. For example, it can be argued that the state actively established a capitalist society, with its inevitable class distinctions, simply by failing to prohibit corporations from competing for financial capital. This problem can be resolved only by assuming some baseline which exists "naturally," so that changes to this "natural" state of affairs are viewed as active intervention. As discussed above,[131] it is difficult to articulate a theoretically satisfying rationale for choosing one baseline rather than another, and the choice will generally depend on policy judgments. The implicit baseline choices made throughout this note are not arbitrary, in that they reflect assumptions which underlie our current social, economic, and legal system, or, in some cases, reasoned policy judgements, but they are certainly subject to challenge.

Finally, the second element of the underclass test creates problems of implementation. As discussed above,[132] it is not possible to determine whether exaggerated stereotypes justified or obscured the adverse impact of a state action by examining direct evidence of legislative decisionmaking. Instead, a court must ask whether certain stereotypes about a particular group are prevalent in our society, and, if so, whether they are logically related to the challenged state action. The extent to which this inquiry is meaningful will depend on a judge's willingness to accept unusual kinds of evidence. For example, to convince a judge that many people believe that homosexuals are child-molesters, a plaintiff might present copies of the *National Enquirer*, videotapes of comedians who make relevant homophobic jokes to cheering, laughing audiences, and opinion surveys of high school students. Ultimately, to decide whether such stereotypes are sufficiently prevalent to "matter" for purposes of the second element of the underclass test, a judge will have to apply common sense; this gives a judge room to impose her own point of view.

Underclass analysis does not pretend to eliminate discretion from judicial review. Instead, its purpose is to force courts to confront the substantive goals of the Equal Protection Clause, while limiting judicial intervention to correction of political malfunction. It may be that some judges, to serve particular ends, may twist their interpretation of whether political malfunction has occurred in a given situation. However, this should not discourage an attempt to give viable, relevant standards to the majority of judges, who are likely to apply them in good faith.

---

131. *See* text accompanying notes 109-113 *supra*.
132. *See* text accompanying notes 50-52 *supra*.

Contracts

[6]

ESSAY

RESCUING IMPOSSIBILITY DOCTRINE:
A POSTMODERN FEMINIST ANALYSIS OF CONTRACT LAW*

MARY JOE FRUG†

In this Essay, I seek to enrich contract doctrine by using feminist strategies as a means of contesting and restructuring conventional and stalemated understandings. At the same time, I hope to contribute to feminist theory by exposing, on the somewhat unlikely terrain of the common law, how conventional analytical devices are deeply implicated in the construction of our current gender system. In the pursuit of these objectives, I am going to be particularly concerned with three "texts." The "texts" are law review articles written by male legal scholars for a law readership.

I originally chose the doctrinal problem I am going to discuss for a research project as a result of political happenstance. In 1988, a contracts scholar, who was then serving as chair of the Contracts Section of the Association of American Law Schools, declined a proposal for a joint Association program with feminists. In a publicly circulated letter, the chair explained his decision by elaborating his view that the topic of the relationship between feminist theory and contract law was not "developed . . . to a point where it is ready for such a sponsorship," that it does not yet have "a respectable basis."[1] "In contrast," he wrote, the topic upon which the Contracts Section would focus its program, "excuse of

---

* © Copyright 1992, Gerald E. Frug.

† Professor of Law, Villanova Law School, 1974-1981; Professor of Law, New England School of Law, 1981-1991. Mary Joe Frug was murdered on April 4, 1991; this Essay was left in draft at the time of her death. Earlier versions were presented at a program co-sponsored by the Section on Women and Legal Education and the Society of American Law Teachers at the Annual Meeting of the Association of American Law Schools in January, 1989, at the University of Toronto Legal Theory Workshop in March, 1989, and at a conference of the Critical Studies and Human Research Group on "Feminist Theory and the Question of the Subject," held at U.C.L.A. in May, 1990.

[1] Letter from W. David Slawson, Professor of Law, University of Southern California, to Mary Joe Frug, Professor of Law, New England School of Law 1-2 (June 24, 1988) (circulated to the members of Professor Slawson's advisory committee) (on file with the *University of Pennsylvania Law Review*).

(1029)

performance, adjustment of contract and limitation of remedy on account of unexpected events," "has been thoroughly developed in the literature."[2] Feminist theory, he concluded, was unlikely (ever) to contribute significantly to contract law because "the male bias of our society . . . has not had important consequences for contract law."[3]

Since debates regarding different ways of handling doctrinal problems are a staple component of legal scholarship, I immediately decided to challenge his prediction by writing, as a feminist, about whatever doctrinal issue his group was discussing at the time. In a coincidence that may arouse your interest as it did mine, the contract doctrine I blindly assigned myself uncannily resonates with a postmodern stance toward the female subject. "It is *impossible* to dissociate the questions of art, style and truth from the question of the woman,"[4] Derrida writes in *Spurs*.

> Nevertheless the question "what is woman?" is itself suspended by the simple formulation of their common problematic. One can no longer seek her, no more than one could search for woman's femininity or female sexuality. And she is certainly not to be found in any of the familiar modes of concept or knowledge. Yet [he concludes] it is *impossible* to resist looking for her.[5]

"[I]mpossible to dissociate . . ." and "impossible to resist looking . . . ." The contract doctrine which is the subject of the "texts" I will discuss is the doctrine of impossibility.

INTRODUCTION

The "texts" involving impossibility doctrine that I am going to discuss are an essay by Richard Posner and Andrew Rosenfield in the 1977 *Journal of Legal Studies*;[6] Robert Hillman's 1983 *Cornell Law Review* essay;[7] and a second Hillman piece which is in the 1987 *Duke Law Journal*.[8] These articles are important because they

---

[2] *Id.* at 2.

[3] *Id.*

[4] JACQUES DERRIDA, SPURS: NIETZSCHE'S STYLES 71 (Barbara Harlow trans., 1978) (emphasis added).

[5] *Id.* (emphasis added).

[6] Richard A. Posner & Andrew M. Rosenfield, *Impossibility and Related Doctrines in Contract Law: An Economic Analysis*, 6 J. LEGAL STUD. 83 (1977).

[7] Robert A. Hillman, *An Analysis of the Cessation of Contractual Relations*, 68 CORNELL L. REV. 617 (1983).

[8] Robert A. Hillman, *Court Adjustment of Long-Term Contracts: An Analysis Under Modern Contract Law*, 1987 DUKE L.J. 1.

capture the conflict within the academic dispute about the application of impossibility doctrine. I am going to argue that the rhetoric
and analytical characteristics of the Posner/Rosenfield position on
impossibility doctrine are helpfully understood as stereotypically
masculine, both in their strengths and in their weaknesses. In
contrast, the Hillman article is helpfully understood as offering a
feminine alternative version of the doctrine, with the strengths and
weaknesses associated with that stereotypical position.

As Fran Olsen has written in her article, "The Sex of Law," it is
often the case when opposing discourses develop, in law but also
elsewhere, that the relationship between the dichotomies in the
opposing discourses is likely to mirror cultural stereotypes of
women and men.[9] Identifying the gendered character of the
discourses can therefore be a feminist strategy for challenging the
extensive and complicated network of social and cultural practices
which legitimate the subordination of women. The assumption
underlying this strategy is that language is a mechanism of power,
that there is always more at stake in the relationship of gender and
language than "just" a question of literary style—indeed, that style
itself can constitute a powerful socializing apparatus.

There are at least three forms which such a feminist strategy can
take. One form, which I will not pursue in this Essay, focuses on
the specific gender of individuals noted in a text, analyzing the ways
in which male and female characters and even their pronouns are
deployed. This practice is illustrated by some of my argument in
reviewing Dawson, Harvey, and Henderson's fourth edition,[10] such
as the assertion that the disproportionate number of male parties in
the cases reproduced in that text is likely to foster sexist attitudes
in readers regarding the position of women or womanly persons in
the law.

A second form of feminist discourse practice is to examine the
relationship between the dichotomies in a particular discourse and
cultural stereotypes of women and men. Such dichotomies are
often unconsciously but sometimes consciously molded by their
authors to resonate with stereotypical sex differences. In this Essay

---

[9] *See* Frances Olsen, The Sex of Law 1-2 (Dec. 14, 1988) (unpublished manuscript,
on file with the *University of Pennsylvania Law Review*).

[10] *See* Mary Joe Frug, *Re-Reading Contracts: A Feminist Analysis of a Contracts
Casebook*, 34 AM. U. L. REV. 1065 (1985).

I am going to argue that the academic literature on impossibility doctrine can be arranged along such a masculine/feminine axis—indeed, that it is hard to avoid the sense that this work involves unconscious self-stereotyping around gender categories.

A third form of feminist discourse analysis is to show the way meaning can acquire gendered overtones through the use of rhetoric which a reader consciously or unconsciously registers as sexual double entendre. Thus, I am going to argue that the Posner/Rosenfield and the Hillman articles contain rhetoric which is repeatedly suggestive of stereotypical male and female "sex talk."

Before turning to a discussion of the articles themselves, let me state in a generalized way some of the reasons why I believe that analyzing the gender of legal discourse is useful. First, to the extent that there is a cultural compulsion to maintain the gendered integrity of texts, pursuing the gendered character of a particular text is likely to facilitate a reader's understanding of that text. For example, having identified the Posner/Rosenfield piece as stereotypically masculine, my appreciation of the authors' technical argument about impossibility doctrine is likely to be enhanced by using my understanding of masculinity as a stereotyped role, persona, or mask as a guide to its meaning.

Second, because of the relational character of gendered identities, a reader's understanding of opposing discourses can be furthered by using a gendered trait within one discourse to predict, to understand, or to critique the other. In addition, the hierarchical dimension of gender relations can illuminate the positioning of opposing discourses. In legal debates about doctrinal problems it is almost always the case that one line of thought is understood as the standard or dominant approach, and the second line of thought is treated as exceptional or subordinate to the first. Identifying the gender mask an author assumes not only helps predict which hierarchical position a text will occupy but may also help one understand its entrenchment in that position.

Finally, and perhaps most significantly, the gendered character of discourse can expose weaknesses in legal argument. The cultural compulsion to maintain the gendered identity of one's text involves one—inevitably, perhaps—in the vices of one's virtues. Finding ruptures in a text where its gendered character falters is likely to indicate a problem in the line of thought the text is developing.

One last point of introduction might also be useful—a brief definition of two phrases I have already used in this Essay, feminist theory and impossibility doctrine. I am usually reluctant to define feminist theory separately from the broader, more politically charged category of "feminism" on the grounds that this division can lead to a falsely abstracted and misleading unification of feminist projects. Nevertheless, it seems fair to acknowledge that, like other political movements, feminism has a discourse of explanation which can reasonably be called "theory." I am not sure that much feminism will be excluded by my definition of theory as work which seeks to *account for* the condition of women as well as to illustrate it or oppose it, but this definition has the important virtue of being supple enough to include multiple and even inconsistent categories of explanation.

Although categories within feminist theory are imprecise and overlap, the treatment of impossibility doctrine I will offer here is primarily informed by postmodern feminism, the particular blend of psychoanalysis, linguistics, and philosophy which is concerned with sexual difference and which is associated with the writing of French feminists such as Luce Irigaray and Julia Kristeva and American feminists such as Barbara Johnson and Jane Gallop.[11] In acknowledging the influence of postmodern feminist scholarship, I do not mean to imply that I am conforming to an orthodox methodology or line. I doubt that I am. What does link this paper programmatically with postmodern feminism is a shared intention to disrupt cultural dichotomies—especially, and controversially, the dichotomy of male/female.

Other feminist theories, such as socialist feminism, cultural feminism, lesbian feminism, and the feminism of women of color might also inform and affect a doctrinal analysis of impossibility, although they also might not. For the purposes of this Essay I have quite deliberately overlooked the diversity of feminist theory and the conflict within feminist theories, concentrating instead on the assistance which postmodern feminism has been able to offer my undertaking.

---

[11] *See, e.g.*, JANE GALLOP, THE DAUGHTER'S SEDUCTION: FEMINISM AND PSYCHO-ANALYSIS (1982) [hereinafter GALLOP, SEDUCTION]; JANE GALLOP, THINKING THROUGH THE BODY (1988) [hereinafter GALLOP, THINKING]; LUCE IRIGARAY, SPECULUM OF THE OTHER WOMAN (Gillian C. Gill trans., 1985); LUCE IRIGARAY, THIS SEX WHICH IS NOT ONE (Catherine Porter trans., 1985) [hereinafter IRIGARAY, THIS SEX]; BARBARA JOHNSON, THE CRITICAL DIFFERENCE (1980); BARBARA JOHNSON, A WORLD OF DIFFERENCE (1987) [hereinafter JOHNSON, A WORLD]; JULIA KRISTEVA, DESIRE IN LANGUAGE: A SEMIOTIC APPROACH TO LITERATURE AND ART (Thomas Gora et al. trans., 1980); JULIA KRISTEVA, THE KRISTEVA READER (Toril Moi ed., 1986) [hereinafter KRISTEVA, READER].

The term impossibility doctrine has generally been used to refer to a particular subcategory of law relating to cases in which contractual parties seek to escape their contractual responsibilities on account of "extraordinary," "unanticipated," or "disruptive" circumstances. Other subcategories are the doctrines of mistake, frustration of purpose, commercial impracticability, and failure of presupposed conditions. Like others currently writing about these subcategories, I think the commonalities among the doctrines are more usefully examined than the distinctions.[12] Although elsewhere these doctrines have been referred to collectively as excuse, discharge, or cessation law, I am going to use the term impossibility as a unifying name. I have chosen this name to indicate a deliberate break with the gendered character of current scholarship. In order for feminist theory to rescue (re-skew) excuse doctrine from (within) the respectable debate in which it is currently stuck, I intend to argue, descending only for the moment into postmodern jargon, that excuse doctrine is "impossible," that impossibility doctrine is the *différance* of contract law.[13]

II. THE POSNER/ROSENFIELD AND HILLMAN ARTICLES

A. *The Gendered Character of Impossibility Scholarship*

I begin with the gendered character of the position Posner and Rosenfield take on impossibility doctrine. Summarily dismissing prior attempts to predict when performance will be excused—"The foreseeability test . . . is non-operational . . ."[14]—the authors articulate a new standard for deciding when contract performance should be excused. "[D]ischarge should be allowed," they propose, whenever "the promisee is the superior risk bearer."[15] This standard is applied through a three step analysis, in which a

---

[12] *See, e.g.,* FRIEDRICH KESSLER ET AL., CONTRACTS: CASES & MATERIALS 861-976 (1986) (discussing the "jurisprudential misfortune" of courts treating mistakes different from impossibilities or frustrations); Hillman, *supra* note 7, at 617-18 (arguing that the various doctrines for cessation are treated similarly by the courts); Hillman, *supra* note 8, at 31 (arguing that court intervention should be standardized for certain "impracticable" circumstances); Posner & Rosenfield, *supra* note 6, at 85-86 (asserting that the treatment of contract-discharging doctrines alike for purposes of analysis is most useful).

[13] *See generally* JACQUES DERRIDA, *Différance, in* MARGINS OF PHILOSOPHY 1-27 (Alan Bass trans., 1982).

[14] Posner & Rosenfield, *supra* note 6, at 100.

[15] *Id.* at 90.

decision maker determines a) which party can estimate the probability of loss; b) which party can estimate the magnitude of the loss; and c) which party is better situated to insure against the loss.[16] Posner and Rosenfield confidently claim that the "superior risk bearer" standard can explain "the typical outcomes in the major classes of cases."[17] To the extent that decided cases are inconsistent with the standard, the authors are unperturbed. "It is not our purpose to explain or even identify every inconsistent outcome."[18] To the extent that the application of the test points in opposite directions, the authors' confidence in their standard is undiminished; they assert that "empirical studies" will resolve such conflicts.[19]

Like a phallus, this conceptual proposal is singular, daunting, rigid, and cocksure. The purpose of the "superior risk bearer" standard, as they see it, is to permit courts to decide impossibility cases as if the singular legitimate decisional objective is to facilitate efficient contract planning.[20] (In other words, the only purpose of the legal impossibility standard is to guide parties in future cases so that they can minimize drafting time and effort; the standard is unconcerned with parties already in contractual relationships who desire to know what their responsibilities might be should performance begin to seem "impossible.") In pursuit of future contract planning, Posner and Rosenfield treat all contracts as if they fit a particular, abstract model of contractual relations, in which the relationship between the parties is highly delineated and quite historically discrete.[21] Finally, the authors rely on and defend a sharply and cleanly dichotomized system of contractual remedies, according to which contractual obligations must either be performed in full or discharged.[22] Because the proposal is focused on a single goal, because it is confidently predicated on an abstract model of contractual relations, and because of its clearly decisive, on or off remedial implications, the characteristics of the Posner/

---

[16] *See id.* at 90-92.

[17] *Id.* at 100.

[18] *Id.*

[19] *See id.* at 102, 108.

[20] *See id.* at 90.

[21] *See, e.g., id.* at 98 (using the economically-based discharge doctrine "to supply those contract terms that the parties would have adopted if they had negotiated expressly over them").

[22] *See, e.g., id.* at 110 (comparing the breach/discharge dichotomy to the strict/no liability choice).

Rosenfield impossibility standard correspond to stereotypical male virtues.

Hillman's article presents a sharply contrasting approach to impossibility doctrine along all the dimensions I have just mentioned. His approach actually rejects all three characteristics of the "risk bearer" standard. Thus, Hillman proposes that courts apply impossibility doctrine to serve a number of goals besides the facilitation of future contract planning. These goals, which Hillman calls "fairness norms," include favoring the party with greater equities, rewarding efforts to avoid harm to the other party, rewarding reasonable conduct, and achieving reciprocity in a deal.[23] Hillman explicitly grounds his proposal, following Ian Macneil,[24] in a pluralistic, context-sensitive model of contract relations, emphasizing that in the real world many contracts are based on long-term relationships in which the parties rely on good faith, forbearance, and sharing, rather than insisting on a literal interpretation of their contract texts. Finally, Hillman, like Richard Speidel,[25] seeks to modify the rigid dichotomy of performance or discharge, arguing for an examination of the actual harm being caused to a party and urging that a duty of adjustment should be judicially inferred in some situations.[26] Because Hillman's impossibility proposal is characterized by a concern for multiple objectives, by an appreciation of contextualized relationships, and by a desire to achieve flexibility and sharing in the administration of contract remedies, his proposal neatly fits the popular interpretation of Carol Gilligan's depiction of the virtuous feminine attitudes toward justice.[27]

---

[23] *See* Hillman, *supra* note 7, at 629-39.

[24] *See* IAN R. MACNEIL, THE NEW SOCIAL CONTRACT: AN INQUIRY INTO MODERN CONTRACTUAL RELATIONS 44-47 (1980).

[25] *See, e.g.*, Richard E. Speidel, *Court-Imposed Price Adjustments Under Long-Term Supply Contracts*, 76 NW. U. L. REV. 369, 370 (1981) (discussing the appropriateness of court-imposed adjustments of contract terms); Richard E. Speidel, *Excusable Nonperformance in Sales Contexts: Some Thoughts About Risk Management*, 32 S.C. L. REV. 241, 270-71 (1980) (arguing that there is a role for court adjustment in impracticable circumstances).

[26] *See generally* Hillman, *supra* note 8, at 19-33 (describing the circumstances under which court adjustment may be appropriate).

[27] *See* CAROL GILLIGAN, IN A DIFFERENT VOICE: PSYCHOLOGICAL THEORY AND WOMEN'S DEVELOPMENT 18, 30, 62-63 (1982). For an analysis of Gilligan's influence in legal scholarship, see Mary Joe Frug, *Progressive Feminist Legal Scholarship: Can We Claim "A Different Voice"?*, 15 HARV. WOMEN'S L.J. (forthcoming 1992).

The gendered opposition between the Posner/Rosenfield article and Hillman's articles accentuates Hillman's sometimes explicit but often implicit criticism of the masculine impossibility position. Simply by concretizing and disaggregating an abstract model of contractual relations and by pointing out the merit of expanding conventional remedial options, Hillman's articles offer a critique of the male model which is both powerful and also reminiscent of typical feminine criticisms of masculinity. That is, Hillman's equitable approach suggests the element of *arbitrariness* in imposing the "superior risk bearer" standard in situations where it might have little to do with what the parties actually intended. The gendered opposition between the Posner/Rosenfield article and the Hillman articles also suggests the incomplete and partial character of each position.

I turn now to the sexual double entendre of the rhetoric in these articles. The tone of the Posner/Rosenfield article strikes me as markedly masculine. The article bristles with such cockiness that some of the authors' relatively commonplace law review language takes on the overtones of locker-room swagger as I read it. For example, the authors observe that conventional legal categories in this area of law are "empty,"[28] and they comment that even the most promising branch of scholastic commentary is "sterile."[29] In their promise to do something about this situation, they boast that they will "give content" to an economic analysis of the doctrine.[30]

These observations undoubtedly contribute to the suggestive significance I find in the authors' disregard of the phrase "impossibility doctrine" throughout the body of their article. Despite having used the phrase in their title and in subtitles, elsewhere they almost exclusively describe their subject in terms of "discharge," "discharge cases," and "discharge law." In my judgment, the depth of the authors' substantive bias in favor of contract performance and against discharge is emphasized by the contrast between the word "performance" and its association with completed, conventional heterosexual intercourse, and the association between the word "discharge" and its overtones of coitus interruptus, nocturnal emissions, and masturbation. The rhetorical impression of maleness

---

[28] *See* Posner & Rosenfield, *supra* note 6, at 86 ("Since the typology is empty . . . [it] has led legal scholars to despair of generalizing fruitfully about the discharge problem.").

[29] *See id.* at 87-88 ("[T]hus far the insight has been a sterile one.").

[30] *See id.* at 88.

this article conveys is partly derived from the sense that these two contrasting categories of sexual activities define the authors' limited, stereotypically masculine erotic universe.

In contrast to the Posner/Rosenfield article, the structure, tone, and language of the Hillman articles have feminine overtones. Hillman's tone is unintimidating, accommodating, and unassuming, not cocksure. His position on impossibility is set forth in *two* articles and developed through *four* fairness norms; it has multiple parts. In contrast to the daunting Posnerian tone, Hillman modestly describes his impossibility standard as "supplement[al]" to the principle of "freedom of contract";[31] he deferentially places his standard regarding excuse of performance after a discussion of the express and implied desires of contract parties.[32] Read in comparison with the Posnerian rhetoric, Hillman's tropes, the figurative language he uses, evoke a stereotypically female description of sexual relations. Hillman's unifying name for impossibility doctrine is "cessation" rather than "discharge," and rather than promising to "give content" to an analysis or erect a "framework" he uses the language of display: he promises to "present," to "demonstrate" his thesis.[33]   His frequently stated and principal concern is the application of impossibility law where parties have left "gaps" in their contracts.[34]

B. *Disrupting the Gendered Opposition of Impossibility Scholarship*

Like other postmodern theorists, postmodern feminists use deconstructive analytical strategies to expose contradictory and repressed elements embedded within and supporting the deceptively coherent message on the surface of a text. The strategy I will use here—a strategy inspired by Jane Gallop's most recent book, *Thinking Through the Body*[35]—consists of identifying what I call a critical rupture in a passage; a rupture which, in Barbara Johnson's words, "encounters and propagates the surprise of otherness" or

---

[31] *See* Hillman, *supra* note 7, at 620.

[32] *See id.* at 620-29 (discussing express and implied desires of contracting parties); *id.* at 629-42 (describing a model of "fairness in contract cessation").

[33] *See id.* at 620 ("In the conclusion, I present some brief observations based on the survey in Part II."); *id.* at 617 ("My first goal is to demonstrate that the courts generally have taken a common approach to the issue of cessation.").

[34] *See id.* at 627 (discussing, under the subheading "Gaps," failures of certain contracts to "consider and plan for contingencies that will arise").

[35] *See* GALLOP, THINKING, *supra* note 11.

difference.[36] In each of the texts I examine, the critical rupture is
a point where analytical cogency is sacrificed to the gendered
integrity of the authors' positions.

A critical rupture in the Posner/Rosenfield article occurs at the
moment two-thirds of the way into the article when the authors
briefly discuss "doubtful cases."[37] "Doubtful cases" are defined as
those in which the "superior risk bearer" test "will fail to yield a
definite answer."[38] In singling out "doubtful cases" for separate
treatment Posner and Rosenfield seem about to face a critique of
their own proposal. They seem about to stray from the firm and
confident masculinity that has characterized their argument.
Doctrinally the authors could have chosen one of at least three
solutions for cases which the risk bearer standard does not explain.
They could have recommended discharge; they could have recommended, as they did, that parties be required to perform; or they
could have recommended that "doubtful cases" be subject to an
equitable approach, such as the one Hillman proposed. That is,
they could have chosen a solution that would have broken the
absolutism of the "superior risk bearer" standard by taking into
account the situation of the parties after the contract had been
formed.

The authors reject a Hillman-like solution. Their solution is
decisive but largely unexplained. "Pending definitive empirical
study," they say that the appropriate resolution of doubtful cases is
to reject the application of impossibility doctrine and reaffirm the
principle of strict liability in contract.[39]

By rejecting an equitable approach, with its attendant uncertainty, Posner and Rosenfield refuse an open solution that would have
been inconsistent with the closure they seek. An equitable approach, as Hillman himself points out, is subject to criticism because
it pursues fairness at the cost of certainty.[40] By rejecting discharge
and requiring parties to perform, Posner and Rosenfield choose an
authoritarian rather than a permissive solution for "doubtful cases."
Confronting a threat to the logic of their argument (confronting,
one might also say, difference, or woman), their response exhibits
the weaknesses stereotypically associated with masculinity: they are

---

[36] JOHNSON, A WORLD, *supra* note 11, at 15.
[37] *See* Posner & Rosenfield, *supra* note 6, at 110-11.
[38] *Id.* at 110.
[39] *See id.*
[40] *See* Hillman, *supra* note 7, at 659.

arbitrary, rigid, and authoritarian. They are unable to claim what Keats called "Negative Capability"—the capacity "of being in uncertainties, Mysteries, doubts, without any irritable reaching after fact & reason."[41]

Although there is much to admire in Hillman's impossibility proposal, analyzing the feminization of his work similarly helps reveal the problems that adhere in his approach. A critical rupture in Hillman's proposal occurs in a short section where he concludes his presentation of the "fairness norms." Although he has earlier claimed that the "fairness norms" can "explain" impossibility decisions[42] and has minimized the Posnerian standard as "only of limited help,"[43] here he acknowledges the significance of the Posnerian proposal, admitting that "[c]ourts sometimes justify cessation decisions . . . on the economic and social policies of avoiding economic waste and promoting the economy through contract formation."[44] Hillman seems about to analyze the relationship between his standard and the "superior risk bearer" principle; he seems about to confront a masculine challenge to the feminine virtues of his proposal.

This moment in Hillman's piece, the point when a tough question is raised in the text, parallels the Posner/Rosenfield examination of "doubtful cases." But unlike their decisive, if arbitrary, resolution, Hillman is contradictory and conciliatory. Stating at first that he must avoid the question, because the relationship between the two standards is "complex" and "beyond the scope of this paper,"[45] he immediately reverses this decision, allowing himself "some brief observations."[46] Among these observations is the disingenuous claim that the two standards "generally dictate the same result" since the two standards "correspond."[47] Hillman introduces this latter claim with a conventional feminine disclaimer. "*Intuitively*," he begins. "*Intuitively*, waste-avoidance and preserving the benefits of contract-

---

[41] Letter from John Keats to George and Tom Keats (Dec. 22, 1818), *in* 1 THE LETTERS OF JOHN KEATS: 1814-1821, at 193 (Hyder Edward Rollins ed., 1958).

[42] *See* Hillman, *supra* note 7, at 618-19 ("My second goal is to explain the common approach to cessation. . . . Four interrelated fairness norms figure prominently in such analysis.").

[43] *Id.* at 626.

[44] *Id.* at 640.

[45] *Id.* at 640-41.

[46] *Id.* at 641.

[47] *Id.*

ing through 'keeping the deal together' correspond with protecting the substantial reliance interest of a party on harm-avoidance grounds."[48]

The Posnerian and Hillman standards are concerned with different kinds of unexpected losses. The Posnerian standard implements the allocation of estimated losses behind the veil of history. It seeks to determine what the parties should have decided about allocation before the unexpected event occurred. In contrast, Hillman's standard is concerned with the distribution of actual losses. There is no reason to believe the standards would yield the same outcomes. To reconcile his standard with the Posnerian version Hillman *misstates* the efficiency standard by linking it with *his* goal of "keeping the deal together." The feminine virtue of Hillman's article thereby ruptures in this passage: confronting the threat of difference between his argument and another's, Hillman's response exhibits the stereotypical weaknesses associated with femininity: he appeals to intuition to cover a slight misrepresentation, using misrepresentation as it is commonly deployed to mitigate the feminine terror of confrontation, argument, and autonomy.

Although the texts I have been discussing seek to provide a useful legal standard by which to determine how impossibility doctrine is applied, they therefore fail in their objectives. Just as Hillman's legal argument fails when the gendered persona of his text falters and is reasserted, so Posner and Rosenfield's attempt to develop a legal standard for impossibility fails at a point of crisis in the gender role of their text. By asserting that "doubtful cases" should not be excused, they avoid discharge and call on the parties for performance. Masculine cockiness thus identifies the point at which Posner and Rosenfield abruptly abandon the project of delineating a legal standard for impossibility doctrine and arbitrarily reinstate the principle of strict liability in its place.

C. *The Gendered Context of Impossibility Doctrine*

Thus far my analysis of current impossibility literature has used reading strategies inspired by postmodern feminism in order to expose shortcomings in current approaches to the problem of impossibility. Let me now indicate briefly how feminist theory might yield constructive insights regarding the generation of persuasive doctrinal argument in impossibility cases.

---

[48] *Id.* (emphasis added) (citation omitted).

One idea is to explore the striking parallels between impossibility doctrine and the character and development of divorce and annulment law. Like impossibility doctrine, the function of annulment and divorce is specifically to excuse performance of obligations imposed by the contractual relations of the parties.[49] But the analogies between these fields have historically been foreclosed to contract disputes because of the segregation of the legal subject areas. Because of women's historical links to and dependence on the domestic sphere, the segregation of these areas has a decidedly sex-based character. This sex-segregated character seems particularly pronounced in the context of the nineteenth century, when impossibility doctrine was purportedly "formed."[50] At that time the contracting activity of married women was largely confined to their marriage contracts. Until the reforms begun in the mid-nineteenth century by the Married Women's Property Acts, the law relating to the contracts most *women* entered was separated from the law of other contracts.[51]

I think it would be useful for feminists to elaborate the historically gendered roots of current impossibility doctrine, seeking to determine the effect on impossibility doctrine of placing it in a broader context.[52] One could, for example, track the parallels of the changing remedial consequences of divorce and impossibility over time, seeking—with some caution—to determine the significance of the historical separation between these two similar doctrinal areas. Like impossibility doctrine of the same period, the law of

---

[49] *See* 1 THEOPHILUS PARSONS, THE LAW OF CONTRACTS 384 (1980) (impossibility defense); 11 *id.* at 556 (marriage contracts).

[50] Impossibility doctrine was purportedly "formed" in the early or mid-nineteenth century. *See* GRANT GILMORE, THE DEATH OF CONTRACT 138 n.206 (1974) (crediting Tarling v. Baxter, 108 Eng. Rep. 484 (1827), as the early leading case); Leon E. Trakman, *Winner Take Some: Loss Sharing and Commercial Impracticability*, 69 MINN. L. REV. 471, 475 (1985) (crediting Taylor v. Caldwell, 122 Eng. Rep. 309 (1863)). Paradine v. Jane, 82 Eng. Rep. 897 (1647), is conventionally cited as evidence that impossibility doctrine did not exist earlier. *See, e.g.*, KESSLER ET AL., *supra* note 12, at 913. This case raises for me, however, the possibility that the doctrine in fact predates the nineteenth century, since such a "rejection" could be understood as a recognition of the doctrine coupled with a refusal to utilize it.

[51] *See* Frances Olsen, *Statutory Rape: A Feminist Critique of Rights Analysis*, 63 TEX. L. REV. 387, 399 n.56 (1984) ("Until the passage of the married women's property acts in the late 19th century, married women were legally incompetent to bind themselves by contract.").

[52] The methodology of this section is consistent with the long-standing feminist practice of analyzing the consequences for a particular discourse of omitting women or topics which particularly interest or involve women.

divorce in mid-nineteenth century American legal history offered parties narrower opportunities for excuse of contract performance than is true today. Unlike the consequences of impossibility doctrine, however, the use of divorce did not always fully discharge marital contracts, in that alimony awards functioned in many cases to extend a husband's duties of marital support after divorce had terminated his marital status.[53]

In this century Ian Macneil and others have argued that contract doctrine ought to take into account, rather than suppress, the interest which contract parties may have in preserving their relationship beyond the event giving rise to an impossibility dispute.[54] Indeed, Macneil is often cited by those, like Hillman and Speidel, who seek to encourage a duty of adjustment in certain impossibility situations. There is a remarkable similarity between Macneil's description of "relational" contract law and its remedial consequences and the typical descriptions of marriage and divorce law which preceded the divorce reforms of the early 1970s. Despite the warm reception that Macneil's proposals have received among some contract scholars, there is a remarkable silence regarding his work among others, including, not surprisingly, Posner and Rosenfield.

Another potentially fruitful comparison between the law of divorce and impossibility doctrine in the mid-nineteenth century is likely to be the acknowledged interest of the state in divorce suits. In the classical treatment of impossibility issues, the public interest was so decisively banished from explicit consideration that courts often heavily and unsubtly deployed the device of an invented "implied condition" to determine whether excuse was warranted, a device subjected to increasing criticism after the turn of the century.[55] In contrast, a marriage and divorce treatise writer of the mid-nineteenth century describes the public interest in divorce litigation as the "one great controlling principle running through all matrimonial suits, and bringing into subserviency all other law on the subject."[56] Indeed, in at least two states a public prosecuting

---

[53] See JOEL P. BISHOP, COMMENTARIES ON THE LAW OF MARRIAGE AND DIVORCE, AND EVIDENCE IN MATRIMONIAL SUITS §§ 548-590 (Boston, Little, Brown 1852).

[54] See supra note 24 and accompanying text.

[55] See 5 SAMUEL WILLISTON, A TREATISE ON THE LAW OF CONTRACTS §§ 668-669 (Walter Jaeger ed., 3d ed. 1961) ("Where . . . the law itself has imposed the condition . . . it can . . . shap[e] the boundaries of the constructive condition in such a way as to do justice and avoid hardship.").

[56] BISHOP, supra note 53, § 297.

officer was required to participate in divorce proceedings along with the parties.[57]

Although the public interest in divorce continues to hover over even the most liberal no-fault divorce jurisdictions,[58] the public interest in such proceedings is considerably more subtly manifested than it was in the last century; parties enjoy the appearance of more individualized control over divorce. In contrast, the public interest in impossibility disputes is more overt than it was in the last century, in part because impossibility disputes seem to arise more frequently today as a result of governmental regulatory changes than seems to have been the case in the past. The task here will be to analyze, again exercising caution, the significance of the changing roles of public interest in the separated yet analogous areas involving claims to excuse contract performance.

III. RESCUING (RE-SKEWING) IMPOSSIBILITY DOCTRINE

The gendered integrity that I have argued Posner/Rosenfield and Hillman tenaciously preserve in their essays is incompatible with the approach I attribute to postmodern feminists regarding sexual difference. There is, in fact, an illuminating parallel between the postmodern feminist desire to challenge the borders that define us as men and women and a re-skewed, cogent impossibility doctrine which is neither masculine, nor feminine, nor some confused, androgynous mixture.

Although lesbian feminists and women of color have begun to unravel the imperialistic claims many feminists make regarding women,[59] postmodern feminists have theorized these challenges. They maintain that replacing male values with female values simply reallocates power between the poles of an axis; it does not challenge the confining structure of the (gendered) axis.[60] Male-

---

[57] *See id.*

[58] *See, e.g.*, CAL. CIV. PROC. CODE § 1760 (West 1982) (providing that the family conciliation court shall have jurisdiction over "any controversy . . . between spouses [who have a minor child in their household whose welfare might be affected by the controversy] . . . which may . . . result in the dissolution or annulment of the marriage"); MASS. ANN. LAWS ch. 208, § 1A (Law. Co-op. 1981 & Supp. 1991) (providing that in deciding on a couple's efforts to obtain divorce on the ground of irretrievable breakdown of their marriage, "the court shall . . . make a finding as to whether or not an irretrievable breakdown of the marriage exists").

[59] *See, e.g.*, THIS BRIDGE CALLED MY BACK: WRITINGS BY RADICAL WOMEN OF COLOR (Cherríe Moragan & Gloria Anzaldúa eds., 1983) (challenging feminist claims from the perspective of both lesbian feminists and women of color).

[60] *See generally* GALLOP, SEDUCTION, *supra* note 11, at 124 (noting that female

ness and femaleness therefore persevere as confining and restraining consequences of biological data because of the oppositional framework in which we locate them.

Postmodern feminists seek to alter this oppositional structure by grounding their analyses of sexual difference on the structuralist insight that meaning depends on non-meaning. Maleness is not just the opposite of femaleness. Instead, maleness depends on femaleness. Unlike Posner, Rosenfield, and Hillman, postmodern feminists are willing to confront the differences *within* maleness or femaleness.[61] At the same time, despite current claims to the contrary,[62] postmodern feminists also *accept* sexual difference.[63] Postmodern feminists are thus able to treat women as historically situated individuals with commonalities *at the same time* that they are challenging the link between femininity and biological femaleness.

Transposing their paradoxical approach toward sexual difference to impossibility doctrine, a postmodern feminists' observation would be that the meaning of strict liability or performance depends on the concept of what non-performance or excuse of performance would mean. Contract law is constituted by the idea that parties can count on allocating today the risks of tomorrow. By claiming that *some* unexpected circumstances are *not* allocated by contract, the doctrine of impossibility affirms the ability of contract to protect against those risks that *are* allocated. Impossibility doctrine is thus located at the margins of strict liability, where it constantly threatens to disrupt expectations of performance—just as postmodern feminists both acknowledge and challenge the borders that define us as men and women. Indeed it is because of this location at the margins that impossibility doctrine can perform its constituting and liberating function within contract doctrine.

---

theorists merely reverse the bipolar gender characterization of male theorists); KRISTEVA, READER, *supra* note 11, at 81-82 (discussing the Marxist view of wealth as resulting from the bipolar elements of work, which is male, and matter, which is female).

[61] *See, e.g.*, IRIGARAY, THIS SEX, *supra* note 11, at 81-85 (discussing how "the double demand—for both equality and difference—[can] be articulated").

[62] Postmodern feminists are increasingly charged with claims that their work is depolitical, or anti-political, or post-feminist. *See, e.g.*, Karen Offen, *The Use and Abuse of History*, WOMEN'S REVIEW OF BOOKS, April 1989, at 15-16 (asking "Must the postmodernist be necessarily post-feminist?"). *But see* JOHNSON, A WORLD, *supra* note 11, at 25-31 (discussing whether "writerliness" is "conservative").

[63] Jane Gallop is particularly adept at challenging the male/female opposition at the same time she disrupts it. *See generally* GALLOP, SEDUCTION, *supra* note 11.

In their efforts to subject the problem of unexpected contract conditions to predictable standards, Posner, Rosenfield, and Hillman segregate impossibility from strict liability. This instinct toward segregation is understandable, in that oppositional relationships tend to produce hierarchies. And the value of impossibility doctrine to contracting parties would be jeopardized if the doctrine were subordinated to strict liability, just as the value of contracting would be drastically undermined if the principle of strict liability were subordinated to the doctrine of impossibility. As we have seen, however, these authors' segregating efforts devolve into yet another oppositional structure, the genderization of impossibility, and this genderization defeats the project of articulating a predictable standard of impossibility doctrine application.

I think that the quest for a predictable standard is misguided—that impossibility doctrine must be articulated in relationship to but not in opposition to the principle of strict liability. This obligation makes the doctrine of impossibility doctrine "impossible." But I do not believe that claiming the impossibility of impossibility doctrine requires the doctrine to be consigned to the realm of the subjective, the irrational, the nihilistic, or the non-legal. My suggested feminist approach to impossibility adopts the approach postmodern feminists have used in confronting the problem of sexual difference. Postmodern feminists do not seek to help women be more like men or to replace male values with female values, or to achieve an androgynous reconstruction and unification of male and female. Postmodern feminists attempt to overcome the male/female opposition by accepting it and at the same time disrupting it.

Can feminist critical scholars claim a different voice in analyzing contract law doctrine? I hope I have conveyed that we can, in so far as the use of gender stereotypes is useful in legal analysis. I also hope I have indicated that we cannot.

"Who are *we*" is a penetrating question to turn on my discussion here. The feminine text I analyzed was written by a man. The stereotypes I associated with gender may not be every woman's or every feminist's. The negative stereotypes associated with Hillman's text distinguish his "voice" and mine from the upbeat version of femininity popularly attributed to Gilligan's book.[64] Indeed, I am willing to admit that the particular traits I associate with masculine and feminine stereotypes are undoubtedly a product of my cultural

---

[64] *See* GILLIGAN, *supra* note 27.

position as a white woman, a midwesterner, a heterosexual daughter of the fifties, a law professor who entered the profession when patriarchy was virtually unchallenged. Like Hillman, I speak in sexual drag. If "we" can claim "a different voice" it must be understood, like impossibility doctrine, to lack a coherent essence.

Criminal Law

[7]

International Journal of the Sociology of Law 1989, **17**, 445–463

The Effect of Entrenching a Bill of Rights upon Political Discourse: Feminist Demands and Sexual Violence in Canada

JUDY FUDGE*

Osgoode Hall Law School, York University, Canada

Introduction

The struggle which led to the guarantee of equality rights within Canada's recently entrenched *Charter of Rights and Freedoms* was heralded as a political victory both by and for feminists. However, the effect of this struggle is ambiguous. Whilst the struggle itself both mobilised and radicalised women's groups across Canada, the actual results of *Charter* litigation have been much less positive. This paper attempts to evaluate the *Charter*'s impact on political discourse by examining both its mobilising effect on women's groups and its impact upon a concrete area in which it has been invoked. To this end, the paper examines how the general claim that the entrenchment of constitutionally guaranteed rights has a progressive mobilising effect for political movements by looking at the concrete struggle of Canadian feminists to obtain equality rights in the Canadian *Charter*. The paper then examines how the *Charter* has been used to challenge the *Criminal Code* provisions which are designed to protect women and children from sexual violence and victimisation. Whilst the paper focuses on an area which underscores the problematic and contradictory results the entrenchment of a *Charter of Rights* has had on feminist demands, the broader object of this study is to provide a basis for evaluating the impact an entrenched charter of rights has on political discourse.

* I would like to thank my colleagues Shelley Gavigan, Harry Glasbeek and Michael Mandel for their helpful comments and suggestions.

0194–6595/89/040445 + 19 $03.00/0

The Struggle to Entrench Equality Rights

In 1982 the *Charter of Rights and Freedoms* was entrenched in the Canadian constitution. Significantly, neither a groundswell demand for judicial protection of fundamental rights and freedoms by the Canadian population in general nor identifiable minorities in particular marked the political process leading up to the entrenchment of the *Charter*. Rather, this process of constitutional renewal was initiated by the federal government in response to the nationalist aspirations of the people of the predominantly francophone province of Quebec (Glasbeek & Mandel, 1985; Mandel, 1989). Thus, the entrenchment of a justiciable charter of rights in the Canadian constitution was not a response to the demands of popular struggle, but was instead an essential element in the central government's response to a popular struggle.

It is in this context that Canadian feminist organisations mobilised to secure the guarantee of sex equality rights in the *Charter*. Once faced with the federal government's agenda of entrenching a charter of rights it was incumbent upon feminist organisations to respond. Experience with the *Canadian Bill of Rights*, a federal statute which was not entrenched and which applied only to the federal government, clearly demonstrated to women's groups the significance of legislative language when it came to judicial protection of sex equality rights. In two decisions, *Lavell*, [1974] 1 S.C.R. 1349 and *Bliss*, [1979] 1 S.C.R. 183, the Supreme Court of Canada exhibited its willingness to exploit legislative language to deny equality rights to women. In *Lavell* a native woman challenged the provision in the *Indian Act* which deprived Indian women, but not Indian men, of Indian status for marrying non-Indians. She argued that it violated her right to equality before the law. Distinguishing between inequality *in the law itself* and inequality in its *administration* the Supreme Court of Canada held that the *Bill of Rights* only prohibited the latter and, thus, that Mrs Lavell's right to equality had not been infringed since the law discriminated and the government's administration did not. In *Bliss* the Supreme Court of Canada held that requirements under the *Unemployment Insurance Act* governing a pregnant woman's entitlement to unemployment insurance benefits did not contravene the equality provisions of the *Bill of Rights*. While the Court held that the maternity benefit provisions of the *Unemployment Insurance Act* had an unequal impact on women and men, it stated that this was due to "nature", and not a result of the statute. Since pregnant women were not similarly situated to other claimants, different treatment did not constitute unequal treatment.

Thus, at the outset of the process of constitutional renewal the initial concern of feminist organisations was to ensure that the courts should have as little discretion as possible, lest they used it to limit women's equality rights once they were enshrined in the *Charter*. According to a prominent member of one of the main feminist lobby groups "[g]iven the sorry record of the courts on women's rights cases, this is not a matter to be left to judicial discretion"

(Mandel, 1989: 257). Consequently, the first stage of the equality campaign was dominated by lawyers who attempted to negotiate changes to the language used to express equality rights. However, political developments quickly changed this. In order to make the *Charter* palatable to the provinces the federal government added a legislative override clause which would enable the federal Parliament or a provincial legislature to declare that a "an Act of Parliament or of the legislature shall operate notwithstanding" that it infringed a right or freedom otherwise guaranteed by the *Charter*. The possibility that equality rights might be subjected to legislative override radically altered the nature of the feminist campaign. What initially consisted of a series of negotiations over legal language conducted under the auspices of well-established feminist umbrella organisations was transformed into a campaign of mass mobilisation (Kome, 1983). The struggle to preserve sex equality rights from the legislative override expanded to include grass roots women's groups as well as individual women who had never identified themselves as feminists. Moreover, the perceived antipathy of the politicians to the entrenchment of unqualified equality rights radicalised the nature of the feminist critique. Radical critiques of the state which emphasised the absence of women's groups from the process of constitutional renewal and the opposition of vested interests to equality demands tended to replace the liberal feminist analysis which dominated the earlier expert, negotiation stage (Gotell, 1989).

The politicians responded to the mass mobilisation for equality rights by giving the feminist lobby the language that it wanted in section 15, the general guarantee of equality rights, and by providing that section 28, the clause guaranteeing that the rights and freedom under the *Charter* applied equally to women and men, was not subject to legislative override. Thus, the struggle for the entrenchment of equality rights was a resounding political victory for feminists in Canada, particularly in light of the failure of repeated campaigns by American feminists to obtain an equal rights amendment to the American *Bill of Rights* (Hosek, 1983).

The entrenchment of equality rights in the Canadian *Charter* says more about the relative ease with which the Canadian political process responded to formal equality claims, particularly when contrasted with the United States, than it does about the value of the inclusion of such rights as part and parcel of the legal process. From one perspective, the ability of feminist organisations to get this included in the *Charter* and to secure what they considered to be adequate constitutional protection for equality rights became the litmus test of the political strength of the women's movement. The constitutional entrenchment of equality rights became a symbol of profound political significance around which many disparate feminist organisations and women's groups were able to coalesce. As one activist involved in the process reflected "the greatest achievement of the women's constitutional struggle may not have been the rewriting of the law, but the process of strengthening mass collective action whereby the anger of women crystallized into law" (Billings, 1983: 13).

The Assertion of Constitutional Rights as a Mobilising Strategy

But, how are we to evaluate the impact of the *Charter*'s guarantee of equality rights on the mobilisation of the women's movement in Canada? Does the fact that a wide variety of feminist organisations and women's groups coalesced around the struggle for constitutionally guaranteed equality rights imply that such rights are *per se* progressive? Or does the fact that such rights functioned as important symbols for political mobilisation suggest instead something about the abstract and under-determined nature of the demand for general legal rights?

According to Schneider, the assertion of constitutional and other general legal rights is an extremely important and positive political act. Maintaining a strict agnosticism regarding the actual results of constitutional litigation sponsored by feminist organisations, Schneider emphasises the positive aspect of the "way in which the assertion or 'experience' of rights can express a political vision, affirm a group's humanity, contribute to an individual's development as a whole person, and assist in the collective political development of a social or political movement, particularly in its early stages" (Schneider, 1986: 589). For her it is possible to divorce the positive influence the assertion of legal rights has on the political mobilisation of social movements from the results of litigation. In contrast to Schneider's position, I want to propose an alternative, less sanguine, analysis which focuses on the *nature of the political discourse* generated by the assertion of abstract legal rights. Schneider's analysis ignores the impact this form of politics has upon the nature of political discourse. Rather than regarding the fact of mass mobilisation as positive *per se*, it is important to examine how abstract legal rights function as the basis for coalitions or mobilisation. It is possible that women's organisations were able to rally around the struggle for a constitutional guarantee of equality rights *precisely* because such an abstract demand did not require concrete articulation or illustration.

Eric Hobsbawm has pointed out that throughout history members of movements which have challenged the status quo "spoke the language of *rights* (and still do), if only because this is the natural language of anyone who sets up a model of morality and justice ... and makes claims in the light of this model" (Hobsbawm, 1984: 308). It is also, as he notes, "the natural language of politics, since it provides a built-in moral backing for any demand or action" (ibid: 308). Thus, the significance of the assertion of a right depends upon the social vision or politics which informs it. According to Hobsbawm "rights in the sense of wide-ranging claims to a good or a tolerable life, are not ends in themselves, but broad aspirations which can be realized only through complex and changing social strategies, on which they throw no specific light" (ibid: 310). In the struggle for the entrenchment of equality rights in Canada, feminists' organisations were never required to assert a positive vision of what legal equality for women entailed. What they did was respond to an agenda set by the federal government, defining their goals in terms of the shortcomings of the government's proposals. In the words of a prominent participant in the entrenchment struggle

> [w]omen's involvement in Canadian constitution making ... arose logic-
> ally out of the women's movement's historic tendency to work on short-
> term, specific reformist goals, not necessarily tested against their long-term
> impact and not necessarily rising out of any widely held structural under-
> standing of the nature of oppression (Billings, 1983: 13).

Thus, feminist organisations which may have adopted profoundly different analyses of the causes of women's oppression and, consequently, incommensurable visions of what substantive equality rights for women entails were never required to confront their differences.

This essential indeterminacy regarding the concrete social policies entailed by constitutional equality rights for women is made even clearer by the fact that almost immediately following the entrenchment of the *Charter* "organizations started sprouting up vowing to use the Charter to oppose laws giving advantages to women" (Mandel, 1989: 258). Various anti-feminist groups have employed the *Charter* as a political symbol to mobilise opposition to affirmative action for women, to win fathers a say in abortion, to protect the rights of the foetus, and to secure more rights for those accused of sexual assault. This suggests that to the extent that the *Charter* can be used as a symbol for political mobilisation by feminists, it can also be used by groups and organisations which are directly opposed to a feminist political agenda. There is nothing in the *Charter*, or rights rhetoric in general, which precludes its use as a political symbol by a wide variety of groups which seek to attack state intervention designed to meliorate hardships imposed by market ordering or socially embedded racist or sexist attitudes. Any positive evaluation of abstract legal rights which rests on the ability of feminist and other social movements to exploit abstract rights as political symbols must account for the fact that these same symbols can be exploited by groups with opposing political agendas.

Consequently, it is not possible to evaluate the impact of the entrenchment of equality rights in the *Charter* solely in terms of the mobilising effect it has played. However, there are other criteria which can be used to evaluate the impact of the *Charter*. The ultimate goal of the feminist struggle was to provide institutional recognition of women's equality claims and to provide women with a legal remedy if their equality claims were not respected. It is obvious, however, that the actual enjoyment of equality of rights is clearly not part of a self-implementing process. Initially, feminists relied upon the federal and provincial legislatures to remedy statutory or other governmental violations of women's constitutional equality rights. The *Charter* provided a three year moratorium on the operation of the equality rights in order to give both levels of government ample time to conduct audits of statutory instruments for possible equality rights violations and to bring forth amending legislation. However, the various governments' legislative reviews focused almost exclusively on issues of formal equality and, consequently, have identified and remedied only the most overtly discriminatory aspects of legislation (Eberts, 1985; Shofrel, 1985). This narrow focus can be linked to the methodology of the audits which ignored those aspects of women's oppression which are not found in the express statutory wording, but that which, rather, are perpetuated by laws which have an indirect and disproportionate impact on women (Gotell, 1989).

Because of the government's failure to use proactive means to remedy legislation which has contributed to the systematic discrimination of women, many feminist lawyers and activists turned to the courts. They recognised, however, that it was necessary to develop a litigation strategy if the case-by-case articulation of equality rights was to benefit women. In April 1985 the Women's Legal Action and Education Fund (LEAF) was formed to assist women with important test cases and to ensure that equality rights litigation is undertaken in a planned, responsible and expert manner (Women's Legal Education and Action Fund, 1987; Atcheson *et al.*, 1984).

Thus, the most publicised battle for substantive equality rights for women in Canada is now being fought in the courts. But the terrain of the courtroom and the weapon of *Charter* litigation is not the exclusive possession of feminist organisations. Possibly because of the fact that of the few remaining explicit uses of gender-based classification in the statute books most benefit women, men have brought a great many of the equality challenges. Moreover, men are also arguing that other rights guaranteed in the *Charter*, such as the rights to natural justice, to the freedom of association, and to a full and fair hearing, ought to take precedence over women's equality rights in the event of a conflict. Men have used the *Charter* to challenge welfare legislation providing benefits to sole support mothers, child support provisions, the procedures regulating the adoption of children born to single women, and sexual assault provisions in the *Criminal Code* (Fudge, 1987). And an astonishing number of the challenges brought by men have been successful; male complainants are making and *winning* ten times as many equality claims as women (Lahey, 1987).

Can these results be explained in terms of the peculiarities of the lower court decisions? Perhaps. Or are they reducible to the peculiarities of the Canadian political and/or legal contexts? Again, this is a possible explanation of such seemingly perverse results. However, I want to suggest that the impact of entrenching general and abstract rights in a constitutional document must be evaluated not only in terms of its potential mobilising effect and the actual results of litigation, but also with reference to the form of *political discourse* constitutional litigation generates (Glasbeek & Mandel, 1984; Mandel, 1989). Moreover, this form of political discourse is not confined to the courts, but has imperialistic tendencies which both requires and enables it to invade other political institutions. Only once the hegemonic capacity of abstract legal discourse is recognised is it possible to evaluate whether the entrenchment of abstract and general legal rights will facilitate or impede the struggle to transform oppressive social and legal relations.

The Charter and Legislation Designed to Protect Women and Children from Sexual Violence or Victimisation

Many feminists have long regarded the criminal regulation of sexual activity, and rape in particular, as a symbol of the state's collusion in male control of female sexuality [1] (Brownmiller, 1975; Clark & Lewis, 1977; MacKinnon, 1983). Since the 1970s feminists in Canada have engaged in a process of law reform which culminated in 1983 with the passage of amending legislation which was based upon the coincident, but not completely congruent, interests of feminists and law enforcement agencies (Snider, 1985). The amendments abolished rape and substituted gender neutral sexual assault provisions, eased the evidentiary requirements for convictions on sexual assault, narrowed the opportunities for the defence to question a victim on her past sexual conduct and placed restrictions on the publication of a victim's name (Statutes of Canada, 1980–81–82–83, c.125). In addition, maximum penalties were increased and several defences for sexual misconduct with young adults from 14 to 16 years old were dropped. With the advent of the *Charter*, however, male defendants have sought to invoke their constitutional rights to invalidate aspects of the sexual assault legislation which both predated and antedated the 1983 reforms. This, in turn, has provoked another round of legislative reforms and more are likely to result from the continuing flurry of constitutional litigation attacking aspects of the sexual assault legislation. This has led many feminists to denounce what they perceive to be the use of the *Charter* by men to enhance men's rights at the expense of women's sexual autonomy (Lahey, 1987; Women's Legal Education and Action Fund, 1987).

Paradoxically, some of the first equality cases to be argued before the courts consisted of attempts by male defendants to invoke the guarantees of sex equality contained in section 15 of the *Charter*. They sought to invalidate provisions in the *Criminal Code* which were designed to protect young women from sexual victimisation by older men. The greatest number of such cases involved challenges to two sections of the *Criminal Code*; section 146, which provided that every male person who has intercourse with a female person who is under the age of fourteen years and who is not his wife is guilty of an offence, and section 153, which provided that every male person who had illicit sexual intercourse with his stepdaughter, foster daughter or female ward was guilty of an offence. Lower courts have been unanimous in accepting the argument that section 153 infringes the guarantee of formal legal equality provided by section 15 of the *Charter* and have invalidated section 153 [2]. By contrast, the sex equality challenges to section 146, known as the statutory rape provision, have met with mixed results. Primarily this is because different courts have provided competing characterisations of the provision. Those courts which have characterised section 146 as designed to prevent the sexual victimisation of young children have invalidated the provision on the grounds that it does not protect young male children [3]. This has led to the absurd result of revoking the legislative protection afforded to young women on the grounds that similar protection is not provided for young men. However, the majority of courts have upheld the provision, characterising section 146 as an attempt to prevent teenage pregnancies [4]. Relying upon special dangers which befall a young woman who engages in sexual intercourse, such as teenage pregnancy, the likelihood of abortion, physical and emotional harm, wantonness and prostitution, the Ontario Court of Appeal held that it was "neither unfair nor irrational for Parliament to conclude that it was a much more serious offence for a male to have sexual intercourse with a female under fourteen than a female to have sexual intercourse with a male under fourteen, and to enact the specific offence in section 146(1)" (*R.* v. *Boyle* (1988), 40 C.C.C. 202).

Whilst some, but not all, feminists might applaud the fact that section 146 has withstood this constitutional challenge, most would not accept the reasons employed by the courts to validate the provision (Olsen, 1984). Where the courts were willing to uphold the legislation, they did so not for the reason that feminists urged upon them, namely, that such criminal provisions are necessary to counteract the widespread and pervasive sexual victimisation of women in our society, but rather on the paternalistic grounds that it was necessary to protect young women from their own biological capacities or on the basis of some insultingly tenuous connection between early sexual activity, wantonness and prostitution.

Equality rights have also been invoked by male defendants to challenge section 246.1 of the *Criminal Code* which provided that where an accused is charged with sexually assaulting a person under the age of 14 years, "it is not a defence that the complainant consented to the activity that forms the subject-matter of the charge unless the accused is less than three years older than the complainant." As the provision is expressed in gender neutral language, defendants have asserted that section 246.1 discriminates on the basis of age, since it deprives those of them who are more than three years older than a victim who is under 14 of arguing that the activity was consensual. The courts have, however, upheld the provision, either on the basis that distinctions on the basis of age in the area of sexual activity do not constitute discrimination, or relying on the argument that such distinctions, although discriminatory, are reasonable [5].

But the equality rights guarantees are not the only grounds upon which male defendants have launched constitutional challenges to sections 146 and 246.1. The guarantee of natural justice contained in section 7 of the *Charter* has proven to be a much more potent form of challenge. Defendants have argued that these provisions create absolute liability offences in that an honest and reasonable mistake regarding the age of a young girl with whom they had sexual intercourse is irrelevant to a finding of guilt. This is, they argue, contrary to the principles of natural justice.

This argument has met with mixed results in the Canadian courts. In *R. v. Ferguson* [(1987), 36 C.C.C. (3d) 507] the British Columbia Court of Appeal upheld section 146 on the grounds that the infringement could be justified because young women who engaged in sexual intercourse ran unique risks and that an absolute liability offence would deter men from having sexual intercourse with women who might be younger than 14 years old. This rationale was explicitly rejected by three members of the Supreme Court of Canada in *R. v. Stevens* [(1988), 41 C.C.C. (3d) 193]. Whilst a four member majority of that Court refused to rule on the argument on the grounds that the application of section 7 of the *Charter* to the particular case would give it retrospective effect, three members of the Court addressed the constitutionality of section 146. Writing on behalf of these dissentients, Wilson J., a woman, opined that section 146 violated the principles of natural justice which require, at a minimum, that a due diligence defence is available to accused. Refusing to accept the rationale adopted by the British Columbia Court of Appeal in *Ferguson*, Wilson J. was adamant that a *mens rea* component was an essential element of a criminal offence and that the failure to provide a mistake of fact defence with respect to a central element of the offence was a violation of an accused's right to natural justice.

The dissenting decision of the Supreme Court of Canada in *Stevens* has been adopted by subsequent courts which have been called upon to decide the constitutionality of section 146 [6]. This is not surprising given the common law courts' unwillingness to impose criminal liability in the absence of the requisite *mens rea* on the part of the accused. In *R. v. Roche* [(1985), 46 C.R. (3d) 160] the Ontario Court of Appeal held that section 246.1 had to be construed to accord with the fundamental principles of penal liability and fundamental principles of section 7 of the *Charter*. Thus, the accused was entitled to rely on the common law defence of an honest belief in the existence of facts which, if true, would make the act innocent. The implication of allowing the accused to raise a mistake of fact defence regarding the 'victim's' [7] age is that the accused's belief as to whether or not the victim consented was crucial to a finding of guilt.

These constitutional arguments have spilled over into the legislative forum. The federal government introduced a series of amendments to the *Criminal Code* which were specifically designed to bring the impugned provisions in line with the *Charter*. The federal government proposed to abolish all of the existing gender specific sexual offences such as section 146 and section 153 and replace them with gender neutral provisions which included sexual interference and were not limited to sexual intercourse. In addition, the amendments provided a due diligence defence to the accused person who had taken all reasonable steps to discover the victim's age. Thus, the issue of consent would be relevant, albeit indirectly, in cases where the young person was under 14 years old.

Throughout the Parliamentary committee's discussion of the proposed amendments, the Minister of Justice repeatedly asserted that although the government preferred an absolute liability offence for a person engaging in sexual activity with a young person under the age of 14, the government did "not want to offend any provision of the Charter" (Canada, 1986–87, 1:40). The introduction of a mistake of fact defence with respect to the 'victim's' age was strongly supported by various lawyers' groups representing the criminal defence bar. However, these groups argued that a due diligence defence would offend the *Charter* and that the prosecution should be required to prove that the defendant knew that the young person was under 14 years old (Canada, 1986–87, 7:29). Starting from the opposite position, the National Association of Women and the Law (N.A.W.L.) strongly objected to the due diligence defence on the grounds that it would ultimately "bring the inquiry down to consent" (Canada, 1986–87, 7:29). The government also proposed to narrow the disparity between the ages of the accused and the victim for determining when consent is a relevant issue so as to limit the possibility of *Charter* challenges on the basis of age discrimination. By contrast, women's groups and child protection lobbies recommended that in attempting to balance the need for protection against the desire not to criminalise consensual sexual activity between adolescents, the government should err on the side of protection. They hoped that "the wheels of prosecutorial discretion would serve to ensure" those cases involving consensual sexual activity between adolescents would not come up (Canada, 1986–87, 7:22, 7:75). But the government met each of the criticisms of its liberalising reforms with the refrain that the *Charter* required it, provoking a member of the opposition to complain:

> the more we lie back on these things because of our fears of having our legislation invalidated, the less relevant our legislation is to the needs of Canadian society. It is a new kind of conservatism, if I can put it that way, to stand back and say let us not take risks to do what we think is right for the young people of our country (Canada, 1986–87, 10:14).

In the end, the *Charter* arguments won out and legislation which was specifically designed to accommodate what the judiciary regarded as the imperatives of the constitution was proclaimed (Statutes of Canada, 1987, c.24). The principle of gender neutrality in the drafting of sexual assault legislation was affirmed, despite the fact that since the 1983 reforms many feminists had reconsidered the political value associated with abolishing gender specific offences such as rape and providing gender neutral offences such as sexual assault. There is a growing apprehension amongst feminists that gender neutrality serves to obfuscate the gendered relations of social power that are manifested in sexual assault (Cohen & Backhouse, 1980; Chase, 1983–84). The *Charter*'s guarantee of sex equality appears to have foreclosed the reintroduction of gender specificity in sexual assault offences. More importantly perhaps, the *Charter* seems to have had an impact on feminist demands themselves. In

1983 N.A.W.L. recommended that the law not be used to criminalise sexual experimentation between adolescents (Snider, 1985). However, during the last round of reforms N.A.W.L. urged the government to criminalise a broader range of consensual sexual experimentation between adolescents. N.A.W.L.'s reliance on prosecutorial discretion as the method of preventing abuse is somewhat astonishing, given the fact that feminists have long complained that the criminal process is riven with judicial and prosecutorial discretion which is biased against women (Boyle, 1984; Minch & Linden, 1984; Clark & Lewis, 1977). Essentially what distinguished this round of reforms from that of 1983 was the fact that the federal government was able to respond to feminist demands by absolving itself of responsibility and pointing to the *Charter*. Thus, another paradox of the *Charter* emerges; in the area of sexual assault legislation, feminists may no longer be able to call upon the legislature to constrain the courts, whilst the legislature may be able to rely upon the courts to absolve itself of political responsibility.

This is particularly troubling in light of the fact that in the 1970s Canadian feminists turned to the legislatures precisely because the courts were not responsive to their concerns about the way in which victims of rape and sexual assault were being treated within the criminal justice process. Central elements of the 1983 reforms were directed to lessening the ordeal experienced by victims of sexual assault who chose to come forth to testify [8]. According to the federal government, such restrictions would not only protect the victim's privacy, they would facilitate the prosecution of sexual offenders.

The issue of whether the past sexual conduct of the victim with others than the accused is relevant in a sexual assault trial has provoked a deep split between civil libertarian criminal lawyers and feminists. The former argue that sexual assault should be treated like any other crime and that, according to the title of a recent article, "'Sparing' the Complainant 'Spoils' the Trial" (Dougherty, 1985). By contrast, feminists argue that the assumption that the past sexual conduct of the victim is relevant either to her general credibility or to the accused's belief in her consent both derives from and reinforces a social image of women which equates sexual activity with lack of integrity and licenses man's views that women say no to sexual activity when they really mean yes (Dawson, 1987–88). As such, they assert that evidence regarding the victim's past sexual conduct should not be admitted. But despite the existence of legislative prophylactics which sought to restrict questions regarding the complainant's past sexual conduct, courts invariably have continued to allow such questions (Boyle, 1984). Thus, a centre piece of of the 1983 reforms was the imposition of restrictions on the court's discretion to allow the victim to be questioned by the defence about her past sexual conduct.

The *Charter* has, however, changed this. To date, only one court has decided not to tamper with the legislative restrictions on the grounds that the probative value of the evidence of the victim's past sexual conduct does not outweigh its prejudice to the victim [*R. v. Bird* [*Man.*] (1984), 40 C.R. (3d) 41 (Man.

Q.B.)]. And whilst the majority of the courts have found that prohibiting the use of sexual reputation evidence to undermine the victim's credibility did not violate the defendant's right to natural justice, virtually all of them have decided that such evidence is relevant to the question of the defendant's belief about the victim's consent and that the legislative prohibition against admitting such evidence violated the *Charter* [9]. Thus, evidence of the victim's past sexual conduct is considered to be relevant by the judiciary to the extent that it is probative of the accused's belief that the victim consented. But judicial disagreement has arisen over the issue of the appropriate remedy. Upholding the 'rape shield' provisions in general, the Ontario Court of Appeal stated that there may well be exceptions wherein the court ought to exercise its residual discretion to allow cross-examination [*Re Seaboyer and the Queen* (1987), 37 C.C.C. (3d) 53)]. The Alberta Court of Appeal has, however, specifically disagreed with the reasoning of the Ontario Court of Appeal in this respect, stating that the entire provision should be struck down as a constitutional exemption does not guarantee the defendant's right to natural justice (*R.* v. *Wald*, [1989] A.J. No. 140). Despite the fact that *Seaboyer* has been touted as a partial victory by feminists, the result of the decision is to encourage attempts to fashion exceptions which will invite the courts to exercise their discretion favourably, so as to help the accused and embarrass the victim. The ease with which this may be done is suggested by the Ontario Court's hackneyed, but predictable, suggestion of what might be the exception. They referred to the complainant who is a prostitute and the importance of the past sexual conduct of the complainant known to the accused to a just determination of a case [*Seaboyer* (1987) at 305]. Ultimately, this issue will be decided by the Supreme Court of Canada, where feminist organisations have already successfully sought leave to intervene in the appeal from the Ontario decision [10]. And, despite the possibility that the damage will be controlled, it is unlikely that the judiciary will give up its jealously guarded discretion to admit evidence which it has always believed to be probative.

The second type of protection offered to victims of sexual assault is the provision enabling them to request a mandatory court order which prohibits the publication of material which will lead to the disclosure of the victim's identity. In *Canadian Newspapers Co. Ltd.* v. *A.G. of Canada* ([1987] 2 S.C.R. 122) the appellant, a newspaper publisher, attempted to argue that the blanket prohibition against publishing the name of complainants in sexual assault cases constituted a *prima facie* violation of the *Charter*'s guarantee of freedom of expression. Whilst acknowledging that the mandatory ban constituted a *prima facie* violation of the freedom of expression, a unanimous Supreme Court of Canada went on to assert that the interests protected by the ban (the complainant's willingness to come forward) overrode the minimal restriction imposed on the media's freedom of expression. But the Court was careful to emphasise that the case involved an application made by a *newspaper* on the basis of freedom of expression, and not by an *accused*. The decision "side-stepped and expressly left open the question of what the result would be if an accused person's interest in a 'fair trial' were in the balance. In such cases the general tendency of the Supreme Court of Canada, too, is to rely heavily on judicial discretion to reconcile conflicting interests" (Mandel, 1989: 262).

Cases such as *Seaboyer* and *Canadian Newspapers* have increasingly demanded the attention and resources of groups like L.E.A.F. which were originally formed to use the *Charter* to further feminist struggles for equality. As a result of the *Charter*, feminist organisations are having to spend precious time, energy and money in the courts defending legislation that it took many women many years to achieve. Perhaps this is the ultimate paradox of the *Charter*: whilst feminists organisations are attempting to develop situated and contextual theories of equality which will address women's social and historical subordination, simultaneously innumerable other litigants, including defendants charged with sexual assault offences and right-to-life organisations, are invoking the *Charter* to claim a formal equality which may well erode victories which feminists believed they had already won.

Feminists have been heartened by a recent decision of the Supreme Court of Canada which appears to preclude the use of the equality rights guaranteed by the *Charter* to strike down legislation, including the *Criminal Code* sexual assault offences, designed specifically to protect or benefit women. In *Andrews* v. *Law Society of British Columbia* [[1989] S.C.R. 143], the Supreme Court of Canada seems to have accepted LEAF's argument that the equality rights guaranteed by section 15 of the *Charter* should not be read formalistically so as to protect only "similarly-situated" groups, but rather should be given a remedial interpretation so as to protect those groups which have historically suffered disadvantage. This interpretation would appear to eliminate claims to equality brought by male defendants accused of sexual assault. However, this decision has come too late for those arguing for the sexual specificity of sexual offences, since, as we have seen, the last vestiges of sexual specificity were amended in response to the first round of successful challenges.

It is possible, however, that this interpretation of the equality rights provision could be used to justify legislation such as the 'rape shield' provisions which would otherwise infringe other constitutional protections. LEAF has argued, for instance, that since by far the majority of victims of sexual assault are women, rape shield legislation is necessary if women are to participate in society on an equal basis with men. Because the law does not protect the privacy of sexual assault victims, women do not complain to the police and sexual offenders are not prosecuted or punished, with the result that women are intimidated from participating in public life. According to this analysis, women's equality rights under the *Charter* should trump male defendants' rights to natural justice and a fair trial (LEAF Factum in *Canadian Newspapers Co.* v. *A.G. Canada, October, 1987*). Of course, it would be up to the judiciary to weigh these competing constitutional rights.

But there is something very peculiar about this argument. Instead of directly confronting the issue of how best to balance the competing social interests and policies, as the federal government did during the 1983 amendments to the sexual assault provisions of the *Criminal Code*, the argument is cast in the form of competing constitutional rights. In effect, when a defendant raises the issue that the impugned provision violates his constitutional rights, he is asking the court to substitute its judgment for that of the legislature. Ignoring for the moment the actual outcome of the court's decision, it is important to attend to the form of the argument. It is essentially dishonest. What the *Charter* does is detach form from substance (Mandel, 1989: 310). Instead of directly addressing the question of how best to promote women's sexual autonomy under social relations which result in women's sexual subordination, feminists who invoke the *Charter* must couch their arguments in terms of the rhetoric of equality rights. Whilst it is true that social conditions will figure in their argument, they will figure only indirectly and to the extent that it is necessary to establish the rights claim. In this way the feminist discourse about power is translated into a discourse of rights. Moreover, the legislature need no longer provide a respite from the abstraction and detachment of the courts, for, as we have seen, inconvenient discussions of competing social analyses, visions and interests can now be swept away by invoking the *Charter*.

But the effect of the *Charter* on the political debate surrounding sexual assault extends beyond its detachment and dishonesty. By reconstituting the political discourse in terms of rights, the *Charter* has polarised and narrowed the debate without challenging prevailing practices. The focus is on how the state ought to respond to coercive sexual practices and the sexual victimisation of women and children. Although this emphasis predates the entrenchment of the *Charter*, the *Charter* reinforces it since its scope is limited to government action, thereby hardening the ideological separation between the "public" political sphere and the "private" economic and social spheres of life (Gotell, 1989; Fudge, 1987). And even though the equality rights guarantees of the *Charter* are available for use when incidents of discrimination are alleged by people who can show that they are victims of systemic discrimination because the world of private ordering has made them so, their equality claim only arises where a govenmental law perpetuates this (Glasbeek, 1989). Thus, feminists are drawn increasingly into the state's agenda, working hand in hand with the state to implement their commitment to women (Findlay, 1988).

Working with the state is not, *per se*, a criticism of the effect of the *Charter* on political discourse. Rather, the problem arises when both an unproblematic understanding of the state is employed and the focus on the state leads to an obfuscation of the social relations of power which constitute the problem of coercive sexuality. The problem with the *Charter* is that it tends both to select and reinforce exactly these kinds of political discourses.

The dominant feminist demands around the problem of sexual violence have tended to link up both with the state's agenda of increasing its control over all aspects of sexual practices and sexuality (Snider, 1985; Lowman *et al.*,

1986), as well as the new right's agenda to criminalise an ever increasing ambit of sexuality which falls outside that condoned by traditional family values (Eisenstein, 1984; Petchesky, 1984: 241–285). This coincidence between such antagonists is not fortuitous. It emerges from a shared understanding of the nature of the state and sexuality. The assumptions shared by feminists on the one hand and new right activists on the other are that the state's role is exclusively instrumental and that sexuality must be controlled. Where these two groups disagree is over the aspects of sexuality and sexual practices which the state ought to control. And even civil libertarians, typically associated with the criminal defence bar, accept the assumption that the role of the state is almost exclusively instrumental. Where civil libertarians part company with feminists and the new right is that they seek to minimise the scope of the state's instrumental control of sexuality and sexual practices.

Charter litigation is premised on an assumption of the instrumental nature of the state. And it is this view of the state which informs both liberal and radical feminist demands, as well as conventional liberal and libertarian analysis (Vega, 1988). Each interest group seeks to influence the state, which is seen as comprising the legislature, bureaucracy and executive, by the assertion of right in the autonomous arena of the courts. Thus, not only are the courts seen as separate from the state, but successful rights claims are seen as unproblematically self-executing, rather than as typically dependant on further state action for their implementation (Petter, 1988; Hasson, 1988).

In addition, *Charter* litigation also tends to reinforce the prevailing discourse about sexuality. Instead of challenging how we traditionally think about consent, the cases illustrate that both feminists and civil libertarians who have invoked the *Charter* have accepted that the discourse on sexuality is lodged between the opposing poles of consent and coercion. Whilst liberal feminists merely reassert the consent/coercion dichotomy, radical feminists collapse it by denying the possibility of consent under conditions of sexual subordination (Vega, 1988). Civil libertarians, by contrast, have merely attempted to redraw the dichotomy in terms of the defendant's belief in consent and evidence of physical coercion. Thus, none of the participants in *Charter* litigation have sought to transform the discourse itself. Consequently, the shifting boundaries of coercion have been ignored (Coward, 1987).

By resorting to the *Charter*, feminists have focused on the law, particularly legislatively created law, as the source of the problem of sexual violence, with the result that the social construction of sexuality and the social relations of power in which sexual practices take place fade into the background. Sexual practices occur within socially constructed power relations which are in a constant process of redefinition, challenge, retrenchment and struggle (Vega, 1988). *Charter* litigation, which takes place within an adversarial setting with peculiar forms of style, proof and address, lends itself to a reductionist analysis which is not sensitive to the modulations of history or the contradictions embedded in social relations (Scott, 1988). Such a reductionist analysis of sexual violence is particularly dangerous, not only on account of the strange alliances it promotes (Weir & Casey, 1984; Eisenstein, 1984: 246–254; Segal, 1987: 70–116), but also because it reinforces, rather than tackles, the ideology of male sexual needs.

Conclusion

This paper has attempted to show that rights are not inherently progressive, but rather depend upon the politics informing them. The struggle for the entrenchment of equality rights in the Canadian constitution mobilised women's groups in opposition to the state's agenda, but it did not provide a substantive vision of the social relations and policies that such rights entailed. Instead, feminists were forced to articulate their substantive demands through litigation, often in response to challenges invoked by defendants seeking to undermine victories feminist thought they had already won. This has had the effect of narrowing and reinforcing the prevailing discourse concerning sexual violence against women and children.

In Canada, the discussion of sexual violence against women and children is predominantly located within a particular discourse which is reinforced by its articulation within a set of institutions. This discourse, as I have attempted to show, rests upon two central premises, a conception of the instrumental nature of the state and a view of sexuality organised around the coercion/consent dichotomy. The articulation of this discourse within the institution of *Charter* litigation further reinforces, even if it does not require, these premises. Thus, the courts, as the institutions of judicial review and rights interpretation and application within liberal societies, become the dominant institutions through which relations of subordination are organised and reproduced. And as the *Charter* comes to dominate political discourse it defines the universe within which political struggle occurs. The *Charter* and the discourse on sexual violence and the state it selects and reinforces exercises a hegemonic sway over other forms of politics. Thus, critics who question the possibility of a positive role for the *Charter* are characterised as having stepped outside the prevailing discourse and their cry for a different type of politics are marginalised. This could prove very costly, since social transformation depends upon the expansion of political discourse, rather than upon its legalisation.

Notes

1 Here I am referring to liberal and radical feminist analyses of male sexual violence against women since they have tended to dominate (Boyd & Sheehy, 1986: 18–22). Until fairly recently socialist feminists have been noticeably absent from the discourse concerning sexual violence. This is attributable in part, I would suggest, to the fact that operating assumptions of the prevailing discourse render it virtually impossible for them to participate.

2 *R.* v. *Howell* (1986), 26 C.R.R. 267 (Nfld. Dist. Ct.); *R.* v. *Paquette* (1988) 14 C.R.D.
   350. 70–01 (B.C.S.C.).

3 *R.* v. *Lucas* (1985), 16 C.R.R. 1 (Ont. Dist. Ct.) rev'd on other grds (1986), 27
   C.C.C. (ed) 229 (Ont. C.A.); *R.* v. *Porier* (1985) 69 N.B.R. (2d) 1 (N.B. Prov. Ct.).

4 *R.* v. *Monk* (1985), 43 Sask, L.R. 318 (Sask. Q.B.); *R.* v. *Bearhead* (1986), 27 C.C.C.
   (ed) 546 (Alta. Q.B.); *R.* v. *M.E.D.* (1985), 47 C.R. (3d) 382 (Ontario Prov. Ct.);
   R. v. *Boyle* (1988), 40 C.C.C. (3d) 193 (Ont. C.A.); *R.* v. *S(R)*, [1987] B.C.J. No.
   1255 (B.C. Co. Ct.); *R.* v. *Drybones* (1985), 23 C.C.C. (3d) 457 (N.W.T.S.C.).

5 The Canadian *Charter of Rights and Freedoms* involves a two stage process for those
   seeking to impugn legislation. First, the party seeking to rely on the *Charter* must
   demonstrate that a protected right has been infringed. Second, the party seeking to
   uphold the legislation, typically the Crown, must demonstrate that the infringement constitutes a reasonable limitation that is demonstrably justified in a free and
   democratic society.
   R. v. *Ladouceur* (1988), 14 C.R.D. 350. 10–02 (Ont. Prov. Ct); *R.* v. *LeGallant*
   (1985), 18 C.R.R. 362 (B.C.C.A.); *R.* v. *Halleran* (1987), 39 C.C.C. (3d) 177 (Nfld.
   C.A.).

6 *R.* v. *Perkins* [1987] N.W.T.J. No. 82 (N.W.T.S.C.); *R.* v. *Brooks*, [1989] A.J. No. 2,
   Appeal No. 8703–1035–A (Alta. C.A.).

7 I have sued the term 'victim' because of the limited options available. 'First witness'
   or 'complainant' does not suggest how both feminist and liberal discourse characterise the victim of a sexual offence.

8 The 1983 amendments limited the circumstances under which a victim of sexual
   assault could be questioned about her past sexual conduct with others than the
   accused and prohibited the publication of information which might disclose the victim's identity.

9 *R.* v. *Coombs* (1985), 23 C.C.C. (3d) 356 (Nfld. S.C.); *R.* v. *Oquataq* (1985), 18
   C.C.C. (3d) 440 (N.W.T.S.C.); *R.* v. *Brun* (1986), 28 C.C.C. (3d) 397 (N.B.Q.B.);
   R. v. *LeGallant* (1985), 47 C.R. (3d) 170 (B.C.C.A.); *R.* v. *J.W.B.* (1986) 173
   A.P.R. 123 (N.S.Y.Ct.); *R.* v. *Wald* [1989] A.J. No. 140 (Alta. C.A.). *Re: Seaboyer
   and the Queen* (1987), 37 C.C.C. (3d) 53 (Ont. C.A.).

10 Leave to appeal to the Supreme Court of Canada was granted 16 May, 1988 and
   LEAF was granted intervenor status in the appeal.

References

Atcheson, M. E., Symes, B. S. & Eberts, M. (1984) *Women and Legal Action: Precedents,
Resources and Strategies for the Future.* Canadian Advisory Council on the Status of
Women: Ottawa.

Billings, R. (1983) Introduction. In *The Taking of Twenty-Eight.* Women's Educational
Press: Toronto, pp. 13–31.

Boyd, S. & Sheehy, E. (1986) Feminist Perspectives on Law: Canadian Theory and
Practice. *Canadian Journal of Women and Law* 2, 1–52.

Boyle, C. (1984) *Sexual Assault.* Carswell: Toronto.

Brock, D. & Kinsman, S. (1986) Patriarchal Relations Ignored: An Analysis and Critique of the Badgley Report on Sexual Offenses Against Children and Youths. In
Regulating Sex: An Anthology of Commentaries on the Findings and Recommendations of the

Badgley and Fraser Reports (Lowman, J., Jackson, M. T., Polys, T. S. & Gavigan, S., Eds) School of Criminology, Simon Fraser University: Burnaby, B.C. pp. 107–125.

Brownmiller, S. (1975) *Against Our Will: Men, Women and Rape.* Penguin: New York.

Burstyn, V. (1985) Political Precedents and Moral Crusades: Women, Sex and the State. In *Women Against Censorship.* Douglas McIntyre: Vancouver, pp. 4–31.

Canada (1986–87) *Minutes of Proceeding and Evidence of the Legislative Committee in Bill C 15, Criminal Code and Canada Evidence Act (amdt.)* Ottawa: House of Commons, 33rd Part., 2nd Sess. Issues 1–12.

Chase, G. (1983–84) An Analysis of the New Sexual Assault Laws. *Canadian Woman Studies* 4, 53.

Clark, L. S. & Lewis, D. (1977) *Rape: The Price of Coercive Sexuality.* The Women's Press: Toronto.

Cohen, L. S. & Backhouse, C. (1980) Desexualizing Rape: Dissenting View on the Proposed Rape Amendments. *Canadian Woman Studies* 2, 99.

Coward, R. (1982) Sexual Violence and Sexuality. In *Sexuality: A Reader* (Feminist Review, Ed.) Virago: London, 1987, pp. 307–325.

Dawson, T. (1987–88) Sexual Assault Law and Past Sexual Conduct of the Primary Witness: The Construction of Relevance. *Canadian Journal of Women and the Law* 2, 310–334.

Dougherty, D. (1985) "Sparing" the Complainant "spoils" the Trial. 40 *Criminal Reports* (3d) 55–67.

Eberts, M. (1985) Sex-based Discrimination and the Charter. In *Equality Rights and the Canadian Charter of Rights and Freedoms.* (Bayefsky, A. & Eberts, M. Eds) Carswell: Toronto, pp. 183–229.

Eisenstein, Z. (1984) *Feminism and Sexual Equality.* Monthly Review Press: New York.

Findlay, S. (1988) Feminist Struggles with the Canadian State: 1966–1988. *Resources for Feminist Research* 17, 5.

Fudge, J. (1987) The Public/Private Distinction: The Possibilities of and the Limits to the Use of Charter Litigation to Further Feminist Struggles. *Osgoode Hall Law Journal* 25, 485–554.

Glasbeek, H. & Mandel, M. (1984) The Legalization of Politics in Advanced Capitalism. *Socialist Studies* 2, 84.

Glasbeek, H. (1980) A No-Frills Look at the Charter of Rights and Freedoms or How Politicians and Lawyers Hide Reality. *University of Ottawa Law Review*, forthcoming.

Gotell, L. (1989) The Canadian Women's Movement, Equality Rights and the Charter. *Canadian Research Institute for the Advancement of Women.* Ottawa.

Hasson, R. A. (1988) The Charter and Social Legislation. Presented at the Conference on the Canadian Charter or Rights and Freedoms, Edinburgh, May 20–21, 1988.

Hobsbawm, E. (1984) *Workers: Worlds of Labor.* Pantheon: New York.

Hosek, C. (1983) Women and the Constitutional Process. In *And No One Cheered* (Banting, K. S. & Simeon, R., Eds). Methuen: Toronto, p. 280.

Kome, P. (1983) *The Taking of Twenty-Eight.* Women's Educational Press: Toronto.

Lahey, K. (1987) Feminist Theories of Inequality. In *Equality and Judicial Review* (Martin, S. & Mahoney, K., Eds). Carswell: Toronto, pp. 71–85.

Lowman, J., Jackson, M. A., Palys, T. S. & Gavigan, S. (1986) *Regulating Sex: An Anthology of Commentaries on the Findings and Recommendations of the Badgley and Fraser Reports.* School of Criminology, Simon Fraser University: Burnaby, B.C.

The Effect of Entrenching a Bill of Rights upon Political Discourse 463

MacKinnon, C. (1983) Feminism, Marxism, Method and the State: Toward Feminist Jurisprudence. *Signs* **8**, 634–658.

Mandel, M. (1989) *The Charter of Rights and the Legalization of Politics in Canada*. Wall and Thompson: Toronto.

Minch, C. S. & Linden, R. (1987) Attrition and the Processing of Rape Cases. *Canadian Journal of Criminology* **29**, 389–404.

Olsen, F. (1984) Statutory Rape: A Feminist Critique of Rights Analysis. *Texas Law Review* **63**, 387–432.

Petchesky, R. (1984) *Abortion and Woman's Choice*. Longman: New York.

Petter, A. (1988) *Backwards March: The Political Wrongs of the Charter of Rights*. Presented at the Conference on the Canadian Charter of Rights and Freedoms, Edinburgh, May 20–21, 1988.

Schneider, E. (1986) The Dialectic of Rights and Politics: Perspectives from the Women's Movement. *New York University Law Review* **61**, 589–652.

Scott, J. (1988) Deconstructing Equality – Versus – Difference: Or, the Uses of Post-structuralist Theory for Feminism. *Feminist Studies* **14**, 33–48.

Segal, L. (1987) *Is the Future Female: Troubled Thoughts on Contemporary Feminism*. Virago: London.

Shofrel, S. (1985) Equality Rights and Law Reform in Saskatoon. *Canadian Journal of Women and the Law* **1**, 108.

Snider, L. (1985) Legal Reform and Social Control: The Dangers of Abolishing Rape. *International Journal of the Sociology of Law* **13**, 337–356.

Vega, J. (1988) Coercion and Consent—Classical Liberal Concepts in Texts on Sexual Violence. *International Journal of the Sociology of Law* **16**, 75–89.

Weir, L. S. & Casey, L. (1984) Subverting Power in Sexuality. *Socialist Review* **139**, 157.

Women's Legal Education and Action Fund (1987) *Litigation Works: A Report on LEAF Litigation Year Two*. Carswell: Agincourt.

Statutes Cited

An Act to Amend the Criminal Code and the Canadian Evidence Act, S.C. 1987, C.24.

Canadian Charter of Rights and Freedoms, Pt. 1 of the *Constitution Act, 1982* being Schedule B of the *Canada Act 1982* (U.K.), 19872. C-11.

Canadian Bill of Rights, S.C. 1960, c. 44 reprinted in R.S.C. 1970, App. III.

Criminal Law Amendment Act, S.C. 1980-801-82-83 C.125.

Criminal Code, R.S.C. 1970, C-34.

Indian Act, R.S.C. 1970, I-6.

Unemployment Insurance Act, 1971, R.S.C. 1971, c. 48.

Date accepted: June 1989

[8]

Describing and Changing: Women's Self-Defense Work and the Problem of Expert Testimony on Battering

*ELIZABETH M. SCHNEIDER**

I. INTRODUCTION

In the years since *State v. Wanrow*[1] was decided, the article *Representation of Women Who Defend Themselves in Response to Physical and Sexual Assault*[2] was published, and the Women's Self-Defense Law Project[3] was founded, many courts[4] and commentators[5] have been sensitized

©Elizabeth M. Schneider 1986.

*The author worked with the Women's Self-Defense Law Project, was co-counsel on appeal in *State v. Wanrow*, 88 Wash. 2d 221, 559 P.2d 548 (1977) and co-counsel for *amicus curiae* in *State v. Kelly*, 97 N.J. 178, 478 A.2d 364 (1984), described in this article.

The research and writing of this article was completed with the generous support of Brooklyn Law School Faculty Summer Research Stipends. Earlier versions were presented at the Fourteenth and Fifteenth National Conferences on Women and the Law (1984, 1985), the Feminist/Critical Legal Studies Conference (1985) and as a Clara Brett Marshall lecture at the University of Toronto Law School (1985).

I am grateful to many people who gave me comments on an early draft and shared their ideas with me: Julie Blackman, Rhonda Copelon, Marjorie Fields, Nan Hunter, Ann Jones, Sylvia Law, Betty Levinson, Holly Maguigan, Isabel Marcus, Martha Minow, Susie MacPherson, Nadine Taub, Lenore Walker and Ellen Yaroshefsky. Ann Jones was a particular source of encouragement and editorial support. Scott Pollock, Judith Chananie, Kathleen Turley and Linda Feldman, former and present students at Brooklyn Law School, provided helpful research and editorial assistance.

1. 88 Wash. 2d 221, 559 P.2d 548 (1977).

2. Schneider & Jordan, *Representation of Women Who Defend Themselves in Response to Physical or Sexual Assault*, 4 WOMEN'S RTS. L. REP. 149 (1978). A slightly different version was published as Schneider, Jordan & Arguedas, *Representation of Women Who Defend Themselves in Response to Physical or Sexual Assault*, 2 AM. J. OF TRIAL ADVOC. 19 (1978), reprinted in WOMEN'S SELF-DEFENSE CASES: THEORY AND PRACTICE (E. Bochnak ed. 1981).

3. The Women's Self-Defense Law Project was jointly founded by the Center for Constitutional Rights and the National Jury Project in April 1978 to assist lawyers around the country to more effectively represent women victims of violence who had defended themselves. The Project consulted on more than 100 of these cases, working closely on case analysis, the development of defense theory, preparation of witnesses, and development of expert testimony. The Project developed legal and educational materials, led training sessions for lawyers and other groups and served as a public education resource on women's self-defense issues. It also developed an attorney questionnaire which was completed for 50 cases. A fuller description of the Project's work, examples of the casework strategy that the Project developed and a chart with the results of the attorney questionnaire are in WOMEN'S SELF-DEFENSE CASES: THEORY AND PRACTICE, *supra* note 2.

4. *See, e.g.,* Borders v. State, 433 So. 2d 1325 (Fla. Dist. Ct. App. 1983) (admitted expert testimony); Hawthorne v. State, 408 So. 2d 801 (Fla. 1982) (same); State v. Hundley, 236 Kan. 461, 693 P.2d 475 (1985) (modified jury instruction); State v.

WOMEN'S RIGHTS LAW REPORTER [Vol. 9:195 (1986)]

to issues of sex-bias in the law of self-defense. The overwhelming number of cases in which courts have addressed issues of women's self-de-

fense have involved battered women charged with killing men who battered them.[6] The primary legal issue relating to sex-bias in the law of self-

Kelly, 97 N.J. 178, 478 A.2d 364 (1984) (admitted expert testimony); State v. Leidholm, 334 N.W.2d 811 (N.D. 1983) (modified jury instruction); Commonwealth v. Zenyuh, 307 Pa. Super. 253, 453 A.2d 338 (1982) (rejects traditional equal force rule); State v. Kelly, 102 Wash. 2d 188, 685 P.2d 564 (1984) (admitted expert testimony); State v. Allery, 101 Wash. 2d 591, 682 P.2d 312 (1984) (admitted expert testimony); State v. Dozier, 163 W. Va. 192, 255 S.E.2d 552 (1979) (modified jury instruction).

5. *See, e.g.,* Crocker, *The Meaning of Equality for Battered Women Who Kill Men in Self-Defense,* 8 HARV. WOMEN'S L.J. 121 (1985); Donovan & Wildman, *Is the Reasonable Man Obsolete? A Critical Perspective on Self-Defense and Provocation,* 14 LOY. L.A. L. REV. 435 (1981); Eber, *The Battered Wife's Dilemma: To Kill or to be Killed,* 32 HASTINGS L.J. 895 (1981); Eisenberg and Seymour, *The Self-Defense Plea and Battered Women,* 14 TRIAL 34 (1978); Fabricant, *Homicide in Response to a Threat of Rape: A Theoretical Examination of the Rule of Justification,* 11 GOLDEN GATE U.L. REV. 945 (1981); Freeman, *Violence Against Women: Does the Legal System Provide Solutions or Itself Constitute the Problem?,* 3 CAN. J. FAM. L. 377 (1980); Kates and Engberg, *Deadly Force: Self-Defense Against Rape,* 15 U.C.D.L. REV. 873 (1982); Rittenmeyer, *Of Battered Wives, Self-Defense and Double Standards of Justice,* 9 J. CRIM. JUST. 389 (1981); Robinson, *Defense Strategies for Battered Women Who Assault Their Mates: State v. Curry,* 4 HARV. WOMEN'S L.J. 161 (1981); Schneider, *Equal Rights to Trial for Women: Sex Bias in the Law of Self-Defense,* 15 HARV. C.R.-C.L. L. REV. 623 (1980); Schneider and Jordan, *supra* note 2; Walker, Thyfault, Browne, *Beyond the Juror's Ken: Battered Women,* 7 VT. L. REV. 1 (1982); Commentary, *Expert Testimony and Battered Women: Conflict Among the Courts and a Proposal,* 3 J. LEGAL MEDICINE 267 (1982); Wasik, *Cumulative Provocation and Domestic Killing,* 1982 CRIM. L. REV. 29 (1982); Note, *Legal and Psychiatric Concepts and the Use of Psychiatric Evidence in Criminal Trials,* 73 CALIF. L. REV. 411 (1985); Note, *Self-Defense: Battered Woman Syndrome on Trial,* 20 CAL. W.L. REV. 485 (1984); Note, *The Admissibility of Expert Testimony on the Battered Woman Syndrome in Support of a Claim of Self-Defense,* 15 CONN. L. REV. 121 (1982); Survey, *Self-Defense,* 13 GONZ. L. REV. 278 (1977); Survey, *Criminal Law: Defenses,* 20 GONZ. L. REV. 325 (1984-85); Comment, *Battered Wives Who Kill: Double Standard Out of Court, Single Standard In?,* 2 LAW & HUM. BEHAV. 133 (1978); Note, *Battered Woman Syndrome: Admissibility of Expert Testimony for the Defense: Smith v. State,* 47 MO. L. REV. 835 (1982); Comment, *Criminal Law—Self-Defense—Jury Instructions Given on Subjective Standard of Reasonableness in Self-Defense Do Not Require a Specific Instruction on Battered Woman Syndrome,* 60 N.D. L. REV. 141 (1984); Note, *The Admissibility of Expert Testimony on Battered Wife Syndrome: An Evidentiary Analysis,* 77 N. U.L. REV. 348 (1982); Comment, *State v. Thomas: The Final Blow to Battered Women?,* 43 OHIO ST. L.J. 491 (1982); Note, *The Battered Wife Syndrome: A Potential Defense to a Homicide Charge,* 6 PEPPERDINE L. REV. 213 (1978); Note, *Limits on the Use of Defensive Force to Prevent Intramarital Assaults,* 10 RUT.-CAM. L.J. 643 (1979); Note, *Battered Woman's Syndrome and Premenstrual Syndrome: A Comparison of Their Possible Use as Defenses to Criminal Liability,* 59 ST. JOHN'S L. REV. 558 (1985); Comment, *Expert Testimony on the Battered Wife Syndrome: A Question of*

Admissibility in the Prosecution of the Battered Wife for the Killing of Her Husband, 27 ST. LOUIS U.L.J. 407 (1983); Note, *Criminal Law—Evidence—Expert Testimony Relating to Subject Matter of Battered Women Admissible on Issue of Self-Defense—Ibn-Tamas v. United States,* 407 A.2d 626 (D.C. 1979), 11 SETON HALL L. REV. 255 (1980); Note, *Partially Determined Imperfect Self-Defense: The Battered Wife Kills and Tells Why,* 34 STAN. L. REV. 615 (1982); Note, *The Use of Expert Testimony in the Defense of Battered Women,* 52 U. COLO. L. REV. 587 (1981); Comment, *A Woman, A Horse, and a Hickory Tree: The Development of Expert Testimony on the Battered Woman Syndrome in Homicide Cases,* 53 UMKC L. REV. 386 (1985); Note, *The Expert as Educator: A Proposed Approach to the Use of Battered Woman Syndrome Expert Testimony,* 35 VAND. L. REV. 741 (1982); Comment, *The Battered Spouse Syndrome as a Defense to a Homicide Charge Under the Pennsylvania Crimes Code,* 26 VILL. L. REV. 105 (1980-81); Comment, *Evidence: Admitting Expert Testimony on the Battered Woman Syndrome,* 21 WASHBURN L.J. 689 (1982); Note, *Women's Self-Defense Under Washington Law—State v. Wanrow,* 54 WASH. L. REV. 221 (1978); Note, *Does Wife Abuse Justify Homicide?,* 24 WAYNE L. REV. 1705 (1978); MacKinnon, *Toward Feminist Jurisprudence* (Book Review), 34 STAN. L. REV. 703 (1982) (reviewing ANN JONES, WOMEN WHO KILL (1980)).

6. *See* Moran v. Ohio, 105 S. Ct. 350 (1984) (Brennan J., dissenting from denial of *certiorari*); Meeks v. Bergen, 749 F.2d 322 (6th Cir. 1984); Fennell v. Goolsby, 630 F. Supp. 451 (E.D. Pa. 1985); Ibn-Tamas v. United States, 407 A.2d 626 (D.C. 1979), *remand aff'd,* 455 A.2d 893 (D.C. 1983); Ward v. State, 470 So. 2d 100 (Fla. Dist. Ct. App. 1985); Terry v. State, 467 So. 2d 761 (Fla. Dist. Ct. App. 1985); Cannon v. State, 464 So. 2d 149 (Fla. Dist. Ct. App. 1985); Borders v. State, 433 So. 2d 1325 (Fla. Dist. Ct. App. 1983); Hawthorne v. State, 408 So. 2d 801 (Fla. Dist. Ct. App. 1982), *remand rev'd on other grounds* 470 So. 2d 770 (Fla. Dist. Ct. App. 1985); State v. Bobbitt, 389 So. 2d 1094 (Fla. Dist. Ct. App. 1980), *vacated and remanded* 415 So. 2d 724 (1982); Ledford v. State, 254 Ga. 656, 333 S.E.2d 576 (1985); Strong v. State, 251 Ga. 540, 307 S.E.2d 912 (1983); Mullis v. State, 248 Ga. 338, 282 S.E.2d 334 (1981); Smith v. State, 247 Ga. 612, 277 S.E.2d 678 (1981); Wisecup v. State, 157 Ga. App. 853, 278 S.E.2d 682 (1981); State v. Griffiths, 101 Idaho 163, 610 P.2d 522 (1980); People v. Minnis, 118 Ill. App. 3d 345, 455 N.E.2d 209 (1983); People v. Adams, 102 Ill. App. 3d 1129, 430 N.E.2d 267 (1981); People v. White, 90 Ill. App. 3d 1067, 414 N.E.2d 196 (1980); Fultz v. State, 439 N.E.2d 659 (Ind. App. 1982); State v. Nunn, 356 N.W.2d 601 (Iowa Ct. App. 1984); State v. Hundley, 236 Kan. 461, 693 P.2d 475 (1985); State v. Lynch, 436 So. 2d 567 (La. 1983); State v. Edwards, 420 So. 2d 663 (La. 1982); State v. Burton, 464 So. 2d 421 (La. Ct. App. 1985); State v. Necaise, 466 So. 2d 660 (La. Ct. App. 1985); State v. Anaya, 438 A.2d 892 (Me. 1981); May v. State, 460 So. 2d 778 (Miss. 1984); State v. Martin, 666 S.W.2d 895 (Mo. Ct. App. 1984); State v. Kelly, 97 N.J. 178, 478 A.2d 364 (1984); State v. Branchall, 101 N.M. 498, 684 P.2d 1163 (Ct. App. 1984); People v. Emick, 103 A.D.2d 643, 481 N.Y.S.2d 552 (App. Div. 1984); People v. Torres, 128 Misc. 2d 1048, 488 N.Y.S.2d 358 (Sup.Ct. 1985); People v. Powell, 102 Misc. 2d 775, 424 N.Y.S.2d 626 (Sup. Ct. 1980), *aff'd,* 83 A.D.2d 719, 442 N.Y.S.2d 645 (App. Div. 1981); State v. Leidholm, 334 N.W.2d 811 (N.D. 1983); State v. Thomas, 66 Ohio St. 2d 518, 423 N.E.2d 137 (1981), *habeas*

defense which courts have addressed[7] and on which public attention has focused[8] has been the issue of admissibility of expert testimony on "battered woman syndrome." A significant number of important legal victories have been won in the general area of what has become known as women's self-defense work[9] and on the particular issue of the admissibility of expert testimony on battered woman syndrome.[10]

Several cases which have admitted this testimony, such as the important 1984 decision of the New Jersey Supreme Court in *State v. Kelly*,[11] have done so on the basis of an extraordinary acceptance of and insight into the feminist theoretical premises of women's self-defense work. Nevertheless, the main approach litigators developed and courts adopted on the issue of expert testimony on battering, the battered woman syndrome perspective, reflects ongoing tensions and paradoxes within women's self-defense work. The goal of women's self-defense work has been to overcome sex-bias in the law of self-defense and to equalize treatment of women in the courts. This goal was to be achieved by recognizing women's different experiences and the different circum-

stances in which women kill, and by explaining those different experiences and circumstances in the trial process. In theory, expert testimony on battering is the logical extension of this idea; but in fact, the expert testimony cases pose troubling questions about the degree to which these goals have been realized.

First, cases involving expert testimony on battered woman syndrome resound with the very sex-stereotypes of female incapacity which women's self-defense work has sought to overcome.[12] Second, on the level of theory, the cases appear to revive a set of doctrinal oppositions which *Wanrow* challenged.[13] Third, on the level of practice, appellate cases on the issue suggest that expert testimony is not being admitted where it is most needed—where the woman's experiences and the circumstances of the homicide are indeed most "different."[14] This article explores these problems and examines the first two in depth. After an overview of the problem of expert testimony on battering, the article turns to the decision of the New Jersey Supreme Court in *State v. Kelly*, followed by consideration of the implications of the work on expert testimony for

---

petition denied sub nom. Thomas v. Arn, 728 F.2d 813 (6th Cir. 1984), *aff'd*, 106 S. Ct. 466 (1985); State v. Moore, 72 Or. App. 454, 695 P.2d 985 (1985); Commonwealth v. Zenyuh, 307 Pa. Super. 253, 453 A.2d 338 (1982); Fielder v. State, 683 S.W.2d 565 (Tex. Ct. App. 1985); State v. Kelly, 102 Wash. 2d 188, 685 P.2d 564 (1984); State v. Allery, 101 Wash. 2d 591, 682 P.2d 312 (Wash. 1984); State v. Wanrow, 88 Wash. 2d 221, 559 P.2d 548 (1977); State v. Walker, 40 Wash. App. 658, 700 P.2d 1168 (Ct. App. 1985); State v. Dozier, 163 W. Va. 192, 255 S.E.2d 552 (1979); State v. Felton, 106 Wis. 2d 769, 318 N.W.2d 25 (1981), *aff'd in part, rev'd in part*, 110 Wis. 2d 485, 329 N.W.2d 161 (1983); Buhrle v. State, 627 P.2d 1374 (Wyo. 1981).

7. Appellate cases that have addressed the admissibility of expert testimony on battered woman syndrome and declined to admit this testimony include: State v. Edwards, 420 So. 2d 663 (La. 1982); State v. Burton, 464 So. 2d 421 (La. Ct. App. 1985); State v. Necaise, 466 So. 2d 660 (La. Ct. App. 1985); State v. Thomas, 66 Ohio St. 2d 518, 423 N.E.2d 137 (1981), *habeas petition denied sub nom.* Thomas v. Arn, 728 F.2d 813 (6th Cir. 1984), *aff'd*, 106 S. Ct. 466 (1985); Fielder v. State, 683 S.W.2d 565 (Tex. Ct. App. 1985); State v. Buhrle, 627 P.2d 1374 (Wyo. 1981). Appellate cases which have admitted testimony on battered woman syndrome include: Terry v. State, 467 So. 2d 761 (Fla. Dist. Ct. App. 1985); Borders v. State, 433 So. 2d 1325 (Fla. Dist. Ct. App. 1983); Smith v. State, 247 Ga. 612, 277 S.E.2d 678 (1981); People v. Minnis, 118 Ill. App. 3d 345, 455 N.E.2d 209 (1983); State v. Anaya, 438 A.2d 892 (Me. 1981); State v. Kelly, 97 N.J. 178, 478 A.2d 364 (1984); State v. Branchall, 101 N.M. 498, 684 P.2d 1163 (Ct. App. 1984); State v. Allery, 101 Wash. 2d 591, 682 P.2d 312 (1984).

8. *See generally* Margolick, *When Battered Wives Kill Does the Law Treat Them Fairly?*, N.Y. Times, Dec. 11, 1985, at C8; *Use of Experts in Battering is Upheld on Women's Trials*, N.Y.

Times, July 25, 1984, at A1; Margolick, *Battered Woman Tells of Torture That Led to Killing*, N.Y. Times, Dec. 3, 1983, at B1; Schmiekle, *Outcome Unpredictable in Cases Where Wives Kill Battering Husbands*, Minneapolis Tribune, March 18, 1984, at A1; *Battered Women: Understanding the Problem*, Trial Magazine, Jan. 1986, at 75; Moses, *Wife Acquitted in Man's Death*, Newsday, May 10, 1985, at 1; Fox, *Battered Woman Claim Aids Acquittal in Murder Trial*, N.Y.L. J., Apr. 26, 1985, at 1, col. 3-4.

9. The term "women's self-defense work" which is used throughout this article has been used to describe legal work on issues of sex-bias in the law of self-defense and criminal defenses generally. The term was first used as the name of a project jointly sponsored by the Center for Constitutional Rights and the National Jury Project to consult on these problems, The Women's Self-Defense Law Project. *See supra* note 3. Women's self-defense work is now commonly used as a shorthand characterization of these issues. *See supra* note 3.

10. Appellate cases that have ruled on and recognized the relevance of expert testimony on battered woman syndrome to women's claims of self-defense include: Terry v. State, 467 So. 2d 761 (Fla. Dist. Ct. App. 1985); Borders v. State, 433 So. 2d 1325 (Fla. Dist. Ct. App. 1983); Smith v. State, 247 Ga. 612, 277 S.E.2d 678 (1981); People v. Minnis, 118 Ill. App. 3d 345, 455 N.E.2d 209 (1983); State v. Anaya, 438 A.2d 892 (Me. 1981); State v. Kelly, 97 N.J. 178, 478 A.2d 364 (1984); State v. Branchall, 101 N.M. 498, 684 P.2d 1163 (N.M. Ct. App. 1984); State v. Allery, 101 Wash. 2d 591, 682 P.2d 312 (1984).

11. 97 N.J. 178, 478 A.2d 364 (1984).

12. *See infra* note 17 and accompanying text.

13. *See infra* notes 106-81 and accompanying text.

14. *Id.*

WOMEN'S RIGHTS LAW REPORTER [Vol. 9:195 (1986)]

feminist legal theory and suggestions of some practical ways to remedy problems which arise.

This article is motivated by several concerns. As a litigator, co-counsel for defendant in *Wanrow*[15] and co-counsel for *amicus curiae* in *Kelly*,[16] I have argued for the admissibility of expert testimony as the logical extension of *Wanrow*. Yet as a feminist legal theorist and now, an academician, I believe it is important to confront some of the contradictions that the expert testimony cases reveal within women's self-defense work. Women's self-defense work was conceived of as a way to remedy unequal treatment for women that results from application of the male norms and standards of the criminal justice system. It was developed to assist women in speaking in our own voices in the courtroom, to describe the differences and complexity of our experience, and to expand the legal options available in defending ourselves against charges of homicide or assault beyond the traditional insanity and incapacity pleas.

Historically, views of women as being unreasonable, sex-bias in the law of self-defense, and myths and misconceptions concerning battered women have operated to prevent battered women from presenting acts of homicide or assault committed against batterers as reasonable self-defense. Expert testimony on battered woman syn-

drome was developed to explain the common experiences of, and the impact of repeated abuse on, battered women. The goal was to assist the jury and the court in fairly evaluating the reasonableness of the battered woman's action and to redress this historical imbalance, at least where the testimony was proffered as relevant to self-defense. The notion of expert testimony was predicated on an assumption that battered women's voices would not be understood or were not strong enough to be heard alone in the courtroom.

Examination of the expert testimony cases involving battered women underscores the complexity of the task of expanding defense options for battered women faced with homicide or assault. These cases reveal the tenacity of sex-stereotyping for, despite the purpose for which this legal strategy was conceived, old stereotypes of incapacity are replicated in a new form. Judicial opinions suggest that lawyers who have submitted expert testimony have had this testimony focus primarily on the passive, victimized aspects of battered women's experience, their "learned helplessness," rather than circumstances which might explain the homicide as a woman's necessary choice to save her own life. Even if lawyers are not emphasizing this aspect, judges are hearing the testimony in this way.[17] For both lawyers and

---

15. I was co-counsel for Yvonne Wanrow (with Nancy Stearns) on appeal to the Washington Supreme Court. *See* State v. Wanrow, 88 Wash. 2d 221, 559 P.2d 548 (1977).

16. I was co-counsel to *amicus curiae* American Civil Liberties Union of New Jersey and New Jersey Coalition for Battered Women (with Stephen Latimer) in State v. Kelly, 97 N.J. 178, 478 A.2d 364 (1984). We filed an *amicus* brief in the New Jersey Supreme Court. *See* Brief and Appendix of *Amici Curiae*, [this issue at 245]. Subsequently, I was granted leave to participate in the oral argument of the case.

17. *See, e.g.,* Fennell v. Goolsby, 630 F. Supp. 451, 456 (E.D. Pa. 1985) ("The continued cycle of violence and contrition [sic] results in the battered woman living in a state of learned helplessness. Because she is financially dependent on the batterer, she may feel partly responsible for the batterer's violence, she may believe that her children need a father, or fear reprisal if she leaves. The battered woman lives with constant fear, coupled with a perceived inability to escape. Eventually she comes to believe that her only options are enduring the abuse, striking back, or committing suicide."); Ibn-Tamas v. United States, 407 A.2d 626, 634 (D.C. 1983) (The expert "testified that women in this situation typically are low in self esteem, feel powerless, and have few close friends . . . [they also believe that] they themselves are somehow responsible for their husbands' violent behavior. . . ." The expert's contribution, according to the court, "would have been akin to the psychiatric testimony admitted in the case of Patricia Hearst 'to explain the effects kidnapping, prolonged incarceration and

physical abuse may have had on the defendant's mental state at the time. . . .' "); Smith v. State, 247 Ga. 612, 614, 277 S.E.2d 678, 680 (1981) (The expert testified "that it is not unusual for a battered woman who has been abused over a long period of time to remain in such a situation, that a battered woman's self-respect is usually very low and she believes she is a worthless person . . . and that the primary emotion of a battered woman is fear."); State v. Hundley, 236 Kan. 461, 467, 693 P.2d 475, 479 (1985) ("The abuse is so severe, for so long a time and the threat of bodily harm so constant, it creates a standard mental attitude in its victims. Battered women are terror-stricken people whose mental state is distorted and bears a marked resemblance to that of a hostage or a prisoner of war. The horrible beatings they are subjected to brainwash them into believing there is nothing they can do. They live in constant fear of another eruption of violence. They become disturbed persons from the torture."); State v. Anaya, 456 A.2d 1255, 1266 (Me. 1983) (The expert testified that battered women "typically stay with their men out of economic dependency, and that they most frequently . . . react with passivity to the violence of their mates."); People v. Emick, 103 A.D.2d 643, 654, 481 N.Y.S.2d 552, 559 (App. Div. 1984) (The expert "described the battered wife syndrome as a multistage form of family 'disease' . . . the abused wife undergoes a personality change as the abuse increases. She becomes frightened and unable to project her thinking into the future. She lives her life from one beating to the next and her thoughts relate solely to her efforts to avoid the next beating. . . . [T]he wife eventually judges the term "syndrome" and the psychological description of battered women that predominates in battered woman syndrome descriptions appears to conjure up images of a psychological defense—a separate defense and/or an impaired mental state defense.[18] Moreover, although the rationale for admission of expert testimony on battered woman syndrome was to counteract stereotypes of battered women as solely responsible for the violence, testimony is being presented, heard and sometimes misheard, that goes to the other extreme of depicting battered women as helpless victims and failing to describe the complexity and reasonableness of why battered women act. Courts are reflecting these perspectives in opinions on expert testimony on battered woman syndrome that resonate with familiar stereotypes of female incapacity.

Judicial perceptions of battered woman syndrome as a form of incapacity have problematic consequences for defense of battered women. The critical defense problem in representing battered women who kill and assert self-defense is how to explain the woman's *action* as reasonable. The woman's experience as a battered woman and her inability to leave the relationship—her victimization—is the context in which that action occurs. When battered woman syndrome is presented or heard in a way that sounds like passivity or incapacity, it does not address the basic fact of the woman's action and contradicts a presentation of reasonableness. Indeed, the overall impact of the battered woman syndrome stereotype may be to limit rather than expand the legal options of women who cannot conform to these stereotypes. Judges are not likely to recognize the need for expert testimony in those cases where the woman's

---

feels that she cannot escape her tormentor and that she will be tracked down if she attempts to flee the situation. Her self esteem vanishes and her confidence is shattered. She feels that no one would believe her if she told them about the abuse and, thus, she keeps it to herself."; People v. Torres, 128 Misc. 2d 129, 132, 488 N.Y.S.2d 358, 361 (Sup. Ct. 1985) ("Among the characteristics of such abused women are a decrease in self-esteem, an emotional dependence upon the dominant male and a type of psychological 'learned' helplessness arising out of an inability to predict or control the violence directed against them. Numbed by a dread of imminent aggression, these women are unable to think clearly about the means of escape from this abusive family existence; and this emotional paralysis is often reinforced by their traditional beliefs about the sanctity of home and family and their false hopes that things will improve."); People v. Powell, 102 Misc. 2d 775, 780-81, 424 N.Y.S.2d 626, 630 (1980), *aff'd*, 83 A.D.2d 719, 442 N.Y.S.2d 645 (App. Div. 1981) (" 'Learned helplessness' is identified by defendant as a recently documented theory which explains the psychological paralysis that maintains the victim status of the battered wife. . . . When someone becomes prey to the psychological condition of learned helplessness, it distorts their feelings, beliefs and behavior so that they react as though they do not have the ability to control what happens to them; that a battered woman does not like the beatings but likes the loving behavior which occurs after the beating and she becomes submissive and passive."); State v. Leidholm, 334 N.W.2d 811, 819 (N.D. 1983) ("Such testimony generally explains the 'phenomenon' as one in which a regular pattern of spouse abuse creates in the battered spouse low self-esteem and a 'learned helplessness,' i.e., a sense that she cannot escape from the abusive relationship she has become a part of."); State v. Allery, 101 Wash. 591, 596, 682 P.2d 312, 315 (1984) ("Psychologists describe a phenomenon known as 'learned helplessness', a condition in which the woman is psychologically locked into her situation due to economic dependence on the man, an abiding attachment to him, and the failure of the legal system to adequately respond to the problem."); State v. Kelly, 102 Wash. 2d 188, 192, 685 P.2d 564, 567 (1984) ("The expert described behavioral characteristics which Mrs. Kelly exhibited. These included: frustration; stress disorders; depression; economic and emotional dependence on her husband; hopes that the

marriage would improve; poor self image; isolation, and learned helplessness. 'Isolation' was described as a loss of contact with family or friends. 'Learned helplessness' was deemed explanatory of why a battered woman would remain in a harmful relationship. It was said to arise because of the woman's fear and the unpredictability of batterings, which would lead to a feeling of surrender and a failure to realize or know options available to escape the relationship.").

18. *See, e.g.,* Ledford v. State, 254 Ga. 656, 657, 333 S.E.2d 576, 577 (1985) ("The trial court ordered that appellant 'be remanded to the custody of the Georgia Department of Human Resources and that she be examined by professionals from the Forensic Services Program to determine her competency to stand trial and her degree of criminal responsibility in relation to the offense with which she is charged.' This order contemplates an examination that could relate to battered woman syndrome."); State v. Hundley, 236 Kan. 461, 463, 693 P.2d 475, 479 (1985) ("Battered women are terror-stricken individuals whose mental state is distorted and bears a marked resemblance to that of a hostage or a prisoner of war."); State v. Necaise, 466 So.2d 660, 665 (La. Ct. App. 1985) ("We believe that allowing testimony which would attempt to prove the defendant a victim of 'battered woman syndrome' and which would seek to establish her 'state of mind' at the time of the shooting, absent a plea of 'not guilty and not guilty by reason of insanity,' would be, in effect, condoning the concept of 'partial responsibility'—the allowing of proof of mental derangement short of insanity as evidence of lack of deliberate or premeditated design."); State v. Martin, 666 S.W.2d 895, 900 (Mo. Ct. App. 1984) ("[C]ounsel on appeal . . . argues that the failure to interrogate the witnesses regarding the effect of appellant's mental disease, the battered woman syndrome, on her capacity to deliberate and premeditate constituted ineffective assistance of counsel."); and see cases cited *infra* note 148. *See also* Acker & Toch, *Battered Women, Straw Men, and Expert Testimony: A Comment on State v. Kelly,* 21 CRIM. L. BULL. 125 (1985) ("The battered wife syndrome is yet another new defense seeking the attention of criminal law specialists."); Price, *Battered Woman Syndrome: A Defense Begins to Emerge,* 194 N.Y.L.J. 1 (Nov. 1985); Price, *Battered-Woman Syndrome: A Defense Begins to Emerge; part 2—cases,* 194 N.Y.L.J. 3 (1985).

WOMEN'S RIGHTS LAW REPORTER [Vol. 9:195 (1986)]

actions significantly depart from both the traditional "male" model of self-defense and the passive "battered woman" model.[19] If they do admit the testimony they may see its relevance in terms that, even unwittingly, conform to or reinforce these stereotypes.

For feminist theorists and practitioners the issue of expert testimony is also important because it highlights a broader problem that we face in many different contexts. How do we describe and name a legal problem for women—describe it in detail, in context—and translate it to unsympathetic courts in such a way that it is not misheard and, at the same time, does not remain static? How do we develop legal theory and practice that is not only accurate to the realities of women's experience but also takes account of complexity and allows for change?

The expert testimony cases manifest this problem on the issue of the characterization of battered women's experience in terms of victimization, for battered woman syndrome has been presented, interpreted and heard as victimization. Yet the expert testimony cases by definition pose the dilemma of how we describe *both* victimization and agency in women's lives. How do we translate women's experiences honestly to courts without falling into extremes of victimization *or* fault that can be misheard? In describing what has appeared to be an accurate picture of battered

women in order to remedy sex-bias, have we emphasized the victimized, passive, helpless aspects of the battered woman's experience in order to counteract the disabling stereotypes that solely blame her for the violence? In so doing, have we permitted courts to limit the utility of women's self-defense and constrained its theoretical impact as well?

II. THE PROBLEM OF EXPERT TESTIMONY

The question of the admissibility of expert testimony on battered woman syndrome has been the primary legal issue which appellate courts have addressed in the area of women's self-defense work. There are several reasons for this. First, most women's self-defense cases have involved battered women.[20] The work of the Women's Self Defense Law Project stressed the particular utility of expert testimony in this context, depending on the facts of the case.[21] Many lawyers defending these women have sought to introduce expert testimony on battered woman syndrome at trial.[22] While trial judges appear to have admitted this testimony in the majority of cases,[23] where courts have excluded it and the women have been convicted, the question of the admissibility of expert testimony has frequently become the major issue on appeal.[24] Thus the question of expert testimony has received a great

---

19. *See infra* text accompanying notes 106-81.

20. *See* cases cited *supra* note 6.

21. Early work on women's self-defense stressed the positive role that expert testimony might play at trial. *See generally* Schneider and Jordan, *supra* note 2, at 43-44 but cautioned that it should not be reflexively proffered; Schneider, *supra* note 5, at 645; MacPherson, Ridolfi, Sternberg and Wiley, *Expert Testimony* in WOMEN'S SELF-DEFENSE CASES: THEORY AND PRACTICE (E. BOCHNAK, ED.), *supra* note 2, at 88-90. This work also emphasized that the need for experts ought to be evaluated based on the facts in each particular case, and that "[t]he task of the expert is to provide the jury with information that complements the defendant's testimony and makes her particular experience plausible to them." MacPherson, Ridolfi, Sternberg and Wiley, *id.* at 89.

22. Apart from the appellate cases which have reviewed trial court exclusions of expert testimony, or appellate cases reviewing some other trial issue which mention whether expert testimony was proffered, there is no authoritative record of lawyers' efforts to introduce expert testimony on battered woman syndrome. For several years, Dr. Lenore Walker, the most widely known expert in this field, had kept a count of those cases which had come to her attention. As of the Fall 1982, there were 50 cases around the country in which lawyers had attempted to get the testimony admitted. The testimony was excluded in only four cases, and two of those four were overturned on appeal. List of cases involving expert testimony

prepared by Dr. Lenore Walker (on file with author). My own experience consulting with lawyers and discussing these issues with the media leads me to believe that there are now several hundred cases around the country in which this testimony has been proffered.

23. For example, as of December 1982 Dr. Lenore Walker had been qualified and testified as an expert in 24 cases. *See* Affidavit of Dr. L. Walker, Dec. 15, 1982, State v. Kelly, 97 N.J. 178, 478 A.2d 364 (1984). *See also* the chart of 50 women's self-defense cases organized by jurisdiction, charge, disposition, sentence, appeal and admission of expert testimony in WOMEN'S SELF-DEFENSE CASES—THEORY AND PRACTICE (E. Bochnak, ed.), *supra* note 2, at 289-300. This chart shows that expert testimony was admitted in 10 cases, excluded in six and admitted at sentencing in one. Appellate opinions that report that the testimony was admitted at trial include: People v. Emick, 103 A.D.2d 643, 481 N.Y.S.2d 552 (1984); People v. Torres, 128 Misc. 2d 129, 488 N.Y.S.2d 358 (Sup. Ct. 1984); State v. Leidholm, 334 N.W.2d 811 (N.D. 1983); State v. Kelly, 102 Wash. 2d 188, 685 P.2d 564 (1984); State v. Felton, 106 Wis. 2d 769, 318 N.W.2d 25 (1981); *aff'd in part, rev'd in part,* 110 Wis. 2d 485, 329 N.W.2d 161 (1983). For those appellate cases which have ruled that it is admissible, see *supra* note 10.

24. Fennell v. Goolsby, 630 F. Supp. 451 (E.D. Pa. 1985); Ibn-Tamas v. United States, 407 A.2d 626 (D.C. 1979), *remand aff'd,* 455 A.2d 893 (D.C. 1983); Terry v. State, 467 So. 2d 761, (Fla. Dist. Ct. App. 1985); Borders v. State, 433 So. 2d 1325

deal of attention from courts[25] and commentators.[26] Most appellate courts have ruled that this testimony is admissible,[27] and commentators have almost unanimously supported admissibility.[28]

It is now well-established that homicide or assault cases involving battered women who killed their assailants pose serious problems to traditional self-defense. Women's self-defense work, beginning with *State v. Wanrow*,[29] has developed the perspective that self-defense requirements of reasonableness, imminent danger and equal force are sex-biased.[30] A woman who kills her husband is viewed as inherently unreasonable because she is violating the norm of appropriate behavior for women.[31] A battered woman who kills her batterer has to overcome special myths

and misconceptions about battered women. She must particularly explain why she stayed in the relationship and did not leave her home; why she did not call the police or get other assistance before acting; and why she believed that at the time she responded the danger she faced was imminent, posed a threat to her life, and was therefore different and more serious than other times when she had been beaten, had not acted, and had survived.[32]

The purpose of expert testimony has been to educate the judge and jury about the common experiences of battered women, to explain the context in which an individual battered woman acted, so as to lend credibility and provide a context to her explanation of her actions.[33] Expert

---

(Fla. Dist. Ct. App. 1983); Hawthorne v. State, 408 So. 2d 801 (Fla. Dist. Ct. App. 1982), *remand rev'd.* 470 So. 2d 770 (Fla. Dist. Ct. App. 1985); Mullis v. State, 248 Ga. 338, 282 S.E.2d 334 (1984); Smith v. State, 247 Ga. 612, 277 S.E.2d 678 (1981); People v. Minnis, 118 Ill. App. 3d 345, 455 N.E.2d 209 (1983); People v. White, 90 Ill. App. 3d 1067, 414 N.E.2d 196 (1980); State v. Burton, 464 So. 2d 421 (La. Ct. App. 1985); State v. Anaya, 438 A.2d 892 (Me. 1981); State v. Martin, 666 S.W.2d 895 (Mo. App. 1984); State v. Kelly, 97 N.J. 178, 478 A.2d 364 (1984); State v. Branchall, 101 N.M. 498, 684 P.2d 1163 (Ct. App. 1984); State v. Thomas, 66 Ohio St. 2d 518, 423 N.E.2d 137 (1981); State v. Moore, 72 Or. App. 454, 695 P.2d 985 (1985); Fielder v. State, 683 S.W.2d 565 (Tex. Ct. App. 1985); State v. Allery, 101 Wash. 2d 591, 682 P.2d 312 (Wash. 1984); Buhrle v. State, 627 P.2d 1394 (Wyo. 1981).

25. *See supra* note 4.

26. *See supra* note 5.

27. For appellate courts that have accepted the admissibility of expert testimony on battered woman syndrome, see cases cited *supra* note 10. Appellate courts that have declined to admit expert testimony on battered woman syndrome include: State v. Edwards, 420 So. 2d 663 (La. 1982) (expert testimony inadmissible to negate specific intent); State v. Burton, 464 So. 2d 421 (La. Ct. App. 1985) (expert testimony inadmissible to show insanity); State v. Necaise, 466 So. 2d 660 (La. Ct. App. 1985) (expert testimony inadmissible to show state of mind); State v. Thomas, 66 Ohio St. 2d 518, 423 N.E.2d 137 (1981) (expert testimony not relevant to a claim of self-defense); Fielder v. State, 683 S.W.2d 565 (Tex. Ct. App. 1985) (expert testimony inadmissible where defendant failed to show she was a battered woman); State v. Buhrle, 627 P.2d 1374 (Wyo. 1981) (expert testimony inadmissible on facts presented).

28. Crocker, *supra* note 5; Donovan & Wildman, *supra* note 5; Eber, *supra* note 5; Eisenberg & Seymour, *supra* note 5; Robinson, *supra* note 5; Schneider, *supra* note 5; Schneider & Jordan, *supra* note 2; Walker, Thyfault, Browne, *supra* note 5; Walter, *supra* note 5; Note, 73 CALIF. L. REV. 411 (1985), *supra* note 5; Note, 20 CAL. W.L. REV. 485, *supra* note 5; Note, 15 CONN. L. REV. 121 *supra* note 5; Survey, 20 GONZ. L. REV. 325, *supra* note 5; Comment, 2 LAW & HUM. BEHAV. 133, *supra* note 5; Comment, 60 N.D.L. REV. 141, *supra* note 5; Note, 77 NW. U.L. REV. 348, *supra* note 5; Comment, 43 OHIO ST. L.J. 491, *supra* note 5; Note, 6 PEPPERDINE L. REV. 213, *supra* note 5; Note, 59 ST. JOHN'S L. REV. 558, *supra* note 5; Comment, 27 ST. LOUIS U.L.J. 407, *supra* note 5; Note, 11

SETON HALL L. REV. 255, *supra* note 5; Note, 52 U. COLO. L. REV. 587, *supra* note 5; Comment, 53 UMKC L. REV. 386, *supra* note 5; Note, 35 VAND. L. REV. 741, *supra* note 5; Comment, 26 VILL. L. REV. 105, *supra* note 5; Comment, 21 WASHBURN L.J. 689, *supra* note 5; MacKinnon, *supra* note 5.

29. 88 Wash. 2d 221, 559 P.2d 548 (1977).

30. WOMEN'S SELF-DEFENSE CASES—THEORY AND PRACTICE (E. Bochnak, ed.), *supra* note 2; Crocker, *supra* note 5; Donovan & Wildman, *supra* note 5; Fabricant, *supra* note 5; MacKinnon, *supra* note 5; Schneider, *supra* note 5; Schneider & Jordan, *supra* note 2; Schneider, Jordan & Arguedas, *supra* note 2; Walker, Thyfault & Browne, *supra* note 5.

31. Schneider & Jordan, *supra* note 2; Schneider, Jordan & Arguedas, *supra* note 2.

32. *See supra* note 31. *See also* Crocker, *supra* note 5; Note, 35 VAND. L. REV. 741 (1982); Note, 20 CAL. W.L. REV. 485 (1984).

33. *See, e.g.,* State v. Kelly, 97 N.J. at 201-02, 478 A.2d at 375. ("As can be seen from our discussion of the expert testimony, Dr. Veronen would have bolstered Gladys Kelly's credibility. Specifically, by showing that her experience, although concededly difficult to comprehend, was common to that of other women who had been in similarly abusive relationships. Dr. Veronen would have helped the jury understand that Gladys Kelly could have honestly feared that she would suffer serious bodily harm from her husband's attacks, yet still remain with him. This, in turn would support Mrs. Kelly's testimony about her state of mind (that is, that she honestly feared serious bodily harm) at the time of the stabbing."); Ibn-Tamas v. United States, 407 A.2d at 634 ("Dr. Walker's testimony, therefore, arguably would have served two functions: (1) it would have enhanced Mrs. Ibn-Tamas' general credibility in responding to cross-examination designed to show that her testimony with her husband was implausible; and (2) it would have supported her testimony that on the day of the shooting her husband's actions had provoked a state of fear which led her to believe she was in imminent danger . . . and thus responded in self defense."); People v. Torres, 128 Misc. 2d 129, 134, 488 N.Y.S.2d 358, 363 (Sup. Ct. 1985) (The court will "permit the use of expert testimony about the battered woman's syndrome to help substantiate defendant's claim of self-defense.") *See* Note, 20 CAL. W.L. REV. 485 (1984); Crocker, *supra* note 5; Note, 11 SETON HALL L. REV. 255, *supra* note 5; Comment, 53 UMKC L. REV. 386; Walker, Thyfault &

202   WOMEN'S RIGHTS LAW REPORTER   [Vol. 9:195 (1986)

testimony can give the judge and jury information concerning the common experiences and characteristics of battered women in order to refute widely held myths and misconceptions concerning battered women that would interfere with judge or juror ability to evaluate the woman's action fairly.[34] Judges and jurors may accept the appropriateness of woman abuse as part of the marital relationship, assume the woman deserved or was responsible for the brutality, and blame her for not ending the relationship.[35] Expert testimony can present a different picture by demonstrating that the battered woman was a victim. Introduction of expert testimony is important because a battered woman who explains a homicide as a reasonable and necessary response to abuse in the home, threatens deeply held stereotypes of appropriately submissive female conduct and of patriarchal authority.[36] Expert testimony on the experiences of battered women can also answer specific questions that are in judges' and jurors' minds of why the battered woman didn't leave her home, why she may not have reported the battery to the police, and, most importantly, why she believed that the danger she faced on the par-

ticular occasion was life-threatening. In short, it can show that her conduct was reasonable.[37]

In most of the cases in which expert testimony on battering has been presented, the expert has testified concerning battered woman syndrome, a pattern of severe physical and psychological abuse inflicted upon a woman by her mate.[38] Dr. Lenore Walker, the leading researcher in this field, breaks down the pattern of abuse into a three-stage cycle of violence: a tension-building stage characterized by discrete abusive events; an acute battering stage characterized by uncontrollable explosions of brutal violence by the batterer; and a loving respite stage characterized by calm and loving behavior and pleas for forgiveness.[39] In the classic description, the battered woman lives in a constant state of fear that anything she does may precipitate another beating. She may be paralyzed by "learned helplessness," a sense of loss of predictability and control over her life, although she often has survival strategies. She may also have such a sense of low self-esteem and so few real and/or perceived options that she cannot leave the abusive relationship.[40]

Battered woman syndrome can also include a

Browne, *supra* note 5; See Note, 35 VAND. L. REV. 741, *supra* note 5; Comment, 15 CONN. L. REV. 121, *supra* note 5.

34. Smith v. State, 247 Ga. 612, 619, 277 S.E.2d 678, 683 (1981) ("We . . . find that the expert's testimony explaining why a person suffering from battered woman's syndrome would not leave her mate, would not inform police or friends and would fear increased aggression against herself, would be such conclusions that jurors could not ordinarily draw from themselves."); People v. Torres, 128 Misc. 2d 129, 134, 488 N.Y.S.2d 358, 362 (Sup. Ct. 1985) ("[S]pecialized knowledge would properly assist the jury in understanding the unique pressures which are part and parcel of the life of a battered woman, and, in this manner, enable the jury to disregard their prior conclusions as being common myths rather than informed knowledge."); State v. Allery, 101 Wash. 2d 591, 597, 682 P.2d 312, 316 (1984) ("[T]he defense has the option to explain her feelings to enable the jury to overcome stereotyped impressions about women who remain in abusive relationships."). *See also* Walker, Thyfault & Browne, *supra* note 5; Survey, 20 GONZ. L. REV. 325, *supra* note 5; Note, 52 U. COLO. L. REV. 587, *supra* note 5.

35. *See, e.g.,* People v. Emick, 103 A.D.2d 643, 658 n.3, 481 N.Y.S.2d 552, 561 (App. Div. 1984) (Expert testimony would "rebut the common perception that defendant could have left the decedent and their turbulent domestic setting."); People v. Torres, 128 Misc. 2d 129, 134, 488 N.Y.S.2d 358, 362 (Sup. Ct. 1985) (". . . the proffered expert evidence would also serve to dispel the ordinary lay perception that a woman who remains in a battering relationship is free to leave her abuser at any time."). *See also* Crocker, *supra* note 5; Robinson, *supra* note 5; Schneider, *supra* note 5; Walker, Thyfault & Browne, *supra* note 5; Walter, *supra* note 5; Note, 52 U. COLO. L. REV. 587, *supra* note 5; Note, 21 WASHBURN L.J. 689, *supra* note 5.

36. *See generally* Schneider, *supra* note 5, at 627-29.

37. People v. Minnis, 118 Ill. App. 3d 345, 356, 455 N.E.2d 209, 219 (1983) ("Those courts which have allowed expert evidence on the syndrome have done so only for the purpose of explaining why the abuse a woman suffered causes her to reasonably believe that her life is in danger and that she must use deadly force to escape her batterer."); People v. Torres, 128 Misc. 2d 129, 134, 488 N.Y.S.2d 358, 362 (Sup. Ct. 1985) ("[I]t is apparent that the proffered expert evidence is admissible as having substantial bearing on the defendant's state of mind at the time of the shooting and is, therefore, relevant to the jury's evaluation of the reasonableness of her perceptions and behavior at the time."); State v. Leidholm, 334 N.W.2d 811, 820 (N.D. 1983) ("[T]he facts of a particular case requires it to consider expert testimony, once received in evidence, describing battered woman syndrome and the psychological effects it produces in the battered spouse when deciding the issue of the *existence* and *reasonableness* of the accused's belief that force was necessary to protect herself from imminent harm."); State v. Kelly, 102 Wash. 2d 188, 195, 685 P.2d 564, 570 (1984) ("[T]he expert testimony was offered to aid the jury in understanding the reasonableness of Mrs. Kelly's apprehension of imminent death or bodily injury."); State v. Allery, 101 Wash. 2d 591, 597, 682 P.2d 312, 316 (1984) (Expert testimony would allow the defense "[t]o effectively present the situation as perceived by the defendant, and the reasonableness of her fear."); Donovan and Wildman, *supra* note 5; Eber, *supra* note 5; Eisenberg and Seymour, *supra* note 5; Comment, 27 ST. LOUIS U.L.J. 407, *supra* note 5; Comment, 53 UMKC L. REV. 386, *supra* note 5.

38. *See* cases cited *supra* note 10. *See also* State v. Kelly, 102 Wash. 2d 188, 655 P.2d 1202 (1982).

39. L. WALKER, THE BATTERED WOMAN 55-70 (1979).

40. *Id.*

description of the psychological impact of the common social and economic problems which battered women face. These problems have also been widely documented:[41] the police and the courts fail to protect women from abuse;[42] battered women may not be able to leave their mates because they may have no job,[43] child care, adequate housing[44] or community social services;[45] battered women suffer severe isolation and shame which strengthens their belief that they have no safe alternative;[46] and that lack of alternatives and

the cycle of battering in which the men promise to reform leads battered women to cling to the illusion that the men will change.[47] When the violence recurs and escalates, battered women realize that they lack control over the situation and they deteriorate into depression and "learned helplessness," expecting unpredictable, more severe and increasingly frequent beatings.[48]

Lawyers representing battered women have sought to introduce expert testimony to explain women's claims of self-defense[49] and to show that

---

41. *See supra* note 28. *See also* Comment, *The Battered Spouse Syndrome as a Defense to a Homicide Charge Under the Pennsylvania Crimes Code, supra* note 5. *See generally* R. DOBASH & R. DOBASH, VIOLENCE AGAINST WIVES (1979); R. GELLES, THE VIOLENT HOME (1982); R. LANGLEY & U. R. LEVY, WIFE BEATING (1977); D. MARTIN, BATTERED WIVES (1976); E. PIZZEY, SCREAM QUIETLY OR THE NEIGHBORS WILL HEAR (1974); S. STEINMETZ, THE CYCLE OF VIOLENCE (1977); U.S. COMM'N ON CIVIL RIGHTS, BATTERED WOMEN: ISSUES OF PUBLIC POLICY (1978); VIOLENCE IN THE FAMILY (S. Steinmetz & M. Straus eds. 1974); L. WALKER, *supra* note 39; Barden, *Wife Beaters: Few of Them Ever Appear Before a Court of Law*, N.Y. Times, Oct. 21, 1974, § 2, at 38, col. 1; Durbin, *Wife-Beating*, LADIES HOME J., June 1974, at 62; Eisenberg & Micklow, *The Assaulted Wife: "Catch-22" Revisited*, 3 WOMEN'S RTS. L. REP. 138 (1977); Straus, *Wife Beating: How Common and Why?*, 2 VICTIMOLOGY 443 (1978); Woods, *Litigation on Behalf of Battered Women*, 5 WOMEN'S RTS. L. REP. 7 (1978).

42. D. MARTIN, *supra* note 41, at 87-118; Barden, *supra* note 41, at 38; Eisenberg, *An Overview of Legal Remedies for Battered Women—Part I*, TRIAL, Aug. 1979, at 28; Eisenberg & Micklow, *supra* note 41, at 159; Fields, *Representing Battered Wives or What to Do Until the Police Arrive*, 3 FAM. L. REP. 4025, 4027-28 (1977); Truninger, *Marital Violence: The Legal Solutions*, 23 HASTINGS L.J. 259, 262 (1971); Woods, *supra* note 41, at 9-11.

43. Eber, *supra* note 5, at 902; Robinson, *supra* note 5, at 165-66, 173; Schneider, *supra* note 5, at 626; Walter, *supra* note 5, at 273; Note, 52 U. COLO. L. REV. 588; Note, 35 VAND. L. REV. 743.

44. *See supra* note 43.

45. *See supra* note 43.

46. Eber, *supra* note 5, at 901; Robinson, *supra* note 5, at 166; Schneider, *supra* note 5, at 627; Walker, Thyfault & Browne, *supra* note 5, at 11; Note, 35 VAND. L. REV., *supra* note 5, at 743, n.13.

47. Walker, *supra* note 39, at 532.

48. Robinson, *supra* note 5, at 172; Walker, *supra* note 39, at 532; Walker, Thyfault & Browne, *supra* note 5, at 6; Walter, *supra* note 5, at 276; Note, 52 U. COLO. L. REV., *supra* note 5, at 588; Note, 35 VAND. L. REV., *supra* note 5, at 742; Note, 21 WASHBURN L.J., *supra* note 5, at 689, n.3.

49. While expert testimony has been used primarily to explain women's self-defense claims, *see supra* note 10, it may also be relevant to other issues. In a letter to the author Dr. Lenore Walker describes a range of possible other uses:

As I see it, areas where explaining about battered women to the court will make a difference are broader than the simple self-defense homicide situations. And, in any such cases, having a psychological term to explain state of mind is important.

Some examples I can think of include:

1. A battered woman in New Mexico broke windows and set their rented home on fire after being coerced into cashing checks for which there were insufficient funds, beaten and threatened with abandonment (which meant no opportunity to deposit funds from his next paycheck to cover the debts). Since she didn't directly attempt to harm the batterer, self-defense isn't really appropriate while an insanity defense is. However, New Mexico law doesn't include temporary insanity. Without the long standing history of the battered woman syndrome, it couldn't rise above the diminished capacity issue.

2. In Westchester County, Pennsylvania, the battered woman and her daughter shot and killed her battering husband in self-defense. Then, they set fire to his body and the house. The state contended they did so to create an alibi while the defense asserts that the psychosocial stressors pushed her to her breaking point resulting in a brief reactive psychosis. While such a state of temporary insanity can be explained without the battered woman syndrome, using it is more effective. My admissibility was challenged and the testimony admitted because of my credentials as a clinical psychologist.

3. In a recent Missouri case the prosecution used approximately one million dollars in insurance as evidence of motive for first degree murder. Evidence of the battered woman syndrome could have been used to counter that motive as well as claim self-defense even though the battered woman hired a man to kill her battering husband. Expert testimony was not allowed even though I tried to argue that hiring a hired gun to kill a hired gun met the equal force test in self-defense. The case is on appeal.

4. In Kansas, the Supreme Court just ruled that evidence of rape trauma syndrome is admissible to rebut the defense of consent. I foresee use of evidence of battered woman syndrome in much the same way. In fact, a case in Illinois has done so, resulting in conviction of the batterer.

Letter from Dr. Lenore Walker to Elizabeth M. Schneider (Fall 1982) (discussing relevant uses of expert testimony in battered women cases). *See also*, Neeley v. State, No. 7 Div. 145 (Ala. Crim. App. March 12, 1985) (expert testimony admitted to prove defendant acted under extreme duress and coercion equal to brainwashing); Morrison v. Bradley, 622 P.2d 81 (Colo. App. 1980) *rev'd on the amount of damages*, 655 P.2d 385 (1982) (expert testimony admitted on wrongful death claim); People v. Minnis, 118 Ill. App. 3d 345, 455 N.E.2d 209 (1983) (error to exclude expert testimony offered to rebut prosecution's claim that dismemberment proved consciousness of guilt); State v. Anaya, 438 A.2d 892, 894 (Me. 1981) (expert testimony admit-the woman acted reasonably because she was in imminent danger of death or great bodily harm. The expert witness usually begins by explaining what is known about battering relationships and then describing battered woman syndrome and its effects on a woman's state of mind. The expert then points out the similarities between the battered woman syndrome model and the facts in the defendant's case. Finally, she will render an opinion as to whether the defendant was a victim of battered woman syndrome in order to explain why the defendant was in fear for her life.[50] Of course, the facts of the case must support defendant's claim that she was a battered woman in order to make the expert testimony relevant.[51]

Admissibility of expert testimony at trial depends on a judicial finding that the testimony is both relevant to the issue at hand—either self-defense or some other issue—and that it meets the general standards governing the admissibility of expert testimony. In order for the testimony to be relevant to self-defense the court must determine that the testimony renders the desired inference— that the defendant reasonably believed she was in imminent danger and that the deadly force was necessary to avoid this danger—more probable than it would be without this evidence.[52] In order

for the expert's testimony to be deemed admissible it must meet the jurisdiction's particular standard for admissibility of expert testimony generally.[53] The traditional formulation, as set forth in *State v. Dyas*,[54] is that (1) the subject matter "must be so distinctively related to some science, profession, business or occupation as to be beyond the ken of the average layman"; (2) the expert witness "must have sufficient skill, knowledge or experience in that field or calling as to make it appear that his opinion or inference will probably aid the trier in his search for truth"; and (3) "the state of the pertinent art or scientific knowledge [must permit] a reasonable opinion to be asserted by . . . an expert."[55] Jurisdictions that have effectively adopted the Federal Rules of Evidence have a broader standard.[56]

Significantly, the majority of appellate courts that have ruled on the trial court's exclusion of expert testimony have determined that expert testimony on battered woman syndrome is relevant to a claim of self-defense.[57] However, even where it is found relevant, the trial court must find that it has met the general standard for admissibility of expert testimony. In several cases, this requirement has proven to be a substantial hurdle.[58] Moreover, even if the trial court admits the expert

---

ted where ". . . the record clearly shows that [defendant] was relying on a theory of self-defense or provocation to mitigate or justify her conduct."); State v. Baker, 120 N.H. 773, 424 A.2d 171 (1980) (expert testimony admitted to rebut batterer's claim of insanity in prosecution for attempted murder of his wife); State v. Lambert, 312 S.E.2d 31 (W. Va. 1984) (lay testimony on battering provides basis for duress defense to conviction for welfare fraud).

50. *See* Ibn-Tamas v. United States, 407 A.2d 626, 631 (D.C. 1979); State v. Anaya, 438 A.2d 892, 894 (Me. 1981); State v. Kelly, 102 Wash. 2d 188, 655 P.2d 1202, 1203 (1982).

51. Dr. Lenore Walker has suggested that sometimes the expert will have to testify when the facts are not available from the woman because the woman has been unable to testify in her own behalf.

52. C. McCORMICK, EVIDENCE, § 185 (E. Cleary ed. 3d ed. 1984).

53. Jurisdictions exhibit minor variations in their standards for admission of expert testimony. *Compare* State v. Kelly, 97 N.J. 178, 208, 478 A.2d 364, 379 (1984) ("Evidence Rule 56(2) provides that an expert may testify 'as to matters requiring scientific, technical, or other specialized knowledge, if such testimony will assist the trier of the fact to understand the evidence or determine a fact in issue.' In effect, this Rule imposes three basic requirements for the admission of expert testimony: (1) the intended testimony must concern a subject matter that is beyond the ken of the average juror; (2) the field testified to must be at a state of the art such that an expert's testimony could be sufficiently reliable; and (3) the witness must have sufficient expertise to offer the intended testimony. *See* N.J. Rules of Evidence (Anno. 1984), Comment 5 to Evid. R.

56.") *with* State v. Allery, 101 Wash. 2d 591, 596, 682 P.2d 312, 315 (1984) ("ER 702 provides 'If scientific, technical, or other specialized knowledge will assist the trier of the fact to understand the evidence or to determine a fact in issue, a witness qualified as an expert by knowledge, skill, experience, training, or education, may testify thereto in the form of an opinion or otherwise.' The admissibility of expert testimony under this rule depends upon whether (1) the witness qualifies as an expert, (2) the opinion is based upon an explanatory theory generally accepted in the scientific community, and (3) the expert testimony would be helpful to the trier of the fact. State v. Canady, 90 Wash. 2d 808, 585 P.2d 1185 (1978). *See generally* 5A TEGLAND, WASH. PRAC., *Evidence* § 288 (2d ed. 1982)").

54. Dyas v. United States, 376 A.2d 827, 832 (D.C. 1977), *cert. denied*, 434 U.S. 973 (1977).

55. C. McCORMICK, *supra* note 52, § 13.

56. FED. R. EVID. 702 provides that "[I]f scientific, technical or other specialized knowledge will assist the trier of fact to understand the evidence or to determine a fact in issue, a witness qualified as an expert by knowledge, skill, experience, training or education, may testify thereto in the form of an opinion or otherwise."

57. *See* cases cited *supra* note 10.

58. Ibn-Tamas v. United States, 455 A.2d 893, 894 (D.C. 1983) ("The trial court has stated on remand that it did consider the relevant factors as outlined by this court in its original ruling. It concluded, *inter alia* 'that defendant failed to establish a general acceptance by the expert's colleagues of the methodology used in the expert's study of battered women.' . . . We hold that the trial judge was not compelled, as a matter of

testimony proffered by the defense, the prosecution may be permitted to have an expert testify to counter the assertion that the woman is battered or has battered woman syndrome.[59]

Expert testimony on battered woman syndrome has had a substantial impact on the criminal process. Expert testimony has been admitted at trial in a large number of cases around the country,[60] not only in cases involving claims of self-defense.[61] Defense lawyers have also proffered it at other stages of the criminal process, such as the grand jury, on motions to dismiss, and at sentencing.[62] In general the expert testimony cases have demonstrated significant judicial recognition of the depth and severity of the problems of sex-stereotyping in the trial process for battered women claiming self-defense.[63] These cases

---

law, to admit the evidence."); Buhrle v. State, 627 P.2d 1374, 1378 (Wyo. 1981) ("We are not saying that this type of testimony is not admissible; we are merely holding that the state of the art was not adequately demonstrated to the court, and because of the inadequate foundation the proposed opinions would not aid the jury").

The court may rule that the expert has insufficient qualifications to render an opinion on battered woman syndrome. For example in State v. Moore, 72 Or. App. 454, 459, 695 P.2d 985, 987-88 (1985), the appellate court affirmed the trial court's disqualification of the expert stating:

The particular aspects of this complex defense require that the expert be qualified to evaluate the literature and the various phases of the syndrome and to apply the syndrome to the particular facts of the case before an opinion can be rendered whether the defendant was responding in self-defense. The witness here had been employed as a crisis center counselor and as a private counselor to abused women. She had taken college courses and was in the process of obtaining a Bachelor's degree and a Master's degree concurrently. She had no degrees. The trial court ruled that she did not have the requisite qualifications to testify as an expert witness or to give an opinion on the self-defense issue. We are not faced here with the availability of the defense, but *only* with the qualifications of the witness as an expert.

See Ward v. State, 470 So. 2d 100 (Fla. Dist. Ct. App. 1985). The court may decline to admit expert testimony on battered woman syndrome where the proffered expert did not identify the defendant as a battered woman. In Fielder v. State, 683 S.W.2d 565 (Tex. App. 1985), expert testimony on battered woman syndrome was held to be inadmissible when the expert was unfamiliar with the facts of the case. There the expert had not interviewed the defendant. Testimony of two other experts was also ruled inadmissible because the experts were deemed not qualified to render an opinion on whether the defendant was a battered woman.

Experts on the battered woman syndrome have also been attacked for holding feminist beliefs. Dr. Lenore Walker describes her experience in one case in the following way:

In Joyce Hawthorne's third trial in 1982, the judge again ruled on the issues of admissibility of expert testimony. The handling of the case illustrates the subjectivity of the process of ascertaining credibility in the courtroom. My own testimony, which was partially based on my research on battered women, was ruled unacceptable. Although my research was funded by the Nattional Institute of Mental Health (NIMH) and had thus passed the scrutiny of peer review, at an admissibility hearing the court chose to believe the testimony given by a male sociologist and a male political scientist who charged that my research was biased because of my feminist political views. These professors, who admitted never having any personal contact with NIMH, told the court that the NIMH system of scientific peer review does not operate according to the stated policy,

but rather awards grants to favored researchers. Thus they argued, the scientists who found my research methodology appropriate should not be believed. Those "experts" also misinterpreted another researcher's published article on domestic violence, necessitating calling him to testify in rebuttal. In addition, the court ruled that the field was not sufficiently accepted by the scientific community to support the delivery of an expert opinion.

Walker, *Battered Women, Psychology, and Public Policy*, AMERICAN PSYCHOLOGIST, Oct. 1984, at 1178, 1180. *See also* Ibn-Tamas v. United States, 455 A.2d 893, 894 (D.C. 1983) (Gallagher, Assoc. Judge, retired, concurring, referring to Dr. Walker's testimony, "[i]t appears that the Doctor's approach would require tracing the man-woman relationship back to the roots of civilization—a subject which would require a little pondering, I should think").

59. This is becoming a serious problem in many cases involving battered women. For example, in Gladys Kelly's remand trial, the defense called Dr. Lenore Walker, and the prosecution put on an expert witness who testified that Gladys Kelly did not have battered woman syndrome. Gladys Kelly was convicted at her second trial. Her trial attorney, Charles Lorber, believes that the prosecution's rebuttal use of expert testimony created serious obstacles to acquittal. Telephone conversation with Charles Lorber (November 14, 1985).

60. *See* cases cited *supra* notes 4, 10, 22.

61. Neelley v. State, No. 7 Div. 145 (Ala. App. March 12, 1985) (brainwashing); Morrison v. Bradley, 622 P.2d 81 (Colo. Ct. App. 1980), *rev'd. as to the amount of damages,* 655 P.2d 385 (1982) (wrongful death); People v. Minnis, 118 Ill. App. 3d 345, 455 N.E.2d 209 (1983) (rebut consciousness of guilt); State v. Baker, 120 N.H. 773, 424 A.2d 171 (1980) (rebut insanity defense).

62. *See* discussion of case referred to as State v. Green (expert testimony presented in grand jury) in Blackman, *Innovative Involvements for an Expert Witness: Ideas Toward the Representation of Battered Women Who Kill* [this issue at 227]; People v. Livingston (expert testimony presented on motion to dismiss) in Blackman, *id.* at 234; People v. Salerno and Commonwealth v. Devore (expert testimony admitted at sentencing hearing) in Blackman, *id.* at 238. *See also* Neelley v. State, No. 7 Div. 145 app. 2 (Ala. App. March 12, 1985) (expert testimony presented at motion for retrial); Wisecup v. State, 157 Ga. App. 853, 278 S.E.2d 682 (1981) (presented in brief of *amicus curiae* on appeal); Fennell v. Goolsby, No. 84-1351 (E.D. Pa. Aug. 28, 1985) (presented on petition for writ of *habeas corpus*); People v. Powell, 83 A.D.2d 719, 442 N.Y.S.2d 645 (1981) (presented on post-trial motion to set aside verdict on grounds of newly discovered evidence of expert testimony).

63. *See* sources cited *supra* notes 5 and 10; *see also* Thomas v. Arn, 728 F.2d 813, 815 (6th Cir. 1984) (Jones, C.J. concurring) ("In my view, the trial court's exclusion of expert testimony impugned the fundamental fairness of the trial process thereby depriving Thomas of her constitutional right to a fair trial. There is sufficient literature which suggests that the

WOMEN'S RIGHTS LAW REPORTER [Vol. 9:195 (1986)

acknowledge the important role expert testimony can play in presenting the woman's defense.[64] Even in those cases in which expert testimony on battered woman syndrome has been held inadmissible, courts have largely ruled that there was an insufficient basis on which to find it admissible on the facts presented.[65]

From the beginning, literature on women's self-defense work has emphasized that expert testimony should not be used in isolation; expert testimony should be integrated with overall defense

strategy, tied to the particular facts of the case and focused on the particular defense problems in the case. Commentators cautioned that an emphasis on expert testimony on battered woman syndrome, as the sole or even primary vehicle for remedying sex-bias in the trial process, was problematic because lawyers might not use the testimony carefully and tie it to the particular facts of the woman's case,[66] because defense strategy might focus on evidence of battering rather than the reasonableness of the woman's act,[67] and be-

---

public and thus, juries, do not understand the scope of the problem concerning battered women. . . . The law cannot be allowed to be mired in antiquated notions about human responses when a body of knowledge is available which is capable of providing insight."), *aff'd*, 106 S. Ct. 466 (1985); State v. Hundley, 236 Kan. 461, 467, 693 P.2d 475, 479, (1985) ("Carl's threat was no less life-threatening with him sitting in the motel room tauntingly playing with his beer bottle than if he were advancing toward her. The objective test is how a reasonably prudent battered woman would perceive Carl's demeanor. Expert testimony is admissible to prove the nature and effect of wife-beating just as it is admissible to prove the standard mental state of hostages, prisoners of war, and others under long-term life-threatening conditions."); State v. Anaya, 438 A.2d 892, 894 (Me. 1981) ("We agree with the District of Columbia Court of Appeals, and various commentators, that where the psychologist is qualified to testify about the battered wife syndrome, and the defendant establishes her identity as a battered woman, expert evidence on the battered wife syndrome must be admitted since it 'may have . . . a substantial bearing on her perceptions and behavior at the time of the killing, . . . [and is] central to her claim of self defense.' "); State v. Branchall, 101 N.M. 498, 506, 684 P.2d 1163, 1169 (Ct. App. 1984) ("We appreciate the trial judge's concern that in giving a self-defense instruction he would be condoning shootings by angry spouses under no threat of imminent harm. But we also believe that when a defendant has introduced evidence that he, or she, is about to be attacked, evidence concerning all of the relevant facts known to the defendant which affected his or her action should be considered by a jury. We hold that, under the facts of this case, the defendant was entitled to a self-defense instruction."); State v. Allery, 101 Wash. 2d 591, 597, 682 P.2d 312, 316 (1984) ("To effectively present the situation as perceived by the defendant, and the reasonableness of her fear, the defense has the option to explain her feelings to enable the jury to overcome stereotyped impressions about women who remain in abusive relationships. It is appropriate that the jury be given a professional explanation of the battering syndrome and its effects on the woman through the use of expert testimony.")

64. Smith v. State, 247 Ga. 612, 619, 277 S.E.2d 678, 683 (1981) ("[T]he expert's testimony explaining why a person suffering from battered woman's syndrome would not leave her mate, would not inform police or friends, and would fear increased aggression against herself, would be such conclusions that jurors could not ordinarily draw for themselves."); People v. Torres, 128 Misc. 2d 129, 134, 488 N.Y.S.2d 358, 362 (Sup. Ct. 1985) ("Expert testimony is admissible as having a substantial bearing on the defendant's state of mind at the time of the shooting and is, therefore, relevant to the jury's evaluation of the reasonableness of her perceptions and behavior at that time."); State v. Leidholm, 334 N.W.2d 811,

820 (N.D. 1983) ("The jury's use of a subjective standard of reasonableness in applying the principles of self-defense to the facts of a particular case requires it to consider expert testimony, once received in evidence, describing battered woman syndrome and the psychological effects it produces in the battered spouse when deciding the issue of the *existence* and *reasonableness* of the accused's belief that force was necessary to protect herself from imminent harm.")

65. Ibn-Tamas v. United States, 455 A.2d 893, 894 (D.C. 1983) (methodology of the expert was not generally accepted by the expert's colleagues in the field); Hawthorne v. State, 470 So. 2d 770, 773 (Fla. Dist. Ct. App. 1985), (the facts of the case were insufficient to support an expert's opinion); State v. Burton, 464 So. 2d 421 (La. Ct. App. 1985) (facts could not support a self-defense claim); State v. Martin, 666 S.W.2d 895, 899 (Mo. Ct. App. 1984) (same); Fielder v. State, 683 S.W.2d 565, 595 (Tex. Ct. App. 1985) (expert testimony inadmissible when defendant failed to establish her identity as a battered woman); *see also* Mullis v. State, 248 Ga. 338, 339, 282 S.E.2d 334, 337 (1981) (expert testimony would not aid the trier of fact); State v. Griffiths, 101 Idaho 163, 165, 610 P.2d 522, 524 (1980) (same); State v. Thomas, 66 Ohio St. 2d 518, 521, 423 N.E.2d 137, 139 (1981) (same).

66. Schneider, *supra* note 5, at 645; MacPherson, Ridolfi, Sternberg & Wiley, *Expert Testimony* in WOMEN'S SELF-DEFENSE CASES: THEORY AND PRACTICE (K. Bochnak, ed.), *supra* note 2, at 88-90. A case that poses troubling questions about the appeal of battered woman syndrome for lawyers and the need for lawyers to consider the facts of the particular case and alternative defense theories is State v. Felton, 110 Wis. 2d 485, 329 N.W.2d 161 (1983) Rita Felton was charged with first-degree murder for the shooting death of her husband while he slept. At trial the defense put on an expert on the "battered spouse syndrome" as relevant to the defense of self-defense, and the defendant was convicted. Defendant's appellate counsel filed a motion for new trial on the theory that trial counsel was ineffective because he had withdrawn a mental disease or defect defense on the day of trial, and had failed to consider a heat of passion defense that would have reduced the crime to manslaughter. The Wisconsin Supreme Court reversed the conviction and granted a new trial. From the opinion, it is hard to evaluate the defense strategy in the case. It appears that Rita Felton's defense lawyer may have focused too much on battered woman syndrome minimizing the hard facts in the case and alternative strategies. On the other hand, the Supreme Court's willingness to find a defense lawyer's use of a self-defense approach as the basis for ineffective assistance of counsel, to the exclusion of the more familiar impaired mental state and heat of passion strategies, is troubling.

67. *See* discussion of the Carol Gardner case in WOMEN'S SELF-DEFENSE CASES: THEORY AND PRACTICE (E. Bochnak, ed.), *supra* note 2, at 179-202. In this case "post-trial interviews

cause there were risks that the substance of the expert testimony on battered woman syndrome would be presented or heard in a way that would unwittingly reinforce sex-stereotypes.[68]

Virtually all of the cases that have considered the issue of expert testimony have done so in the context of testimony on battered woman syndrome and they have focused on Dr. Lenore Walker's work in her book *The Battered Woman*.[69] The fact that the substance of the proffered or admitted testimony has been on battered woman syndrome has shaped judicial treatment of the issue in problematic ways. The phrase "battered woman syndrome" was intended to simply describe common psychological and social characteristics of battered women. Research on battered woman syndrome emerged from an effort to counteract the myths and misconceptions that women initiated, provoked and enjoyed the violence; it suggested that battered women were

truly victims. Thus the initial focus of battered woman syndrome was a psychological analysis of battered women's victimization, their sense of paralysis or "learned helplessness."[70] Although the term is purely descriptive, its psychological content and the language and import of the term carry a different message. Regardless of its more complex meaning,[71] the term "battered woman syndrome" has been heard to communicate an implicit but powerful view that battered women are all the same, that they are suffering from a psychological disability and that this disability prevents them from acting "normally."

Recent experience with cases of expert testimony on battered woman syndrome confirms these early concerns. Precisely because expert testimony on battered woman syndrome has been commonly understood by lawyers and judges as the primary, perhaps even shorthand, way to solve the problem of sex-bias in the trial process

---

revealed that over-reliance on the theme of battering prevented the defense team and the jurors from focusing on the legal elements of self-defense." *Id.* at xvii.

Reliance on testimony by experts on battering served to shift the focus of attention away from the events of that evening to a theoretical notion of a prior history of abuse. The theories about battering did not explain Ms. Gardner's perceptions of what was going on that evening because her life history did not conform to the testimony about patterns of abuse. Moreover, her own intense fear on the witness stand made her incapable of communicating the emotional impact of either her past experience with Mr. Gardner's violence or her past experience with burns, although these factors were probably very significant to the fear she felt that night.

Id. at 198-99.

68. [E]xpert testimony not clearly tied to the individual woman defendant's circumstances and perspective should be used with care. Such testimony may suggest to the trier of fact that there is a "battered woman's syndrome" defense, which could encourage sexual stereotyping. Thus, the use of expert witnesses is often prudently forgone, especially where the defendant is credible and articulate.

Schneider, *supra* note 5, at 646.

69. L. WALKER, THE BATTERED WOMAN (1979); Fennel v. Goolsby, No. 84-1351, n.1 (E.D. Pa. Aug. 28, 1985); Ibn-Tamas v. United States, 407 A.2d 626, 631-39 (D.C. 1983); Hawthorne v. State, 408 So. 2d 801, 805 (Fla. Dist. Ct. App. 1982), *remand rev'd*, 470 So. 2d 770 (Fla. Dist. Ct. App. 1985); State v. Martin, 666 S.W.2d 895, 900, n.2 (Mo. Ct. App. 1984); State v. Kelly, 97 N.J. 178, 188-96, 478 A.2d 364, 369-72 (1984); People v. Torres, 128 Misc. 2d 129, 132-33, 488 N.Y.S.2d 358, 361 (Sup. Ct. 1985); People v. Powell, 102 Misc. 2d 775, 779-82, 424 N.Y.S.2d 626, 629-31 (Sup. Ct. 1980), *aff'd*, 83 A.D.2d 719, 442 N.Y.S.2d 645 (App. Div. 1981); State v. Moore, 72 Or. App. 454, 461, 695 P.2d 985, 989 (1985) (Newman, J., concurring); Fielder v. State, 683 S.W.2d 565, 589, n.3 (Tex. Ct. App. 1985); Buhrle v. State, 627 P.2d 1374, 1376-78 (Wyo. 1981); *and see* Affidavit of Dr. L. Walker, *supra* note 23.

70. L. WALKER, *supra* note 69, at 42-55.

71. Recently Dr. Walker has published a new book which reevaluates her early findings using updated empirical studies. L. WALKER, THE BATTERED WOMAN SYNDROME, 1-4 (1984). In this book she acknowledges criticism of the term "battered woman syndrome".

There are some who have criticized the concept of a battered woman syndrome on the grounds that it "clinicalizes" women, and thus perpetuates sexism inherent in the field of mental health. Why not call it the batterer's syndrome? Women do adopt the feelings, thoughts, and behaviors which constitute this syndrome as a reaction to a man's violence. Other feminists have rejected the construct of learned helplessness because of the political implications that women are helpless to stop being battered, rather than understanding the psychological changes that occur which make it more difficult to terminate such a relationship.

The effects of labeling have been shown to have the potential of having a generally negative effect within the clinical professions. However, there is also research which demonstrates the need to organize new knowledge refuting older misconceptions in a way that draws cognitive connections to the existing knowledge base. So, I have chosen to organize the data presented here in such a way that is easily familiar to most professionals for whom it is intended. However, I urge each of you to utilize it with great caution, to help battered women and their families. I share it with that purpose in mind.

Id. at xi.

Some of the findings in the new book support a more complex and less victimized view of battered women, through an analysis of battered woman's self-perceptions. For example, Dr. Walker suggests that "[t]he issue of the woman's response to violent attacks by the man who loves her has been further clouded by the mythology that she behaves in a manner which is either extremely passive or mutually aggressive. Rather these data suggest that battered women develop survival or coping skills that keep them alive with minimal injuries." *Id.* at 33.

Feminist Legal Theory II

for battered women and to include battered women's voice in the courtroom, it is critical to examine both its importance and its risks. The New Jersey Supreme Court's opinion in *State v. Kelly* highlights both.

III. *STATE v. KELLY*

In *State v. Kelly*, the New Jersey Supreme Court held that expert testimony concerning battered woman syndrome was admissible. The court ruled that the testimony was relevant under New Jersey's standard of self-defense,[72] and that the testimony met the standards of New Jersey's rules for admissibility of expert testimony.[73]

In *Kelly*, the defendant was charged with second degree murder of her husband.[74] Gladys Kelly had been battered by her husband throughout their seven-year marriage.[75] The beatings had begun on the day after her marriage, when she was beaten in public. On the day of the homicide, Mr. Kelly had been drinking and started beating her in public. During the physical struggle that ensued, she wounded him with a pair of scissors.[76] She claimed that he was biting and clubbing her, and that she responded in self-defense.

At trial, defense counsel attempted to introduce the expert testimony of a clinical psychologist[77] to explain why Gladys Kelly, as a battered woman, had a reasonable belief that she was in imminent danger of death or serious bodily harm and needed to act in self-defense.[78] The trial judge conducted a lengthy examination of the expert,[79] but held that the testimony was not relevant under New Jersey's standard of self-defense[80] and did not reach the issue of scientific reliability. On appeal, the Appellate Division affirmed the trial court's ruling on relevance[81] and ruled that admission of the testimony was cumulative and unnecessary in light of the defendant's testimony of prior abuse.[82] An *amicus curiae* brief on behalf of the New Jersey Civil Liberties Union and the New Jersey Coalition on Battered Women was submitted in support of admissibility in the New Jersey Supreme Court and counsel was granted leave to argue.[83] In addition, the American Psychological Association filed a brief in support of admissibility which focused on the issue of scientific reliability.[84] In the Supreme Court, defendant and *amici* argued that the testimony was relevant and that it met New Jersey's standards for admissibility of expert testimony.[85]

The testimony presented at trial focused on

---

72. State v. Kelly, 97 N.J. 178, 197, 478 A.2d 364, 373 (1984). The New Jersey Supreme Court ordered the case remanded for a new trial to determine whether the proffered expert testimony would satisfy New Jersey's standard of acceptability for scientific evidence. *Id.* at 212, 478 A.2d at 381. One judge dissented from the remand on the issue of scientific acceptability, finding that defendant Kelly had sufficiently demonstrated both scientific acceptance and reliability. *Id.* at 220, 478 A.2d at 385 (Handler, J., concurring in part and dissenting in part).

73. *Id.* at 211, 478 A.2d at 380.

74. *Id.* at 188, 478 A.2d at 368.

75. *Id.* at 189, 478 A.2d at 369.

76. *Id.* at 190, 478 A.2d at 369.

77. *Id.* at 197, 478 A.2d at 372-73.

78. *Id.* at 201, 478 A.2d at 375.

79. *Id.* at 188, 478 A.2d at 368.

80. The trial court ruled that New Jersey's standard of self-defense as set forth in State v. Bess, 53 N.J. 10, 247 A.2d 669 (1968), did not permit admission of evidence concerning defendant's state of mind. The trial court stated:

I will assume arguendo that [the expert] is eminently qualified as a psychologist, that the state of research and art of her profession is such that there, and I could find that there is a battered wife syndrome, that this defendant falls well within the purview of the guidelines of that battered wife syndrome, that that syndrome has been plausibly and reasonably determined by reasonable scientific efforts on her part, notwithstanding that she herself has had, she being this witness has had what we might call in a quantitative sense a limited number of

subject women that those tests are plausible, findings are plausible.

That she would be appropriate to give testimony to a lay Jury as to the consequences of the syndrome, but that's not the bottom line. The bottom line is, to put it vulgarly, so what? Because, under our law what can it go to and that's what I want to ask you. What would that evidence go to? It does not go to self-defense.

Trial Transcript at 2T, 126, *Kelly*.

81. The Appellate Division affirmed the trial court's ruling stating:

We agree with the ruling below barring Dr. Veronen's testimony, both on the authority . . . of *State v. Bess*, and on the ground that its exclusion was not clearly capable of producing an unjust result, R. 2:10-2, and did not beyond a reasonable doubt lead the jury to a result it otherwise might not have reached, *State v. Macon*, 57 N.J. 325, 336 (1971).

State v. Kelly, No. A-2256-80-T4, slip op. at 4 (App. Div. July 6, 1982).

82. *Id.*

83. Brief of *Amici Curiae*, American Civil Liberties Union of New Jersey and New Jersey Coalition on Battered Women, State v. Kelly, 97 N.J. 178, 478 A.2d 364 (1984); order of court granting leave to argue, State v. Kelly, No. A-2256-80-T4 (App. Div. July 6, 1982) dated April 18, 1983.

84. Brief of *Amicus Curiae*, American Psychological Association in Support of Appellant, State v. Kelly, 97 N.J. 178, 478 A.2d 364 (1984).

85. *See* Briefs of *Amici Curiae*, State v. Kelly, 97 N.J. 178, 478 A.2d 364 (1984).

the battered woman syndrome.[86] The expert emphasized the traditional components of the syndrome, as did the briefs on appeal, including the *amicus* briefs.[87] The briefs submitted to the Supreme Court emphasized the broad need for admissibility of this evidence on the issues of why Gladys Kelly did not leave her husband and the reasonableness of her perception of danger.[88]

The Supreme Court's analysis of relevance reveals much about the dilemmas of using battered woman syndrome in women's self-defense work and the gains and limits of judicial understanding of the inherent issues. First, the court exhaustively and sensitively documented the severity of the problem of woman-abuse and the pervasiveness of stereotypes and myths concerning battered women. The vehicle for this discussion was the battered woman syndrome. The court described the experiences of battered women based upon the battered woman syndrome as "a series of common characteristics that appear in women who are abused physically and psychologically over an extended period of time by the dominant male figure in their lives,"[89] and analyzed Dr. Walker's three stages of the battering cycle.[90] The court discussed both these "psychological impacts of battery" and the external social and economic factors which make it difficult for women to extricate themselves from the battering relationship: lack of money and support systems, primary responsibility for child care, and the fear and well-grounded belief that if the woman leaves the man will follow her and subject her to an even more brutal attack.[91] Nonetheless, the court also recited the "symptoms" of the syndrome and the common personality traits of the battered woman:[92] "low self-esteem, traditional beliefs about the home, the family, and the female sex role, tremendous feelings of guilt that their marriages are failing and the tendency to accept responsibility for the batterer's actions."[93]

Second, the court's understanding of the relevance and importance of this testimony was expansive. The court suggested that admission of the testimony was important because it would

bolster Gladys Kelly's credibility in the eyes of the jury by demonstrating that her experiences, which the jury would find difficult to comprehend, were in fact common to women in abusive situations.[94] The court ruled that in light of its interpretation of New Jersey's standard of self-defense, the expert testimony would be central to the *honesty* of Gladys Kelly's belief that she was in imminent danger of deadly harm, and it would aid the jury in determining whether a reasonable person could have believed that there was imminent danger to her life.[95] The court characterized this as relevant under the "objective" standard of self-defense.[96]

Third, the court held that the testimony was relevant because the expert could have responded to myths and misconceptions about battered women, particularly that the battered woman was free to leave, with information concerning battered women's inability to leave, "learned helplessness," and the lack of alternatives.[97] The court emphasized that:

> The crucial issue of fact on which this expert's testimony would bear is why, given such allegedly severe and constant beatings, combined with threats to kill, defendant had not long ago left decedent. . . . The expert could clear up these myths, by explaining that one of the common characteristics of a battered wife is her inability to leave despite such constant beatings her "learned helplessness"; her lack of anywhere to go; her feeling that if she tried to leave, she would be subject to even more merciless treatment, her belief in the omnipotence of her battering husband; and sometimes her hope that her husband will change his ways.[98]

Yet, significantly, the court's analysis of relevance appears to focus on the woman's inability to leave. Indeed, the court contrasts the crucial nature of the expert testimony to rebut myths concerning why the battered woman does not leave with the relevance of the expert's testimony

---

86. *See* Trial Transcript at 2T, *Kelly.*
87. *Id. See also* Briefs of *Amici Curiae, supra* notes 83-84.
88. *See supra* notes 86-87.
89. *Kelly*, 97 N.J. at 191, 478 A.2d at 370.
90. Dr. Lenore Walker, a prominent writer on the topic of battered women, proposes three stages of the syndrome in her book THE BATTERED WOMAN (1979).
91. *Kelly*, 97 N.J. at 195, 478 A.2d at 372.

92. *Id.*
93. *Id.*
94. *Id.* at 201, 478 A.2d at 375.
95. *Id.* at 204, 478 A.2d at 377.
96. *Id.*
97. *Id.* at 205, 478 A.2d at 377.
98. *Id.*

210   *WOMEN'S RIGHTS LAW REPORTER* [Vol. 9:195 (1986)]

to the jury's determination of the reasonableness of the woman's act.

> The difficulty with the expert's testimony is that it sounds as if an expert is giving knowledge to a jury about something the jury knows as well as anyone else namely, the reasonableness of a person's fear of imminent serious danger. That is not at all, however, what this testimony is directly aimed at. It is aimed at an area where the purported common knowledge of the jury may be very much mistaken, an area where jurors' logic, drawn from their own experience, may lead to a wholly incorrect conclusion, an area where expert knowledge would enable the jurors to disregard their prior conclusions as being common myths rather than common knowledge. After hearing the expert, instead of saying Gladys Kelly could not have been beaten up so badly for if she had, she certainly would have left, the jury could conclude that her failure to leave was very much part and parcel of her life as a battered wife. The jury could conclude that instead of casting doubt on the accuracy of her testimony about the severity and frequency of prior beatings, her failure to leave actually reinforced her credibility.[99]

This is underscored in the portion of the opinion in which the court defines the scope of the expert's testimony for retrial. The court again emphasizes that "the area of *expert* knowledge relates . . . to the reasons for defendant's failure to leave her husband."[100] The court goes on to explain:

> Either the jury accepts or rejects that explanation and, based on that, credits defendant's stories about the beatings she suffered. No expert is needed, however, once the jury has made up its mind on those issues, to tell the jury the logical conclusion, namely, that a person who has in fact been severely and continuously beaten might very well reasonably fear that the imminent beating she was about to suffer could be either life-threatening or pose a risk of serious injury. What the expert could state was that defendant had the battered-wo-

man's syndrome, and could explain that syndrome in detail, relating its characteristics to defendant, but only to enable the jury better to determine the honesty and reasonableness of defendant's belief. Depending on its content, the expert's testimony might also enable the jury to find that the battered wife, because of the prior beatings, numerous beatings, as often as once a week, for seven years, from the day they were married to the day he died, is particularly able to predict accurately the likely extent of violence in any attack on her. That conclusion could significantly affect the jury's evaluation of the reasonableness of defendant's fear for her life.[101]

Kelly exemplifies contradictory themes in the development of the issue of expert testimony. The Supreme Court's opinion reveals both the severity and tenacity of the problem of sex-bias in the law of self-defense. The court acknowledges the importance of this testimony to explain, not merely the woman's "subjective" honesty, but also the "objective" reasonableness of her response. At the same time, the Supreme Court seems to perceive the testimony as primarily relevant to the issue of why Gladys Kelly did not leave, rather than the reasonableness of why she acted.

The language of the court's opinion in the last paragraph cited above is perplexing. On the one hand the court seems to say that admissibility of expert testimony on battering is important precisely because jurors' common sense experience with domestic relationships will give them the illusion of knowledge; jurors will not be aware of how their views have been shaped by common myths and stereotypes and tainted by bias. But the court's primary example is focused on why the battered woman didn't leave. Indeed, the opinion seems to suggest that if the testimony were focused on the issue of "reasonableness" of the woman's fear (and therefore the reasonableness of her *act* of self-defense as opposed to her failure to leave), the jury's perception that the expert was "giving knowledge to a jury about something the jury knows as well as anyone else, namely the reasonableness of a person's fear of imminent serious danger,"[102] would be right.

---

99. *Id.* at 206, 478 A.2d at 378.
100. *Id.*

101. *Id.* at 207, 478 A.2d at 378.
102. *Id.* at 206, 478 A.2d at 378.

Certainly the court is correct that the question of why the battered woman did not leave (so as to avoid the possibility of death) is a threshold issue in the jury's mind. Her failure to leave raises the question of whether the woman was really battered (for if she was, why did she stay?), as well as the question of whether, by staying, she had in a sense "assumed the risk" of death. However, these questions only present the first issue for the jury. The second issue (and the more pressing one in many cases) is the reasonableness of the battered woman's belief that she was in particular jeopardy at the time that she responded in self-defense. A battered woman who has been the victim of abuse for many years and has survived it before must credibly explain why it was necessary to act on that occasion. Expert testimony, admitted for the purpose of explaining why the battered woman did not leave, does not help the jury answer the question whether she was reasonable in acting violently in order to save her life. It thus does not address the basic defense problem that the battered woman faces. Indeed, if the testimony is limited, or perceived as limited to the issue of why the woman does not leave, it highlights a contradiction implicit in the message of battered woman syndrome—if the battered woman was so helpless and passive, why did she kill the batterer?

In fairness to the Supreme Court, the *Kelly* opinion does mention that "the expert's testimony might also enable the jury to find that the battered wife, because of the prior beatings . . . is particularly able to predict accurately the likely extent of violence in any attack on her" and "that conclusion could significantly affect the jury's evaluation of the reasonableness of defendant's fear for her life."[103] This is a crucial point, indeed in most cases this is the real importance of the testimony. Yet the court seems to minimize the importance of this broader and more central understanding of relevance by its statement that the expert testimony is not relevant to the jury's determination of the reasonableness of a person's fear of imminent severe danger because this is "something the jury knows as well as anyone else."[104]

Expert testimony submitted in *Kelly* and briefs and arguments presented to the Supreme

Court claimed that the testimony was important to assist the jury in understanding the crucial components of reasonableness: the reasonableness of Gladys Kelly's perception of the danger, and the imminence of that danger. Yet the court appears to both accept and minimize that broader view. In this sense, the opinion only focuses on part of the problem. The reasonableness of the woman's fear and the reasonableness of her act are *not* issues which the jury knows as well as anyone else. The jury needs expert testimony on reasonableness precisely because the jury may not understand that the battered woman's prediction of the likely extent and imminence of violence is particularly acute and accurate.

The court's lack of emphasis on this aspect of the relevance of the testimony is puzzling, particularly in light of its insightful and expansive explanation of the problems that expert testimony must address. One possible explanation is that the court finds it easier to focus on those aspects of the testimony which characterize the woman as passive and helpless (i.e., her inability to leave) rather than active and violent but reasonable. This highlights the dilemma of battered woman syndrome: explanation of the battered woman's actions from a solely victimized perspective cannot fully explain why she believed it was necessary to act.

In this sense, although *Kelly* is an extraordinary opinion, it reflects larger problems. Perhaps the fact that the substance of the proffered testimony submitted in many courts has been on battered woman syndrome and "learned helplessness" has unwittingly allowed even sensitive courts to emphasize individual psychological incapacity by admitting the testimony but then perceiving its relevance in a more limited way. Courts appear to be willing to recognize the importance of expert testimony when the rationale for admission is women's individual and collective psychological "weakness."[105] Judicial willingness to find the battered women's perspective acceptable may relate to the fact that the perspective that courts are hearing and to which they are responding is that of damaged women, not of women who perceive themselves to be, and may in

103. *Id.*
104. *Id.*
105. In contrast, those courts that have rejected the admissibility of expert testimony have not focused on the

woman's victimization. *See, e.g.,* State v. Thomas, 660 Ohio St. 2d 518, 423 N.E.2d 137 (1981); People v. White, 90 Ill. App. 3d 1067, 414 N.E.2d 196 (1980).

212

fact be, acting competently, assertively and rationally in light of the alternatives.

IV. EXPERT TESTIMONY: DILEMMAS FOR FEMINIST LEGAL THEORY

The issue of the admissibility of expert testimony on battering, as in *State v. Kelly*, reveals tensions and contradictions which have been implicit in legal work on women's self-defense since *State v. Wanrow*. The judicial opinions which have admitted this testimony are, like *Kelly*, in a certain sense astounding. They have accepted the basic assumptions of sex-bias in the law of self-defense[106] and they have adopted explicitly feminist perceptions of a distinct and shared women's experience.[107] They have ruled on the basis of a

heightened consciousness of women's self-defense[108] and understandings of the pervasiveness and severity of domestic violence.[109] They have acknowledged that there is sex-bias in the concept of reasonableness,[110] that myths and misconceptions concerning battered women are widely shared and interfere with juror determinations,[111] and that full and fair consideration of self-defense is impaired by juror bias.[112] Thus, on one level, these cases constitute an advance for feminist legal work. At the same time, these cases highlight dilemmas and contradictions which need to be confronted and addressed.

The arguments first raised in *Wanrow* and accepted by the plurality opinion of the Washington Supreme Court were based on several as-

---

106. Terry v. State, 467 So. 2d 761, (Fla. Dist. Ct. App. 1985); Smith v. State, 247 Ga. 612, 277 S.E.2d 678 (1981); *See* People v. Minnis, 118 Ill. App. 3d 345, 455 N.E.2d 209 (1983); State v. Anaya, 438 A.2d 892 (Me. 1981).

107. *See, e.g.,* State v. Kelly, 97 N.J. 178, 192-93, 478 A.2d 364, 371 (1984) ("As the problem of battered women has begun to receive more attention, sociologists and psychologists have begun to focus on the effects a sustained pattern of physical and psychological abuse can have on a woman. The effects of such abuse are what some scientific observers have termed 'the battered-woman's syndrome,' a series of common characteristics that appear in women who are abused physically and psychologically over an extended period of time by the dominant male figure in their lives.")

108. *See, e.g.,* State v. Kelly, 97 N.J. 178, 478 192-93 A.2d 364 (1984), discussed at notes 72-105 and accompanying text; State v. Allery, 101 Wash. 2d 591, 682 P.2d 312, 316 (1984) ("To effectively present the situation as perceived by the defendant, and the reasonableness of her fear, the defense has the option to explain her feelings to enable the jury to overcome stereotyped impressions about women who remain in abusive relationships. It is appropriate that the jury be given a professional explanation of the battering syndrome and its affects on the woman through the use of expert testimony.")

109. *See, e.g.,* State v. Kelly, 97 N.J. 178, 478 A.2d 364 (1984):
In the past decade social scientists and the legal community began to examine the forces that generate and perpetuate wife beating and violence in the family. What has been revealed is that the problem affects many more people than had been thought and that the victims of the violence are not only the battered family members (almost always either the wife or the children). There are also many other strangers to the family who feel the devastating impact, often in the form of violence, of the psychological damage suffered by the victims.
Due to the high incidence of unreported abuse (the FBI and other law enforcement experts believe that wife abuse is the most unreported crime in the United States), estimates vary of the number of American women who are beaten regularly by their husband, boyfriend, or the dominant male figure in their lives. One recent estimate puts the number of women beaten yearly at over one million. See *California Advisory Comm'n on Family Law, Domestic Violence,* app. F at 119 (1st report 1978). The

state police statistics show more than 18,000 *reported* cases of domestic violence in New Jersey during the first nine months of 1983, in 83% of which the victim was female. It is clear that the American home, once assumed to be the cornerstone of our society, is often a violent place.
Id. at 190-91, 478 A.2d at 369-70 (footnotes omitted). *See also* People v. Torres, 128 Misc. 2d 129, 132, 488 N.Y.S.2d 358, 361 (Sup. Ct. 1985) ("According to Dr. Blackman's hearing testimony, a recognition by social scientists of the high incidence of wife beating has produced in the past decade intensive research. . . ").

110. State v. Kelly, 97 N.J. 178, 478 A.2d 364 (1984); Terry v. State, 467 So. 2d 761, (Fla. Dist. Ct. App. 1985); People v. Minnis, 118 Ill. App. 3d 345, 455 N.E.2d 209 (1983); State v. Anaya, 438 A.2d 892 (Me. 1981); State v. Allery, 101 Wash. 2d 591, 682 P.2d 312 (1984).

111. *See, e.g.,* State v. Kelly, 97 N.J. 178, 192, 478 A.2d 364, 370 (1984) ("Some popular misconceptions about battered women include the beliefs that they are masochistic and actually enjoy their beatings, that they purposely provoke their husbands into violent behavior, and most critically, as we shall soon see, that women who remain in battering relationships are free to leave their abusers at any time."); People v. Torres, 128 Misc. 2d 129, 134, 488 N.Y.S.2d 358, 362 (Sup. Ct. 1985) ("[T]he average layman has numerous misconceptions concerning the options available to a victim of domestic abuse. Thus, Dr. Blackman's specialized knowledge would properly assist the jury in understanding the unique pressures which are part and parcel of the life of a battered woman, and in this manner, enable the jury to disregard their prior conclusions as being common myths rather than informed knowledge").

112. State v. Kelly, 97 N.J. 178, 209, 478 A.2d 364, 379 (1984) ("As previously discussed, a battering relationship embodies psychological and societal features that are not well understood by law observers. Indeed, these features are subject to a large group of myths and stereotypes. It is clear that this subject is beyond the ken of the average juror and thus is suitable for explanation through expert testimony."); People v. Torres, 128 Misc. 2d 129, 134, 488 N.Y.S.2d 358, 362 (Sup. Ct. 1985) ("[T]he proffered expert evidence is admissible as having a substantial bearing on the defendant's state of mind at the time of the shooting and is, therefore, relevant to the jury's evaluation of the reasonableness of her perceptions and behavior at that time.").

sumptions which have become basic: first, that women act in self-defense under different circumstances and in different ways than men;[113] second, that the law of self-defense incorporates sex-bias;[114] and third, that sex-stereotypes of women as a group generally, and battered or raped women specifically, interfere with juror determinations of women's claims of self-defense.[115] *Wanrow* and the substantial work on women's self-defense which flowed from it resulted from efforts to have the reasonableness standard of self-defense expand to include women's different experience and adjust to include sex-bias in the law.

On the level of practice, *Wanrow* and subsequent women's self-defense work sought to expand the legal options available to women defending against charges of homicide or assault for killing men who battered or raped them. By explaining the different circumstances in which women acted to save their own lives, women's acts which had previously been viewed as outside the purview of self-defense, and viewed as appropriate for insanity, heat of passion of manslaughter, could now be viewed as within self-defense. But the impact was not limited to self-defense. The goal was for individual women to have a wider range of defense options and for lawyers to be able to evaluate and present to courts women's

situations and circumstances free from stereotypes and sex-bias.

On the level of theory, as other commentators have noted,[116] *Wanrow* posed a radical challenge to a number of dichotomies in legal thought: the dichotomy of differences and sameness in equality theory; the dichotomy of excuse and justification in criminal law jurisprudence; and the dichotomies of individual and group determination, including those perceptions which were the subjective and objective standards generally. Examination of the theoretical dilemmas which this work poses raises hard questions about whether *Wanrow*'s goals have been furthered.

A. Differences/Sameness

Wanrow squarely raised the issue of the different circumstances in which women killed in self-defense,[117] the different means by which they killed,[118] and the different factual contexts,[119] as well as the history and experience of sex-discrimination.[120] Women's self-defense work since *Wanrow* has emphasized those differences in the particular context of battered women.

Wanrow attempted to use acknowledgement of these different circumstances and experiences as the basis for accommodation to the same stan-

---

113. State v. Wanrow, 88 Wash. 2d 221, 559 P.2d 548, 558 (1977). ("In our society, women suffer from a conspicuous lack of access to training in and the means of developing those skills necessary to effectively repel a male assailant without resorting to the use of deadly weapons"). *See also* Zimring, Mukherjee and Van Winkle, *Intimate Violence: A Study of Intersexual Homicide in Chicago*, 50 U. CHI. L. REV. 910, 920 (1983) ("As one might expect, weapons other than the omnipresent American firearm and knife play a more important role in killings by males than by females"). For sources supporting the view that most persons killed by women were men with whom the women had familial relationships, and that the killings were "often in self-defense or in a victim-precipitated interaction," *see* Schneider, *supra* note 5, at 624, n.3. One recent study of spousal homicide concluded that homicides committed by women were more commonly in response to physical violence, while homicides committed by men were precipitated by "sex-role threat," threat of female infidelity, desertion or abandonment. Bernard, Vera, Vera and Newman, *Till Death Do Us Part: A Study of Spousal Murder*, 10 AM. ACAD. OF PSYCHIATRY AND THE LAW BULL. 271 (1982). *See also* Browne, *Assault and Homicide at Home: When Battered Women Kill*, in 3 ADVANCES IN APPLIED SOCIAL PSYCHOLOGY (M.J. Sakes and L. Saxe, eds. 1985).

114. Schneider and Jordan, *supra* note 2, at 159; The *Wanrow* opinion explains this insight in the following way:

The second paragraph of instruction No. 10 not only establishes an objective standard, but through the persistent use of the masculine gender leaves the jury with the impression the objective standard to be applied is that

applicable to an altercation between two men. The impression created—that a 5'4" woman with a cast on her leg and using a crutch must, under the law, somehow repel an assault by a 6'2" intoxicated man without employing weapons in her defense, unless the jury finds her determination of the degree of danger to be objectively reasonable—constitutes a separate and distinct misstatement of the law and, in the context of this case, violates the respondent's right to equal protection of the law. The respondent was entitled to have the jury consider her actions in the light of her own perceptions of the situation, including those perceptions which were the product of our nation's 'long and unfortunate history of sex discrimination.' *Frontiero v. Richardson*, 411 U.S. 677, 684 . . . (1973). Until such time as the effects of that history are eradicated, care must be taken to assure that our self-defense instructions afford women the right to have their conduct judged in light of the individual physical handicaps which are the product of sex discrimination. To fail to do so is to deny the right of the individual woman involved to trial by the same rules which are applicable to male defendants (citations omitted). State v. Wanrow, 559 P.2d at 558-59.

115. Schneider and Jordan, *supra* note 2, at 31.

116. *See generally* MacKinnon, *supra* note 5; Crocker, *supra* note 5.

117. *See supra* note 113.

118. *Id.*

119. *Id.*

120. *See supra* note 114.

WOMEN'S RIGHTS LAW REPORTER [Vol. 9:195 (1986)

dard of self-defense.[121] The court's opinion emphasized that failure to accommodate the law to these differences had consequences under the equal protection clause of the Fourteenth Amendment.[122] Women could be denied equal rights to trial.[123]

At the time *Wanrow* was litigated, only a few feminist litigators and legal scholars questioned the appropriateness of a formal equality model of analysis—an analysis which emphasized the sameness or similarity of men and women, as opposed to women's differences.[124] There was fear of acknowledging difference in any sphere either "real" or "socially constructed,"[125] or of arguing a need for different legal treatment, because women would then be subject to the "patriarchal protectionism" which constituted lesser and unequal treatment.[126] Today many feminist thinkers and litigators are challenging formal models of equality.[127] Much criticism has been raised about the extent to which formal equality models rest on a male standard and do not allow for accommodation of women's experiences and perspectives.[128] This debate has recently centered on legal treatment of pregnancy, particularly state laws which single out pregnancy and maternity for special and more favorable treatment.[129] Proponents of these laws have asserted the need to accommodate the law to women's physical differences and socially constructed discrimination.[130] Yet the fear persists for many that acknowledgement of "difference" in the law necessarily implies unequal treatment.[131]

In *Wanrow*, this concern over whether acknowledgement of difference necessarily implies inferiority is heightened by the Washington Supreme Court's use of the word "handicaps" to describe the effect of sex discrimination.[132] Sex discrimination is disabling to women as a class

and to individual women. Nonetheless the court's use of the word "handicaps" to describe this effect was troubling. It played on the stereotype of victimized and mistreated women that has historically limited women's claims for equal treatment and suggested that the court's responsiveness to Yvonne Wanrow's claim was shaped by patriarchal solicitude.

The expert testimony cases are the natural result of the "differences" approach—the goal of the expert testimony is to explain the content of battered women's *different* experiences and perceptions so that juries can fairly apply the *same* legal standards to them. But the question which the expert testimony cases squarely pose is this: if battered women's experiences are explained as different, can they ever be genuinely incorporated into the traditional standard and understood as equally reasonable? Are these different experiences inevitably perceived as inferior, as "handicaps"? If so, is it necessary to alter the traditional standard?

These tensions are heightened by the fact that the substance of the testimony is on battered woman syndrome. Description of the battered women's common experiences has become encapsulated in the phrase "battered woman syndrome." Theoretically, it is a vehicle to set apart and describe battered women's "different" but common experiences. However, like the word "handicaps" in *Wanrow*, "battered woman syndrome" carries with it stereotypes of individual incapacity and inferiority which lawyers and judges may respond to precisely because they correspond to stereotypes of women which the lawyers and judges already hold. Battered woman syndrome does not mean, but can be heard as reinforcing stereotypes of women as passive, sick, powerless and victimized. Although it was devel-

---

121. *Id.*

122. *Id.*

123. *Id.*

124. *See generally* Brown, Emerson, Falk and Freedman, *The Equal Rights Amendment: A Constitutional Basis for Equal Rights for Women,* 80 YALE L.J. 871 (1971); Williams, *The Equality Crisis: Some Reflections on Culture, Courts and Feminism,* 7 WOMEN'S RTS. L. REP. 175 (1982).

125. Williams, *supra* note 124.

126. *Id.*

127. *See generally* C. MACKINNON, SEXUAL HARASSMENT OF WORKING WOMEN (1979); Krieger & Cooney, *The Miller-Wohl Controversy: Equal Treatment, Positive Action and the Meaning of Women's Equality,* 13 GOLDEN GATE L. REV. 513 (1983); Scales, *Towards A Feminist Jurisprudence,* 56 IND. L.J.

375 (1981); Note, *Toward a Redefinition of Sexual Equality,* 95 HARV. L. REV. 487 (1981).

128. *See supra* note 127.

129. *Compare* Krieger & Cooney, *supra* note 127 *with* Williams, *Equality's Riddle: Pregnancy and the Equal Treatment/Special Treatment Debate,* 13 N.Y.U. REV. L. & SOC. CHANGE 325 (1984-85).

130. Krieger & Cooney, *supra* note 127.

131. Williams, *supra* note 129.

132. "Until such time as the effects of that history are eradicated, care must be taken to assure that our self-defense instructions afford women the right to have their conduct judged in light of the *individual physical handicaps which are the product of sex discrimination.*" State v. Wanrow, 559 P.2d at 559 (emphasis added).

oped to merely *describe* the common psychological experiences and characteristics which battered women share, and it is undoubtedly an accurate description of these characteristics, battered woman syndrome can be misused and misheard to enshrine the old stereotypes in a new form. This repeats an historic theme of treatment of women by the criminal law—women who are criminals are viewed as crazy or helpless or both.[133] Thus the description of battered women's "different" experiences, although purely categorical in intent, carries with it the language and baggage of familiar stereotypes of female incapacity.

B. Excuse/Justification

Wanrow and subsequent women's self-defense work have been premised on the view that the traditional boundaries and definitions of self-defense, as a form of justification, were sex-biased and shaped by male experience. Assertion of self-defense was therefore not viewed as an available legal option, and women were more often shunted into some defense of incapacity; either insanity, heat of passion or extreme emotional disturbance. Although the line between justification and excuse is often not entirely clear,[134] justification and excuse have different emphases.[135] Self-defense as justification focuses on the act of defending oneself; it rests on a determination that the act was right because of its circumstances.[136] In contrast, a finding of excuse, like insanity or heat of passion, focuses on the actor; it is a finding that the act, although wrong, should be tolerated because of the actor's characteristics or state of mind.[137] Traditionally, since women's acts of violence

could not be viewed as reasonable, the inquiry shifted to excuse; women were viewed as incapable.[138] Women's self-defense work has attempted to redraw the lines between justification and excuse,[139] to challenge the stereotypes which might prevent women, lawyers, and judges from viewing the woman's acts as justified. The goal of expert testimony is also to challenge these stereotypes and make it possible for the jury to identify with and understand the circumstances of the act and to thereby see the act as reasonable.

However, the danger of the battered woman syndrome approach is that it revives concepts of excuse. Even the New Jersey Supreme Court's thoughtful and comprehensive analysis of battered woman syndrome in *Kelly* has elements of a classic excuse description; it focuses on the woman's defects, the woman subject to the "syndrome." It implies that she is limited because of *her* weakness and *her* problems.[140] It does not appear to affirm the circumstances of her act. The opinion seems to suggest that admission of expert testimony is primarily important because the battered woman "suffers" from the syndrome and could not be expected to leave her home, not because it is relevant to the reasonableness of her act. The court is willing to extend its "protection" and admit the testimony because the battered woman is perceived as weak. Although the purpose of expert testimony on battered woman syndrome is to explain the reasonableness of the woman's action, the psychological aspect of the description sounds like incapacity and excuse.

By emphasizing a strain of excuse, battered woman syndrome tends to rigidify other dichoto-

---

133. *See* A. JONES, WOMEN WHO KILL 158-166 (1980); E. SHOWALTER, THE FEMALE MALADY: WOMEN, MADNESS AND ENGLISH CULTURE (1985); *The Insanity Plea: For Women Only*, Psychology Today, March 1985, at 16 (report of study that concludes that jurors are less likely to believe a plea of not guilty by reason of insanity from a man than a woman); *see also* sources cited in Schneider, *supra* note 5, at 638, nn.82 & 83.

134. *See generally* G. FLETCHER, RETHINKING CRIMINAL LAW 855 (1978); Greenawalt, *The Perplexing Borders of Justification and Excuse*, 84 COLUM. L. REV. 1897 (1984); Robinson, *A Theory of Justification: Societal Harm as a Prerequisite to Criminal Liability*, 23 U.C.L.A. L. REV. 266 (1975); Note, *Partially Determined Imperfect Self-Defense: The Battered Wife Kills and Tells Why*, 34 STAN. L. REV. 615, 630-34 (1982).

135. *See supra* note 134.

136. FLETCHER, *supra* note 134, at 855-57; Robinson, *supra* note 134, at 275.

137. *See supra* note 136.

138. Schneider, *supra* note 5, at 638; Crocker, *supra* note 5, at 130-31.

139. Schneider, *supra* note 5, at 638; Crocker, *supra* note 5, at 130-31; MacKinnon, *supra* note 5, at 717, n.73. (MacKinnon suggests that "a feminist perspective tends to undermine the traditional distinction between justification and excuse").

140. This characterization may somewhat overstate the psychological description in *Kelly*. In describing the expert's testimony, the court states that Dr. Veronen "described in general terms the component parts of the battered woman's syndrome and its effects on a woman's physical and mental health. The witness then documented, based on her own considerable experience in counseling, treating and studying battered women, and her familiarity with the work of others in the field, the feelings of anxiety, self-blame, isolation, and, above all, fear that plagues these women and leaves them prey to a psychological paralysis that hinders their ability to break free or seek help." Kelly, 97 N.J. at 195-97, 478 A.2d at 372-73. This theme is even more prevalent in other cases, *see* cases cited *supra* note 17.

WOMEN'S RIGHTS LAW REPORTER [Vol. 9:195 (1986)]

mies which, as others have suggested, are roughly correlated with excuse and justification.[141] Excuse suggests that the act is personal to the defendant, a private act, in contrast with a more public and common sense of rightness which justification reflects.[142] Excuse suggests a sense of the subject, while justification implies a more objective statement.[143] Redrawing the boundaries of justification and excuse means recasting the boundaries of the private/public and subjective/objective oppositions, making women's experiences generally, and battered women's experiences and perceptions specifically, more public and legitimate, and also more objective.

The notion of battered woman syndrome contains the seeds of old stereotypes of women in new form—the victimized and the passive battered woman, too paralyzed to act because of her own incapacity.[144] From a defense standpoint, this perspective is potentially counterproductive in that it explains why the woman did not leave but not why she acted. It is in tension with the notion of reasonableness necessary to self-defense since it emphasizes the woman's defects and incapacity. It also does not adequately describe the complex experiences of battered women.[145] The effect is that women who depart from this stereotype, because of their own life situations or because the facts of their cases do not fit this perspective, are not likely to be able to take advantage of judicial solicitude. This has already presented serious defense problems in several cases.[146] The stereotype of the reasonable battered woman who suffers from battered woman syndrome creates a new and equally rigid classification, which has the potential to exclude battered women whose circumstances depart from the model and force them once again into pleas of insanity or manslaughter rather than expanding our understandings of reasonableness. It thus reinforces and rigidifies the traditional boundaries of justification and excuse, rather than redrawing them.

From the standpoint of the jury's determination of whether the woman acted reasonably in self-defense, the explanation of battered woman syndrome is only partial. Giving commonality to an individual woman's experience can make it seem less aberrational and more reasonable. Yet, to the degree that the explanation is perceived to

---

141. For example, MacKinnon suggests that justification and excuse are correlated with a dichotomy of personal/individual v. universal/social. MacKinnon, *supra* note 5, at 717, n.73. Greenawalt suggests that justification and excuse are correlated with objective/subjective and general/individual. Greenawalt, *supra* note 134, at 1915.

142. MacKinnon, *supra* note 5, at 717, n.73; Crocker, *supra* note 5, at 130-31.

143. Greenawalt, *supra* note 134, at 1915.

144. Phyllis Crocker calls this "the battered woman syndrome stereotype." She describes it in the following way:

A stereotype about battered women's behavior is emerging that threatens to create a separate standard of reasonableness for battered women. Some courts seem to treat battered woman syndrome as a standard to which all battered women must conform rather than as evidence that illuminates the defendant's behavior and perceptions. As a result, a defendant may be considered a battered woman only if she never left her husband, never sought assistance, and never fought back. Unless she fits this rigidly-defined and narrowly-applied definition, she is prevented from benefiting from battered woman syndrome testimony. Simultaneously, the prosecution characterizes her actions as unreasonable under the rubric of the reasonable man. Under that standard, the defendant must explain why her act of self-defense does not resemble a man's. The result is that the claims of the individual woman get caught between two conflicting stereotypes: the judicial construct of the battered woman based on the syndrome testimony, and the prosecutorial model that uses myths about battered women to prove their unreasonableness. Neither of these stereotypes allows a battered woman to portray the reasonableness of her actions accurately to the jury.

The double bind of the two stereotypes is most apparent in the reactions to a defendant's physical response to prior abuse. If the defendant has tried to resist in the past, the court accepts this as evidence that rebuts her status as a battered woman. On the other hand, if the defendant has never attempted to fight back, the prosecution argues that the defendant did not act as a "reasonable man."

Crocker, *supra* note 5, at 144-45.

145. For a description of the complex experiences of battered women, see WALKER, *supra* note 71.

146. *See generally* Crocker, *supra* note 5. Crocker suggests that in "non-traditional confrontation cases, in which the battered woman kills either in anticipation of or following a physical attack," expert testimony is often excluded "because the court views the battered woman's act as unreasonable." Even in "traditional confrontation cases, where the battered woman's act of self-defense seems to fit the traditional self-defense model, courts will admit battered woman syndrome expert testimony apparently because they doubt the reasonableness of the battered woman's perception of danger." Crocker, *supra* note 5, at 138-39. Barbara Hart, an attorney in Pennsylvania, raised a similar issue in a letter describing the problems in a battered woman self-defense case involving a black woman who did not conform to the battered woman syndrome stereotype. She raises the question whether the battered woman syndrome was developed through interviews with women from middle- or upper-income families for whom the concept of self-defense was relatively unknown." Letter from Barbara Hart to author dated November 30, 1984 (on file with author). For a discussion of the Carol Gardner case, see WOMEN'S SELF-DEFENSE CASES: THEORY AND PRACTICE, *supra* note 2, at 179-203.

focus on her suffering from a "syndrome," a term which suggests a loss of control and passivity, the testimony seems to be inconsistent with the notion of reasonableness, and the substance of the testimony appears to focus on incapacity.

In addition, battered woman syndrome has sounded to many lawyers and judges like either a separate defense[147] or a defense akin to impaired mental state.[148] Some courts have assumed that expert testimony on battered woman syndrome was being proffered as relevant to an impaired mental state defense.[149] This is undoubtedly not merely the problem of the term itself—which, again, intends to be simply descriptive—but of the stereotypes that it triggers for lawyers and judges. Courts are more likely to hear and respond to a perception of women as damaged than as reasonable, so presentation of testimony on battered woman syndrome responds more to and plays on patriarchal attitudes which courts have exhibited toward women and women defendants generally.

C. Individual/Group

Wanrow emphasized the importance of the individual's perspective as shaped by her experience as a woman. In *Wanrow* the court recognized the importance of the individual woman's own perspective as the standard of self-defense,[150] but at the same time the court recognized that this perspective had a distinct and collective component to it.[151] The court in *Wanrow* emphasized that a central aspect of the individual woman's perception was "those perceptions which were the product of our nation's long and unfortunate history of sex-discrimination."[152] The individual woman's experience thus was shaped by the history of sex discrimination. The court sees it as a *particular* experience (i.e. separate from that of men) and a *common* experience, an experience which women share together. Thus women share a common experience that is "different."

Wanrow challenged the dichotomy between individual and group perspective. Indeed, it stressed the necessary interrelationship between the individual and social perspective. *Wanrow's* suggestion that an individual woman's distinct experience is a crucial aspect of her perspective set the foundation for the admission of testimony concerning the content of that woman's experience.[153]

In the expert testimony area, courts have recognized that the experiences of battered women are distinct and shared,[154] that these experiences are outside the common experience of jurors,[155]

---

147. *See, e.g.,* Price, *supra* note 18.

148. For example, some courts have characterized the testimony as evidence of extreme emotional disturbance, misunderstanding the purpose for which the testimony was offered. *See generally* Ledford v. State, 254 Ga. 656, 333 S.E.2d 576 (1985) (upon application for funds to hire expert witness to testify on battered woman syndrome the court ordered competency hearing, which on appeal was found not to be abuse of discretion); State v. Edwards, 420 So. 2d 663 (La. 1982) (battered woman syndrome seen as evidence of mental disease or defect); State v. Martin, 666 S.W.2d 895 (Mo. Ct. App. 1984) (appellate counsel claims that trial counsel was ineffective for failure to present battered woman syndrome to show diminished capacity); People v. Powell, 102 Misc. 2d 775, 424 N.Y.S.2d 626 (Tompkins County Ct. 1980), *aff'd*, 83 A.D.2d 719, 442 N.Y.S.2d 645 (App. Div. 1981) (testimony on battered woman syndrome may be relevant to diminished capacity); State v. Kelly, 102 Wash. 2d 188, 685 P.2d 564 (1984) (court denied prosecutor's request to admit defendant's prior acts under theory analogizing battered woman syndrome to insanity defense); State v. Hundley, 236 Kan. 461, 693 P.2d 475 (1985) (battered woman syndrome characterized as "malady"); State v. Felton, 110 Wis. 2d 485, 329 N.W.2d 161 (1981) (trial counsel's use of defense of self-defense and reliance on expert testimony on battered woman syndrome rather than impaired mental state or heat of passion/provocation held to be ineffective assistance of counsel); *but see*, People v. Torres, 128 Misc. 2d 1129, 488 N.Y.S.2d 358 (Sup. Ct. 1985) (battered woman syndrome specifically not offered for mental disease or defect).

149. *See, e.g.,* Neelley v. State, No. 7 Div. 145 (Ala. App. Ct.

March 12, 1985) (battered woman syndrome proffered as proof that the defendant was not "responsible for her acts by reason of a mental disease or defect induced by the abuse she endured at the hands of her husband."); Ledford v. State, 254 Ga. 656, 333 S.E.2d 576 (1985); State v. Edwards, 420 So. 2d 663 (La. 1982); State v. Necaise, 466 So. 2d 660 (La. Ct. App. 1985) (expert testimony on battered woman syndrome held inadmissible as proof of "mental derangement short of insanity"); State v. Burton, 446 So. 2d 421 (La. Ct. App. 1984) (evidence of prior hostile acts inadmissible in connection with defense of insanity and battered woman syndrome); State v. Felton, 110 Wis. 2d 485, 329 N.E.2d 161 (1981).

150. State v. Wanrow, 88 Wash. at 240, 559 P.2d at 559.

151. *Id.*

152. *Id.*

153. Of course, *Wanrow* did not involve the issue of the admissibility of expert testimony. *But see* State v. Allery, 101 Wash. 2d 591, 597, 682 P.2d 312, 316 (1984) (where the Washington Supreme Court relies on *Wanrow* for the admissibility of expert testimony).

154. *See supra* note 107.

155. *See, e.g.,* Smith v. State, 247 Ga. 612, 619, 277 S.E.2d 678, 683 (1981) ("We . . . find that the expert's testimony explaining why a person suffering from battered woman's syndrome would not leave her mate, would not inform police or friends, and would fear increased aggression against herself, would be such conclusions that jurors could not ordinarily draw for themselves."); State v. Kelly, 97 N.J. 178, 209, 478 A.2d 364, 379 (1984) ("As previously discussed, a battering relationship embodies psychological and societal features that are not well understood by lay observers. Indeed, these features

and that it is necessary for the jury to learn about these experiences in order to overcome myths and misconceptions concerning battered women in order to evaluate whether the woman was acting in self-defense.[156] This view is based on a recognition that the common ways that battered women have acted in self-defense (i.e. in not being able to leave, and in attacking assailants while asleep) will not be otherwise understandable to jurors.

Many courts have accepted the need for expert testimony. But consider what judicial acceptance of this testimony implies. It emphasizes the profound gap between the experiences of battered women and those of the rest of society; it reaffirms the notion of a woman's viewpoint *and* separate experience. It suggests that psychological and social factors are interrelated and that individual experience is necessarily shaped by group identity. It also suggests that women's own description of their experiences lacks credibility, because these experiences differ from the male norm, and because women generally are not viewed as believable.[157]

Courts are effectively recognizing that an expert, a professional, someone not a battered woman, is needed to translate the experiences of large numbers of women in this society[158] to the rest of society's representatives. It is arguable

that expert testimony may be necessary only for a transitional period, until women's voices are strong enough to be heard on their own. But experience with the use of experts in the women's movement suggests that there may be risks. Courts may find experts particularly useful in cases involving women not as a complement to, but as a substitute for, women's voices.[159]

On a theoretical level, judicial acceptance of expert testimony has a profound impact because it affirmatively recognizes the substantive experience and content of sex discrimination and validates a "woman-centered" perspective.[160] This collapses the dichotomy between individual experience and group experience[161] by describing the experience as not just the individual's, but that of all battered women generally. At the same time, it is disturbing, for it suggests that only experts can bridge the gap between the individual and collective experience of women and counsel jurors and society that an individual woman's experience has a social validity and commonality and might be reasonable.[162]

D. Subjective/Objective

The development of women's self-defense work from *Wanrow* to *Kelly* reveals change in

---

are subject to a large group of myths and stereotypes. It is clear that this subject is beyond the ken of the average juror and this is suitable for explanation through expert testimony."); State v. Torres, 128 Misc. 2d 129, 134, 488 N.Y.S.2d 358, 363 (Sup. Ct. 1985) ("[T]he subject matter of the battered woman is one outside of the common knowledge of the trier of fact"); State v. Allery, 101 Wash. 2d 591, 597, 682 P.2d 312, 316 (1984) ("We find that expert testimony explaining why a person suffering from the battered woman syndrome would not leave her mate, would not inform police or friends, and would fear increased aggression against herself would be helpful to a jury in understanding a phenomenon not within the competence of an ordinary lay person").

156. *See supra* note 111.

157. Frieze, Parsons, Johnson, Ruble, Zellman, Women and Sex Roles: A Social Psychological Perspective 280-85 (1978).

158. One study estimated that one million women are physically abused by their husbands or male companions each year. California Advisory Commission on Family Law, Domestic Violence, *cited in* State v. Kelly, 97 N.J. 178, 191, 478 A.2d 364, 370 (1984).

159. For a discussion of the historical and social role of experts in the women's movement, see B. Ehrenreich & D. English, For Her Own Good: One Hundred Fifty Years of Expert's Advice to Women (1978). Although experts can assist women so that courts can hear women's voices, experts may also be a more acceptable source of information than "ordinary" women. The dangers of

professionalization of decision-making are serious, particularly where the realm of expertise is scientific or based on a medical model. For example, in Roe v. Wade, 410 U.S. 113 (1973), the Supreme Court discusses the decision to terminate a pregnancy as one to be made between a woman and her doctors. As subsequent cases unfold, courts seem to place the reproductive decision more in the hands of doctors. *See* Asaro, *The Judicial Portrayal of the Physician in Abortion and Sterilization Decisions: The Use and Abuse of Medical Discretion*, 6 Harv. Women's L.J. 51 (1983). For an interesting analysis of the changing social contexts in which the use and type of expert testimony relied upon by courts should be viewed, see Weisberg, *The Discovery of Sexual Abuse: Expert's Role in Legal Policy Formulation*, 18 U.C.D. L. Rev. 1 (1984). Further analysis of the role and social implications of "experts" in the women's movement generally and in women's rights litigation specifically is important, but is outside the scope of this article.

160. *See generally*, Rich, *A Women-Centered University*, in On Lies, Secrets, and Silence: Selected Prose 1966-1978 (1979).

161. MacKinnon, *supra* note 5, at 717 n.73.

162. Of course there are also other ways to educate jurors and translate women's experiences within the court process. For example *voir dire* is important in these cases. For a full discussion of defense strategies, see Women's Self-Defense Cases: Theory and Practice (Bochnak, ed.), *supra* note 2; Robinson, *supra* note 5; Schneider, *supra* note 5; Schneider and Jordan, *supra* note 2.

our perspectives on the content of the standard of self-defense.

Traditionally courts and commentators have distinguished "subjective" from "objective" standards of self-defense.[163] The objective standard—the traditional "reasonable man standard"—looked at reasonableness from the perspective of the hypothetical reasonable man[164] while the subjective standard looked at reasonableness from the individual's own perspective.[165] It has been recognized that these characterizations of subjective and objective are poles on a continuum, since the jury must find that the actor acted reasonably under either approach.[166]

The objective reasonable man standard of self-defense has been criticized from many perspectives,[167] for failing to take account of complex social reality,[168] for embodying a rigid view of individual responsibility[169] and for resulting in sex-bias.[170] Recently objective standards in general have been criticized by feminist legal theorists who have argued that these standards inherently embody male values.[171] Our understandings of what is "objective" have been based largely on male experience,[172] and stereotypes of men as objective and analytical have also been contrasted with stereotypes of women as subjective and emotional.[173]

Wanrow arose in the context of a subjective individualized standard of self-defense[174] and the arguments developed there about the need for an individualized perspective responded to the traditional "reasonable man" formulation. However, *Wanrow*, and the women's self-defense work which has developed from it, did not rest on the traditional subjective formulation.[175] The content of the individualized perspective which *Wanrow* emphasized was clearly social and not simply psy-

---

163. 40 Am. Jur. 2d *Homicide* § 154 (1968); Donovan & Wildman, *supra* note 5, at 444-45; Eber, *supra* note 5, at 919-20; Comment, 60 N.D. L. REV. 141, *supra* note 5, at 146-47.

164. 40 Am. Jur. 2d *Homicide*, § 154 (1985); W. LAFAVE & A. SCOTT, HANDBOOK ON CRIMINAL LAW, § 53, at 391 (1972); Crocker, *supra* note 5, at 125; Donovan, *supra* note 5, at 444; Eber, *supra* note 5, at 919-20; Comment, 60 N.D. L. REV. 141, *supra* note 5, at 146.

165. 40 Am. Jur. 2d *Homicide*, § 154 (1968); MODEL PENAL CODE § 3.04(1) (Tent. Draft No. 8, 1958); R. PERKINS, CRIMINAL LAW, at 1113-14 (3d ed. 1982); Donovan, *supra* note 5, at 445; Eber, *supra* note 5, at 919; Comment, 69 N.D. L. REV. 141, *supra* note 5, at 147. Others have characterized the distinction somewhat differently. Crocker for example suggests that the objective standard is one in which the jury considers how "an ordinary intelligent and prudent person in the position of the defendant under the circumstances existing at the time of the alleged offense would have responded." Under a subjective standard, "a defendant's conduct is to be judged by what the defendant himself believed and has reasonable grounds to believe was necessary." Crocker, *supra* note 5, at 125.

166. Schneider & Jordan, *supra* note 2, at 30.

167. *See generally*, G. Fletcher, *supra* note 134, § 10.1, at 759; Donovan & Wildman, *supra* note 5; Schneider & Jordan, *supra* note 2.

168. Donovan & Wildman, *supra* note 5.

169. *Id.* at 465.

170. Schneider & Jordan, *supra* note 2, at 30-31.

171. *See generally*, MacKinnon, *Feminism, Marxism, Method and the State: Toward Feminist Jurisprudence*, 8 SIGNS 635 (1983).

172. MacKinnon, *supra* note 171; Schneider, *supra* note 5, at 635.

173. *See* sources cited at Schneider, *supra* note 5, at 636.

174. The court in *Wanrow* discussed the issue of the standard in the following way:

The second paragraph of instruction No. 10 contains an equally erroneous and prejudicial statement of the law. That portion of the instruction reads:

However when there is no reasonable ground for the person attacked to believe that *his* person is in imminent

danger of death or great bodily harm, and it appears to *him* that only an ordinary battery is all that is intended, and all that *he* has reasonable grounds to fear from *his* assailant, *he* has a right to stand *his* ground and repel such threatened assault, yet *he* has no right to repel a threatened assault with naked hands, by the use of a deadly weapon in a deadly manner, unless *he* believes, *and has reasonable grounds* to believe, that *he* is in imminent danger of death or great bodily harm.

(Italics ours).

In our society women suffer from a conspicuous lack of access to training in and the means of developing those skills necessary to effectively repel a male assailant without resorting to the use of deadly weapons. Instruction No. 12 does indicate that the "relative size and strength of the persons involved" may be considered; however, it does not make clear that the defendant's actions are to be judged against her own subjective impressions and not those which a detached jury might determine to be objectively reasonable. . . . The applicable rule of law is clearly stated in *Miller*, at page 105, 250 P. at page 645:

If the appellants, at the time of the alleged assault upon them, as reasonably and ordinarily cautious and prudent men, honestly believed that they were in danger of great bodily harm, they would have the right to resort to self-defense, and their conduct is to be judged by the condition appearing to them at the time, not by the condition as it might appear to the jury in light of testimony before it.

Wanrow, 88 Wash. 2d at 239-40, 559 P.2d at 558.

175. Given the blurred lines between objective and subjective standards of self-defense, the theory in *Wanrow* is applicable even where the standard is more objective. A critical aspect of sex-bias in the law of self-defense is the notion of reasonableness in general as problematic for women. The more individualized the standard, the easier it may be for women. *See* Schneider, *supra* note 5, at 639-40. But it is possible that individualization may not go far enough because "while it considers individual characteristics, it may not recognize their significance." Crocker, *supra* note 5, at 125, n.11.

WOMEN'S RIGHTS LAW REPORTER   [Vol. 9:195 (1986)]

chological.[176] It was the woman's individual perspective shaped by her experience as a woman within the collective and historical experience of sex discrimination.[177] At the time, it seemed difficult enough to convince a jury that the woman might be reasonable even when applying a standard emphasizing the woman's own perspective. It was even more difficult to imagine arguing woman's experiences as objectively reasonable.

However, the expert testimony cases suggest that perhaps the *Wanrow* approach was too cautious. Expert testimony on battered woman syndrome necessarily challenges the dichotomy of subjective versus objective, as did *Wanrow*. The individual woman seeks expert testimony about the characteristics of the larger group of which she is a member to show that she acted reasonably both as an individual and as a member of that group. The very notion of expert testimony about the common character of battered women contains a subjective (individualized) component and an objective (group) component. The substance of the testimony describes experience which in some sense can be considered as objective. Courts have held that this testimony is relevant in jurisdictions with both objective and subjective standards.[178]

Kelly demonstrates this development. The very issue in *Kelly* was whether the expert testimony was relevant under New Jersey's standard of self-defense.[179] The trial court interpreted it as a traditional objective standard; counsel argued that under either standard the testimony was relevant.[180] The court held that the testimony was relevant to the objective reasonableness of the de-

fendant's belief as to whether she "reasonably believe(d) deadly force to be necessary to prevent death or serious bodily harm."[181] This recognition of a woman's and battered woman's experiences and perceptions as objectively reasonable is vitally important. The court thereby accords a woman's experience a group-based "public" dimension rather than merely an individual, "private" subjective one. At the same time, perhaps it is not surprising that the content of what is deemed "objective" is an image of a victimized, passive battered women. Perhaps this is the reason the court sees it as objective and acceptable.

V. DESCRIBING AND CHANGING: THE UNDERLYING THEME OF VICTIMIZATION AND AGENCY

The underlying theme throughout this discussion of the expert testimony cases is the dilemma that the notion of victimization poses for feminist legal theory. Examination of the expert testimony cases on battering has suggested that a perspective like battered woman syndrome, which either emphasizes victimization or which is susceptible to being characterized as victimization, raises serious problems for women in theory and practice.

Over the last several years, victimization has increasingly become a powerful, pervasive and seductive theme in the women's movement and the women's legal rights movement.[182] It is a theme that has had wide appeal. While I believe that women are victims, and that this perspective on women's experience is important and useful, particularly on issues concerning violence against

---

176. The *Wanrow* court emphasizes that sex discrimination is the social context in which the individual woman's experience is to be evaluated. The notion of individualization was not intended to discount social factors since "the circumstances of the act and the characteristics and perceptions of the individual defendant are shaped by social experience." Schneider, *supra* note 5, at 640. For a discussion of the interrelationship of social and individual factors in these cases, see generally, MacKinnon, *supra* note 5.

177. Schneider, *supra* note 5, at 640; MacKinnon, *supra* note 5.

178. For cases that have admitted expert testimony on battered woman syndrome with a standard that the court has characterized as "subjective," see People v. Torres, 128 Misc. 2d 1129, 488 N.Y.S.2d 358 (Sup. Ct. 1985); State v. Kelly, 33 Wash. App. 541, 655 P.2d 1202 (1982); State v. Allery, 101 Wash. 591, 682 P.2d 312 (1984). For cases that have admitted expert testimony with a standard that the court has characterized as "objective," see State v. Kelly, 97 N.J. 178, 478 A.2d 364 (1984). Some of the courts admitting expert

testimony do not characterize their own standards of self-defense. *See, e.g.,* People v. Minnis, 118 Ill. App. 3d 345, 455 N.E.2d 209 (1983); State v. Anaya, 438 A.2d 892 (Me. 1981), *aff'd on other grounds,* 456 A.2d 1255 (Me. 1983).

179. The trial court in *Kelly* held that the expert testimony was not relevant under New Jersey's objective standard of self-defense.

180. *See* Appellant's Brief, State v. Kelly (Appellate Division), and Brief of *Amici Curiae* American Civil Liberties Union of New Jersey *et al* in State v. Kelly, *supra* notes 16 and 84 [this issue at 245].

181. Schneider, *supra* note 5, at 638; Crocker, *supra* note 5, at 130-31; State v. Kelly, 97 N.J. 178, 478 A.2d 364 (1984).

182. Many of the ideas raised in this section developed from discussion in a workshop that Isabel Marcus, Rhonda Copelon, Nan Hunter and I jointly led at the Feminist/Critical Legal Studies Conference in Boston in May 1985. Our dialogue helped me articulate my own concerns more clearly and strengthened me to express them more directly.

women, the virtually exclusive focus on victimization by the women's movement in recent years has been problematic. Portrayal of women as solely victims or agents is neither accurate nor adequate to explain the complex realities of women's lives. It is crucial for feminists and feminist legal theorists to understand and explore the role of both victimization and agency in women's lives, and to translate these understandings into the theory and practice that we develop.

As we have seen, expert testimony on battered woman syndrome describes common experiences of battered women and has had an important educational effect on courts and assisted women in getting justice from the courts. At the same time, it is problematic and susceptible to misuse because it is likely to be misheard. Expert testimony which emphasizes or is heard to emphasize only battered women's helplessness or victimization is necessarily partial and incomplete because it does not address the crucial issue of the woman's action, or her agency[183] in a prosecution for homicide—namely, why the battered woman acted. It can lock lawyers and judges into stereotypical thinking which does not force them to genuinely understand the reasonableness of an individual battered woman's act. Juries evaluating the claims of battered women who have killed their batterers are looking at women who have been both victims and actors. These women have acted to save their own lives. Our explanation of the reasonableness of their claims of self-defense has to take both their victimization and their agency into account. The woman's action has to be put in the context of her victimization.

Other feminist theorists and legal thinkers have questioned the women's movement's reliance on victimization in a range of contexts,[184] including divorce[185] and pornography.[186] In the specific context of battered women, Susan Schechter has emphasized the dangers of an analysis premised on victimization. She suggests that the characterization of victim has been viewed as posing a complicated political problem for the battered women's movement

> because the focus on victimization helps to blur the insight that the struggle for battered women's rights is linked to the more general fight for women's liberation. When activists view battering as victimization rather than as an aspect of oppression, they have a tendency to see individual problems rather than collective ones.[187]

In addition, she observes that "victim" may be a label that battered women reject because "it fails to capture their complexity and strength."[188]

At the same time, a notion of the importance of women's agency without a social context of victimization is equally unsatisfactory. The no-

---

183. Perhaps using the words *action* and *agency* as parallels here is problematic. The woman has acted, but she has also been, as Catharine MacKinnon acutely observes, "acted upon." MacKinnon, *supra* note 5, at 734. It is not fair to say that she has been "self-acting" or really an agent, in the sense of free agent. Yet there is a sense in which the notion of victimization in its extreme form seems to deny any agency, the possibility of individual action, or the fact of action altogether.

184. *See generally* S. SCHECHTER, WOMEN AND VIOLENCE, THE VISIONS AND STRUGGLES OF THE BATTERED WOMEN'S MOVEMENT (1982); A. JAGGAR, FEMINISM AND HUMAN NATURE (1983); K. FERGUSON, THE FEMINIST CASE AGAINST BUREAUCRACY (1984); Duggan, Hunter and Vance, *False Promises: Feminist Antipornography Legislation in the United States* in WOMEN AGAINST CENSORSHIP (V. Burstyn ed. 1985); Fineman, *Implementing Equality: Ideology, Contradiction and Social Change, A Study of Rhetoric in the Regulation of the Consequences of Divorce*, 1983 WIS. L. REV. 789; *Feminist Discourse, Moral Values and the Law—A Conversation*, 31 BUFFALO L. REV. 1 (1985).

185. *See generally*, Martha Fineman's discussion of the theme of victimization in feminist divorce reform work, Fineman, *supra* note 184.

186. *See generally*, Duggan, Hunter and Vance, *supra* note 184. Lisa Duggan, Nan Hunter and Carole Vance critique the feminist strategy of anti-pornography ordinances on the ground that they are premised on a view of sexuality as victimization, and do not take account of women's agency as sexual actors.

The proposed ordinances are also dangerous because they seek to embody in law an analysis of the role of sexuality and sexual images in the oppression of women with which even all feminists do not agree. *Underlying virtually every section of the proposed laws there is an assumption that sexuality is a realm of unremitting unequaled victimization for women. Pornography appears as the monster that made this so.* The ordinances' authors seek to impose their analysis by putting state power behind it. But this analysis is not the only feminist perspective on sexuality. Feminist theorists have also argued that the sexual terrain, however power-laden, is actively contested. *Women are agents, and not merely victims, who make decisions and act on them, and who desire, seek out and enjoy sexuality.*

Duggan, Hunter and Vance, *supra* note 184, at 151 (emphasis supplied).

187. Schechter, *supra* note 184, at 252.

188. *Id.* For an insightful analysis of the complex reasons that individuals who have been discriminated against do not want to experience themselves as victims, *see also* Bumiller, *Anti-Discrimination Law and the Enslavement of the Victim: The Denial of Self-Respect by Victims Without a Cause* (Working Paper, Disputes Processing Research Program, University of Wisconsin—Madison Law School).

222   WOMEN'S RIGHTS LAW REPORTER [Vol. 9:195 (1986)

tion of agency carries with it assumptions of lib-eral visions of autonomy, individual action, indi-vidual control and mobility that are also inadequate and incomplete. But women do act, we have acted in history,[189] we act to make choices and shape our lives, we act even when there are few and terrible options. Sometimes, like battered women who kill, we act if only in order to survive.

In the battered woman context, recognition of the need to transcend the dichotomy and exclu-sivity of characterizations of victim versus agent and develop a theory and practice which encom-passes both has consequences for the way we ap-proach and handle the use of expert testimony in battered women's cases. Defense efforts should focus on the battering experience as well as the reasonableness of the woman's actions. Expert testimony on battering should be proffered and admitted, but lawyers should be sensitive to the way in which they understand, characterize and explain the testimony and its relevance, and they should not rely on it to the exclusion of other de-fense strategies. Battered women who kill need not be portrayed solely as victims with the focus on the battering, but as actors and survivors whose acts are reasonable. The psychological mechanisms that battered women develop, as in battered woman syndrome, can be explained as ways for battered women to cope and survive.[190] If killing in self-defense can be understood as a reasonable act in terms of the context of victimi-zation and other options, both the victimization and agency aspects of battered women's exper-iences are included. If battered women who kill are described as women who are victims but have

fought back in order to survive, their actions in killing their batterers may be more effectively un-derstood as reasonable.

Defense lawyers and experts must emphasize the common experiences of battered women, but must describe both the particular experiences of the individual woman and be sensitive to the sex-stereotypical implications of the testimony. De-fense lawyers and experts should emphasize the common aspects of the battered women's experi-ence, both her helplessness and her behavioral ad-justments that allow her to survive, her desperate coping, her unique insight and ability to know and anticipate the degree of violence she faces, and her painful understanding of the paucity of alternatives available to women in this culture.[191] This fuller description of battered women's exper-iences is both more accurate and better explains to judges and juries why a battered woman doesn't leave the house and why she kills to save her own life.

Explanation of aspects of both victimization and agency makes it possible for expert testimony to more accurately describe the complexity of bat-tered women's experiences, respond to the hard defense problems presented in these cases, and al-low for change by transcending static stereotypes. Feminist legal work must both describe and allow for change. As lawyers for battered women we must take account of battered women's exper-iences in being acted upon and acting.[192] Our work must simultaneously capture the reality of battered women's lives, translate this reality more fully and effectively to courts, and push toward transforming this reality.

---

189. Feminist Discourse, supra note 184, at 60 (Feminist historian Ellen C. DuBois stated "[T]he basic discovery of the discipline of women's history is that women act in history: they create history and that includes their own oppression as well as their own liberation. If they don't create history, then there is no possibility for change in their position").
190. The work of both Drs. Julie Blackman and Lenore

Walker expresses these approaches. See Blackman, Battered Women Who Kill Their Husbands, New Perspectives On Self-Defense (paper presented at the American Psychological Association meeting, Toronto 1984); WALKER, supra note 71, at 33.
191. See supra note 190.
192. See supra note 183.

Family Law

[9]

THE MYTH OF STATE
INTERVENTION IN THE FAMILY

Frances E. Olsen*

Most people concede that there are times when state officials should intervene in the private family. Doctrines of family privacy are no longer thought to justify societal neglect of beaten wives or abused children. Yet society continues to use the ideal of the private family to orient policy. It seems important therefore to examine the concept of state intervention in the private family. In this essay, I argue that the private family is an incoherent ideal and that the rhetoric of nonintervention is more harmful than helpful.

Although most people accept in general the assertion that the state should not intervene in the family, they qualify the assertion with the caveat that the state should sometimes intervene in order to correct inequality or prevent abuse. I refer to this widely-accepted caveat as the "protective intervention argument" against nonintervention in the family.

This essay presents a different argument against the policy of nonintervention in the family. It suggests that the terms "intervention" and "nonintervention" are largely meaningless. The terms do not accurately describe any set of policies, and as general principles, "intervention" and "nonintervention" are indeterminate. I refer to this argument as the "incoherence argument."

A useful comparison can be drawn between arguments against a policy of nonintervention in the private family and arguments against a policy of nonintervention in the free market.[1] The pol-

* Acting Professor of Law, University of California at Los Angeles. B.A., 1968, Goddard College; J.D., 1971, University of Colorado; S.J.D., 1984, Harvard University.

I am grateful to Mary Joe Frug, Grace Blumberg, and Bill Alford for helpful comments on earlier drafts. I would also like to express my appreciation to the summer, 1984, Fellows of the University of Wisconsin Legal History Colloquium sponsored by the National Endowment for the Humanities for convincing me that more had to be said about state intervention in the family; to the editors of the *University of Michigan Journal of Law Reform* who, with grace and good humor, coaxed and badgered me into writing this essay; to Ken Kimmel for his research assistance; and to the Research Committee of the UCLA Academic Senate for financial support.

1. I originally drew this comparison in Olsen, *The Family and the Market: A Study of Ideology and Legal Reform*, 96 HARV. L. REV. 1497 (1983).

836   Journal of Law Reform   [VOL. 18:4

icy of nonintervention in the free market, often referred to as laissez faire, was pursued by many American courts in the nineteenth and early twentieth centuries. The group of scholars known as legal realists played an important role in discrediting the legal theories that supported laissez faire. Their arguments form a useful contrast and resource for the arguments I present in this essay.

The protective intervention argument applies in a similar manner to both laissez faire and nonintervention in the family: whenever either the market or the family misfunctions, the state should intervene to correct inequality and protect the defenseless. The most common and easily accepted argument against laissez faire is that the free market sometimes breaks down or works to the serious disadvantage of particular individuals or groups; state intervention is then necessary to protect the interests of the weaker economic actors and of society in general. This parallels the protective intervention argument regarding the family. Sometimes the family misfunctions; instead of being a haven that protects and nurtures family members, the family may become a center of oppression and exploitation.[2] When this happens the state should step in to prevent abuse and to protect the rights of the individual family members. Both the market version and the family version of this protective intervention argument presuppose that it would be possible for the state to remain neutral, but present reasons that the state should not do so.

The incoherence argument against nonintervention in the family parallels the legal realists' argument against laissez faire. Both laissez faire and nonintervention in the family are false ideals. As long as a state exists and enforces any laws at all, it makes political choices. The state cannot be neutral or remain uninvolved, nor would anyone want the state to do so. The staunchest supporters of laissez faire always insisted that the state protect their property interests and that courts enforce contracts and adjudicate torts.[3] They took this state action for granted and chose not to consider such protection a form of state intervention. Yet the so-called "free market" does not function except for such laws; the free market could not exist independently of the state. The enforcement of property, tort, and contract law requires constant political choices that may

---

2. *See* Minow, *Beyond State Intervention in the Family: For Baby Jane Doe,* 18 U. MICH. J.L. REF. 933, 948-50 (1985).

3. *See* Cohen, *The Basis of Contract,* 46 HARV. L. REV. 553, 561-62 (1933).

benefit one economic actor, usually at the expense of another. As Robert Hale pointed out more than a half century ago, these legal decisions "are bound to affect the distribution of income and the direction of economic activities."[4] Any choice the courts make will affect the market, and there is seldom any meaningful way to label one choice intervention and the other laissez faire. When the state enforces any of these laws it must make political decisions that affect society.

Similarly, the staunchest opponents of state intervention in the family will insist that the state reinforce parents' authority over their children. Familiar examples of this reinforcement include state officials returning runaway children and courts ordering incorrigible children to obey their parents or face incarceration in juvenile facilities. These state actions are not only widely supported, they are generally not considered state intervention in the family. Another category of state policies is even less likely to be thought of as intervention. Supporters of nonintervention insist that the state protect families from third-party interference. Imagine their reaction if the state stood idly by while doctors performed non-emergency surgery without the knowledge or permission of a ten-year-old patient's parents, or if neighbors prepared to take the child on their vacation against the wishes of the parents, or if the child decided to go live with his fourth grade teacher. Once the state undertakes to prevent such third-party action, the state must make numerous policy choices, such as what human grouping constitutes a family and what happens if parents disagree. These choices are bound to affect the decisions people make about forming families, the distribution of power within the family, and the assignment of tasks and roles among family members. The state is responsible for the background rules that affect people's domestic behaviors. Because the state is deeply implicated in the formation and functioning of families, it is nonsense to talk about whether the state does or does not intervene in the family. Neither "intervention" nor "nonintervention" is an accurate description of any particular set of policies, and the terms obscure rather than clarify the policy choices that society makes.

---

4. Hale, *Coercion and Distribution in a Supposedly Non-Coercive State*, 38 POL. SCI. Q. 470 (1923). *See* Kennedy, *Form and Substance in Private Law Adjudication*, 89 HARV. L. REV. 1685, 1748-49 (1976).

I. THE PROTECTIVE INTERVENTION ARGUMENT

To understand the incoherence argument, it is useful to examine in more detail the protective intervention argument—the argument that nonintervention would be possible but is not always a good idea. The protective intervention argument is an argument in favor of selective intervention.[5] In exceptional situations, the state should intervene in the family to protect the interests of society and of the family members who may be at risk; aside from such exceptional situations, state intervention should ordinarily be limited to routine matters such as setting formal requirements for marriage licenses and providing public schooling for children.[6]

According to the usual version of the protective intervention argument, state intervention beyond routine matters should be carefully limited. Excessive or unnecessary intervention jeopardizes people's freedom and interferes with family intimacy. Because of the risks inherent in state intervention, say proponents of protective intervention, safeguards should be devised to protect against government abuse and to prevent unnecessary expansion of state intervention. As long as proper safeguards exist, however, state intervention can be useful—an important force for good.

---

5. The protective intervention argument presupposes that the concept of state intervention in the family is coherent and meaningful. I argue that the concept is instead incoherent and meaningless.

First, it makes no logical sense to consider the policies referred to as "nonintervention" any less interventionist than many policies referred to as "intervention." By and large, policies supporting the status quo are referred to as nonintervention and attempts to change the status quo are called intervention; "intervention" and "nonintervention" are inappropriate and misleading terms to use to characterize these policies. Moreover, the policies referred to as "intervention" and "nonintervention" have a wide range of overlap; the same policy will be referred to as intervention by some and nonintervention by others. There is no objective or rational basis upon which to determine who is correct, because there is no logical basis for considering any particular set of policies nonintervention.

The protective intervention argument, however, presupposes that there is a basis for distinguishing intervention from nonintervention and that the terms have meaning. In my discussion of the protective intervention argument, I find it convenient occasionally to use the term "intervention" as though it had meaning. When I use the term, I intend for it to convey the range of contradictory meanings that people assign in everyday use of language.

6. As I argue *infra*, pp. 848-54, these "routine" matters can have an important influence on family roles and power relations within the family.

A. *Families Can Malfunction*

The argument in favor of selective state intervention is based on the notion that although families ought to be safe, supportive, and loving, some families at some times are not.[7] The family is supposed to be a warm, nurturant enclave governed by an ethic of altruism and caring—a haven protecting its members from the dangers of an authoritarian state and from the anarchistic intrusions of private third parties. Proponents of protective intervention recognize that in some unfortunate situations, the family can cease to be a haven and become instead, "a center of oppression, raw will and authority, violence and brutality, where the powerful economically and sexually subordinate and exploit the powerless."[8]

B. *State Protection of Individuals*

When a family malfunctions it may be important for the state to protect an individual from the private oppression that members of families sometimes inflict on each other. The protective intervention argument justifies state intervention in the family to protect children from abuse or serious neglect. State officials can remove children from their families if the children have been physically or sexually abused. In cases of child neglect, the state may send social workers into the children's homes or remove the children, temporarily or permanently, for their protection. Such state protection can include ordering medical care, even against the parents' religious scruples. These policies are generally considered to be a form of state intervention in the family, but accepted as intervention that is justified, indeed necessary.

Until recent years, state protection for battered wives was also considered state intervention in the family—again, perhaps justified intervention, but intervention nonetheless. The protective intervention argument characterizes such state protection as a

---

7. A more radical strand of criticism might argue that the nuclear family is a seething hothouse or an oppressive structure that will *often* become destructive of individual members.

8. Minow, *supra* note 2, at 948. Professor Gerald Frug describes the city similarly as an enclave protecting individual freedom or alternatively a threat jeopardizing individual freedom. *See* Frug, *The City as a Legal Concept*, 93 HARV. L. REV. 1057, 1121 (1980). He suggests that "any form of group power intermediate between a centralized state and the individual" may have a precarious existence in a liberal political state. *See id.*

beneficial and necessary form of intervention into a family that
has problems. Few people today would openly oppose state enforcement of rape and battery laws against spouses.[9] If providing
shelter houses and legal aid to battered wives constitutes state
intervention, many argue that such intervention is fully justified
to protect individual wives from being oppressed by their husbands. In the exceptional cases in which families misfunction,
the state should step in to protect the powerless.

This protective intervention argument begins to blend into
the incoherence argument when people dispute whether such
protection should be considered intervention at all. Some people
would assert that when the family relationship has broken down,
so has any justifiable claim to family privacy, and that state protection of the individual no longer constitutes intervention into
the family. Indeed, proponents of this view might argue that it
would be state intervention to try to keep the family together—for example, not to allow estranged spouses to get a divorce. In such arguments, the idea that the privacy of the family
unit should be protected from state intervention begins to be
replaced by the notion that what merits protection is the privacy
of the individual regarding sexuality, procreation, and the formation of intimate, family-like relationships.[10] I consider this

---

9. People struggling to eliminate the marriage exemption from rape laws tell me,
however, that they find a great many people who *do* oppose the enforcement of rape laws
against husbands. The National Clearinghouse on Marital Rape sent me a packet of
newspaper clippings from all over the country that are filled with amazing quotations
from state legislators. Opposition to marital rape laws range from assertions that "sex is
part of the [marriage] contract," Tex. Rep. Patricia Hill, *quoted in* the Times-Herald,
May 21, 1985 (Dallas, Tex.), and "I don't know how you can have a sexual act and call it
forcible rape in a marriage situation," Alaska Sen. Paul Fischer, *quoted in* Daily News,
Mar. 21, 1985 (Juneau, Alaska), to concerns with false charges and "blackmail." Legislators argue that the "state shouldn't be going behind the bedroom doors," Tex. Rep. Patricia Hill, *quoted in* Times-Herald, *supra. See also* S.D. Rep. Joe Barnett, *reported in*
Argus Leader, Mar. 2, 1985 (Sioux Falls, S.D.) (keep government out of the bedroom).
Spousal rape laws are "an absolute intrusion into family life," S.D. Sen. Thomas Ruby,
quoted in Capital Journal, Mar. 15, 1985, (Pierre, S.D.). They would pit family members
against one another, S.D. Rep. Bernie Christenson, *reported in* Capital Journal, Feb. 14,
1985 (Pierre, S.D.) and "erode at family life," S.D. Sen. Harold Halverson, *quoted in*
Argus Leader, Feb. 28, 1985 (Sioux Falls, S.D.). "I still believe in the old traditional bond
of marriage," Alaska Sen. Paul Fischer, *quoted in* Daily News, *supra* (copies of all clippings on file with U. Mich. J.L. Ref.).

10. This shift from the concept of a private family into which the state should not
intervene to the concept of individual privacy regarding intimate relationships corresponds to a more general shift I have referred to as the "liberalization of the family." *See*
Olsen, *The Politics of Family Law,* 2 Law and Inequality 1, 6-8 (1984). There I discuss
the shift that has taken place from seeing the family as an organic group to seeing it as a
contract among individuals. *See id.* at 11-12.

For an argument that this individual privacy right should be grounded in individual
autonomy and not in marriage and family, see Eichbaum, *Towards an Autonomy-Based*

concept of individual privacy to be part of the protective intervention argument—that state intervention is sometimes justified—because although the privacy argument redefines state intervention, it still considers intervention and nonintervention coherent, meaningful concepts.

C. Safeguards Against Excessive Intervention

The protective intervention argument usually treats nonintervention as the norm and intervention as an exception.[11] As one jurist put it: "The normal behavior of husband and wife or parents and children towards each other is beyond the law—as long as the family is 'healthy.' The law comes in when things go wrong."[12]

People who support selective state intervention often assert that safeguards are necessary to protect families from excessive state intervention—attempts by the state to offer protection when it is not really necessary. Child abuse and neglect statutes typically provide that until behaviors pass some threshold, the family is to remain private and the state should not intrude. The Constitution has been held to supply additional protection to family privacy by requiring a clear and convincing showing of abuse or neglect before parental rights may be severed.[13] Physical or sexual abuse or serious neglect is usually necessary to trigger state intervention. This possibility of state intervention, even if it actually occurs only in rare exceptional cases, can play a significant role in keeping family behavior within reasonable bounds of decency.[14]

Divorce or legal separation may also be considered a sufficient trigger to justify state intervention that would otherwise not be allowed. For example, many people who would oppose such policies in an ongoing family believe that if parents separate, the

---

Theory of Constitutional Privacy: Beyond the Ideology of Familial Privacy, 14 HARV. C.R.-C.L. L. REV. 361 (1979).

11. A more radical version of the protective intervention argument might maintain that state intervention is frequently or always necessary to protect individuals from the inherent oppressiveness of the nuclear family. *See supra* note 7.

12. Kahn-Freund, *Editorial Foreword* to J. EEKELAAR, FAMILY SECURITY AND FAMILY BREAKDOWN at 7 (1971), *quoted in* Freeman, *Violence Against Women: Does the Legal System Provide Solutions or Itself Constitute the Problem?,* 3 CAN. J.F.L. 377, 387 (1980).

13. Santosky v. Kramer, 455 U.S. 745, 768-70 (1982).

14. The possibility of state action in more extreme cases can have a significant influence on everyday behavior within the family. *See, e.g.,* Minow, *supra* note 2, at 952-53.

state should order the noncustodial parent to provide financial support for his or her child in case the parent would not do so without a court order.[15] As long as they see safeguards, such as thresholds of family misbehavior or breakdown, to protect against excessive intervention, most people today support a certain level of protective intervention by the state.

II. THE INCOHERENCE ARGUMENT

The incoherence argument goes further and I believe is more fundamental than the protective intervention argument. The protective intervention argument treats nonintervention as a fully possible but sometimes unwise choice; the incoherence argument questions the basic coherence of the concepts intervention and nonintervention. The state defines the family and sets roles within the family; it is meaningless to talk about intervention or nonintervention, because the state constantly defines and redefines the family and adjusts and readjusts family roles. Nonintervention is a false ideal because it has no coherent meaning.

For example, suppose a good-natured, intelligent sovereign were to ascend the throne with a commitment to end state intervention in the family. Rather than being obvious, the policies she should pursue would be hopelessly ambiguous. Is she intervening if she makes divorces difficult, or intervening if she makes them easy? Does it constitute intervention or nonintervention to grant divorce at all? If a child runs away from her parents to go live with her aunt, would nonintervention require the sovereign to grant or to deny the parents' request for legal assistance to reclaim their child? Because complete agreement on family roles does not exist, and because these roles undergo change over time, the state cannot be said simply to ratify preexisting family roles. The state is continuously affecting the family by influencing the distribution of power among individuals.

The incoherence argument is more complex with regard to the family than with regard to the market. Because nonintervention in the family has been understood as a variety of things, demon-

---

15. *Compare, e.g.,* Anderson v. Anderson, 437 S.W.2d 704 (Mo. Ct. App. 1969) (ordering divorced father to pay for daughter's college education) *with* Roe v. Doe, 29 N.Y.2d 188, 272 N.E.2d 567, 324 N.Y.S.2d 71 (1971) (refusing to order father to support daughter's college education). In McGuire v. McGuire, 157 Neb. 226, 59 N.W.2d 336 (1953) the court refused to order spousal support for the wife in an ongoing marriage, although the circumstances of the parties were such that the court might well have awarded spousal support had there been a legal separation.

strating its incoherence becomes more complicated than demonstrating that laissez faire is incoherent with respect to the market. Laissez faire is incoherent because no apolitical or neutral way exists to enforce property, contract, or tort law; once the state undertakes to enforce any of these laws, courts are forced to make political choices that cannot help but have important effects on the market and on the direction of economic activities. The alternative of not enforcing any property, contract, and tort law—creating a "state of nature"—is unacceptable in the marketplace. Once one rules out a state of nature, the government can no longer keep "hands off" the market; the question becomes simply which particular policies the government shall support.

The greater complexity of the incoherence argument with respect to the family than with respect to the market makes it initially easier to see that the state is not a neutral arbiter when it deals with the family. Historically, the state bolstered the power of the father over his family. A policy-based refusal to bolster this power might well be considered "intervention"—whether justified under the protective intervention argument or considered obtrusive and unjustified.[16] Even today the state is often expected to enforce parents' authority over their children. To many who endorse hierarchical family relations, "nonintervention" seems to mean simply state support for the family member with power. "Nonintervention" loses much of its appeal if one thinks of it as mere reinforcement of the status quo. Moreover, because the status quo undergoes continual change, nonintervention in the hierarchical family cannot be coherent. Even if state officials attempted simply to support the status quo they would still be forced to make political choices that have important effects on the distribution of roles and power within a family.

In recent years, the state has been expected to treat the members of the family—especially the husband and wife—more as equals. With increasing juridical equality within the family, the parallel between laissez faire with respect to the market and nonintervention with respect to the family becomes closer. Complete juridical equality would require a new concept of state intervention and nonintervention. At least two radically different concepts are possible, though neither would be acceptable to most people and, as I will demonstrate, neither is coherent. One possibility, which I refer to as the Market Model, is based on

16. *See infra* p. 850.

enforcement of all laws, just as they are enforced in the market. Under this model, all rights and obligations would be enforced between family members the same way laws are enforced between strangers. In this manner the state could avoid direct support for family hierarchy. Nonintervention under the Market Model would be incoherent for the same reasons laissez faire is incoherent: enforcement of any property, tort, or contract law, whether between family members or strangers, requires political choices that necessarily affect the power of the individuals and groups involved and the direction of both their intimate and their commercial relations.

A second possible model of state "nonintervention" in a juridically equal family is non-enforcement or delegalization—no rights or obligations to be enforced between family members. I refer to this construct as the State of Nature Model. Unlike the situation regarding the market,[17] something approaching this model is acceptable to many as a form of "nonintervention" in the family. It can be demonstrated, however, that nonintervention under the State of Nature Model is also incoherent. First, because the "state of nature" would exist only within the family, the state would have to decide the boundaries of family. In addition, if the state of nature within the family were partial instead of complete, the state would have to decide which rights and obligations it would enforce within the family. These decisions require political choices that necessarily affect the roles and power within a family. Once the state undertakes to enforce some but not all rights and obligations, the state cannot avoid policy choices that will affect family life. No logical basis exists for identifying these state choices as either intervention or nonintervention.

A. Introduction: Laissez Faire and Nonintervention

As I have suggested, the incoherence argument against nonintervention in the family is both simpler and more complex than the corresponding argument against laissez faire in the market. An important claim of laissez faire was that the state could and should treat market actors as juridical equals and enforce evenhandedly uncontroversial neutral ground rules that would en-

---

17. In the market, virtually no one would find a state of nature acceptable. People insist that some form of tort, contract, and property law be enforced. *See supra* p. 836.

sure the protection of all.[18] The incoherence argument against laissez faire demonstrated that the ground rules were not and could not be made neutral and that they could not be enforced even-handedly. Opponents of laissez faire showed that policy issues arose constantly within every aspect of tort and contract law doctrine—that the kind of apolitical legal system that laissez faire envisioned and depended upon was a myth.[19]

In the case of the market, laissez faire seemed at least to produce a kind of state neutrality, because courts treated people as juridical equals. Workers and bosses were said to have identical rights to freedom of contract.[20] Legal formalism or conceptualism presupposed that it was possible for a legal system to be rational, objective, and principled—scientific rather than political. The failure of legal formalism or conceptualism rendered laissez faire incoherent.[21] Had it really been true that law could be apolitical, that contract law could simply enforce the will of the parties, and tort law simply require those at fault to compensate their victims, laissez faire might well have been coherent.[22] No one has come up with any plausible method for removing the need for political choice from law, however, and I consider it highly unlikely that any such method exists or could be devised.[23]

B. Nonintervention and the Hierarchical Family

The notion of nonintervention in the family is in a sense less plausible than laissez faire in the market. The ideal laissez-faire state would treat market actors as juridical equals; the state does not treat members of a family as juridical equals. Further,

---

18. I refer to laissez faire in the past tense because I am speaking of its classical form, which came to seem implausible many years ago. *See* Kennedy, *supra* note 4, at 1746-48.

19. *See id.* at 1748-49.

20. *See, e.g.,* Lochner v. New York, 198 U.S. 45, 52-58 (1905).

21. *See* Kennedy, *supra* note 4, at 1731-32.

22. Under these circumstances, the incoherence argument would fall, and the important question would be the one raised by the protective intervention argument—whether the free market led to injustice and needless suffering in particular cases that could properly be relieved through selective state intervention.

23. My agnosticism regarding the possible existence of an apolitical jurisprudence is based primarily on the difficulty of proving a negative. It is relatively easy to show that particular attempts to ground judicial decision-making on apolitical bases fail—for example, that the law-and-economics field does not offer such a basis, *see* Horwitz, *Law and Economics: Science or Politics?*, 8 HOFSTRA L. REV. 905 (1980) (arguing that law-and-economics claims to present such an apolitical basis but cannot)—but it would be very difficult to prove that all possible attempts are bound to fail.

the constitutive role of law in creating the market is less obvious than law's constitutive role in creating and defining the family. Laws establish who is married to whom and who shall be considered the child of whom.

The existence of this "legal-positivist" view of the family should not, however, obscure the coexisting and competing "natural law" belief that the family exists as a natural human formation, not created but merely recognized (or not recognized) by the state. Such a notion is implicit in the sense shared by most of us that some families exist that are not legally recognized. In fact, a great deal of family law doctrine can be seen as a response to the problems caused by the disjunction between legally recognized or de jure families and "natural" or de facto families—the gap between the legal definition of family and the sense people have of what a family really is.[24]

Although the state defines and reinforces specific roles and a particular hierarchy within the family, these policies are often considered nonintervention; indeed, a refusal to bolster family hierarchy has sometimes been considered state intervention in the family.[25] The idea that the state can intervene or not intervene in the family, and particularly that the state practices a policy of nonintervention when it bolsters family hierarchy, would seem to depend upon the belief that a natural family exists separate from legal regulations, and that the hierarchy the state enforces is a natural hierarchy, created by God or by nature, not by law.[26]

---

24. Common law marriage, putative marriage, and a variety of presumptions that legitimate bigamous second or third marriages all serve to enable courts to treat established (real) families like legal families. *See also, e.g.,* Stanley v. Illinois, 405 U.S. 645, 651-52 (1972) (invalidating state law denying unwed father legal rights of parent); Glona v. American Guar. & Liab. Ins. Co., 391 U.S. 73, 75-76 (1968) (limiting state's discretion to base wrongful death law on legal rather than biological relationships).

25. *See infra* p. 850.

26. In response, it might be argued that the state can adopt a meaningful policy of "nonintervention" even towards a "family" that it plays the major part in defining. Proponents of this view might acknowledge that their policy of selective nonintervention departs from the literal meaning of the term but assert that a distinction between the roles the state must play before the family can be legally recognized and other roles it might play lends coherence to their use of the term. On this view, the state plays one role as ground rule maker—policing the borders of the definition of "family" and protecting that family from intruding third parties. This role might be said to be sufficiently noncontroversial that it may be distinguished from numerous other roles—such as providing contraception or abortion—that the state may choose to avoid under a policy of "nonintervention."

The standard and most obvious difficulty with this approach appears when one tries to select which functions are so "noncontroversial" that they come within the state's role as ground rule maker, and which functions are objectionable enough that the state should abjure them under its general policy of "nonintervention." While there may be some

1. The concept of a natural family— Last century the idea that wives were naturally dependent upon their husbands was believed by some people as firmly as the idea that children are naturally dependent upon their parents is believed now. The state was expected to bolster the husband's power over his wife whenever it was threatened. The husband chose the family domicile and the wife was essentially forced to live there, just as children are today. As expressed in a nineteenth-century treatise on domestic relations: "The domicile of the wife follows that of the husband; the domicile of the infant may be changed by the parent. Thus does the law of domicile conform to the law of nature."[27] Natural law or "Divine Providence" was thought to be the origin of our laws regarding the family.[28] "[P]ositive law but enforces the mandates of the law of nature, and develops rather than creates a system."[29] Although there have been changes in what is considered natural within the family, the basic notion that family relations are natural relations has not changed that much. Today women may no longer be considered naturally dependent on their husbands, but children are still considered naturally dependent on their parents.[30]

A similar concept of a natural family finds expression in constitutional law. At least since 1944, the Supreme Court has recognized a constitutionally-protected right of family privacy—a "private realm of family life which the state cannot enter."[31]

---

functions—for example, requiring blood tests of marrying couples—that most would agree fit the first category, the great bulk of decisions will be objectionable to a number of putative "family" members. Given the inevitability of substantial disagreement over which family policies are neutral ground rules and which are objectionable intervention, labelling any such set of policies "nonintervention" robs the term of any sensible meaning. These family policies in fact arise from politics and do not flow logically from neutral principles.

A second and more fundamental difficulty defeats the project of distinguishing the establishment of neutral ground rules from other state activities. Any ground rules that are sufficiently noncontroversial that they might plausibly be considered neutral would be too general to settle concrete disputes. Policies may well be internally consistent but still be indeterminate. No policies "flow logically" from principles, even if principles could be neutral. This argument parallels the arguments of some legal realists that laissez faire was incoherent because the state could not enforce even-handedly uncontroversial neutral ground rules. *See supra* pp. 844-45.

27. J. SCHOULER, A TREATISE ON THE LAW OF THE DOMESTIC RELATIONS § 3, at 9 (5th ed. 1895). The author later criticizes as "judicial interference" the policy of some courts to relieve the wife of her obligation to follow her husband where his choice of domicile is unreasonable. *See id.* § 38, at 69.

28. *See id.* §/3, at 8.

29. *Id.* § 2, at 5.

30. *See infra* pp. 851-52 & note 46.

31. Prince v. Massachusetts, 321 U.S. 158, 166 (1944). The right to family privacy is often traced back to Meyer v. Nebraska, 262 U.S. 390 (1923) and Pierce v. Society of

The source of this family privacy has recently been said to be
"not in state law, but in intrinsic human rights."[32] The Supreme
Court clearly envisions a concept of family relationship that is
not dependent upon state law: "Nor has the [Constitution] refused to recognize those family relationships unlegitimized by a
marriage ceremony."[33] The family has its "origins entirely apart
from the power of the State."[34] Thus, for purposes of constitutional adjudication, "[t]he legal status of families has never been
regarded as controlling."[35] The nineteenth century concept of a
natural family has continued into the twentieth century. We
now recognize law's important role in creating the nineteenth-
century family. I would hope we will not have to wait until the
twenty-first century to recognize the constitutive role of law in
the twentieth-century family.

   2. *State enforced hierarchy: Not intervention?*— Nonintervention would seem to have meaning against a backdrop of preexisting prescribed social roles within the family. State-created
background rules shape and reinforce these social roles by as-
signing power and responsibility within the family. These background rules are not usually thought of as state intervention, but
they implicate the state in the prescribed family roles and undermine claims of nonintervention. The setting of the roles requires political choices that can hardly be considered nonintervention. The state whose policy choices have had such a great
effect upon these family roles certainly cannot be considered
neutral, nor should the label "nonintervention" be used to conceal or confuse the political nature of the choices society makes.

   Moreover, the enforcement of these family roles, which is
what many people mean by "nonintervention," requires the
state to make continual policy choices about the scope and

Sisters, 268 U.S. 510 (1925). *Meyer* invalidated a statute that forbade the teaching of any
modern language other than English in the first eight grades. and *Pierce* overruled a law
that required children to attend public schools. Both statutes were found to be unwar-
ranted intrusions into parents' liberty to raise their children. The cases were decided on
the basis of the individual right to liberty, once granted substantive protection by the
due process clause of the fourteenth amendment. Although the Court has abandoned
many of its substantive due process cases from the same period, it has reaffirmed *Meyer*
and *Pierce. See Developments in the Law—The Constitution and the Family,* 93 HARV.
L. REV. 1157, 1161-63 (1980).

   32. Smith v. Organization of Foster Families. 431 U.S. 816. 845 (1977) (footnote
omitted).

   33. Stanley v. Illinois, 405 U.S. 645. 651 (1972). The *Stanley* Court was dealing with
the biological father-child relationship, but it also emphasized Mr. Stanley's role in *raising* his children.

   34. Smith v. Organization of Foster Families, 431 U.S. 816. 845 (1977).

   35. *Id.* at 845 n.52.

meaning of the roles it is enforcing. The content of family roles has changed over the years and there has never been complete agreement about the authority husbands and parents have over wives and children or about the responsibilities that go along with the authority. State officials must determine borderline questions about the nature and extent of family hierarchy on a case-by-case basis, and pursuing a policy of "nonintervention" cannot relieve state officials from having to make ad hoc political decisions about the family.

   a.   The Family Head Model: Direct empowerment of superior— Last century some people believed that by empowering the head of the family—the husband and father—to act for the family and to settle intrafamily disputes, the state could avoid intervening in the family. I refer to this policy as the Family Head Model. In theory, this model would relieve the state of making case-by-case decisions regarding the family.

   During the early nineteenth century, the husband was the juridical head of the family, entitled to control the wife and children. He was also the financial head of the family. The common law, enforced by the state, provided that a wife's property belonged to her husband. Any personal property to which the wife held legal title was transferred automatically, by operation of law, to her husband; and the husband was given a life estate in her real property.[36] He was entitled to the services of his wife and children. If they received wages, these wages belonged to him; even if they worked without pay, the father could recover the value of services they provided to third parties.[37] Although he could not legally sell the sexual services of his wife and minor

---

36. This dramatic imposition was not considered state intervention. The transfer of the wife's property was sometimes characterized as a "gift," *see* J. SCHOULER, *supra* note 27, § 80, at 132, but the wife had no choice about conferring it. Even if the couple agreed that the wife could keep her property, their contract would have been invalid. Complicated rules applied to certain incorporeal interests of the wife. The husband's title to choses in action and certain real property interests was considered conditional and he would have to complete certain acts in order to appropriate the choses to himself or to carry out his right of reduction into possession. *See id.* §§ 80-159, at 131-248.

37. *See* Benson v. Remington, 2 Mass. 113 (1806) (ordering neighbors who had allowed a teenager to live with them to pay her father wages for the value of the services she performed or might have performed for them). Probably the neighbors would not have resisted the father's claim and appealed the decision in his favor had it not been for the peculiar facts of the *Benson* case. Several years before, the father had abandoned his family and left them in "extreme poverty." *Id.* at 113. The neighbors found the daughter in a "very helpless condition," *id.*, and took her into their home. Three years before he brought the lawsuit, the father had returned and made a similar demand of money from the neighbors, but community pressure forced him to compromise his claim. This history suggests that in the *Benson* case, the state was empowering the father and not just enforcing the agreed norms of society.

850   Journal of Law Reform   [VOL. 18:4

daughters, he could recover money from any man who had sexual intercourse with them without his permission.[38] Some people objected to these policies, but there is no evidence that anyone considered the policies state intervention.

Moreover, the nineteenth-century concept of nonintervention might require the state to bolster the authority of the father. If the wife were to leave and take the children with her, the courts would ordinarily be expected to grant a habeas corpus writ ordering her to return them to him. For courts to refuse to issue such a writ would be considered state intervention in the family.[39]

Today courts are less expected to bolster the power of the husband over the wife, but they are still expected to reinforce parents' authority over children. Many states have a procedure whereby courts can label a child "incorrigible" or "in need of supervision" and order the child to obey the parents or be locked up in the functional equivalent of jail.[40] Parents also have considerable power over whether their child will be institutionalized as mentally defective or troubled.[41] My point is not that such situations are very common, but that these state policies that empower parents are not considered state intervention in the family.

In more subtle ways, also, the state directly authorizes parents to act on behalf of the child. The parents are empowered by the state, as well as by custom, to name the child and to change its name if they wish. They determine the state of which the child shall be a legal citizen. They enroll the child in school. These powers are established by state regulations, regulations that define family roles but are hardly noticed and certainly not considered state intervention.

b. Creating economic dependence— The social interaction within a family can be significantly affected by the economic dependence of wives on husbands and of children on parents. It is obvious to us today that laws and regulations in force early last century made the wife economically dependent upon the husband, and an adolescent economically dependent on his father,

---

38. The husband's action would be for "criminal conversation" if the man had intercourse with his wife and for loss of services if with the daughter. Many commentators have considered this action for loss of the daughter's services to be a legal fiction that allowed the father to recover for his loss of honor or hurt feelings.

39. *See* Olsen, *supra* note 1, at 1505 & n.30.

40. *See* Katz & Teitelbaum, *PINS Jurisdiction, the Vagueness Doctrine, and the Rule of Law.* 53 IND. L.J. 1 (1977-1978).

41. *See* Parham v. J.R., 442 U.S. 584, 600-04 (1979).

typically until age twenty-one. Neither married women nor minors could carry on a trade or business except under the authority of the husband and father; their services belonged to him and he could collect any wages they might earn. Last century this dependency seemed natural to many people.

Today the state's role in reinforcing economic dependency is less obvious but it is still significant. Although state laws no longer require women to perform unpaid work for their husbands as part of the marriage contract, as in previous centuries, federal tax laws still provide a significant economic incentive for domestic labor to remain unpaid.[42] An additional basis for women's economic dependency is low pay; statistically, women's wages are only sixty-one percent of men's.[43] Although state laws that in the past encouraged or required sex discrimination in employment have been preempted by federal antidiscrimination laws,[44] a number of government agencies save many thousands of dollars by paying lower salaries for jobs held mainly by women than for jobs of comparable worth that men perform.[45]

A child's economic dependence on her parent reinforces and increases the parent's power over the child. Although young children might not be capable of independence,[46] as children grow

---

42. If a taxpayer pays to have housework done, the cost is generally not a tax deduction. If, however, he marries someone who keeps house for him, he can file a joint return with her and they need not include as income the value of her housekeeping services. Or, suppose two taxpayers each did paid housework for the other. Their tax liabilities would be greater than if they each did their own housework.

43. National Committee on Pay Equity & National Institute for Women of Color, Women of Color and Pay Equity, *reprinted in Women in the Workforce: Pay Equity: Hearings Before the Joint Economic Committee*, 98th Cong., 2d Sess. 190, 198 (1984).

44. *See* Olsen, *supra* note 1, at 1548, 1555-59.

45. A number of state governments have undertaken studies and have found that it would be very expensive to enact a program of "comparable worth." Thus they would seem to be reaping a significant economic benefit from taking advantage of women's lower pay. In AFSCME v. State of Washington, Nos. 84-3569, 84-3590 (9th Cir. Sept. 4, 1984) (available September 18, 1985 on Lexis, Genfed Library, Cases file), the Ninth Circuit struck down a District Court decision that would have required Washington State to make comparable worth payments.

46. It is easy to assume that young children are naturally dependent on their parents. Upon closer examination, however, this assumption seems unjustified. Certainly, human offspring would appear to be as defenseless as other primate young, and in this sense can be said to be naturally dependent. But, in this sense, children would be naturally dependent upon their mother, possibly on their father, and probably upon the larger community. In many parts of the world a mother and infant or a mother, father, and infant could not survive alone.

In civilized society, young children remain dependent. That this dependency is on the child's *parents* is surely based on laws. Laws ensure that most children remain with their parents, although in spite of the law, large numbers of children are separated from their parents. Presumably more children would be taken from their parents were it not for the

older, their dependence is increasingly attributable to state regulations. Child labor laws, however wise as policy, are state regulations that make it difficult for children to gain economic independence.[47] And the state goes further. State laws not only limit a child's opportunity for paid employment, they also require her to attend school—work for which she receives no pay.[48] Finally, when a state pays welfare benefits for a child or orders one parent to pay support for a child, the money does not go to the child herself, but to a custodian, usually the other parent. This maintains the child's economic dependency on her custodian. If we are concerned about the state intervening in the family if it provides free contraceptives to girls without telling their parents, we should not overlook the fact that state policies have made it difficult for girls to pay for contraceptives or to get them any other way.[49]

c. *Eliminating alternative sources of support or nurturance*— Last century a woman was required to live in the home of her husband. He could choose to live anywhere, and she was obliged to follow him. One method of enforcing this requirement was to eliminate alternative living possibilities. Anyone who offered lodging to a runaway wife could be charged with harboring her. Although her father might, as a practical matter, get by with this infraction, it would be difficult for anyone else to do so. Most women would be unable to help her and most men ill-advised to do so.[50] If a runaway wife formed a close relationship with a man, they could be suspected of adultery and treated very harshly. If she actually had sexual relations with another man, she could be recaptured and forced home by her

---

legal (as well as social) disapproval of kidnapping.

Moreover, the period of dependency could be considerably shortened if, for example, property laws were not enforceable against children. One could have a society in which children were allowed to take whatever they needed and to eat food they found as freely as many children eat at home. My point is not that this plan would produce a better society or healthier children, but simply that it would be possible.

47. *See, e.g.,* CAL. LABOR CODE §§ 1290-1311 (West 1971 & Supp. 1985); Youth Employment Standards Act, MICH. COMP. LAWS §§ 409.101-.124 (1979) (restricting and regulating the hours and types of employment for minors).

48. *See, e.g.* Compulsory Education Law, CAL. EDUC. CODE §§ 48200-48324 (West 1978 & Supp. 1985); Michigan Compulsory School Attendance Law, MICH. COMP. LAWS ANN. §§ 380.1561.-1599 (West 1979). Of course, it can be argued that school attendance is non-productive labor and should be considered a benefit rather than a burden. In some societies, however, being a student is considered gainful employment and people are paid to attend school. My point is simply that these state policies are not natural or inevitable and they implicate the state in the economic dependency of youngsters.

49. *See infra* p. 860; Olsen, *supra* note 1, at 1506 & n.33.

50. *See* J. SCHOULER, *supra* note 27, § 41, at 71-72.

husband.[51] The husband could bring a civil suit and recover money damages from the man for "criminal conversation." The husband would continue to own his wife's property and to be entitled to her services, but he would no longer have to support her. In many cases he could take their children away from her and perhaps even bar her from visiting them.[52]

Today the state will ordinarily not penalize third parties who offer lodging or friendship to a woman without the permission of her husband, but laws continue to penalize those who offer the same to children without the permission of their parents. The state is implicated in the power and role distribution within the family when its laws prevent children from looking to third parties for support. Yet the state is not accused of intervening in the family when it forces children to live with their parents or when it prohibits doctors from treating minors without the parents' knowledge and approval. The child may be required to associate or forbidden from associating with people, at the whim of the parents. Statutes permitting courts to issue grandparent visitation orders that may limit this parental prerogative in certain egregious cases are themselves sometimes criticized as state "intervention" in the family.[53] The state gives parents considerable coercive power over children and then characterizes its refusal to monitor this power as "nonintervention."

   d.   *Limiting state protection*— Last century the father was permitted to discipline his wife and children, and this permission often extended to corporal punishment. Behavior that would constitute a criminal offense if directed at a stranger was fully legal against one's children and mere grounds for separation or divorce if directed against one's spouse. Doctrines of intrafamily tort immunity protected the husband and father from civil suits by his beaten wife or children.[54]

---

51. *See id.* § 45, at 76. If a husband discovered his wife in bed with another man and killed them, his crime would be a misdemeanor, not a felony. *See id.* § 45, at 76, n.5.

52. Lord Talfourd's Act, an 1839 reform bill in England that gave courts power to grant mothers child custody and visitation, specifically excluded from its provisions adulterous mothers; and some Lords who opposed the bill still argued that the *risk* that an adulterous mother could benefit from the reform if her adultery could not be proven was so unacceptable that the bill should be defeated. *See* 44 PARL. DEB. (3d ser.) 772, 789 (1838).

53. *See, e.g.,* Olds v. Olds, 356 N.W.2d 571, 574 (Iowa 1984). In some situations, grandparent visitation orders may coerce a child to continue unwanted contact with the grandparents.

54. The same doctrine would, of course, protect the wife and child from civil suit if they were to assault or batter the husband and father, but usually it did not work that way.

Today, intrafamily tort immunity has been widely abolished, but a great deal of behavior that would be criminal or tortious between strangers may still be done with impunity within a family. In many states, the husband may legally force sexual intercourse upon his wife. In most states, spouse abuse is treated differently from other forms of personal violence—sometimes better, often worse. Children are offered limited state protection against their parents. Usually, crimes and torts will be recognized only if a child is badly abused; and even this occasional enforcement is often thought to constitute state intervention—justified, but intervention nonetheless. In theory, parents can be prosecuted for homicide, sexual abuse, serious physical assaults, and child neglect. In practice, however, a child's dependency is so extensive that many crimes, including assault and sexual abuse, often go unprosecuted.

3. *Changes in family hierarchy over time*— The nature and degree of power that the state allows one family member to exercise over another has changed over time and is regularly contested. Reforms that have claimed to provide for juridical equality between men and women have tended to modify the legal role expectations placed on husbands and wives. The role relationship between parent and child has also undergone considerable change over time. Because parents' power over their children is incomplete, the state must adjudicate borderline cases and in doing so necessarily influences the family. At one extreme, state prosecution of a father for intentionally killing his child is universally approved and is unlikely to be considered state intervention in the family; at the other extreme, charging a father with kidnapping for sending a child to her room as a form of punishment would strike most people as serious state intervention in the family. Courts must frequently draw a line between protecting the individual family member and promoting family authority, and different courts would draw the line closer to one or the other of these extremes. Exactly where a court draws the line, or where it would be expected to draw the line, will affect power relations within the family. The choices that courts make will be based on policy considerations and the state cannot avoid making decisions that will influence family relations.

Moreover, when parents disagree, the state has to decide which of the two to empower or to refuse to empower. This choice will in turn influence relations between the parents. Thus, what is frequently referred to as "nonintervention" involves an initial policy choice regarding family roles, followed by further policy choices regarding the details of those roles.

Because nonintervention is understood with reference to specific family roles and the state is expected to take these roles into account in settling disputes, courts must make one choice after another regarding the content and nature of these roles. As long as they do not ratify and enforce *all* assertions of authority by a husband or parent—for example, they prosecute intrafamily murder—courts must decide which behavior they will sanction and which they will not. These decisions require courts to take a stand on complex issues of intergenerational conflict and gender politics. The simple claim that the state should not intervene in the family tends to obscure the genuine problems of ethics and policy that continually arise.

C. Nonintervention and the Egalitarian Family

In theory it would be possible for the state to avoid taking a stand in favor of juridical hierarchy within the family. There are at least two ways the state could settle lawsuits involving families that would avoid ratifying family hierarchy. One would be to treat the family as a miniature state of nature by refusing to enforce any lawsuits between family members; the other would be to treat marriage as nothing more than an express contract and parentage as irrelevant, and enforce all lawsuits between family members just as though the litigants were not related. A consideration of these two contrasting extremes will further illustrate the difficulty with the concept of "nonintervention."

1. State of Nature Model— The state might seem to be able to remain neutral among family members by steadfastly refusing to enforce any tort, contract, or criminal law between members of a family. This approach, if carried to the extreme, would create a "state of nature" within the family, and could be said to take seriously the notion that families should work out their own problems. If a wife were being beaten, it would be up to her to deal with the problem; the state would not "intervene." If she dealt with the problem by shooting her husband, the state would be expected to continue its policy of "nonintervention." If a person were indicted for murder, it would be a sufficient defense to prove that the defendant and the victim were members of the same family. The killing would then be considered a family matter into which the state should not intrude.

As in any imagined state of nature, this approach would seem to benefit the stronger and prejudice the weaker members of a family. In fact, though, it might disempower the physically weak less than the system that seems to operate in some communities—a system that treats intrafamily battery as private, but leaves homicide fully outlawed. Such a system is especially disempowering to wives if spouse abuse is not recognized as a justification for or defense to homicide.[55]

The State of Nature Model would not really enable the state to remain neutral or uninvolved in the family. Even if the state of nature were complete within the family, the state would still have to decide who constituted a family and how to deal with lawsuits involving third parties and members of the family. Also, a complete state of nature would not fit contemporary views of nonintervention in the family. A partial state of nature within the family might be acceptable to many people; but if the state of nature were partial, decisions about what laws to enforce among family members would require additional political choices that would affect authority and roles within families.

2. *Market Model*— A second way the state might seem to be neutral among family members is based on the opposite strategy of enforcement. The state could treat each member of a family as a juridical equal and treat their family status as irrelevant. Marriage and parentage would become private relationships, not recognized by the state. Courts would treat as irrelevant the fact that litigants were married to one another or that one was the parent of the other, and enforce lawsuits as between any unrelated people or strangers. This approach essentially ignores the family relationship and treats family members just as strangers are treated. Such a policy would not fit contemporary views of nonintervention in the family, especially as regards children. For example, under the Market Model, parents who disciplined their children by sending them to their rooms might be guilty of kidnapping and the children could have a valid cause of action for false imprisonment. Parents would have neither an obligation to support children nor a right to keep them from living away from home. Children and parents would be free to cut their own deals. Contracts entered into between children and their parents, or between any other family members, would be just as enforceable as contracts between any unrelated individuals.

The concept of nonintervention based on the Market Model is not only unacceptable to most people, but it is also no more coherent than laissez faire. All the arguments put forth by the legal realists to show the incoherence of laissez faire apply to nonintervention under the Market Model. The neutrality of the

---

55.   *See* Olsen, *supra* note 1, at 1509.

Market Model would be formal neutrality only, even as between adults. The particular tort, contract, and criminal laws the state chose to create and enforce would affect the relative power of individuals and thus the bargains they could negotiate with their spouses, children, or other relatives. For example, strong battery laws are likely to help wives and children; weakened self-defense doctrines limit their ability to protect themselves, and would seem to help husbands.[56]

To illustrate further, consider the laws that forbid prostitution and nullify contracts when sexual services constitute all or part of the consideration on one side of the agreement. In our present society, the effect of nullifying such contracts usually enriches the male at the expense of the female.[57] The public policy against prostitution might have something to do with refusing to reduce women to sex objects, but it might have as much or more to do with preserving for men the economic resources that rein-

---

56. Popular television programs have recently presented sympathetic portrayals of abused wives and children who, unable to enlist police protection against an abusive husband or father, killed their abuser. *See, e.g.,* "The Burning Bed" (dramatized account of abused wife killing husband); "60 Minutes" (news special on boy who shot his abusive father).

57. The case of Marvin v. Marvin, 18 Cal. 3d 660, 557 P.2d 106, 134 Cal. Rptr. 815 (1976), has been widely praised and blamed for the many things it held and refused to hold, but few if any commentators have paid attention to the court's insistence that a contract for sexual services is unenforceable. This seemingly neutral rule is likely in practice to hurt occasional unsophisticated women. Men, sophisticated or unsophisticated, are likely to be benefited or left untouched.

The anti-prostitution rule also limits the right to contract, and it limits it in a way more likely to hurt women than men. It is one thing to say that we will not assume that men necessarily get more out of sexual intercourse than women do, but it is quite another thing to say that courts may not consider and couples may not contract about any differential benefit that may accrue. Given the statistics on present satisfaction with sexual intercourse, I would suggest that this clearly harms women. *See* Leerhsen, Jackson & Bruno, *Ann Landers and 'The Act,'* NEWSWEEK, Jan. 28, 1985, at 76 [hereinafter cited as *Ann Landers*] (reporting survey results that 72% of women were dissatisfied with sex as practiced).

One criticism sometimes made of the *Marvin* case is that it invites courts to inquire into the intimate details of a couple's life. *See, e.g.,* Chambers, *The "Legalization" of the Family: Toward a Policy of Supportive Neutrality,* 18 U. MICH. J L. REF. 805 (1985). To make "whisperings across the pillows," *id.* at 825, sacred, private, and unrepeatable is to support the sexual status quo. Sex as currently practiced seems to be startlingly more satisfactory to men than to women. *See Ann Landers, supra.* Privatizing sex reduces discussion that might lead to change. Sex is private in part because the state makes it private and because keeping sex private seems to serve the interests of those with power. The taboo on inquiring into the quality of male-female relationships may be based more on a fear of exposing systematic inequality than on anything else. Child custody cases often involve inquiry into the quality of parent-child relationships. Although commentators may criticize courts' ability to judge intimate relationships, child custody cases do suggest that courts can examine intimate relationships without any devastating effects.

force their prestige and power.[58] The result of policies that enrich men and impoverish women is that even if the law were to refuse to permit "family" defenses to contract, tort, or criminal actions, wives would still often bring to the marriage a position lower in the social and economic hierarchy, and thus a weaker bargaining position vis-à-vis their husbands.

III. THE EXPERIENCE OF STATE INTERVENTION

The assertion I have made—that the concepts of state intervention and nonintervention in the family are essentially meaningless—might ring hollow to an impoverished mother struggling to keep the state from taking her children away from her. More tragically, my assertion could sound absurd or seem totally meaningless to many innocent children who live in fear of the juvenile authorities. Hundreds of youngsters, the quality of whose lives has already been diminished by poverty and neglect, have been forced into silence and concealment. The specter of state intervention in the family denies to many of them even the partial relief they might get from sharing their pain and humiliation with a friendly neighbor or sympathetic teacher. Many such children exist, and to them state intervention can seem real and frightening.

There are many other examples of situations in which people experience themselves to be victims of state intervention. In the 1960's a husband and wife in Connecticut were denied legal access to contraceptives until they sued and appealed their case to the United States Supreme Court.[59] Earlier in the century, Lillie and O.B. Williams were prosecuted for bigamous cohabitation and sentenced to jail terms when state officials in North Carolina decided to challenge the Nevada divorces they had obtained from their previous spouses.[60] They too took their case to the United States Supreme Court and won, only to lose on a retrial and second appeal.[61] To both these couples state intervention would seem to be a very real concern.

State intervention may also have considerable meaning to the lover who, upon the death of his beloved, finds himself with no

---

58. For an elaboration of these ideas, see F. Olsen, Prostitution: The Stigma of Money (Apr. 16, 1985) (transcript of talk given at UCLA Law School) (copy on file with U. MICH. J.L. REF.).

59. *See* Griswold v. Connecticut, 381 U.S. 479 (1965).

60. *See* Williams v. North Carolina, 317 U.S. 287 (1942).

61. *See* Williams v. North Carolina, 325 U.S. 226 (1945).

status, their jointly shared property snatched away by the beloved's long-estranged parents. The lover has no say about funeral arrangements and cannot even attend services without the permission of the parents. Even if the couple drew up wills, the beloved's testament would once have been routinely set aside for presumed undue influence.[62]

The parents, however, might well consider their family intruded upon if the state were to limit their rights for the sake of their child's lover. Lillie and O.B. Williams's first spouses may have resented the courts of Nevada intervening in their family affairs by granting divorces against them when, under their own state law, they had committed no wrong and would expect to have a right to remain married.[63]

The experience of state intervention in the family can involve either affirmative coercive behavior by state officials, such as physically forcing a child away from his or her parent, or a refusal by state officials to come to the aid of one claiming a family right, such as the state's failure to order foster parents to relinquish a child to her natural parent.[64] From the child's perspective, the transfer of custody to natural parents the child barely knows would seem to be as serious intervention as it would be to take her away from a natural parent.

The experience of intervention depends upon having some expectation disappointed or some sense of entitlement violated. Disappointment and violation are very real experiences. Unfortunately, they cannot be avoided by a simple policy of nonintervention in the family. Moreover, disappointment and violation of hopes and dreams may be as distressing as the disappointment and violation of expectations and entitlements. It is not clear, in the example above, that the state should sacrifice the interests of a lover for the sake of the beloved's parents, just because the parents, under present law, have more settled expectations and entitlements.

Because the notion of state intervention depends upon a conception of proper family roles and these roles are open to dispute, almost any policy may be experienced by someone as state

---

62. *See In re* Kaufman's Will, 20 A.D.2d 464, 247 N.Y.S.2d 664 (1964), *aff'd*, 15 N.Y.2d 825, 205 N.E.2d 864, 257 N.Y.S.2d 941 (1965). *See also* Sherman, *Undue Influence and the Homosexual Testator*, 42 U. PITT. L. REV. 225, 239-48 (1981) (asserting that homosexuals' wills are subjected to heightened scrutiny for undue influence).

63. For a discussion of the difficulties with such conflicting rights, see Olsen, *Statutory Rape: A Feminist Critique of Rights Analysis*, 63 TEX. L. REV. 387 (1984).

64. *See* Bennet v. Jeffreys, 40 N.Y.2d 543, 356 N.E.2d 277, 387 N.Y.S.2d 821 (1976) (finding long period of separation from natural parent an extraordinary circumstance that can "trigger" the best interests of the child test).

intervention. In many situations, someone's expectations will be disappointed or sense of entitlement violated no matter what action the state takes or refuses to take. One can often argue that in a particular case nonintervention really means whatever one wants the state to do; any policy one dislikes might be labeled intervention.

For example, from one perspective, the state intervenes in the family when it provides contraceptives to minors. The "squeal rule" proposed by the Reagan administration, although not preventing the distribution of contraceptives, would have required that parents be notified that contraceptives had been given to their children.[65] This was supposed to reduce state intervention in the family and to enable parents to counsel their children about the problems of adolescent sex. Opponents feared it would deter the youngsters from obtaining contraceptives (but not from engaging in sex), and argued that this particular intervention in the family was justified.

From another perspective, the "squeal rule" does not reduce state intervention (whether for good or ill), but is itself a crude, abusive form of intervention. The state achieves a virtual monopoly on effective birth control by impoverishing young women and forbidding inexpensive over-the-counter sales of prescription contraceptives.[66] It then proposes to use this monopoly to intrude into the parent-child relationship and pass along information to the parents that the parents have neglected to obtain the old-fashioned way—by talking with their children. The state thus rewards neglectful parents and removes from them an incentive to maintain supportive communication with their children. It encourages parents to neglect their child's sex education and to ignore the pressures put upon their child until after the child has become sexually active and the state so notifies them.

---

65. *See* 48 Fed. Reg. 3600 (1983) (to be codified at 42 C.F.R. §§ 59.2, 59.5). *See also* N.Y. Times, Feb. 20, 1983, at E5, col. 4. The rule was found unlawful on statutory grounds. *See* Planned Parenthood Fed'n of Am. v. Schweiker, 712 F.2d 650 (D.C. Cir. 1983). Some people have opposed the "squeal rule" on the grounds that certain fathers might demand sex from their daughters if they found out that the daughters were sexually active. Others fear fathers would respond with physical abuse of their daughters.

66. The state's role seems even more intensive and insidious when we consider how reluctant state officials are to prosecute date rape. The state permits unsafe streets that limit a woman's choices: she may stay home (statistically, a remarkably dangerous location for women), go out in a group of people, or go out with one man. Especially if she chooses the one-man option, the female may find herself faced with the further choice of consenting to sexual intercourse or being raped by him without recourse. Thus, women cannot really be said to have the option of refraining from sexual intercourse. Abstinence is not a reliable form of birth control for many women.

Nonintervention arguments can be leveled against laws and regulations that refuse to treat unmarried couples enough like a family[67] or against laws that treat them too much like a family.[68] Nonintervention arguments can be used to keep children from being put into foster care, to remove them from foster care, or to keep them from being removed from foster care.[69] Nonintervention arguments can even be leveled against a policy of enforcing contracts between unwed couples.[70] While one can sympathize with anyone who is disappointed by a state policy, it is hard to see that anything is actually gained by characterizing the cause of that disappointment as state intervention.[71]

IV. WHY IT MATTERS

The protective intervention argument, that the state should intervene in the family when necesary, has gained so much acceptance—just as the protective intervention argument against laissez faire has gained widespread acceptance—that one might wonder why we need the incoherence argument, that intervention and nonintervention are meaningless concepts. First, it is not the case that the exception has swallowed the rule. Under the protective intervention argument, the state is treated as having a policing function—to detect and correct those rare circumstances that disturb and disrupt the family, without questioning any of the basic individualistic foundations of society. The assertion that the state can and should avoid "intervention" in the family plays an important but generally unrecognized ideological role.[72] Further, focusing on "nonintervention" tends to mush and confuse the ethical and political choices we make. It directs our attention to a false issue and obscures genuine issues of ethics and policy. Finally, both laissez faire and nonintervention in

---

67. *See* Chambers, *supra* note 57.

68. *See id.*; Burt, *Coercive Freedom: A Response to Professor Chambers*, 18 U. MICH. J.L. REF. 829 (1985).

69. *See* Smith v. Organization of Foster Families, 431 U.S. 816 (1977) (acknowledging, but refusing to accept, argument).

70. *See* Burt, *supra* note 68.

71. This is not to deny the ideological significance of the concern, however. To complain that the hassling of your living arrangement (whether through zoning laws, fornication laws, or any other law or regulation) constitutes state intervention in the family is an ideological claim, a claim of entitlement to live the way you choose. For example, successfully characterizing state laws against homosexual relations as state "intervention" in the family tends to legitimate same-sex relationships.

72. For an interesting discussion of the ideological role of family law, see Freeman, *supra* note 12, at 387-401. *See also* Olsen, *supra* note 10.

the family have sprung up in modern versions—law-and-economics in place of laissez faire and the individual right to privacy in place of nonintervention in the family. These new forms, one labeled conservative, the other liberal, are flawed in the same way the originals—laissez faire and nonintervention—are flawed. The standard liberal criticism of law-and-economics and the standard conservative criticism of the right to privacy are both versions of the protective intervention argument. In each instance, I believe the incoherence argument presents a more important critique.[73]

---

73. In the case of privacy, liberals argue that the fundamental principle of individual privacy offers a rational justification or grounding for a great many policies—ranging from access to contraceptives to a disapproval of surveillance over sexual choices. Conservatives often respond by pitting public morality against individual privacy. This is parallel to the protective intervention argument regarding the family. The conservatives assume that privacy is a coherent concept and that the rational elaboration of this principle would lead to the policies supported by the liberals. The argument of the conservatives that public morality justifies limiting privacy is like the argument that the state should intervene in the private family to protect against abuse.

The stronger and more important answer to the liberals' claim would be like the incoherence argument. Privacy is not a coherent concept and it does not lead to any indisputable policy choices. The state is implicated in privacy just as it is in family. Although I support many of the policies they advance in the name of "privacy," I believe the liberals are mistaken to think that they can ground or justify these policies on any rational or apolitical basis.

In the case of law-and-economics, conservatives argue that the concept of efficiency offers a rational justification for a great many policies. In particular, law-and-economics purports to demonstrate that many economic policies supported by liberals simply fail objectively—they will not produce the results the liberals hope to achieve. Liberals often respond by pitting equality, justice, or fairness against efficiency. This is parallel to the protective intervention argument against laissez faire policies toward the free market. Liberals often assume that efficiency is a coherent concept and that a relentless focus on efficiency would lead to the policies supported by the conservatives.

The stronger and more important answer to the conservatives' claim would be like the incoherence argument against laissez faire. "Efficiency" is indeterminate and does *not* lead to the policy choices that conservatives claim it does. Liberals do not have to resort to arguments that pit other goals against efficiency, but can challenge the basic underlying premises of conservative law-and-economics. *See* Kennedy, *Distributive and Paternalist Motives in Contract and Tort, with Special Reference to Compulsory Terms and Unequal Bargaining Power*, 41 MD. L. REV. 563 (1982); Kennedy, *Cost-Benefit Analysis of Entitlement Programs: A Critique*, 33 STAN. L. REV. 387 (1981); Kelman, *Misunderstanding Social Life: A Critique of the Core Premises of Law and Economics*, 33 J. LEGAL EDUC. 274 (1983); Kelman, *Consumption Theory, Production Theory and Ideology in the Coase Theorem*, 52 S. CAL. L. REV. 669 (1979); Kelman, *Choice and Utility*, 1979 WIS. L. REV. 769. *See also* Horwitz, *supra* note 23; Kennedy & Michelman, *Are Property and Contract Efficient?*, 8 HOFSTRA L. REV. 711 (1980).

CONCLUSION

State intervention in the family is an ideological, not an analytic concept. The incoherence argument demonstrates that neither intervention nor nonintervention has a coherent meaning. The protective intervention argument, that the state should intervene in the family whenever necessary to defend the interests of society or of individual oppressed family members, does not go far enough. First, it presupposes that nonintervention is a possible choice; and second, it usually accepts nonintervention as a norm or as an ideal.

The protective intervention argument misperceives the problems caused by unfortunate social policies. For example, the problem with state officials taking children away from poor parents is not really a problem of state "intervention," but a problem of the substance of that state behavior. What the state does is sometimes *so bad* that people would rather it did nothing—which of course is not possible. The effort to get the state to do nothing, even if it were possible, misfocuses attention. It is misguided to treat freedom as the polar opposite of state "intervention" or of government regulation. As Morris Cohen noted in another context, real freedom depends upon opportunities supplied by institutions that involve legal regulation.[74] The attempt to criticize state "intervention" instead of criticizing the particular policies pursued may be especially limiting for poor people, who often have to rely on various government programs and are thus less likely to benefit from any political strategy based on the myth of nonintervention.[75]

Sexual abuse of children provides an example of the inadequacy of the rhetoric of nonintervention. It also illustrates problems with the state giving adults so much authority and power over children.[76] A child's failure to report sexual abuse

---

74. *See* Cohen, *supra* note 3, at 591.

75. *Cf.* MacKinnon, *The Male Ideology of Privacy: A Feminist Perspective*, 17 RADICAL AMERICA, July-Aug. 1983, at 23, 32 (noting that abortion rights are particularly easy to deny to poor women because the right is based on privacy).

76. The state establishes a situation of dependency and then allows as the only alternative a complete severing of the relationship. If you watch television ads for toilet paper and blue jeans, the puzzling question is not why incest is so widespread but rather that sexual abuse of children has any limits. If we make children totally dependent upon one or two adults and allow helplessness and dependency to be eroticized, we should not pretend surprise and outrage at child abuse. The state empowers adults and gives tax deductions for advertising that eroticizes domination. *See generally* J. Kilbourne, Killing Us Softly: Advertising's Image of Women (Cambridge Documentary Films, Inc. 1979) (film examining use of sex in advertising as reflective and partially constitutive of

may often be her best response to a bad situation. Incest deprives a child of autonomy and corrupts the protection the abusing parent offers the child. And when abuse is discovered, instead of empowering the child and making it possible for him or her to resist the adult, state officials tend to move in and take over—sometimes making matters worse. After revealing sexual abuse the child is all too likely to have even less autonomy and fewer options for dealing with his or her vulnerability and hurt. The child may be summarily denied the opportunity to maintain any relationship with the abusing adult, even if the child wants desperately to maintain a relationship. In cases of child abuse, including sexual abuse, state policy should end the abuse or empower the child to end it, not force the child to leave home.[77]

If we think in terms of intervention versus nonintervention, and consider our options to be thus limited, we are less likely to devise effective alternatives.[78] As we become less preoccupied with the myth of state intervention, perhaps we can focus proper attention on the realities of people's lives.

---

culture).

77.   How to empower children to end their abuse is a topic for another article. Most of us are not accustomed to thinking about ways to empower victims. For some early thoughts, see Olsen, *supra* note 63, at 407-09, 424, 431. It seems important to explore creative ways to improve the options available to children in difficult home situations. For example, modern technology might enable children to summon help quickly enough that it would be safe for them to stay with abusive parents to whom they are deeply attached.

78.   While this essay has focused on the family, its thesis is general. The state cannot be neutral, nor can it be a neutral arbiter of rights. *See* Olsen, *supra* note 63; *Symposium: A Critique of Rights*, 62 TEX. L. REV. 1363 (1984).

[10]

LEGAL STORIES, CHANGE, AND INCENTIVES— REINFORCING THE LAW OF THE FATHER*

MARTHA ALBERTSON FINEMAN**

I. INTRODUCTION

This article addresses the problems for women and children latent in recent suggestions to use the law to create incentives for men to use birth control.[1] It examines these problems in the context of exploring the ways in which various "stories"[2] or narratives about the family are generated and used as society confronts changes in intimate behavior. The search for incentives is undertaken as part of a contemporary reexamination of what constitutes responsible male sexuality and fatherhood. It is only one aspect of a much larger contemporary reconstruction of the traditional family narrative in the wake of pressures generated by changing patterns of behavior and altered expectations for the family as a social institution.

In contemporary society, it is no longer clear what constitutes appropriate family role behavior—who is acting as a good mother or father. In fact, it is no longer clear who or what constitutes a family. One aspect of the reconstruction of the family narrative currently underway involves the creation of a generic category of family relationship—parenthood—from the previously differentiated roles of mother and father and a corresponding redefinition of the social and cultural understandings of fatherhood and its legal implications.[3] This reconstruction of the family narrative has been undertaken largely in response to women resisting their historically assigned roles as wives and mothers in the traditional family story.[4]

Changes quite often generate controversy and resistance. Traditional stories are met with alternative visions and, as a result, are modified, restated, and reintroduced into the ongoing debates. Ultimately, the collected and conflicting stories we tell about families in our society reveal

---

* ©Copyright by Martha A. Fineman 1993. Adrienne Hiegel imposed order to the footnotes in this article—a task for which she has gained my admiration and thanks.

** Maurice T. Moore Professor of Law, Columbia University.

1. This suggestion was an explicit part of the discussion in a "by invitation only" seminar I attended in Washington, D.C., in the spring of 1992, sponsored by the National Institute of Health.

2. *See* discussion *infra* part II.A.

3. *See* Martha L. Fineman, *The Neutered Mother*, 46 U. MIAMI L. REV. 653, 660-62 (1991).

4. *See id.* at 665.

a great deal about how we view and understand the world in which we operate.

Despite the existence of alternative stories, it is important to remember that not all stories can be equally verified by empirical observations. For example, the dominant spousal story for the past decade has been one of *equality*; yet, there continues to be great gender *inequality* in the allocation of the burdens and costs associated with reproduction.[5] This difference is only one aspect of a much larger pattern of ingrained and persistent gender inequality that characterizes the functioning of intimate entities in our culture. The burdens associated with intimacy and the maintenance of intimacy have always been disproportionately allocated to women. Furthermore, given the cultural and market structures built upon this fundamental division of family labor, this inequality is going to be very difficult to change. If we were serious about redistributing these burdens, it would require an ideological and structural reorientation of society that does not seem likely to occur any time within the near future.

A final cautionary note is necessary to those prone to place too much faith in the potential power of alternative stories. Even if one believes in the possibility of change, it is unlikely that it will occur through legal restructuring. Law is more reflective than constitutive of social realities, tracking closely existing power alignments. Historically, real change has been difficult to achieve. In particular, legal reforms in the area of intimate relations have tended to be misdirected, addressing the wrong questions and neglecting certain significant issues.[6] This has resulted in actions that reinforce, rather than alleviate, existing gender inequalities.

II. RETHINKING THE CONCEPT OF FAMILY

A. *The Struggle over the Family*

The retelling of family narratives is a process that deserves some initial attention to put the reproduction and male-incentive story into context. The contemporary family is a social and cultural construct with multiple valuations. In recent years there have been significant shifts in the

---

5. *See generally* MARTHA A. FINEMAN, THE ILLUSION OF EQUALITY: THE RHETORIC AND REALITY OF DIVORCE REFORM (1991) (noting that there have been various backlashes generated by the women's movement's push for family and workplace equality, including formation of fathers'-rights groups); VICTOR R. FUCHS, WOMEN'S QUEST FOR ECONOMIC EQUALITY (1988) (concluding that the constant conflict between simultaneously maintaining family and career arises much more for women than for men, persistently frustrating women's goal of attaining economic equality).

6. *See* Martha L. Fineman, *Images of Mothers in Poverty Discourses*, 1991 DUKE L.J. 274, 295.

importance attached to the family as a cultural icon, as well as reconsideration of it as a functional institution. It seems that family in our society is viewed as such a simple and undisputed institution that a mere reference to it serves as a full definition of widely shared values and norms and, at the same time, as a complex, changing site of ongoing struggle over basic ideological divisions in our society.[7]

The family is an increasingly important object of study, however, generating federal grants and volumes of sociological, psychological, and political literature. The family is both overvalued on a symbolic and metaphoric level and systematically devalued in terms of the allocation of societal resources. A cultural and political schizophrenia exists about the institution.[8]

Fundamental changes in the way many Americans organize their day-to-day family lives have contributed to that schizophrenia. Social movements such as feminism and children's rights, organized in part to bring the existence of the exploitive potential within traditional family roles to political light, have set the stage for a collective reimagining of the family.[9] As a result, there is a great deal of cultural negotiation around the ways that we have traditionally organized intimacy in American society.

The evolutionary dialogue associated with such negotiation reveals the inescapably political (in the largest sense of that word) and ideological nature of change. The arguments for and against change are largely carried on through the use of stories or narratives, which are generated in a variety of ways. These narratives come in multiple guises. They may be cast as social science or case studies, illuminated and buttressed by "scientific" or other designated objective means; framed as legislative or judicial fact-finding, legitimated because it is asserted that they were democratically produced within a stylized system of legal processes; or merely selected for dramatization because it is recognized that they will attract an audience when reported in the media or represented in fiction

---

7. See Martha A. Fineman, *Intimacy Outside of the Natural Family*, 23 CONN. L. REV. 955, 969 (1991).

8. See Susan M. Okin, *Change in the Family: Change in the World*, UTNE READER, Mar.–Apr. 1990, at 74 (stating that the family in modern theory seems to be considered as a background institution—the real focus being on the individual). A related phenomenon is that typically any legal feminist who writes about the family has been cast as a "cultural feminist" and marginalized as being primarily domestically oriented, even if the focus of the analyses of the family is on concepts such as power and domination. See Patricia A. Cain, *Feminism and the Limits of Equality*, 24 GA. L. REV. 803, 835-38 (1990). See generally Robin West, *Feminism, Critical Social Theory and Law*, 1989 U. CHI. LEGAL F. 59 (defending the choice of some feminists to discuss the law without employing the framework suggested by critical social theorists).

9. See Fineman, *supra* note 7, at 969.

or film.[10] There may be different forms to the stories—some are horror stories, others more like sentimental visions—but typically they seem to offer both explanations for the status quo, as well as normative direction for the future.

Rethinking the family has led to the discovery of ignored or suppressed family stories. These alternative family stories become part of the dialogue, more successfully embraced when confined to individuals and defined as choosing a lifestyle. The acceptance and integration of the changes on a general or a political level, however, have been impeded by the political treatment of the family and its exploitation as a changing institution in transition. In fact, the traditional stories gain potency in the context of attack.

B. *Fathers and Families*

Rethinking the family on a grand scale is rightly recognized as a significant ideological endeavor. The societal nature of this core institution means that potential changes to it cannot be viewed in isolation from their impact on other institutions. Belying the traditional dichotomy between public and private spheres is the assertion that if the family changes, so will the market.[11] There is unease with the increasingly unavoidable conclusion that there are no independent, unconnected choices.[12]

The family as an institution has historically served important practical and ideological functions in our society. For centuries, it stood alone as the formal and institutionalized manifestation of condoned sexual intimacy, a cultural monopoly currently under attack. It has also operated as the social institution in which the dependency of the very young and,

---

10. This list, by no means exhaustive, tacitly recognizes the validity of the postmodern claim that all texts are narrative and hence can be productively deconstructed.

11. *See* Fineman, *supra* note 3, at 661.

12. Increasingly, scholars and policymakers have recognized the relationship between such "unconnected" issues as the divorce rate and the increase in applications for Aid to Families with Dependent Children (AFDC), and the falseness of the dichotomy between work and family. *See generally* LENORE J. WEITZMAN, THE DIVORCE REVOLUTION: THE UNEXPECTED SOCIAL AND ECONOMIC CONSEQUENCES FOR WOMEN AND CHILDREN IN AMERICA (1985). The grand rethinking of the "family," however, will and must occur. The pressure of the growing numbers of untraditional families mandates that such rethinking proceed. One interesting question will be how explicitly political or ideological the rethinking will be. Many resist the application of ideological terms to their personal experiences. Women who support equal rights in work and at home are careful to indicate that they are not "feminists," and "alternative" families struggle to analogize their same-sex or non-marital cohabitation situations with the traditional norm of formal heterosexual marriage. *See* Fineman, *supra* note 7, at 969-72. People shun the characterization of their behavior as deviant and seek the safety of normality.

sometimes, the elderly and ill can be referred, confined, and thereby hidden and ignored.[13] The family functions as a complementary institution to the state, alleviating it from direct economic responsibility for its citizens.

These important social functions are premised on a division of labor within the family. This division has historically confined women to the private or family sphere, thus making them bear directly the burdens of intimacy and dependency in our society. Men, as fathers and husbands, have had the corresponding responsibility of economic support for the family. This gendered division of labor has been the dominant casting script for family stories. As more and more people are resisting their assigned roles, however, society experiences the emergence of alternative family narratives.

Fatherhood, for example, has certainly gained stature as more than a mere biological classification with certain legal consequences. But, the revised role must still be understood as an ideological construct implicated in and fashioned by traditional power relationships within the institutions of the family and the state. The historic organization and operative assumptions about traditional family relationships obscured the state-sanctioned power imbalance inherent in the family institution. The status of father, husband, and head of household needed no formal explication of the power the status held.

As adherence to the traditional family form has begun to wither away, the complementary power relationships embedded in it had to be made explicit to be preserved. New stories are fashioned. The emerging alternative narratives, however, do not always challenge the basic operation of the status quo.[14] In divorce law, newly wrought designations of the rights and/or responsibilities associated with the status of spouse and parent ensure that male control will survive the end of the marriage relationship. Traditional assumptions, refashioned for a no-fault-divorce world, are articulated as ongoing economic support obligations, along with coerced access to, and control over, ex-wife and child.

The contemporary challenges to traditional patriarchal family forms, however, are not limited to the divorce context. Divorce at least assumes an initial adherence to traditional heterosexual formal marriage. There are more profoundly deviant family forms gaining adherents and emerging as fundamental challenges to the traditional narrative. Increasing numbers of never-married women are becoming mothers, creating the perception of a social "crisis" for family traditionalists in our society. To many

---

13. *See* Fineman, *supra* note 7, at 969-72.

14. *See, e.g.*, Fineman, *supra* note 3, at 658 (providing an example of this in the context of alterations, labeled "reforms," in the area of custody at divorce and poverty-law rules).

observers of the contemporary scene, it seems clear that women are not behaving as they should. Furthermore, many men seem to welcome the reprieve from enforced economic responsibility for families. The old roles are ignored.

III. LEGAL INCENTIVES AND THE MORAL TALE OF RESPONSIBLE FATHERHOOD

In recent years, as the institution of fatherhood has been transformed on an ideological and rhetorical level, there has been a lot of popular and political attention to the *new man*. Initially, the calls for change came from a feminist community convinced that the ideals of sharing and equality could be implemented in the family, as well as in the market context. More recently, however, the portends of change are not feminist rhetoric, but the statistically constructed stories of real-life mothering that seem to call into question the continued relevance of traditional fatherhood. In its extreme form, the new motherhood seems to reject men altogether. Many more women are living large segments of their lives as single mothers. The category of never-married mothers increases with each *new* governmental report, causing alarm in some circles.[15]

An essential part of the never-married or newly single mothers' story has become the failure of biological fathers to assume responsibility for their offspring. Currently, there are considerations of the potential role of the law in creating incentives for men to use contraception, pay child support, and marry their children's mothers. Given that feminists and liberal policymakers have long sought to distribute more evenly the burdens associated with reproduction and child rearing, one might inquire, "What is wrong with that goal?" I want to try to answer that question by examining the implications of the search for ways to provide legal incentives for male use of birth control and for exposing the potential for adding even more burdens to the load mothers carry.[16]

A. *Incentives and Punitive Potential*

My basic concern with proposals for using law to encourage male responsibility for birth control is that the question of how to provide incentives inevitably will slip into a discussion of how to create disincentives. This discussion will really be a debate about the appropriate

---

15. *See* Fineman, *supra* note 6, at 275 n.1; *see also* Fineman, *supra* note 3, at 665 (noting that the birth rate to unmarried women has increased continuously since 1980).

16. Other incentive proposals should be considered separately, although there are common threads that accompany child-support and other single-mother tales in the stories about irresponsible fathers.

form of punishment for irresponsible reproduction. Furthermore, in regard to reproductive issues, typically it is women who are punished, even in those cases in which men were the initial focus of the incentive–disincentive system.[17] Perhaps this is due to an implicit realization that, because of their "unique" position regarding reproduction, women are likely to be more effective targets for coercive social policy reforms.

Asking the wrong questions regarding incentives and reproduction in areas other than contraception has meant that the issue of how best to support women and children in society is relatively neglected. The concern with child poverty in welfare debates, for example, is subsumed into the debate on nonmarital reproduction and how to curtail it.

One basic problem with a consideration of incentives is that the wrong issues are often addressed due to the inherent limitations of law and the process of lawmaking. Law is a very crude instrument with which to fashion and further social policy. For one thing, law is much better at fashioning prohibitions and determining punishments than creating affirmative incentives for behavior. In either case, whether developed to structure incentives or to define punishments for certain behavior, law is most effective when it tracks societal norms and values about which there is strong agreement.[18] Attempts to use law to transform society by imposing norms on an unreceptive population, however, are seldom successful.[19]

In addition, when societal norms are in a state of flux, as they certainly are in relation to matters of sexual intimacy, contraception, and reproductive rights, the law tends to be identified as a site of contest. Warring societal factions seek to codify their world view, thereby giving legitimacy to their stories about what are appropriate ideals and values. Policy formation and law reform in this regard are political or, at least, tend to develop in a politicized environment. This is significant because it means that the lawmaking process often becomes a highly charged, symbolic endeavor. In such instances, the explicit subject matter under consideration is merely the tip of a larger, ideologically potent iceberg. The political nature of policy formation also means that lawmaking occurs in the context of compromise and conciliation, activities that may undermine specific, controlled steps in a well-considered strategy to accomplish certain goals. Furthermore, it is important to remember that quite often the weaker, underrepresented members of society—women, children, and the poor—are those whose interests are first sacrificed in the

---

17. *Cf.* Fineman, *supra* note 6, at 294-95.

18. *See* Fineman, *supra* note 3, at 662.

19. *See id.*

spirit of compromise, or whose version of the story is never heard in the first place.

These warnings about the nature of law are relevant in considering how skeptical we should be about the quest for legal incentives for male use of contraception. In the abstract, such an endeavor may be worthwhile, but, because incentive has tended historically to be perceived and implemented as punishment,[20] we should be concerned about the ultimate punitive possibilities of any specific incentive-directed outcomes.

B. *Men Who Are Cast as Responsible Reproducers*

The focus on incentives for men is shaped by and reflective of a story laden with values and norms about the appropriate contexts for reproduction that needs further exploration and refinement. Regarding the question of existing incentives, for example, the fundamental premise of the reproduction story seems to be that women have a natural incentive to use birth control because the context of their decision making is defined by the potential for pregnancy and the resulting social role they will play as mothers. For men, however, the incentive must be artificially manufactured through the creation of economic consequences using the legal system.

The conclusion that legal changes are necessary to provide contextual incentives for men, as an *undifferentiated* group, to use birth control is not an obvious one for someone familiar with existing family law and policy. Because of the existing, well-established set of legal obligations that adhere to the marital status, a more careful consideration reveals a reproductive story in which men are divided into two distinct categories with regard to the incentive question.[21] Some men are responsible

---

20. *See* JAMES Q. WILSON, THINKING ABOUT CRIME 118 (1983) (stating that "[t]o a psychologist, deterring persons from committing crimes or inducing persons to engage in noncriminal activities are but special cases of using 'reinforcements' (or rewards) to alter behavior"); *see also* HERBERT L. PACKER, THE LIMITS OF THE CRIMINAL SANCTION 37-39 (1968). For Packer, the notion of retribution is also significant as an underlying rationale for deterrence arguments for sanctions. Although atonement through suffering has historically been a major theme in religious thought, it doubtless plays a role in thought about secular punishment as well. The retribution view of punishment shifts the emphasis from deterrence to demands that the criminal take it upon himself or herself to become reconciled with the social order. *Id.* It is precisely this notion of punishment for failure to conform to the social order that this article explores.

21. This process of categorization is consistent with much of the "we/them" distinction that characterizes criminal law. Commentators differ on the degree of "difference" between normal and criminal individuals. For example, James Wilson has stated that

potential reproducers, while others are not. The legal institution of marriage provides the context of responsibility for some men. Men who are neatly and securely tied to the nuclear family by marriage have plenty of legal and economic incentives to plan families—to engage in responsible reproduction.

The incentives that married men experience in regard to reproduction are not biologically compelled. They are derivatively compelled, however, because the status of being married ties the economic future of husbands to their wives' reproductive fortunes. It is well known that married men are legally responsible for child support, an obligation that extends beyond the marital tie should there be a divorce. Therefore, from a policy perspective, married men can be comfortably presumed to be responsible reproducers, not in need of further incentives regarding birth control. Married men's reproductive potential is contained and contextualized within an institution that has well-defined legal expectations and obligations for them and their relationship to their children.

Of course, it could be that, as a policy matter, we are not satisfied by the incentive for male *participation* in decision making about contraception that marriage provides. Some policymakers may want to use law to enhance male *control* over reproduction in the nuclear-family context. Perhaps some people feel that men would make better, more responsible decisions about reproduction than women do. A few men have expressed dismay about their perception that men have lost control (or perhaps they never had control) over reproduction.[22] These men believe that women unfairly exercise a monopoly over the reproductive decision.[23] This attitude is reflected in the rhetoric of spokesmen for several men's rights groups who strongly endorsed the idea of an oral male contraceptive because, as Dan Logan, Executive Director of the men's rights group Free Men stated:

> [W]e always treat reproductive rights as a women's subject and something they control[.] I think the fact that women carry a

---

to assert that "deterrence doesn't work" is tantamount to either denying the plainest facts of everyday life or claiming that would-be criminals are utterly different from the rest of us. They may well be different to some degree—they most likely have a weaker conscience, worry less about their reputation in polite society, and find it harder to postpone gratifying their urges—but these differences of degree do not make them indifferent to the risks and gains of crime.

WILSON, *supra* note 20, at 119.

22. *See* Jean Marbella, *Men Offer Mixed Opinions on Male Birth Control Pill*, L.A. TIMES, May 14, 1990, at E3.

23. *See id.*

womb in their body is an accident of biology. It could just as
easily have been men. We have just as much at stake in
reproductive subjects as women do.[24]

In addition, Fredric Hayward, executive director of Men's Rights,
Inc. believes it is important for men to get equal access to better
contraceptive options because under the current system of reproductive
roles, men have been excluded from full parenthood. He stated that a
woman's "[i]dea that, 'It's my body, I'm bearing the risk, therefore I'm
the one who will make the decisions,' that's the female chauvinism version
of men who think women shouldn't have the vote because they weren't the
ones who fought in the fields to get democracy. . . ."[25]

In regard to the desire to increase married men's participation and
control in the reproductive area, it is interesting to note that one of the
issues of first impression in the Pennsylvania abortion case, recently
decided by the Supreme Court, was spousal notification.[26] The Third
Circuit recognized that existing Supreme Court doctrine precluded viewing
any requirement of spousal notification as an expression of the State's
interest in protecting a husband's interest in a pre-viable fetus.[27] The
judges determined that what the Pennsylvania legislature must have sought
to preserve was something considerably more modest—the preservation for
the husband of "the *possibility of participating* in a decision his wife is
constitutionally privileged to make on her own for her own reasons."[28]
For the Third Circuit, this possibility did not constitute the kind of
compelling state interest that could justify substantial burdens on the wife's
right to abortion.[29]

Although a majority of the Supreme Court ultimately agreed on the
impermissibility of spousal notification,[30] one thing that remains apparent
is that segments of society are very concerned with protecting a role for
married men regarding abortion.[31] Furthermore, this concern may be
gaining adherents. One of the dissenting Third Circuit judges in *Casey*

---

24. *Id.* (quoting Dan Logan, Executive Director, Free Men).

25. *Id.* (quoting Fredric Hayward, Executive Director, Men's Rights, Inc.)

26. *See* Planned Parenthood v. Casey, 112 S. Ct. 2791 (1992).

27. *See* Planned Parenthood v. Casey, 947 F.2d 682, 709-15 (3d Cir. 1991), *aff'd
in part and rev'd in part*, 112 S. Ct. 2791 (1992).

28. *Id.* at 715 (emphasis added).

29. *See id.*

30. *See Casey*, 112 S. Ct. at 2796.

31. *See* Kay Miller, *How Do Married Men Feel About Ruling on Abortion?*, STAR
TRIB. (Minneapolis), July 6, 1992, at 1E.

stated that the Court had already determined that

> a man has a fundamental interest in preserving his ability to father
> a child. . . . [A] husband who is willing to participate in raising
> a child has a fundamental interest in the child's welfare. . . . It
> follows that a husband has a "legitimate" interest in the welfare
> of a fetus he has conceived with his wife. . . . This interest may
> be legitimately furthered by state legislation. . . . The
> Pennsylvania legislature could have rationally believed that some
> married women are initially inclined to obtain an abortion without
> their husbands' knowledge because of perceived problems—such
> as economic constraints, future plans, or the husbands' previously
> expressed opposition—that may be obviated by discussion prior
> to the abortion.[32]

C. *The Tale of the Irresponsible Reproducer*

While furthering male control over reproductive decisions made in the
context of marriage may be of some concern, most law-reform efforts
have focused on controlling the conduct of the unmarried man, presumed
to be an irresponsible potential reproducer.[33] It is with regard to *this*
group of men that the reason for the use of law in the search for
incentives becomes clear. Recent changes in the law are attempts to
replicate the derivative incentives for reproductive responsibility that
marriage provides—to tie legally the father to the mother and the child.
While the paternity proceeding, the particular device to accomplish this

---

32. *Casey*, 947 F.2d at 725-26 (Alito, J., concurring in part and dissenting in part).

33. *See generally* GORDON H. LESTER, U.S. DEP'T OF COMMERCE, SERIES P-60,
CURRENT POPULATION REPORTS, CHILD SUPPORT AND ALIMONY: 1989 (listing the
statistics, according to demographics, of alimony and child-support awards). This
presumption about differentiated responsibility has concrete implications. Unmarried
fathers are not held to the same economic standards as married fathers, even by courts.
As of 1989, for example, the child-support award rate for never-married mothers was
24%, while the rate for ever-married mothers, by contrast, was 72%, or three times that
of never-married women. Of the women due child support, the percentages of women
who received some payments in 1989 were not significantly different for the two
groups—72% of never-married mothers entitled to it received some support, while about
73% of ever-married mothers received payments. *Id.* at 6. The mean child-support
amount differed greatly, however, depending on status. In 1989, divorced women
received a mean child-support payment of $3,268, while the payments to never-married
women averaged $1,888. *Id.* at 7. Such differences undoubtedly contribute to the high
rate of never-married women who live below the poverty level (53.9%). *Id.* at 2.

goal, has been with us a long time, recent measures greatly increase its use and direct its consequences.[34]

Theoretically, through the paternity proceeding, irresponsible reproducers are burdened with the same economic and legal consequences that men within traditional marriage relationships would have. The logic is that they will then have the same incentive to be responsible. The use of the term incentive in this context, however, is disingenuous. To a great extent, the social policy search is really for an effective *deterrent* for irresponsible potential reproducers. In this case, therefore, the legal response should be viewed as creating disincentives or punishment —punitive responses to socially unacceptable behavior and its consequences.

A punitive model is consistent with history. At common law, criminal sanctions were imposed for indulgence in nonmarital sex.[35] Disincentives for irresponsible reproduction included bastardy proceedings and the use of the criminal process to coerce marriage by designating marriage as a defense to criminal proceedings for fornication or nonmarital cohabitation.[36] Such starkly punitive responses seem out-of-date in our more sexually permissive era. But while most states have abolished criminal regulation of nonmarital heterosexual relations, noncriminal consequences exist that are still enforced by the legal system. The criminal process has been replaced with civil proceedings that assign financial responsibility for nonmarital children, thereby coupling the single mothers' economic needs with presumed economically viable fathers. Theoretically these fathers will assume the financial obligations for their nonmarital children.

---

34. *See infra* part III.D.

35. *See generally* Martha L. Fineman, *Law and Changing Patterns of Behavior: The Sanctions on Non-Marital Cohabitation*, 1981 WIS. L. REV. 275, 278-80 (stating that in Wisconsin, criminal prohibition on cohabitation without formal marriage dates back to 1839).

36. *See* Hendrik Hartog, *The Public Law of a County Court: Judicial Government in 18th Century Massachusetts*, 20 AM. J. LEGAL HIST. 282, 299-300 (1976). Fornication accounted for over 40% of prosecutions in a Massachusetts court in the 18th century. The number of men and married women prosecuted for fornication fell after 1740, and it was primarily single women who were brought before the court on charges of criminal fornication in the latter half of the century. Men continued, however, to be sued for bastardy. *Id.*

D. *Paternity Proceedings:*
Transformation of Irresponsible Reproduction

The paternity proceeding is typically classified as civil in nature; yet, it is viewed by many public-interest advocates as akin to a criminal trial.[37] The imposition of a child-support award is considered to be the equivalent of an eighteen-year sentence.[38] There are constant efforts to secure criminal-process-type protections for putative fathers in these proceedings, such as the right to counsel, the imposition of higher burdens of proof, and other reforms.[39] Paternity proceedings, from a State's perspective, however, are far more remedial than punitive in nature. Perhaps most significantly, they are for the purpose of restitution—to restore to the State public funds expended on the nonmarital child.[40]

The frequency of paternity proceedings, prompted by state and federal reforms, has greatly increased during the past several years. Reliance on this process is an essential step in assuring private or family responsibility for children, and it has been a mainstay of recent welfare reforms. These reforms seek to ensure that children are firmly anchored financially, morally, and legally to a father. Cynically, one might observe that the paramount welfare reform objective of paternity actions is letting the State off the economic hook by substituting paternal-support obligation for State funds.[41]

---

37. *See* Mark D. Esterle, *Indigents in Paternity Actions*, 24 J. FAM. L. 1, 9-10 (1985).

38. *See id.* at 3.

39. See Victoria S. Williams & Robert G. Williams, *Identifying Daddy: The Role of the Courts in Establishing Paternity*, 28 JUDGES' J. 2, 3 (1989). The criminal roots of paternity proceedings may account for the complex procedures that attend the process. Some states continue to use criminal terminology, such as "arraignment" and "paternity warrant," in the judicial processing of paternity cases. *Id*; *see also* Reynolds v. Kimmons, 569 P.2d 799, 801 (Alaska 1977) (finding that although paternity proceedings will not result in immediate incarceration, a parent of a child under 16 who intentionally fails to provide support may be held criminally liable).

40. *See generally* Harry D. Krause, *Child Support Reassessed: Limits of Private Responsibility and the Public Interest*, 24 FAM. L.Q. 1 (1990) (exploring the mounting tension between "(1) society's continuing need for a functioning family infrastructure, (2) the modern 'Me Generation's' emphasis on individual's *rights* . . . , (3) traditional financial responsibility for dependents . . . , and (4) the care-giving capacity of the one parent family"); Williams & Williams, *supra* note 39, at 3. Only a small fraction of paternity establishment cases are brought to the court by private plaintiffs. *Id.*

41. *See* Hartog, *supra* note 35, at 302. It is interesting to note that early fornication prosecutions served a similar purpose. Because most New England towns had the right after 1758 to bind into servitude any woman with an illegitimate child who refused to reimburse or "procure the reimbursement" for the public expense of raising the child,

The objective of paternity proceedings is the creation of a legal tie between the single father and the dependent single mother and child. Unlike the consensual nature of the relationship between a married couple, neither the mother's nor the father's wishes regarding the establishment of such a tie are considered relevant. This tie is essential for the incentive or sanction of child support to apply in a nonmarital situation.

Child support as a sanction for irresponsible reproduction (reproduction outside of marriage) is part of the structure of the Family Support Act of 1988 (FSA),[42] the first major legislation addressing

---

fornication prosecutions became a method of forcing women to name the putative father in an effort to obtain support. The fornication prosecutions ultimately functioned as an administrative procedure to reallocate the costs of illegitimacy. *Id.*

42. *See* Pub. L. No. 100-485, 102 Stat. 2343 (codified as amended in scattered sections of 42 U.S.C. (1988)). Subtitle A, entitled "Child Support" provides in § 101 that the wages of an absent parent shall be subject to withholding in enforcing payment of child-support orders and that the Secretary of Health and Human Services will conduct a study to determine the feasibility of requiring immediate income withholding of all child-support awards in a state. Exceptions are allowed when both parties agree to other arrangements or when one party shows good cause. *Id.* § 101, 102 Stat. at 2344-45.

Section 102 clarifies that a family receiving public assistance will not have the first $50 of each month's child-support payment counted against their entitlement, even if that payment is made more than once in a single month; e.g., payments made for prior months. *Id.* § 102, 102 Stat. at 2346.

Section 103 provides that the state must establish support payment guidelines and that there must be a judicial "rebuttable presumption" that such guidelines are correct. This presumption may be overcome by showing that enforcement of such standards would be "unjust or inappropriate in a particular case." *Id.* § 103, 102 Stat. at 2346-48.

Subtitle C, entitled "Improved Procedures for Child Support Enforcement and Establishment of Paternity," provides various standards for States' support enforcement mechanisms. It provides that States must establish time limits for response to requests for investigations and time limits by which payments must be made of support money collected by the State. Section 123 requires that States have either automated data processing and information retrieval systems or a system that the State can show is equivalent. *Id.* § 123, 102 Stat. at 2352-53.

Section 125 provides that "each State shall require each parent to furnish to such State . . . the social security account number issued to the parent unless the State (in accordance with regulations prescribed by the Secretary) finds good cause for not requiring the furnishing of such number." *Id.* § 125, 102 Stat. at 2353-54.

Section 126 established the Commission on Interstate Child Support, which makes recommendations to Congress for improving interstate child support and holds at least one conference on interstate child support to assist in formulating these recommendations. *Id.* § 126, 102 Stat. at 2354-55.

Section 128 requires the Secretary of Health and Human Services to
conduct a study of the patterns of expenditures on children in two-parent families, in single-parent families following divorce or separation, and in single-parent families in which the parents were never married, giving

poverty to pass Congress in several decades. The FSA reflects the belief that welfare dependency is a significant problem requiring dramatic reorientation of welfare policy.[43] Provisions of the FSA mandate stricter

---

particular attention to the relative standards of living in households in which both parents and all of the children do not live together.
Id. § 128, 102 Stat. at 2356. The Secretary is also required to submit policy recommendations based on this study. *Id.*

43. *See* 42 U.S.C. § 602 (1988). The primary objective seems to be the insertion of welfare recipients into the workforce. This is accomplished for the single mother either by mandating her to work or train for work and/or by substituting the employed father as the child's primary source of support instead of the State. The new legislation's focus on reinforcing the work ethic and dominant individualistic norms of self-sufficiency through the imposition of "workfare" provisions for mothers of young children has been the major emphasis of most commentators. The Job Opportunities and Basic Skills (JOBS) component of the reform legislation represents the latest instance in the long history of welfare to promote work and discourage welfare dependency among the poor. Most often the term "workfare" has been reserved for the requirement that recipients work off their benefits, usually by accepting some form of public or community work assignment. The JOBS program has been called the "new workfare" in that, while requiring work, it also offers opportunities for education, job training, skill development, job counseling, and placement in the private sector, along with other support services such as extended child care and health insurance. Fineman, *supra* note 6, at 277 n.4. The JOBS program, then, is workfare with support services. The JOBS program replaces the Work Incentive Program (WIN), 42 U.S.C. § 602 (1967), which was initiated in 1967. *See* Fineman, *supra* note 6, at 277 n.4.

Prior to the passage of the Family Support Act, policy discussions emphasized research that highlighted the effectiveness of "new workfare" programs in moving people from welfare to work. *See* JUDITH M. GUERON, REFORMING WELFARE WITH WORK (Occasional Paper Number Two, Ford Foundation Project on Social Welfare and the American Future, 1987); LAWRENCE M. MEAD, BEYOND ENTITLEMENT (1986) (stressing that low-cost programs emphasizing work requirements as a general norm are cost-efficient and likely to provide considerable movement from welfare to work); Lawrence M. Mead, *The Potential for Work Enforcement: A Study of WIN*, 7 J. POL. ANALYSIS & MGMT. 264 (1988). *But see* Christopher Jencks & Kathryn Edin, *The Real Welfare Problem*, 1 AM. PROSPECT 31 (1990). Increased employment through workfare programs, however, was hardly a solution to the poverty problems of poor, female-headed families if we take into account the earnings needed by these families to get out of poverty. Mothers in these particular families would, on average, need jobs that pay in the vicinity of two to three times the minimum wage before they could be reasonably expected to leave welfare and meet their expenses, including child and health care.

The essence of the so-called "welfare trap" is not that welfare warps women's personalities or makes them pathologically dependent, though that may occasionally happen. The essence of the "trap" is that while welfare pays badly, low-wage jobs pay even worse. Most welfare mothers are quite willing to work if they end up with significantly more disposable income as a result. But they are not willing to work if working will leave them as poor as they were when they stayed home.

enforcement of child-support orders, including wage withholding.

While federal provisions help collect support from divorced fathers thereby insuring continuation of responsible reproduction, it is in relation to unmarried men that major efforts were undertaken. States are required to meet federal standards for establishing paternity for children born out of wedlock as a means of obtaining child support from absent fathers.[4] The provisions mandating paternity proceedings reflect the idea of responsible reproduction and, by legally tying the father to the mother–child unit, reinforce traditional norms of male economic responsibility for children that are typically expressed in the context of the nuclear family.

The political rhetoric surrounding the reforms evidences the assumed desirability of the traditional family form. In addressing the FSA in the Senate, for example, Senator Moynihan began his comments by commending President Bush for his remarks at the United Nations World Summit for Children. Senator Moynihan stated that

> [o]ne sentence [of Bush's remarks is] especially notable. "We want to see the day when every American child is part of a strong and stable family." The importance of this statement is elemental. Unlike the problems of children in much of the world, age-old problems of disease, new problems of ecological disaster, the problems of children in the United States are overwhelmingly

---

. . .

All these calculations lead inexorably to one conclusion. An unskilled single mother cannot expect to support herself and her children in today's labor market either by working or by collecting welfare. If she wants to make ends meet, she must either get help from someone else (usually an absent father, parent, or boyfriend) or she must combine work and welfare. At present, the only way she can combine work and welfare is to collect AFDC and then work without telling the welfare department.

Id. at 43-45.

44. *See* 42 U.S.C. § 666(a)(5)(A) (1988). The FSA imposes standards of compliance on the States, requiring that, as of 1991, each State's "paternity establishment percentage for such fiscal year equals or exceeds" a requisite amount. The "paternity establishment percentage" is the ratio of the total number of children born out of wedlock who are receiving some form of public assistance and for whom paternity has been established, to the total number of children born out-of-wedlock who are receiving some sort of public assistance. This section also requires the child and all other parties in contested paternity cases to submit to genetic tests, except where good cause has been shown that this is not in the best interest of the child. Those not in receipt of AFDC may be charged for such tests. The statute encourages the State to adopt simple civil procedures for voluntary acknowledgement of paternity and for establishing paternity in civil cases. Pub. L. No. 100-485, § 111(a), 102 Stat. at 2348-50 (codified at 42 U.S.C. § 652(g)(2)(A) (1988)).

associated with the strength and stability of their families. Our problems do not reside in nature, nor yet are they fundamentally economic. Our problems derive from behavior.[45]

Having established his basic premise, Moynihan continued that

[t]here is a mountain of scientific evidence showing that when families disintegrate, children often end up with intellectual, physical, and emotional scars that persist for life . . . . We talk about the drug crisis, the education crisis, and the problems of teen pregnancy and juvenile crime. But all these ills trace back predominantly to one source: broken families.[46]

Moynihan's rhetoric, which attributes the problems of the poor to their own behavior, tracks the simplistic tendency in poverty discourses to categorize mothers negatively—single mothers and their children seem to be cast as merely a by-product of the real concern that is male irresponsibility.

IV. SINGLE MOTHERS AND THE "COSTS" OF RESPONSIBILITY

The connection between irresponsibility and marital status is even more explicit in the stories told in the recently enacted welfare reforms in New Jersey.[47] The New Jersey reform has two basic thrusts. First, it encourages marriage formation by creating economic *incentives*, thereby demonstrating a preference for responsible family formation. Married

---

45. 136 CONG. REC. S14,416 (daily ed. Oct. 3, 1990) (statement of Sen. Moynihan) (quoting President George Bush).

46. 136 CONG. REC. S14,418 (daily ed. Oct. 3, 1990) (statement of Sen. Moynihan) (introducing to the record an article by Sen. Moynihan); *see also* 134 CONG. REC. S7730 (daily ed. June 14, 1988) (statement of Sen. Specter) (discussing the hand-in-hand relationship between poverty and crime, and the need to reform welfare from a hand-out to a hand-up system); 134 CONG. REC. S4712 (daily ed. Apr. 26, 1988) (statement of Sen. Cochran) (discussing the need to reform the welfare program from a system of reliance to a ladder of self-dependency, calling for requirements that all able-bodied welfare recipients work and that absent fathers pay child support, thus strengthening family cohesion); 134 CONG. REC. S3069 (daily ed. Mar. 25, 1988) (statement of Sen Cochran) (noting that two-thirds of those classified as "poor" are single mothers and children, resulting in their long-term dependence on public assistance).

47. *See* N.J. STAT. ANN. §§ 44:10-19, -20 (West Supp. 1992) The statute's purpose is to go beyond economic aid to the recipient alone by offering the recipient assistance in obtaining higher academic and vocational training.

couples would be allowed to live together without losing a portion of their welfare benefits, as would have happened under the earlier law.[48]

Second, the reform both escalates and defuses the punishment or sanctions for irresponsible reproduction. The sanctions are justified by the rhetorical linking of reforms in public assistance with the assumption of personal responsibility. The punitive paternity proceeding is present,[49] of course, but the legislation goes further than this in its imposition of sanctions. Mothers and children are *directly punished* by the removal of economic incentives for irresponsible reproduction. The new statute denies a sixty-four-dollar monthly increase for each additional child born into a welfare family.[50]

As the New Jersey reforms indicate, the logic behind economic incentives in conjunction with reproduction ultimately leads to sanctions (disguised as incentives) on the single mother and her child. Justification for the escalation and expansion of disincentives is couched in terms of incentives—translated into an attempt at weaning people off welfare by forcing them to "be responsible for their actions."[51]

In fact, it may be that even if fathers are also a source of concern, the mothers' behavior is more easily brought within the incentives conceptualization, simply because they are the ones who actually give birth and assume care for the children. The State of Maryland recently announced welfare reforms designed to reduce benefits for welfare mothers who fail to exhibit responsible behavior regarding their children's school attendance and health care.[52] In California, Governor Wilson's deputy press secretary commented on reforms to limit or deny aid if a variety of behaviors, including having additional children, were engaged in by welfare mothers: "We're not asking them to get off aid and seek a 40 hour-a-week job; we're asking [the welfare mother] to start taking responsibility for [her] life, to do something positive and constructive to increase self-esteem, to go out and start earning on [her] own."[53]

Even liberal commentators, such as Irwin Garfinkel of the Institute for Poverty Research, have concluded that it is the potential for maternal deterrence or incentive that is relevant to welfare reforms. He stated that the problem with providing more aid to single-parent families is that doing so creates incentives for the formation and preservation of single-parent

---

48. *See id.* § 44:10-3.5.

49. *See id.* § 44:4-1.04.

50. *See id.*

51. Paul Taylor, *Carrots and Sticks of Welfare Reform*, WASH. POST, Feb. 4, 1992, at A13.

52. *See* Julie Kosterlitz, *Behavior Modification*, NAT'L J., Feb. 1, 1992, at 271.

53. *Id.* (quoting James Lee).

families. Garfinkel, unlike some conservative commentators, recognizes that single-mother families may not be all bad:

> Of course, it is possible that society is better off—or at least no worse off—as a result of whatever additional single-parent families are created by more favorable treatment of those groups. Not all marriages are made in heaven. Some men beat their wives and children . . . . In some of these cases, all the parties may be better off separate rather than together.[54]

Nonetheless, he concludes that "[d]espite the fact that increases in single parenthood may not be socially pernicious, prudence would suggest that in the face of ignorance we should seek to minimize incentives for single parenthood."[55]

If it is in fact easier to structure arguments for incentives directed at mothers because they will be considered potentially more effective, this is likely to produce more mean-spirited and parsimonious reforms like those in New Jersey. As a political matter, these women and their children are the weakest members of society, the most dependent, and the least immediately dangerous. And, if contraception fails, punishment seems to be ideologically justified in contemporary welfare rhetoric.

There is a second concern, however, about the potential for the use of law to provide economic incentives for male use of birth control. Even if incentives or reforms are conceived of as exclusively aimed at fathers, they will inevitably affect mothers negatively as a group.

This negative effect on mothers is the reason paternity proceedings raise concern. For instance, aspects of the process itself are objectionable. Single mothers lose their privacy.[56] They are asked questions about their

---

54. Irwin Garfinkel, The Role of Child Support in Anti-Poverty Policy, Institute for Research on Poverty, Discussion Paper #713-82, at 12 (1982) (unpublished paper, on file with the author).

55. Id.

56. To support an alleged father's denial of paternity at a contested hearing, attorneys will often subpoena all men with whom the woman had sexual relations during the period in question. *See* Stenzel v. Bennett, 374 N.Y.S.2d 175 (App. Div. 1975) (using the testimony of the petitioner's landlord regarding the number of men going in and out of her apartment helped cast doubt on the asserted paternity of the child by inferring sexual relations with other men); Russo v. Hardy, 328 N.Y.S.2d 888, 889 (Fam. Ct. 1972) (finding that social-services records concerning statements made by the mother about her relations with men are admissible). *But see* Margaret B. v. Gilbert W., 382 N.Y.S.2d 306 (App. Div. 1976) (illustrating that the intrusiveness of the hearing to the putative father may be significantly less and that answers to interrogatories by the alleged father and income-tax records may not be admissible at a hearing), *rev'd*, 363 N.E.2d 712 (N.Y. 1977).

intimate lives and potentially are subject to penalties, including incarceration.[57] Benefits may be withheld if they refuse to cooperate.[58]

It is the mothers, and ultimately the children, who are now, and will continue to be, sanctioned in pursuit of incentives for male responsibility for birth control. Not only will single mothers lose their privacy, but also many will find themselves exposed to possible violence and abuse as a result of the establishment of an unwanted paternity tie.[59] Furthermore, there may be other long-term implications because along with paternity obligations come visitation rights and, perhaps, claims for custody.[60]

Even non-AFDC[61] single mothers are vulnerable to the sanctioning resulting from this incentive-conferring process. In Wisconsin, for example, under a rhetorical bludgeon that dictates that every child has a right to a father or at least to a father's name on a birth certificate, legislation has been passed that requires *all* single mothers to participate in paternity proceedings.[62] These proceedings are mandated even if the State is not likely to be asked to become a source of economic support for the child. The major architect of the legislation has stated that

> [w]e have now in Wisconsin a law that I authored that will become the model for the nation regarding paternity. It has as its foundation that every child born in Wisconsin has a legal right to a father. Children without legal fathers have started down a slippery slope that leads to poverty. Our new paternity law is a

---

57. *See* Fineman, *supra* note 6, at 295.

58. *See* Tomas v. Rubin, 926 F.2d 906, 910 (9th Cir.), *clarified on denial of reh'g*, 935 F.2d 1555 (9th Cir. 1991). The requirement of cooperation may include the willingness to: talk, provide information, give complete answers, maintain a pleasant tone, and give the names of others who can provide information regarding the absentee parent. The requirement may also include friendliness, interest, sincerity, and the maintenance of eye contact.

59. *See, e.g.*, Waller v. Carlton Co. Hum. Servs. Dep't, No. C6-89-1116, 1989 WL 145393 (Minn. Ct. App. Dec. 5, 1989). The court denied a request of the good cause exception to the cooperation requirement in light of anticipated physical and emotional abuse to the applicant. The court held that the mother had failed to substantiate her allegation that the child was the product of rape with legal documentation. The applicant had, however, presented affidavits from her social worker and a friend attesting to the violent nature of the putative father. *Id.*

60. *See* Helen Donigan, *Calculating and Documenting Child Support Awards Under Washington Law*, 26 GONZ. L. REV. 13, 20 (1990). In a survey of Washington attorneys and judges, 61% of attorneys and 71% of judges indicated that women may trade lower child support in exchange for a promise not to contest custody. *See id.*

61. *See* Aid to Families with Dependent Children, 42 U.S.C. § 602 (1988).

62. *See* WIS. STAT. ANN. §§ 767.45-.53 (West 1988).

radical departure in that the interests of the child will become equal if not paramount to the interests of the natural parents. The law seeks to ensure that at the time of birth the state and the mother will pursue, for non-marital birth, the establishment of paternity and the subsequent collection of support.

But the philosophy of the law is not punitive. Rather, it assumes that families are natural and that it is not appropriate to have laws that have as their result that in one out of every two births outside of marriage the child will have no legal father—paternity will never be established.

Under our new law the birth certificate will be the vehicle to establish paternity early on. A presumption of paternity will be created with the filing of a statement. It will go with the birth certificate in most cases when the baby leaves the hospital. It will provide the basis for courts to order child support. But most important, it will give that child a legal father.

Both our child support law and our new paternity law are designed to ensure parental responsibility and to help families form and most importantly give new rights to children.[63]

The legislator seems unconcerned that the mother's cooperation, which will require her to reveal details of her sexual and personal life, will be compelled under the potential sanction of incarceration by use of the contempt power. Nor does he take note of the fact that the legal father's paternal involvement with the child will not be mandated by the court beyond, *perhaps*, payment of child support. Also absent is any mention of the fact that a legal father can exercise legal rights, becoming an unwanted, perhaps abusive, presence in the mother's and child's lives merely because he fathered the child.[64]

V. CONCLUSION—THE META-NARRATIVE: THE PRIVATIZATION OF INTIMACY

The story of responsible reproduction and the role of incentives has significant social consequences that are perhaps even more important than the potential for individual harm. The focus on paternity proceedings designed to tie men to single mothers and their children financially is a moral to the story, which has significant ideological implications. Most important is that it obscures the magnitude and dimensions of the

---

63. Speaker Tom Loftus of the Wisconson State Legislature, Remarks at the National Child Support Enforcement Association, New Orleans, La. (Aug. 23, 1988) (on file with the author).

64. *See* Fineman, *supra* note 6, at 294-95.

economic deprivations that make it difficult for women who make decisions to reproduce or to raise their children.[65] Rather than addressing the needs of existing single mothers, disincentive reforms take the form of either punishing them for reproducing or pushing them into a nuclear family form—a model of family life increasingly discredited, even in the middle class from which it arose.

A legal anthropologist might view the paternity proceeding as a ritual. The State, in its orchestration and performance of the proceeding, reinforces, recreates, and reiterates several fundamental societal values. Paramount among these is, of course, the strong preference for formally celebrated heterosexual marriage as the core social unit upon which all else is founded. This preference places responsible reproduction within the context of the traditional family—a context in which the legal consequences are clear and the decisions will be considered and controlled.

For far too long and to too great an extent, family policy in this country has been fashioned and formulated with this dominant ideological construct in mind. The nuclear-family ideal, and the policy based on it, foster the assumption that the maintenance of intimacy, from contraception to responsibility for the day-to-day care of children, is primarily a private task. Intimacy and the costs it generates are placed within the confines of the traditional family structure—a unit that is self-sufficient, and independent, in which independent gender roles function to assure reproduction and nurturing. This type of thinking has allowed the withdrawal of governmental assistance from *all* families in the past decade, not only the poor.

---

65. *See* LESTER, *supra* note 33, at 7. Of all women living with children under 21 years of age whose father is not living in the household, only 58% were awarded child-support payments. *Id.* at 10. Only about half of these women received the full amount of payments they were due, leaving 32% of all such families below the poverty level. *Id.* at 1. Of the 4.2 million women who were never awarded child-support payments, 64% wanted an award but did not obtain one. *Id.* at 10. Furthermore, there is significant doubt whether the provisions of the reforms are effective measures of increasing child-support payments from absent fathers. The detailed requirements for wage withholding call for accurate records; when the forms were enacted, States were faced with large backlogs of delinquent cases which "compounded startup problems." *Id.* Delays in States' institution of wage withholding, in approval of federal funding for automated child-support systems, and in the issuing of federal guidelines for the systems have contributed to a low rate of collection of payment under the reforms. Eighty-one percent of advocates questioned indicated that enforcement of payment through use of liens was "poor," and used phrases like "never done," "non-existent," and "refuses to do this" when commenting on these provisions. In one case, an advocate was told by the IV-D agency that personnel did not know the procedure for enforcing payment through liens.

For these reasons, the idea of using law to provide incentives for male use of birth control presents difficulties. It seems to be that the logic of this particular reproductive story will inevitably contribute to the creation and furtherance of associated myths about the idealized private family and its relationships that should be challenged. The stories we are telling about our families, whether traditional or reconfigured, continue to justify sanctions and punitive reforms that create disadvantages for women and children.

[11]

Marriage

Ruth Colker[†]

I don't believe in restricted clubs,[1] yet I belong to one by virtue of being married. Five years ago, when I was intimately involved with a woman, I could not imagine that I would ever want to get married. In this essay, I will explore some of the coercive elements of our society that would compel even me, a committed feminist, to marry. I will also discuss to what extent lesbian and gay people should be seeking to extend marriage to include their relationships. I will first briefly summarize the marriage debate that has been occurring within the lesbian and gay community and then provide my own position on this issue. Because the personal is political, I will relate some of my life history to explain my position.

Lesbian and gay people in our society cannot attain a legally recognized marriage.[2] Virtually no one in the lesbian and gay community believes that society should exclude lesbian and gay people from marriage. An impassioned debate, however, exists as to whether lesbian and gay activists should be seeking to extend marriage to people in same-sex relationships as a top priority.[3]

Opponents of same-sex marriage as a high priority argue that marriage is a sexist, patriarchal institution that lesbian and gay people should not be seeking to enter.[4] Entering that institution would simply contribute to our

---

† Ruth Colker is the C.J. Morrow Professor of Law, Tulane University. This essay was delivered at the Gay and Lesbian Legal Issues panel at the Frontiers of Legal Thought Conference held at Duke Law School in January, 1991. It was also delivered at the University of Tennessee in April, 1991. I would like to thank Dana Lesseman, a student at Duke Law School, and Kelly Bryson, a student at the University of Tennessee, for inviting me to deliver this paper at their institutions.

1. I borrow this phrase from Lindsey Van Gelder. *See* Lindsey Van Gelder, *Marriage as a Restricted Club*, Ms. MAGAZINE, Feb. 1984, at 59.

2. Some people mistakenly believe that lesbian or gay people in San Francisco or in Denmark can enjoy all of the privileges of marriage. There is, however, no jurisdiction that currently offers all of the privileges of marriage to lesbian or gay couples. Denmark has gone the farthest but, even under Danish law, lesbian and gay people are not provided with the privilege of adopting children. *See* Nan Hunter, *Marriage, Law, and Gender: A Feminist Essay*, 1 LAW & SEXUALITY: A REVIEW OF LESBIAN AND GAY LEGAL ISSUES (forthcoming 1991). Although several cities in the United States have passed partnership registration programs, these programs are powerless to provide lesbian and gay people with the privileges of marriage that are traditionally offered at the federal and state level. Partnership registration programs may be beneficial; however, they do not accord lesbian and gay people the full privileges of marriage.

3. Many of the ideas that I develop in this paper were formed in response to a Lesbian and Gay Rights Symposium held at Tulane Law School in October, 1990. My brief summary of many of the positions taken in that symposium cannot adequately describe the depth of the authors' analyses; I therefore strongly encourage the reader of this essay to read a longer discussion of the marriage debate in volume one of LAW & SEXUALITY: A REVIEW OF LESBIAN AND GAY LEGAL ISSUES. LAW & SEXUALITY is a student-run journal at Tulane Law School. It is one of the only journals in the United States devoted exclusively to lesbian and gay legal issues. The first issue will appear in July, 1991.

4. *See, e.g.*, Mary Dunlap, *The Lesbian/Gay Marriage Debate: A Microcosm of Our Hopes and*

subordination at the hands of the state. Moreover, opponents argue that there is no reason to assume that same-sex relationships would actually gain social legitimacy by receiving this token state sanction. Instead, lesbian and gay people would sacrifice some of their anonymity, making them even easier targets for discrimination.[5] Finally, some opponents argue that if marriage is available, lesbian and gay people would be under strong pressure to marry, because benefits would be available only on that basis.[6] Thus, they argue that we should fight for recognition of a broader definition of family but not tie that recognition to the institution of marriage.

Advocates of lesbian and gay marriage as a high priority argue that as long as lesbian and gay people are denied this privilege, they are denied full citizenship.[7] While they recognize the possible problems with embracing marriage, because of its patriarchal history, they also suggest that allowing lesbian and gay people to enter marriage would transform the institution. Marriage could become an institution of intimacy between equals if same-sex couples could marry.[8] Thus, attaining marriage for lesbian and gay people should be a priority, because that step would make marriage-dependent benefits available to lesbian and gay people while radicalizing the institution of marriage.

I will now tell you where I personally fit into this debate, since the personal is political. I will then apply an anti-essentialist[9] perspective to this debate. One reason that I am providing some personal history is to get to one of my sub-issues: labelling. I get tired of rigid gay/straight labels, which certainly do not apply to my life. I, therefore, increasingly find it useful to come out of the closet as a bisexual in order to question those rigid labels.

I was involved in an intimate, sexual relationship[10] with a woman for seven years from 1980 to 1987. During that time, I really hated the institution of marriage. I would refuse to go to weddings of my straight[11] friends, be-

---

Troubles in the Nineties, 1 LAW & SEXUALITY (forthcoming 1991).

   5. *See id.*

   6. *See* Nitya Duclos, *Some Complicating Thoughts About Same-Sex Marriage*, 1 LAW & SEXUALITY (forthcoming 1991).

   7. *See* Kenneth Karst, *The Freedom of Intimate Association*, 89 YALE L.J. 624 (1980).

   8. *See* Hunter, *supra* note 2.

   9. *See generally* Angela Harris, *Race and Essentialism in Feminist Legal Theory*, 42 STAN. L. REV. 581 (1990); ELIZABETH SPELMAN, INESSENTIAL WOMAN: PROBLEMS OF EXCLUSION IN FEMINIST THOUGHT (1988); Nitya Duclos, *Lessons of Difference: Feminist Theory in Cultural Diversity*, 38 BUFF. L. REV. 325 (1990); Maria Lugones & Elizabeth Spelman, *Have We Got a Theory for You! Feminist Theory, Cultural Imperialism and the Demand for "The Woman's Voice,"* 6 WOMEN'S STUD. INT'L F. 573 (1983).

   10. I should note that I don't know what the word "sexual" means in the context of an intimate relationship with a woman. My use of the word "sexual" is not intended to suggest any particular activities; it is only intended to indicate the high degree of intimacy in the relationship. I agree with Catharine MacKinnon's suggestion that we have no idea what the word sexual would mean if male-domination did not exist. *See* CATHARINE MACKINNON, TOWARD A FEMINIST THEORY OF THE STATE 126-54 (1989). Thus, I don't know what the word "sexual" should or does mean in any context, and, in particular, in the context of an intimate relationship with a woman. Nevertheless, I persist in using the word without intending to endorse its conventional meaning.

   11. I have trouble knowing what labels to use to describe my friends. Some of my friends who got married were committed heterosexuals who could not imagine a relationship with a person of the same sex. Others were bisexual and had been in intimate relationships with people of the same sex. I use the word

cause I felt that their marriages contributed to my own subordination. When straight friends got married, I usually contributed money in their name to the Louisiana Sexual Privacy Project,[12] telling them that I was contributing this money so that lesbian and gay people could ultimately enjoy the privileges that they enjoy. At that time, I thought that the best strategy for attaining equality from a feminist as well as a lesbian perspective was to get straight people to stop marrying rather than to change the law to permit lesbian and gay people to be able to marry. I was quite baffled as to why so many of my straight friends got married when they knew that marriage was an exclusive private club that didn't want me as a member.

About a year and a half later, in late 1988 (when I was no longer intimately involved in a relationship with a woman), I decided to spend a semester at the University of Toronto. I met a man during that time with whom I became intimately involved, and we began to explore how we could both live in the same country together. Canadian universities have a Canada-first policy with respect to permanent positions, so that it became clear that the University could probably hire me only if I married my male partner, and thereby became a Canadian. The United States has very restrictive immigration rules so that, again, we could only readily enter the United States together if we got married.[13] I had told my partner that I would never get married so long as lesbian and gay people could not get married. Although he is not a lawyer, my partner started to follow the news and learned that the Canadian Charter of Rights and Freedoms was being interpreted in ways that suggested that lesbian and gay people might soon be able to marry in Canada.[14] As we began to talk about

---

"straight" only to communicate that they were not same-sex couples. (Language is difficult; I don't want to call them opposite sex couples because the adjective "opposite" suggests a false bipolarization. In addition, "same sex" applies a false uniformity.)

12. The Louisiana Sexual Privacy Project is a project of the Louisiana affiliate of the American Civil Liberties Union. It was created sometime in 1985 to help provide funding for lesbian and gay rights cases.

13. When we were discussing how to live in the same country, we discovered the doubly coercive nature of our immigration laws. Had my partner been a woman, the United States, at one time, could have excluded him from entry for being a "homosexual." *See, e.g.*, Boutlier v. Immigration and Naturalization Service, 387 U.S. 118 (1967) (affirming exclusion of homosexuals under Immigration and Nationality Act of 1952). By contrast, if my male partner and I were to marry, he would be entitled to first-preference admission as a spouse. *See* Immigration and Nationality Act of 1952, as amended, 8 U.S.C. 1151(a)&(b) (1988) (spouses are immediate relatives who are not covered by numerical limitations). Thus, lesbian and gay people were excluded while married heterosexuals were given first preference. The Immigration Laws, therefore, encouraged people to be both heterosexual and married. In the past year, some modest progress to eliminate this coercion has occurred. The Immigration and Naturalization Act has been amended so that homosexuality is no longer a ground for exclusion. *See* Act of Nov. 29, 1990, Pub. L. No. 101-649, which no longer contains "sexual deviation" as a ground for exclusion. For further explanation, see H.R. No. 101-723(I), which states that "in order to make it clear that the United States does not view personal decisions about sexual orientation as a danger to other people in our society, the bill repeals the 'sexual deviation' exclusion ground." Although lesbian and gay people are no longer subject to absolute exclusion, they still are not permitted to enter the United States under the first preference for married people.

14. More recent court decisions, however, are not so promising. *See, e.g.*, R. v. Andrews, 65 O.R. 161 (2d) (Ct. App. 1988) (holding that Ontario Health Insurance Plan did not violate Canadian Charter of Rights and Freedoms by defining family so as not to include gay families). Nevertheless, changes may soon be occurring in Ontario under the leadership of the new premier, Bob Rae, who is a member of the New Democratic Party. Rae has already modified Ontario legislation so that public employees receive benefits without regard to sexual orientation. I do not know whether he plans to modify the marriage laws.

having a child, with my partner possibly staying home to look after the child on a part-time or full-time basis, it also became clear to me that society would treat us and the child coercively if we did not marry. For example, my partner would lose his health insurance in the United States if he went to less than full-time paid employment, and I could not cover him under my plan at work unless we were married. I talked to lots of my lesbian and gay friends who told me not to be a martyr on principle and go ahead and get married.[15] Thus, because of our society's coercive practices with respect to immigration and children, we got married in May 1990, and immigrated to the United States in August 1990. (Unfortunately, our plans to have children have been delayed as I have had two miscarriages.[16])

My own personal experience has confirmed my skepticism about embracing the institution of marriage. Marriage was not simply an available option for us—to be freely chosen. Instead, it was the only alternative available to us that would allow us to live together in the same county. It makes more sense to change institutions so that their benefits are not marriage-dependent rather than make lesbian and gay people eligible for these benefits only by getting married. If we eliminate marriage-dependent benefits then people can choose to embrace marriage for symbolic rather than legal or utilitarian reasons. For example, if benefits were available to self-defined family units, then handicapped people who live together and poor women with children who live together to share babysitting and household expenses could qualify for family-related benefits irrespective of whether they wanted to marry or even engage in intimate sexual activity.

A successful example of that strategy recently occurred in New York. Miguel Braschi had been evicted from his rent-controlled apartment after his male lover, Leslie Blanchard, died.[17] A state statute prohibited the eviction

---

15. To the extent that the reactions of my lesbian and gay friends have been negative, that reaction has more to do with the sex of my partner than with my embracing the institution of marriage. Some friends, for example, told me that they could no longer trust me or feel comfortable with me socially if I were involved with a man. Other friends said that I could no longer be a good role model for lesbians. Those of my friends who stood by me while I dated men were generally supportive of my marriage. They wanted me to be able to live and work in the United States on feminist and gay issues in a supportive personal environment. Nevertheless, I have never felt comfortable with my decision to enter the institution of marriage. Because I did not feel comfortable asking them to embrace this public institution with me and to take on the expenses of travelling to Canada, I chose not to invite any of my friends to our marriage ceremony. Interestingly, one of my lesbian friends told me that she wished that I had invited her to the ceremony because she would then have felt more certain that she was still part of my life. We have, however, subsequently spent a lot of private time together which, I believe, was a more meaningful way to demonstrate to her that she is still a major part of my life.

16. Many people may consider it inappropriate for me to share news about those miscarriages. I have done so quite deliberately because I think that our silence about the early stages of women's pregnancies is often destructive to women. Although half of all women apparently experience miscarriages and fifteen to twenty percent of all pregnancies end in miscarriages, there is enormous silence about this phenomenon. Women are told not to tell anyone that they are pregnant until the second trimester, thereby causing them to suffer in silence during the first trimester of their pregnancy if they are sick and nauseous or experience a miscarriage. By publicly sharing my own miscarriages, I hope to encourage other women to share their first-trimester pregnancy experiences and break the silence.

17. *See* Braschi v. Stahl Assoc.'s Co., 74 N.Y.2d 201, 543 N.E.2d 49, 544 N.Y.S.2d 784 (1989).

of a family member who was living with the deceased tenant at the time of the deceased's death. The New York Court of Appeals ruled that Braschi did qualify as a family member, defining a family as "two adult lifetime partners whose relationship is long term and characterized by an emotional and financial commitment and interdependence."[18] This definition was formulated so as to include lesbian and gay couples, as well as handicapped people or poor people who live together in order to share household expenses and responsibilities, whether or not those people engage in an intimate relationship.

Extending the *Braschi* theory, I would, therefore, rather change the immigration laws so that they are not marriage-dependant than work to permit lesbian and gay people to marry so that they can take advantage of that benefit. Similarly, I would like to work to change health care rules to enable workers to cover people other than their legal "spouses."[19]

Turning to an anti-essentialist perspective,[20] one problem with the account of the marriage debate that I have provided so far is that it is based on a middle-class model. Employer-based health insurance is not available to unemployed people; even employment does not guarantee access to insurance or affordable health care. Rent control statutes are only available to people who can afford an apartment. The immigration laws' spousal preference is not available unless you can meet certain financial criteria.[21] Thus, the institution of marriage acted coercively in my life because I had the financial resources to take advantage of the privileges of marriage. Miguel Braschi benefitted from a broad definition of family because he could afford to pay rent on a rent-controlled apartment. For poor people, marriage may offer few economic advantages. It should not surprise us to learn that marriage is a much less popular institution in poor communities than in middle-class communities. Thus, in the lives of poor lesbian and gay people, it is probably more important to talk about creating universal health insurance or housing than it is talk about how lesbian and gay people can get their partner on their health insurance plan.

---

18. *Id.* at 211, 543 N.E. 2d at 54, N.Y.S.2d at 789.

19. Professor Gene Schultz suggested to me that we should even go further—that there is no reason to tie benefits to "families." For example, as a faculty member at Tulane University, I can get free tuition for a member of my immediate family. But why shouldn't I be allowed to get free tuition for any designated member of the community at large? By limiting benefits to family members, we gain the privilege of extending benefits to people of the same socio-economic class as ourselves. A poor high school student in New Orleans is probably more deserving of free tuition to Tulane University than my husband, yet the university rules do not provide me with the option of extending the free tuition to the poor high school student. Just think how much we could improve the provision of health care if we each had the option of adding one non-related individual to our health insurance plans! At this time in our history, however, that kind of extension is virtually unthinkable.

20. This anti-essentialism critique has been strongly influenced by Nitya Duclos. *See* Duclos, *supra* note 6.

21. Because my spouse did not enter under a work permit, I had to file an affidavit of financial support on his behalf. In addition, we both had to promise that he would not seek to use the welfare system of the United States. The Immigration and Nationality Act does not appear, on its face, to require such disclosures; however, it gives discretion to the administrative agency to create certain documentary requirements. *See* 8 U.S.C. 1202(b).

The marriage debate in the lesbian and gay community reminds me a bit of the abortion debate in the feminist community. Many poor women say that they don't want to talk about abortion, they want to talk about how to get the state to stop coercing poor women into being sterilized, how to get the state to provide decent prenatal care for women so that their babies don't suffer from low birth weight.[22] Thus, I could imagine poor women in the lesbian community saying that they don't want to talk about marriage, they want to talk about universal health insurance and state-financed day care for children for whom women, gay or straight, almost always have primary social responsibility.

In sum, I think we should work to change the definition of family and the exclusive class-based ways that our society provides privileges, rather than encourage more people—gay or straight—to enter the institution of marriage. I do not oppose the passage of legislation that would open up marriage to lesbian and gay people; however, I would not encourage the lesbian and gay community to make such legislation a high priority item.

---

22. *See* ANGELA DAVIS, *Racism, Birth Control & Reproductive Rights*, in WOMEN, RACE, AND CLASS 159 (1981).

International Law

[12]

FEMINIST APPROACHES TO INTERNATIONAL LAW

By Hilary Charlesworth, Christine Chinkin and Shelley Wright*

I. INTRODUCTION

The development of feminist jurisprudence in recent years has made a rich and fruitful contribution to legal theory. Few areas of domestic law have avoided the scrutiny of feminist writers, who have exposed the gender bias of apparently neutral systems of rules.[1] A central feature of many western theories about law is that the law is an autonomous entity, distinct from the society it regulates. A legal system is regarded as different from a political or economic system, for example, because it operates on the basis of abstract rationality, and is thus universally applicable and capable of achieving neutrality and objectivity.[2] These attributes are held to give the law its special authority. More radical theories have challenged this abstract rationalism, arguing that legal analysis cannot be separated from the political, economic, historical and cultural context in which people live. Some theorists argue that the law functions as a system of beliefs that make social, political and economic inequalities appear natural.[3] Feminist jurisprudence builds on certain aspects of this critical strain in legal thought.[4] It is much more focused and concrete, however, and derives its theoretical force from immediate experience of the role of the legal system in creating and perpetuating the unequal position of women.

There is no single school of feminist jurisprudence. Most feminists would agree that a diversity of voices is not only valuable, but essential, and that the search for, or belief in, one view, one voice is unlikely to capture the reality of women's experience or gender inequality. "One true story" cannot be told, and the promise is of "the permanent partiality of feminist inquiry."[5] As Nancy Hartsock has

---

* Senior Lecturer, University of Melbourne Law School; Senior Lecturer, University of Sydney Law School; and Lecturer, University of Sydney Law School, respectively. The first version of this paper was presented at the Australian National University's International Law Seminar in May 1989. We thank Graeme Coss of the University of Sydney Law School for his excellent research assistance and our colleagues Hilary Astor, Andrew Byrnes and Jenny Morgan, who all made very helpful comments on our work in progress.

[1] *See, e.g.,* Olsen, *The Family and the Market,* 96 HARV. L. REV. 1497 (1983); Karst, *Women's Constitution,* 1984 DUKE L.J. 447; Lahey & Salter, *Corporate Law in Legal Theory and Legal Scholarship: From Classicism to Feminism,* 23 OSGOODE HALL L.J. 543 (1985); Scales, *The Emergence of Feminist Jurisprudence: An Essay,* 95 YALE L.J. 1373 (1986); Minow, *The Supreme Court October 1986 Term—Justice Engendered,* 101 HARV. L. REV. 47 (1987); Grbich, *The Position of Women in Family Dealing: the Australian Case,* 15 INT'L J. SOC. L. 309 (1987); Bender, *A Lawyer's Primer on Feminist Theory and Tort,* 38 J. LEGAL EDUC. 3, 29–30 (1988); Bartlett, *Feminist Legal Methods,* 103 HARV. L. REV. 831 (1990); R. GRAYCAR & J. MORGAN, THE HIDDEN GENDER OF LAW (1990).

[2] *See generally* D. N. MacCORMICK, LEGAL REASONING AND LEGAL THEORY (1978); J. W. HARRIS, LEGAL PHILOSOPHIES (1980).

[3] *E.g.,* Gordon, *New Developments in Legal Theory,* in THE POLITICS OF LAW 281 (D. Kairys ed. 1982).

[4] For a discussion of the major differences between feminist jurisprudence and the "liberal" and "critical" schools of jurisprudence, see West, *Jurisprudence and Gender,* 55 U. CHI. L. REV. 1 (1988); *see also* West, *Feminism, Critical Social Theory and Law,* 1989 U. CHI. LEGAL F. 59; Polan, *Towards a Theory of Law and Patriarchy,* in THE POLITICS OF LAW, *supra* note 3, at 294, 295–96.

[5] S. HARDING, THE SCIENCE QUESTION IN FEMINISM 194 (1986); *see also* Bartlett, *supra* note 1, at 880–87.

said, "At bottom, feminism is a mode of analysis, a method of approaching life and politics, a way of asking questions and searching for answers, rather than a set of political conclusions about the oppression of women."[6]

International law has thus far largely resisted feminist analysis. The concerns of public international law do not, at first sight, have any particular impact on women: issues of sovereignty, territory, use of force and state responsibility, for example, appear gender free in their application to the abstract entities of states. Only where international law is considered directly relevant to individuals, as with human rights law, have some specifically feminist perspectives on international law begun to be developed.[7]

In this article we question the immunity of international law to feminist analysis —why has gender not been an issue in this discipline?—and indicate the possibilities of feminist scholarship in international law. In the first section, we examine the problems of developing an *international* feminist perspective. We then outline the male organizational and normative structure of the international legal system. We go on to apply feminist analyses developed in the context of domestic law to various international legal principles. Our approach requires looking behind the abstract entities of states to the actual impact of rules on women within states. We argue that both the structures of international lawmaking and the content of the

---

[6] Hartsock, *Feminist Theory and the Development of Revolutionary Strategy*, in CAPITALIST PATRIARCHY AND THE CASE FOR SOCIALIST FEMINISM 56, 58 (Z. R. Eisenstein ed. 1979); *see also* Rhode, *Gender and Jurisprudence: An Agenda for Research*, 56 U. CINN. L. REV. 521, 522 (1987); Gross, *What is Feminist Theory?*, in FEMINIST CHALLENGES: SOCIAL AND POLITICAL THEORY 190, 196–97 (C. Pateman & E. Gross eds. 1986). Some feminists dispute this description of feminism. Catharine MacKinnon, for example, has argued:

> Inequality on the basis of sex, women share. It is women's collective condition. The first task of a movement for social change is to face one's condition and name it. The failure to face and criticize the reality of women's condition, a failure of idealism and denial, is a failure of feminism in its liberal forms. The failure to move beyond criticism, a failure of determinism and radical paralysis, is a failure of feminism in its left forms. . . . As sexual inequality is gendered as man and woman, gender inequality is sexualized as dominance and subordination. . . . The next step is to recognize that male forms of power over women are affirmatively embodied as individual rights in law.

C. MACKINNON, TOWARD A FEMINIST THEORY OF THE STATE 241–44 (1989).

Some continental European, particularly French, feminists have pursued a different set of concerns from those of Anglo-American feminists. They have undertaken the task of deconstructing the dominant masculine modes of speech and writing. "We must reinterpret the whole relationship between the subject and discourse, the subject and the world, the subject and the cosmic, the microcosmic and the macrocosmic," writes Luce Irigaray. "And the first thing to say is that, even when aspiring to a universal or neutral state, this subject has always been written in the masculine form . . . ." Irigaray, *Sexual Difference*, in FRENCH FEMINIST THOUGHT: A READER 118, 119 (T. Moi ed. 1987). Although male language and social structures have also concerned Anglo-American feminists, they have generally not approached the issue by focusing on a wholly new type of discourse in which new feminine meanings, associated with the undiscovered potential of the female body, are seen as the potential source of a reconstructed world. *Id.* at 129. A brief introduction to French feminist thought can be found in Dallery, *The Politics of Writing (The) Body: Ecriture Feminine*, in GENDER/BODY/KNOWLEDGE 52 (A. M. Jaggar & S. R. Bordo eds. 1989).

[7] *E.g.*, Holmes, *A Feminist Analysis of the Universal Declaration of Human Rights*, in BEYOND DOMINATION: NEW PERSPECTIVES ON WOMEN AND PHILOSOPHY 250 (C. Gould ed. 1983); A. Byrnes, *Can the Categories Fit the Crimes? The Possibilities for a Feminist Transformation of International Human Rights Law* (paper delivered at Conference on International Human Rights and Feminism, New York, Nov. 18, 1988); Neuwirth, *Towards a Gender-Based Approach to Human Rights Violations*, 9 WHITTIER L. REV. 399 (1987); Bunch, *Women's Rights as Human Rights: Toward a Re-vision of Human Rights*, 12 HUM. RTS. Q. 486 (1990).

rules of international law privilege men; if women's interests are acknowledged at all, they are marginalized. International law is a thoroughly gendered system.

By challenging the nature and operation of international law and its context, feminist legal theory can contribute to the progressive development of international law. A feminist account of international law suggests that we inhabit a world in which men of all nations have used the statist system to establish economic and nationalist priorities to serve male elites, while basic human, social and economic needs are not met. International institutions currently echo these same priorities. By taking women seriously and describing the silences and fundamentally skewed nature of international law, feminist theory can identify possibilities for change.

II. DIFFERENT VOICES IN INTERNATIONAL LAW

In this section we examine the notion of a "different voice" in the international context: first, the relationship between feminist and Third World challenges to international law; and second, whether the voices of women from the developed and developing worlds have anything in common.

Much feminist scholarship has been concerned with the identification of a distinctive women's voice that has been overwhelmed and underestimated in traditional epistemologies.[8] Rehabilitation of this voice challenges the objectivity and authority of male-designed disciplines. Feminist legal scholars have drawn in particular on the work of psychologist Carol Gilligan[9] to investigate whether there is a distinctively feminine way of thinking or solving problems: do women have a "different voice," a different way of reasoning, from that of men?

Gilligan's research into childhood development indicates that young girls, when asked to solve a moral dilemma set in a hypothetical problem, typically think about, and react to, the problem differently than boys.[10] Girls tend to invoke an "ethic of care"[11] and see things in terms of relationships, responsibility, caring, context, communication; boys rely on an "ethic of rights" or "justice"[12] and analyze problems in abstract terms of right and wrong, fairness, logic, rationality, winners and losers, ignoring context and relationships. Traditional psychological theory has regarded the male type of reasoning as more "advanced" than the female pattern.

Gilligan's work has been useful to a critical analysis of legal reasoning, which lays claim to abstract, objective decision making. If legal reasoning simply reproduces a masculine type of reasoning, its objectivity and authority are reduced. Feminists have been able to describe the possibility of an equally valid "feminine" reasoning based on factors usually considered irrelevant to legal thinking.[13] Alter-

---

[8] *See, e.g.,* E. SHOWALTER, A LITERATURE OF THEIR OWN: BRITISH WOMEN NOVELISTS FROM BRONTË TO LESSING (1977); R. RUETHER, SEXISM AND GOD-TALK: TOWARD A FEMINIST THEOLOGY (1983).

[9] C. GILLIGAN, IN A DIFFERENT VOICE: PSYCHOLOGICAL THEORY AND WOMEN'S DEVELOPMENT (1982).

[10] *Id.* at 25–51.   [11] *Id.* at 164.

[12] *Id.* at 164, 174.

[13] *See, e.g.,* Menkel-Meadow, *Portia in a Different Voice: Speculations on Women's Lawyering Process,* 1 BERKELEY WOMEN'S L.J. 39 (1985); idem., *Excluded Voices: New Voices in the Legal Profession Making New Voices in the Law,* 42 U. MIAMI L. REV. 29 (1987); Sherry, *Civic Virtue and the Feminine Voice in Constitutional Adjudication,* 72 VA. L. REV. 543 (1986). *Cf.* Bartlett, *supra* note 1, at 854–58. For an argument that Hans Morgenthau's influential work in international relations, with its hierarchical ordering of morality, parallels the work of the psychologist Lawrence Kohlberg, which is challenged by Carol

native, nonlitigious, dispute resolution and nonconfrontational negotiation techniques are sometimes proposed as examples of such an approach.[14]

The notion of women's "different voice" has been criticized by some feminist scholars.[15] Although Gilligan attributes the difference in masculine and feminine voices primarily to gendered child-rearing practices,[16] the identification of women with caring, conciliation and concern with personal relationships, writes Carol Smart, "slides uncomfortably and exceedingly quickly into socio-biologism which merely puts women back in their place."[17] And Catharine MacKinnon argues: "For women to affirm difference, when difference means dominance, as it does with gender, means to affirm the qualities and characteristics of powerlessness."[18] Our concern here with women's voices, however, is to identify not so much a distinctive feminine morality as distinctive women's experiences, which are factored out of the international legal process and thus prevent this discipline from having universal validity.

Feminist and Third World Challenges to International Law

Are women's voices and values already present in international law through the medium of the Third World? The divisions between developed and developing nations (and between socialist and nonsocialist states) have generated a lively debate over the universality of principles of international law.[19] One consequence of decolonization has been the great increase in the number of independent states, particularly in Africa and Asia. These states have challenged both substantive norms of international law and the traditional lawmaking processes as either disadvantageous to them or inadequate to their needs.[20] The impact of this challenge to assumptions about the objective neutrality of norms by showing them to support western values and interests has been substantial.[21] Developing states have also emphasized decision making through negotiation and consensus, and through the use of nontraditional methods of lawmaking such as the "soft law" of General Assembly resolutions.[22] These techniques find some parallel in the types

---

Gilligan, see Tickner, *Hans Morgenthau's Principles of Political Realism: A Feminist Reformulation,* 17 MILLENNIUM 429, 433 (1989).

[14] *See, e.g.,* Menkel-Meadow, *Towards Another View of Legal Negotiation: The Structure of Problem Solving,* 31 U.C.L.A. L. REV. 754 (1984); Rifkin, *Mediation from a Feminist Perspective,* 2 LAW & INEQUALITY 21 (1984). Not all legal feminists support such an approach. *E.g.,* Bottomley, *What is happening to family law? A feminist critique of conciliation,* in WOMEN IN LAW 162 (J. Brophy & C. Smart eds. 1985); Shaffer, *Divorce Mediation: a Feminist Perspective,* 46 U. TORONTO FAC. L. REV. 162 (1988).

[15] For a critical analysis of the empirical work of Gilligan and her notion of a dichotomy between male and female moral reasoning, see Mednick, *On the Politics of Psychological Constructs,* 44 AM. PSYCHOLOGIST 1118, 1119–20 (1989); *see also* C. FUCHS EPSTEIN, DECEPTIVE DISTINCTIONS: SEX, GENDER, AND THE SOCIAL ORDER 76–83 (1988).

[16] C. GILLIGAN, *supra* note 9, at 171; *see generally* N. CHODOROW, THE REPRODUCTION OF MOTHERING: PSYCHOANALYSIS AND THE SOCIOLOGY OF GENDER (1978).

[17] C. SMART, FEMINISM AND THE POWER OF LAW 75 (1989).

[18] C. MACKINNON, FEMINISM UNMODIFIED: DISCOURSES ON LIFE AND LAW 38–39 (1987). *Compare* Gilligan, *Reply [to Critics],* 11 SIGNS 324 (1986).

[19] *See, e.g.,* A. CASSESE, INTERNATIONAL LAW IN A DIVIDED WORLD 105–25 (1986).

[20] *See generally* THIRD WORLD ATTITUDES TOWARD INTERNATIONAL LAW: AN INTRODUCTION (F. Snyder & S. Sathirathai eds. 1987).

[21] *See* A. CASSESE, *supra* note 19, at 105–25.

[22] *See* Chinkin, *The Challenge of Soft Law: Development and Change in International Law,* 38 INT'L & COMP. L.Q. 850 (1989); Bedjaoui, *Poverty of the International Legal Order,* in INTERNATIONAL LAW: A CONTEMPORARY PERSPECTIVE 152, 157–58 (R. Falk, F. Kratochwil & S. Mendlovitz eds. 1985).

of dispute resolution sometimes associated with the "different voice" of women. In his study of American diplomacy in the first half of this century, George Kennan implied that nonwestern views of international relations and the feminine were linked:

> If . . . instead of making ourselves slaves of the concepts of international law and morality, we would confine these concepts to the unobtrusive, almost feminine function of the gentle civilizer of national self-interest in which they find their true value—if we were able to do these things in our dealings with the peoples of the East, then, I think, posterity might look back upon our efforts with fewer and less troubled questions.[23]

This apparent similarity between the perspective culturally identified with women and that of developing nations has been studied in a different context. In *The Science Question in Feminism*, Sandra Harding notes the "curious coincidence of African and feminine 'world views' "[24] and examines them to determine whether they could be the basis of a "successor," alternative view of science and epistemology. Harding observes the association of the feminine with the second half of the set of conceptual dichotomies that provide the essential framework for traditional, Enlightenment science and epistemology: "Reason vs. emotion and social value, mind vs. body, culture vs. nature, self vs. others, objectivity vs. subjectivity, knowing vs. being."[25] In the generation of scientific truth, the "feminine" parts of these dichotomies are considered subordinate. Harding then notes the similarity of this pattern and the description of the "African world view" identified by scholars in other disciplines. This world view is characterized by "a conception of the self as intrinsically connected with, as part of, both the community and nature."[26] The attribution to women and Africans of "a concept of the self as dependent on others, as defined through relationships to others, as perceiving self-interest to lie in the welfare of the relational complex," permits the ascription to these groups of an ethic based on preservation of relationships and an epistemology uniting "hand, brain and heart." These perceptions contrast with the "European" and male view of the self as autonomous, separate from nature and from others, and with its associated ethics of "rule-governed adjudication of competing rights between self-interested, autonomous others" and its view of knowledge as an entity with a separate, "objective" existence.[27]

There are problems in identifying these subordinate voices. For example: How far are these world views the product of colonial and patriarchal conceptual schemes?[28] Are they in fact generally held by the groups they are ascribed to?[29] How accurate are contrasting schemata in capturing reality?[30] Harding argues that the linkage of the two discourses may nevertheless be useful as providing "categories of challenge"—that is, naming "what is absent in the thinking and

---

[23] G. KENNAN, AMERICAN DIPLOMACY, 1900–1950, at 53–54 (1953); *cf.* Jaquette, *Power as Ideology: A Feminist Analysis,* in WOMEN'S VIEWS OF THE POLITICAL WORLD OF MEN 9, 22 (J. Stiehm ed. 1984) (noting the similarity between the "female" strategy of persuasion rather than confrontation and the strategies of small states in a weak position in the international system).

[24] S. HARDING, *supra* note 5, at 165.   [25] *Id.*

[26] *Id.* at 170.   [27] *Id.* at 171.

[28] *Id.* at 172–73; *see also* C. MACKINNON, *supra* note 18, at 39–40.

[29] S. HARDING, *supra* note 5, at 173–74.   [30] *Id.* at 174–76.

social activities of men and Europeans" and stimulating analysis of how social orders based on gender and race can come into being.[31]

More general analogies have been drawn between the position of Third World states and that of women. Both groups are said to encounter the paternalist attitude that they must be properly trained to fit into the world of developed countries and men, respectively.[32] Both feminists and developing nations have also resisted assimilation to prevailing standards and have argued for radical change, emphasizing cooperation rather than individual self-advancement.[33] Both groups have identified unilinear structures that allow their systematic domination and the development of apparently generally applicable theories from very narrow perspectives.[34]

Thus far, however, the "different voice" of developing nations in international law has shown little concern for feminist perspectives. The power structures and decision-making processes in these societies are every bit as exclusive of women as in western societies and the rhetoric of domination and subjugation has not encompassed women, who remain the poorest and least privileged.[35] Thus, at the United Nations Mid-Decade for Women Conference in Copenhagen in 1985, an Indian delegate could argue that since he had experienced colonialism, he knew that it could not be equated with sexism.[36] Although the developing nations' challenge to international law has been fundamental, it has focused on disparities in economic position and has not questioned the silence of half the world's population in the creation of international law or the unequal impact of rules of international law on women.[37] Indeed, this challenge to the European origins of international law and many of its assumptions may have had an adverse effect on the development of a gender-based analysis of international law precisely because of the further level of confrontation it is assumed such an analysis would cause.

Feminism in the First and Third Worlds

An alternative, feminist analysis of international law must take account of the differing perspectives of First and Third World feminists.[38] Third World femi-

---

[31] *Id.* at 186.

[32] Brock-Utne, *Women and Third World Countries—What Do We Have in Common?*, 12 WOMEN'S STUD. INT'L F. 495, 496–97 (1989).

[33] *Id.* at 497.   [34] *Id.* at 500–01.

[35] K. JAYAWARDENA, FEMINISM AND NATIONALISM IN THE THIRD WORLD *passim* (1986); C. EN-LOE, MAKING FEMINIST SENSE OF INTERNATIONAL POLITICS: BANANAS, BEACHES AND BASES 42–64 (1989).

[36] *Quoted in* C. BUNCH, PASSIONATE POLITICS 297 (1987). Another example of this gender-blind focus is the comment of Nehru cited by Cassese to exemplify the developing world's rejection of the traditional legal order: "The spirit of the present age is opposed to any kind of domination of one over the other, whether it is national domination, economic, class or racial. There is a strong urge to resist this kind of domination." T. MENDE, CONVERSATIONS WITH MR NEHRU 44 (1956), *quoted in* A. CASSESE, *supra* note 19, at 56.

[37] In her study of the "curious coincidence" between African and feminine world views, Sandra Harding also notes that neither Africanists nor feminists have acknowledged the parallels in each other's epistemologies. S. HARDING, *supra* note 5, at 177–79.

[38] There are, of course, significant differences *within* the "First" and "Third" World feminist movements. Although the discussion here is on a general level, these differences need to be studied in any detailed examination of international law. *See* Lazreg, *Feminism and Difference: The Perils of Writing as a Woman on Women in Algeria*, 14 FEMINIST STUD. 81 (1988); Mohanty, *Under Western Eyes: Feminist Scholarship and Colonial Discourses*, 30 FEMINIST REV. 61 (1988); Strathern, *An Awkward Relationship: The Case of Feminism and Anthropology*, 12 SIGNS 276 (1987).

nists operate in particularly difficult contexts. Not only does the dominant European, male discourse of law, politics and science exclude the kind of discourse characterized by the phrase "a different voice," both female *and* non-European, but also feminist concerns in the Third World are largely ignored or misunderstood by western feminists.[39] Western feminism began as a demand for the right of women to be treated as men. Whether in campaigns for equal rights or for special rights such as the right to abortion, western feminists have sought guarantees from the state that, as far as is physically possible, they will be placed in the same position as men. This quest does not always have the same attraction for nonwestern women. For example, the western feminist preoccupation with a woman's right to abortion is of less significance to many Third World women because population-control programs often deny them the chance to have children.[40] Moreover, "nonpositivist" cultures, such as those of Asia and Africa, are just as masculinist, or even more so, than the western cultures in which the language of law and science developed.[41] In the context of international law (and, indeed, domestic law), then, Third World feminists are obliged to communicate in the western rationalist language of the law, in addition to challenging the intensely patriarchal "different voice" discourse of traditional non-European societies. In this sense, feminism in the Third World is doubly at odds with the dominant male discourse of its societies.

The legacy of colonial rule has been particularly problematic for many women in the Third World. Local women were seen as constituting a pool of cheap labor for industries, agriculture and domestic service, and local men were often recruited to work away from their families. Local women also provided sex to the colonizers, especially where there was a shortage of women from home.[42] To local men, the position of their women was symbolic of and mirrored their own domination: while colonialism meant allowing the colonial power to abuse colonized women, resistance to colonialism encompassed reasserting the colonized males' power over their women.[43]

Nationalist movements typically pursued wider objectives than merely to transfer power from white colonial rulers to indigenous people: they were concerned with restructuring the hierarchies of power and control, reallocating wealth within society, and creating nothing less than a new society based on equality and nonexploitation. It was inevitable that feminist objectives, including the restructuring of society across gender lines, would cause tension when set beside nationalist objectives that sounded similar but so frequently discounted the feminist perspective.

Nevertheless, local women were needed in the fight against colonialism, which imposed numerous restrictions on them. The Sri Lankan feminist Kumari Jayawardena has shown that for many nationalists the objective of overthrowing

---

[39] The tension between some First and Third World feminists over the correct approach to the issue of female genital mutilation is an example. *See* Savane, *Why we are against the International Campaign*, 40 INT'L CHILD WELFARE REV. 38 (1979); R. MORGAN, SISTERHOOD IS GLOBAL 1–37 (1984); Boulware-Miller, *Female Circumcision: Challenge to the Practice as a Human Rights Violation*, 8 HARV. WOMEN'S L.J. 155 (1985).

[40] *See* C. Bulbeck, Hearing the Difference: First and Third World Feminisms 3–6 (paper delivered at Women's Studies Conference, University of Melbourne, September 1990).

[41] *See* Narayan, *The Project of Feminist Epistemology: Perspectives from a Nonwestern Feminist*, in GENDER/BODY/KNOWLEDGE, *supra* note 6, at 256.

[42] C. ENLOE, *supra* note 35, at 65–92.   [43] *Id.* at 44.

colonial rule required both the creation of a national identity around which people could rally and the institution of internal reforms designed to present themselves as western and "civilized," and therefore worthy of self-rule.[44] Thus, both the colonizers and the local men demanded that local women be modeled on western women. On the one hand, "ladylike" (western) behavior was regarded as a "mainstay of imperialist behavior," as "feminine respectability" taught the colonized and colonists alike that "foreign conquest was right and necessary."[45] On the other hand, many local males believed that "women needed to be adequately Westernized and educated in order to enhance the modern and 'civilized' image of their country."[46] Of course, the model handed down by western civilization embraced all the restrictions imposed on western women.

The need to rally around a national identity, however, required that local women, even while being groomed on the western model, also take it upon themselves to be "the guardians of national culture, indigenous religion and family traditions."[47] These institutions in many instances repressed women. Halliday points out that, despite the belief that the spread of nationalism and nationalist ideas is beneficial to women, "nationalist movements subordinate women in a particular definition of their role and place in society, [and] enforce conformity to values that are often male-defined."[48] Women could find themselves dominated by foreign rule, economic exploitation and aggression, as well as by local entrenched patriarchies, religious structures and traditional rulers.

These conflicting historical perspectives highlight a significant problem for many feminists in the developing world.[49] Feminist and women's movements have been active in numerous developing countries since at least the late nineteenth and early twentieth centuries,[50] but too often women in nationalist movements have had to choose between pressing their own concerns and seeing those concerns crushed by the weight of the overall struggle against colonial rule.[51] Feminists in nonwestern countries and, before independence, in the nationalist movements, were open to attack from their own people for accepting decadent western capitalism, embracing the neocolonialism of a foreign culture, and turning away from their own culture, ideology and religion. The explicit or implicit addition was that their acceptance of western feminist values was diverting them from the revolutionary struggle against the colonial power. In other contexts, the emanci-

---

[44] "Western secular thought is a crucial factor in fashioning a consciousness and devising structures that would make possible an escape from the domination of Western political power." K. JAYAWARDENA, *supra* note 35, at 6.

[45] C. ENLOE, *supra* note 35, at 48.   [46] K. JAYAWARDENA, *supra* note 35, at 8.

[47] *Id.* at 14.

[48] Halliday, *Hidden from International Relations: Women and the International Arena*, 17 MILLENNIUM 419, 424 (1988).

[49] *See* Chinkin, *A Gendered Perspective to the International Use of Force,* 12 AUSTL. Y.B. INT'L L. (1992, forthcoming).

[50] K. JAYAWARDENA, *supra* note 35, gives accounts of feminist movements in Turkey, Egypt, Iran, Afghanistan, India, Sri Lanka, Indonesia, the Philippines, China, Vietnam, Korea and Japan. Cf. J. CHAFETZ & A. DWORKIN, FEMALE REVOLT: WOMEN'S MOVEMENTS IN THE WORLD AND HISTORICAL PERSPECTIVE (1986), especially chapter 4, which describes, inter alia, "first wave" women's movements in China, Japan, India, Indonesia, Persia/Iran, Egypt, the Caribbean islands, Mexico, Argentina, Brazil, Chile, Peru and Uruguay.

[51] This is not an experience unique to Third World women. See the account of attitudes toward women of the revolutionary movements in the United States in the 1960s, in R. MORGAN, GOING TOO FAR: THE PERSONAL CHRONICLE OF A FEMINIST (1977).

pation of women has been regarded as a Communist tactic to be resisted by resort to traditional values.[52] Problems of loyalty and priorities arise in this context that do not exist for western feminists. Many Third World feminist movements either were begun in cooperation with nationalistic, anticolonial movements or operate in solidarity with the process of nation building.[53] Overt political repression is a further problem for feminism in the Third World. In nonwestern cultures there may be a much greater fear and hatred of the feminine, especially when it is not strictly confined to the domestic sphere, than is apparent or expressed in western society.[54]

Despite differences in history and culture, feminists from all worlds share a central concern: their domination by men. Birgit Brock-Utne writes: "Though patriarchy is hierarchical and men of different classes, races or ethnic groups have different places in the patriarchy, they are united in their shared relationship of dominance over their women. And, despite their unequal resources, they are dependent on each other to maintain that domination."[55] Issues raised by Third World feminists, however, require a reorientation of feminism to deal with the problems of the most oppressed women, rather than those of the most privileged. Nevertheless, the constant theme in both western and Third World feminism is the challenge to structures that permit male domination, although the form of the challenge and the male structures may differ from society to society. An international feminist perspective on international law will have as its goal the rethinking and revision of those structures and principles which exclude most women's voices.

III. The Masculine World of International Law

In this section we argue that the international legal order is virtually impervious to the voices of women and propose two related explanations for this: the organizational and normative structures of international law.

The Organizational Structure of International Law

The structure of the international legal order reflects a male perspective and ensures its continued dominance. The primary subjects of international law are states and, increasingly, international organizations. In both states and international organizations the invisibility of women is striking. Power structures within

---

[52] An example is the position of women in Afghanistan since 1979. *See, e.g., An Afghan Exile, Her School and Hopes for Future*, N.Y. Times, June 12, 1988, §1, at 14, col. 1:

> Westerners who have studied Afghan society, as well as many Afghan men, say education for women has been damaged by its association with the Communist coup and the subsequent Kabul regimes. . . .
>
> The Government that took power after the coup in April 1978 immediately associated itself with feminism . . . . Women's groups became propaganda tools for the Kabul regime . . . .

[53] This problem now may also arise in Central and Eastern Europe, where feminists face unique problems in their own search for development and democracy.

[54] *See, e.g.*, H. AFSHAR, WOMEN, STATE AND IDEOLOGY: STUDIES FROM AFRICA AND ASIA 4 (1987). Examples of women who are politically active, often regarding issues that would be characterized in the West as feminist, and who have been punished for it through arrest, torture and detention are found in Singapore and Malaysia in 1987. On Singapore, see ASIA WATCH, SILENCING ALL CRITICS (1989). On Malaysia, see AMNESTY INTERNATIONAL, "OPERATION LALLANG": DETENTION WITHOUT TRIAL UNDER THE INTERNAL SECURITY ACT (1988).

[55] Brock-Utne, *supra* note 32, at 500.

governments are overwhelmingly masculine: women have significant positions of power in very few states, and in those where they do, their numbers are minuscule.[56] Women are either unrepresented or underrepresented in the national and global decision-making processes.

States are patriarchal structures not only because they exclude women from elite positions and decision-making roles, but also because they are based on the concentration of power in, and control by, an elite and the domestic legitimation of a monopoly over the use of force to maintain that control.[57] This foundation is reinforced by international legal principles of sovereign equality, political independence and territorial integrity and the legitimation of force to defend those attributes.

International organizations are functional extensions of states that allow them to act collectively to achieve their objectives. Not surprisingly, their structures replicate those of states, restricting women to insignificant and subordinate roles. Thus, in the United Nations itself, where the achievement of nearly universal membership is regarded as a major success of the international community, this universality does not apply to women.

Article 8 was included in the United Nations Charter to ensure the legitimacy of women as permanent staff members of international organizations. Article 8 states: "The United Nations shall place no restrictions on the eligibility of men and women to participate in any capacity and under conditions of equality in its principal and subsidiary organs." While there was no overt opposition to the concept of gender equality at the 1945 San Francisco Conference, which drafted the Charter, some delegates considered the provision superfluous and said that it would be "absurd" to put anything so "self-evident" into the Charter. However, at the insistence of the Committee of Women's Organizations, Article 8 was included. It was phrased in the negative, rather than as an affirmative obligation to include women, as the right to choose delegates and representatives to international organizations was thought to belong to nation-states, whose freedom of choice was not to be impeded in any way.[58] In reality, women's appointments within the United Nations have not attained even the limited promise of Article 8.[59] The Group on Equal Rights for Women in the United Nations has observed

---

[56] In March 1991, women headed their country's government in 4 of the 159 member states of the United Nations. In mid-1989, at cabinet level only 3.5% of the ministries in 155 countries were held by women, and 99 nations had no women ministers. UN DEP'T OF PUBLIC INFORMATION, UNITED NATIONS FOCUS: WOMEN IN POLITICS: STILL THE EXCEPTION?, November 1989. *See generally* Halliday, *supra* note 48. States are slow to make women permanent representatives to the United Nations: in March 1990, 4 out of 149 were women. The four states represented by women were Barbados, New Zealand, Senegal and Trinidad and Tobago. The names of the permanent representatives of ten nations were not available.

[57] *See* B. REARDON, SEXISM AND THE WAR SYSTEM 15 (1985).

[58] *See* R. B. RUSSELL, A HISTORY OF THE UNITED NATIONS CHARTER 793–94 n.24 (1958); Editorial, *The United Nations' Women at 40*, EQUAL TIME, 40th Special Anniversary Issue, 1985, at 1.

[59] In 1946 the Commission on the Status of Women was established to promote the equal rights of women and to eliminate sex discrimination. ESC Res. 2/11 (June 21, 1946). By 1975, the level of female participation in professional positions within the United Nations and its specialized agencies was so low that one of the goals of the United Nations Decade for Women (1976–1985) was to improve female representation in the sought-after professional posts subject to geographic distribution. "It is on these geographic posts which most of the attention of the General Assembly's Fifth Committee is focused because with these jobs goes the power." EQUAL TIME, July 1985, at 5. On the "renewed commitment by the international community to the advancement of women and the elimination of gender bias," see Forward-Looking Strategies for the Advancement of Women to the Year

that "gender racism" is practiced in UN personnel policies "every week, every month, every year."[60]

Women are excluded from all major decision making by international institutions on global policies and guidelines, despite the often disparate impact of those decisions on women. Since 1985, there has been some improvement in the representation of women in the United Nations and its specialized agencies.[61] It has been estimated, however, that "at the present rate of change it will take almost 4 more decades (until 2021) to reach equality (i.e.: 50% of professional jobs held by women)."[62] This situation was recently described as "grotesque."[63]

The silence and invisibility of women also characterizes those bodies with special functions regarding the creation and progressive development of international law. Only one woman has sat as a judge on the International Court of Justice[64] and no woman has ever been a member of the International Law Com-

---

2000 (adopted by the World Conference of the UN Decade for Women, Nairobi, Kenya, July 15–26, 1985), UN Doc. A/CONF. 116/12 (1985).

In 1978 a target of 25% women in professional UN posts by 1982 was established. It had not been reached by 1986. Stephen Lewis, then Ambassador and Permanent Representative of Canada to the United Nations, said in the Fifth Committee of the General Assembly: "Progress in the field of women's opportunities and rights in this arena . . . is so minutely incremental, it's like a parody of social change." EQUAL TIME, July 1985, at 5. The target was subsequently reformulated by the General Assembly to 30% by 1990, and then to 35% by 1995.

[60] EQUAL TIME, March 1986, at 8–9. A few of the UN agencies deserve special mention. Women are the primary suppliers of child care throughout the world, yet in 1989 the United Nations Children's Fund, the agency responsible for the welfare of children, had 4 senior women officials out of a total of 29. More than half the food grown in Africa is produced by women (*see* S. CHARLTON, WOMEN IN THIRD WORLD DEVELOPMENT 61 (1984)), yet the Food and Agriculture Organization had no women senior officials out of 51 positions in 1989. Health issues, especially infant and child mortality rates, are a major concern of women, yet in 1989 the World Health Organization employed at most 4 senior female officials out of 42 overall. In all situations of economic dysfunction, women and children suffer the most (*see* Riley, *Why are Women so Poor?*, EQUAL TIME, March 1987, at 18; *cf.* A. DWORKIN, RIGHT WING WOMEN 151–52 (1983)); yet there were no senior women decision makers in the International Monetary Fund in 1989. The majority of the world's refugees are women, but in 1989 only 1 of the 28 senior posts in the Office of the United Nations High Commissioner for Refugees was held by a woman. In 1990 the first woman High Commissioner, Professor Sadako Ogata, was appointed.

[61] In 1985 the Secretary-General appointed a Co-ordinator for the Improvement of the Status of Women to a term of 12 months. This period was subsequently extended. The Secretary-General's report, Review and Appraisal of the Implementation of the Nairobi Forward-Looking Strategies for the Advancement of Women, UN Doc. E/CN.6/1990/5 [hereinafter Nairobi Review], indicates that between 1984 and 1988 the total increase in the representation of women in professional and management positions in the United Nations was 3.6%, to a total of 21% of the professional staff. At the senior management level in 1988, however, only 4% of the staff were women. *Id.* at 84–86. In March 1990 the figure for women in posts subject to geographical distribution was 27.7%. UN REV., August 1990, at 4. Although by the mid-eighties over 40% of the Secretariat staff were women, they were mainly in lower-status secretarial and clerical positions. UNITED NATIONS, DEP'T OF INTERNAT'L ECONOMIC AND SOCIAL AFFAIRS, COMPENDIUM OF STATISTICS AND INDICATORS ON THE SITUATION OF WOMEN 1986, at 558–77 (Statistical Office Social Statistics and Indicators Series K, No. 5, 1989). The important and prestigious positions of Under-Secretary-General and Assistant Secretary-General are almost entirely held by men. In 1990 two women held the position of Under-Secretary-General and no women were Assistant Secretaries-General.

[62] EQUAL TIME, July 1985, at 5.

[63] B. URQUHART & E. CHILDERS, A WORLD IN NEED OF LEADERSHIP: TOMORROW'S UNITED NATIONS 29 (1990); *see also id.* at 61.

[64] Mme. Suzanne Bastid was a judge *ad hoc* in Application for Revision and Interpretation of the Judgment of 24 February 1982 in the Case concerning the Continental Shelf (Tunisia/Libyan Arab Jamahiriya) (Tunisia v. Libya), 1985 ICJ REP. 192 (Judgment of Dec. 10).

mission. Critics have frequently pointed out that the distribution of judges on the Court does not reflect the makeup of the international community, a concern that peaked after the decision in the *South West Africa* cases in 1966.[65] Steps have since been taken to improve "the representation of the main forms of civilization and of the principal legal systems of the world"[66] on the Court, but not in the direction of representing women, half of the world's population.

Despite the common acceptance of human rights as an area in which attention can be directed toward women, they are still vastly underrepresented on UN human rights bodies.[67] The one committee that has all women members, the Committee on the Elimination of Discrimination against Women (CEDAW Committee), the monitoring body for the Convention on the Elimination of All Forms of Discrimination against Women (Women's Convention),[68] has been criticized for its "disproportionate" representation of women by the United Nations Economic and Social Council (ECOSOC). When it considered the CEDAW Committee's sixth report, ECOSOC called upon the state parties to nominate both female and male experts for election to the committee.[69] Thus, as regards the one committee dedicated to women's interests, where women *are* well represented, efforts have been made to decrease female participation, while the much more common dominance of men in other United Nations bodies goes unremarked. The CEDAW Committee in fact rejected ECOSOC's recommendation on various grounds, including the fear that it might open the gates to a flood of men, diluting the women's majority and undermining the committee's effectiveness. The representatives believed that the state parties and ECOSOC should direct their attention to equality of representation elsewhere before seeking to interfere with the membership of this committee.[70]

---

[65] South West Africa, Second Phase (Ethiopia v. S. Afr.; Liberia v. S. Afr.), 1966 ICJ REP. 6 (Judgment of July 18).

[66] Statute of the International Court of Justice, Art. 9. On the changes in the composition of the Court, see E. McWHINNEY, THE INTERNATIONAL COURT OF JUSTICE AND THE WESTERN TRADITION OF INTERNATIONAL LAW 76–83 (1987).

[67] In 1991, as in 1989, there were 2 women (out of 18) on the Economic, Social and Cultural Rights Committee, 1 (out of 18) on the Committee on the Elimination of Racial Discrimination, 2 (out of 18) on the Human Rights Committee, and 2 (out of 10) on the Committee against Torture. *See* Byrnes, *The "Other" Human Rights Treaty Body: The Work of the Committee on the Elimination of Discrimination Against Women,* 14 YALE J. INT'L L. 1, 8 n.26 (1989). The Sub-Commission on Prevention of Discrimination and Protection of Minorities has 6 women out of 26 members. Thus, there is a total of 13 women out of 90 "independent experts" in the UN human rights system, apart from the CEDAW Committee.

[68] GA Res. 34/180 (Dec. 18, 1979) (entered into force Sept. 3, 1981). *See also* Declaration on the Elimination of Discrimination against Women, GA Res. 2263 (XXII) (Nov. 7, 1967).

[69] A. BYRNES, REPORT ON THE SEVENTH SESSION OF THE COMMITTEE ON THE ELIMINATION OF DISCRIMINATION AGAINST WOMEN AND THE FOURTH MEETING OF STATES PARTIES TO THE CONVENTION ON THE ELIMINATION OF ALL FORMS OF DISCRIMINATION AGAINST WOMEN (FEBRUARY–MARCH 1988), at 13 (International Women's Rights Action Watch 1988).

[70] *Id.* Another reflection of the low status of women's concerns within the United Nations system is the apparently low priority the Women's Convention is given on the human rights agenda. At its seventh session in 1987, the CEDAW Committee claimed to have been provided with far worse working conditions than other human rights committees. *Id.* at 16. *See also* Byrnes, *supra* note 67, at 56–59. Byrnes has observed:

> The fact that CEDAW has been given less time than other comparable bodies while covering economic and social rights as well as civil and political rights is perhaps the reflection of a less than full commitment to the pursuit of the goals of the Convention or at least a serious underestimate of the extent of the work to be done.

A. BYRNES, *supra* note 69, at 20.

Why is it significant that all the major institutions of the international legal order are peopled by men? Long-term domination of all bodies wielding political power nationally and internationally means that issues traditionally of concern to men become seen as general human concerns, while "women's concerns" are relegated to a special, limited category. Because men generally are not the victims of sex discrimination, domestic violence, and sexual degradation and violence, for example, these matters can be consigned to a separate sphere and tend to be ignored. The orthodox face of international law and politics would change dramatically if their institutions were truly human in composition: their horizons would widen to include issues previously regarded as domestic—in the two senses of the word. Balanced representation in international organizations of nations of differing economic structures and power has been a prominent theme in the United Nations since the era of decolonization in the 1960s. The importance of accommodating interests of developed, developing and socialist nations and of various regional and ideological groups is recognized in all aspects of the UN structure and work. This sensitivity should be extended much further to include the gender of chosen representatives.

The Normative Structure of International Law

Since the primary subjects of international law are states, it is sometimes assumed that the impact of international law falls on the state and not directly on individuals. In fact, the application of international law does affect individuals, which has been recognized by the International Court in several cases.[71] International jurisprudence assumes that international law norms directed at individuals within states are universally applicable and neutral. It is not recognized, however, that such principles may impinge differently on men and women; consequently, women's experiences of the operation of these laws tend to be silenced or discounted.

The normative structure of international law has allowed issues of particular concern to women to be either ignored or undermined. For example, modern international law rests on and reproduces various dichotomies between the public and private spheres, and the "public" sphere is regarded as the province of international law. One such distinction is between public international law, the law governing the relations between nation-states, and private international law, the rules about conflicts between national legal systems. Another is the distinction between matters of international "public" concern and matters "private" to states that are considered within their domestic jurisdiction, in which the international community has no recognized legal interest.[72] Yet another is the line drawn between law and other forms of "private" knowledge such as morality.[73]

[71] See, e.g., Legal Consequences for States of the Continued Presence of South Africa in Namibia (South West Africa) notwithstanding Security Council Resolution 276 (1970), 1971 ICJ REP. 16, 56, para. 125 (Advisory Opinion of June 21), where it was stated that the nonrecognition of South Africa's administration in South West Africa should not be allowed to have an adverse impact on the people of Namibia. In the Anglo-Norwegian Fisheries case (UK v. Nor.), 1951 ICJ REP. 116 (Judgment of Dec. 18), and Fisheries Jurisdiction (UK v. Ice.), Merits, 1974 ICJ REP. 3 (Judgment of July 25), the impact of changed fishing zones on the livelihood of people in the various states who engaged in fishing was taken into account by the Court.

[72] UN CHARTER Art. 2(7).

[73] E.g., South West Africa, Second Phase, 1966 ICJ REP. 6 (Judgment of July 18). Cf. Western Sahara Case, 1975 ICJ REP. 12, 77 (Advisory Opinion of Oct. 16): "economics, sociology and human geography are not law" (Gros, J., sep. op.).

626   THE AMERICAN JOURNAL OF INTERNATIONAL LAW   [Vol. 85

At a deeper level one finds a public/private dichotomy based on gender.[74] One explanation feminist scholars offer for the dominance of men and the male voice in all areas of power and authority in the western liberal tradition is that a dichotomy is drawn between the public sphere and the private or domestic one. The public realm of the work place, the law, economics, politics and intellectual and cultural life, where power and authority are exercised, is regarded as the natural province of men; while the private world of the home, the hearth and children is seen as the appropriate domain of women. The public/private distinction has a normative, as well as a descriptive, dimension. Traditionally, the two spheres are accorded asymmetrical value: greater significance is attached to the public, male world than to the private, female one. The distinction drawn between the public and the private thus vindicates and makes natural the division of labor and allocation of rewards between the sexes. Its reproduction and acceptance in all areas of knowledge have conferred primacy on the male world and supported the dominance of men.[75]

Feminist concern with the public/private distinction derives from its centrality to liberal theory. Explanations for the universal attribution of lesser value to women and their activities have sometimes proposed a variation of the public/private dichotomy: women are identified with nature, which is regarded as lower in status than culture—the province of men.[76] As Carole Pateman has pointed out, however, this universal explanation for the male domination of women does not recognize that the concept of "nature" may vary widely among different societies. Such an analysis can be reduced easily to a simple biological explanation and does not explain particular social, historical or cultural situations.[77] Women are not always opposed to men in the same ways: what is considered "public" in one society may well be seen as "private" in another. But a universal pattern of identifying women's activities as private, and thus of lesser value, can be detected.[78]

How is the western liberal version of the public/private distinction maintained? Its naturalness rests on deeply held beliefs about gender. Traditional social psychology taught that the bench marks of "normal" behavior for men, on the one hand, and women, on the other, were entirely different. For men, normal and natural behavior was essentially active: it involved tenacity, aggression, curiosity, ambition, responsibility and competition—all attributes suited to participation in the public world. "Normal" behavior for women, by contrast, was reactive and passive: affectionate, emotional, obedient and responsive to approval.[79]

---

[74] For a fuller discussion, see Charlesworth, *The Public / Private Distinction and the Right to Development in International Law*, 12 AUSTL. Y.B. INT'L L. (1992, forthcoming).

[75] H. EISENSTEIN, CONTEMPORARY FEMINIST THOUGHT 11–26 (1984); Rosaldo, *Women, Culture, and Society: a Theoretical Overview*, in WOMEN, CULTURE, AND SOCIETY 17 (M. Z. Rosaldo & L. Lamphere eds. 1974); J. ELSHTAIN, PUBLIC MAN, PRIVATE WOMAN (1981); THE PUBLIC AND THE PRIVATE (E. Gamarnikow et al. eds. 1983); Pateman, *Feminist Critiques of the Public / Private Dichotomy*, in PUBLIC AND PRIVATE IN SOCIAL LIFE 281 (S. I. Benn & G. F. Gaus eds. 1983).

[76] Ortner, *Is Female to Male as Nature is to Culture?*, in WOMEN, CULTURE, AND SOCIETY, *supra* note 75, at 72.

[77] Pateman, *supra* note 75, at 288. *See also* Rosaldo, *The Use and Abuse of Anthropology: Reflections on Feminism and Cross-Cultural Understanding*, 5 SIGNS 409 (1980); Goodall, *"Public and Private" in Legal Debate*, 18 INT'L J. SOC. L. 445 (1990).

[78] Imray & Middleton, *Public and Private: Marking the Boundaries*, in THE PUBLIC AND THE PRIVATE, *supra* note 75, at 12, 16.

[79] *See* H. EISENSTEIN, *supra* note 75, at 8; K. MILLETT, SEXUAL POLITICS 228–30 (1970).

Although the scientific basis of the public/private distinction has been thoroughly attacked and exposed as a culturally constructed ideology,[80] it continues to have a strong grip on legal thinking. The language of the public/private distinction is built into the language of the law itself: law lays claim to rationality, culture, power, objectivity—all terms associated with the public or male realm. It is defined in opposition to the attributes associated with the domestic, private, female sphere: feeling, emotion, passivity, subjectivity.[81] Moreover, the law has always operated primarily within the public domain; it is considered appropriate to regulate the work place, the economy and the distribution of political power, while direct state intervention in the family and the home has long been regarded as inappropriate.[82] Violence within the home, for example, has generally been given different legal significance from violence outside it; the injuries recognized as legally compensable are those which occur outside the home. Damages in civil actions are typically assessed in terms of ability to participate in the public sphere. Women have difficulty convincing law enforcement officials that violent acts within the home are criminal.[83]

In one sense, the public/private distinction is the fundamental basis of the modern state's function of separating and concentrating juridical forms of power that emanate from the state. The distinction implies that the private world is uncontrolled. In fact, the regulation of taxation, social security, education, health and welfare has immediate effects on the private sphere.[84] The myth that state power is not exercised in the "private" realm allocated to women masks its control.

What force does the feminist critique of the public/private dichotomy in the foundation of domestic legal systems have for the international legal order? Traditionally, of course, international law was regarded as operating only in the most public of public spheres: the relations between nation-states. We argue, however, that the definition of certain principles of international law rests on and reproduces the public/private distinction. It thus privileges the male world view and supports male dominance in the international legal order.

The grip that the public/private distinction has on international law, and the consequent banishment of women's voices and concerns from the discipline, can be seen in the international prohibition on torture. The right to freedom from torture and other forms of cruel, inhuman or degrading treatment is generally accepted as a paradigmatic civil and political right. It is included in all international catalogs of civil and political rights[85] and is the focus of specialized United

---

[80] *E.g.*, E. JANEWAY, MAN'S WORLD, WOMEN'S PLACE: A STUDY IN SOCIAL MYTHOLOGY (1971); J. ELSHTAIN, *supra* note 75.

[81] Olsen, *Feminism and Critical Legal Theory: An American Perspective*, 18 INT'L J. SOC. L. 199 (1990); Thornton, *Feminist Jurisprudence: Illusion or Reality?*, 3 AUSTL. J. L. & SOC'Y 5, 6–7 (1986).

[82] K. O'DONOVAN, SEXUAL DIVISIONS IN LAW (1986); Stang Dahl & Snare, *The coercion of privacy*, in WOMEN, SEXUALITY, AND SOCIAL CONTROL 8 (C. Smart & B. Smart eds. 1978).

[83] *See* CRIMES AGAINST WOMEN: PROCEEDINGS OF THE INTERNATIONAL TRIBUNAL 58–67, 110–75 (D. Russell & N. Van de Ven eds. 1984).

[84] K. O'DONOVAN, *supra* note 82, at 7–8.

[85] *E.g.*, International Covenant on Civil and Political Rights, Dec. 16, 1966, Art. 7, 999 UNTS 171; European Convention for the Protection of Human Rights and Fundamental Freedoms, Nov. 4, 1950, Art. 3, 213 UNTS 221 [hereinafter European Convention]; American Convention on Human Rights, Nov. 22, 1969, Art. 5, *reprinted in* ORGANIZATION OF AMERICAN STATES, HANDBOOK OF EXISTING RULES PERTAINING TO HUMAN RIGHTS IN THE INTER-AMERICAN SYSTEM, OEA/Ser.L/V/II.65, doc. 6, at 103 (1985).

Nations and regional treaties.[86] The right to be free from torture is also regarded as a norm of customary international law—indeed, like the prohibition on slavery, as a norm of *jus cogens*.[87]

The basis for the right is traced to "the inherent dignity of the human person."[88] Behavior constituting torture is defined in the Convention against Torture as

> any act by which severe pain or suffering, whether physical or mental, is intentionally inflicted on a person for such purposes as obtaining from him or a third person information or a confession, punishing him for an act he or a third person has committed or is suspected of having committed, or intimidating or coercing him or a third person, or for any reason based on discrimination of any kind, when such pain or suffering is inflicted by or at the instigation of or with the consent or acquiescence of a public official or other person acting in an official capacity.[89]

This definition has been considered broad because it covers mental suffering and behavior "at the instigation of" a public official.[90] However, despite the use of the term "human person" in the Preamble, the use of the masculine pronoun alone in the definition of the proscribed behavior immediately gives the definition a male, rather than a truly human, context. More importantly, the description of the prohibited conduct relies on a distinction between public and private actions that obscures injuries to their dignity typically sustained by women. The traditional canon of human rights law does not deal in categories that fit the experiences of women. It is cast in terms of discrete violations of rights and offers little redress in cases where there is a pervasive, structural denial of rights.[91]

The international definition of torture requires not only the intention to inflict suffering, but also the secondary intention that the infliction of suffering will fulfill a purpose. Recent evidence suggests that women and children, in particular, are victims of widespread and apparently random terror campaigns by both governmental and guerrilla groups in times of civil unrest or armed conflict.[92] Such suffering is not clearly included in the international definition of torture.

A crucial aspect of torture and cruel, inhuman or degrading conduct, as defined, is that they take place in the public realm: a public official or a person acting officially must be implicated in the pain and suffering. The rationale for this limitation is that "private acts (of brutality) would usually be ordinary criminal offenses which national law enforcement is expected to repress. *International* concern with torture arises only when the State itself abandons its function of protecting its citizenry by sanctioning criminal action by law enforcement personnel."[93]

---

[86] United Nations Convention against Torture and Other Cruel, Inhuman or Degrading Treatment or Punishment, GA Res. 39/46 (Dec. 10, 1984), *draft reprinted in* 23 ILM 1027 (1984), *substantive changes noted in* 24 ILM 535 (1985) [hereinafter Torture Convention]; Inter-American Convention to Prevent and Punish Torture, Dec. 9, 1985, *reprinted in* 25 ILM 519 (1986); European Convention for the Prevention of Torture and Inhuman or Degrading Treatment or Punishment, Nov. 26, 1987, Council of Europe Doc. H (87) 4, *reprinted in* 27 ILM 1152 (1988).

[87] *See* Filartiga v. Pena-Irala, 630 F.2d 876 (2d Cir. 1980).

[88] Torture Convention, *supra* note 86, Preamble.

[89] *Id.*, Art. 1(1).

[90] *See* J. BURGERS & H. DANELIUS, THE UNITED NATIONS CONVENTION AGAINST TORTURE 45–46 (1988).

[91] A. Byrnes, *supra* note 7, at 10.

[92] *See* AMNESTY INTERNATIONAL, WOMEN IN THE FRONT LINE: HUMAN RIGHTS VIOLATIONS AGAINST WOMEN 45–46 (1991).

[93] Rodley, *The Evolution of the International Prohibition of Torture*, in AMNESTY INTERNATIONAL, THE UNIVERSAL DECLARATION OF HUMAN RIGHTS 1948–1988: HUMAN RIGHTS, THE UNITED NATIONS AND AMNESTY INTERNATIONAL 55, 63 (1988).

Many women suffer from torture in this limited sense.[94] The international jurisprudence on the notion of torture arguably extends to sexual violence and psychological coercion if the perpetrator has official standing.[95] However, severe pain and suffering that is inflicted outside the most public context of the state—for example, within the home or by private persons, which is the most pervasive and significant violence sustained by women—does not qualify as torture despite its impact on the inherent dignity of the human person. Indeed, some forms of violence are attributed to cultural tradition. The message of violence against women, argues Charlotte Bunch, is domination:

> [S]tay in your place or be afraid. Contrary to the argument that such violence is only personal or cultural, it is profoundly political. It results from the structural relationships of power, domination, and privilege between men and women in society. Violence against women is central to maintaining those political relations at home, at work, and in all public spheres.[96]

States are held responsible for torture only when their designated agents have direct responsibility for such acts and that responsibility is imputed to the state. States are not considered responsible if they have maintained a legal and social system in which violations of physical and mental integrity are endemic.[97] In its draft articles on state responsibility, the International Law Commission did not widen the concept of imputability to incorporate such acts.[98] A feminist perspective on human rights would require a rethinking of the notions of imputability and state responsibility and in this sense would challenge the most basic assumptions of international law. If violence against women were considered by the international legal system to be as shocking as violence against people for their political ideas, women would have considerable support in their struggle.

The assumption that underlies all law, including international human rights law, is that the public/private distinction is real: human society, human lives can be separated into two distinct spheres. This division, however, is an ideological construct rationalizing the exclusion of women from the sources of power. It also makes it possible to maintain repressive systems of control over women without interference from human rights guarantees, which operate in the public sphere. By extending our vision beyond the public/private ideologies that rationalize limiting our analysis of power, human rights language as it currently exists can be used to describe serious forms of repression that go far beyond the juridically narrow vision of international law. For example, coercive population control tech-

---

[94] *See* AMNESTY INTERNATIONAL, *supra* note 92, *passim*.

[95] Violent attacks resulting in permanent physical damage have been held to meet the requisite level of severity. *E.g.*, The First Greek Case, 12 Y.B. EUR. CONV. ON HUM. RTS. 499 (1969); Bassano Hernandez & Massera v. Uruguay, Report of the Human Rights Committee, 35 UN GAOR Supp. (No. 40), Ann. VII, at 124, UN Doc. A/35/40 (1979). Rape and sexual assault may not, however, be provable in the same way as other physical harm, and the allegation of such abuse itself stigmatizes the victim. *See* AMNESTY INTERNATIONAL, *supra* note 92, at 3.

[96] Bunch, *supra* note 7, at 490–91.   [97] *See* A. Byrnes, *supra* note 7, at 10.

[98] *See* [1979] 2 Y.B. INT'L L. COMM'N 90, UN Doc. A/CN.4/SER.A/1979/Add.1; [1980] 2 *id.* at 14, 70, UN Doc. A/CN.4/SER.A/1980/Add.1. Article 19(3)(c) does state that an international crime may result from "a serious breach on a widespread scale of an international obligation of essential importance for safeguarding the human being, such as those prohibiting slavery, genocide, apartheid." Historically, however, oppression of women has not been regarded in this light. *See also* INTERNATIONAL CRIMES OF STATE: A CRITICAL ANALYSIS OF THE ILC'S DRAFT ARTICLE 19 ON STATE RESPONSIBILITY (J. Weiler, A. Cassese & M. Spinedi eds. 1989); UNITED NATIONS CODIFICATION OF STATE RESPONSIBILITY (M. Spinedi & B. Simma eds. 1987).

niques, such as forced sterilization, may amount to punishment or coercion by the state to achieve national goals.[99]

Another example of the failure of the normative structure of international law to accommodate the realities of women's lives can be seen in its response to trafficking in women. Trafficking in women through prostitution, pornography and mail-order-bride networks is a pervasive and serious problem in both the developed and the developing worlds.[100] These practices do not simply fall under national jurisdiction, as the ramifications of the trafficking and exploitative relationships cross international boundaries. They involve the subordination and exploitation of women, not on the simple basis of inequality or differences among individuals, but as a result of deeply engrained constructs of power and dominance based on gender. Catharine MacKinnon's observation that women's "material desperation" is connected to violence against women[101] is even more powerful in the international context. To a large extent, the increase in trafficking in women in the Third World stems from growing economic disparities on the national and international levels.[102] Once caught up in the trafficking networks, penniless women in foreign countries are at the mercy of those who arrange and profit from the trade.

Existing norms of international law could be invoked to prohibit at least some of the international exploitation of women and children.[103] The international law on this issue, however, is incomplete and limited in scope. Just as the prohibition of the slave trade, and subsequently of slavery itself, did not occur until economic considerations supported its abolition,[104] so a real commitment to the prevention of sexual trafficking in women is unlikely to be made unless it does not adversely affect other economic interests. As Georges Scelle has written:

> The struggle against slavery, the protection of the bodily freedom of individuals only begin in international law when it is clearly demonstrated that slave labour has *economic* drawbacks and that the progress of modern technology allows it to be *replaced*. Whenever human manpower has not been replaced, slave labour and forced labour still exist, despite all efforts made to proscribe it. This proves that a *moral conviction*, even if of a general character, does not override the necessities of economic life in the formation of legal rules.[105]

---

[99] An example at the opposite extreme was the demand of the Ceausescu regime in Romania that all married women undergo regular medical examinations by public health officials to determine whether they were pregnant or had had an abortion. The purpose was to achieve an explicit state goal: for each married woman to have at least four children.

[100] See K. BARRY, FEMALE SEXUAL SLAVERY (1984); Kappeler, *The International Slave Trade in Women, or, Procurers, Pimps and Punters,* 1 LAW & CRITIQUE 219 (1990); C. ENLOE, *supra* note 35, at 19–41, 65–92.

[101] C. MACKINNON, *supra* note 18, at 40–41.

[102] See EQUAL TIME, March 1989, at 22–23 (report on UNESCO Conference on the Elimination of Trafficking in Women and Children, New York, 1988).

[103] Article 6 of the Women's Convention, *supra* note 68, provides that state parties should "take all appropriate measures, including legislation, to suppress all forms of traffic in women and exploitation of prostitution of women." *See also* B. WHITAKER, SLAVERY: REPORT 11–20, UN Doc. E/CN.4/Sub.2/1982/20/Rev.1, UN Sales No. E.84.XIV.1 (1984); Convention for the Suppression of the Traffic in Persons and of the Exploitation of the Prostitution of Others, Mar. 21, 1950, 96 UNTS 271; Reanda, *Prostitution as a Human Rights Question: Problems and Prospects of United Nations Action,* 13 HUM. RTS. Q. 202 (1991).

[104] For a brief history of the international prohibition of slavery, see A. CASSESE, *supra* note 19, at 52–54.

[105] 2 G. SCELLE, PRÉCIS DE DROIT DES GENS 55 (1934), *translated and quoted in id.* at 53.

No technological advances have succeeded in replacing the many services of women, and the economic benefits of pornography and trafficking are immense.[106] The role and stake of the media "in sensationalizing, exploiting and commercializing women's bodies" also cannot be ignored as contributing factors.[107]

Some branches of international law have recognized and addressed issues relating to women. Various International Labour Organisation Conventions focus on women.[108] A growing literature on these conventions examines the assumptions they make about the role of women, the topics they cover, and their approach to the position of women.[109]

The Women's Convention is the most prominent international normative instrument recognizing the special concerns of women. But the terms of the Convention and the way it has been accepted by states prompt us to ask whether it offers a real or chimerical possibility of change.

The Women's Convention has been ratified or acceded to by almost two-thirds of the members of the United Nations.[110] Article 1 defines "discrimination against women" as

> any distinction, exclusion or restriction made on the basis of sex which has the effect or purpose of impairing or nullifying the recognition, enjoyment or exercise by women, irrespective of their marital status, on a basis of equality of men and women, of human rights and fundamental freedoms in the political, economic, social, cultural, civil or any other field.[111]

Although the Convention goes further than simply requiring equality of opportunity and covers the more contentious concept of equality of result, which justifies affirmative action programs and protection against indirect discrimination, the underlying assumption of its definition of discrimination is that women and men are the same. Most international commentators treat this model of equality as uncontroversial.[112] But the notions of both equality of opportunity and equality of result accept the general applicability of a male standard (except in special circum-

---

[106] C. MacKinnon, *supra* note 18, at 179.   [107] Equal Time, *supra* note 102, at 22.

[108] For a list of these Conventions, see Hevener, *An Analysis of Gender Based Treaty Law: Contemporary Developments in Historical Perspective*, 8 Hum. Rts. Q. 70, 87–88 (1986).

[109] One author has analyzed the Conventions dealing with women according to whether their purpose is protective (viewing women as in need of special protection), corrective (redressing previous gender imbalance) or nondiscriminatory (aiming at formal equality between the sexes). Hevener, *supra* note 108. Some of the earlier Conventions that were intended to be protective of women's roles as child bearers and rearers are now being reappraised. For example, in 1988 the Australian Government announced its withdrawal from ILO Convention (No. 45) concerning the Employment of Women on Underground Work in Mines of all Kinds, June 21, 1935, *as modified by* Final Articles Revision Convention, 1946, 40 UNTS 63, which was originally regarded as protective, on the basis that the Convention now appears discriminatory because it denies women access to certain forms of employment. The instrument of denunciation was deposited by Australia on May 20, 1988, to take effect a year later. Commonwealth of Australia, Treaty List 1988, at 28 (1989).

[110] As of May 1991, 105 states had ratified or acceded to the Convention, according to the UN Information Office, Sydney, Australia. For a helpful guide to the literature on the Convention, see Cook, *Bibliography: The International Right to Nondiscrimination on the Basis of Sex*, 14 Yale J. Int'l L. 161 (1989).

[111] Women's Convention, *supra* note 68, Art. 1.

[112] *See, e.g.,* M. Halberstam & E. DeFeis, Women's Legal Rights: International Covenants an Alternative to ERA? (1987); D'Sa, *Women's rights in relation to human rights: a lawyer's perspective*, 13 Commonwealth L. Bull. 666, 672–74 (1987).

stances such as pregnancy) and promise a very limited form of equality: equality is defined as being like a man.[113] "[M]an," writes Catharine MacKinnon, "has become the measure of all things."[114] On this analysis, equality can be achieved in a relatively straightforward way by legally requiring the removal of identifiable barriers to the rise of women to the same status as men: equality is achievable within the social and legal structures as they are now. This assumption ignores the many real differences and inequities between the sexes and the significant barriers to their removal.[115]

The phenomenon of male dominance over women is above all one of power. Sexism is not a legal aberration but a pervasive, structural problem. MacKinnon says, "[Gender] is [a question] of hierarchy. The top and the bottom of the hierarchy are different all right, but that is hardly all."[116] On this basis, the most productive analysis of inequality is in terms of domination and subordination. Thus, equality is not freedom to be treated without regard to sex but freedom from systematic subordination because of sex.

Certainly, the separate focus on women in the Women's Convention is beneficial in some respects. Attention is drawn to issues of distinct concern to women (for example, trafficking in women and prostitution)[117] and to the fact that not all women have the same problems (for example, rural women have special needs).[118] The reporting provisions require that state parties focus on the steps they have taken to implement the goals of the Convention so that discrimination against women does not become submerged in general human rights issues.[119] The Convention also provides an important mix of civil, political, economic and social rights.

The Women's Convention, however, establishes much weaker implementation procedures than those of other human rights instruments of apparently universal applicability such as the International Convention on the Elimination of All Forms of Racial Discrimination[120] and the Covenant on Civil and Political Rights.[121] More generally, the specialized nature of the Women's Convention has been used by "mainstream" human rights bodies to justify ignoring or minimizing women's perspectives. They can assure themselves that, since these problems are scrutinized elsewhere, their organizations are relieved from the task. Yet the impact on women and men of many provisions of, for example, the Covenant on Civil and Political Rights may not be the same.

States have made a significant number of reservations and declarations of understanding when becoming parties to the Women's Convention. Article 28(1) permits ratification subject to reservations, provided the reservations are not "in-

---

[113] For a discussion of this approach, see Lacey, *Legislation Against Sex Discrimination: Questions from a Feminist Perspective*, 14 J. L. & SOC'Y 411 (1987).

[114] C. MACKINNON, *supra* note 18, at 34.

[115] *See* Dowd, *Work and Family: The Gender Paradox and the Limitation of Discrimination Analysis in Restructuring the Workplace*, 24 HARV. C.R.-C.L. L. REV. 79 (1989).

[116] MacKinnon, *Feminism, Marxism, Method and the State: Toward Feminist Jurisprudence*, 8 SIGNS 635 (1983).

[117] Women's Convention, *supra* note 68, Art. 6.

[118] *Id.*, Art. 14.   [119] *Id.*, Art. 18.

[120] *Opened for signature* Mar. 7, 1966, 660 UNTS 195, *reprinted in* 5 ILM 352 (1966).

[121] *Supra* note 85. For an analysis of these differences, see Reanda, *Human Rights and Women's Rights: The United Nations Approach*, 3 HUM. RTS. Q. 11 (1981); Meron, *Enhancing the Effectiveness of the Prohibition of Discrimination against Women*, 84 AJIL 213 (1990).

compatible with the object and purpose of the present Convention" (Article 28(2)). No criteria are given for the determination of incompatibility. Over 40 of the 105 parties to the Convention have made a total of almost a hundred reservations to its terms.[122] Many of these reservations were motivated by the conflict between some interpretations of Islam and the notion of sexual equality. They take the form of limiting the reserving state's obligations under the Convention to the taking of steps compatible with Islamic law and customs. Both general reservations and reservations to specific provisions[123] have been made that are regarded by other state parties as incompatible with the overall object and purpose of the Convention.[124] Other reservations concern national religious or customary laws that restrict women's inheritance and property rights;[125] nationality laws that do not accord women the same rights as men to acquire, change or retain their nationality upon marriage;[126] and laws limiting women's economic opportunities, freedom of movement and choice of residence.[127]

The pattern of reservations to the Women's Convention underlines the inadequacy of the present normative structure of international law. The international community is prepared to formally acknowledge the considerable problems of inequality faced by women, but only, it seems, if individual states are not required as a result to alter patriarchal practices that subordinate women. Members of the CEDAW Committee, which monitors the implementation of the Convention but does not have jurisdiction to determine the compatibility of reservations with it, have questioned representatives of state parties about their reservations.[128] The biennial meetings of the state parties, however, have not taken action to obtain an authoritative determination on the compatibility of the reservations with the object and purpose of the Convention.[129] The numerous reservations made to the Women's Convention stand in stark contrast to the four substantive reservations made to the Convention on the Elimination of All Forms of Racial Discrimina-

---

[122] MULTILATERAL TREATIES DEPOSITED WITH THE SECRETARY-GENERAL: STATUS AS AT 31 DECEMBER 1989, at 170–79, UN Doc. ST/LEG/SER.E/8 (1990) [hereinafter MULTILATERAL TREATIES]. For a discussion of reservations generally in the context of the Women's Convention, see Byrnes, *supra* note 67, at 51–56; Cook, *Reservations to the Convention on the Elimination of All Forms of Discrimination Against Women*, 30 VA. J. INT'L L. 643 (1990); Clark, *The Vienna Convention Reservations Regime and the Convention on Discrimination against Women*, 85 AJIL 281 (1991).

[123] E.g., the reservations made by Egypt to the Women's Convention. With respect to Article 2, which condemns all forms of discrimination against women, the general reservation states that "Egypt is willing to comply with the content of this article, provided that such compliance does not run counter to the Islamic Sharia." Egypt made a particular reservation to Article 16, which requires parties to take steps to eliminate discrimination against women with respect to marriage and family relations during marriage and on its dissolution, on the ground that the *Shari'a* requires a man to pay "bridal money" to his wife, to maintain her during marriage and to make a payment on divorce, whereas women do not have any parallel obligations. For this reason the *Shari'a* promotes "complementarity" between spouses by restricting a wife's right to divorce to judicial proceedings, while not so restricting that of a husband. MULTILATERAL TREATIES, *supra* note 122, at 172–73.

[124] See the statements of objection to the Islamic reservations by the Federal Republic of Germany, Mexico and Sweden in *id.* at 179–84.

[125] *See* Cook, *supra* note 122, at 701.   [126] *See id.* at 693–96.

[127] *See id.* at 696–702.   [128] *Id.* at 708 nn.303, 304.

[129] The 1986 meeting of state parties expressed concern about the compatibility of some reservations with the Convention and asked the Secretary-General to seek the views of state parties. Subsequent meetings have not pursued this issue. *See id.* at 708; Clark, *supra* note 122, at 283–85.

tion[130] and suggest that discrimination against women is somehow regarded as more "natural" and acceptable than racial discrimination.

In sum, the Women's Convention, the international legal flagship with respect to women, is an ambiguous offering. It recognizes discrimination against women as a legal issue but is premised on the notion of progress through good will, education and changing attitudes and does not promise any form of structural, social or economic change for women. The limited scope of the Convention is further restricted by the international community's general tolerance of reservations to it by the state parties.

IV. Toward a Feminist Analysis of International Law

How can feminist accounts of law be applied in international law? Feminist legal theory can promote a variety of activities. The term signifies an interest (gender as an issue of primary importance); a focus of attention (women as individuals and as members of groups); a political agenda (real social, political, economic and cultural equality regardless of gender); a critical stance (an analysis of "masculinism" and male hierarchical power or "patriarchy"); a means of reinterpreting and reformulating substantive law so that it more adequately reflects the experiences of all people; and an alternative method of practicing, talking about and learning the law.[131] Feminist method must be concerned with examining the fundamentals of the legal persuasion: the language it uses; the organization of legal materials in predetermined, watertight categories; the acceptance of abstract concepts as somehow valid or "pure"; the reliance in practice on confrontational, adversarial techniques; and the commitment to male, hierarchical structures in all legal and political organizations.

Christine Littleton has said, "Feminist method starts with the very radical act of taking women seriously, believing that what we say about ourselves and our experience is important and valid, even when (or perhaps especially when) it has little or no relationship to what has been or is being said *about* us."[132] No single approach can deal with the complexity of international legal organizations, processes and rules, or with the diversity of women's experiences within and outside those structures. In this section we look at two interconnected themes developed in feminist accounts of the law that suggest new ways of analyzing international law.

Critique of Rights

The feminist critique of rights questions whether the acquisition of legal rights advances women's equality.[133] Feminist scholars have argued that, although the search for formal legal equality through the formulation of rights may have been politically appropriate in the early stages of the feminist movement, continuing to focus on the acquisition of rights may not be beneficial to women.[134] Quite apart

---

[130] *See* Cook, *supra* note 122, at 644 n.5; Clark, *supra* note 122, at 283.

[131] Wishik, *To Question Everything: The Inquiries of Feminist Jurisprudence*, 1 BERKELEY WOMEN'S L.J. 64 (1985).

[132] Littleton, *Feminist Jurisprudence: The Difference Method Makes* (Book Review), 41 STAN. L. REV. 751, 764 (1989).

[133] Some members of the critical legal studies movement have engaged in a parallel, but distinct, critique of rights. *See, e.g.,* Tushnet, *An Essay on Rights*, 62 TEX. L. REV. 1363 (1984); Hyde, *The Concept of Legitimation in the Sociology of Law*, 1983 WIS. L. REV. 379.

[134] Gross, *supra* note 6, at 192; C. SMART, *supra* note 17, at 138–39.

from problems such as the form in which rights are drafted, their interpretation by tribunals, and women's access to their enforcement, the rhetoric of rights, according to some feminist legal scholars, is exhausted.[135]

Rights discourse is taxed with reducing intricate power relations in a simplistic way.[136] The formal acquisition of a right, such as the right to equal treatment, is often assumed to have solved an imbalance of power. In practice, however, the promise of rights is thwarted by the inequalities of power: the economic and social dependence of women on men may discourage the invocation of legal rights that are premised on an adversarial relationship between the rights holder and the infringer.[137] More complex still are rights designed to apply to women only such as the rights to reproductive freedom and to choose abortion.[138]

In addition, although they respond to general societal imbalances, formulations of rights are generally cast in individual terms. The invocation of rights to sexual equality may therefore solve an occasional case of inequality for individual women but will leave the position of women generally unchanged.[139] Moreover, international law accords priority to civil and political rights, rights that may have very little to offer women generally. The major forms of oppression of women operate within the economic, social and cultural realms. Economic, social and cultural rights are traditionally regarded as a lesser form of international right and as much more difficult to implement.[140]

A second major criticism of the assumption that the granting of rights inevitably spells progress for women is that it ignores competing rights: the right of women and children not to be subjected to violence in the home may be balanced against the property rights of men in the home or their right to family life.[141] Furthermore, certain rights may be appropriated by more powerful groups: Carol Smart relates that provisions in the European Convention on Human Rights on family life[142] were used by fathers to assert their authority over ex nuptial children.[143] One solution may be to design rights to apply only to particular groups. However, apart from the serious political difficulties this tactic would raise, the formulation of rights that apply only to women, as we have seen in the international sphere, may result in marginalizing these rights.

A third feminist concern about the "rights" approach to achieve equality is that some rights can operate to the detriment of women. The right to freedom of religion,[144] for example, can have differing impacts on women and men. Freedom to exercise all aspects of religious belief does not always benefit women because many accepted religious practices entail reduced social positions and status for

---

[135] C. SMART, *supra* note 17, at 139.   [136] *Id.* at 144.

[137] *Id.*

[138] *Id.* at 146–57. For a discussion of the feminist ambivalence toward gendered laws such as statutory rape laws, see Olsen, *Statutory Rape: A Feminist Critique of Rights Analysis*, 63 TEX. L. REV. 387 (1984).

[139] *See, e.g.*, C. SMART, *supra* note 17, at 145; Lacey, *supra* note 113, at 419.

[140] *See, e.g.*, Cranston, *Are There Any Human Rights?*, DAEDALUS, No. 4, 1983, at 1, 12.

[141] C. SMART, *supra* note 17, at 145; E. Kingdom, The right to reproduce (paper delivered at 13th Annual Conference of the Association for Legal and Social Philosophy, Leeds, Apr. 4–6, 1986), *quoted in id.* at 151; *see also* Fudge, *The Public / Private Distinction: The Possibilities of and the Limits to the Use of Charter Litigation to Further Feminist Struggles*, 25 OSGOODE HALL L.J. 485 (1987).

[142] European Convention, *supra* note 85, Art. 8.

[143] C. SMART, *supra* note 17, at 145.

[144] *E.g.*, International Covenant on Civil and Political Rights, *supra* note 85, Art. 18.

women.[145] Yet attempts to set priorities and to discuss the issue have been met with hostility and blocking techniques. Thus, at its 1987 meeting the CEDAW Committee adopted a decision requesting that the United Nations and the specialized agencies

> promote or undertake studies on the status of women under Islamic laws and customs and in particular on the status and equality of women in the family on issues such as marriage, divorce, custody and property rights and their participation in public life of the society, taking into consideration the principle of El Ijtihad in Islam.[146]

The representatives of Islamic nations criticized this decision in ECOSOC and in the Third Committee of the General Assembly as a threat to their freedom of religion.[147] The CEDAW Committee's recommendation was ultimately rejected. The General Assembly passed a resolution in which it decided that "no action shall be taken on decision 4 adopted by the Committee and request[ed that] the Committee . . . review that decision, taking into account the views expressed by delegations at the first regular session of the Economic and Social Council of 1987 and in the Third Committee of the General Assembly."[148] CEDAW later justified its action by stating that the study was necessary for it to carry out its duties under the Women's Convention and that no disrespect was intended to Islam.[149]

Another example of internationally recognized rights that might affect women and men differently are those relating to the protection of the family. The major human rights instruments all have provisions applicable to the family. Thus, the Universal Declaration proclaims that the family is the "natural and fundamental group unit of society and is entitled to protection by society and the State."[150] These provisions ignore that to many women the family is a unit for abuse and violence; hence, protection of the family also preserves the power structure within the family, which can lead to subjugation and dominance by men over women and children.

The development of rights may be particularly problematic for women in the Third World, where women's rights to equality with men and traditional values may clash. An example of the ambivalence of Third World states toward women's concerns is the Banjul Charter, the human rights instrument of the Organization of African Unity.[151]

The Charter, unlike "western" instruments preoccupied with the rights of individuals, emphasizes the need to recognize communities and peoples as entities

[145] *See, e.g.,* Arzt, *The Application of International Human Rights Law in Islamic States,* 12 HUM. RTS. Q. 202, 203 (1990). *See generally* A. SHARMA, WOMEN IN WORLD RELIGIONS (1987). *Cf.* Sullivan, *Advancing the Freedom of Religion or Belief through the UN Declaration on the Elimination of Religious Intolerance and Discrimination,* 82 AJIL 487, 515–17 (1988).

[146] UN Doc. E/1987/SR.11, at 13, *quoted in* A. BYRNES, *supra* note 69, at 6. *Cf.* An-Na'im, *Rights of Women and International Law in the Muslim Context,* 9 WHITTIER L. REV. 491 (1987).

[147] A. BYRNES, *supra* note 69, at 6.   [148] GA Res. 42/60, para. 9 (Nov. 30, 1987).

[149] A. BYRNES, *supra* note 69, at 6–7. On these events, see also Clark, *supra* note 122, at 287–88.

[150] Universal Declaration of Human Rights, GA Res. 217A (III), Art. 16(3), UN Doc. A/810, at 71 (1948). *Cf.* International Covenant on Economic, Social and Cultural Rights, Dec. 16, 1966, Art. 10(1), 993 UNTS 3; International Covenant on Civil and Political Rights, *supra* note 85, Art. 23. *See* Holmes, *supra* note 7, at 252–55.

[151] African Charter on Human and Peoples' Rights, *adopted* June 27, 1981, OAU Doc. CAB/LEG/ 67/3/Rev.5, *reprinted in* 21 ILM 59 (1982) [hereinafter Banjul Charter]. *See* Wright, *Economic Rights and Social Justice: A Feminist Analysis of Some International Human Rights Conventions,* 12 AUSTL. Y.B. INT'L L. (1992, forthcoming).

entitled to rights, and it provides that people within the group owe duties and obligations to the group. "Peoples' " rights in the Banjul Charter include the right to self-determination,[152] the right to exploit natural resources and wealth,[153] the right to development,[154] the right to international peace and security,[155] and the right to a generally satisfactory environment.[156]

The creation of communal or "peoples' " rights, however, does not take into account the often severe limitations on the rights of women within these groups, communities or "peoples." The Preamble to the Charter makes specific reference to the elimination of "all forms of discrimination, particularly those based on race, ethnic group, colour, sex, language, religion or political opinion." Article 2 enshrines the enjoyment of all rights contained within the Charter without discrimination of any kind. But after Article 2, the Charter refers exclusively to "his" rights, the "rights of man." Articles 3–17 set out basic political, civil, economic and social rights similar to those contained in other instruments, in particular the International Covenants, the Universal Declaration of Human Rights (which is cited in the Preamble) and European instruments. Article 15 is significant in that it guarantees that the right to work includes the right to "receive equal pay for equal work." This right might be useful to women who are employed in jobs that men also do. The difficulty is that most African women, like women elsewhere, generally do not perform the same jobs as men.

Articles 17 and 18 and the list of duties contained in Articles 27–29 present obstacles to African women's enjoyment of rights set out elsewhere in the Charter. Article 17(3) states that "[t]he promotion and protection of morals and traditional values recognized by the community shall be the duty of the State." Article 18 entrusts the family with custody of those morals and values, describing it as "the natural unit and basis of society." The same article requires that discrimination against women be eliminated, but the conjunction of the notion of equality with the protection of the family and "traditional" values poses serious problems. It has been noted in relation to Zimbabwe and Mozambique that

> [t]he official political rhetoric relating to women in these southern African societies may be rooted in a model derived from Engels, via the Soviet Union, but the actual situation they face today bears little resemblance to that of the USSR. In Zimbabwe particularly, policy-makers are caught between several ideological and material contradictions, which are especially pertinent to women-oriented policies. The dominant ideology has been shaped by two belief-systems, opposed in their conceptions of women. Marxism vies with a model deriving from pre-colonial society, in which women's capacity to reproduce the lineage, socially, economically and biologically, was crucial and in which lineage males controlled women's labour power.[157]

This contradiction between the emancipation of women and adherence to traditional values lies at the heart of and complicates discussion about human rights in relation to many Third World women. The rhetoric of human rights, on both the national and the international levels, regards women as equal citizens, as "individ-

---

[152] Banjul Charter, *supra* note 151, Art. 20.   [153] *Id.*, Art. 21.
[154] *Id.*, Art. 22.   [155] *Id.*, Art. 23.
[156] *Id.*, Art. 24.
[157] Jacobs & Tracy, *Women in Zimbabwe: Stated Policies and State Action,* in WOMEN, STATE IDEOLOGY: STUDIES FROM AFRICA AND ASIA 28, 29–30 (H. Afshar ed. 1988).

uals" subject to the same level of treatment and the same protection as men. But the discourse of "traditional values" may prevent women from enjoying any human rights, however they may be described.[158]

Despite all these problems, the assertion of rights can exude great symbolic force for oppressed groups within a society and it constitutes an organizing principle in the struggle against inequality. Patricia Williams has pointed out that for blacks in the United States, "the prospect of attaining full rights under the law has always been a fiercely motivational, almost religious, source of hope."[159] She writes:

> "Rights" feels so new in the mouths of most black people. It is still so deliciously empowering to say. It is a sign for and a gift of selfhood that is very hard to contemplate restructuring . . . at this point in history. It is the magic wand of visibility and invisibility, of inclusion and exclusion, of power and no power . . . .[160]

The discourse of rights may have greater significance at the international level than in many national systems. It provides an accepted means to challenge the traditional legal order and to develop alternative principles. While the acquisition of rights must not be identified with automatic and immediate advances for women, and the limitations of the rights model must be recognized, the notion of women's rights remains a source of potential power for women in international law. The challenge is to rethink that notion so that rights correspond to women's experiences and needs.

The Public/Private Distinction

The gender implications of the public/private distinction were outlined above.[161] Here we show how the dichotomy between public and private worlds has undermined the operation of international law, giving two examples.

The Right to Development.[162] The right to development was formulated in legal terms only recently and its status in international law is still controversial.[163] Its proponents present it as a collective or solidarity right that responds to the phenomenon of global interdependence, while its critics argue that it is an aspiration rather than a right.[164] The 1986 United Nations Declaration on the Right to Development describes the content of the right as the entitlement "to participate

---

[158] In particular contexts, some black and Asian feminists have argued that the family should be the rallying point for struggle. For example, Valerie Amos and Pratibha Parmar write: "In identifying the institution of the family as a source of oppression for women, white feminists . . . reveal[] their cultural and racial myopia, because for Asian women in particular, the British state through its immigration legislation has done all it can to destroy the Asian family . . . ." Amos & Parmar, *Challenging Imperial Feminism*, 17 FEMINIST REV. 3, 15 (1984).

[159] Williams, *Alchemical Notes: Reconstructing Ideals from Deconstructed Rights*, 22 HARV. C.R.-C.L. L. REV. 401, 417 (1987).

[160] *Id.* at 431. *See also* Schneider, *The Dialectic of Rights and Politics: Perspectives from the Women's Movement*, 61 N.Y.U. L. REV. 589 (1986). *Compare* Hardwig, *Should Women Think in Terms of Rights?*, 94 ETHICS 441 (1984).

[161] *See* text at notes 74–86 *supra*.

[162] For a fuller analysis of this theme, see Charlesworth, *supra* note 74.

[163] Alston, *Making Space for New Human Rights: The Case of the Right to Development*, 1 HARV. HUM. RTS. Y.B. 3 (1988); Rich, *The Right to Development: A Right of Peoples*, in THE RIGHTS OF PEOPLES 39 (J. Crawford ed. 1988).

[164] *E.g.*, Brownlie, *The Rights of Peoples in Modern International Law*, in THE RIGHTS OF PEOPLES, *supra* note 163, at 1, 14–15.

in, contribute to, and enjoy economic, social, cultural and political development, in which all human rights and fundamental freedoms can be fully realized."[165] Primary responsibility for the creation of conditions favorable to the right is placed on states:

> States have the right and the duty to formulate appropriate national development policies that aim at the constant improvement of the well-being of the entire population and of all individuals, on the basis of their active, free and meaningful participation in development and in the fair distribution of the benefits resulting therefrom.[166]

The right is apparently designed to apply to all individuals within a state and is assumed to benefit women and men equally: the preamble to the declaration twice refers to the Charter exhortation to promote and encourage respect for human rights for all without distinction of any kind such as of race or sex. Moreover, Article 8 of the declaration obliges states to ensure equality of opportunity for all regarding access to basic resources and fair distribution of income. It provides that "effective measures should be undertaken to ensure that women have an active role in the development process."

Other provisions of the declaration, however, indicate that discrimination against women is not seen as a major obstacle to development or to the fair distribution of its benefits. For example, one aspect of the right to development is the obligation of states to take "resolute steps" to eliminate "massive and flagrant violations of the human rights of peoples and human beings." The examples given of such violations include apartheid and racial discrimination but not sex discrimination.[167]

Three theories about the causes of underdevelopment dominate its analysis: shortages of capital, technology, skilled labor and entrepreneurship; exploitation of the wealth of developing nations by richer nations; and economic dependence of developing nations on developed nations.[168] The subordination of women to men does not enter this traditional calculus. Moreover, "development" as economic growth above all takes no notice of the lack of benefits or disadvantageous effects this growth may have on half of the society it purports to benefit.

One aspect of the international right to development is the provision of development assistance and aid. The UN General Assembly has called for international and national efforts to be aimed at eliminating "economic deprivation, hunger and disease in all parts of the world without discrimination" and for international cooperation to be aimed, inter alia, at maintaining "stable and sustained economic growth," increasing concessional assistance to developing countries, building world food security and resolving the debt burden.[169]

Women and children are more often the victims of poverty and malnutrition than men.[170] Women should therefore have much to gain from an international right to development. Yet the position of many women in developing countries has deteriorated over the last two decades: their access to economic resources has

---

[165] GA Res. 41/128, Art. 1(1) (Dec. 4, 1986).   [166] *Id.*, Art. 2(3).
[167] *Id.*, Art. 5.
[168] Thomas & Skeat, *Gender in Third World Development Studies: An Overview of an Underview,* 28 AUSTL. GEOGRAPHICAL STUD. 5, 11 (1990); *see also* J. HENSHALL MOMSEN & J. TOWNSEND, GEOGRAPHY OF GENDER IN THE THIRD WORLD 16 (1987).
[169] GA Res. 41/133 (Dec. 4, 1986).
[170] *See* M. WARING, COUNTING FOR NOTHING 134 (1988).

been reduced, their health and educational status has declined, and their work burdens have increased.[171] The generality and apparent universal applicability of the right to development, as formulated in the UN declaration, is undermined by the fundamentally androcentric nature of the international economic system and its reinforcement of the public/private distinction. Of course, the problematic nature of current development practice for Third World women cannot be attributed simply to the international legal formulation of the right to development. But the rhetoric of international law both reflects and reinforces a system that contributes to the subordination of women.

Over the last twenty years, considerable research has been done on women and Third World development.[172] This research has documented the crucial role of women in the economies of developing nations, particularly in agriculture. It has also pointed to the lack of impact, or the adverse impact, of "development" on many Third World women's lives. The international legal order, like most development policies, has not taken this research into account in formulating any aspect of the right to development.

The distinction between the public and private spheres operates to make the work and needs of women invisible. Economic visibility depends on working in the public sphere and unpaid work in the home or community is categorized as "unproductive, unoccupied, and economically inactive."[173] Marilyn Waring has recently argued that this division, which is institutionalized in developed nations, has been exported to the developing world, in part through the United Nations System of National Accounts (UNSNA).[174]

The UNSNA, developed largely by Sir Richard Stone in the 1950s, enables experts to monitor the financial position of states and trends in their national development and to compare one nation's economy with that of another. It will thus influence the categorization of nations as developed or developing and the style and magnitude of the required international aid. The UNSNA measures the value of all goods and services that actually enter the market and of other nonmarket production such as government services provided free of charge.[175] Some activities, however, are designated as outside the "production boundary" and are not measured. Economic reality is constructed by the UNSNA's "production boundaries" in such a way that reproduction, child care, domestic work and subsistence production are excluded from the measurement of economic productivity and growth.[176] This view of women's work as nonwork was nicely summed up in 1985 in a report by the Secretary-General to the General Assembly, "Overall socio-economic perspective of the world economy to the year 2000." It said: "Women's productive and reproductive roles tend to be compatible in rural areas of low-income countries, since family agriculture and cottage industries keep women close to the home, permit flexibility in working conditions *and require low investment of the mother's time.*"[177]

---

[171] *See* UNITED NATIONS, WORLD SURVEY ON THE ROLE OF WOMEN IN DEVELOPMENT 19–20 (1986); J. HENSHALL MOMSEN & J. TOWNSEND, *supra* note 168, at 15; Nairobi Review, *supra* note 61, at 8–10.

[172] The first major study was E. BOSERUP, WOMAN'S ROLE IN ECONOMIC DEVELOPMENT (1970). For a valuable survey of this literature, see Thomas & Skeat, *supra* note 168.

[173] M. WARING, *supra* note 170, at 13.   [174] *Id.* at 83.

[175] *Id.* at 27.   [176] *Id.* at 25.

[177] UN Doc. A/40/519, para. 210, at 99 (1985), *quoted in id.* at 177 (emphasis added).

The assignment of the work of women and men to different spheres, and the consequent categorization of women as "nonproducers," are detrimental to women in developing countries in many ways and make their rights to development considerably less attainable than men's. For example, the operation of the public/private distinction in international economic measurement excludes women from many aid programs because they are not considered to be workers or are regarded as less productive than men.[178] If aid is provided to women, it is often to marginalize them: foreign aid may be available to women only in their role as mothers,[179] although at least since 1967 it has been recognized that women are responsible for as much as 80 percent of the food production in developing countries.[180] The failure to acknowledge women's significant role in agriculture and the lack of concern about the impact of development on women mean that the potential of any right to development is jeopardized from the start.

Although the increased industrialization of the Third World has brought greater employment opportunities for women, this seeming improvement has not increased their economic independence or social standing and has had little impact on women's equality. Women are found in the lowest-paid and lowest-status jobs, without career paths; their working conditions are often discriminatory and insecure.[181] Moreover, there is little difference in the position of women who live in developing nations with a socialist political order.[182] The dominant model of development assumes that any paid employment is better than none[183] and fails to take into account the potential for increasing the inequality of women and lowering their economic position.

As we have seen, the international statement of the right to development draws no distinction between the economic position of men and of women. In using the neutral language of development and economics, it does not challenge the pervasive and detrimental assumption that women's work is of a different—and lesser —order than men's. It therefore cannot enhance the development of the group within developing nations that is most in need. More recent UN deliberations on development have paid greater attention to the situation of women.[184] Their concerns, however, are presented as quite distinct, solvable by the application of special protective measures, rather than as crucial to development.[185]

---

[178] An example is the aid program of the United States foreign aid agency, USAID, after a Sahelian drought. The herds were reconstituted, but only by replacing cattle owned by heads of family, i.e., men. Cattle owned by the nomadic women, used in dowry and bride wealth payments, were not replaced, which reduced the independence of the women. M. WARING, *supra* note 170, at 144.

[179] A World Bank report on development projects it sponsored acknowledged that it had supported women's projects almost exclusively in the areas of "health, hygiene, nutrition and infant care." WORLD BANK, WORLD BANK EXPERIENCE WITH RURAL DEVELOPMENT, 1965–1986, at 89 (1987).

[180] S. CHARLTON, *supra* note 60, at 61.   [181] Thomas & Skeat, *supra* note 168, at 8.

[182] *See* Molyneux, *Women's Emancipation under Socialism: A Model for the Third World*, 9 WORLD DEV. 1019 (1982).

[183] *See* Thomas & Skeat, *supra* note 168, at 11.

[184] *E.g.*, Analytical compilation of comments and views on the implementation of the Declaration on the Right to Development prepared by the Secretary-General, UN Doc. E/CN.4/AC.39/1988/L.2, paras. 59–63; Report prepared by the Secretary-General on the Global Consultation on the Realization of the Right to Development as a Human Right, UN Doc. E/CN.4/1990/9, paras. 15, 42, 51, 52, 59 [hereinafter 1990 Report].

[185] The section of the Secretary-General's report entitled "Obstacles to the implementation of the right to development as a human right," for example, mentions failure to respect the right of peoples to self-determination, racial discrimination, apartheid, foreign occupation, restrictions on transfers of

The Right to Self-Determination. The public/private dichotomy operates to reduce the effectiveness of the right to self-determination at international law. The notion of self-determination as meaning the right of "all peoples" to "freely determine their political status and freely pursue their economic, social and cultural development"[186] is flatly contradicted by the continued domination and marginalization of one sector of the population of a nation-state by another. The treatment of women within groups claiming a right to self-determination should be relevant to those claims. But the international community's response to the claims to self-determination of the Afghan and Sahrawi people, for example, indicates little concern for the position of women within those groups.

The violation of the territorial integrity and political independence of Afghanistan by the Soviet Union when it invaded that country in 1979, and other strategic, economic, and geopolitical concerns, persuaded the United States of the legality and morality of its support for the Afghan insurgents.[187] In deciding to support the rebels, the United States did not regard the policies of the *mujahidin* with respect to women as relevant.[188] The mujahidin are committed to an oppressive, rural, unambiguously patriarchal form of society quite different from that espoused by the socialist Soviet-backed regime. Indeed, Cynthia Enloe notes that "[o]ne of the policies the Soviet-backed government in Kabul pursued that so alienated male clan leaders was expanding economic and educational opportunities for Afghanistan's women."[189] A consequence of the continued support for the insurgents was the creation of a vast refugee flow into Pakistan. Of these refugees, 30 percent were women and 40 percent were children under thirteen.[190] The mullahs imposed a strict fundamentalist regime in the refugee camps, which confined women to the premises, isolated them, and even deprived them of their traditional rural tasks. There is no indication that any different policy would be followed if the mujahidin were successful and able to form a government in Afghanistan. Indeed, this marginalization and isolation of Afghan women is being projected into the future, as the educational services provided by the UN High Commissioner for Refugees are overwhelmingly for boys.[191] The vital impact of education on women and its effect in undermining male domination have been well documented.[192]

Morocco's claims to Western Sahara and the Polisario resistance to those claims have led to the establishment of Sahrawi refugee camps in Algeria that are mainly occupied by women and children. In these camps, however, women have been able to assert themselves: they have built hospitals and schools, achieved high rates of literacy, and supported "the right of the woman and the mother," as well as the

---

technology and the consumption patterns of industrialized countries as serious barriers to the realization of the right to development, but it contains no reference to sex discrimination. 1990 Report, *supra* note 184, paras. 27–35. Compare the detail of Article 14 of the Women's Convention, *supra* note 68.

[186] International Covenant on Civil and Political Rights, *supra* note 85, Art. 1; International Covenant on Economic, Social and Cultural Rights, *supra* note 150, Art. 1.

[187] *See* Reisman, *The Resistance in Afghanistan Is Engaged in a War of National Liberation*, 81 AJIL 906 (1987).

[188] By contrast, the United States used the repression of women in Iran after the 1979 revolution as an additional justification for its hostility to the Khomeini regime.

[189] C. ENLOE, *supra* note 35, at 57.

[190] N.Y. Times, Mar. 27, 1988, §1, at 16, col. 1.

[191] *Id.* The total enrollment in UN schools is 104,000 boys and 7,800 girls.

[192] *See, e.g.,* K. JAYAWARDENA, *supra* note 35, at 17–19.

"fight for independence."[193] The international community, through the International Court of Justice and the General Assembly, has reiterated the right of the people of Western Sahara to self-determination.[194] Despite this legal support, the Sahrawis' only backing comes from Algeria, while Morocco is backed, inter alia, by France and the United States. The determination of these women to keep alive a "democracy, based on proportional representation, with centralised and equal distribution, full employment, [and] social and political parity between the sexes" in the adverse conditions of refugee camps has received little international support.[195]

The international community recognizes only the right of "peoples" to self-determination, which in practice is most frequently linked to the notion of the independent state. Women have never been viewed as a "people" for the purposes of the right to self-determination. In most instances, the pursuit of self-determination as a political response to colonial rule has not resulted in terminating the oppression and domination of one section of society by another.

States often show complete indifference to the position of women when determining their response to claims of self-determination; the international invisibility of women persists. Thus, after the Soviet Union vetoed a Security Council resolution on the invasion of Afghanistan, the General Assembly reaffirmed "the inalienable right of all peoples . . . to choose their own form of government free from outside interference" and stated that the Afghan people should be able to "choose their economic, political and social systems free from outside intervention, subversion, coercion or constraint of any kind whatsoever."[196] The General Assembly's concern was with "outside" intervention alone. Women arguably suffer more from "internal" intervention: women are not free to choose their role in society without the constraints of masculine domination inside the state and are constantly subject to male coercion. The high-sounding ideals of noninterference do not apply to them, for their self-determination is subsumed by that of the group. The denial to women of the freedom to determine their own economic, social and cultural development should be taken into consideration by states in assessing the legitimacy of requests for assistance in achieving self-determination and of claims regarding the use of force.[197]

V. CONCLUSION

The feminist project, it has been said, has the "twin aims of challenging the existing norms and of devising a new agenda for theory."[198] This paper emphasizes the need for further study of traditional areas of international law from a perspective that regards gender as important. In a review of two Canadian legal textbooks on remedies, Christine Boyle points out that they simply do not address

---

[193] As demonstrated by the objectives of The Women's Union, founded in 1974. Cumming, *Forgotten Struggle for the Western Sahara,* NEW STATESMAN, May 20, 1988, at 14 ("Women are at the heart of the revolution; their own struggle for rights doesn't have to wait until the war is over, the two are indivisible").

[194] Western Sahara Case, 1975 ICJ REP. 12 (Advisory Opinion of Oct. 16).

[195] Cumming, *supra* note 193, at 15. Whether the electoral victory in Algeria of a fundamentalist party in 1990 will change the situation in these camps remains to be seen.

[196] GA Res. ES–6/2 (Jan. 14, 1980).

[197] For further discussion of the relevance of the position of women to the international law on the use of force, see Chinkin, *supra* note 49.

[198] Thornton, *supra* note 81, at 23.

the concerns and interests of women.[199] She criticizes this great silence and concludes: "Men and Law" is tolerable as an area of intellectual activity, but not if it is masquerading as "People and Law."[200] International legal structures and principles masquerade as "human"—universally applicable sets of standards. They are more accurately described as international men's law.

Modern international law is not only androcentric, but also Euro-centered in its origins, and has assimilated many assumptions about law and the place of law in society from western legal thinking. These include essentially patriarchal legal institutions, the assumption that law is objective, gender neutral and universally applicable, and the societal division into public and private spheres, which relegates many matters of concern to women to the private area regarded as inappropriate for legal regulation. Research is needed to question the assumptions of neutrality and universal applicability of norms of international law and to expose the invisibility of women and their experiences in discussions about the law. A feminist perspective, with its concern for gender as a category of analysis and its commitment to genuine equality between the sexes, could illuminate many areas of international law; for example, state responsibility, refugee law, use of force and the humanitarian law of war, human rights, population control and international environmental law.[201] Feminist research holds the promise of a fundamental restructuring of traditional international law discourse and methodology to accommodate alternative world views. As Elizabeth Gross points out, this restructuring will not amount to the replacement of one set of "truths" with another: "[feminist theory] aims to render patriarchal systems, methods and presumptions unable to function, unable to retain their dominance and power. It aims to make clear how such a dominance has been possible; and to make it no longer viable."[202]

The centrality of the state in international law means that many of the structures of international law reflect its patriarchal forms. Paradoxically, however, international law may be more open to feminist analysis than other areas of law. The distinction between law and politics, so central to the preservation of the neutrality and objectivity of law in the domestic sphere, does not have quite the same force in international law. So, too, the western domestic model of legal process as ultimately coercive is not echoed in the international sphere: the process of international law is consensual and peaceful coexistence is its goal. Finally, the sustained Third World critique of international law and insistence on diversity may well have prepared the philosophical ground for feminist critiques.

A feminist transformation of international law would involve more than simply refining or reforming existing law. It could lead to the creation of international regimes that focus on structural abuse and the revision of our notions of state responsibility. It could also lead to a challenge to the centrality of the state in international law and to the traditional sources of international law.

The mechanisms for achieving some of these aims already exist. The Covenant on Economic, Social and Cultural Rights and the Women's Convention could be used as a basis for promoting structural economic and social reform to reduce

---

[199] Boyle, Book Review, 63 CAN. B. REV. 427 (1985).

[200] *Id.* at 430–31.

[201] Papers given at a conference on gender and international law held at the Centre for International and Public Law, Australian National University, August 1990, dealt with some of these areas. The papers will be published in the *Australian Year Book of International Law* (1992). *See also* Greatbatch, *The Gender Difference: Feminist Critiques of Refugee Discourse,* 1 INT'L J. REFUGEE L. 518 (1989).

[202] Gross, *supra* note 6, at 197.

some of the causes of sexual and other abuse of women. The notion of state responsibility, however, both under these Conventions and generally, will have to be expanded to incorporate responsibility for systemic abuse based on sexual discrimination (broadly defined) and imputability to the state will have to be extended to include acts committed by private individuals. An international mechanism to hear complaints of individuals or groups, such as a protocol to the Women's Convention allowing for individual or representative petitions to the CEDAW Committee, could give women's voices a direct audience in the international community.

Is a reorientation of international law likely to have any real impact on women? Feminists have questioned the utility of attempts at legal reform in domestic law and warn against attributing too much power to law to alter basic political and economic inequalities based on sex.[203] Could this reservation be made a fortiori with respect to international law, whose enforcement and efficacy are in any event much more controversial? Would an altered, humanized international law have any capacity to achieve social change in a world where most forms of power continue to be controlled by men?

Like all legal systems, international law plays an important part in constructing reality. The areas it does not touch seem naturally to belong within the domestic jurisdiction of states. International law defines the boundaries of agreement by the international community on the matters that states are prepared to yield to supranational regulation and scrutiny. Its authority is derived from the claim of international acceptance. International legal concerns have a particular status; those concerns outside the ambit of international law do not seem susceptible to development and change in the same way. To redefine the traditional scope of international law so as to acknowledge the interests of women can open the way to reimagining possibilities for change and may permit international law's promise of peaceful coexistence and respect for the dignity of all persons[204] to become a reality.

---

[203] *E.g.*, C. SMART, *supra* note 17, at 25, 81–82.
[204] UN CHARTER, Preamble.

[13]

Female Subjects of Public International Law: Human Rights and the Exotic Other Female*

Karen Engle**

Mary Joe Frug greatly influenced my thinking about the categories discussed in this essay. She did so through her own work and through specific comments and inquiries about a related project, both of which have pushed me to clarify many of the assumptions and distinctions I present here. Mary Joe's enthusiasm and her engagement with issues of gender identity made doing this type of work exciting, challenging and fun. While she endeavored to open space for more "play" in our thinking and acting about gender, Mary Joe never lost sight of the very serious impact that these issues have on women's lives. More than anyone I have encountered, Mary Joe devoted her energy to understanding all types of people, attempting to learn what made them tick. This essay is for Mary Joe, with her enthusiasm and engagement in mind.

For centuries, several societies—primarily located in Muslim Africa—have engaged in a practice that is often, perhaps euphemistically, referred to as female circumcision.[1] Some call it genital mutilation. Others use more specific and technical language to describe the partic-

---

   *   Copyright © 1992 by Karen Engle. Reprinted by permission.
   ** Associate Professor of Law, University of Utah.

For their helpful comments and suggestions on earlier drafts of this essay, I am grateful to Abe Chayes, Dan Danielsen, Marcella David, Rainer Forst, David Kennedy, Duncan Kennedy, Martha Minow and Ileana Porras. Thanks also to participants of the Legal Theory Circle at the University of Helsinki Faculty of Law and the Dutch/American Critical Legal Studies Summer Camp for reacting to this work in its early stages. An earlier version of this essay is published in Finnish as *Nainen kansainvalisen oikeuden subjektina: Esimerkkina klitorodektomia*, 3 OIKEUS 214 (1991).

   1. Although this procedure is today most commonly performed in parts of Africa that are predominantly Muslim, it is neither exclusively performed in those areas nor done in all countries of the region. History of the practice in the Sudan indicates that the operation antedates both the arrival of Islam and of Christianity. Janice Boddy, *Body Politics: Continuing the Anticircumcision Crusade*, 5 MED. ANTHROPOLOGY Q. 15, 15 (1991). While Muslim clerics generally insist that clitoridectomy in any of its various forms is not an Islamic religious custom, "most rural Sudanese believe some form of pharaonic circumcision is to be required on religious grounds." *Id.*

ular form the practice takes, such as clitoridectomy or infibulation.[2]

The subjects (some would say objects) of this procedure are young girls ranging in age from several days just prior to marriage, depending on the particular cultural practices of the region involved. Clitoridectomy serves largely as a prerequisite, if not a direct rite of passage, to a girl's adulthood, or womanhood. A woman who has not participated in the ritual is likely to be denied the possibility of marriage and is thereby foreclosed access to certain privileges of her society. The procedure is almost universally performed by women, either trained or lay. It often proves to be dangerous, sometimes fatal, because it is not always done in hygienic circumstances.

As might be expected, many feminists have attacked this custom, and pointed to it as one more, yet quite extreme, example of misogyny and (male) societal control over female bodies. Many Western feminists have reacted with outrage, calling for an abrupt end to the practice. Their outrage has been fueled, or at least justified, by the condemnation of the practice by some women within societies that engage in it, such as Egyptian Nawal El Saadawi.[3] Some African women who oppose the practice encourage Western women to condemn it, in the belief that Western women have more clout to pressure governments to put an end to it.

For others, including other feminists, clitoridectomy poses a more complex set of issues. The complexity arises in part from the fact that women perform the operation on other females and that girls, if old enough to consider it, often claim to desire the procedure. That the

---

2. For (varied) descriptions of the practice, see Halima Warzazi, *Report of the Working Group on Traditional Practices Affecting the Health of Women and Children*, U.N. ESCOR, Commission on Human Rights, 42d Sess., Prov. Agenda item 19, U.N. Doc. E/CN.4/1986/42 (1986) [hereinafter *U.N. Report on Traditional Practices*]; OLAYINKA KOSO-THOMAS, THE CIRCUMCISION OF WOMEN: A STRATEGY FOR ERADICATION 16-17 (1987); Alison Slack, *Female Circumcision: A Critical Appraisal*, 10 HUM. RTS. Q. 437, 440-42 (1988). The different types of practice often account for variations in the language used to describe it. Other language differences stem from a wide range of, and often opposing, views about the practice.

I generally use the term clitoridectomy because of its anatomical specificity, its particular reference to the clitoris. I also use it because of its technicality, as a way of avoiding the sometimes rhetorical extremes of "circumcision" and "mutilation." In applying the term, however, I realize that I am failing to accurately portray many of the procedures, both those that are more akin to male circumcision in that they excise only a small portion of the clitoris and those that remove and operate on much more than the clitoris, such as infibulation. The former is often performed in Egypt while the latter is most common in the Sudan. For a more thorough description of practices in those countries, see Daniel Gordon, *Female Circumcision and Genital Operations in Egypt and the Sudan: A Dilemma for Medical Anthropology*, 5 MED. ANTHROPOLOGY Q. 3 (1991).

3. *See generally* NAWAL EL SAADAWI, THE HIDDEN FACE OF EVE: WOMEN IN THE ARAB WORLD (Sherif Hetata ed. & trans., 1980); NAWAL EL SAADAWI, WOMAN AT POINT ZERO (Sherif Hetata trans., 1983).

practice is deeply rooted in culture also poses difficulties. One Western feminist has suggested that Western women ought not be so shocked by the practice, given our own forms of bodily self mutilation, through, for example, plastic surgery, incessant dieting, or wearing shoes that are too small.[4] In a similar vein, Gayatri Spivak has discussed what she calls "symbolic clitoridectomy," which "has always been the 'normal' accession to womanhood and the unacknowledged name of motherhood."[5]

As the practice has become more widely known throughout the world, many have begun to talk about it as an international human rights violation. The last decade has paved the way for this kind of analysis, as public international law has expanded—at least formally— to include issues specifically pertaining to women.

With this expansion, a body of literature has developed that advocates women's rights as international human rights. Three broad approaches have emerged within that literature which I have labeled doctrinalist, institutionalist and external critique. The three approaches represent different feminist attitudes toward law, ranging from liberal to radical, as well as different approaches to rights discourse in general and to human rights law in particular.[6]

In this essay, I explore some of the ways that these different approaches confront, or would confront, clitoridectomy. I do so with an eye toward the various notions of women's subjectivity the approaches display. Specifically, as Western women's rights advocates attempt to use universal international human rights law, institutions, and discourse as means for eradicating clitoridectomy,[7] I am interested in the ways and extent to which the advocates recognize and respond to differences among women. I focus particularly on their assumptions about and reactions to what might be considered the Exotic Other Female.

---

4. *See* Rhoda E. Howard, *Health and the Social Degradation of Dishonored Groups*, paper presented at Conference on Human Rights in the 21st Century, in Banff, Alberta, Canada (Oct. 24, 1990) (on file with the *New England Law Review*); *see also* Ruth Rosen, *Perspective on Women's Health: Draw the Line at the Knife*, L.A. TIMES, Nov. 17, 1991, at M5 (describing breast implant surgery as "barbaric" and similar to other "mutilations" that are considered violations of human rights, such as footbinding, dowry deaths, and clitoridectomies).

5. Gayatri C. Spivak, *French Feminism in an International Frame, in* IN OTHER WORLDS: ESSAYS IN CULTURAL POLITICS 134, 151 (1987).

6. I have set forth and defined these approaches in detail in Karen Engle, *International Human Rights and Feminism: When Discourses Meet*, 13 MICH. J. INT'L L. 517 (1992).

7. While many women's rights advocates are not from the "West," those I discuss or allude to in this essay live, as far as I know, in North America or Europe. I believe that the positions they take, however, are due more to the fact that they rely on universal international human rights law and discourse than that they are Western. But I am not certain.

I use Exotic Other Female here to signify collectively those women within a culture that practices clitoridectomy, who through their action (or inaction) condone the practice. Implicit in this label is the assumption that the Exotic Other Female, or at least her needs and desires, are not totally accessible to someone outside her culture.

I name and discuss the Exotic Other Female in an attempt to introduce her overtly into the discourse about women's human rights. Even though women's human rights advocates usually fail to acknowledge openly—much less engage—the Exotic Other Female, I argue that they nevertheless imagine her and in doing so make many assumptions about her. The existence of the Exotic Other Female (as something "out there") seems to guide much of their analysis.

In discussing the Exotic Other Female, I do not mean to essentialize her; she is only that when she is merely imagined and not engaged. Once engaged, *she* will become *they*—many and complex—which might be one reason many have for not engaging her (and for not allowing her to engage them). One of the questions I hope to begin to address in this essay is how it would be possible to move beyond merely imagining this Other.[8]

Exploring the various ways that women's human rights advocates imagine the Exotic Other Female as they approach the issue of clitoridectomy yields some surprising and paradoxical results. It might seem, for example, due to the universalizing nature of international human rights doctrine, that liberal feminists, who are most committed to using legal doctrine to eradicate clitoridectomy, would be least likely to acknowledge differences among women. In fact, doctrinal advocates turn out to be the most overt in taking account of the Exotic Other Female. That they take account of her, however, does not mean that they engage her; rather, they attempt to change her mind about the practice by choosing a doctrinal position with which she might agree.

A similar paradox unfolds through exploration of the radical feminist positions taken by women's human rights advocates. It might seem that those advocates most critical of what they see as the "maleness" of the international human rights framework would be most able to take into account women's differences, since they would not be tied to formal universal norms as embodied in "male" international human rights doctrine. It happens, though, that the radical feminists are much less likely than the liberal feminists to confront the fact that some women defend and practice clitoridectomy. Indeed, the radical feminists do not generally even acknowledge the existence of the Exotic Other Female. The failure to acknowledge her is due largely, I believe, to their radical focus on a male/female dichotomy that they identify in human

---

8. For a provocative discussion of a similar question in the context of sati in India, see Gayatri C. Spivak, *Can the Subaltern Speak? Speculations on Widow-Sacrifice*, 7/8 WEDGE 120 (1985).

rights discourse, which they see as the primary obstacle to achieving women's human rights.

I. The Doctrinalist Approach

Doctrinalists generally approach international human rights law by focussing on one practice that they believe violates a particular right, here the practice of "female circumcision" (as they label it).[9] They then attempt to demonstrate doctrinally how the practice ought to be eradicated on the basis of rights derived from international law. Because no legal provisions specifically mention clitoridectomy or female circumcision, those who advocate its end go through one human rights instrument after another to show that the practice is prohibited by the existence of rights such as "rights of the child,"[10] "the right to sexual and corporal integrity,"[11] and the "right to health."[12]

In attempting to assimilate a particular woman's right to the dominant human rights framework, doctrinalists tend to make liberal feminist assumptions. That is, they do not indicate that bringing women into the human rights structure would radically change or disrupt the structure; indeed, their arguments assume that the positive law already includes women by providing, if indirectly, the right they advocate.

Although doctrinalists basically rely on the assimilation of women's rights to positive human rights law, they recognize that international human rights law is difficult to enforce. Enforcement seems particularly tough in the case of women's human rights, since those claims are plagued by a counter-claim of cultural relativism. So strong is the counter-claim that Alison Slack frames the purpose of her article as determining "at what point the 'tradition' [of] female circumcision becomes a human rights violation justifying pressure from foreign cultures to end this 'tradition.'"[13]

While those who take other approaches to women's human rights do not openly confront this counter-claim of cultural relativism, doctrinalists often do. Although in the end they reject a cultural relativist perspective as they argue for "universal" human rights, they are nevertheless acutely aware that disagreements about the scope and shape of women's rights exist, particularly in the case of clitoridectomy. These disagreements are not just between men and women or between cultures; they actually exist between women. The acknowledgement of

---

9. In describing this approach to clitoridectomy, I rely primarily on articles by Kay Boulware-Miller and Alison Slack. *See* Kay Boulware-Miller, *Female Circumcision: Challenges to the Practice as a Human Rights Violation*, 8 HARV. WOMEN'S L.J. 155 (1985); Slack, *supra* note 2.

10. *See* Boulware-Miller, *supra* note 9, at 165-69.

11. *See id.* at 169-72.

12. *See id.* at 172-76; Slack, *supra* note 2, at 485-86.

13. Slack, *supra* note 2, at 439.

disagreements among women is, in my mind, a strength of the doctrinalists' feminist approaches. It allows them to engage women's differences to a greater extent than those who take the other approaches, which tend to assume, albeit to different degrees, a monolithic or essential "woman."

Although doctrinalists acknowledge these differences among women's attitudes, they eventually attempt to work around them. They seem to imagine the existence of the Exotic Other Female, the one who opposes abolition of the practice she might even help perpetuate, as something that must be reckoned with. For the doctrinalists, this imagined Other is a reminder that the right, no matter how enshrined in public international law, is not universally accepted. Rather than denying the existence of the Exotic Other Female, doctrinalists propose strategies for changing her mind and thus for removing an obstacle to universal recognition of the right. In choosing among strategies, they express sensitivity to cultural differences.

At this stage, doctrinalists engage in what I call strategic positivism. Although a number of rights exist in positive law that would seemingly prohibit clitoridectomy (right to corporal and sexual integrity, rights of children, right to health), those who oppose the practice do not stress them all. Instead, they make a strategic decision about which right to pursue, depending on which rights rubric governments and the Exotic Other Female (as victim, and often as victimizer) are most likely to accept. Alison Slack and Kay Boulware-Miller agree that governments are most likely to accept a right to health argument, since, as Boulware-Miller puts it, they "are more concerned with basic health and economic problems than with the arguably more elitist rights they associate with Western countries, such as political rights and fundamental freedoms."[14] Boulware-Miller believes women, too, will be most likely to accept an end to the practice based on a health argument, because, unlike the other potential rights arguments, it avoids an "imposing and judgmental approach."[15]

Doctrinalists, therefore, deal with the tension between cultures by acknowledging the tension and then working around it. While a

---

14. Boulware-Miller, *supra* note 9, at 173; *see also* Slack, *supra* note 2, at 486.

15. Boulware-Miller, *supra* note 9, at 166-67, 171-72. Health arguments have been the most common means of attempting to eradicate clitoridectomy, both by intergovernmental and nongovernmental actors. *See, e.g.,* Halima Warzazi, *Study on Traditional Practices Affecting the Health of Women and Children,* U.N. ESCOR, Commission on Human Rights, 43d Sess., Prov. Agenda item 4, U.N. Doc. E/CN.4/ Sub.2/1991/6 (1991); *U.N. Report on Traditional Practices, supra* note 2; Koso-Thomas, *supra* note 2. Even those who have taken a more radical approach to clitoridectomy, calling it "genital mutilation" for example, have responded favorably to the health approach. *See, e.g., Progress Report: WIN News Grass Roots Campaign to Eradicate GM [Genital Mutilation],* 18 WOMEN'S INT'L NETWORK NEWS 38-39 (1992).

strength of their approach is that they recognize and even take account of differences among women, they neither engage those women that practice clitoridectomy nor confront the practice itself. Rather than finding out why women defend the practice, they try to convince them to change their minds, by phrasing the issue as one of health. They do so despite the United Nations own research on "traditional practices affecting the health of women and children," which indicates that women who oppose clitoridectomy within those cultures where it is practiced rarely cite health as a reason.[16]

By approaching the issue as one of health, doctrinalists seem to have avoided taking any overtly "political" stance on the issue of clitoridectomy. For them, international human rights law, by guaranteeing a right to health, demands an end to the practice. Approaching clitoridectomy as a health issue raises another concern. If the practice could be done without negative health consequences, international law might actually become complicit in the practice, obligating states to ensure that it is performed under better health conditions. This possibility is one the doctrinalists do not address.[17]

II. THE INSTITUTIONALIST APPROACH

The institutionalist approach to women's human rights concentrates on the institutions that have been created by international law to enforce human rights.[18] Those who take this approach do not generally advocate particular rights, and they are not concerned with which international instruments guarantee which rights. They believe that if posi-

---

16. *See U.N. Report on Traditional Practices, supra* note 2, at 15 (discussing reasons women give for opposing the practice as "violation of fundamental human rights," "violation of women's image," "social complications," and "cultural conformism"); *see also id.* at 14 (Of the "sample of persons opposed to female circumcision," only 12.72 per cent gave "illnesses and accidents" as a reason, as opposed to 43.63 per cent who said the practice is pointless and 32.72 per cent who listed "diminution of sensitivity" for the reason.).

17. The possibility is not as remote as it might seem. Gordon reports that in urban parts of the Sudan, there is already an official policy of using the health care system to perform the procedures in order to reduce complications and health risks. Moreover, trained medical personnel with drugs and equipment have been disseminated and used to perform clitoridectomies and other genital operations. *See* Gordon, *supra* note 2, at 12 (citing ASMA EL DAREER, WOMEN, WHY DO YOU WEEP? (1982); FRAN P. HOSKEN, THE HOSKEN REPORT: GENITAL AND SOCIAL MUTILATION OF FEMALES 47, 287 (1982)).

18. I primarily base my description of this approach on Margaret E. Galey, *International Enforcement of Women's Rights*, 6 HUM. RTS. Q. 463 (1984) and Laura Reanda, *Human Rights and Women's Rights: The United Nations Approach*, 3 HUM. RTS. Q. 11 (1981). More recent literature takes very similar approaches. *See, e.g.,* Theodor Meron, *Editorial Comments: Enhancing the Effectiveness of the Prohibition of Discrimination Against Women*, 84 AM. J. INT'L L. 213 (1990); Andrew C. Byrnes, *The "Other" Human Rights Treaty Body: The Work of the Committee on the Elimination of Discrimination Against Women*, 14 YALE J. INT'L L. 1 (1989).

tive law or doctrine guaranteeing women's rights is to be meaningful, institutions must transform that law or doctrine into action, through pragmatic, meaningful enforcement mechanisms. To the extent that transformation has not occurred, they largely hold responsible the (primarily male) actors that deploy human rights discourse through international institutions. Institutionalists do not attack the international institutional framework per se. Instead, they argue either that mainstream institutions—those institutions that see themselves as enforcing all human rights, not differentiating between women and men—need to rearrange their priorities to include issues of women, or that specialized women's institutions—meant specifically to enforce women's rights and generally comprised of women—must be given power equal to mainstream ones.

Because of their reliance on existing institutional structures to assimilate women's rights, I also consider these advocates liberal feminists. Their approaches, however, could be understood as more radical than those of the doctrinalists, as the institutionalists are critical of the present (male) deployment of the system. The difficulties the institutionalists point to are more directly attributed to a male dominated structure than those identified by the doctrinalists. These advocates provide useful insights into the power plays within the institutional framework that keep men in control and women's rights at the periphery.

Although institutionalists do not generally focus on particular human rights violations, we can imagine a way that they might approach clitoridectomy. They would likely start by taking for granted that the practice is in violation of international human rights law (although a brief discussion with a doctrinalist might be required to convince them). Their task would then be to see international institutions enforce the rights the doctrinalists derive.

As they make proposals for greater enforcement of women's rights, institutionalists—unlike doctrinalists—are not concerned with the possibility that women might disagree about particular rights. Rather, they focus on what they see as male/female disagreements, which manifest themselves in the bureaucratic structures of international institutions, both mainstream and specialized. In this context, institutionalists often act as if international institutional actors are largely free from the cultures from which they hail (except that male actors are obvious products of patriarchy). The Exotic Other Female never enters into the sterile institutional framework because within that framework there is nothing to be other to but the male actors who have power to deploy and control international institutions.

Applying their analysis to clitoridectomy, institutionalists would argue that international institutions could in theory, and partly within their present structure, address the issue. For the institutional framework to be effective in combatting the practice, however, they would contend that either mainstream institutions must expand their (presently male) focus or specialized women's institutions must be granted power equal to the mainstream ones. Institutionalists would generally pursue the second possibility, implying that were the specialized institutions given sufficient power, clitoridectomy could be brought to an end. Hence, although the Commission on Human Rights, through its Sub-commission on the Protection of Minorities, has investigated clitoridectomy as a practice affecting women's health, institutionalists might argue that the issue could be addressed more effectively and directly by a specialized institution, such as the Commission on the Status of Women. But, they would point out, the Commission on the Status of Women could only even potentially do so if it were granted investigatory powers equal to the Commission on Human Rights.

Within the institutionalists' discussions and proposals, however, lies the very real possibility that even if women's institutions were given the power needed to pursue their agendas, women comprising those institutions might reject that power. Margaret Galey, for example, has discussed a meeting of the Commission on the Status of Women where some members were reluctant to accept responsibility for investigating individual cases, a power she sees as essential to enforcing women's rights, because they "recognized that this would involve investigation of allegations, a politically sensitive matter, and a considerable expense, which the Commission's membership was unlikely to support."[19] Although the Commission eventually passed the resolution, its members have continued to debate whether to increase their capacity to receive communications.[20] They have also rejected possibilities for greater power in other areas.[21]

The reality that women, even within specialized women's institutions might disagree about "what they want," poses a very real, although largely unacknowledged, obstacle to actualizing the solutions these advocates propose. Hence, while those who pursue women's rights institutionally offer a powerful analysis of the workings and priorities of the international institutional framework, as well as of the

---

19. Galey, *supra* note 18, at 469.

20. Even as recently as the 1991 meeting of the Commission, members were unable to agree on a resolution that purported to grant greater power to receive or investigate complaints. Indeed, a draft resolution on "Communications concerning the status of women," *Monitoring the Implementation of the Nairobi Forward-Looking Strategies for the Advancement of Women*, U.N. ESCOR, Commission on the Status of Women, 35th Sess., Agenda item 4, U.N. Doc. E/CN.6/1991/L.14 (1991), did not even make it to the floor.

21. In 1988, for example, the Commission chose not to request an increase in the length of its meetings, even though the General Assembly encouraged it to do so. Sandra Colliver, *United Nations Machineries on Women's Rights: How Might They Better Help Women Whose Rights are Being Violated*, in NEW DIRECTIONS IN HUMAN RIGHTS 25, 29 (Ellen L. Lutz et al. eds., 1989).

often gendered nature of presumably neutral bureaucratic structures, they are prevented from fully exploring the changes they seek by only focussing on, and in turn reinforcing, male/female differences.

III. External Critiques

Other women's human rights advocates begin by situating themselves outside the human rights system looking in at the discourse. From their (initial) external perches, they raise questions about whether human rights discourse can really assimilate women's issues/demands/rights.

In this section, I identify and discuss three external critiques, each of which suggests a different level of belief in the ability of international rights discourse and the human rights framework to address issues of women. Unlike the doctrinalists and institutionalists, who believe that the human rights framework can assimilate women's rights, the external critics believe structural changes—whether in human rights theory, doctrine, institutions or language—are needed to accommodate women's concerns.

For the most part, I consider those who take these approaches to be radical feminists because they critique the human rights system for the ways it perpetuates women's subordination.[22] To a certain extent, they also approach women's human rights as if all women were essentially the same.

The radical feminist positions of these critics do not, I believe, make them incapable of accepting that women disagree, even about clitoridectomy. Rather, they focus so much on the subordination of women by men that they tend to generalize the extent to which all women have an interest in overcoming men's power, the assumption here being that "genital mutilation" (as they call the practice) is a clear exercise of male power. This near exclusive focus on subordination, I maintain, is largely responsible for the failure of radical feminists to engage the Exotic Other Female. Were the external critics to confront the fact that females disagree about clitoridectomy, they would likely assign "false consciousness" to those whom they consider do not recognize their own oppression.

A. *Integration*

The integrationist approach to international human rights challenges human rights advocates to accept a coherent or integrated theory of *human* rights—one that represents the rights of both women and men—and to realize "human rights which are genuinely human."[23]

---

22. *See* Alison M. Jaggar, Feminist Politics and Human Nature 83-85 (1983).
23. Fran P. Hosken, *Toward a Definition of Women's Human Rights*, 3 Hum. Rts. Q. 1, 10 (1981).

Those who take this approach often refer to the rights of "half of humanity."[24] For them it is because women are human, not just women, that their human rights should be protected. That they are not protected is not directly due to women's differences from men (or from each other) but to the failure of the human rights system to pay attention to women's (human) situation.

Although this approach might sound similar to the doctrinalist approach, since it suggests an underlying belief in a human rights framework that can incorporate women's rights, it differs in an important respect. While the doctrinalists assume that the framework already assimilates women, the integrationists argue that the human rights system must change its focus to accommodate women's rights. And even though the integrationists do not stress women's differences from men—hoping that both male and female can be dealt with under the human rubric—they do have some sense of a gender struggle. The problem with human rights practice, they argue, is that it has focussed on men's rights.

Integrationists begin their critique of the international human rights system by noting rampant violations of what they assume to be women's human rights. One example of such violations is "genital mutilations of women which still kill, maim, and blight the physical and psychological health of millions of women and little children every year."[25] They then argue that the international human rights system is disingenuous because it does not declare clitoridectomy a human rights violation and aim to end the practice.

To the extent that those who take this approach confront the issue of cultural relativism, they see the relativist claim as false and inconsistent, made by those who simply want to exclude practices such as clitoridectomy from human rights analysis. Riane Eisler, for example, abruptly dismisses the argument that "the enactments and enforcement of laws prohibiting genital mutilation would be improper interference with ethnic traditions, constituting merely one more form of 'Western cultural imperialism' "[26] with the following response: "All institutionalized behavior, including cannibalism and slavery, are cultural traditions. And surely no human rights advocate . . . would today dare to justify cannibalism or slavery . . . on cultural or traditional grounds."[27] Implicit in this rejection of the claim is that clitoridectomy is analogous to cannibalism and slavery. Referring to the practice as mutilation makes this analogy more likely; no one would *choose* to be eaten, enslaved, or mutilated.

---

24. *See, e.g.*, Riane Eisler, *Human Rights: Toward an Integrated Theory of Action*, 9 HUM. RTS. Q. 287, 287, 289 (1987).

25. *Id.* at 295.

26. *Id.*

27. *Id.* at 296.

Integrationists believe that the difficulty in bringing women's rights into the human rights arena lies not with international human rights discourse per se, but rather with its presently exclusive male focus. That focus, which is not only not endemic to human rights theory but in opposition to it, must be changed if the practice of clitoridectomy is to be brought to an end.

Integrationists provide important insights into the often inconsistent claims that keep women's rights at the periphery of international human rights law and discourse.[28] The refusal of the integrationists to see human rights theory as preventing the protection of women's rights allows them to pursue possibilities for using international rights as a site for struggling for the improvement of women's condition. The question they do not explore, however, is what it means to improve women's condition. For them, ending "genital mutilation" is only a matter of changing the focus of the international human rights system. These advocates do not confront the possibility that "culture" might really be an obstacle to achieving change. In particular, they do not consider that resistance to ending the practice, and even to labeling it "mutilation," might come from (some) women themselves. For integrationists, the Exotic Other Female is not to be engaged.

B.   *Reconceptualization/Redefinition*

Human rights critics who take this approach do not have as much faith as the integrationists in the ability of human rights theory to merely expand its focus to accommodate women's rights. For them, international human rights theory is seriously flawed because it is centered on a "male" definition of human rights. Hence, to accommodate women's rights, the theory would require reconceptualizing and redefining. Specifically, women would have to define their own rights.

This approach differs from the integrationist approach, then, in a subtle way. Avoiding the possibility that women might need any special rights, the integrationists aim to normalize or universalize women's rights, making them an essential part of human rights (hence the discussion of the *human* rights of women). Those who call for reconceptualization, on the other hand, embrace women's differences from men, through their call upon women to define their own rights.[29]

---

28. The integrationists' undermining of the public/private distinction is perhaps a better example of the inconsistency of the claims than their response to cultural relativism. *See infra* note 30.

29. *See, e.g.*, Noreen Burrows, *International Law and Human Rights: The Case of Women's Rights, in* HUMAN RIGHTS: FROM RHETORIC TO REALITY 80, 89-96 (Tom Campbell et al. eds., 1986). In describing this approach, I rely largely on this article by Noreen Burrows and a lecture by Felice Gaer. *See* Felice Gaer, Address at 1988 Harvard Human Rights Program Symposium on Women's Rights and Human Rights: Possibilities and Contradictions (Apr. 16, 1988) (videotape on file with the *New England Law Review*).

If they were to talk about "genital mutilation," reconceptualists might argue that the human rights system has not begun to deal with the issue because women have not defined the rights necessary to end the practice. Without such definition, human rights law regarding women, with its present focus on discrimination, is bound to respond insufficiently to the issue.

For these advocates, once women define their rights, it will become clear that human rights must be reconceptualized. Essential to this reconceptualization is the entry of human rights law into the traditional private sphere. The reconceptualist position assumes a distinction between public and private realms and takes for granted that international human rights, as presently theorized, excludes from its purview the private sphere.[30] From that perspective, clitoridectomy—because it is a "private" (not officially state conducted) practice—cannot be seen as a violation of international human rights until the human rights field has been reconceptualized to include the private.

By calling for women to define their rights, the reconceptualist position, unlike that of the integrationists, in principle opens itself up to the possibility of listening to a multiplicity of women's voices and even to engaging the Exotic Other Female. Yet, one of the central assumptions of this position seems to be that women will agree about what are or should be their rights. The goal of the reconceptualist is, if not to shift from the male vision of human rights, at least to supplement that vision with a female one. Male and female are, for these purposes, static notions.

The reconceptualist position is not, however, unaware of claims of cultural relativism. Noreen Burrows, for example, sees cultural differences as posing difficulties to the process of achieving recognition of women's rights: "Given the diversity in the forms of interpersonal relations and cultural variations which exist, say in the structure of the family, it may prove difficult to specify with sufficient precision those rights which the international community would recognize as being the rights of women."[31] Even as Burrows expresses this concern, however, she never suggests that women themselves might disagree about which rights they have; rather, her concern is that the "international community" might have trouble accepting or properly interpreting the rights because of its apparent sympathy with cultural variations. That women might be a part of that conflictual international community is not an issue she addresses.

---

30. This approach to the public/private distinction is also a significant departure from the integrationist approach, which argues that the claim that human rights does not enter the private sphere is as irrational and politically determined as the cultural relativism claim. *See, e.g.*, Eisler, *supra* note 24, at 293.

31. Burrows, *supra* note 29, at 85.

C. *Linguistic Critique*

Whether through integration or reconceptualization, those who pose the first two external critiques assume that the international human rights framework can be made to accommodate women's concerns. The problems integrationists and reconceptualists identify with human rights theory turn in large part on the view that it has addressed itself, perhaps exclusively, to the concerns of men. They disagree primarily about whether that focus is endemic to the theory. Another external critique poses what I call a linguistic challenge to human rights discourse. Those who aim this critique at international rights discourse generally explicitly situate themselves outside it, identifying with a particular cause or discipline (for example, feminism or biology) to examine the biases reflected in the discourse. For them, human rights discourse is not just male focussed, controlled or deployed; it is "male."

Here I focus on only one strand of this critique, which poses what it considers to be the feminist critique of rights. Although the critique borrows from communitarianism and early Marxism, and resonates with many of the critiques of rights by critical legal theorists, it does so with a strong cultural feminist perspective. That is, it assumes that there are certain essential values that are female and that cannot be realized through traditional rights discourse.

For these critics, "the concept of 'rights' is masculinist and patriarchal, a concept that came into its own with the rise of capitalism."[32] Adding an essentialist feminist twist to other critiques of rights, they suggest that "in our assertion of rights we [feminists] play a masculinist game."[33] Moreover:

> "[r]ights" language seems to assume . . . that society is a collection of atomic particles in which any given individual's happiness . . . is viewed as mutually disinterested from another's, that communities or love relationships are not ethically relevant in deciding what action ought to be taken. Rights language is fundamentally adversarial and negative . . . . Feminists seek a framework that emphasizes positive values such as helping, cooperating and acting out of love, friendship or relatedness, as well as fairness.[34]

Other problems these advocates identify with rights discourse are that it "fails to resolve moral disputes cohesively" and that it is "static and does not challenge the social structures."[35]

Even after setting forth this harsh critique, these advocates (as with many rights critics) return to rights language. They claim to do so,

---

32. Helen B. Holmes & Susan R. Petersen, *Rights Over One's Own Body: A Woman-Affirming Health Care Policy*, 3 HUM. RTS. Q. 71, 73 (1981).
33. *Id.*
34. *Id.*
35. *Id.*

however, "in a nonabsolutist fashion . . . affirm[ing] other moral criteria than rights—such as duty, loyalty, friendship, responsibility, goodness, and justice—as the basis of moral action."[36] In the end, then, they accept rights language by adding to their use of it what they consider to be essential women's values.

Although these advocates raise a number of important issues about the lack of neutrality of language and the role(s) that language plays in social struggles, their critique eventually relies on a deeply entrenched male/female dichotomy. Even though all the other advocates, save the doctrinalists, also rely to some extent on this dichotomy, this one is most based on essential, and thereby presumably unchangeable, differences between men and women. Along with their notion that men and women fundamentally differ comes a strong sense that all women are the same. Hence, in their assumption and even promotion of an essential woman's culture, the linguistic critics come the closest of any women's rights advocates to erasing the experiences/beliefs/desires of the Exotic Other Female. Their theory cannot accommodate any recognition of disagreements among women; it would disrupt their totalizing scheme.

* * *

All the authors who challenge human rights discourse from the outside—never assuming that it was meant to protect or assimilate their feminist demands—eventually defend the discourse in some form. Their greatest strength, I believe, is their self-conscious approach and insightful understanding of the nuances of language and of power. With all the potential obstacles to achieving women's human rights these advocates identify, however, they fail to consider seriously the possibility that women are not all the same and that legitimate differences might exist among them, particularly regarding issues such as clitoridectomy. The extent to which that failure problematizes their position differs with the various approaches.

IV. CONCLUSION: BEYOND IMAGINATION

At first glance, it would appear that approaching the practice of clitoridectomy as a violation of human rights would prohibit any discussion of cultural relativism. It seems that universal and international human rights implicitly represent a denial of the validity of any cultural difference that might stand in opposition to the declared universal norm. If this were the case, one might expect the debate about clitoridectomy in the international rights context to differ significantly from the debate among feminists described at the beginning of this essay.

It turns out, though, that as with the debate about clitoridectomy in other contexts, some women's rights advocates are sensitive to the de-

---

36. *Id.* at 74.

sire of the Exotic Other Female to maintain and participate in the practice of her culture, while other women's rights advocates refuse to engage the Other's "desires," presumably because they are mere products of false consciousness. Hence, the possibility or impossibility of taking account of "real" cultural differences and beliefs informs much of how women's rights advocates approach clitoridectomy.

Another puzzle has emerged. Just as it seems that a universal human rights approach would prohibit discussion of cultural relativism, it also would seem that those advocates most committed to formal international legal doctrine would be less sensitive to discussion of cultural difference than those advocates who appear to have a sophisticated understanding of the nuances of legal doctrine. I maintain, however, that at least in the context of women's human rights advocacy, the opposite happens. The more doctrinally oriented the advocate is, the more open she is to recognizing differences among women. And the more she moves outside the formal legal structures, the more she assumes an essential woman's voice.

This puzzle is due in part, I believe, to the differing attitudes that women's rights advocates display toward rights. While the doctrinalists stake their universal claims in liberal positive rights agreed to by sovereigns, those who apply an external critique often rely on some inherent moral basis, generally rights, for their claims. Positive law seems to free up the doctrinalists, allowing them to choose any doctrinally derived right they believe to be effective in persuading the Exotic Other Female. Those who claim moral rights do not experience the same type of liberty; a right is a right regardless of whether those they entitle want to claim it.

The puzzle is also related to the different feminist postures assumed by the advocates. While the most formalist advocates tend to be liberal (tolerant) feminists, those most external to the formal structures tend to be radical (in this case often essentialist) feminists. To the extent that liberal feminists are concerned with increasing women's choices and radical feminists are concerned with increasing women's power,[37] it makes sense that the liberals would be more open to a variety of women's views and desires. The radicals, by concentrating on women's power (versus men's power), are invested in making women one cohesive group.

As advocates move from the more liberal to the more radical positions, they become progressively more concerned about changing the power dynamics, and they move further outside the formal legal structures to try to achieve that change. Hence, institutionalists play the perfect middle-ground, assuming the institutional structures can eventually assimilate their feminist demands but nevertheless recognizing

---

37. *See* Robin L. West, *The Difference in Women's Hedonic Lives: A Phenomenological Critique of Feminist Legal Theory*, 3 WIS. WOMEN'S L.J. 81, 87 (1987).

that the male domination of the structure makes the assimilation difficult. The further they move outside doctrine, the more advocates work within a dichotomous male/female framework. That dichotomy seems to keep women's differences, or different women, at bay.

Whether they work inside or outside the doctrinal and institutional frameworks, most women's rights advocates recognize at some level that women have been marginalized, consciously or not, from those frameworks. But they do not generally recognize that their own pursuit of women's rights is also marginalizing. Just as human rights advocates might keep women at the periphery, if not exclude them altogether, women's rights advocates keep the Exotic Other Female at the margins. The Exotic Other Female, however, apparently present or not, affects women's rights advocacy. Whether or not advocates openly acknowledge or engage her needs and desires, she is always just below the surface or around the corner, even as a potential disruption to their critiques and proposals. Perhaps it is to avoid that potential disruption, increased exponentially and possibly infinitely, that she is kept at bay.

I do not mean to suggest in this essay that the "male" side of the male/female split is unproblematic. I believe that it is largely because so many of the women's rights advocates readily accept a stereotypical and essentialist view of men that they are unable to problematize the female side. Being caught in the male/female dichotomy prevents further exploration of either "male" or "female."

Doctrinalists seem to have avoided this trap by assuming that women can assimilate to the (gender-neutral) human rights doctrine. They are able to take account of the existence of the Exotic Other Female through their attempts at persuading her (which requires using doctrine strategically). But through their concentrated effort at bringing all females into the realm of human rights doctrine, they fail to recognize the very biases reflected in that doctrine, as well as in human rights institutions and discourse, that might keep women outside its scope.

It appears, then, that even though each approach provides some valuable insights into the workings of the international human rights framework, none actively engages the Exotic Other Female. Either the advocates maternalistically try to change her mind or they seem to ignore or not believe her desires, often dissipating her by attributing to her false consciousness. Either way, advocates' imagined constructs of her guide their strategies for gaining recognition of women's rights.

Gayatri Spivak has said that "[b]etween patriarchy and imperialism, subject-constitution and object-formation, the figure of the woman disappears, not into pristine nothingness, but into a violent shuttling which is the displaced figuration of the 'Third World Woman' caught between tradition and modernization."[38] The failure of advocates to engage the Exotic Other Female does not erase her; she is not absent. The task ahead for women's human rights advocates is to acknowledge the presence of the Exotic Other Female, even in her sometimes apparent absence, and to use some of those insights already provided by their varied approaches to begin to move from imagination to engagement.

---

38. Spivak, *supra* note 8, at 128.

Jurisprudence

[14]

Essay

The Book of "A"

Linda R. Hirshman[*]

I. Introduction

I suppose that, in light of Harold Bloom's claim that a woman wrote the Bible, my contention that Aristotle was a feminist should be positively uncontroversial.[1] Nonetheless, as in Bloom's work, it is the apparent perversity and actual richness of the juxtaposition between feminism and the ancient understandings that I wish to explore. This effort springs from the contemporary revision of moral philosophy, which poses a morality of virtue—particularly as expressed in Aristotle's ethical writings—against the modern tradition of a morality of rules.[2] As set forth below, contemporary feminism powerfully invokes and instantiates that revision; it is a puzzle that the relationship to the Aristotelian source has not been more fully explored. The role of Aristotelian misogyny must not be underestimated, but the effort is eminently worth making, because Aristotle's writings on virtue ethics are the most ambitious work in the philosophical tradition addressing the critical question facing feminism—and contemporary political theory generally—today: the purpose and limits of equality.

* Professor of Law and Norman and Edna Freehling Scholar, IIT Chicago-Kent College of Law. J.D. 1969, University of Chicago Law School; Ph.D. Candidate, University of Illinois. Thanks to Professors Ronald Allen, John Ayer, Randy Barnett, Richard Kraut, Jane Larson, and Richard Posner for reading and criticizing the drafts, and to the participants in the New York University Law School Legal Theory Workshop, the University of Chicago Law School Legal Theory Workshop, and the Arizona State Law School Faculty Workshop for their communal consideration and individual suggestions. ("[T]he activity of wisdom is admittedly the pleasantest of excellent activities." 2 ARISTOTLE, *Nicomachean Ethics*, in THE COMPLETE WORKS OF ARISTOTLE X.7.1177a23-24, at 1729, 1861 (Bollingen Series No. 71, Jonathan Barnes ed., 1984) (Revised Oxford Translation)).

1. *See* HAROLD BLOOM, THE BOOK OF J (David Rosenberg trans., 1990). Of course, the assumption of human authorship of the Bible is already heresy. For the most recent of the several millennia of authority, see Richard Bernstein, *A Perennial Scrapper Takes on God and the Bible*, N.Y. TIMES, Oct. 24, 1990, at C11.

2. The beginning of the development is generally attributed to the path-breaking work of G.E.M. Anscombe. *See* 3 G.E.M. ANSCOMBE, *Modern Moral Philosophy*, in THE COLLECTED PHILOSOPHICAL PAPERS OF G.E.M. ANSCOMBE 26, 26-42 (Basil Blackwell ed., 1981).

Accordingly, I will first try to draw feminism and Aristotelianism together by emphasizing the similarity in their assumptions about human nature and philosophical method. Next, I will try to draw some insights from classical philosophy, specifically from Aristotle's work, for contemporary issues of law and feminist jurisprudence, particularly the issues like surrogacy and the selective service, which have puzzled—if not stymied—liberal theorists. In the end, I will focus on the hard differences between a philosophy characterized by overt misogyny and by the affirmative positing of answers on the one hand and a jurisprudence of liberation and the tolerance of differences on the other. I will conclude that Aristotelian "tough-mindedness"[3] on the varieties of the human condition, coupled with the unifying classical vision of citizenship, breaks the liberal frame and provides a model of a good life unavailable in other moral traditions, a model from which answers to the puzzles of modern feminism may be drawn.

II. Feminist Jurisprudence and Classical Philosophy

Can a study of Aristotle's writings add to feminist jurisprudence? I think the answer is clearly "yes," in at least three ways. First, Aristotle's methods and the attendant epistemology presage and support feminist methods and epistemology; each is also importantly linked to the recent revival of interest in moral learning from the methods of literary analysis. Second, Aristotle's writings make explicit and defend a view of the human condition as naturally political that is central to most important contemporary feminist thought. Finally, and I hope most interestingly, the Aristotelian vision of an ideal of the good life for citizens may be the best source of substantive answers about politics and the political community to which liberal equality has been inadequate and which feminism, like any normative theory, must ultimately produce.

A. Feminist Methods and Classical Methods

To take the easy subject first, consider feminist methods. Since Catharine MacKinnon's pathbreaking work ten years ago,[4] feminist jurisprudence has pursued several avenues of analysis, reasoning, and criticism. First, and perhaps earliest, feminists began "asking the 'woman question,'" meaning challenging legal doctrines and methods on the

---

3. The phrase is from William James through Margaret Jane Radin. *See* Margaret J. Radin, *The Pragmatist and the Feminist,* 63 S. CAL. L. REV. 1699, 1713 (1990).

4. *See* Catharine A. MacKinnon, *Feminism, Marxism, Method, and the State: An Agenda for Theory,* 7 SIGNS 515 (1982) [hereinafter MacKinnon, *Agenda for Theory*]; Catharine A. MacKinnon, *Feminism, Marxism, and the State: Toward Feminist Jurisprudence,* 8 SIGNS 635 (1985) [hereinafter MacKinnon, *Toward Feminist Jurisprudence*].

grounds that they disadvantage women.[5] Having found legal doctrines and methods that purported to be just and appeared to be neutral, but produced results that grossly disadvantaged women, feminists perceived a hidden male viewpoint first in the rules and then in the process of liberal legalism itself.[6] Feminist scholars countered with methods of feminist practical reasoning, which resembles traditional practical reasoning,[7] in approaching problems "with multiple perspectives, contradictions, and inconsistencies"[8] which precludes as undesirable the "reduction of contingencies to rules by which all disputes can be decided in advance."[9] In order to be able to gather the information necessary for feminist practical reason, feminists turned to the well-established social feminist method of

---

5. MacKinnon, *Toward Feminist Jurisprudence, supra* note 4, at 638; *see* Katharine T. Bartlett, *Feminist Legal Methods,* 103 HARV. L. REV. 829, 837 (1990).

6. Scratch the consciousness of any female law school graduate since the publication of Betty Friedan's *The Feminine Mystique* in 1963, and you will hear a story to illustrate this. Mine involves "vital heat." *See infra* text accompanying note 59. Sometime around the middle of my first year at (we'll call it the University of Chillcago) law school in the mid-sixties, I noticed that I was freezing all the time I was in the school building and suffering from an unusual number of colds. A preliminary inquiry into the matter sent me to, we'll call him Shel B. Nameless, a senior faculty member whose specialty and institutional role did not immediately suggest him as a candidate for control of the thermostat.

"Professor Nameless," I inquired, "why is it always so cold in the law school?"

"Well," he replied, "it's actually just the right temperature. If you'd wear a jacket and vest like a real law student, you wouldn't be cold at all."

* * *

"Plus ça change, plus c'est la même chose." A woman of my acquaintance was being considered for appointment to the faculty of one of the twenty "top ten" law schools this year. In urging his colleagues not to appoint, a faculty member (since he conflates the relevant norm with resemblance to himself, we'll call him Professor Moral) attempted to discount the publication of two of her scholarly articles in two top ten law reviews during the previous two years. "Not analytical enough," he explained. "If she'd write doctrinal scholarship like a real law professor, she might be good enough for our faculty."

It is this confusion of the species with the particular speaker—the replacement of the purported neutrality of liberalism with what I will hereafter call "limoralism"—that has fueled so much of the feminist disenchantment with the project generally. *See* Drucilla Cornell, *Sexual Difference, the Feminine, and Equivalency: A Critique of MacKinnon's* Toward a Feminist Theory of the State, 100 YALE L.J. 2247, 2258-59 (1991) (maintaining that feminist arguments, which suggest that the impact of gender hierarchy limits thinking about equality, are not given the weight they deserve). For very recent expositions of the phenomenon in legal academe, see Peter M. Shane, *Why Are So Many People So Unhappy? Habits of Thought and Resistance to Diversity in Legal Education,* 75 IOWA L. REV. 1033 (1991); Margaret J. Radin, *Affirmative Action Rhetoric,* 85 SOC. PHIL. & POL'Y 130 (1991). For a further explanation of limoralism, see *infra* text accompanying note 98.

7. Bartlett explicitly refers to "a classic Aristotelian model of practical deliberation." Bartlett, *supra* note 5, at 850.

8. *Id.* at 851; *see* Radin, *supra* note 3, at 1706-07 (invoking "feminism and pragmatism," meaning the "theory that truth is inevitably plural, concrete, and provisional" and noting that the two share "the commitment to finding knowledge in the particulars of experience").

9. Bartlett, *supra* note 5, at 853.

consciousness raising:[10] "collaborative or interactive engagements with others based upon personal experience and narrative."[11]

Feminist methodology also implicates and invokes feminist epistemology. As feminist scholar Katharine Bartlett points out, methods must ultimately be evaluated according to the defensibility, and even rightness of the answers they generate.[12] Here, too, there are several schools of thought. The first, rational empiricism, pretty much tracks traditional modes of truth-finding.[13] Corresponding to the liberal assumptions of the "early contemporary legal feminists," rational empiricism is a tool for bringing women up to the purported neutrality of equal treatment.[14] When rational empiricism failed to address the truth claims of women with different life experiences than men,[15] feminists responded to the inadequacy of rational empiricism with theories of standpoint epistemology, which challenges rational empiricism as hopelessly tied to the existing male power structure, and with claims for women's unique access to understanding, based on their particular life-experiences.[16] A third school, corresponding to trends of deconstruction in other disciplines, sees each of the prior claims to knowledge as fatally foundationalist and asserts the pure social, local, and provisional nature of all truth.[17]

Recently, several feminist scholars have been trying to modify the parochial epistemologies of postmodernism and standpoint epistemology.[18] Bartlett, for example, calls her more general epistemology

---

10. *See id.* at 831; MacKinnon, *Agenda for Theory, supra* note 4, at 519; Nancy Hartsock, *Fundamental Feminism: Process and Perspective*, 2 QUEST 67, 71 (1975).

11. Bartlett, *supra* note 5, at 831; *see* Radin, *supra* note 3, at 1707; Martha L. Fineman, *Challenging Law, Establishing Differences: The Future of Feminist Legal Scholarship*, 42 FLA. L. REV. 25, 38 (1990).

12. Bartlett, *supra* note 5, at 867.

13. *See id.* at 868.

14. Wendy W. Williams, *Equality's Riddle: Pregnancy and the Equal Treatment/Special Treatment Debate*, 13 N.Y.U. REV. L. & SOC. CHANGE 325, 370-74 (1984-85) (discussing the merits of equal protection as opposed to special treatment for women in the workplace).

15. *See, e.g., supra* note 6.

16. *See* Deborah L. Rhode, *Feminist Critical Theories*, 42 STAN. L. REV. 617, 622 (1990); Bartlett, *supra* note 5, at 868-87.

17. *See* Bartlett, *supra* note 5, at 878; *see also* Rhode, *supra* note 16, at 620-21 (discussing the irony of how feminist adherents of deconstruction may acknowledge gender oppression exists, but because of the tenets of deconstruction such oppression would not be able to be documented); DRUCILLA CORNELL, *The Feminist Alliance with Deconstruction, in* BEYOND ACCOMMODATION: ETHICAL FEMINISM, DECONSTRUCTION, AND THE LAW 79, 79-82 (1991) (discussing the implications of deconstruction for Lacan's foundationalist framework of the feminine and arguing for an alternative approach to the feminine as an allegory rather than as a fact). In her recent essay, *Sexual Difference*, Cornell seems to be proposing a more compelling vision of true concerns, defending the claims of female sexuality as essential to any proper "conception of the person," asserting affirmatively that "we cannot rise above our empirical selves of the flesh in order to be *free*." Cornell, *supra* note 6, at 2267 (emphasis in original). Robin West is currently offering an epistemology of "empathy." *See* Robin West, *Taking Preferences Seriously*, 64 TUL. L. REV. 659, 701 (1990).

18. *See, e.g.,* Bartlett, *supra* note 5, at 880 (discussing "positionality," which acknowledges the

"positionality."[19] Positionality recognizes the existence but situated and partial quality of truth, which emerges from relationships and involvements and is subject to variation depending on the social context, a variation which is the product of an effort to examine truth, particularly in light of other viewpoints.[20] Within this realist, yet flexible, approach to knowledge, feminists ask the next question, which Deborah Rhode characterizes as "the difference makes."[21] In answering this question, she makes an epistemological claim similar to Bartlett's: "To disclaim objective standards of truth is not to disclaim all value judgments. We need not become positivists to believe that some accounts of experience are more consistent, coherent, inclusive, self-critical, and so forth."[22]

Margaret Radin similarly seeks a middle ground by linking feminism to the revived interest in pragmatism.[23] As a result of her confrontation with the "double bind"[24] of lost freedom or bad choices in the context of commodified sexuality,[25] she sees pragmatic choice of the "less bad" alternative (and constant revision of choice) as the only path to a positive outcome.[26] According to Radin, pragmatism, like feminism, is characterized by a strong linkage to actual experience and a capacity to seek workable choices rather than an idealized hypothetical.[27]

Radin's feminism is greatly strengthened by its linkage with pragmatism: one of the founders of pragmatism, William James, cogently articulated the linkage between the idealization of rationalism and weak-mindedness. Instead he claimed the (male language) superior ground of "toughness" for people who can live with incompleteness and uncertainty.[28]

---

existence of empirical knowledge and its contingency, as a modification of postmodernist and standpoint epistemology); Martha Minow, *The Supreme Court 1986 Term—Foreword: Justice Engendered*, 101 HARV. L. REV. 10, 74-82 (1987) (arguing against impartiality and standpoint theories in favor of an epistemology which will embrace multiple alternative realities); Rhode, *supra* note 16, at 626 (discussing the different theoretical approaches employed by feminists, while noting that each theorist's desire to locate judgments within the patterns of social practice served as a unifying commitment).

19. Bartlett, *supra* note 5, at 880.

20. *See id.* at 880-83.

21. Rhode, *supra* note 16, at 625.

22. *Id.* at 626.

23. Radin, *supra* note 3, at 1706.

24. *See id.* at 1699-1704. Radin defines the double bind to be the fact that "both commodification and noncommodification may be harmful." *Id.* at 1700.

25. *See* Margaret J. Radin, *Market-Inalienability*, 100 HARV. L. REV. 1849, 1921-36 (1987).

26. *See* Radin, *supra* note 3, at 1700.

27. *See id.* at 1706-09.

28. *See* Radin, *supra* note 3, at 1712 (citing WILLIAM JAMES, PRAGMATISM 13 (1975)). For tough-minded tolerance of uncertainty, see, *e.g.*, Robert C. Post, *The Constitutional Concept of Public Discourse: Outrageous Opinion, Democratic Deliberation, and Hustler Magazine v. Falwell*, 103 HARV. L. REV. 601 (1990) (finding tensions between unbridled expression and the community necessary for discourse both fruitful and troubling); Cass R. Sunstein, *Pornography and the First Amendment*, 1986 DUKE L.J. 589 (suggesting the revival of a sliding scale of protection with less deference for speech of low value, such as pornography). Compare, for example, the intolerance of

The converse is also true since pragmatism, dependent as it is on real experience, is often criticized for its epistemological and normative conservatism.[29]   Linked to feminism in Radin's vision, however, pragmatism must include the viewpoints and experience of persons rather removed from the social-epistemological hegemony, who provide a much-needed source of alternative vision.[30]

Bartlett's positionality and Radin's pragmatism are hardly a breakthrough in epistemology; the solution to epistemological regression by the social positing of knowledge is at least as old as *On Certainty*[31] and as new as the work of Charles Taylor.[32]   Indeed, I am going to claim that feminism actually instantiates methods and answers dating back to antiquity.   Yet, as set forth below, this linkage of late contemporary legal feminism to Aristotelianism, while not assuming to create the world anew,[33] is actually quite a political and epistemological asset.[34]

How do these feminist methods recapitulate classical methods?   For these answers, I turn to the work of one of the leading scholars of the classical revival, Martha Nussbaum.   Nussbaum's writings bring together two of the strands in the tapestry I wish to weave herein: the analysis of classical philosophy and the moral role of fiction.[35]   Nussbaum has long written from the joint perspective of a classical scholar and a student of fiction,[36] but her recent work has focused increasingly on the latter.[37]

---

uncertainty in Martin H. Redish & Gary Lippman, *Freedom of Expression and the Civic Republican Revival in Constitutional Theory: The Ominous Implications*, 79 CAL. L. REV. 267, 304 (1991) (arguing that Post's variety of civic republicanism is "the equivalent of communitarian vigilantism," and that "[o]nce one accepts the basic premise that the violation of communitarian sensibilities may be grounds for the punishment of expression, it is difficult to find *any* principled stopping point for application of that premise" (emphasis added)).

29. *See* Radin, *supra* note 3, at 1708-09.

30. *See id.* at 1719-20.

31. LUDWIG WITTGENSTEIN, ON CERTAINTY (G.E.M. Anscombe & G.H. von Wright eds. & G.E.M. Anscombe & Dennis Paul trans., 1969).

32. CHARLES TAYLOR, SOURCES OF THE SELF: THE MAKING OF THE MODERN IDENTITY (1989).

33. *Cf.* Joan C. Williams, *Deconstructing Gender*, 87 MICH. L. REV. 797 (1989) (stating that pragmatism is the product of male philosophy and thus not attributable to feminism).

34. *See infra* text accompanying notes 182-95.

35. I have explored these ideas previously. *See* Linda R. Hirshman, *Brontë, Bloom, and Bork: An Essay on the Moral Education of Judges*, 137 U. PA. L. REV. 177 (1988) [hereinafter Hirshman, *Moral Education*]; Linda R. Hirshman, *The Virtue of Liberality in American Communal Life*, 88 MICH. L. REV. 983 (1990) [hereinafter Hirshman, *Virtue of Liberality*].   For the explicit tie between literary morality and feminism, see Carolyn Heilbrun & Judith Resnick, *Convergences: Law, Literature, and Feminism*, 99 YALE L.J. 1913 (1990).

36. MARTHA C. NUSSBAUM, FRAGILITY OF GOODNESS: LUCK & ETHICS IN GREEK TRAGEDY AND PHILOSOPHY (1986) [hereinafter NUSSBAUM, FRAGILITY]; Martha C. Nussbaum, *Non-Relative Virtues: An Aristotelian Approach*, in ETHICAL THEORY: CHARACTER AND VIRTUE 32 (Midwest Studies in Philosophy Vol. 13, Peter A. Finch et al. eds., 1988) [hereinafter Nussbaum, *Non-Relative Virtues*]; Martha C. Nussbaum, *Shame, Separateness, and Political Unity: Aristotle's Criticism of Plato*, in ESSAYS ON ARISTOTLE'S ETHICS 395 (Amélie O. Rorty ed., 1980) [hereinafter Nussbaum, *Separateness*].

37. *See, e.g.*, MARTHA C. NUSSBAUM, LOVE'S KNOWLEDGE: ESSAYS ON PHILOSOPHY AND

As I will show, each perspective embraces and illuminates contemporary feminism.[38]

First, in the method of consciousness raising, feminists are using two very traditional Aristotelian methods: canvassing the appearances and conversing about justice with people who speak the same language about justice the questioner does.[39] As in consciousness raising, the appearances are also set forth in their confusion and disarray,[40] and, in trying to order them, thinkers must avoid the seduction of abstract theorizing[41] but ultimately come to see the fundamental quality of our everyday behaviors, or, as Nussbaum puts it, to the "ability to give accounts."[42]

In her recent essay *The Literary Imagination in Public Life*,[43] Nussbaum described the process in rich detail:

> When we read a novel such as *Hard Times*, reading not as literary theorists asking about theories of interpretation, but as human beings

---

LITERATURE (1990); Martha C. Nussbaum, The Literary Imagination in Public Life, Alexander Rosenthal Lectures, Northwestern University Law School (April 8-10, 1991) [hereinafter Nussbaum, Literary Imagination].

38. It is certainly no coincidence that feminist Robin West articulates the case for legal paternalism in terms almost identical to Nussbaum's. *See* West, *supra* note 17, at 664-65 (arguing that the "moral as well as motivational basis for paternalistic judicial intervention . . . is the judge's sympathetic understanding of the subjective well-being, aspirations, goals, values, and plights of the litigants before her").

39. Nussbaum quotes Aristotle's description of his philosophical method in the *Nicomachean Ethics*:

[W]e must set down the appearances (*phainomena*) and, first working through the puzzles (*diaporēsantas*), in this way go on to show, if possible, the truth of all the beliefs we hold (*ta endoxa*) about these experiences; and, if this is not possible, the truth of the greatest number and the most authoritative. For if the difficulties are resolved and the beliefs (*endoxa*) are left in place, we will have done enough showing.

NUSSBAUM, FRAGILITY, *supra* note 36, at 240 (quoting and translating Aristotle, *Nicomachean Ethics* VII.1.1145b1-8); *cf.* RICHARD KRAUT, ARISTOTLE ON THE HUMAN GOOD 343 n.27 (1989) ("In defending the political and the philosophical lives, Aristotle is not simply recording 'Common Sense Morality,' for both lives were objects of criticism, and Aristotle's response to these criticisms is not merely an appeal to what most people think." (citations omitted)).

40. NUSSBAUM, FRAGILITY, *supra* note 36, at 246.

41. *See* Daniel A. Farber, *The Case Against Brilliance*, 70 MINN. L. REV. 917, 929 (1986) (arguing that brilliant, counterintuitive theories are undesirable in fields such as law and economics, which are dedicated to "understanding purposive human behavior"); Suzanna Sherry, *An Essay Concerning Toleration*, 71 MINN. L. REV. 963, 964 (1987) (noting that the adoption of a rights-based legal system has adversely affected society, encouraging the use of an entirely abstract method of discourse and creating a moral vacuum with serious practical consequences); Daniel A. Farber, *Brilliance Revisited*, 72 MINN. L. REV. 367, 376-81 (1987) (arguing that too much emphasis is placed on abstract theorizing in current scholarly standards and maintaining that common sense and truth may be of primary importance).

42. NUSSBAUM, FRAGILITY, *supra* note 36, at 251.

43. Nussbaum, Literary Imagination, *supra* note 37. A revised version of the first of these three lectures was recently published as Martha C. Nussbaum, *The Literary Imagination in Public Life*, 22 NEW LITERARY HIST. 877 (1991). As the title indicates, Nussbaum is discussing not Aristotelianism and feminism, but Aristotelianism and the literary imagination—but the similarities are striking.

who are moved and delighted, we are not skeptics . . . we are, in
effect, being constituted by the novel as judges of a certain sort—as
Aristotelian equitable women and men . . . [The ensuing judgments]
are not based on transcendent standards; indeed, our experience as
readers leads us to think that such standards would be both unnecessary for and irrelevant to our search. For as concerned readers we
search for a human good that we are trying to bring about in and for
the human community; . . . we move back and forth, as readers,
between concrete experience and general principle, seeking for the
best and most comprehensive fit between principles and concrete
perceptions, sorting out all the "appearances," as Aristotle said, and
producing a view that will "save the greatest number and the most
basic." We attempt, in effect, to know ourselves, and what is deepest in ourselves, regarding the novel as *about us*, our hopes and
fears.[44]

Not only is the Aristotelian judge sensitive to the human, as compared
to the transcendent, she is also anchored to the concrete, as opposed to the
abstract. Thus, "the novel also directs our attention to the historical and
local particularities of the characters' world, making us see ways in which
it differs from our own. We think about human flourishing not abstractly,
but in relation to that concrete context, asking about the material and
social conditions of the characters' daily lives, and the relation of those
concrete conditions to their hopes and fears."[45]

The second and most obvious parallel between the classical methods
and feminist methods is the feminist invocation of practical reason—a
concept inextricably intertwined with the Aristotelian method—as it emerges from the procedure linked to consciousness raising set forth above.
Thus, assuming that the appearances are all we have to deal with,[46] ethics

---

44. Nussbaum, Literary Imagination, *supra* note 37 lecture 3 (emphasis in original).

45. *Id.* lecture 1. *Compare id. with* West, *supra* note 17, at 684 ("By seeing the individuality,
the particularity, of the other, we can assume the feel of her burdens and by doing so we come to
sympathetically understand them.").

46. *See* NUSSBAUM, FRAGILITY, *supra* note 36, at 240, 291. This is, of course, one of the crucial
points on which philosophies, including ancient philosophies, divide. Compare the Aristotelian method
described here with, for example, the theory-building Socrates in the *Protagoras* or Book VI of the
Republic. *See* NUSSBAUM, FRAGILITY, *supra* note 36, at 241 ("The appearances—by which Plato and
his predecessors usually mean the world as perceived, demarcated, interpreted by human beings and
their beliefs—are taken to be insufficient 'witnesses' of truth. Philosophy begins [according to Plato]
when we acknowledge the possibility that the way we pre-philosophically see the world might be
radically in error."); *see, e.g.,* PLATO, THE REPUBLIC 176 (Benjamin Jowett trans., 1901) (asserting
that, in Book VI, Socrates argues that "philosophers only are able to grasp the eternal and unchangeable, and those who wander in the region of the many and variable are not philosophers").

One might argue that the fault line doesn't even run between ancient and modern philosophy.
Compare JOHN RAWLS, A THEORY OF JUSTICE 1-17 (1971) ("My aim is to present a conception of
justice which generalizes and carries to a higher level of abstraction the familiar theory of social
contract. . . . [T]he guiding idea is that the principles of justice for the basic structure of society are

must be centered in human discourse, as well. From this immersion in the human, Nussbaum elicits the basic structure of what she calls Aristotle's "non-scientific deliberation."[47] Like human situations, rules must be particular enough to be concrete and flexible. Thus,

> the good judge is one who regards general principles as summaries of wise decisions in the past, whose judgment respects that tradition of judgment, but who is also keenly perceptive of the concrete context and prepared to extend her historical tradition in order to meet the new context in an appropriate way.[48]

In order to do so, we must take account of the changeability, context-dependency, and variety of life.[49] Nussbaum invokes Aristotle's image of the flexible ruler: one cannot use a straight edge to measure a fluted column.[50] She contrasts this Aristotelian methodology with

> the aim of the law to become a simple and systematic science—an aim that has been around since Bentham, . . . a mistaken aim, . . . a simple pseudo-scientific algorithm (or a deductive system) represent[ing] not the achievement of order and rationality, but a falling off from the order and the rationality that are there to be found in human life.[51]

All of this sounds very like the description of feminist practical reason set forth above.

The hardest fit is of course asking the woman question. Actually, as some recent Straussian[52] rereadings of the works reflect, Aristotle did ask

---

the object of the original agreement.") *with* John Rawls, *Justice as Fairness: Political not Metaphysical*, 14 PHIL. & PUB. AFF. 223, 225 (1985) ("Whether justice as fairness can be extended to a general political conception for different kinds of societies existing under different historical and social conditions, or whether it can be extended to a general moral conception, or a significant part thereof, are altogether separate questions. I avoid prejudging these larger questions one way or the other."). Insofar as *A Theory of Justice* is an exercise in the Aristotelian method of theorizing from the observed human condition in Rawls's world—as Rawls seems to be suggesting in his later work—Rawls's subject, in his metaphysical autonomy and separateness, seems like a powerful example of the solipsism of l*imoralism*, which feminism has so powerfully unveiled. I am indebted to Lawrence Sager for reminding me of this Aristotelianism of (at least) late Rawls.

47. NUSSBAUM, FRAGILITY, *supra* note 36, at 290; *see id.* at 290-317; *see also* Nussbaum, *supra* note 43, at 902-03 (distinguishing between the pseudo-science of economic rationalism and the truth claims of novelistic complexity).

48. Nussbaum, Literary Imagination, *supra* note 37, lecture 3.

49. *See* NUSSBAUM, FRAGILITY, *supra* note 36, at 298-306.

50. *Id.* at 301.

51. Nussbaum, Literary Imagination, *supra* note 37, lecture 3. In rejecting the pure, but thin, air of liberal philosophy, feminism adopts one part of the communitarian critique of the metaphysics of liberalism. *See, e.g.*, MICHAEL J. SANDEL, LIBERALISM AND THE LIMITS OF JUSTICE (1982). See *supra* notes 6 and 46 for the critique of the solipsism, as well as the descriptive inadequacy of the enterprise.

52. "Straussian" refers to the (now quite various and even gender-integrated) followers, students, and interpreters of the works of Leo Strauss. Strauss was, for twenty-five years, the Robert Maynard Hutchins Distinguished Service Professor at the University of Chicago. For the most thorough review

the woman question;[53] like most feminists, I just don't like the answer he gave. Yet, asking the question remains constant. Like the feminists of the current generation, he noticed the differences between women's lives and men's lives and asked why they were different. He noted that women resemble men in their capacity for speech and hence for justice. As a contemporary feminist described it, "judging by the number of references to the question, Aristotle considered the existence and nature of women to be one of the features of life that most compellingly called for an explanation."[54] His answers were physical, ethical, and political. Now, obsession can hardly qualify as support, or Hitler would be considered a Jewish scholar. But within the parameters of rational discourse on the range of matters that attracted Aristotle's attention, his concern with the issue is noteworthy and, compared with modern treatments, the complexity of his answers commendable. The value of Aristotle's approach might be described as taking the subject seriously, even if getting it somewhat wrong, as opposed to treating it as of no moment.[55]

For example, recent work on the construction of human gender highlights the difference between the two approaches and illuminates Aristotle's inquiry about women with much new light. In the opening words of *Making Sex*,[56] historian Thomas Laqueur lays out the issue: "The first thing that strikes the careless observer is that women are unlike men. They are "the opposite sex" (though why "opposite" I do not know; what is the "neighboring sex"?). But the fundamental thing is that women are more like men than anything else in the world."[57]

---

of his role in modern political philosophy, see *Special Issue on Leo Strauss*, 53 REV. POL. 3 (1991).

53. *See* Steven G. Salkever, *Women, Soldiers, Citizens: Plato & Aristotle on the Politics of Virility*, 19 POLITY 232, 238-42 (1986); Harold L. Levy, *Does Aristotle Exclude Women From Politics?*, 52 REV. POL. 397 (1990).

54. Lynda Lange, *Woman is Not a Rational Animal: On Aristotle's Biology of Reproduction*, in DISCOVERING REALITY: FEMINIST PERSPECTIVES ON EPISTEMOLOGY, METAPHYSICS, METHODOLOGY AND PHILOSOPHY OF SCIENCE 1, 2 (Sandra Harding & Merrill B. Hintikka eds., 1983) [hereinafter DISCOVERING REALITY].

55. Modern American jurisprudence may not have progressed so far. *See, e.g.*, Geduldig v. Aiello, 417 U.S. 484, 496 n.20 (1974) (holding that California's failure to include pregnancy in its disability insurance scheme did not violate the Equal Protection Clause because it did not exclude women from coverage on the basis of gender but "merely removes one physical condition—pregnancy—from the list of compensable disabilities. While it is true that only women can become pregnant, it does not follow that every legislative classification concerning pregnancy is a sex-based classification"); Personnel Administrator of Massachusetts v. Feeney, 442 U.S. 256, 275 (1979) (holding that a statute which favored veterans for civil service jobs was not discriminatory even though it excluded "significant numbers of women from preferred state jobs," since it excluded them not as women but as nonveterans).

56. THOMAS LAQUEUR, MAKING SEX: BODY AND GENDER FROM THE GREEKS TO FREUD (1990).

57. *Id.* at 1 (quoting Dorothy L. Sayers, *The Human-Not-Quite-Human*, in ARE WOMEN HUMAN? (1971)).

Laqueur musters an impressive array of evidence to demonstrate that the opposition of the genders is substantially modern, a construct of the eighteenth century.

> For two millennia the ovary, an organ that by the early nineteenth century had become a synecdoche for woman, had not even a name of its own. Galen refers to it by the same word he uses for the male testes, *orcheis*, allowing context to make clear which sex he is concerned with. Herophilus had called the ovaries *didymoi* (twins), another standard Greek word for testicles, and was so caught up in the female-as-male model that he saw the Fallopian tubes—the spermatic ducts that led from each "testicle"—as growing into the neck of the bladder as do the spermatic ducts in men. They very clearly do not. Galen points out this error, surprised that so careful an observer could have committed it, and yet the correction had no effect on the status of the model as a whole. Nor is there any technical term in Latin or Greek, or in the European vernaculars until around 1700, for vagina as the tube or sheath into which its opposite, the penis, fits and through which the infant is born.[58]

Under the old model, "men and women were arrayed according to their degree of metaphysical perfection, their vital heat, along an axis whose telos was male."[59] Here, as in so much of human learning, Aristotle is a critical source. As I will set forth in more detail below,[60] Aristotle of course recognized the existence of men and women and their differences. The critical points are two: first, much of Aristotle's vision of the two genders is based on the naturalness of social behavior (passivity, householding, etc.)—not solely or even primarily the naturalness of physical or biological fact.[61] Second, as to physical-biological fact there is serious textual evidence that:

> though Aristotle certainly regarded male and female bodies as specifically adapted to their particular roles, he did not regard these adaptations as the signs of sexual opposition. The qualities of each sex

---

58. *Id.* at 4-5 (emphasis in original) (footnote omitted).

59. *Id.* at 5-6.

60. *See infra* text accompanying notes 146-54.

61. *See* LAQUEUR, *supra* note 56, at 28-29 ("What we would take to be ideologically charged social constructions of gender—that males are active and females passive . . . were for Aristotle indubitable facts, 'natural' truths. What we would take to be the basic facts of sexual differences . . . males have a penis and females a vagina . . . were for Aristotle contingent and philosophically not very interesting."); SUSAN M. OKIN, JUSTICE, GENDER, AND THE FAMILY 14 (1989) (arguing that "Aristotle, whose theory of justice has been so influential, relegated women to a sphere of 'household justice'—populated by persons who are not fundamentally equal to the free men who participate in political justice, but inferiors whose natural function is to serve those who are more fully human"). Laqueur's claims are, of course, not incontestable. *See, e.g.*, Katharine Park & Robert A. Nye, *Destiny is Anatomy*, THE NEW REPUBLIC, Feb. 18, 1991, at 53, 54 (noting that the "distinction between the [one sex and two sex models] blurs into a haze of contradictions"). Yet even Laqueur's success in blurring the modern dichotomy is instructive.

> entailed the comparative advantage of one or the other in minding
> the home or fighting . . . . But these adaptations were not the basis
> for ontological differentiation. In the flesh, therefore, the sexes
> were more and less perfect versions of each other.[62]

Accordingly, Aristotle not only asked the "woman question," he asked it
with a particular intensity, because the answers were:

> framed . . . to valorize the extraordinary cultural assertion of patri-
> archy, of the father, in the face of the more sensorially evident claim
> of the mother. The question for the classical model is not what it
> explicitly claims—why woman?—but the more troublesome ques-
> tion—why man?[63]

Laqueur's presentation of Aristotle's inquiry is most interesting
because it stands in such marked contrast to the modern view. Compare
it, for instance, to Susan Okin's description of contemporary theories of
justice:

> superficial appearances can easily lead to the impression that they
> are inclusive of women. In fact, they continue the same "separate
> spheres" tradition, by *ignoring* the family, its division of labor, and
> the related economic dependency and restricted opportunities of most
> women.[64]

As the deep contextualization and concrete orientation of Aristotelian
methods suggest, Aristotle's epistemology also turns out to be markedly
similar to the modified contextuality of the recent feminist world view.
Aristotle's theories of education begin with early childhood and emphasize
heavily the role of parents in habituating children to virtuous behavior:[65]
his virtues are largely social virtues.[66] Of great importance—and as yet
undervalued by contemporary feminism—Aristotle made an important
point of expressing the social or learned component not only of reason, but
of emotions.[67] To take just one of numerous examples, as Aristotle saw
it, an emotion like anger includes a judgment about the objects for anger

---

62. LAQUEUR, *supra* note 56, at 29.

63. *Id.* at 20.

64. OKIN, *supra* note 61, at 9 (emphasis added).

65. *See* M.F. Burnyeat, *Aristotle on Learning to Be Good*, *in* ESSAYS ON ARISTOTLE'S ETHICS, *supra* note 36, at 69, 74 (noting that for Aristotle, parents play a role in telling the child what is "noble and just" and in guiding his conduct "so that by doing the things [he is] told are noble and just [he] will discover that what [he has] been told is *true*" (emphasis in original)).

66. *See* NANCY SHERMAN, THE FABRIC OF CHARACTER: ARISTOTLE'S THEORY OF VIRTUE 1 (1989).

67. *See* WILLIAM W. FORTENBAUGH, ARISTOTLE ON EMOTION 45-49 (1975). Bartlett distinguish-es as particularly feminist the recognition of diverse human experiences and the role of emotion or passion. *See* Bartlett, *supra* note 5, at 857-58.

and a belief that the object injured the angry person in a relevant way.[68] Distinguishing offenses suitable for anger, for example by criteria of intentionality, from those which are not is an obvious exercise of judgment and is easily distinguishable from more primal urges like hunger.[69] Aristotle's clear expression of the social construction of belief, combined with his methods of exploring ethics through the device of looking first at the appearances of familiar, or at least accessible, societies, supports the particularity of Aristotelian positionality.

Yet, as Martha Nussbaum has pointed out in a recent essay, there are strong indications of an ultimate recognition of the limits on relativism throughout Aristotle's work.[70] Here, the parallel to Radin's and Bartlett's work is illuminating. First, and most importantly, Aristotle's ethics delineates those aspects of human life to which any system of ethics must apply, regardless of the cultural context. The "list" is characterized by the possibility of choice (for instance, no discussion of the possibility of choosing immortality plays a role) and, usually, the debatability of the choices; that is, no one right answer immediately emerges. The relativism is immediately limited, Nussbaum notes, because all ethical systems at least have these spheres of choice in common.[71]

The ensuing debate over choices may produce competing versions of the good life for human beings, but the allowable answers will not be completely open-ended, either. At least some solutions will be discarded entirely, leaving at most a plurality of competing solutions.[72] An exam-

---

68. *See* FORTENBAUGH, *supra* note 67, at 14-15.

69. *See* Nussbaum, Literary Imagination, *supra* note 37, lecture 2.

70. *See* Nussbaum, *Non-Relative Virtues*, *supra* note 36, at 33. Philosopher Rosalind Hursthouse recently described cabined Aristotelian relativism:

> We should not automatically assume that it is impossible that some other communities could be morally inferior to our own; maybe some are, or have been . . . [b]ut in communities in which life is a great deal tougher for everyone than it is in ours, having the right attitude to human life and death, parenthood, and family relationships might well manifest itself in ways that are unlike ours.

Rosalind Hursthouse, *Virtue Theory and Abortion*, 20 PHIL. & PUB. AFF. 223, 240 (1991).

71. Nussbaum, *Non-Relative Virtues*, *supra* note 36, at 32-36. Nussbaum's list of Aristotle's spheres of choice includes (1) fear of important damages; (2) bodily appetites; (3) distribution of limited resources; (4) management of personal property where others are concerned; (5) management of personal property where hospitality is concerned; (6) attitudes and actions with respect to one's own worth; (7) attitudes to slights and damages; (8) association and living together and the fellowship of words and actions; (9) attitudes to the good and ill fortune of others; (10) intellectual life; and (11) planning of one's life and conduct. *Id.* at 35-36.

72. Readers familiar with the monism of the liberal legalist position in, for example, the debate over pornography or the regulation of campus hate speech will recognize the utility of the Aristotelian middle ground of a plurality of approaches. *See supra* text accompanying note 28. For some other recent work on the range of possible middle grounds, see Kenneth L. Karst, *Boundaries and Reasons: Freedom of Expression and the Subordination of Groups*, 1990 U. ILL. L. REV. 95, 117 (arguing that members of a subordinated group "need the freedom to express their liberation in ways that are likely to fall outside the [F]irst [A]mendment's most generous interpretations"); Mari J. Matsuda, *Public*

ple of this is Aristotle's writing on the issue of management of one's property where others are concerned. Noting the human tendency to neglect the common on the one hand, yet committed to the concept of the superiority of citizenship to mere productivity on the other, he suggests a variety of virtuous schemes for sharing property.[73] His discussion excludes, however, Platonic communism on the one hand and unbridled dominion on the other. Nussbaum acknowledges the objection that immediately arises to examples such as this: that even the human tendency to neglect the common is grounded in a bedrock of human experiences that are themselves socially shaped.[74] Nonetheless, here again there is no need to choose between moral authoritarianism and moral anarchy. Indeed, after the long exercise in the *Politics* of examining the appearances of existing states, Aristotle ultimately devotes the last two chapters of the book to the ideal state and the even more abstract question of the best human life.[75]

This purchase, however tenuous, is essential, if feminism is going to defend itself against legitimate claims of unmanageable particularism.[76] Robin West's recent work exalting contextual empathy in defense of paternalistic judging reflects the problem. Although she carefully confines herself to decisions in particular cases,[77] more and more legal governance is statutory.[78] Moreover, although she notes the resemblance between the act of empathic recognition and the recognition of precedent,[79] she does

---

Response to Racist Speech: Considering the Victim's Story, 87 MICH. L. REV. 2320, 2321 (1989) (stating that in an effort to protect both the victim and the First Amendment, "formal criminal and administrative sanction . . . is an appropriate response to racist speech"); Richard Delgado, *Campus Antiracism Rules: Constitutional Narratives in Collision*, 85 NW. U. L. REV. 343, 383 (1990) (arguing that "speech by which society 'constructs' a stigma picture of minorities may be regulated consistently with the [F]irst [A]mendment"); and Thomas C. Grey, *Civil Rights and Civil Liberties of a Discriminatory Verbal Harassment*, 8 SOC. PHIL. & POL'Y 81, 83 (1991) (arguing for a harassment policy which recognizes the concerns of civil rights and civil liberties).

73. 2 ARISTOTLE, *Politics*, *in* THE COMPLETE WORKS OF ARISTOTLE I.4.1253b24-.1254a17, at 1986, 1989 (Bollingen Series No. 71, Jonathan Barnes ed., 1984) (Revised Oxford Translation) [hereinafter *Politics*].

74. *See* Nussbaum, *Non-Relative Virtues*, *supra* note 36, at 41-42. We have already seen how vulnerable even the physical facts of gender are to this kind of construction. *See supra* text accompanying notes 56-64.

75. *See Politics*, *supra* note 73, VII.1.1323a15-VIII.7.1342b34, at 2100-29.

76. *See* Frederick Schauer, *Harry Kalven and the Perils of Particularism*, 56 U. CHI. L. REV. 397, 413 (1989) (noting that "law's traditional aversion to contextualism is contingent and not inexorable, and that it involves political and psychological presuppositions that ought to be exposed to more critical analysis"); Frank J. Michelman & Margaret J. Radin, *Pragmatist and Post-Structuralist Critical Legal Practice*, 139 U. PA. L. REV. 1019, 1049 (1991) (noting that "feminists can be tempted into disabling radical particularism").

77. West, *supra* note 17, at 693 (focusing on a contract dispute and a person affected by an anti-sodomy statute).

78. *See* GUIDO CALABRESI, A COMMON LAW FOR THE AGE OF STATUTES 1 (1982) (noting that statutes are the primary source of law in the legal system).

79. West, *supra* note 17, at 701 (arguing that the decision to follow precedent is a sympathetic

not confront the fact that decisions in particular cases still play a role in predicting what future decisions will be; in that context, the empathic judge of the present will be influencing outcomes for persons not before her in any guise. By contrast to pure contextuality, Aristotle's ethical theory provides the possibility for preliminary assessments of preferred reality; cross-cultural comparison is also available to test the reality.[80]

Thus, as I will set forth more fully below, Aristotelian epistemology, like feminist positionality, limits the possibilities of idealism and its earthly companion, radical social change.[81] Whether that similarity is good or bad, and I will contend its desirability, it is sufficient at this point to note the effect.

B. *Feminist Politics and Classical Politics*

Having described the parallels between Aristotle's philosophy and feminist jurisprudence, I turn to the substantive inquiry. I thought to make scholarly history by being the first feminist writer in a decade to produce a whole article without citing Carol Gilligan's book, but here it is.[82] Gilligan opened the hottest debate in contemporary human psychology by differing with Lawrence Kohlberg's taxonomy of moral development, which culminates in the capacity for justice,[83] by accusing him of reproducing male norms for the morality of the whole species. Gilligan asserted that women grow up and develop a moral voice that emphasizes, at its fullest, relational values, seeking to maintain the community ties, rather than to satisfy abstract notions of justice.[84] Catharine MacKinnon, at the other pole of feminist theory, has been noteworthy for her relentless emphasis on the power of the existing social relationships of male domination, exposing "'woman' as a social construction."[85] This includes the

---

choice: "[w]e must understand the subjectivity, the equities, and the 'feel' of the parties involved" in the case relied upon before declaring it is a controlling precedent for the case at hand).

80. *See* Nussbaum, *Non-Relative Virtues, supra* note 36, at 45-46.

81. *See id.* at 50 ("Aristotle likes to point out that an inquiry into the human good cannot . . . end up describing the good of some other being, say a god, a good, that on account of our circumstances, it is impossible for us to attain." (citation omitted)).

82. CAROL GILLIGAN, IN A DIFFERENT VOICE (1982).

83. Lawrence Kohlberg, *Stages of Moral Development as a Basis for Moral Education, in* MORAL DEVELOPMENT, MORAL EDUCATION, AND KOHLBERG 15, 62-66 (Brenda Munsey ed., 1980) (arguing that the final stage of development is "recognizing the primacy of justice over all other moral considerations"); *see* LAWRENCE KOHLBERG ET AL., MORAL STAGES: A CURRENT FORMULATION AND A RESPONSE TO CRITICS 122 (Contributions to Human Development Vol. 10, John A. Meacham ed., 1983) (noting that Gilligan pointed out "the possibility of sex bias in Kohlberg's theory" and postulated "a second moral obligation different from a justice orientation").

84. *See* GILLIGAN, *supra* note 82, at 24-63.

85. MacKinnon, *Agenda for Theory, supra* note 4, at 530. Here, Laqueur's work powerfully buttresses, as well as draws on, MacKinnon's insight. *See supra* text accompanying note 58; *infra* text accompanying notes 174-75.

construction of Gilligan's appealing nurturing female, and MacKinnon is admittedly "agnostic" on what female moral development would look like in a transformed world.[86]

Two interesting insights emerge from these two leading schools of feminist thought. First, if male moral norms and behaviors of separateness support a political philosophy of people as naturally separate with the attendant consequences, including the liberal ideal of the "non-aggression treaty,"[87] the Gilligan model supports (at least for half of humanity) the philosophy of people as naturally social. Or, as Aristotle put it twenty-four hundred years ago, man is a political animal.[88]

Second, there is a deep level at which Gilligan and MacKinnon agree; if people are naturally political, it is predictable and understandable that they establish morality socially. (And vice versa. That is, if they create their morality socially, there is at least one sense in which sociability is natural and prior: in the creation of reality.) Where else would naturally political creatures get their norms?

Not surprisingly, Aristotle, also believing people to be naturally sociable, consistently asserted the social element of important aspects of the human self:

> But he who is unable to live in society, or who has no need because he is sufficient for himself, must be either a beast or a god: he is no part of a state.[89]

There are numerous examples of Aristotle's position, and each one of them corresponds to a current claim of feminist politics. In education, children must be told to engage in virtuous behaviors.[90] After long years of such coerced or shamed behaviors, they may become habituated to such behavior, which, for Aristotle, was the foundation of a virtuous character.[91] For students of good character, of course, virtue can be studied

---

86. *See Feminist Discourse, Moral Values, and the Law—A Conversation*, 34 BUFFALO L. REV. 11, 27 (1985) (remarks of Catharine A. MacKinnon).

87. *See* BERNARD WILLIAMS, ETHICS AND THE LIMITS OF PHILOSOPHY 103-04 (1985).

88. *Politics, supra* note 73, I.2.1253a3, at 1987. Actually, unlike his translator, Aristotle didn't even get the gender completely wrong. The Greek word is ἄνθρωπος, meaning human being, although most translators regard it as most comparable to the pre-feminist English usage of "man" to include both genders. SUSAN M. OKIN, WOMEN IN WESTERN POLITICAL THOUGHT 77 (1979). I am indebted to Richard Kraut for help with the usage.

89. *Politics, supra* note 73, I.2.1253a28-30, at 1987.

90. 2 ARISTOTLE, *Nicomachean Ethics, in* THE COMPLETE WORKS OF ARISTOTLE, *supra* note 73, X.9.1180a1-5, at 1729, 1864 [hereinafter *Nicomachean Ethics*]; *Politics, supra* note 73, VIII.1.1337a10-32, at 2121; *see* Matsuda, *supra* note 72, at 2350 (noting the importance of education in the battle to combat racism).

91. *Nicomachean Ethics, supra* note 90, I.4.1095a31-b13, at 1731; *id.* II.4.1105b5-11, at 1746. This is, of course, the answer to Jon Macey's astute (but pessimistic) criticism of the civic republican revival of concepts of public virtue, that only the virtuous can deliberate virtuously. *See* Jonathan R. Macey, Comment, *The Missing Element in the Republican Revival*, 97 YALE L.J. 1673, 1674 (1988).

through philosophy, including Aristotle's lectures.[92]   Moreover, and here is a critical core of Aristotle's ethics, friendship of good persons enhances one's self-understanding,[93] providing "another self before us whose similar actions and traits we can study."[94]

Much less familiar to modern and feminist ears, however, is Aristotle's (and the general classical) belief that even private and familial efforts do not suffice; Aristotle explicitly and repeatedly invokes the laws as the necessary and proper source of moral tutelage.[95]   Indeed, it is to enable its citizens to lead a virtuous life that the city exists.[96]

III. So What?

Although many feminist theorists have broken the assumption of the neutrality of private orderings and revealed that the private-public distinction preserves the hegemony of private oppression, most of their work has sought to invoke the public authorities in the interests of equality, rather than virtue.[97]   But, as recent feminist writings so powerfully reveal, equality—which always contains a more or less hidden image of the actual norm—constantly threatens to collapse into l*imoral*ism,[98] the introduction of the male norm in the guise of a universal neutral norm. Moreover, and as the debates over issues like abortion and the draft reveal, there are real differences related to gender which generate real social costs to a political effort to construct a genuinely egalitarian regime.[99]   Where equality is

---

Macey distinguishes rationality from virtue, a profoundly modern assumption. Reason, construed classically as including the reason of the emotions, *see supra* text accompanying note 67, and the cabined moral pluralism of practical reason would probably be all the virtue required for a civic republic. But I have suspected Macey for some time of virtuous longings. *See* Linda R. Hirshman, *Postmodern Jurisprudence and the Problem of Administrative Discretion*, 82 Nw. U. L. Rev. 646, 704 (1988) (citing Jonathan R. Macey, *Promoting Public-Regarding Legislation Through Statutory Interpretation: An Interest Group Model*, 86 COLUM. L. REV. 223, 224 (1986)). (Macey's canons of statutory construction support the role of the judiciary as leading society to a public-regarding outcome in regulatory matters. Macey, *An Interest Group Model, supra*, at 262.).

92. *See* Burnyeat, *supra* note 65, at 81.

93. *Nicomachean Ethics, supra* note 90, IX.9.1170a13-b18, at 1849-50.

94. SHERMAN, *supra* note 66, at 143.

95. *See Nicomachean Ethics, supra* note 90, X.9.1179b4-80a21, at 1864-65.

96. *Politics, supra* note 73, III.9.1280a24-.1281a6, at 2031-33; *Nicomachean Ethics, supra* note 90, V.1.1129a7-12, at 1781.

97. The intransigence of gender inequality under a liberal regime is most graphically expressed in the work of Catharine MacKinnon, *see* MacKinnon, *Agenda for Theory, supra* note 4, and as collected in CATHARINE A. MACKINNON, FEMINISM UNMODIFIED (1987); ANDREA DWORKIN & CATHARINE A. MACKINNON, PORNOGRAPHY AND CIVIL RIGHTS (1988); and CATHARINE A. MACKINNON, TOWARD A FEMINIST THEORY OF THE STATE (1989).

98. *See supra* note 6.

99. I have dealt with this problem elsewhere. *See* Hirshman, *Moral Education, supra* note 35, at 223 (noting that in the abortion debate "the hard question [is] whether, against all of these contrary indications of [equality], an upright state must still intervene because of a moral claim on behalf of the potential life"). Even the authors of the bold egalitarian defense of the Equal Rights Amendment

seen as a social construct,[100] the discussion should change, and issues of political virtue and the definition of a good common life are unavoidable.[101]   It is at this point that contemporary feminist jurisprudence stops.

As will be set forth immediately below, this hesitation at the door of substance is understandable, yet, as Drucilla Cornell's recent dissent from MacKinnon's vision makes explicit, both l*imoral*ism and feminist oppositionism suffer from the same flaw: a failure to articulate a flourishing life suitable for women.[102]   Cornell invokes the recent work of welfare economist Amartya Sen—a theory Sen calls equality of "capability and well being"[103]—to enrich the discussion.   The problem is that the focus has been on equality rather than on the much harder and more important work of describing well-being.

The publication of Cornell's essay signifies, I hope, the beginning of an explicit acknowledgement that feminism cannot be neutral on the good, and it is at this point that the classical tradition, long neglected in legal philosophy, can play such a powerful role.   Evidence of dissatisfaction with this failure has been surfacing in many places.   For instance, in the recent literature, it is the moral claim against commodification of childbearing, not just the inequality claim, that supports withholding enforcement of or even criminalizing the act.[104]

Both Radin and Nussbaum articulate the problem, and in almost the same way, by comparing their solutions to Dworkin's superficially pragmatic-Aristotelian method of legal decision making as expressed in *Law's Empire*.[105]   Dworkin's Herculean judge, the reader may recall, tries to

would only assert that there would be "many" women capable of meeting the weight requirements of armed combat eligibility.   Barbara A. Brown et al., *The Equal Rights Amendment: A Constitutional Basis for Equal Rights for Women*, 80 YALE L.J. 871, 977 (1971).   The most recent manifestation of the phenomenon is United Automobile Workers v. Johnson Controls, 111 S.Ct. 1196, 1206-07 (1991) (holding that Johnson Controls' fetal-protection policy which excluded fertile female employees from jobs with a high risk of exposure to lead violated the Civil Rights Act of 1964, because it was not justified as a bona fide occupational qualification).

100.   It is interesting to note how this insight has lagged behind the widely accepted concept of the social construction of property.

101.   The notion of constructed equality comes from Hannah Arendt.   *See* HANNAH ARENDT, ON REVOLUTION (1963).

102.   *See* Cornell, *supra* note 6, at 2248-51 (criticizing MacKinnon's inability to view "feminine sexual difference as other than victimization" as a stumbling block to her program for reform through state intervention into traditional gender hierarchy and identity, and proposing instead a program for "equivalent rights").

103.   Amartya Sen, *Inequality Reexamined: Capability and Well-Being* (paper delivered at Conference on Quality of Life, Helsinki, Finland, July 1988), *cited in* Cornell, *supra* note 6, at 2251. Martha Nussbaum also relies on the same source.   *See* Nussbaum, *supra* note 43, at 910.

104.   *See* Radin, *supra* note 25, at 1925-27 (suggesting that society's aversion to the selling of babies may be based upon "a moral prohibition on market treatment of . . . babies").

105.   Indeed, both Radin and Nussbaum articulate this imperative in nearly identical terms.   *See* Radin, *supra* note 3, at 1723; Nussbaum, Literary Imagination, *supra* note 37, lecture 3.

find an interpretation of new events coherent with the previous products of the legal system after the fashion of the authors of a chain novel.[106] Critics since *Law's Empire* have used this conservative technique to tag Dworkin with impotence before the claims like those ultimately vindicated in *Brown v. Board of Education*.[107] In essence, the critique is that the legal system cannot be a source of change toward the ideal; it usually simply carries forward the past. In the best of circumstances it only brings legal institutions into conformity with social change from the outside.[108]

As noted above, Radin invokes the dialogic solution strongly associated as well with the Minow-Michelman school.[109] Bring the voices of the oppressed into discourse in the legal system, and change can occur consistent with conceptual coherence, because the social concept of a legal system includes the as yet unreconciled claims of the oppressed. Nussbaum's answers from the Aristotelian tradition are much more substantive about the good:

> My reader/judge operates with a general conception of the human being and human flourishing, treating some aspects of the person and some activities as essential, others as more peripheral. She has, in connection with this, a rich conception of human agency that she brings to bear in concrete cases . . . . I see no such clear guidance emerging from Dworkin's commitment to general ethical principles—and indeed it is clear from other writings that Dworkin's liberalism makes him suspicious of having any such conception of the human being and the human good, even at a very high level of generality.[110]

---

106. *See* RONALD DWORKIN, LAW'S EMPIRE 228-32 (1986).

107. 347 U.S. 483 (1954); *see* Radin, *supra* note 3, at 1723; *cf.* Allan C. Hutchinson, *Indiana Dworkin and Law's Empire*, 96 YALE L.J. 637, 659-60 (1987) (criticizing Dworkin's analysis of legal integrity in the face of precedent perceived as immoral).

108. *See* DWORKIN, *supra* note 106, at 379-89. Ronald Dworkin has added greatly to the bootstrap effect of his already conservative technique by advocating in the New York Review of Books—a non-technical forum for the formation of social opinion—outcomes dictated by positive law, as if they were thereby entitled to moral weight. *See* Ronald Dworkin, *Liberty and Pornography*, N.Y. REV. BOOKS, Aug. 15, 1991, at 12, 15 (arguing that "[f]reedom of speech, conceived and protected as a fundamental negative liberty, is the core of the choice modern democracies have made" and that it is "a choice we must now honor").

109. *See* Frank J. Michelman, *Law's Republic*, 97 YALE L.J. 1493, 1524-32 (1988) (arguing for a move to a dialogic constitutionalism); Minow, *supra* note 18, at 90-95 (stating that one can decide when moved by competing views because "immersion in the particulars does not require the relinquishment of general commitments"); Frank J. Michelman, *The Supreme Court 1985 Term—Foreword: Traces of Self Government*, 100 HARV. L. REV. 3, 73-77 (1986) (arguing that "[o]ne can usefully describe, and significantly criticize, particular judicial performances in terms of their apparent degrees of commitment to the pursuit of mediative practical reason through normative dialogue").

110. Nussbaum, Literary Imagination, *supra* note 37, lecture 3.

Furthering Nussbaum's project, I hope that by showing the methodological and epistemological similarities between Aristotle's work and
contemporary feminist thought, I have made legitimate an inquiry into the
substantive answers about the human good Aristotle provided for feminist
legal issues in particular. Rather than letting this important move rest on
implication, however, let me reiterate in a nutshell how Aristotle's virtues
reflect and support the substance of contemporary feminism. Since Aristotle, like many contemporary feminists, assumes the natural sociability of
the species, his teleological virtues are directed to the end of society.
Thus: "Since the end of individuals and of states is the same, the end of
the best man and of the best constitution must also be the same . . . .
Courage and endurance are required for business and philosophy for
leisure, temperance and justice for both . . . ."[111]

How might a canvas of Aristotle's political virtues illuminate issues
confronting contemporary feminism? Two examples come immediately to
mind. They are not only the two most visible contemporary feminist
issues; they are and have been, I would claim, issues at the core of human
ethics since ethical theory began. They are but current variations of the
old questions of citizenship.[112] In present terms, we ask whether feminists should press for the inclusion of women in mandatory military service and why, and whether feminists should support women's freedom to
contract for surrogate motherhood or should resist state enforcement of
such contracts, or, at the other extreme, contend for the criminality of
such arrangements.

A. The Garden of the Finzi-Contini

In an extraordinary movie[113] a few years ago, director Vittorio
deSica depicted the last years before the extermination of the centuries-old
Jewish community in Italy. The movie takes place after Mussolini had
ascended to power but before the Jews were deported. In what was for
me the most telling scene of the movie, the young, draft-age boy in the

---

111. *Politics, supra* note 73, VII.15.1334a11-15, at 2116-17.

112. *See* Susan Rose-Ackerman, *Inalienability and the Theory of Property Rights*, 85 COLUM. L.
REV. 931, 967-68 (1985) (discussing military service and jury duty as inalienable duties of citizenship);
Kenneth L. Karst, *The Pursuit of Manhood and the Desegregation of the Armed Forces*, 38 UCLA L.
REV. 499, 523-24 (1991) (discussing military service as an aspect of citizenship); Hirshman, *Moral
Education, supra* note 35, at 180 (discussing freedom to control reproduction as an aspect of citizen-
ship).

113. THE GARDEN OF THE FINZI-CONTINI (Columbia Pictures 1980). Jean Elshtain suggests that
movies are the bearers of the war culture in our time. *See* JEAN B. ELSHTAIN, WOMEN AND WAR 12
(1987). It may be that this relationship is explainable by the linkage between the flowering of the
novel form and the feminization of culture. *See, e.g.*, ANN DOUGLAS, THE FEMINIZATION OF
AMERICAN CULTURE (1977). *But see* NORMAN MAILER, THE NAKED AND THE DEAD (1948). I am
indebted to Richard Posner for reminding me of the male war novels of World War II.

Jewish family is riding somewhere on a train when a group of soldiers—all boys of a similar age and in uniform—gets on. Nothing overtly violent or even threatening happens, but the juxtaposition of that Jewish boy in his civilian clothes to the community of soldiers chillingly foreshadowed the fate of those excluded from the community's norms and rites of citizenship.

In his recent Nimmer lectures, Professor Kenneth Karst articulated the liberal egalitarian claims for women (and gays and racial minorities) to be fully included in military service, as a part of their overall claim for equal citizenship under the Fourteenth Amendment.[114] The article, a noteworthy example of the possibilities for a liberalism free of l*imoral*ism, systematically dismantles the supposedly neutral arguments of efficiency against integration of the armed services, leaving bare the actual dynamic of a military establishment in the service of the social construction of gender.

As with so much of Karst's writing, his insights and proposals would do most of the work on any feminist political agenda.[115] I seek to add to his invaluable work a different perspective: I am asking why feminists should support the full participation in the armed services from without, not why a sincere liberal of any gender should from within. In the context of that inquiry, I am asking how concepts of virtuous citizenship inform that enterprise—not how concepts of equality of citizenship do. As set forth above, my theory of equality constructed for citizenship would support gender integration of the armed services, even against appealing claims of efficient screening or diminished effectiveness.

---

114. The concept of equal citizenship is the heart of Karst's constitutional jurisprudence and comes as close as any modern liberal theory to articulating a rich claim to political life. *See* KENNETH L. KARST, BELONGING TO AMERICA: EQUAL CITIZENSHIP AND THE CONSTITUTION 2 (1989) [hereinafter KARST, BELONGING TO AMERICA]; *see also* Kenneth L. Karst, *The Supreme Court 1976 Term—Foreword: Equal Citizenship Under the Fourteenth Amendment*, 91 HARV. L. REV. 1, 5 (1977) [hereinafter Karst, *Equal Citizenship*] (defining the "essence of equal citizenship [as] the dignity of full membership in the society" and including within this principle "not only . . . equality of legal status, but also . . . a greater equality of . . . rank on a scale defined by degrees of deference or regard"). For a recent vindication of Karst's instrumentalist version of military service, see Charles Moskos, *How Do They Do It? Why the Military is the Only Truly Integrated Institution in America*, NEW REPUBLIC, Sept. 5, 1991, at 16, 20 (concluding from a look at the military that "race relations can best be transformed by an unambiguous commitment to non-discrimination coupled with uncompromising standards of performance" and that the change in the military was motivated by a realization that the military's race problem "was so critical that it was on the verge of self-destruction").

115. This is so even when Karst comes out in opposition to the main line of contemporary feminist politics, as for instance when Karst opposes regulation of pornography by articulating the advantage to the oppressed group of not restraining passionate and unreasoning speech. *See* Karst, *supra* note 72, at 138-39 (suggesting that "[i]t is dangerous for . . . women in particular . . . to define expressive behavior [pornography] outside the freedom of expression because the behavior is effective in conveying its message" because women, as an oppressed group, use this type of speech to further their cause).

Courage is a personal virtue, in Aristotle, the mean between fear and confidence.[116] But tempting as it is to translate classical concepts of military virtue into things like courage in the face of disease or loss of status,[117] Aristotle quite clearly directs our attention to the concerns of the classical order:

> With what sort of terrible things, then, is the brave man concerned?
> Surely with the greatest; for no one is more likely than he to stand
> his ground against what is dreadful. Now death is the most terrible
> of all things; for it is the end, and nothing is thought to be any
> longer either good or bad for the dead. But the brave man would
> not seem to be concerned even with death in *all* circumstances, e.g.
> at sea or in disease. In what circumstances, then? Surely in the
> noblest. Now such deaths are those in battle; for these take place in
> the greatest and noblest danger. And this agrees with the ways in
> which honours are bestowed in city-states and at the courts of mon-
> archs.[118]

Courage in defense of the city, moreover, is so central to the community that it even supports the claim of the many to political justice based on their sharing in the risk of defending it. In Aristotle's polity form of regime, for example, citizens are defined as those who can bear heavy arms.[119] This is, of course, another example of the linkage between personal virtue and political virtue described above.[120]

Interestingly, critical as participation in defending the city in battle is, ultimately Aristotle is going to relegate war to the category of the neces-sary, rather than the good in itself.[121] This diminution of enthusiasm is among the most important evidence for what many scholars regard as the role of classical philosophy in moderating the war culture of Homeric Greece.[122] Aristotle supports this argument in his usual way, by refer-

---

116. *Nicomachean Ethics*, *supra* note 90, III.6.1115a7-8, at 1760.

117. *See* Salkever, *supra* note 53, at 244 (discussing Plato's treatment of *andreia* (virility) in the *Republic* and Plato's statement that "[t]rue courage . . . has nothing to do with soldiering or citizen-ship; it is best seen as persistence in following abstract arguments wherever they lead (*Republic* 6, 503b-504a)").

118. *Nicomachean Ethics*, *supra* note 90, III.6.1115a23-32, at 1760 (emphasis in original).

119. *See Politics*, *supra* note 73, III.7.1279b3-4, at 2030. Karst picks up this important point, too, although he does not trace it back to Aristotle. *See* Karst, *Equal Citizenship*, *supra* note 114, at 1.

120. *See supra* text accompanying notes 97-101.

121. *Politics*, *supra* note 73, VII.2.1325a6-7, at 2103.

122. *See* TERENCE IRWIN, PLATO'S MORAL THEORY: THE EARLY AND MIDDLE DIALOGUES 15-19 (1977); *see also* ELSHTAIN, *supra* note 113, at 54 (observing that a "tempering of the warrior ideal occurs in the work of Aristotle"). In his extraordinary essay on the *Iliad*, J.B. White has suggested quite another interpretation: that the revision of attitudes toward war begins in the last book of the *Iliad*, with the voice of Homer as the source. *See* JAMES B. WHITE, WHEN WORDS LOSE THEIR MEANING 50-58 (1984). *But see* SIMONE WEIL, THE ILIAD, OR, THE POEM OF FORCE 3 (Mary

ring to the experience before his readers—the defeat of the warlike Spar-
ta[123]—as well as to common sense arguments, like the riskiness of an
expansionist policy[124] and ultimately to moral claims like the injustice of
subordinating people to slavery (unless, of course they are natural
slaves).[125]

The critical thing to notice here, however, is that military virtue is not
abandoned; it is simply transferred from the individualistic honor culture
to the collectivity. Political theorist Jean Elshtain expresses the transition
well:

> When Socrates steps onto the stage, a new discourse—cast in the
> form, first, of Plato's dialogues, then of Aristotle's sustained analy-
> ses—takes shape as the pre-eminent narrative of and for the city, the
> real and the ideal polis. The shift thus marked as the polites super-
> sedes the warrior is not one from war to peace. What is at stake
> instead is collective understandings of war as a human undertaking
> and an object of reflection. . . . War may bind the body politic, but
> only as a regularized collective activity, undertaken from civic
> necessity, not from an individual search for glory or vengeance or
> lust to annihilate. There is not room in Plato's Republic for the war
> lover. But there is ample space and need for the Guardian-warrior,
> a zealous defender of the autonomy of the city, wholly devoted to its
> good and cut off from "selfish" pursuits.[126]

If additional evidence were needed of the linkage of military virtue and
communal life, the crucial claim of community (and against the individualism of private property that pervades the Politics)—the common table—is
an ancient Homeric war custom.[127]

Interestingly, in the debate among feminists before the Supreme Court
turned away the equality challenge to the single sex draft law,[128] this
argument never really got made. Instead, the debate centered on an
assimilationist versus alienationist ground in which no one was willing to
speak up for the military virtues. The alienationist position was that
women should reject the draft as a part of a fundamental critique of Amer-

---

McCarthy trans., Pendle Hill 1956) ("The true hero, the true subject, the center of the *Iliad* is
force. . . . In this work, at all times, the human spirit is shown as modified by its relations with
force.").

123. *Politics, supra* note 73, VII.14.1333b21-23, at 2116.

124. *Id.*

125. *Id.* VII.14.1333b39-43, at 2116.

126. ELSHTAIN, *supra* note 113, at 53.

127. *See id.* at 54. Elshtain refers to the role of the common table in the Republic, which is, of
course, far removed from Aristotle's views on private property. The significance of the practice in
Aristotle's writings seems much greater, since the presumption is against sharing. *See* Hirshman,
Virtue of Liberality, supra note 35, at 1024-25.

128. Rostker v. Goldberg, 453 U.S. 57 (1981).

ican foreign and domestic policy and "reject the war reflex as an instance of male hysteria; in its essence, feminism is opposed to violence."[129] The assimilationist position, as well articulated by liberal feminist Wendy Williams, tracks the basic argument of liberal autonomy:

> To me, *Rostker* never posed the question of whether women should be forced as men now are to fight wars, but whether we, like them, must take the responsibility for deciding whether or not to fight, whether or not to bear the cost of risking our lives, on the one hand, or resisting in the name of peace, on the other.[130]

Now there are things that could be said. For instance, feminists who believe in the abstract primacy of community might argue that they will not serve a society that is oppressive root and branch. Or communitarian feminists might defend their consistency by asserting that the community, whether of women or all humanity, is not defined by national borders and thus they are being faithful to their communitarianism in refusing to participate in rending the community with arms.

But for those who invoke, as many—perhaps most—American feminists do, the ideals of equality[131] and of a share in American prosperity,[132] the absence of serious discussion of the virtues of service is troublesome,[133] and the common features of feminist and classical assumptions quite helpful. Thus, when military service is seen as one of the rites by which the moral force of the law is brought to command the

---

129. The opposition is contained in *A Feminist Opposition to the Draft* (authors unidentified), collected in Catharine MacKinnon's unpublished materials for a course taught at the Stanford Law School, Fall 1980, and reported in Wendy W. Williams, *The Equality Crisis: Reflections on Culture, Courts, and Feminism*, 7 WOMEN'S RIGHTS L. RPTR. 175 (1982); *see also* CYNTHIA ENLOE, DOES KHAKI BECOME YOU? THE MILITARISATION OF WOMEN'S LIVES 7 (1983) (stating that women's groups opposing militarism "have deliberately devised actions that have avoided top-down relationships . . . because they saw the qualities of equality, spontaneity, and connectedness as the opposites of the quintessential characteristics of both patriarchy and militarism" (citation omitted)).

130. Williams, *supra* note 129, at 190.

131. *See* Ann C. Scales, *Feminist Jurisprudence*, 95 YALE L.J. 1373, 1402-03 (1988) ("My admission that feminism is result-oriented does not import the renunciation of all standards. In a system defined by constitutional norms such as equality, we need standards to help us make connections among norms, and to help us see 'family resemblances' among instances of domination.").

132. *See* Williams, *supra* note 129, at 175 (asserting that women must look to legislatures rather than courts if they wish to share fully in American prosperity).

133. Elshtain sees some pro-military stance in the bellicose writings of the feminist separatists and in the National Organization for Women's brief on behalf of the petitioners in *Rostker*. *See* ELSHTAIN, *supra* note 113, at 238-39. A decade earlier, the most influential piece of legal scholarship supporting the Equal Rights Amendment included some references to the connection between military service and citizenship. *See* Brown et al., *supra* note 99, at 968-69. The separatist writings are, of course, utopian, and of limited interest to an inquiry into community on this earth. The NOW brief, like the Brown article, basically instantiates the liberal claim to equality, stressing the importance of military service to equality, but not addressing in any meaningful way the virtue-citizenship issues of substance. In this, Karst's work is the best example of the genre. *See* KARST, BELONGING TO AMERICA, *supra* note 114 and accompanying text.

shaping of a virtuous self, the classical and feminist recognition of the role
of the state in creating norms of self would lead feminists to address the
larger question of the value of such service in the shaping of a self. Then,
when military service is seen as the quintessence of participation in the
community, the common ground of the primacy of the political would urge
feminists in the direction of mandatory military service.[134]

Nor is this the only way in which consideration of the issue would
change. Jean Elshtain speculates that the historical construction of war has
left room for only two characters: the male "just warriors" and the female
"beautiful souls," who suffer and support and sometimes protest, but are
always the "other."[135] Within this dichotomy, there is no room for any
moderate stance. Women are caught in a double bind of participating in
acts of military aggression they feel to be wrong or of being found unfit to
defend their country.[136] In the world of the double bind, one must seek
the second-best solution. Elshtain sees the escape for women as resting on
a revitalization of civic identity and connection in the defense of the state.
The concept would include the role of private conscience and the recognition of incommensurability and conflicting claims in the making of military
policy.[137] Like Nussbaum's Aristotle, Elshtain's politician would see the
morality on large issues, but preserve decision making for a flexible
measure that includes irony about the prospects of war and the tolerance
of defeat in its engagement.[138] Under this measured view, the admixture
of Aristotle's householding, life-preserving female would moderate the
Athenian military norm to one more like a "large, dreamy beast. . . .
Real courage has nothing of savagery about it, but goes 'rather with the
gentler and more lion-like characters.'"[139]

B. *The Case of Baby S(emen)*

Laqueur asserts that Aristotle, like most thinkers before the eighteenth
century, posits a model of the species as "one sex." "What we would take
to be the basic facts of sexual difference . . . were for Aristotle contingent
and philosophically not very interesting observations about particular

---

134. Note how this discussion differs from Karst's recitation of the virtues of combat service for
women: "access to 'society's legitimate, organized, planned, rewarded, technological use of force' is
a historically validated road to power in society." Karst, *supra* note 112, at 525. Women's voices are
habitually denied authority, which comes automatically with military roles. *Id.* at 528.

135. ELSHTAIN, *supra* note 113, at 3-13.

136. *See generally* Radin, *supra* note 3.

137. ELSHTAIN, *supra* note 113, at 248.

138. *Id.* at 251-52.

139. Salkever, *supra* note 53, at 251 (quoting Aristotle, *Politics* VIII.4.1338b19). Compare, for
instance, the supposed liberal "tough-mindedness" about war portrayed in DAVID HALBERSTAM, THE
BEST AND THE BRIGHTEST (1976), with pragmatic tough-mindedness about the nuances and limits of
power. *See* Radin, *supra* note 3.

species under certain conditions."[140]   Thus, Aristotle discounted the
identity of maleness and the existence (or size) of sexual organs, aligned
the sex organs with the alimentary system, common to all species, and
used a term for sex organs (kaulos) that was the same for both genders.[141]   Even semen and menstrual fluid, so important for the hierarchy
of reproduction, were, for Aristotle, but levels on a common hierarchy of
blood.[142]

As reflected in the description of Aristotle's reproductive theory
herein, Aristotle's thought is substantially less consistent than Laqueur's
thesis permits.[143]   While assuming at least proximity to the genders, if
not identity as Laqueur would have it still, Aristotle is also the author of
the most hierarchical of theories about reproduction—and hierarchy of
necessity implies some distinction. Aristotle's theory centers on "semen,"
defined not as the fluid which is its carrier, but as whatever it is that
initiates the growth of a new life sort of in the way that a craftsman molds
matter.[144]   For reasons that do not matter here, he concludes that semen
must come from one parent or the other, rather than both.[145]   He further
concludes that it comes from the male, because, *inter alia*, "the emission
of even a small quantity of semen is exhausting."[146]   Because women
exist, however, and produce a sort of fluid, and because nature makes
nothing in vain, according to Aristotle, the woman must also contribute
something; Aristotle concludes that the something is the material of the
child.[147]

This theory had some pitfalls for Aristotle, because, insofar as the
semen contains no material, all the material elements of the new entity
would need be in the material, and this provides a potentially preemptive
role for the female. But Aristotle resolves this problem, too, in favor of
the male, on the ground that the rational soul exists separate from the
body. Thus, the father, producer of the semen, can be responsible for

---

140. LAQUEUR, *supra* note 56, at 28-29.

141. *Id.* at 34.

142. LAQUEUR, *supra* note 56, at 42. Laqueur refers chiefly to the *Generation of Animals* and
the *History of Animals*. His references are accurate; although he acknowledges some debate about the
authenticity of Book X of the *History of Animals*, Barnes reflects none. *See* Jonathan Barnes, *Note to
the Reader* to 1 ARISTOTLE, *supra* note 73, at xiii, xiii.

143. *See supra* note 61.

144. Lange, *supra* note 54, at 3.

145. *See* 1 ARISTOTLE, *Generation of Animals*, *in* THE COMPLETE WORKS OF ARISTOTLE, *supra*
note 73, I.19.727a26-30, b6-11, at 1129 [hereinafter *Generation of Animals*].

146. Lange, *supra* note 54, at 4 (citing Aristotle, *Generation of Animals*, I.18.725b6-8). I kid
you not. Other reasons are that semen is more "concocted," which I take to mean concentrated, and
that women have less vital heat than men. *Id.*

147. *See Generation of Animals*, *supra* note 145, I.20.729a29-31, at 1132.

ensouling the mother's material contribution into the new individual. And is.[148]

Many things follow from this assertion. As the soul is higher than the body, which it shares with the lower animals, the male is higher than the female in Aristotle's taxonomy. Because the male is higher, the female exists to facilitate sexual (rather than hermaphroditic) reproduction. She is instrumental to species reproduction: "The actuality of her human potential is the incubation of a male child."[149] Thus, Aristotle's writings on reproduction contain the seeds of both the hierarchy and proximity of the genders. A lot of Aristotle's biology is clearly circular or nonsense or both. Aristotle is severely hampered by his lack of a microscope, to say nothing (since his semen theory also rests heavily on a notion of vital heat) of the lack of a thermometer. Commentators of this school, of whom Thomas Laqueur is the latest, claim that Aristotle assumed the inferiority of women and from this assumption drew his biology and his politics separately.[150] This still leaves the task of dealing with the politics intact, but at least jettisons the scientific-looking part of the enterprise. By this way of thinking, Aristotle's characterization of women as inferior natural instruments of the material of reproduction is neither necessary nor sufficient for his political misogyny. Not necessary, because Aristotle's debasement of the status of women, including his science, was the result of his methodology of reproducing as truth the opinions about virtue common in his society. And not sufficient, because his science was nonsense. So, until recently, Aristotle lay safely twice buried by the Enlightenment.

About fifteen years ago, people in the United States began engaging—not in great numbers, but in increasing numbers and with increasing visibility—in the practice of hiring surrogate "mothers"[151] to bear children to be taken away and raised in a separate family unit. The practice has generated enormous controversy, and there are numerous responses ranging from proposals to criminalize the practice, to treating it like a protected constitutional right.[152]

---

148. *Id*. II.3.737b27-32, at 1144.

149. Lange, *supra* note 54, at 12.

150. Lange, *supra* note 54, at 13. For much of this line, we are indebted to the pathbreaking work of Michel Foucault. MICHEL FOUCAULT, HISTORY OF SEXUALITY (Robert Hurley trans., 1985). But Laqueur expands the social positing of sexuality with a lot of impressive research revealing the social construction of the body—a much less flexible notion, one would think, than sexuality. He thus strongly buttresses Foucault's insights. *See generally* LAQUEUR, *supra* note 56.

151. To judge from the readings and responses to drafts of this paper, vocabulary is critical in this debate. Readers have suggested "so-called" surrogacy, "contracted pregnancy," and "surrogate wombs." As Martha Field points out, however, in most surrogacy situations, the women are actual mothers, contributing both egg and womb. MARTHA FIELD, SURROGATE MOTHERHOOD 5 (2d ed. 1990). I'll use the popular term, as Field does, for ease, if not clarity.

152. *Id*. at 7-9.

That's the thing about Aristotle. Just when his critics think they have him safely buried in a liberal overcoat of Enlightenment assumptions about equality and Enlightenment discoveries about science, up he pops. Before embarking upon what insights, if any, can be drawn from Aristotle's views on the production of offspring and gender relationships, I will make two preliminary points. First, unlike the discussion of courage set forth above,[153] the lessons from Aristotle's hierarchical biology for the politics of surrogacy bear largely not on the ends of a good human life, but on a preliminary issue for feminists: the means to claim such a life. If any lesson about the teleological concept of citizenship emerges from a return to the ancient writings, it is such assumption as existed of similarity between the genders. Second, I will discuss the moral-political wisdom of surrogacy from the standpoint of women's interests in aspiring to full citizenship separate from the question of whether and to what extent the coercive power of the state should be used to enforce an outcome. This disclaimer is not because classical learning has no wisdom on the role of the state as a force for virtue. As set forth above, this is one of the most neglected, but important, aspects of the classical revival.[154] Rather, it is because the role of the state in surrogacy arrangements has been much discussed in the last few years,[155] while the citizenship aspects of the undertaking have been less extensively explored. Insofar as they have been explored, it has been within a debate framed by liberal assumptions of sale and exchange, concerns that reflect the liberal focus on freedom rather than the classical focus on virtue.[156] Perhaps once the virtue issues are raised to the surface, the debate about avenues of effectuating the superior arrangement will go easier.[157]

In the debates about the wisdom of the practice of surrogacy, feminists on both sides of the issue have argued about a lot of things: whether surrogacy turns women into a commodity, thus debasing them in some unspecified commercial way or whether commodification is desirable, because women should be glad to make money from their childbearing capacities, otherwise sadly undervalued in the market place; whether reproductive technologies simply treat women as walking wombs, caring much more expensively and elaborately for the fetus than the woman,

---

153. *See supra* notes 116-20 and accompanying text.

154. *See supra* text accompanying notes 95-96.

155. *See* FIELD, *supra* note 151, at 229-38. Field's citation of writings on the subject occupies ten pages in the book. *Id.*

156. For an interesting recent instance of this methodology with more evidence of the relationship between feminism and virtue ethics, see Hursthouse, *supra* note 70.

157. Unless, of course, one buys into the "ominous" totalitarian scenarios of liberal legalism, in which case, of course, issues of the good life are too scary to consider. See *supra* note 6 for the hidden agendas of liberalism.

which could be solved by changing the power relationships with the medical establishment; whether claiming rearing rights would relegate women to the home again or raise them from the abased state in which children were entirely the father's domain,[158] as part of the common-law unity between man and wife, being man.[159] But, in all of the discussion of surrogacy—even the feminist debates over surrogacy—no one seems to have noticed that modern science has managed to reproduce the most oppressive parts of both classical and modern biology: the hierarchy of classical thought and the dualism of the modern.

1. The Hierarchy of Surrogacy.—In both common forms of surrogacy, a woman submits herself to a man's reproductive plans. In ordinary surrogacy, a man who wishes to "have"[160] a baby (reproduce himself) may obtain a female womb and material for his purposes. In gestational surrogacy, where the surrogate does not contribute the egg, two women contribute to the man's child.

As Aristotle's writings make clear, it is the soul of the new human that matters. Although we products of modern science now know that both genetic parents contribute to all aspects of the new human, insofar as we moderns also recognize the possibility of contributing by choice to the development of a human soul, it is in the form of rearing and educating the child. By taking it away at birth, the father can claim that domain exclusively. The best illustration of this dynamic is the paradigmatic surrogacy case, *In re Baby M.*[161] There, as the opinion reflects, "the family's only survivor [William Stern] very much wanted to continue his bloodline."[162] That end was accomplished the day Baby M was born. Yet he fought relentlessly—not for his physical "bloodline"—but to gain custody and raise the child. Interestingly, the hierarchy of the spiritual-intellectual over the physical also replicated the hierarchy, long familiar to feminist critics of liberalism, of the public over the private.[163] Thus, the production of the child in the hidden womb is valued less than the visible education and rearing.

The counterarguments on behalf of surrogacy do not overcome this fundamental political lesson. Insofar as the father delegates his authority

---

158. I am indebted to John Ayer for reminding me of the importance of this point; rearing children is indeed a two edged sword in gender relationships; it is traditionally private, yet critical to the public enterprise. *Compare* PLATO, *supra* note 46, *with* NANCY CHODOROW, THE REPRODUCTION OF MOTHERING: PSYCHOANALYSIS AND THE SOCIOLOGY OF GENDER (1978).

159. *See* FIELD, *supra* note 151, at 25-32.

160. Radin, *supra* note 25, at 1929-30 (noting that "the would-be father is 'producing' a baby of his 'own'").

161. 537 A.2d 1227 (N.J. 1988).

162. *Id.* at 1235.

163. I am grateful to Cass Sunstein for suggesting this alternative reading of the hierarchy.

to a woman not the mother he is simply exercising his judgment about the efficient way to accomplish his ends. Insofar as he is sharing the child with the egg donor, he is claiming at least half of the surrogate's service, which leaves the proportion of women to men in the enterprise at two to one, with one female still functioning entirely as the material cause.

Now simply replicating Aristotle's misogynistic biology is perhaps not a "discussion stopper"[164] about the wisdom of the procedure. But it should at least make one pause. This is so, because, as set forth above, the allocation of roles in reproduction is at least circular with, if not causal of, a powerful analogy with every other political role. For all of these reasons, the resemblance between the present fad for surrogacy and Aristotle's picture of the female providing the physical matter for a male to endow with a soul in the *Generation of Animals* is chilling.

2. *The Dualism of Surrogacy.*—In defense of the regime, liberals would say, that between members of opposite sexes the most optimistic prospect is sale—the nonaggression treaty.[165] In this market economy, the argument goes, selling what you have and purchasing what you want is the quintessential autonomous act. The emphasis on the dignity of the exchange is critical, because, without such a show of respect, being an instrument to someone else's purposes is an abased posture, with political consequences not only for the individual involved, but for all who resemble her in the relevant way.[166] Opponents of surrogacy have made the counterarguments against sale, of course:[167] arguments over freedom of will[168] and arguments over appropriate political limitations on free will, such as those contained in the Civil Rights Act of 1964.[169] In response,

---

164. Lange, *supra* note 54, at 10.

165. *See supra* note 156 and accompanying text.

166. That's one reason why the oft-cited hypothetical about the altruistic surrogate bearing the sister's child is flawed. If the surrogate gives the child to her sister to raise, the instrumentalization factor is reduced a lot; in part, it's her own family history and line she's serving. *See* Shari O'Brien, *Commercial Conceptions: A Breeding Ground for Surrogacy*, 65 N.C. L. REV. 127, 131, 152-53 (1986) (using examples of this "altruistic surrogacy" to argue that it does not carry the same risks of exploitation and commodification as the commercial version, and therefore should not be regulated).

167. FIELD, *supra* note 151, at 151-52 (arguing that the choice by a pregnant surrogate to break the birthing contract and keep the baby as her own must be respected, trumping the prior autonomous acts of selling and purchasing the birthing services).

168. *See, e.g.*, Anita L. Allen, *Privacy, Surrogacy, and the Baby M Case*, 76 GEO. L.J. 1759, 1786 (1988) (arguing that economic duress, among other factors, makes the "role of individual free will in the formation of legal obligation in modern life . . . easily exaggerated"); Robin West, *Authority, Autonomy, and Choice: The Role of Consent in the Moral and Political Visions of Franz Kafka and Richard Posner*, 99 HARV. L. REV. 384, 386 (1985) ("[G]ood and evil, and right and wrong, lose all meaning when all that matters is whether and to what extent people get exactly what they think they want.").

169. *See, e.g.*, Margaret D. Townsend, Comment, *Surrogate Mother Agreements: Contemporary Legal Aspects of a Biblical Notion*, 16 U. RICH. L. REV. 467, 476-77 (1982) (addressing but ultimate-

proponents of unregulated surrogacy also invoke the superficial equality of the sperm bank and all its variations like testicular implants.[170]

One conclusion to the argument is that the issue does not exist in the ideal world. The reports reflect that there is almost no controversy over sperm banks.[171] One assumes that sperm banks don't get anyone excited in part because the imposition on the male is so much less onerous, but also because these scenarios just don't happen all that often. And the reason they don't is the same one that supports confronting surrogacy as it exists. In American society, women are in a reduced position of social, political, and economic power. In that framework, surrogacy is a practice that disadvantages women for the symbolic and political reasons set forth above. If, in an Amazonian never-never-land, the larger purpose were truly a shared one, like the well-being of the city in which all live, the alienation and instrumentalism discussion would change. So probably would so many other factors that the discussion becomes science fictional.

But Laqueur's work fuels a much more powerful attack on the liberal defense of surrogacy: that it rests not on a fact of the matter, but on a social construct imposed upon the natural world and therefore subject to revision. As Laqueur describes the development, "[S]ometime in the eighteenth century, sex as we know it was invented. The reproductive organs went from being paradigmatic sites for displaying hierarchy, resonant throughout the cosmos, to being the foundation of incommensurable difference . . . ."[172] Moreover, and most interestingly, the new paradigm did not rest on breakthroughs in natural science: important techniques in the measurement of hormones are a twentieth-century phenomena; there was no consensus on the functions of sperms and eggs until the nineteenth, and the two-sex model predicted all sorts of unprovable consequences, like qualitative differences in skeletal formation or uniform sexuality throughout nature (including, for example, plants).[173]

Cultural historians speculate, and it seems difficult to refute, that the newly-discovered sexual difference was invented to justify continued male domination of the public sphere, after the universalistic claims for liberty

---

ly rejecting a suggestion by the Assistant Attorney General of Virginia that surrogacy agreements violate the Thirteenth Amendment and the Civil Rights Act).

170. *See* Marjorie M. Shultz, *Reproductive Technology and Intent-Based Parenthood: An Opportunity for Gender Neutrality*, 1990 WISC. L. REV. 297, 330 n.93. (This source relates the story of a testicular implant in Europe. But the report is hearsay, and it may be apocryphal.).

171. Radin, *supra* note 25, at 1930 n.277, 1932 n.285 (noting that, given the present gender structure, men are less likely to be considered "fungible" in carrying on the female genetic line, despite the practice of artificial insemination).

172. LAQUEUR, *supra* note 56, at 149. Laqueur's critics, Park and Nye, are substantially less critical of Laqueur's reading of the modern literature than the ancient. *See* Park & Nye, *supra* note 61, at 54.

173. LAQUEUR, *supra* note 56, at 152-73.

and equality characteristic of the Enlightenment.[174]   Many writers have examined the politics of liberal exclusion, which Laqueur sums up as follows:

> Social-contract theory at its most abstract postulated a body that, if not sexless, is nevertheless undifferentiated in its desires, interests, or capacity to reason.   In striking contrast to the old teleology of the body as male, liberal theory begins with a neuter individual body: sexed but without gender, in principle of no consequence to culture, merely the location of the rational subject that constitutes the person. The problem for this theory is how to legitimate as "natural" the real world of male dominion of women, of sexual passion and jealousy, of the sexual division of labor and of cultural practices generally from such an original state of no-gender.   The answer to making their "natural beings recognizable," . . . was for social-contract theorists to "smuggle social characteristics into the natural condition."   However the argument works in detail, the end result is that women are absent from the new civil society for reasons based in "nature."   A biology of sexual incommensurability offered these theorists a way of explaining—without resorting to the natural hierarchies of the one-sex model—how in the state of nature and prior to the existence of social relations, women were already subordinated to men.   Therefore the social contract could then be created between men only, an exclusively fraternal bond.   Ironically, the genderless rational subject engendered opposite, highly gendered sexes.[175]

Then, as now, absent such an explanation, liberal equality would have threatened profoundly the other critical item of the liberal agenda: limited government.[176]

The construction of the sexes as opposites is essential to the defense of commodification.   For, as Radin so graphically expresses it, universal commodification is the default drive of even liberal pluralism:

> Prominent principles in liberal pluralism include negative liberty, the person as abstract subject, and a conceptual notion of property. These principles are basic to the free market and its institutions, private property, and free contract.   Negative liberty and the subjectivity of personhood underlie convictions that inalienable things are internal to the person, and that inalienabilities are paternalistic. Conceptualism finds alienability to be inherent in the concept of

---

174. *See id.* at 194.

175. *Id.* at 196-97 (footnote omitted) (quoting CAROLE PATEMAN, THE SEXUAL CONTRACT 41 (1988)); *see supra* note 6.

176. For a good discussion of the sources of modern liberalism in this context, see JULES STEINBERG, LOCKE, ROUSSEAU, AND THE IDEA OF CONSENT: AN INQUIRY INTO THE LIBERAL-DEMOCRATIC THEORY OF POLITICAL OBLIGATIONS 23-51 (1978).

property. These convictions make the case for liberal pluralism uneasy, always threatening to assimilate to universal commodification.[177]

The most important lesson to draw from this recital is that the arguments about surrogacy are good arguments, but they all exist within the "double bind" choice between free alienation and political disfigurement,[178] a choice which stems directly from the dichotomization of the genders themselves.

What the classical revival does here is break the liberal frame within which the debate has been waged in a way that even the arguments against commodification have failed to accomplish. The classical revival can do so because it reveals that the commodification of reproduction simply locks in the construct of opposite sexes; it shows that the more women behave and/or are categorized as distant and exotic variations on the species, the harder it's going to be to claim citizenship in the common polity. Already founded on a biology of little epistemological legitimacy, a regime of distance from all the social and emotional ties that can surround somewhat more intimate[179] reproduction is just widening the liberally (and li*moral*ly) constructed gulf between women and men. One alternative is of course the relationships of love and altruism associated with the family.[180] But critics of the family model have rightly pointed to its inadequacy as a matrix for free personal development[181] and for the resolution of conflict.[182]

Here, too, the revival of classical learning offers visions of an alternative world, long repressed under the li*moral* regime. Martha Nussbaum teases out the balance between separateness and unity in the political state, where the Aristotelian flexible measure can reflect degrees of difference and contexts of difference free of the Manicheanism of modern thought.[183] More specifically, Aristotle writes of political friendship: the relationship between citizens equal in important ways and valuing one

---

177. Radin, *supra* note 25, at 1887-88.

178. *See supra* note 166.

179. Hirshman, *Moral Education, supra* note 35.

180. *See, e.g.,* ALLEN E. BUCHANAN, MARX AND JUSTICE: THE RADICAL CRITIQUE OF LIBERALISM 13, 86 (1982) (arguing that "Marx cannot appeal to the family as a model for . . . communist society because for him the family as it has existed throughout the history of class-divided society is a microcosm of alienation and exploitation").

181. *See* Jeremy Waldron, *When Justice Replaces Affection: The Need for Rights,* 11 HARV. J.L. & PUB. POL'Y 625, 645 (1988) (arguing that the ability to distance oneself from, analyze and even sometimes repudiate intimate relationships is a good thing because it can often enhance individual autonomy and lead to social change).

182. *See, e.g.,* WILL KYMLICKA, CONTEMPORARY POLITICAL PHILOSOPHY (1990).

183. *See* Nussbaum, *Separateness, supra* note 36, at 396-97, 410, 421 (discussing Aristotle's "attack" on Plato's vision of unity, and criticizing Plato's denial of the importance of separateness).

another for the good in each other.[184]   Such citizens are separate, but
intimate in spending time together and knowing one another, even to the
concrete details of their existence.[185]   Such a friendship, even though
linked to mutual advantage and thus not of the elevated nature of virtue
friendship, still approaches a mean between the indifference of commercial
relationships[186] and the authoritarianism of the family.[187]   As the classi-
cist John Cooper expressed it:

> civic friendship involves mutual good will, trust, and well-wishing,
> and the mutual interest that fellow-citizens have in one another's
> characters is part of that good will and well-wishing. . . .   Each
> expects his fellow-citizens in their dealings with him (political,
> economic, and social) to be motivated not merely by self-interest (or
> other private particular interest) but also by concern for his good for
> his own sake . . . .[188]

Although Aristotle clearly associated gender relationships with the household, he explicitly included them in his descriptions of kinds of friendships:

> Betweeen man and wife friendship seems to exist by nature; for man
> is naturally inclined to form couples . . . .   [B]oth utility and plea-
> sure seem to be found in this kind of friendship.   But this friendship
> may be based also on excellence, if the parties are good . . . .[189]

Drucilla Cornell's recent dissent from MacKinnon's vision of hopeless
alienation between the genders may mark the birth of such a vision in legal
feminism.[190]   Steven Salkever has also started to explore the implications
of Aristotle's wisdom for the genders specifically, with an eye to constructing relationships of neither hierarchy nor alienation.[191]   The good

---

184. *See Nicomachean Ethics, supra* note 90, VIII.1.1155a1-IX.12.2.1172a16, at 1825-52
(concluding that the most perfect friendship occurs where both persons are good and resemble each
other in their virtue); *see also* Salkever, *supra* note 53, at 242 (arguing that Aristotle understood
political relationships as facilitating the development of the potential values that are peculiar to each
sex); Carnes Lord, *Aristotle, in* HISTORY OF POLITICAL PHILOSOPHY 118, 129-30 (Leo Strauss &
Joseph Cropsey eds., 1987) (asserting that for Aristotle, "[t]he political significance of friendship
consists fundamentally in its mitigation of men's attachment to their private interests in favor of a
spontaneous sharing with others of external goods").

185. *See Nicomachean Ethics, supra* note 90, IX.12.1171b29-.1172a8, at 1851-52; *id.*
IX.10.1170b33-.1171a11, at 1850-51.

186. *Politics, supra* note 73, III.9.1280a25-b12, at 2031-32.

187. *See supra* notes 181-82.

188. John Cooper, *Political Animals and Civic Friendship, in* ARISTOTELES' POLITIK AKTEN DES
XI 220-41 (Symposium Aristotelicum, 1990).

189. *Nicomachean Ethics, supra* note 90, VIII.12.1162a16-29, at 1836 (cited in ARLENE W.
SAXONHOUSE, WOMEN IN THE HISTORY OF POLITICAL THOUGHT: ANCIENT GREECE TO MACHIAVELLI
84 (1985)).

190. *See supra* note 102 and accompanying text.

191. *See infra* notes 223-24 and accompanying text.

news is that the debate over surrogacy may open the way for revision of the relationship between the genders on a much broader front.

IV. The Dog at the Gate

A. Opposition

As my two examples reflect, both the structure and the substance of the classical tradition[192] contain familiar modes of thought and much wisdom for the issues of feminist legal theory. However, there is surprisingly little evidence of this richness in contemporary writing. Although a feminist scholar, Katharine Bartlett disclaims the assertion of complete originality,[193] and her references at this point are all to the liberal underpinnings of feminist theory.[194] Thereafter, with the exception of one brief reference to Aristotle as the source of practical reasoning, one might read Bartlett's entire essay and conclude that the feminist modes and orders sort of sprang full-armored from the forehead of Catharine MacKinnon.

One exception would seem to be Suzanna Sherry's *Civic Virtue and the Feminine Voice in Constitutional Adjudication*, which broke very important ground in illuminating the similarities between the civic republican revival of classical concepts of community and feminist psychology.[195] Even Sherry's excellent work, however, emphasizes heavily (and, one assumes, consciously) the later civic republican tradition rather than the classical sources. Moreover, in her consideration of substantive outcomes (the article is about Justice O'Connor's decisions), she focuses on the divergent results produced by a feminine sensibility in cases with no feminist substantive implications, rather than addressing her classical insights to the woman question.

There are at least three explanations for the feminist neglect of classical theory. One is that the revived interest in classicism has been highly overrated. Another is that, in fact, there is little or nothing to be gained from tracing a philosophical tradition to its roots. Finally, one might conjecture that the association of classical philosophy with the aforemen-

---

192. *See* William A. Galston, *The Use and Abuse of the Classics in American Constitutionalism*, 66 CHI.-KENT L. REV. 47 (1990).

193. *See* Bartlett, *supra* note 5, at 834 ("Feminists acknowledge that some important aspects of their methods and theory have roots in other legal traditions. Although permeated by bias, these traditions nonetheless have elements that should be taken seriously.").

194. *See id.* at 834 n.10 ("Although existing legal tools limit the scope of possible change, I think it important not only to critique our traditions, but to acknowledge their useful—and in some respects subversive—features." (citations omitted)).

195. *See* Suzanna Sherry, *Civic Virtue and the Feminine Voice in Constitutional Adjudication*, 72 VA. L. REV. 543, 584-87 (1986).

tioned bias is so poisonous that it reduces the utility of the relationship, indeed, perhaps, renders it counterproductive.

As to the first explanation—ignorance—the philosophical and political literature is replete with evidence of the depth and breadth of the revived interest in ancient philosophy.[196] In any case, the explanation of ignorance is the least interesting one because it is remediable. If, on the other hand, either one of the other explanations—irrelevance or indigestibility—holds true, education in the classics will still be of no moment.

Addressing the second objection—that a relationship to ancient philosophy sheds no light on current thought—there are at least four arguments for exploring the relationships between ancient philosophy and any contemporary discussions of the good life. First, as I hope the above discussion of substance reflects, ancient philosophy may have answers, even right answers according to some epistemology, as to how to lead a good life. Aristotle's theory is "rich in practical consequences as well as in theoretical insights."[197]   Second, as is powerfully illustrated by Laqueur's exploration of the history of gender, there is the critical and comparativist function of exotic subjects. Scholars have returned to Aristotle out of "a sense of the impoverishment of recent moral philosophy."[198]   An ancient tradition can serve as a point from which to criticize an otherwise solipsistic intellectual regime.[199] Third, the unsinkability of the tradition is interesting. Assuming the wide spread of the process of reflective equilibrium, a two and one half millennium survival of a body of philosophic work has a certain market appeal. And finally, there is the aspect of stability. As feminist theorist Jean Elshtain put it, one must "forge links between the Western tradition and feminist thinking" in order to avoid "[w]ildly visionary futures" with "no cogent way to move from the horror of the present to the heaven of the future."[200] If feminism, which seems in so many ways to be prescribing an entirely new regime, can be shown to have its roots in familiar traditions that did not have either uniformly disruptive nor uniformly negative consequences, the risks inherent in revising society from above according to a theoretical formula are reduced.

---

196. *See, e.g.*, Ronald Dworkin, *The Foundations of Liberal Equality*, *in* THE TANNER LECTURES ON HUMAN VALUES 3 (Grethe B. Peterson ed., 1990); GEORG HENRIK VON WRIGHT, THE VARIETIES OF GOODNESS (1963); PETER GEACH, THE VIRTUES (1977); NUSSBAUM, FRAGILITY, *supra* note 36; ALASDAIR MACINTYRE, AFTER VIRTUE (1981); WILLIAMS, *supra* note 87.

197. Amelia O. Rorty, *Introduction* to ESSAYS ON ARISTOTLE'S ETHICS, *supra* note 36, at 1, 3.

198. *Id.* at 1.

199. *See generally* Ronald Beiner, *The Liberal Regime*, 66 CHI.-KENT L. REV. 73, 86-92 (1990).

200. JEAN B. ELSHTAIN, PUBLIC MAN, PRIVATE WOMAN: WOMEN IN SOCIAL AND POLITICAL THOUGHT 298-99 (1981).

Now it is true that "[w]hen we turn to the great tradition of Western political thought with questions about the justice of the treatment of the sexes in mind, it is to little avail."[201]   But perhaps this is to ask the wrong questions. The issue addressed here is what the ancient traditions have to say about the deeper structure of feminist thought and social thought, structures which, when separated from the immediate context of the answers they produced in ancient times, illuminate contemporary feminism with quite a different light.

But, as is so often the case in the Greek world, there is a dog at the gate: the third objection referenced above. Unlike liberal modernity, which basically defined women away or at best ignored us,[202] Aristotle is the original bad actor. The conservatism of his method, which dictated that he start with the prevailing moral views, the functionalism of his theory, according to which things had value only in relationship to their ends, and his assumption that certain social ends were superior—the enabling of some of society to live the good life—are all blamed for producing his explicit conclusion that women are naturally inferior and for setting in motion twenty-four-hundred years of philosophical misogyny.[203]   If this is true, and if Aristotle's philosophy cannot be separated from its objectionable associations, perhaps its similarity to contemporary feminist theory is reason for concern, rather than celebration.[204] Or at least for irony.

Starting with the core problem of classical misogyny, one must ask whether the linkage can be broken. What of Aristotle's structure depends upon its misogyny? Even if the misogyny is a product, rather than a process, are there elements critical to Aristotle's structure that inevitably produce that result?

B.   Reconciliation

In contrast to feminist legal theorists, as the above discussion reflects, feminist philosophers have been wrestling with Aristotle for quite a while[205]—holding on, perhaps, for a blessing. The problem is set forth

---

201. OKIN, *supra* note 61, at 14.

202. *See id.* at 74-109; *see also* OKIN, *supra* note 88, at 198-202.

203. *See* OKIN, *supra* note 88, at 73-96; OKIN, *supra* note 61, at 52-55.

204. *See* Thomas R. Pangle, *The Classical Challenge to the American Constitution*, 66 CHI.-KENT L. REV. 145 (1990).

205. *See, e.g.*, OKIN, *supra* note 88, at 73-96; ELSHTAIN, *supra* note 200, at 41-54; ARLENE W. SAXONHOUSE, WOMEN IN THE HISTORY OF POLITICAL THOUGHT 63-91 (1985); Arlene Saxonhouse, *Aristotle: Defective Males, Hierarchy and the Limits of Politics, in* FEMINIST INTERPRETATIONS AND POLITICAL THEORY 32 (Mary L. Shanley & Carole Pateman eds., 1991) [hereinafter Saxonhouse, *Aristotle*]; GENEVIEVE LLOYD, THE MAN OF REASON: 'MALE' AND 'FEMALE' IN WESTERN PHILOSOPHY 7-10 (1984); Lange, *supra* note 54, at 1-14; Elizabeth V. Spelman, *Aristotle and the Politicization of the Soul, in* DISCOVERING REALITY, *supra* note 54, at 17, 17-30.

quite graphically by Susan Okin: "Aristotle asserts that women are 'naturally' inferior to men, and that they are therefore 'naturally' ruled by them."[206] As Okin describes the problem, what is natural to any entity in Aristotle's world is inextricably intertwined with its function. Thus, an eye is to see; in its natural condition, it will perform this function. In society, according to Aristotle, a woman's function is to reproduce and to run the family men need for their well-ordered political life. Those aspects of her being compatible with that function are natural.[207] The whole structure rests, in turn, upon the superiority of the Greek political life and the essentiality of subordinating women to it. Once that hierarchy is established, the virtues can be allocated according to function; thus, for instance, women's virtues will be seen as subordination and industrious habits, and men's virtues as courage and the capacity to rule. Two things flow from this: the men's virtues will be automatically classified as superior, and any female manifestations of those virtues will be unnatural.

It is easy to see the points of attack. On the grandest level, one might discard, as has so much of modern thought, Aristotle's teleology: his assertion that things, or at least that people, have a purpose. Or one might attack the connection between teleology and nature, asserting the flexibility or social construct of either teleology or nature. Finally, one might get off at the level of hierarchy—a ranking of ends or natures—or at the positing of the hierarchy of virtue from the existing hierarchy of society at any particular social time. All of these techniques and more have been tried.[208] It is also easy to see that, depending on the level of attack, all, most, or only some of Aristotle's structure would have to go.

Most of the work to date focuses on the second and third points—Aristotle's nature and Aristotle's hierarchy. If, for example, as Laqueur has persuasively argued, "nature" is actually a political construct,[209] the whole scheme rests on Aristotle's political decision to assign

---

206. OKIN, *supra* note 88, at 79.

207. *Id.* at 79-88.

208. *See generally* RICHARD SORABJI, NECESSITY, CAUSE, AND BLAME: PERSPECTIVES ON ARISTOTLE'S THEORY 163-65 (1980) (discussing six "[m]odern criticisms of teleological explanation," including "(1) the supposed exclusion of explanation in terms of necessitating causes"; "(2) the idea that [necessitating causes] are not genuinely explanatory"; (3) "the supposition that a teleological explanation must invoke a conscious agent at work"; (4) the "suspicion . . . that teleological explanations are all very well, but only because they are reducible to something else"; (5) the "distinct doubt [as to] whether anything distinctively teleological actually plays a role in explaining the presence of an organ"; and (6) the "final suspicion that teleological explanations are only second best, that they are rendered otiose by purely causal explanations with no teleological element" (citations omitted)).

209. *See* LAQUEUR, *supra* note 56, at 151-52 ("Aristotle did not need the facts of sexual difference to support the claim that woman was a lesser being than man; it followed from the *a priori* truth that the material cause is inferior to the efficient cause. Of course males and females were in daily life identified by their corporeal characteristics, but the assertion that in generation that male was the efficient and the female the material cause was, in principle, not physically demonstrable; it was itself

women (or, more likely, his acceptance of the social reality that women were assigned) to the household and then assign the household to a lower rank in the "natural" hierarchy leading to the polis.[210] Here the concept of "nature" gets fuzzy, because it drifts from physical biology, however ill-conceived, toward a meaning of orderly or good.[211] As to this aspect of Aristotle's theory of the state, Elshtain says, Aristotle is never clear on what should be the orderly relationship of household and state, simply asserting that the household is "prior" to the state and a part of the state.[212] Elshtain further illuminates the disjuncture between Aristotle's misogyny and his larger theory: that Aristotle saw the basis for human political association in the capacity for speech,[213] and yet there is "no evidence that women in Aristotle's time had been struck dumb."[214] Accordingly, Aristotle is reduced to arguing that women lack the capacity for "reasoned" speech, which he supports in a perfectly circular way by their relegation to the (inferior) household, because they lack the capacity for reasoned speech. Arlene Saxonhouse suggests a more positive reading, arguing for Aristotle's recognition of friendship between the genders and his explicit rejection of slavery as the model for gender relationships.[215] She tempers his relegation of women to second best by noting that, to Aristotle, almost everyone was second best.[216]

Nussbaum attempts to use Aristotle's methods to attack the second aspect of classical misogyny—hierarchy. Starting with the fundamentality of the principle of noncontradiction,[217] she postulates a feminist challenging Aristotle's answer to the woman question by showing him that "a progressive position actually preserves certain deep human beliefs about the equal humanity of other human beings better than his own political theory does."[218] But Nussbaum's egalitarian Aristotle[219] is far from the only figure who might emerge. Freed from the misogyny and the false hierarchy of gender, Aristotle would be forced to confront the structural foundations of human hierarchy. Perhaps the work supports Nussbaum's

a restatement of what it *meant* to be male or female." (emphasis in original)).

210. *Nicomachean Ethics*, *supra* note 90, VIII.12.1162a15-30, at 1836; *see Politics*, *supra* note 73, III.4.1277b25, at 2027 (arguing that it is men's role to acquire for the household while women's role is to preserve the household).

211. *See* OKIN, *supra* note 88, at 80-81.

212. *Politics*, *supra* note 73, I.2.1253a19-20, b1-2, at 1988.

213. ELSHTAIN, *supra* note 200, at 48.

214. *Id.*

215. Saxonhouse, *Aristotle*, *supra* note 205, at 40.

216. *Id.*

217. *See* NUSSBAUM, FRAGILITY, *supra* note 36, at 252 (citing Aristotle, *Metaphysics* IV.4.1006a2-5) ("[C]ontradictory predicates cannot belong to the same subject at the same time.").

218. *Id.* at 258.

219. *See, e.g.*, Nussbaum, *Separateness*, *supra* note 36, at 417 (emphasizing Aristotle's claim that political association is an association of peers and equals).

leveling vision. As set forth above, I think that Aristotle would come closer to Hannah Arendt's resolution: that there is an arena in which naturally unequal players construct equality for extrinsic purposes.[220] Much of his writing, including his reference to the superior wisdom of many opinions on issues of governance[221] and the stability of a polity with a large middle class,[222] reflect this inclination. In a post-Enlightenment regime, civil peace might be such an extrinsic purpose.

Steven Salkever suggests a third reading: stripped of its gender hierarchy, Greek philosophy cannot equate virtue with virility, seen as military courage and the associated high-spiritedness, and other virtues, like temperance and ultimately contemplation-philosophy might emerge as the governing political paradigm.[223] Salkever offers this vision as an interesting alternative to the modern dichotomy of classical militarism versus liberal commercialism.[224]

This reading rests on the heavily contested Straussian presumption that a great philosopher, like nature, makes nothing in vain.[225] Be that as it may, the readings that ensue are sufficiently strained so that wholesale adoption of them would, I think, inevitably undermine the larger structure of Aristotle's thought, which does direct our attention to the polis as the final and most self-sufficient end of human enterprise and which does contain explicit descriptions or explanations of at least a moderately privatized and subordinated female role. Yet, as set forth above, these close readings are valuable for highlighting how Aristotle's thought might appear and develop, if the easy assumption of misogyny were removed.[226]

Regardless of which reading one adopts, lacking a grounding in physical biology, the naturalness of the subordination of women must rest on its normative meaning of well-ordered. Here, the Aristotelian picture

---

220. *See* ARENDT, *supra* note 101, at 30-31; *see also* MARGARET CANOVAN, THE POLITICAL THOUGHT OF HANNAH ARENDT 68-69 (1974) (stating that "Arendt sets the view that all that is necessary for the existence of politics is a public space in which men can meet as equals and begin to act").

221. *See Politics, supra* note 73, III.11.1281b1-3, at 2033.

222. *Id.* at III.11.1282a30-41.

223. *See* Salkever, *supra* note 53, at 251-53.

224. *See id.* at 251. The dichotomy is graphically set forth in Galston, *supra* note 192, at 66 ("[T]here *is* no moral equivalent of war." (emphasis in original)).

225. *Cf.* Thomas L. Pangle & Nathan Tarcov, *Epilogue: Leo Strauss and the History of Political Philosophy, in* HISTORY OF POLITICAL PHILOSOPHY 907, 914 (Leo Strauss & Joseph Cropsey eds., 3d ed. 1987) (noting that the most controversial aspect of Strauss's approach to the history of political philosophy was his suggestion that many past philosophers engaged in "exoteric" teachings ("political teachings which were merely desirable or necessary under their particular [historical] circumstances") as well as "esoteric" teachings (those that "they considered to be the political truth always and everywhere")).

226. I am indebted to Ron Allen for suggesting this line of inquiry.

fits together somewhat better, because Aristotelian society needed the household (and the institution of slavery[227]) to support the political activity he saw as best. But if, because of modern claims of equality, which would block the automatic assignment of any group to the subordinated role of household, or, if, as Nussbaum suggests, because of a change in the notion of leisure, or simply because of technological changes, the role of the household in Aristotle's order is no longer needed to support political activity, the foundation for the abased role of women in his philosophy is further undermined.[228] Nor is the opening of these questions the only beneficial result of excising Aristotle's misogyny. As the dialogists correctly assert, women in any society are uniquely both a part of the society and, to the extent that the society is a patriarchal one, not a part of it. If women are to participate in the dialogue over justice, different opinions about justice will no doubt emerge—as recent western political history reflects—if only from their different sizes and their vulnerability to childbearing. Although difference—particularly difference based on separateness—is neither reliable[229] nor inherently valuable, in the Aristotelian mode of inquiry if everyone articulated the same position, there would be little play for philosophy.[230]

Thus, the way is somewhat cleared for the exercise outlined above: to show how these works of feminism generally and feminist jurisprudence, which is the more familiar legal variant, clearly and provocatively raise many of the large issues and are enriched by the answers available from antiquity.

V. Conclusion

[E]verybody knows values are the BMWs of the nineties and that you're just nobody if you don't have some.[231]

It always worries me when my ideas start to crop up in fashion magazines, especially when feminism has already gone through two whole phases (early contemporary and late contemporary) in the current

---

227. This is truly a subject for another paper, if not another lifetime.

228. Whether or which of these developments is either necessary or sufficient for the political changes is beyond the scope of this paper. At this point I assert merely that, as Laqueur has so graphically demonstrated regarding gender, the so-called natural is often less intransigent than the political.

229. MacKinnon quite properly takes on Gilligan, asserting in effect that the different voice may result largely or entirely from having a pillow over one's face. *See* MACKINNON, FEMINISM UNMODIFIED, *supra* note 97, at 38-39; MACKINNON, TOWARD A FEMINIST THEORY OF THE STATE, *supra* note 97, at 51-52. For a graphic illustration of this concept, see GIUSEPPE VERDI, OTELLO, act 4, sc. 2.

230. *See* NUSSBAUM, FRAGILITY, *supra* note 36, at 240.

231. Colin McEnroe, *Was It Ethical for You, Too?*, MIRABELLA, Nov. 1990, at 130, 130.

incarnation, to say nothing of those poor benighted souls around 1920 who
only wanted to vote. Yet there is a sense in which the movement from the
beginning has been driving toward a consistent single goal, well expressed
by the classical writers: the goal of citizenship. Put another way, woman
is a political animal.

Labour Law

[15]

International Journal of the Sociology of Law 1986, **14**, 377–392

The Invisibility of Women in Labour Law: Gender-neutrality in Model-building

JOANNE CONAGHAN

University of Kent, U.K.

1. Introduction

As a feminist and an academic labour lawyer I find myself confronted with the problem of how to make the two converge. Scanning the popular textbooks, browsing through the mainstream law journals I find little to convince me that women are in any way visible in labour law except in a few 'recognised' areas i.e. sex discrimination law, equal pay legislation and the maternity provisions. These areas apart, labour law is a world made up of full-time male bread-winners and the legal rules reflect this conception of the worker. Moreover the models labour lawyers employ to analyse and evaluate the rules are gender-blind in that they fail to recognise that for men and women experiences of work and the workplace may be very different.

As a result, the particular nature of women's oppression in the production process is not revealed, and labour law, by rendering women invisible legitimates patriarchal conceptions of work and workers. Moreover, even in the areas where gender factors have been explicitly recognised by British labour law, in the context of the equality legislation, (i.e. the Sex Discrimination Act, 1975, the Equal Pay Act, 1970 and the maternity provisions embodied in the Employment Protection Consolidation Act, 1978) these areas tend to be marginalised, set aside, characterised as 'women's law' and that part of the labour law course which tokenistically recognises "women's issues".

Yet women are affected by labour law generally, not just by the equality legislation. In any case the evidence that this legislation has failed to bring about any significant changes in women's employment position is well documented (see for example Kahn, 1983, p. 87ff. Scorer & Sedley, 1983). It is necessary, therefore, for the feminist to explore the terrain of labour law as a whole and to examine its differential impact on and relation to men and women workers. A starting point here, and the subject matter of this paper is a feminist critique of current models used in the analysis of labour law.

0000/86/030377+16 $03.00/0

2. Model-building in Labour Law

Although not always made explicit, the rules and decisions which constitute labour law tend to assume particular frames of reference which can to some extent be characterised as models or 'ideal-types'. Such ideal-type analysis, common in sociological studies of industrial relations (see for example Fox, 1974) is becoming increasingly employed in the study of labour law (e.g. Elias, 1981; Collins, 1982; Forrest, 1980). It provides both a method of analysing and understanding labour law and a standard by which to evaluate it. The model thus constructed may be employed both to describe and to prescribe, to explain and to assess with a view to future change.

Bill Rees identifies four perspectives which he maintains, are employed in the context of labour law (Rees, 1982): they are the Unitary, the Traditional Pluralist, the Radical Pluralist and the Marxist frames of reference. My focus in this paper will be directed primarily at the traditional and radical pluralist models because they capture much of contemporary thinking about labour law and characterise mainstream ideological positions, (although it must be added here that present government policies are moving very much in the direction of a unitary perspective, the implications of which I will consider.)

The traditional pluralist model

Unlike the unitary perspective, pluralism recognises the inevitability of conflict in industrial relations; a conflict nevertheless reconcilable through the collective bargaining process. Collective bargaining is also necessary because the pluralist perspective recognises that the relationship between the employer and the employee is necessarily unequal. Indeed as Otto Kahn Freund points out: "The main object of labour law has always been . . . to be a countervailing force to counteract the inequality of bargaining power which is inherent . . . in the employment relationship" (Kahn-Freund, 1983, p. 18). Thus collective bargaining removes the potential for exploitation and, by establishing an equilibrium between the forces of capital and labour, embodies and embraces the values of industrial democracy and joint sovereignty. Law's role in this vision is that of the neutral arbiter, "holding the ring", facilitating the proceedings. Thus it provides a legal framework within which collective bargaining can take place but it does not attempt to intervene to influence the outcome of negotiations. Law reflects procedural justice. This legal abstentionism, characterised by Kahn Freund as "collective *laissez-faire*", is called upon to explain the role of law in Britain in relation to industrial affairs for most of this century. Even the legal intervention of the 1970s for example the growth of employment protection rights, the development of statutory procedures to facilitate bargaining such as the statutory recognition procedure has a "voluntarist" ring in still ascribing to law a facilitative role and still emphasising the primacy of collective bargaining[1].

The fundamental thrust of the pluralist perspective is that industrial relations ultimately are best left to the parties themselves and that the role of law must necessarily be marginal. As Kahn Freund states: "Acts of Parliament however well-intentioned and well designed, can do something but cannot do much to modify the power relation between labour and management" (Kahn Freund, 1984, p. 19).

The radical pluralist critique

In recent years in Britain and more particularly in America, a strong and con-certed attack from the left has been levelled at the pluralist model[2]. Essenti-ally this critique challenges the ideological assumptions which underlie the pluralist model and asserts that these assumptions operate as a legitimating device disguising the hierarchical and oppressive nature of workplace re-lations. So, for example, the radical critique challenges the assumption that management and labour are roughly equal in bargaining power. The "joint sovereignty" which collective bargaining appears to embody is illusory be-cause management and labour negotiation take place only "at the margins" of the industrial enterprise (Stone, 1981).

The radical critique also challenges the autonomy ascribed to law in in-dustrial relations. Law does not operate neutrally but, by virtue of the pro-capital perspective which its rules embody, works in a hidden way, to promote managerial ends (Klare, 1982). Essentially the radical charge amounts to an indictment of pluralism for failing to change in any substantial way the nature of workplace organisation or the power relations between the parties. What is needed therefore, the radical argues, is a new perspective which recognises the hegemonic influence of current labour law and works to construct new models of industrial organisation and new visions of workplace democracy.

Enter feminism

While the radical critique goes some way to exposing the very real inad-equacies of pluralism as a model of industrial relations, it is ultimately incom-plete because it is utterly gender-blind. The radical approach seeks to make ideological perspectives explicit yet it fails to address or even recognise the partriarchal ideology which permeates pluralist thinking. The radical critique rightly recognises the myth of legal autonomy but fails to specify or to begin to explore the ways in which law operates to maintain the subordinate position of women. Furthermore, the radical critique recognises the hierarchical nature of the workplace characterised by capitalist social relations but it fails to reveal the patterns of hierarchy and exploitation determined by gender relations. Ul-timately then its project, the forging of new more democratic forms of work-place organisation, is flawed, because such forms will still be hierarchical, will still be exploitative, unless they recognise the particular nature of women's oppression.

There is a need then to return to the pluralist model and to re-evaluate it from a feminist critical perspective. But first it is necessary to say something about the terrain within which this debate is taking place. I want to look briefly at women's contemporary position in the labour market.

3. Women, Work and the Labour Market

In Davies & Freedland's leading textbook on labour law the authors state that "levels and patterns of employment have an important impact on and interaction with most aspects of labour law" (Davies & Freedland, 1984). They then go on to present a series of statistics on labour market trends which includes some interesting information on the position of women in work. They conclude that "for the time being an awareness is growing among labour lawyers that the body of law with which they are concerned has to be understood and evaluated against that particular social, economic and analytical background". So, it seems that labour law has to be understood within the context of the structure of the labour market, yet in relation to women such an understanding does not appear to be forthcoming. Women remain visible only at the margins of Davies & Freedland's mammoth text despite the fact that their picture of the labour market tells a very different story. Trends over the last 25 years have witnessed the rapid entry of women, (particularly married women) into the labour market so that they now make up about 40% of the workforce and there is evidence that the numerical gap between men and women workers will continue to close. (For example Veronica Beechey (1985) estimates that women will make up 46% of the workforce by 1990). There is then no doubt that the gender compostion of work is changing and that women are becoming numerically a force to be reckoned with.

Conceptions of employment in the labour market are also changing. The full-time male employee is gradually being ousted by a variety of different forms of employment: part-time work, short-term contracts and 'casual' labour. Self-employment has also increased significantly at least since 1979[3]. The growth in part-time work is particularly significant. Veronica Beechey points out that in Britian today one fifth of the labour force works part-time and this is likely to rise to one quarter by 1990 (Beechey, 1985, p. 12). Beechey also points out that the length of the working life is getting shorter both because of late youth entry into the labour market and early retirement schemes (Beechey, 1985, p. 13). These changes in the nature of employment have particular implications for women. The part-time workforce consisting almost entirely of women, accounts for 40% of all working women. (It is interesting to observe here that a much higher proportion of women work part-time in Britain than elsewhere in Europe. For example, compare our 40% to France's 17% of working women. Sylvia Walby argues that the prevalence of part-time work here can be explained by the particularly poor terms and conditions attaching to part-time work in Britain thus making it an attactive option to British employers (Walby, 1983).)

Women also tend to be numerically high among temporary and short-term workers and of course homeworking is traditionally associated with women (see Allen & Wolkowitz, 1986 for an excellent account of the exploitative nature of home-working). In part such work arrangements of women workers can be explained in terms of their actual or expected domestic commitments. This also helps to explain the high casualisation of women's labour: the need for the working mother to strike an individual bargain with the 'understanding employer' who in return for her 'loyal' service takes a sympathetic attitude to her child-care commitments. (The potential for exploitation here is well documented in Freeman, 1982). However the position of women workers can also be understood in terms of the structure of the labour market itself. Women's work tends to constitute those sections of the labour market which are most low paid and least protected. Barron & Norris characterise women's work as occupying the 'secondary sector' of the labour market (Barron & Norris, 1976). Utilising dual labour-market theory they argue that women's work bears all the hallmarks of the secondary sector: low pay, job insecurity, lack of mobility into the primary sector and absence of promotion structures. However, while dual labour market theories, and other economic approaches which reveal the segmented nature of the labour market help us to understand in part the phenomenon of sex segregation in employment they do not of course explain why it is women who should be exploited in this way in the first place.

The fact remains that the combined effect of women's commitments in the private sphere and established structural discrimination in the public sphere, is to maintain women workers in low paid, routine and much-exploited jobs. Ultimately, the reality of the situation is that in the 1980s, despite the existence of equal pay and sex discrimination legislation, women's average pay is still less than two thirds of men's and women are still extremely underrepresented in professional and high-powered positions. This is of course a damning indictment on the equality legislation but it also suggests the need to take a more serious look both at that legislation and the rules and structures which determine and direct the production process.

4. Pluralism Revisited: the Feminist Critique

The picture of work presented above calls for a new perspective on labour law, one which recognises both the prevalence of women's subordination in the labour market and takes account of changing demographic factors which render traditional models redundant. My critique of pluralism will proceed along four broad but related fronts:

Firstly I want to challenge the legal conception of the worker which pluralism reflects;

Secondly, I will explore the pluralist assumption in favour of the primacy of voluntary collective bargaining;

Thirdly and relatedly, I want to examine the pluralist trend towards legal 'abstentionism' and the concomitant assumption of state neutrality;

382   *J. Conaghan*

Fourthly, I want to challenge the pluralist conception of workplace autonomy and the autonomy of industrial relations generally.

The 'pluralist worker'

The pluralist worker is full-time, continuous, and usually skilled: he is historically the male breadwinner, the earner of the family wage. This is no more
apparent than in the concept of 'employee' utilised by most of the employment
protection legislation. This legislation including for example unfair dismissal,
redundancy and maternity provisions, is predominantly confined to full-time
employees: workers under a 'contract of employment' (Employment Protection
Consolidation Act 1978, S153) who satisfy the necessary qualification period
(at present two years for unfair dismissal, redundancy pay and maternity pay).

Yet as the trends identified above suggest this conception by no means captures the variety of workers who make up the labour force. Moreover the irony
is that those most likely to be excluded from the legislation, part-time workers
(if working under 16 hours)[4]. Temporary and short-term workers[5], home-
workers and other 'casual' workers tend to be the lowest paid and the least
organised; in other words they tend to be that part of the workforce most in
need of employment protection.

More to the point, this motley band of 'non-employees' is as we have observed, populated to a large extent with women workers. Recent labour law
writers, such as Davies & Freedland, have recognised the conceptual inad-
equacies of the contract of employment and have argued for a legal framework
which takes account of the variations in work relationships (Davies & Freedland, 1984, p. 80ff.). Moreover, particular concern has been shown for the
plight of individual groups of workers: there is considerable literature for example on the position of part-time workers and both the courts and the EEC
have been active in identifying their problems[6]. Likewise Hepple & Napier
have argued that labour law has failed to take account properly of the problems faced by temporary workers and they call for specific legislative changes
(Hepple & Napier, 1978).

In the context of home-workers, recent case development have opened up
the possibility of at least some home-workers coming within the legal concept
of 'employee' for purposes of employment protection legislation[7] though
arguably the impact of such developments is not likely to be great because
most homeworking is too casual, too far outside legal conceptions of the employment relationship to submit easily to regulation (Allen & Wolkowitz,
1986). However, although the plight of such workers is, as I have acknowledged, well documented, and although movements are afoot to bring about legal
change, the full-time continuous employee still constitutes the central paradigm around which other types of workers plead for recognition.

Protection for the non-paradigmatic employee is not an entitlement: it must
be aimed or at least in some way justified. This is no more apparent than in the

recent Green Paper on Reform of Social Security which argues that maternity pay is "a form of reward for continuous service with one employer for a period of years" (Government Green Paper, 1985, vol. 2, para. 5, p. 22).

Indeed the maternity provisions are an excellent illustration of the inappropriateness of the pluralist conception of the worker. These provisions are indisputably gender-specific, yet the model of employment which the legislation utilised is gender-neutral. The pregnant worker must be full-time (or at least working more than 16 hours per week) and she must have worked for her employee uninterruptedly for two years. Obviously this excludes many women part-time workers, temporary and short-term workers and women whose employment has been interrupted due to child-care/domestic commitments.

Legislation which utilises such a model cannot take seriously the aim of equality. As a result, for a majority of women workers, the maternity provisions are a non-starter. (For a detailed account of the deficiencies in the present legislation including its limited scope see Upex & Morris, 1981 and Mayhew, 1985.)

The primacy of collective bargaining

The pluralist model assumes a picture of industrial relations which consists of two parties, capital and labour, managements and unions, with conflicting interests reconcilable through collective bargaining. As Kahn Freund observes:

> "The functions [of the collective agreement] express the principle expectations of the two sides and it is through reconciling their expectations that a system of industrial relations is able to achieve that balance of power which is one of its main objectives" (Kahn-Freund, 1983, p. 154).

This bifurcated perspective assumes the gender-neutrality of industrial relations: it assumes that gender is not a factor which is of any relevance in determining power relations. A concomitant assumption is that unions can and should represent the interests of the workforce. But do unions represent the interests of women workers, and of what relevance is collective bargaining to the experience of women's work?

At present about one third of all working women are trade unionists and they account for 30% of trade-union membership as a whole, some 3,500,000 women workers (Hunt, 1982, p. 154). These figures demonstrate a significant increase in female unionisation: female union membership has almost doubled since the early 1960s and at present it is increasing at a much greater rate than male membership.

Despite these changes female membership is confined to a very narrow range of industries: Of the 3,500,000 women union members 3,000,000 can be found in only two of the 177 trade unions affiliated to the TUC; moreover women only dominate numerically in 14 of these unions — mostly public-sector unions — a clear reflection of the degree of job segregation in the labour market (Hunt, 1982, p. 154). So, while women unionists numerically are continuing to grow their voices remain confined to a limited range of platforms.

Moreover the fact remains that two thirds of working women are non-unionised: explanations for this phenomenon point to the unskilled nature of the work women do (thus making replacements easy and therefore bargaining power weak), the fact that women tend to work in small disparate workplaces (in bars, in shops, as cleaners and hairdressers and in catering) and are therefore difficult to organise and the fact that most women operate a 'double shift': i.e. they assume responsibilities at home as well as at work which make it difficult for them to participate in union activities. An evening meeting requires a considerable degree of organisation and effort for the working mother.

It is apparent then, that both the segregated structure of the labour market (the public sphere) and the expected domestic role of women (the private sphere) make it difficult for women workers to organise. It is thus somewhat naive simply to encourage women to join trade unions and participate more actively. The slogan "A Woman's Place is in her Union" does not appear to confront the fact that existing social structures belie this assertation. So, while pluralist labour law is premised on the promotion of voluntary collective bargaining between the 'two sides' of industry, this is a picture which does not include the majority of working women. However, not only are women poorly represented in the union movement and therefore to a considerable extent unassisted by collective bargaining, but it cannot be denied that women's interests and union interests do not always coincide.

There is no doubt that the history of trade unionism includes much that is sexist and discriminatory in relation to women workers. Indeed the very segregation which at present prevents women from contributing to the trade-union movement is itself a product, to a large extent, of trade-union practices. A feminist approach to trade unions and collective bargaining must acknowledge these antagonisms, not ignore them. For example, it must be acknowledged that the feminist pursuit of equal pay inevitably conflicts with the union concern to maintain pay differentials. Moreover, insofar as the trade union movement has campaigned in support of equal pay their primary concern has been with the need to protect men's jobs from being undercut by cheaper female labour. The considerable limitations of the Equal Pay Act, for example the confining of comparisons to men and women in the same employment (Equal Pay Act, 1970, S1) reflect this concern. Indeed it has been observed that "In the Equal Pay Act, 1970 can be seen all the hallmarks of the trade-union campaign for pay protection for men" (Atkins & Hoggett, 1984, p. 21). These antagonisms are exacerbated with the impact of new technology and the consequent 'deskilling' of many jobs thus bringing women into new, previously male-dominated industries (Coyle, 1982).

At the same time, the trade-union movement plays an important role in transmitting and perpetuating an ideology which sees women's rightful place as in the home: from Engels down to the present day the labour movement has romanticised mothering, sanctified the family and involved itself in the campaign for the family wage. While not denying the countervailing tendencies which did and still do exist, there remains within unions a strong residue of patriarchal and sexist attitudes. (For evidence of the contemporary prevalence of the attitudes among male trade unionists and their wives, see Porter, 1982).

Fundamental then, to a feminist approach to labour law, is to challenge the assumption that unions represent the interest of the workers. At the same time, this should not involve us in the popular political process of 'union–bashing': As feminists and socalists have pointed out, the sexual division of labour fragments working-class consciousness and is divisive in the struggle against capitalism.

Nevertheless, this feminist recognition of the problematic relationship between trade unions and women's interests does call for a reassessment of the pluralist emphasis on collective bargaining (Campbell, 1980) — after all it is a process which is of little relevance to many women workers — and more particularly it requires us to re-examine the traditional pluralists and union preference for legal abstentionism: Are women better off with or without legal intervention?

Abstentionism v. interventionism

By now it has become clear that insofar as law directly regulates the labour markets, women for the most part appear beyond its scope: The employment protection legislation is confined in effect to a small number of working women while the law and practice of collective bargaining appears marginal insofar as the majority of women workers are not organised. However although labour law may appear to have no *direct* effect on women, feminists have long recongnised that indirect and more subtle forms of legal intervention may operate to women's detriment. In other words law, by its very failure to intervene may have a regulatory effect on women's lives (McIntosh, 1978).

It therefore becomes relevant to examine the pluralist preference for legal 'abstentionism' in order to understand its particular implications for women workers. A preliminary observation must be that 'abstentionism' for pluralists does not necessarily imply an absence of legislation. Industrial relations have been subject in various ways to legislation at least since the last century and the 1970s have witnessed a proliferation of legislation, endowing employees with individual rights and creating a statutory framework for the promotion of collective bargaining. [See in particular the Trade Union and Labour Relations Act, 1974 (TULRA); the Employment Protection Act, 1975 and the Employment Protection (Consolidation) Act, 1978 (EPCA)].

Though the character of this legislation is, as I have earlier observed, subject to considerable controversy it undoubtedly possesses pluralist and abstentionist characteristics: The employment protection legislation for example is envisaged as a 'floor of rights' upon which collective negotiation can build while the collective framework established by the legislation, particularly the statutory recognition provisions (Employment Protection Act, 1975 SS11-16 repealed by Employment Act, 1980 S19) have a thoroughly procedural flavour. The 1970s legislation became acceptable to pluralist interpretations by continuing to cast law in the role of 'facilitator'. So abstentionism does not mean no regulation but a particular form of regulation: How has this form of regulation affected the postion of women in the labour market?

It is arguable that the narrow scope of the employment protection legislation is in part a result of abstentionist influences not just by virtue of the narrow concept of employee it embodies but more particularly because it presupposes the pre-eminence of voluntary collective bargaining. As a result the rights embodied in the legislation are regarded as minimum rights to be imposed by collective negotiation. For women workers in low-paid poorly organised industries, this means that they are confined in effect to those minimum rights (if they can qualify for them) and even then some women workers may be in so poor a bargaining position as to be afraid to assert them. [The high 'casualisation' of women's labour is a particular problem here (Freeman, 1982)].

Arguably too the limited scope of the Equal Pay Act can be explained in part by a prevailing preference among union leaders for 'voluntary' arrangements. Indeed the conflict between the aims of equal pay and the principle of voluntarism is recognised by Kahn Freund: "The principles of autonomy and voluntary regulation — the very foundations of British collective labour law — have been sacrificed to this most urgent need for counteracting discrimination in employment" (Kahn-Freund, 1983, p. 191). Despite the fact that Kahn Freund views the Equal Pay Act as an 'almost revolutionary' piece of legislation (Kahn-Freund, 1983, p. 190) it was from conception limited in impact and scope.

The concept of 'like work', the limitation of comparisons essentially to workers in the same work places, the reliance on job evaluation schemes which are laden with patriarchal prejudices about what constitutes 'skill' all resulted in a piece of legislation which did little to tackle low pay and nothing at all to solve the problem of job segregation. (Atkins & Hoggett argue that the provision of the act 'positively encouraged' sex segregation (Atkins & Hoggett, 1984, p. 21).

Even the provisions allowing for review of collective agreements by the Central Arbitration Committee (CAC)[8] were minimal in their impact beyond eliminating express discrimination, for example 'women's rates'. Indeed Davies & Freedland observed that attempts by the CAC to widen their powers under S3 were discouraged by the courts, in Davies & Freedland's view, specifically because of a preference for voluntarism (Davies & Freedland, 1984, p. 380).

If abstentionism has played some part in limiting the effectiveness of the equality legislation, its influence is even more obvious in the context of minimum-wage legislation. Both Wages Councils and the Fair Wages Resolution, initially conceived of as measures to tackle problems of low pay (and indeed specifically recognised as concerned with the plight of mostly women workers) gradually became regarded within the context of labour law as legislation for the promotion of voluntary collective bargaining.

Thus evaluations of the success or failure of minimum wage legislation (including the now-repealed schedule 11 to the Employment Protection Act, 1975) came to depend as much on principles of abstentionism and voluntarism as on the need to eliminate low pay. Indeed the former issue dominated debate about wages councils in the early 1970s and in fact some unions were actually in favour of their abolition on the grounds that they discouraged voluntary collective bargaining (Davies & Freedland, 1984, p. 149). Needless to say, the abstentionist principle is one of the arguments which the present Government has hijacked to justify both the repeal of schedule II and the rescinding of the Fair Wages Resolution (Lewis & Simpson, 1981, p. 150). Wages councils are of course also under threat of abolition and their inspectorate has been cut considerably thus increasing their ineffectiveness (Kahn, 1985, p. 86).

The point is that legislation initially conceived of in 1910 as concerned with the problem of low pay and sweated industries, legislation campaigned for by women and to a considerable extent for women has been swallowed up in the abstentionist debate so that its original aims have been relegated to a secondary position. A legal approach which took low pay more seriously may well have produced different results. For the time being wages councils, though of minimal effect in eliminating low pay, are the only protection that many women workers have.

My argument so far has been that the abstentionist principle has effectively minimised the potential of various pieces of labour law legislation to protect women workers. The abstentionist principle is also problematic because in the 1980s, and in the context of Government policy 'abstentionism' has merged with 'deregulation'. Present Conservative Government policy, namely dismantling the statutory framework for the promotion of collective bargaining, cutting the substance of employment protection rights and gradually abolishing legislation for the protection of the low paid[9], is not 'abstentionist' in the pluralist sense of a preference for voluntary collective bargaining. 'Thatcher's law' does not present itself as the neutral arbiter, 'holding the ring' while the two sides 'slug it out'; Thatcherism is explicitly premised upon a conception of labour relations which eschews collective bargaining and seeks to minimise the power of trade unions who constitute an 'external interference' in the natural forces of the free market.

This is a form of deregulation which men and women workers should fight together. At the same time feminists should be aware that present Government policies have a particularly damaging effect on women (David, 1983). Firstly, statistics indicate that a higher rate of unemployment is suffered by women than by men: the recession is hitting women workers particularly badly (Walby, 1983). Secondly, policies of privatisation have a particular effect on working women, one third of whom work in the public sector. Privatisation for

example of cleaners in the NHS, tends to lead to lower pay and greater exploitation, which at the same time casualising women's employment status thus
taking them outside employment protection legislation (Coyle, 1985).
Thirdly, Thatcher's 'reorganisation' of social services cannot fail to drive
many working women 'back into the home' because of lack of child-care facilities, and financial exigencies (Land, 1985). Finally, the equal pay and sex
discrimination provisions, though presently under review and pending
amendment, are of minimal effect given the economic conditions currently
existing. In Thatcher's Britain, women, the most vulnerable, least organised
and most exploited of workers are at the forefront of her policies and are in no
position to assert legal rights against the recalcitrant employer.

To conclude this section, I have been arguing that pluralist promotion of
voluntary collective bargaining and the form of legal regulation it has generated has not necessarily benefited women workers. At the same time, given the
current political climate, and the labour law which it is producing, feminists
must recognise that while pluralism offers them very little, Thatcherism offers
nothing at all. If the present struggle in labour law is to direct itself against
current Government policies feminists must participate fully aware of the legal
implications of present legal strategies and proposed alternatives. The issue is
not regulation or no regulation but what form of regulation will best suit the
interests of women workers[10].

The legal autonomy of industrial relations

My final concern with the pluralist model seeks to link its conception of law's
marginality in the context of labour relations with an ideology which views
society as consisting of two separate and distinct spheres: the family and the
market; the private and the public. (For examples of recent legal work based
on this distinction see Olsen, 1983; O'Donovan, 1985).

Industrial sociologists already maintain that this ideology plays an important part in influencing the actors in the industrial scene — management,
union officials, workers — but this perspective is also reflected in law, legal
categories and legal writings. The labour lawyer views his terrain as beginning
and ending with the labour market; he may extend his investigations into social security — the law of the unemployed is beginning to find its way into
labour-law journals and textbooks, but the sphere of the family is still a realm
untouched and unrecognised by conventional labour law thinking. [It is significant that the Sex Discrimination Act explicitly excludes the domestic sphere
— Sex Discrimination Act, 1975 S6(2) (a)].

Against this background feminists presently campaigning through law are
beginning to realise that the liberal pursuit of formal equality in the workplace
will not achieve their liberation while the sphere of the family remains unchanged. Women's expected roles in the domestic sphere do not just affect their
contribution at work by virtue of the 'double shift' which it tends to impose
upon them:

Popular conception of gender roles, social responsibilities and family life actually affect the dynamics of the workplace influencing the hierarchies and power relations which develop within it;

Industrial relations far from being autonomous are the product of and interact with other social forces in society as a whole.

For feminists, then, campaigning through labour law is not enough because labour law does not confront the dichotomy between public and private but rather tends to perpetuate it. The equality legislation and the maternity provisions are mere acts of tokenism because they attempt to reform the public sphere while leaving the private sphere untouched.

At present women work in a climate where public child-care facilities are wholly inadequate and where the law on tax, social security and pensions all conceive of women as to some extent financially dependent on men. (These areas of law too are notably exempted from sex discrimination provisions. So also is protective legislation restricting the number of hours women work).

The problem is particularly acute because the Conservative Government is pursuing a policy which in effect increases women's domestic role even more by proposing to reduce the maternity provisions, freeze child benefit, abolish the maternity grant and Family Income Supplement, to give but a few examples (Government Green Paper, 1985; Land, 1985).

It thus becomes clear that the pluralist view of industrial relations as an autonomous and self-regulating sphere of activity conflicts with the feminist perspective which insists on the importance of recognising the relationship between the dynamics of the family and the dynamics of the market.

5. Conclusion: Confronting Patriarchy?

An exploration of the pluralist perspective on labour law and radical critiques of that perspective reveal that although to varying extent aware of the nature of capitalist social relations, neither of these frameworks have a conception of or a concern with patriarchal power. They thus reflect the left's concern with the relations of production between capital and labour rather than the relations of reproduction between men and women within the family. (For a series of useful critiques of this left perspective see Campbell, 1980; Coote, 1981; Campbell, 1982.)

Marxist–Feminist approaches on the other hand, specifically addressing the issue of gender hierarchy in the labour market maintain that the sexual division of labour is not a product of capitalism alone but is exploited by it (McIntosh, 1981, p. 8ff.; Barrett, 1980, Ch. 5). Such an insight reveals that feminist perspectives, far from being divisive for the left are essential in the struggle to overcome the divisions capitalism seeks to exploit. Radical approaches to labour law are flawed in their basic failure to recognise this home-truth. Bea Campbell points out (Campbell, 1980) that "United we Fall" if "United" implies a failure to address or take seriously women's concerns.

A feminist perspective on labour law must begin by recognising that power relations in the workplace reflect not just the conflict between capital and la-

bour but also patriarchal attitudes and practices. It is this insight which justifies the pursuit of a specifically feminist approach to labour law and labour
relations, an approach which takes women workers as its starting point and
redefines the terrain of labour law, to take account of their particular interests.

The themes in this paper will be developed further in a forthcoming article
in a collection of critical legal papers in the Journal of Law and Society. I
would like to thank Louise Chudleigh for her help, support, and ideas in the
production of this paper.

Notes

1 I am not of course arguing that the 1970s legislation should *necessarily* be
  interpreted in this way. There are some who argue that the legislation was of a
  character differing completely from anything which had gone before (Collins,
  1982). I am maintaining however that the promotion of *voluntary* collective
  bargaining, implying a secondary role for law, was an important theme in the
  legislation.
2 Examples of the British literature include Collins, 1982; Forrest, 1980 and Fox,
  1974. The American literature is extensive: see in particular Klare, 1982 and
  Stone, 1981.
3 During the 1970s self-employment fell, but the rise since 1979 has been quite
  dramatic: Veronica Beechey argues that this change is mostly accounted for by
  casualisation and the growth of sub-contracting (Beechey, 1985, p. 11). For an
  account of the particular effects of these changes on women workers in the cleaning
  industry see Coyle, 1985.
4 Generally, to qualify for 'his' rights an employee must be 'continuously employed',
  i.e. he must work at least 16 hours per week (EPCA, S.151 and Schedule 13).
5 The employment status of temporary workers is ambiguous and therefore they
  may not constitute an "employee" for purposes of employment protection (Hepple
  & Napier, 1978). All short-term workers are disadvantaged by the qualification
  period.
     Moreover fixed-term workers are particularly disadvantaged because, although
  an agreement to waive the rights conferred by the legislation is generally void
  (EPCA, S.140) it is possible to waive one's rights to unfair dismissal and
  redundancy payment at the expiry of a fixed-term contract (S.142, EPCA). Such
  waiver clauses are becoming common practice, e.g. in fixed-term appointments at
  universities.
6 In *Jenkins v. Kingsgate* (1981) Industrial Case Reports (ICR) 715 the Employment
  Appeals Tribunal (EAT) held (on reference back from the ECJ) that differences in
  pay between part-time and full-time workers could breach the Equal Pay Act,
  unless the employer could show that the differences were reasonably necessary to
  achieve some economic objective and were not based on factors indirectly or
  directly relating to sex.
     In *Clark v. Eley IMI Kynock Ltd* (1983) ICR 165 the EAT held that the application
  of the rule "part-timers first" as a criterion for redundancy selection could
  constitute indirect discrimination under the Sex Discrimination Acft, 1975.
  However see also *Kidd v. DRG* (1985) ICR 405. In European EEC Draft Directive
  on voluntary part-time work submitted by the EEC Commission in 1982 is

presently awaiting the approval of the EEC Council.

7 *Airfix Footwear Ltd v. Cope* (1978) ICR 1210; *Nethermere (St Neots) Ltd v. Taverna* (1983) IRLR 103.

8 Equal Pay Act, 1970, S.3. The European Court has held that this provision does not satisify European law (Case 165/82) and changes are pending which may involve closer scrutiny of collective agreements by the courts. Atkins & Hoggett suggest that this may prove to women's advantage insofar as the threat of court action may well persuade unions to introduce positive action measures into collective agreements (Atkins & Hoggett, 1984, p. 58). This illustrates how women can use the tradition of abstentionism to pursue their particular interests.

9 Schedule 11 of the Employment Protection Act (EPA) 1975 (enforcement of recognised terms and conditions) was repealed by Employment Act (EA) 1980, S.19. The Fair Wages Resolution was rescinded in 1982. The debate about abolishing wages councils continues. A bill is presently going through Parliament which removes wages council protection from workers under 21.

10 Protective legislation, limiting for example the hours that women can work in factories (Factories Act, 1961, S.86) is a case in point: what should be the feminist response to 'deregulation' here? On the one hand, the EOC advocate the abolition of such differential treatment not least because it contributes to the problem of pay inequalities between women and men. On the other hand many women trade unionists and the TUC generally are committed to supporting the legislation. This dilemma exemplifies both the problems with using legal regulation to promote women's interests and, more broadly, the debate within feminism as to the value of the equality principle.

Another recent example of the feminist dilemma is thrown up by reports that the Tory provisions for secret ballots embodied in the 1984 Trade Union Act actually benefit women and encourage their representation; therefore to simply reject this legislation is problematic for women trade unionists seeking to improve women's role in the trade-union movement. (Hague, 1986).

References

Allen, S. & Wolkowitz, C. (1986) The control of women's labour: the case of homeworking. *Feminist Review* **22**, 25–51.

Atkins, S. & Hoggett, B. (1984) *Women and the Law*. Basil Blackwell.

Barron, R.D. & Norris, G.M. (1976) Sexual divisions and the dual labour market. In *Dependence and Exploitation in Work and Marriage* (Barker, D.L. & Allen, S. Eds). Longmans: London.

Beechey, V., (1985) The shape of the workforce to come. *Marxism Today* August, p. 11.

Campbell, B. (1980) United We Fall. *Red Rag* August, 18–22.

Campbell, B. (1982) Power not pin money. *New Socialist* July August, 19–21.

Collins, H. (1982) Capitalist discipline and corporatist law. 11, *Industrial Law Journal* **11**, 78–91, 170–176.

Coote, A. (1981) The AES: a new starting point. *New Socialist* (Nov/Dec).

Coyle, A. (1982) Sex and skill in the organisation of the clothing industry. In *Work, Women and the Labour Market* (West, J., Ed.) Routledge and Kegan Paul.

Coyle, A. (1985) Going private: the implications of privatisation for women's work. Feminist Review **21**, 5–23.

David, M. (1983) Thatcherism *is* Anti-feminism. *Trouble and Strife* **1**, 44–48.

392   *J. Conaghan*

Davies, P. & Freedland, M. (1984) *Labour Law: Text and Materials*, 2nd Edit. Weidenfeld and Nicolson.

Elias, P. (1981) Fairness in unfair dismissal: trends and tensions *International Law Journal* **10** 201.

Forrest, H. (1980) Political values in individual employment law *Modern Law Review*, **43**, 361–80.

Fox, A. (1974) *Beyond Contract: Work, Power and Trust Relations*. Faber and Faber.

Freeman, C. (1982) The understanding employer. In *Work, Women and the Labour Market*, (West, J., Ed.). Routledge and Kegan Paul.

Government Green Paper (1985) *The Reform of Social Security* HMSO, Cmnd. 9517, 9518, 9519.

Hague, H. (1986) Women and unions. *Marxism Today* June, 5.

Hepple, B. & Napier, B. (1978) Temporary workers and the law. *International Law Journal* **7**, 84.

Hunt, J. (1982) A woman's place is in her union. In *Work, Women and the Labour Market* (West, J., Ed.). Routledge and Kegan Paul.

Kahn, P. (1985) Unequal opportunities: women, employment and the law. In *Gender, Sex and Law*, (Edwards, S., Ed.). Croom Helm.

Kahn-Freund, O. (1985) *Labour and the Law*, 3rd Edit. Davies, P. & Freedland, M., Eds. Stevens and Son: London.

Klare, K. (1982) Critical Theory and labour relations law. In *The Politics of Law: a Progressive Critiques* (Kairys, D., Ed.). Pantheon Books: New York.

Land, H. (1985) *Fair Means or Fowler. Trouble and Strife* **7**, 35–38.

Lewis, B. & Simpson, B. (1981) *Striking a Balance: Employment Law after the 1980 Act*. Martin Robertson.

Mackintosh, M. (1981) Gender and economics: the sexual division of labour and the subordination of women. In *Of Marriage and the Market* (Young, K., Wolkowitz, C. & McCullah, R., Eds.). Routledge and Kegan Paul.

McIntosh, M. (1978) The State and the oppression of women. In *Feminism and Materialism* (Kuhn, A. & Wolpe, A.M., Eds). Routledge and Kegan Paul.

Mayhew, J. (1985) Pregnancy and employment law. In *Gender, Sex and Law* (Edwards, S., Ed.). Croom Helm.

O'Donovan, K. (1985) *Sexual Divisions in Law*. Weidenfeld and Nicolson.

Olsen, F. (1983) The Family and the Market: a Study of Ideology and Legal Reform. *Harvard Law Review* **96**, 1497–1578.

Porter, M. (1982) Standing on the Edge: *Work, Women and the Labour Market* (West, J., Ed.) Routledge and Kegan Paul.

Rees, B. (1982) Frames of reference and the public interest. In *Labour Law and the Community* (Weddenburn, W. & Murphy, I.T., Eds). London: Institute of Advanced Legal Studies.

Scorer, C. & Sedley, A. (1983) *Amending the Equality Laws*. London: National Council for Civil Liberties.

Stone, K. (1981) The post-war paradigm in American labour law. *Yale Law Journal* **90**, 1509–1580.

Upex, R. & Morris, A. (1981) Maternity rights: illusions or reality. *International Law Journal* **10**, 218–238.

Walby, S. (1983) Patriarchal structures: the case of unemployment. In *Gender, Class and Work* (Garmarnikow, Morgan, D., Purvis, J. & Taylorson, D., Eds.) Aldershot: Gower.

[16]

VICKI SHULTZ, TELLING STORIES ABOUT WOMEN AND WORK

103 Harv.L.Rev. 1750, 1750–1756, 1758–1759, 1769–
1779, 1797–1811, 1815–1831, 1841–1843 (1990).

How do we make sense of that most basic feature of the world of work, sex segregation on the job? That it exists is part of our common understanding. Social science research has documented, and casual observation confirmed, that men work mostly with men, doing "men's work," and women work mostly with women, doing "women's work." [1] We know also the serious negative consequences segregation has for women workers. Work traditionally done by women has lower wages, less status, and fewer opportunities for advancement than work done by men. Despite this shared knowledge, however, we remain deeply divided in our attitudes toward sex segregation on the job. What divides us is how we interpret this reality, the stories we tell about its origins and meaning. Why does sex segregation on the job exist? Who is responsible for it? Is it an injustice, or an inevitability?

In *EEOC v. Sears, Roebuck & Co.*, the district court interpreted sex segregation as the expression of women's own choice. The Equal Employment Opportunity Commission (EEOC) sued Sears under title VII of the Civil Rights Act of 1964. The EEOC claimed that Sears had engaged in sex discrimination in hiring and promotion into commission sales jobs, reserving these jobs mostly for men while relegating women to much lower-paying noncommission sales jobs. Like most employment discrimination plaintiffs, the EEOC relied heavily on statistical evidence to prove its claims. The EEOC's statistical studies showed that Sears had significantly underhired women sales applicants for the more lucrative commission sales positions, even after controlling for potential sex differences in qualifications.

Although the statistical evidence exposed a long-standing pattern of sex segregation in Sears' salesforce, the judge refused to attribute this pattern to sex discrimination. The judge concluded that the EEOC's statistical analyses were "virtually meaningless," because they were based on the faulty assumption that female sales applicants were

---

1. Although the degree of sex segregation declined modestly during the 1970's, work remains highly segregated by sex. Throughout the 1980's, for example, roughly 60% of all men and women workers would have been required to switch to occupations atypical for their sex to achieve sex integrated occupations. As recently as 1985, over two-thirds of working women were employed in occupations in which at least 70% of the workers were female. These estimates of occupational segregation understate the degree of sex segregation, because even workers employed in apparently sex-neutral occupations often work in industries, firms, departments, and jobs that are highly segregated by sex.

as "interested" as male applicants in commission sales jobs. Indeed, the EEOC had "turned a blind eye to reality," for Sears had proved that women sales applicants preferred lower-paying noncommission sales jobs. The judge credited various explanations for women's "lack of interest" in commission sales, all of which rested on conventional images of women as "feminine" and nurturing, unsuited for the vicious competition in the male-dominated world of commission selling. In the court's eyes, Sears had done nothing to segregate its salesforce; it had merely honored the preexisting employment preferences of working women themselves. ...

Title VII promised working women change. But, consciously or unconsciously, courts have interpreted the statute with some of the same assumptions that have historically legitimated women's economic disadvantage. Most centrally, courts have assumed that women's aspirations and identities as workers are shaped exclusively in private realms that are independent of and prior to the workworld. By assuming that women form stable job aspirations before they begin working, courts have missed the ways in which employers contribute to creating women workers in their images of who "women" are supposed to be. Judges have placed beyond the law's reach the structural features of the workplace that gender jobs and people, and disempower women from aspiring to higher-paying nontraditional employment. ...

The story of how courts have dealt with sex segregation in the workplace is necessarily a story about how they have treated statistical evidence in title VII cases. The purpose of statistical evidence is to demonstrate that women or minorities are significantly underrepresented in the employer's workforce or in certain jobs, thereby proving the existence of the patterns of segregation that the plaintiffs seek to dismantle. From the beginning of title VII enforcement, judges recognized that plaintiffs would often be forced to rely on statistical evidence " 'to uncover clandestine and covert discrimination.' " But almost as quickly as plaintiffs began to use statistical evidence, employers began to devise strategies to undermine its probative value.

One central strategy has been the lack of interest argument. Since 1967, employers have sought to justify patterns of sex and race segregation in their workforces by arguing that these patterns resulted not from any actions they had taken, but rather from women's and minorities' own lack of interest in higher-paying nontraditional jobs. The lack of interest argument attacks the meaningfulness even of statistical evidence showing egregious, long-standing patterns of segregation. For if these patterns are the expression of women's or minorities' independent work preferences, then employers cannot be blamed. Whether such preferences are attributable to biological influences or to pre-work socialization, the point is that employers are not responsible. ...

An analysis of lower court decisions shows that the courts have relied on two mutually exclusive explanations for sex segregation in the workplace. The conservative explanation accepts the lack of interest

argument and attributes sex segregation to women workers' own "choice," while the more liberal explanation rejects the lack of interest argument and attributes segregation to employer "coercion." Even though these interpretations lead to different results, the fact that they are conceptualized as mutually exclusive reveals that they share a common assumption that women form their choices about work, independently of employer action or coercion, in private pre-work realms.
. . .

[C]ourts have relied on and reinforced that assumption through their evaluations of the evidence pertaining to the lack of interest argument. Both conservative and liberal courts have refused to acknowledge that segregation has arisen because employers have historically restricted women to lower-paying, female-dominated jobs. Judges' failure to recognize the influence of historical discrimination on women's work aspirations has led them to adopt an anti-institutional, individualistic approach to evaluating evidence and conceptualizing discrimination in sex segregation cases. The definition of discrimination is limited to taking specific actions to bar women from exercising what are imagined to be preexisting preferences for nontraditional work. The role of title VII is limited to ensuring that employers do not place formal barriers in the way of women who have managed to form and express preferences for nontraditional work under existing workplace arrangements. To a large extent, however, the structures of the workworld that disempower most working women from ever aspiring to nontraditional work are left unexamined.

This approach was not inevitable. Before the first sex discrimination case raising the lack of interest argument was decided, the courts had already decided a landmark series of race discrimination cases addressing the same argument. In these early race discrimination cases, the courts applied evidentiary standards that presumed that continuing patterns of racial segregation were attributable to historical labor market discrimination, rather than to minorities' independent preferences for lower-paying, less-challenging jobs. This approach recognized that human choices are never formed in a vacuum and that people's work aspirations are inevitably shaped by the job opportunities that have historically been available to them, as well as by their experiences in the work structures and relations of which they have been a part. ... To counter the lack of interest argument, judges developed a doctrine that I will call the futility doctrine. This doctrine held that even if minorities had failed to apply in representative numbers, this did not signal any lack of interest in the work, but rather a sense of futility created by the employer's history of discrimination.
. . .

Early courts applied the futility doctrine in a way that acknowledged the history of racial disadvantage in the labor market. ... [T]he courts created an almost irrebuttable presumption that any failure by minorities to apply for more desirable jobs was due to the employer's own historically discriminatory practices. ... [T]his body of doctrine reflected a strong judicial commitment to the view that minorities' work aspirations posed no impenetrable barrier to their full integration into jobs traditionally reserved for whites. This commitment, in turn, reflected an underlying assumption that minorities' current work interests were neither permanent nor inevitable, but rather only provisional preferences formed and expressed in the context of a historically racist workworld. If these work interests had been formed by employers' historically discriminatory practices, then they could also be altered through employers' persistent efforts. Courts universally pressed forward in the belief that employers could "persuade the doubtful and the skeptical that the discriminatory bars have been removed," and thus free minorities to aspire to work many had never before dreamed of being able to do. By acknowledging that people's work aspirations and identities are shaped in the context of what larger institutional and legal environments define as possible, early courts refused to allow employers to escape responsibility for the collective history of labor market discrimination by pinning the blame on its victims.

In sex discrimination cases raising the lack of interest argument, the courts have used a different interpretive framework from the one used in the early race discrimination cases. ... Employers ... have framed the lack of interest argument in two different ways. In the weaker form of the argument (the "lack of applicants" argument), the employer asserts only that women have underapplied, leaving the court to fill in the unstated assumption that women have failed to apply because they lack interest in the work. In the stronger form, however, the employer states explicitly that women are not interested in nontraditional work and that they actually prefer lower-paid, lower-status, traditionally female jobs. Although both forms of the argument are premised on the same set of assumptions, there is a rhetorical distinction between the two. In its weaker form, the argument masquerades as a mere observation of statistical "fact": "We don't know why, but women simply aren't applying for this work." But in its stronger form, the argument is cast in terms of an almost ontological description of the "reality" of women's nature: "Women prefer traditional over nontraditional jobs, and (of course) we know why. It's because they are women." ...

The lack of interest argument depends on the proposition that women are systematically less interested than men in nontraditional work. Its purpose is to refute statistical evidence showing that the employer has underhired women relative to their representation among some eligible pool of workers. This statistical evidence is not undermined simply because *some* women in the proposed pool lack interest in the work; *some* men undoubtedly lack interest in it also. The lack of interest assertion undermines the statistical evidence if, and only if, the women in the proposed pool are sufficiently less interested than men in the work to account for the statistical disparity. ... Within the interpretive framework embraced by both conservative and liberal courts, employers' practices are defined as discriminatory only insofar as they prevent individual women from realizing preexisting preferences for nontraditional work—and not because those practices are part of a larger workplace environment in which many women have never been able to dream of the possibility of doing such work. ...

[Below], I examine how judges have used the "choice" and "coercion" explanations to legitimate accepting or rejecting the lack of interest argument. ... I refer to the rhetorical justification used by courts who have accepted the lack of interest argument as the conservative story of choice, and to the one used by courts who have rejected that argument as the liberal story of coercion. ...

The conservative story of choice is the familiar one told by the *Sears* court: women are "feminine," nontraditional work is "masculine," and therefore women do not want to do it. The story rests on an appeal to masculinity and femininity as oppositional categories. Women are "feminine" because that is the definition of what makes them women. Work itself is endowed with the imagined human characteristics of masculinity or femininity based on the sex of the workers who do it. "Femininity" refers to a complex of womanly traits and aspirations that by definition precludes any interest in the work of men. Even though the story always follows this same logic, the story changes along class lines in the way it is told. Cases involving blue-collar work emphasize the "masculinity" of the work, drawing on images of physical strength and dirtiness. Cases involving white-collar work focus on the "femininity" of women, appealing to traits and values associated with domesticity.

In the blue-collar context, the story begins by describing the work in heavily gendered terms. Courts invoke oppositional images of work as heavy versus light, dirty versus clean, and explicitly align the left side of the equation with masculinity (while implicitly aligning the right side with femininity). ... Once the court described the work in reified, masculine terms, women's lack of interest followed merely as a matter of "common sense." "The defendant manufactures upholstered metal chairs," said one court. "Common sense tells us that few women have the skill or the desire to be a welder or a metal fabricator, and that most men cannot operate a sewing machine and have no desire to learn." ... In these blue-collar cases, courts almost never state their specific assumptions about women workers' traits or attitudes. Just what is it about women's "personal interests" that causes them not to want to be welders ...? Interestingly, employers and courts almost never invoke women's family roles as the reason for their lack of interest in male-dominated blue-collar jobs. They appeal instead to a much broader, naturalized conception of femininity that draws on physical images of weakness and cleanliness and applies even to women without family responsibilities.

... In the white-collar context, courts invoke social and psychological characteristics rather than physical images. In particular, employers invoke women's domestic roles to explain their lack of interest in traditionally male white-collar work, and conservative courts accept these explanations. In *Gillespie v. Board of Education,*[199] the court explained why women teachers did not want to be promoted to administrative positions as follows:

> [M]ales who are pursuing careers in education are often the principal family breadwinners. Women ..., on the other hand, have frequently taken teaching jobs to supplement family income and leave when this is no longer necessary or they are faced with the exigencies of raising a family. We regard this as a logical explanation and find as a matter of fact that there has been no discrimination in the North Little Rock School District.

In some cases the appeal to women's domestic roles is less direct, but even broader in its implications. In *Sears*, for example, the court invoked women's experience in the family as the underlying cause of a whole host of "feminine" traits and values that lead them to prefer lower-paying noncommission sales jobs. According to the court:

> Women tend to be more interested than men in the social and cooperative aspects of the workplace. Women tend to see themselves as less competitive. They often view noncommission sales as more attractive than commission sales, because they can enter and leave the job more easily, and because there is more social contact and friendship, and less stress in noncommission selling. ...

In the end, the logic of the story of choice converges in both blue-collar and white-collar cases. It makes no difference that in blue-collar cases gender is described in physical imagery, while in white-collar cases gender is described in social and psychological terms. In both contexts, the story portrays gender as so complete and natural as to render invisible the processes through which gender is socially constructed by employers. The story is powerful because it appeals to the widely held perception that the sexes are different. It extends this perception into an account of gendered job aspirations: if women have different physical characteristics or have had different life experiences from men, then they must have different work interests, too. There is no room for the possibility that women are different from men in certain respects, yet still aspire to the same types of work. If gender is all-encompassing, it is also so natural as to be unalterable. Women's preferences for "feminine" work are so central to the definition of womanhood itself that they remain unchanged (and unchangeable), regardless of what women experience at work. Because there is no room for change, employers do not and cannot contribute to shaping women's job preferences.

The flip side of the coin is that work itself is somehow inherently "masculine" or "feminine," apart from anything employers do to make it that way. With the world neatly compartmentalized into gendered

199. 528 F.Supp. 433 (E.D.Ark.1981), aff'd on other grounds, 692 F.2d 529 (8th Cir.1982).

people and jobs, sex segregation becomes easy to explain. ... Courts ... often describe women's jobs as "more desirable" than men's jobs, even where women's jobs pay lower wages, afford less prestige, and offer fewer opportunities for advancement than men's. The implicit point of reference for evaluating the desirability of the work, is, of course, the courts' own construction of women's point of view: no court would describe women's work as more desirable to men. The moral of the conservative story is that working women choose their own economic disempowerment. ...

Like their conservative counterparts, liberal courts assume that women form their job preferences before they begin working. This shared assumption, however, drives liberal courts to a rhetoric that is the opposite of conservative rhetoric. Whereas the conservative story has a strong account of gender that implies a preference for "feminine" work, the liberal story has no coherent account of gender. To the contrary, liberal courts suppress gender difference, because the assumption of stable, preexisting preferences means that they can hold employers responsible for sex segregation only by portraying women as ungendered subjects who emerge from early life realms with the same experiences and values, and therefore the same work aspirations, as men.

The liberal story centers around the prohibition against stereotyping. ... This anti-stereotyping reasoning is the classic rhetoric of gender neutrality: it invokes the familiar principle that likes are to be treated alike. The problem lies in determining the extent to which women are "like" men. ... Below the surface, ... this reasoning reflects a basic ambiguity (and ambivalence) about the extent of gender differences. For the anti-stereotyping rule may be interpreted to admit that women are *as a group* less interested than men in nontraditional work, and to assert only that some *individual* women may nonetheless be exceptions who do not share the preferences of most women. Under such an individualized approach, the employer is forbidden merely from presuming that *all* women are so "different" from men that they do not aspire to nontraditional work. ...

[A]t a conceptual level, the liberal suppression of gender difference actually reinforces the conservative story. Because the liberal story assumes that women form their job preferences through pre-workworld socialization, it accepts the notion that only women who are socialized the same as men desire such work. To secure legal victory under the liberal approach, women must present themselves as ungendered subjects without a distinctive history, experience, culture, or identity. But this approach only validates the conservative notion that women who are "different" ("feminine") in non-work aspects automatically have "different" ("feminine") work preferences, as well.

The EEOC's position in *Sears* illustrates this dynamic. The EEOC emphasized that contrary to the district court's findings, it had *not* assumed that female sales applicants were as interested as males in commission sales jobs. Instead, the EEOC had recognized that the women were less interested than the men, and it had controlled for sex differences in interest by isolating the subgroup of female applicants who were similar to the males on a number of different background characteristics and who therefore could be presumed to be equally interested in commission sales. The EEOC argued that "men and women who are alike with respect to [these] ... characteristics ... would be similar with respect to their interest in commission sales." Judge Cudahy, in a dissent from the Seventh Circuit's opinion, agreed. Although he condemned the majority and the district court for "stereotyping" women, his acceptance of the EEOC's argument suggests that only women whose job interests were being inaccurately stereotyped were those whose earlier life experiences resembled men's. Judge Cudahy's and the EEOC's position assumed that the women had formed specific preferences for commission or noncommission saleswork before they applied at Sears. Indeed, Judge Cudahy expressed this assumption explicitly, emphasizing that the EEOC's case would have been much stronger if it had produced "even a handful of witnesses to testify that Sears had frustrated their *childhood dreams* of becoming commission sellers." Once this assumption was accepted, it was impossible to analyze seriously the extent to which Sears had shaped its workers' preferences. The only alternative was to identify the illusive group of women whose personal histories were so similar to men's that one might safely presume that they had been socialized to prefer the same jobs.

This liberal approach faces two strategic difficulties that leave working women vulnerable to the conservative explanation for segregation. The first may be termed a credibility problem. Insofar as the liberal story relies on an image of women as "ungendered," it is less believable than the conservative story. Like most people, judges tend to find implausible the suggestion that women have the same characteristics, experiences, and values as men. Employers are able to turn this perception to their advantage by arguing that even feminists have acknowledged that our sexist society socializes girls and women into "feminine" roles. In *Sears,* for example, the historian retained by Sears was able to cite the feminist consciousness-raising movement to the company's advantage, asserting that the very need for consciousness-raising was premised on the "recognition that men and women have internalized different personality traits and different attitudes." In the end, it made no difference that the EEOC had controlled for sex differences in background, for the judge believed that even women whose life experiences resembled men's remained sufficiently "different" that they lacked interest in commission sales jobs. The conservative story thus capitalizes on the widely held perception of sexual difference to imply that, because girls are conditioned to conform to "feminine" sex roles, adult women will automatically aspire to "feminine" work.

This same dynamic emerges more subtly in connection with the "different family roles" explanation for women's underrepresentation in nontraditional jobs. The liberal approach refuses to credit this explanation, but fails to make clear whether this refusal is based on a denial that women have heavier family responsibilities than men or rather a rejection of the notion that women's concededly heavier family responsibilities lead them to choose female-dominated jobs. This ambiguity weakens the liberal story, for women do assume a greater burden than men for sustaining family life. Again, the result is greater credibility for the conservative story, which clearly acknowledges that domestic labor is gendered. The flaw in the conservative story is not that it unfairly "stereotypes" women as family caretakers, but rather that it portrays women's domestic roles as the fulfillment of a broader set of unalterable "feminine" attributes that dictates a preference for low-paying, traditionally female jobs.

This leads to the second, related problem with the liberal story. Because it denies gender difference, the liberal approach misses the ways in which employers draw upon societal gender relations to produce sex segregation at work. The liberal prohibition against stereotyping assumes that the problem is that the employer has inaccurately identified the job interests of (at least some exceptional) women who have already formed preferences for nontraditional work. By stopping at this level of analysis, however, liberal courts fail to inquire into or discover the deeper processes through which employers actively shape women's work aspirations along gendered lines. ...

[A] rich body of recent sociological research ... [presents] an alternative account of sex segregation in the workplace. Unlike the liberal story, this account recognizes the reality of gender in social life. It acknowledges that women and men are subjected to different expectations and experiences growing up, and that, as a result, they tend to express preferences for different types of work early in their lives. But unlike the conservative story, the new account does not find sex-role conditioning so monolithic or so powerful that it dictates irrevocably gendered job aspirations. Girls may be taught to be "feminine," but this does not imply that adult women will aspire only to traditionally female work throughout their adult lives. Rather, women's work preferences are formed, created, and recreated in response to changing work conditions.

This new account traces gendered work attitudes and behaviors to organizational structures and cultures in the workplace. Like all workers, women adapt their work aspirations and orientations rationally and purposefully, but always within and in response to the constraints of organizational arrangements not of their own making. Providing women the formal opportunity to enter nontraditional jobs is a necessary but insufficient condition to empower them to claim those jobs, because deeper aspects of work systems pose powerful disincentives for women to enter and remain in nontraditional employment.

...

The new account suggests a more transformative role for the law in dismantling sex segregation at work. Once we realize that women's work aspirations are shaped not solely by amorphous "social" forces operating in early pre-work realms, but primarily by the structures of incentives and social relations within work organizations, it becomes clear that title VII can play a major role in producing the needed changes. Title VII cases challenging segregation seek to alter (at least indirectly) the very structural conditions that prevent women from developing and realizing aspirations for higher-paid, more challenging nontraditional jobs. ...

The current judicial framework proceeds from the view that women bring to the labor market stable, fixed preferences for certain types of work. ... I will refer to this view as the pre-labor market explanation for workplace segregation by sex. ... [But] workplace segregation cannot be attributed solely to women's pre-labor market preferences. Even if young women's early preferences perfectly predicted the sex-type of their first jobs, the sex-type of the occupations to which they aspire changes substantially over time. Indeed, most young women aspire to both female-dominated and male-dominated occupations at some point or another during their early careers. In addition, women's early aspirations bear almost no relationship to the sex-type of the occupations they hold over time. If sex segregation were attributable to the fact that women emerged from early life experiences with stable preferences for work of a certain sex-type, we would not expect to see so many women moving between female-dominated and male-dominated occupations. ...

If sociological evidence refutes the view that workplace segregation is a function of women's early socialization, it also challenges the theoretical account of gender implicit in that view. By positing that women have chosen traditionally female work, the pre-labor market explanation initially appears to portray women as agents actively involved in constructing their own work aspirations and identities. Instead, this explanation eliminates women's capacity for agency. To explain segregation as a function of women's own choice, one must presume that the content of early sex-role conditioning is so coherent and its hold on women so permanent that it predetermines what they do throughout their lives. ... In fact, the content of early socialization is neither monolithic nor uniform. Girls receive ambiguous and inconsistent signals that encourage them in some stereotypically masculine behavior as well as stereotypically feminine behavior. In addition, children do not always conform to even the clearest parental expectations, but respond to parental and other messages with their own interpretations. In light of these factors, it is not surprising that women emerge from early socialization with work attitudes and preferences that are open and subject to revision. Neither life nor people are static. ...

At one level, these observations seem astonishingly simple. It seems obvious that socialization does not grind to a halt when young women emerge from childhood, but continues behind the office door or factory gate to influence their attitudes and aspirations as adult workers. This simple point has profound implications, however. It challenges much of what has been taken for granted about how gender is reproduced in our society. ... As one researcher put it, early socialization is a necessary but insufficient condition to account for sex segregation at work. Keeping women in their place economically requires a lifelong system of social control that must be exercised powerfully within the workplace itself. ...

The central insight of this perspective is that adults' work attitudes and behavior are shaped by the positions they occupy within larger structures of opportunity, rewards, and social relations in the workplace. Perhaps for this reason, this perspective has been coined "the new structuralism." But it should not be mistaken for deterministic theories that portray people as having no capacity for agency, for it emphasizes that people act reasonably and strategically within the constraints of their organizational positions in an effort to make the best of them. Indeed, this perspective endows people with an ongoing capacity for agency that is missing from early socialization theories. People's work aspirations and behavior are "the result of a sense-making process involving present experiencing and future projecting, rather than of psychological conditioning in which the dim past is a controlling force." ...

Kanter's study of secretaries in a major industrial corporation vividly portrays this point. The corporation recruited its secretaries from parochial high schools, attended mostly by young women who were accustomed to taking orders and who had had little opportunity to develop habits of independence and initiative. Once hired, secretaries had no opportunity to move upward in the organization. They could not switch to the managerial track. Their own ladder was short, with their formal rank derivative of their bosses': climbing to "the top" meant only snaring a boss who was higher up in the managerial hierarchy. Bosses rewarded secretaries for their attitudes instead of their skills and their loyalty instead of their talent. An analysis of their performance evaluations showed that bosses valued them most highly for "enthusiasm" and "personal service orientation." In exchange, secretaries were offered non-utilitarian, symbolic rewards—such as "praise" and "love"—rather than money or career advancement.

The corporation's secretaries tended to display work attitudes and behaviors that are commonly perceived to be attributes of "femininity." Many were narrowly devoted to their individual bosses, timid and self-effacing, dependent on praise, and given to emotionality and gossip. But it was their position within the organization and the structure of incentives attached to their jobs that led them to develop these orientations. To be good secretaries, they were required to display the "feminine" behaviors that are commonly viewed as an extension of women's intrinsic personalities.

Like the blue-collar men studied by an earlier generation of sociologists, Kanter's secretaries adjusted to their realistically nonexistent possibility of advancement by rating the desirability of promotion relatively low. Similarly, they began to value social relations at work over the intrinsic aspects of the job itself, developing close relationships with their peers in a counterculture that valued mutual aid and loyalty over individual mobility and "success." ...

The stories of blue-collar tradeswomen illustrate the converse effect on women's aspirations created by the opportunity to enter nontraditional jobs offering higher wages, challenge, and the chance for advancement. These women's interest and commitment to nontraditional work seemed almost fortuitous, the by-product of being lucky enough to encounter some opportunity to move into a job offering greater personal growth and rewards. However, the fact that they encountered such an opportunity was not mere happenstance, but a direct consequence of the fact that their employers felt legal pressures to hire women. Many of these women cited the significance of affirmative action in influencing them to pursue nontraditional work. For them, sex-neutral recruiting efforts would have been insufficient. It was important for them to hear that the employer was actively seeking *women* workers—not just looking for workers in general (which they would have understood to mean men). When they heard that some nontraditional job was opening up specifically for women or saw other women performing nontraditional work, or made contact with community-based programs designed specifically to attract and support women in nontraditional work, many of them perceived for the first time that they could aspire to nontraditional jobs. ...

If there is tragedy in this account of how work aspirations and behaviors come to be gendered, there is also potential for hope. If women's work orientations are attributable not to their individual "feminine" characteristics, but rather to the structures of mobility and rewards attached to jobs, then the solution is to change the work structures. Classwide title VII suits challenging sex discrimination in promotion hold the promise to do just that. ... Once judges realize that women's preferences are unstable and always potentially in transition depending on work conditions, it will no longer do to imagine that women have a static set of "true" preferences independent of employer action that courts can discover as a factual matter and use to ground legal decisionmaking. Indeed, the notion that women have stable preferences for traditional or nontraditional work becomes a legal fiction that is plausible only by accepting as given the very structural features of the workplace that women seek to challenge through the lawsuit.

The new account of gender and work thus exposes the myths underlying the conservative "choice" explanation. What is more, it does so in a way that moves beyond, and holds more transformative potential than, the existing liberal alternative. The new account has three implications for legal analysis that, taken together, transform the current judicial framework for interpreting sex segregation.

First, the new account frees courts to reject the conservative "choice" explanation without resorting to the liberal suppression of gender difference. Once judges acknowledge that women's early work preferences remain tentative and temporary, they need not deny the force of gender in social life to hold employers responsible for sex segregation in their workforces. ... To put it more positively, courts may acknowledge that women have a distinctive history, culture and identity, without concluding as a corollary that they are marginal workers content to do only unremunerative, unchallenging jobs. The new account thus frees courts to portray "women" and "workers" as involving no contradiction in terms.

Second, the new account demands deeper judicial scrutiny of the way employers have structured their workplaces. Once the assumption that women approach the labor market with fixed job preferences is abandoned, it will no longer do to conceptualize discrimination in terms of whether the employer has erected specific "barriers" that prevent individual women from exercising their preexisting preferences. Employers do not simply erect "barriers" to already formed preferences: they create the workplace structures and relations out of which those preferences arise in the first place. ... Judges should be skeptical about employers' claims to have made efforts to attract women to nontraditional work. Such efforts are likely to be ineffective unless they enlist the participation of community organizations that serve working women and employ creative strategies to describe the work in terms that will appeal to women. Moreover, even extensive recruiting efforts will fail if the firm manages only to convey an all too accurate picture of organizational life that serves more as a warning than a welcome to women. ...

[T]he third and most fundamental implication of the new account is that the judicial system is itself inevitably implicated in creating women's work preferences. Once we understand that women form their job preferences in response to employers' practices, it becomes clear that courts participate in shaping women's work aspirations all the time. Preference shaping is an unavoidable part of the job judges do when they decide title VII cases challenging workplace segregation. Every time a plaintiff brings such a case, the legal system is confronted with a decision whether to affirm or alter the status quo. When courts accept the lack of interest argument, they permit employers to organize their workplaces in ways that disable women from forming an interest in nontraditional work. When courts impose liability instead, they prompt employers to restructure their workplaces in ways that empower women to aspire to nontraditional jobs. Judicial decisions that reject the lack of interest argument also create a climate in which it is more likely that employers not involved in litigation will undertake genuine affirmative action through creative efforts to dismantle old patterns of sexual hierarchy. That such efforts can alter women's aspirations is clear from the reports of nontraditional women workers. Thus, judges' decisions are embedded in the fabric of organizational life through which women's hopes and dreams as workers are woven. ...

[17]

EXIT: POWER AND THE IDEA OF LEAVING IN LOVE, WORK, AND THE CONFIRMATION HEARINGS

MARTHA R. MAHONEY*

> How could she have brought herself to follow Judge Thomas so faith-fully and so long in her career, given the sordid remarks he allegedly made to her?[1]

> On cross-examination, when discussing an occasion when Mr. Kelly temporarily moved out of the house, the State repeatedly asked Ms. Kelly: "You wanted him back, didn't you?" The implication was clear: domestic life could not have been too bad if she wanted him back.[2]

Exit—the door with the glowing red sign—marks the road not taken that proves we chose our path. Prevailing ideology in both law and pop-ular culture holds that people are independent and autonomous units, free to leave any situation at any time, and that what happens to us is therefore in some measure the product of our choice. When women are harmed in love or work, the idea of exit becomes central to the social and legal dialogue in which our experience is processed, reduced, recon-structed and dismissed. Exit is so powerful an image that it can be used both to dispute the truth of our statements and to keep people from hear-ing what we say at all. The image of exit hides oppression behind a mask of choice, forces upon us a discourse of victimization that emphasizes individualism and weakness rather than collectivity and strength, and

* Associate Professor, University of Miami School of Law. Thanks to Jeanne Adelman, Ken Casebeer, Donna Coker, Joan Mahoney, Susan Mann, Rob Rosen and Steve Schnably for their suggestions, and to Dianne Fischer for research assistance. Stephanie Wildman offered extensive and insightful comments very quickly. All errors are my own. For my indebtedness to Lynne Hen-derson on timely exit and on getting this project underway, this essay is my particular thanks.

1. Senator Jim Exon, explaining his vote in favor of the confirmation of Clarence Thomas; Maureen Dowd, *Republicans Gain Edge by Going Nasty Early*, N.Y. TIMES, Oct. 15, 1991, at A18.

2. State y. Kelly, 478 A.2d 364, 377 (N.J. 1984).

conceals the possibility and necessity of alliance and resistance to oppression.

I began writing this essay the week the Senate confirmed the appointment of Clarence Thomas to the Supreme Court. As I type these words, weeks later, images of the hearings are still before me: of Anita Hill testifying—graceful and composed, tiring as the day wears on, maintaining dignity, clarity, directness, honesty.[3] Of Orrin Hatch's face, filling the screen—the Grand Inquisitor, reprocessing her testimony. Of Clarence Thomas, rigid in his chair, claiming he is being lynched for his independence.[4]

The emotional impact of the hearings was profound but hard to capture. The political impact is hard to predict, because it depends in part on what happens next. Intellectually, there is much to assess. Of all that happened in the hearings, this essay addresses the ways in which failure to exit was used against Anita Hill in the Senate and in public discourse. I compare the treatment of exit in the confirmation hearings with cases involving battered women.[5]

Love and work are the most important areas of life, from which life gains meaning, satisfaction and pleasure. Battering and sexual harassment are abuses of power within the relational worlds of love and work. Battering is about power over the lover: the attempt to exercise power and control marked by a pattern of violent and coercive behaviors.[6] Sexual harassment is an abuse of power associated particularly with the workplace and with preparation for work.[7] Battering and harassment happen, therefore, in the course of constructing ourselves in the world in relation to others, especially to those we love, and in relation to the world itself.

The image of exit denies the ongoing construction of relationships— the process that gives them coherence and meaning—by its insistent attention to idealized moments of mutual freedom to enter and leave.

---

3. A survey of judges, who are in the business of hearing testimony and weighing credibility, revealed that two-thirds of them believed Anita Hill's testimony. Scott Armstrong, *Women Seeking Office Quickened by Thomas Flap*, CHRISTIAN SCI. MONITOR, Oct. 22, 1991, U.S. section, at 1.

4. *Cf.* William Raspberry, *Thomas's Credential: Deprivation*, WASH. POST, Sept. 20, 1991, at A27 (quoting Jesse Jackson referring to Clarence Thomas as "the most sponsored black man in American history").

5. Much of my analysis of exit in the context of battering is based on material more fully developed in my recent article, Martha R. Mahoney, *Legal Images of Battered Women: Redefining the Issue of Separation*, 90 MICH. L. REV. 1 (1991).

6. *Id.* at 53-60.

7. Academia, the other notorious site of sexual harassment, is a workplace for its staff and preparation for work for its students.

Also, emphasizing exit directs attention to individual misbehavior and individual response, concealing relations of power in the family and the workplace—male domination of women,[8] and a legal regime of work without rights in a job or protection against most forms of abuse. The first half of this essay discusses what is hidden in, and hidden by, the focus on exit.

Once exit is defined as the appropriate response to abuse, then staying can be treated as evidence that abuse never happened. If abuse is asserted, "failure" to exit must then be explained. When that "failure" becomes the point of inquiry, explanation in law and popular culture tends to emphasize victimization and implicitly deny agency in the person who has been harmed. Denying agency contradicts the self-understanding of most of our society, including many who share characteristics and experiences of oppression with the person who is being harmed. The conservative insistence that we are untrammeled actors plays on this sensibility, merging rejection of victimization with an ideology that denies oppression. The privatization of assaults on women makes it particularly difficult to identify a model of oppression and resistance, rather than one of victimization and inconsistent personal behavior.

Equating exit and agency denies the possibility and legitimacy of resistance against oppression. Since both staying and leaving can be normal acts of resistance, the focus on exit warps inquiry and treats as illegitimate the struggle to make the fundamental areas of life more one's own. To recognize oppression and resistance in the lives of women, we must reject exit as the test of truth or the core of agency. If we emphasize antisubordination in love and work, we will see resistance differently and see different allies as well. The second half of this essay discusses the necessity of choosing legal and social arguments to reveal and facilitate resistance to oppression.

I.   THE IMPORTANCE OF EXIT

[A]n "outraged person" would [not] stay with a mentor who psychologically abused her, until she was secure enough to make her own way. . . .[9]

---

8. CATHARINE A. MACKINNON, FEMINISM UNMODIFIED 3 (1987); CATHARINE A. MACKINNON, SEXUAL HARASSMENT OF WORKING WOMEN 1 (1979) [hereinafter MACKINNON, SEXUAL HARASSMENT].

9. Maureen Dowd, *Republicans Gain Edge By Going Nasty Early*, N.Y. TIMES, Oct. 15, 1991, at A18 (J. Bennett Johnston, Democratic Senator from Louisiana, explaining why he found Anita Hill's testimony implausible).

[O]ne of the common myths, apparently believed by most people, is that battered wives are free to leave. To some, this [suggests masochism] . . . to others, however, the fact that [she] stays on unquestionably suggests that the 'beatings' could not have been too bad for if they had been, she certainly would have left.[10]

During the week of the confirmation hearings, newspapers repeatedly cited studies of working women, including lawyers, who said that they neither filed complaints nor left their jobs when they encountered sexual harassment.[11] Many women said they would just tell the offender to stop ("just say knock it off.")[12] Anita Hill's story generally tracked this course of action: She said she told her supervisor, Clarence Thomas, that she would not go out with him and that she didn't enjoy sexual conversations; she believed she had successfully handled the situation when the harassment stopped, found the recurrence of harassment distressing, and finally left for academic employment.

Nevertheless, those who supported the confirmation discussed Anita Hill's story as if it did *not* follow a plausible course. In particular, the fact that she continued to work for Clarence Thomas was used to discredit her account of harassment: first, she continued to work for him at the Department of Education, then she moved to the EEOC and continued to work for him there. The move to the EEOC lent a heightened sense of affirmative choice, since she continued working with him rather than trying to continue in an unknown job in the same department.

Failure to exit was raised to dispute the truth of her claims of fact, her account of words spoken by Clarence Thomas (if he really said that, why did she follow him to the EEOC?). Failure to exit was also raised to argue that, if he indeed said those things, his statements could not have been entirely unsought and unwelcome. This position allowed listeners to reconcile absolutely contradictory factual claims with centrist agnosticism or cynicism about truth (maybe they were both telling the truth as

---

10. State v. Kelly, 478 A.2d 364, 377 (N.J. 1984).

11. *See, e.g.*, Tamar Lewin, *A Case Study of Sexual Harassment and the Law*, N.Y. TIMES, Oct. 11, 1991, at A17 (women fear reprisals if they sue for sexual harassment; women fear that their careers and reputation will suffer even if they win; most women do not make formal complaints or leave the job); Emily Courie, *Women in the Large Firms: A High Price for Admission*, NAT'L L.J., Dec. 11, 1989, at 3-5 (survey found that at least 60% of women at large firms experienced unwanted sexual attention of some kind); *cf.* LIN FARLEY, SEXUAL SHAKEDOWN: THE SEXUAL HARASSMENT OF WOMEN ON THE JOB 21-22 (1978) (only 9% of women quit immediately upon harassment; most stayed, though many of these did quit eventually when the situation escalated later).

12. Alan Deutschman, *Dealing With Sexual Harassment*, FORTUNE, Nov. 4, 1991, at 32, 33; Peter Applebome, *In Hometowns, Outrage Over the Senate and Adamant Support for Thomas*, N.Y. TIMES, Oct. 15, 1991, at A19.

they saw it, or, they were both lying in part). Failure to exit was seen as an indication of inconsistency between her actions and her report of her feelings, making suspect her overall credibility (she couldn't be telling the truth, because if she felt the disgust she claimed, she would have left). Finally, failure to exit was used in a sort of waiver argument to imply at least political opportunism, if not dishonesty (if it wasn't bad enough to leave or bring charges then, why bring this up now?).

These concepts of exit in the confirmation hearings bear striking similarity to the uses of exit in social and legal discussion of battered women. The woman's very *presence* in the battering relationship is used against her in several ways. Most important, as in the confirmation hearings, failure to exit is raised to dispute the truth of descriptions of physical violence (if it was so bad, why didn't she leave?). The issue of exit also shapes perception of the woman's functionality, as in custody cases (if she didn't leave, how can she be a strong or competent person—or a fit mother?).[13] In self-defense cases when women kill or harm their abusers, other doctrinal points can also hinge on exit (could danger have been imminent if she could have left instead?).[14]

Anita Hill's move to the EEOC was presented in the hearings as a choice of Clarence Thomas as supervisor rather than a choice of particular work or federal department within which to work. The move was then raised to cast doubt upon the truth of her account and, indirectly, to support challenges to her motives or rationality (she had "fantasies"; she was in love with him).[15] Battered women who separate temporarily and return to their partners encounter similar perceptions. Failure to exit comes to include a very high degree of intentionality. Exit is now clearly defined as possible. The woman is seen as choosing to return to a batterer, rather than to a husband; the act of choosing a batterer throws into question either the truth of her claims or her sanity.

---

13. Battered women are disfavored in custody evaluations. Lenore E. A. Walker & Glenace E. Edwall, *Domestic Violence and Determination of Visitation and Custody in Divorce, in* DOMESTIC VIOLENCE ON TRIAL: PSYCHOLOGICAL AND LEGAL DIMENSIONS OF FAMILY VIOLENCE 127, 140-41 (Daniel J. Sonkin ed., 1987). This problem is exacerbated because explanation of battered women emphasizes victimization, as battered woman syndrome and learned helplessness are generally understood by courts. *See* Myra Sun & Elizabeth Thomas, *Custody Litigation on Behalf of Battered Women*, 21 CLEARINGHOUSE REV. 563, 569-70 (1987).

14. When women kill or harm their abusers, the possibility of exit shapes the issue of whether they faced the *imminent* danger of death or great bodily harm that is crucial to establishing the need for self-defense. *See, e.g.*, Kansas v. Stewart, 763 P.2d 572 (Kansas 1988). Exit is also an issue when law imposes a duty to retreat before using deadly force, although only a small number of states impose this duty on someone attacked by another occupant of the home.

15. *Witnesses Support Account by Judge Thomas's Accuser*, N.Y. TIMES, Oct. 13, 1991, at A1, A10.

The image of exit in battering cases is inconsistent with the realities of separation from violent relationships. Half of all marriages may include violence.[16] A significant number of divorced women report that their husbands were physically violent with them.[17] Violence is everywhere; *both* staying and leaving are normal activities when women encounter violence. Women may leave and return, leave and return, unless or until they are convinced that the relationship is over.[18] The question "why didn't she leave" hides the commonality of violence, the ways women actually behave in the face of violence, and the dangers of exit.[19]

Similarly, the image presented in the confirmation hearings —exit as the normal prompt response to harassment—is inconsistent with the actions of the majority of women who neither report harassment nor leave their jobs. In *Meritor Savings Bank v. Vinson*,[20] the leading case on the "hostile work environment" in sexual harassment, the plaintiff had been harassed continually during virtually the entire four years of her employment with the firm. She sued only after she was fired for taking too much sick leave. There was no hint in the opinion that this undermined her claim of harassment, or that staying with the job was anything other than a normal response to harassment. Similarly, a government

---

16. See the discussion of difficulties of estimating violence in marriage in DIANA E.H. RUS-SELL, RAPE IN MARRIAGE 96-101 (1982). The rate of physical abuse in marriage has been estimated by Lenore Walker and other experts at about 50%, though the lowest recent estimate is 12% and the highest is 60%. *See* Mahoney, *supra* note 5, at 10-11; Christine A. Littleton, *Women's Experience and the Problem of Transition: Perspectives on Male Battering of Women*, 1989 U. CHI. LEGAL F. 23, 28 n.19 (1989) (accepting the 50% estimate).

17. In one study of all women seeking divorce through a Legal Aid office in a five-day period, twenty of fifty wives were identified as "battered women" and thirteen more said that their husbands had been violent with them on one occasion—making a total of 66% who had experienced violence by their husbands at least once. Barbara Parker & Dale N. Schumacher, *The Battered Wife Syndrome and Violence in the Nuclear Family of Origin: A Controlled Pilot Study*, 6 AM. J. PUB. HEALTH 760-61. In another study, 37% of women who applied for divorce listed physical abuse among their complaints. RICHARD A. STORDEUR & RICHARD STILLE, ENDING MEN'S VIOLENCE AGAINST THEIR PARTNERS: ONE ROAD TO PEACE 21 (1989) (citing G. THORMAN, FAMILY VIOLENCE (1980)); *see also* RUSSELL, *supra* note 16, at 96 (21% of divorced women in study reported ex-husbands were physically violent with them).

18. R. EMERSON DOBASH & RUSSELL DOBASH, VIOLENCE AGAINST WIVES: A CASE AGAINST THE PATRIARCHY 144-60 (1979); LEWIS OKUN, WOMAN ABUSE: FACTS REPLACING MYTHS 55-56 (1986); Mahoney, *supra* note 5, at 61-63.

19. In many cases in which the woman's "failure" to leave a violent relationship was at issue legally, the woman had repeatedly left the relationship only to be attacked and forced to return by her batterer. *See, e.g.*, People v. Aris, 264 Cal. Rptr. 167 (Cal. App. 1989); State v. Hodges, 716 P.2d 563, 566-67 (1986) (expert testimony allowed in part to "help dispel the ordinary layperson's perception that a woman in a battering relationship is free to leave at any time"; wife had repeatedly left husband but experienced brutal attacks and threats against her family).

20. Meritor Sav. Bank v. Vinson, 477 U.S. 63 (Kan. 1986).

lawyer who successfully sued the Securities and Exchange Commission after enduring several years of sexual harassment on the job recently pointed out that she had not brought suit until she was "forced into it" when her job was threatened.[21]

Exit is also not the norm for many workers who encounter painful choices about work. Workers threatened by plant closings or job cuts make givebacks on wages and working conditions. When women face particularly agonizing choices in relation to work, they often internalize the pain and keep the job. This is why there were sterilized plaintiffs in the fetal protection cases, and why latchkey children care for themselves after school.[22]

So the normal responses to abuse and harassment in love and work conflict with the image of exit. Yet exit retains great rhetorical power. Exit shaped at least the public rationales of several senators for their votes to confirm Clarence Thomas, and it continues to shape doctrine, juror perception, and litigation strategy in many cases involving battered women. Failure to exit promptly can affect the way a woman's account—or even uncontested facts—are heard, remembered, or weighed.

These images of exit are particularly dangerous because they are used against women when analyzing harms that are particular to women. Women's lives are constructed under conditions of inequality, and any gains we make are built on unequal ground. The ideology of exit implicitly denies inequality in relationships by emphasizing mutual freedom to leave. This rhetoric actually *increases inequality* by strengthening the position of the abuser, because it makes suspect the choice most women make—neither leaving nor suing.

Albert Hirschman noted some time ago that exit has a powerful ideological hold on our society: "With the country having been founded on exit and having thrived on it, the belief in exit as a fundamental and beneficial social mechanism has been unquestioning."[23] As Hirschman explained, however, exit effects change only indirectly; voice (any effort

---

21. Nancy Gibbs, *Office Crimes*, TIME, Oct. 21, 1991, at 52, 54 (quoting Catherine Broderick, a lawyer at the Securities and Exchange Commission and successful plaintiff in a sexual harassment suit against the SEC).

22. Elizabeth Iglesias points out that these are examples of what liberation theologians call "structural violence"—in these cases, another form of violence against women. Personal Communication with Professor Elizabeth Inglesias (1991). For a further example of structural violence in the lives of women workers, see *infra* note 55 (loss of job because of high medical bills for infant).

23. ALBERT O. HIRSCHMAN, EXIT, VOICE AND LOYALTY: RESPONSES TO DECLINE IN FIRMS, ORGANIZATIONS, AND STATES 112 (1970). For the ideology of exit in sexual harassment,

to change the situation rather than escape) is important as an option in its own right and particularly important when loyalty or structural barriers make exit difficult or undesirable.[24] In the context of sexual harassment, voice would include, among other actions, telling the perpetrator to "knock it off," filing complaints through company mechanisms, bringing lawsuits, or taking political action.[25]

In sexual harassment, both exit and voice are affected by the abuse itself. The alternatives for exit—the possibilities of new jobs—can be shaped by the good will of the harasser. But the public exercise of "voice" carries a stigma and may also involve traumatic recounting of personal experience, including experience of the abuse itself.[26] The private exercise of voice—the one that women adopt when they tell the harasser to stop—is invisible at the time and is hidden in retrospect in the question "why didn't she leave?" In battering, both loyalty—identification with the family rather than simply as an individual—and the batterer's determination to block exit may create a similarly invisible attempt to effectuate change.

The concept of exit that pervaded the confirmation hearings denied the importance of work. Similarly, exit denies the importance of love in the context of violence that starts during an intimate, loving relationship. Relationships in both love and work are extended and multiple. Working women form ties to the people with whom they work *and* often ties to their work as well. They have pride in their work, or in their capacity for hard work, for holding on to work, for survival.[27] In the context of family, women often have ties to both the relationships with their husbands *and* the relationships between their husbands and their children. As a test of facts or authenticity of response, exit makes all these ties invisible and eliminates from our understanding of agency the time and effort required to shape one's life under adverse conditions.

---

see FARLEY, *supra* note 11, at 24 (most women are advised to quit; quitting is the prevailing social advice).

24. HIRSCHMAN, *supra* note 23, at 33-34.

25. *Id.* at 30 (voice may include individual or collective petition to the management directly in charge, appeal to a higher authority, or various types of actions or protests).

26. MACKINNON, FEMINISM UNMODIFIED, *supra* note 8, at 114.

27. ELLEN ISRAEL ROSEN, BITTER CHOICES: BLUE-COLLAR WOMEN IN AND OUT OF WORK 14-15 (1987) (noting that blue-collar women describe both the pressure of work and also expressions of pride in their trades, strong friendships, and accomplishments at work).

II. EXIT, WORK AND POWER

The work itself was interesting.[28]

There's no doubt a great many people define themselves in terms of
their work. . . . A job or a trade defines who you are and your place in
society. Your network of friends is often related to your job, so it represents a lot of connections with a lot of humanity, all of which we can
lose in one fell swoop.[29]

Recent articles on unemployment tell us with passionate empathy
that job loss strikes skilled workers and professionals as well as less
skilled workers, and is devastating because people get so much of their
identity through work.[30] Most discussion during the hearings emphasized the harm of harassment to women as *women*, not its harm to
women's work. Yet like unemployment, harassment jeopardizes our
work-related sense of ourselves, and the particular coercion of sexual
harassment is the exercise of power attached to work.[31]

The hearings and their public discussion left many questions of
work subsumed in the focus on exit. There was little or no recognition of
the importance of work in human life nor sense of dignity and purpose in
work at least partly distinct from pure (or impure) ambition. In contrast,
there was a great deal of attention to fears about job loss and the availability of jobs; however, framing the issue as jobs led promptly to a focus
on exit and whether it was possible or constrained in Anita Hill's particular circumstances. Completely invisible and undiscussed, sexual harassment also poses questions of the structure of work in our society, of a
culture shaped by the lack of rights in jobs generally and by norms of
abuse in employment and forced internalization of pain by women
workers.

Anita Hill repeatedly described a strong sense of purpose in her
work. At the law firm, she was "not dissatisfied with the quality of the
work, or the challenges of the work,"[32] but she was not very interested in

---

28. Anita Hill, in opening statement. Videotape of Senate Judiciary Committee meetings on
sexual harassment charges against Clarence Thomas, Oct. 11, 1991 [hereinafter Videotape of Hear-
ings] (on file with the *Southern California Law Review*).

29. University of Miami psychology professor Richard Carrera, discussing the suicide, ten
months after Eastern Airlines went out of business, of a woman who had been a flight attendant with
Eastern for 22 years. Patrick May, *Death of a Flight Attendant*, MIAMI HERALD, Dec. 3, 1991, at
1A, 18A.

30. *See, e.g.,* Martin Merzer, *Florida's Jobless Never So Many, Never So Diverse*, MIAMI HER-
ALD, Nov. 28, 1991, at 1A.

31. MACKINNON, SEXUAL HARASSMENT, *supra* note 8, at 208.

32. Videotape of Hearings, *supra* note 28.

private practice in commercial law. When she was offered the opportunity to begin working for Clarence Thomas, she had heard criticisms of the work of the Office of Civil Rights, but she "saw this as an opportunity to do some work that I might not get to do at another time."[33] She described two of her major projects at the Department of Education. Explaining her decision to move to the EEOC, she said, "The work itself was interesting. . . . I was dedicated to civil rights work, and my first choice was to be in that field."[34] She described feeling helpless and troubled by the combination of pressure for dates and explicitly sexual discussion because she "really wanted to do the work I was doing, I enjoyed that work, but I felt that that was being put in jeopardy by the other things that were going on in the office."[35] Later, she feared he "might take out his anger with me by degrading me or not giving me important assignments."[36] She believed he controlled her access to future opportunities, inside and outside the government.

Anita Hill told a story of ambition that was neither careerism and desire for power and status nor a search for security in any slot as a government lawyer. For the work she sought, the EEOC was an extraordinary opportunity for someone less than two years out of law school. But the Senate and the media overlooked her clear sense that her work was important and worthy. The obverse was true: If her work had been poor, she would have been charged with raising sexual harassment to retaliate for criticism or distract attention from her own failings.

There may have been several simultaneous interactive factors that led Anita Hill's account of her work to be overlooked. First, most working people with day jobs never heard Anita Hill's testimony; they heard sound bites, and they heard Orrin Hatch. This was a special effect created by Clarence Thomas's assertion that he had not heard her testimony himself. In order for him to reply, therefore, her edited words were read to him, on Friday night and Saturday, when working people were at home and watching. If her representations about her work reached the working public at all, they arrived through the filters of the media and Senator Hatch. The consistency of her presentation of work, and the absolute lack of reference to it in the quotes from the public and discussions I have heard, suggest to me that this is the part of her testimony

---

33. Videotape of Hearings, *supra* note 28.
34. Videotape of Hearings, *supra* note 28.
35. Videotape of Hearings, *supra* note 28.
36. Videotape of Hearings, *supra* note 28; *see also Hill Tells of Sex Talk in Opening Statement,* MIAMI HERALD, Oct. 12, 1991, at 19A; *Public Still Backs Confirmation of Thomas, Poll Shows,* N.Y. TIMES, Oct. 15, 1991, at A1, A20.

that was effectively eliminated by the double filter of the senators and the media.[37]

Commitment to her work was also unheard because of her race and her gender. Despite her extraordinary record of achievement, the public and the senators could not perceive in this African-American woman a person with a fine mind—and a finely trained mind—who would seek intellectual challenge and feel committed to using her abilities for worthy ends. To the extent she was heard, work was treated as a question of opportunism or careerism, not idealism or substance.

Also, in the context of sexual harassment, work itself became unimportant, as if the *sexual* quality of the abuse ought to take the event out of the framework of work and identity completely. Senator Specter asked why, if she feared retaliation, she never made notes of Clarence Thomas's sexual conversations to provide evidence in the future. She replied that what she had done in this period was document her work: "I was documenting my work so that I could show to a new employer that I had in fact done these things . . . . not [to] defend myself" or bring a claim for harassment. She had wanted to show that she turned her work around quickly in a fast-paced situation. The senators sought to cast her as a victim—an inconsistent victim—of a *sexual* violation. She had chosen to make this primarily an issue of *work* and protected herself against the employer's power over work, source of the particular coercion of sexual harassment, fighting for her status as a productive attorney. Of this exchange, however, only the "failure" to take notes was reported by the media.[38]

Anita Hill's discussion of work was intermixed with discussion of jobs. She spoke of uncertainty about the future of her position at the Department of Education and of the possibilities of other employment in that department. She said she had no expectation of doing the same job for the new incoming head of the office, that Clarence Thomas had considerable influence with the administration and therefore could block access to other jobs, and that because the Department of Education had been slated for closure by the Reagan administration she did not consider further employment there.

---

37. For example, *New York Times'* excerpts of her testimony omitted almost all references to her work. *Excerpts from Senate's Hearings on the Thomas Nomination*, N.Y. TIMES, Oct. 12, 1991, at A12.

38. Videotape of Hearings, *supra* note 28. The *New York Times'* excerpt, *supra* note 37, reported only Senator Specter's questions regarding her failure to take notes since notes would be useful under the law of evidence, and her initial responses that she had not thought of taking notes and had not been interested in litigation.

The ordinary concept of exit in jobs or consumer exchanges is based on the idea of competition, of having somewhere else to go or another choice to make.[39] Sexual harassment affects the possibility of job searches in several ways. The sexually harassed employee may become less productive in other ways (for example, she may be absent from work more often[40]), and then fear that these problems in her work record will now impede her job search. Explaining to a prospective employer that you are fleeing sexual harassment carries a stigma not present when you say you want different hours, or more responsibility, or you want to work closer to public transportation. Also, when the harasser is a supervisor, the person who has abused power is the one whose references will determine your options. There is no neutral market forming a revolving "exit" door when the continued approval of your current employer is a prerequisite to developing somewhere else to go.

Available alternatives in any field are determined by the nature of the job and may depend on the supply of skilled or unskilled jobs in a small geographic area, or on the supply of jobs within a particular craft, or on the market in a professional field. For legal professionals, among others, qualifications are determined by references describing the quality of one's work. Credentials consist of the certification of ability that is performed by former supervisors and colleagues, not merely of the formal training that makes it possible to apply for a job. Also, the legal profession is a relatively small universe.[41] Exit from employment in such a situation involves a necessary management of references—or else it is exit to nowhere. However, in part because closing the Department of Education does not approach the impact of shutting down a factory or large corporation, it was hard for some listeners to credit anxiety about jobs in a lawyer. Therefore, the discussion of jobs was part of what made failure to exit promptly problematic in public opinion.

Harassment has marked both the exploitation of women's traditional fields of work and the resistance to the desegregation of formerly all-male domains of work such as skilled crafts and the legal profession.[42]

---

39. *See, e.g.,* HIRSCHMAN, *supra* note 23, at 58-59; Farley notes that future work is the key for a woman contemplating leaving a situation where she is sexually harassed. FARLEY, *supra* note 11, at 25.

40. FARLEY, *supra* note 11, at 46 (noting that harassment creates a bad employee record by inducing job turnover and describing absenteeism as "a temporary female coping behavior").

41. The continuing contact between present and former employers can therefore also be threatening. "I can speculate that had I come forward immediately after the EEOC . . . I would have lost my job at Oral Roberts." Videotape of Hearings, *supra* note 28.

42. Vicki Schultz describes both crafts and law as formerly all-male arenas where women are subjected to harassment, and includes stories of egregious lack of training and offensive sexual

Catharine MacKinnon's pioneering work on sexual harassment emphasized the coercion inherent in work itself and the way harassment
harmed women as workers.[43] MacKinnon described the "reciprocal
enforcement of two inequalities[:] . . . male sexual dominance of women
and employer's control of workers."[44] However, the "sexual" in harassment received more attention in the hearings and some scholarship than
the "employer control."[45] To protect women from sexual abuse because
it is so particularly harmful and egregious, most argument about sexual
harassment has effectively ceded the inequities, abusiveness and uncertainty of work. In the hearings and in all of the press coverage, there is
no sense of how the legal structure of work facilitates the abuse of
workers.

Law tolerates abuse by supervisors in lower echelon jobs[46] and
upper-echelon and professional jobs as well.[47] Sexual harassment is only
part of the harassment women encounter at work, including in the legal
profession.[48] As I worked on this essay, friends and colleagues told me
stories of being ordered to violate the rules of professional responsibility
while employed as associates in large law firms, of new lawyers treated
contemptuously and personally insulted by partners at firms, of a young
white male associate told by a white male partner to "carry my briefcase,
because shit rolls downhill." Nonsexual abuse is also generally kept
secret: Nobody told me those things for attribution, even though not one
of them now works or expects to work in a large private firm, and each
would be very uncomfortable to have his or her experience identified.

---

behavior on the job. Vicki Schultz, *Telling Stories About Women and Work: Judicial Interpretations
of Sex Segregation in the Workplace in Title VII Cases Raising the Lack of Interest Argument*, 103
HARV. L. REV. 1750, 1835-36 & nn.331-34 (1990). Catharine MacKinnon notes that sexual harassment is facilitated by and helps perpetuate women's presence in sex-segregated spheres of work.
MACKINNON, SEXUAL HARASSMENT, *supra* note 8, at 9.

43.   MACKINNON, SEXUAL HARASSMENT, *supra* note 8, at 216.

44.   *Id.* at 1.

45.   *See* Christine A. Littleton, *Feminist Jurisprudence: The Difference Method Makes*, 41
STAN. L. REV. 751, 773 (1989) (contrasting MacKinnon's view of the workplace as "only one of
many contexts in which society acts upon the social meaning of female sexuality" with scholars who
treat sexual harassment as the use of an *existing* hierarchy (work) to create another hierarchy (sexual
misuse)). I do not imply that *either* sex or work exists as some neutral phenomenon which is coerced
or affected by the other. Rather, I emphasize that work is *also* a fundamental part of a woman's
identity, and that sexual misuse is possible in part because of the amount of abuse and exploitation
(not merely hierarchy) we permit in work.

46.   *See generally* Regina Austin, *Employer Abuse, Worker Resistance, and the Tort of Intentional Infliction of Emotional Distress*, 41 STAN. L. REV. 1 (1988).

47.   *Id.* at 46-49 (discussing abuse in primary sector jobs).

48.   Schultz, *supra* note 42, at 1835-36.

Most workers encountering abuse assert themselves directly or indirectly, but self-assertion need not mean exit. Staying on a job may not mean defeat but victory, or at least successful resistance. Regina Austin describes the ways secondary sector workers deal with employer abuse by finding ways to maintain their identity, continue working, and survive.[49] In the professional world, silence about abusive behavior by superiors is considered prudent and normal.[50] In both situations, the common occurrence of abuse and gender-based nonsexual harassment[51] means that when the harassment is sexual, employees are already accustomed to internalizing some pain or unhappiness at work.

The week of the confirmation, the Miami Herald reported that "most large local employers . . . have adopted strongly worded policies [on sexual harassment] that are prominently posted."[52] Surely these companies also post minimum wages and permissible hours of work on their shop floors, office corridors or cafeteria walls. The exceptions to employer power—the signs on the wall—are all that is visible. It is as if the walls themselves carry a message, built in brick, hidden under institutional paint:

> This place can close at any time. We could be gone with minimal warning to you, and you can't stop us.
> I can fire you any time I want. I don't even need a reason.
> If I do fire you, it will be up to *you* to prove it was not your fault.
> Otherwise, you can't even get any unemployment insurance benefits.

The rules that determine prudent employee response to abuse make power invisible in law and social consciousness. When power is invisible, this facilitates the focus on exit. Exit, in turn, denies structures of power by focusing on termination rather than the nature of power in that relationship, and by pretending exit from this particular situation will mean exit from all abuse.

Free exit from employment is not a new myth; it is the fundamental underlying tenet of American capitalism. Our jurisprudence holds firm notions of formal equality and mutuality. The fiction that employees and employers are equally, mutually free to walk out is a time-honored one in

---

49. Austin, *supra* note 46, at 25-29; *see also* ROSEN, *supra* note 27, at 77 (women learn to devise strategies to protect against the exploitation intrinsic to factory work, manage difficult jobs, and protect themselves on shop floor).

50. *See, e.g.*, Laura Mansnerus, *Don't Tell*, N.Y. TIMES, § 6 (Magazine), Dec. 1, 1991, at 42.

51. Schultz, *supra* note 42, at 1832-39 (describing serious nonsexual harassment of women as women in nontraditional occupations).

52. Beatrice E. Garcia, *How Rules Against Harassment Can Fail*, MIAMI HERALD, Oct. 17, 1991, at 1A. The local companies with posted policies on sexual harassment included a newspaper chain, American Express, utility companies, a bank, and a large grocery store chain. *Id.*

American law.[53] Exit uses the question of mobility to cover up the power dynamic in the mutuality principle. By emphasizing the woman's freedom to leave, we actually vest in her employer the freedom to take actions that can force her out of her work life. Asking why she didn't leave masks the employer's power to force exit for which the doctrine of constructive discharge is an apologetic, partial compensation.

There is enormous impact on women as women and as workers when we internalize the harms imposed by our lack of rights in work. The least obvious are those that appear exceptional or external to work, such as a company that fires a woman because her newborn had high medical costs.[54] While fetal protection policies were being litigated, women at several plants accepted sterilization in order to avoid losing work.[55] In *American Cyanamid*, after the women were sterilized and before the company's right to force this choice under the Occupational Safety and Health Act was upheld on adjudication, the company closed the department after pressure from OSHA to clean up the environment.[56] Rights to a job or to voice in management would have protected the ability of these women to bear children more surely than did the *Johnson Controls* opinion, which followed the logic of mutual freedom to contract or exit by allowing a woman to choose to expose herself to lead to keep a job.[57]

The difficulty of protecting workers from abuse through tort law is one reason that protection through Title VII is so important.[58] In tort

---

53. *See* Kenneth M. Casebeer, *Teaching an Old Dog Old Tricks: Coppage v. Kansas and At-Will Employment Revisited,* 6 CARDOZO L. REV. 765, 783-89 (1985) (discussing the continued vitality of at-will employment discharge and of image of public good as comprised of sum of employers' private needs).

54. Fleming v. Ayers & Assoc., 948 F.2d 993 (6th Cir. 1991) (holding that a company has no duty to reinstate woman terminated because of newborn's high medical costs even though her discharge was unlawful under ERISA).

55. Oil, Chem. & Atomic Workers v. American Cyanamid Co., 741 F.2d 444 (App. D.C. 1984) (holding that a company did not violate Occupational Safety and Health Act by offering jobs only to infertile women); International Union, UAW v. Johnson Controls, 111 S.Ct. 1196 (1991) (holding that an employer policy barring fertile women from jobs with lead exposure was sex discrimination under Title VII of the Civil Rights Act).

56. *Lead Pigments Shop Closes,* WASH. POST, Jan. 16, 1980, at A12. These women were not laid off with their sixty male colleagues, so sterilizations may have paid off with temporary job retention based on the company's fear of publicity.

57. Rights against plant closings would have protected them from possible later actions by the employer that could also have made a mockery of the choice they had made.

58. MACKINNON, SEXUAL HARASSMENT, *supra* note 8, at 168 (noting high standard for sexual harassment in intentional infliction of emotional distress claims when harassing activity consisted solely of sexual propositions); *id.* at 170-71 (arguing that individualization of claim in tort tends to remove sexual harassment from social context of oppression and domination).

law, "every practice or pattern of emotional mistreatment except the out-rageous, atrocious and intolerable is treated as the ordinary stuff of eve-ryday work life."[59] If most abuse of employees is irremediable, then ordinary methods of internalizing stress, coping, and indirect resistance surely shape the response of workers who encounter the types of racist and sexist abuse banned by our anti-discrimination laws.

When at-will employment renders all workers vulnerable, its inter-action with other forms of social dominance such as racism and sexism increases vulnerability to exploitation and abuse. Other structural fea-tures of law also facilitate harassment but conceal the way it is part of abuse of power regarding work. The legal determination that poverty is not a suspect classification tends to focus legal reform on issues that involve suspect classes and leave class itself out of the picture. This diminishes our consciousness of work generally, including among profes-sionals. Charles Reich recently argued that shifts in constitutional inter-pretation of the past few decades are also important: the simultaneous retention of negative constitutional protection of the individual and con-stitutional expansion of affirmative government interrelationship with private enterprise as employer and manager of the economy has created and legitimated profound social exclusion through exclusion from employment.[60]

The social structure of work also hides power. The racial structure of the burdens of unemployment has allowed economic decline to be masked by ascribing blame to alleged cultural characteristics of African-American women and men.[61] Race (or, more accurately, racism) there-fore decreased social consciousness of the uncertainty of work itself. The burdens of unemployment on women have been concealed by the assumption that women are at least somewhat glad to have time off from work.[62] Therefore, debates about work often take place indirectly, cloaked as questions of race and gender.

Diminished consciousness of work in our consciousness of oppres-sion also follows the decline of organized labor. Many unions have fought for civil rights and against gender discrimination. But to the extent that labor leadership remains disproportionately white and male,

---

59. Austin, *supra* note 46, at 7-8.

60. Charles Reich, *Beyond the New Property: An Ecological View of Due Process*, 56 BROOKLYN L. REV. 731, 742 (1991); *see also* Charles Reich, *The Individual Sector*, 100 YALE L. J. 1409, 1424-25 (1991) (arguing for protecting the inclusion of individuals in the economy as part of contempo-rary constitutional thought).

61. *See, e.g.*, WILLIAM JULIUS WILSON, THE TRULY DISADVANTAGED (1987).

62. ROSEN, *supra* note 27, at 129-39.

this may also diminish labor consciousness as part of our consciousness of oppression.[63] When labor leaders perpetuate the vulnerability of women by being dilatory or uncooperative in pursuing sexual harassment complaints,[64] or by committing sexual harassment themselves, this also separates issues of power in sex and work in public consciousness. Finally, labor has no party and no independent political voice in the United States, which helps keep direct debate about work out of national politics.

Sexual harassment harms women as part of male dominance *and* as part of abuse at work. It creates stress and stigma, marginalizes, creates insecurity about the quality of work, and forces women out of work entirely through constructive discharge. It also creates harm that is particular to the *sexual* quality of the abuse: fear, shame and anger that do not attach to many other forms of abuse of workers. In order to make comprehensible women's choice to respond to sexual harassment by holding on to work, we need to see the oppression in work at this intersection of oppression.

III. EXIT AND POWER IN LOVE AND BATTERING

In our society, a woman does not have to take abuse, mental or physical, from her husband; she can leave him. If she stays, it may be because, all things considered, the feasible alternatives are even worse.[65]

The history . . . revealed a four year relationship with her boyfriend in which abuse began very early and escalated over the course of that relationship, [and] that [Jo Smith] continued the relationship for three basic reasons—she loved him, she believed him each time he said that he loved her and that he was never going to repeat the abuse, and she was afraid that if she tried to leave she would be endangering her life.[66]

63. Sexual harassment can be both racial and sexual oppression simultaneously, and the attempt to divide these forms of oppression may misrepresent the nature of exploitation and the experience of oppression. Mary E. Becker, *Needed in the Nineties: Improved Individual and Structural Remedies for Racial and Sexual Disadvantages in Employment*, 79 GEO. L.J. 1659, 1668, 1675-77 (1991).

64. Jennifer Kaylin, *Women Cite Harassment on Road Building Jobs*, N.Y. TIMES, Nov. 24, 1991, § 12CN, at 4; Elvia R. Arriola, *What's the Big Deal? Women in the New York City Construction Industry and Sexual Harassment Law, 1970-85*, 82 COL. HUM. RTS. L. REV. 21, 59 (1991).

65. Richard A. Posner, *The Ethical Significance of Free Choice: A Reply to Professor West*, 99 HARV. L. REV. 1431, 1444 (1986).

66. Smith v. State, 277 S.E.2d 678, 680 (Ga. 1981).

Exit is also important in legal and social treatment of domestic violence. The question "why didn't she leave?" shapes the discourse on battering in ways markedly similar to the questions raised during the discussion of sexual harassment in the confirmation hearings. This "shopworn question"[67] directs attention away from the batterer's quest for power and control, shifting inquiry to the legitimacy of *response* in the person who was harmed. And just as it directs attention away from the importance of work outside the home, the focus on exit obscures the importance of love, home, and family—and the enormous investment of energy to achieve these goals—that form the context within which battered women are harmed.[68]

It is a peculiarity of the abuse of women that we are expected to "leave" the very centers of our lives whether or not we have anywhere else to go. Leaving *itself* is the option. Christine Littleton has shown that law's emphasis on exit in battering denies the commitment to relationship that women recount in their lives: "Jo gave three reasons for staying—love, faith and fear. The law only had a category—self-defense—for the last, and so it heard only fear."[69] When women describe their experience in violent marriages in terms of love and responsibility, they are treated as insane or masochistic.[70] But relationships begin with love and emotional commitment—forged in a context of social inequality, with the strong societal expectation that women should sacrifice to create and maintain them.[71] Leaving becomes the question because we are seeing the harm, not the relationship in which it arises, or because we have decided (though perhaps the woman has not) that the harm has now come to define the relationship.

Economists and others who are attached to the idea of exit as part of a vision of autonomy and choice may object that a focus on exit does not mean we've focused only on the harm. Rather, a person is always choosing between the *entire situation*, including the harm, and a different situation without it—this doesn't deny the relational world. The quote from

---

67. Ann Jones, *The Burning Bed and Man Slaughter*, 9 WOMEN'S RTS. L. REP. 295, 296 (1986) (book review).

68. Of course, for most women, the home represents a workplace as well the locus of family and love, even for those women who also work outside the home. Francis E. Olsen, *The Family and the Market: A Study of Ideology and Legal Reform*, 96 HARV. L. REV. 1497, 1565 (1983).

69. Littleton, *supra* note 16, at 44 (discussing *Smith v. State*).

70. *Id.* at 45-47.

71. For an insightful discussion of both the importance of love and relationships in women's decision making, and of the problems created by the insistence that the woman should leave the relationship, see *id.* at 45-47 (women may stay to save something besides themselves), 53-54 ("Why should the woman leave? It's her home, too—in fact, often it's her home, period.").

Richard Posner at the beginning of this section, an inadvertent caricature of liberal theory on exit and choice, asserts every woman's ability to exit and then treats "staying" as just another preference. Does this make battering the only question and deny love? In Posner's view, a woman can have the relationship with the battering, because she has decided that the feasible alternatives are worse, or she can be without battering and without this relationship.[72]

But women seek relationships without battering. At the start of most marriages and often for some time afterwards, this is in fact the woman's experience.[73] The onset of violence is always atypical—a break from the previous knowledge of one's partner either absolutely (this sort of temper was never demonstrated before) or in quality (he was often angry, but he never did *this*!)[74] The first incident of violence often takes place after marriage, when the relationship has been cemented in law and public ritual with friends and family, or during pregnancy, when women are most vulnerable physically, economically and emotionally, and have undertaken a life-transforming commitment that ties them more closely and deeply to their partner.[75]

A temporary separation is one of the most common responses to a battering incident.[76] This is not because the woman needs time to consider Posner's question ("will I have him with battering, or leave him to be without it") but because her relationship itself has been thrown into question, her trust damaged or shattered. She *had* a relationship—and

---

72. Posner therefore defines the danger to battered women *as themselves*: "We ought to be wary about embracing a system in which government breaks up families to protect wives against themselves." Posner, *supra* note 65, at 1444. Posner claims to be writing as a liberal, not a law and economics scholar, and I believe he has captured the core of traditional argument on battered women: First, freedom to leave is asserted and treated as a solution (of course, this contains two assumptions); therefore, the problem is the decision not to leave.

73. In Lee Bowker's study of women in Milwaukee, there was no premarital violence in 73% of relationships. In all but five of the cases with premarital violence, it occurred only once or twice. LEE H. BOWKER, BEATING WIFE BEATING 40-41 (1983). Since Bowker reports that one-third of the women experiencing premarital violence were pregnant at the time, it is likely that even in these relationships violence did not occur until after a strong commitment to the relationship.

74. DOBASH & DOBASH, *supra* note 18, at 95-96; *see also* LENORE E. WALKER, THE BATTERED WOMAN (1979).

75. Naomi R. Cahn, *Civil Images of Battered Women: The Impact of Domestic Violence on Child Custody Decisions*, 44 VAND. L. REV. 1041, 1047 (1991) (battering begins or becomes more acute during pregnancy). Many of the women in Bowker's study were attacked after the wedding or during pregnancy. BOWKER, *supra* note 73; *see also* Walker, *supra* note 74, at 105-06 (battering during pregnancy).

76. EDWARD GONDOLF & ELLEN FISHER, BATTERED WOMEN AS SURVIVORS: AN ALTERNATIVE TO TREATING LEARNED HELPLESSNESS 77-78 (1988); OKUN, *supra* note 18, at 55; LENORE E. WALKER: THE BATTERED WOMAN SYNDROME 26 (1984).

she wants a relationship—with a person she loves. Her partner expresses regret and promises to reform.[77] If he seeks psychological help or enters a counseling program, she is most likely to decide it is worth another try.[78]

If we *start* with "battering," then making exit the question is easy: "Why didn't she leave?" Love as a reason for staying is introduced in response, which seems paradoxical. Indeed, I believe women do not love "batterers." Women love their husbands, lovers, and partners. The problem is that their loved ones have begun using violence. Violence may be only one betrayal out of many, and relationships involve many efforts to rebuild trust between partners. It may take time and testing to decide whether it is possible to rebuild trust and continue the relationship. One factor in this process is the determination of whether a loved one has been redefined as a "batterer."[79] But the rhetoric of exit and the focus on battering rather than relationship has made addressing the woman's emotional truth almost impossible: the idea of "loving batterers" is incomprehensible to the great majority of listeners except by implying either masochism or self-destruction on the part of the woman.

Lee Bowker studied formerly violent relationships to determine the ways women succeeded in ending violence in their marriages.[80] Most of the women in his study had "successfully solved the violence problem while married," rather than divorcing to solve the problem.[81] For many of the women in Bowker's study, a threat to end the relationship or the act of taking shelter proved a helpful strategy in ending the violence.[82] In more than half of the relationships, husbands ended violence because they feared divorce or wanted to reestablish the relationship.[83] Many of the narratives in Bowker's study involve either filing for divorce, a threat of separation, or a temporary separation. But at the moment that these

---

77. OKUN, *supra* note 18, at 55 (citing several studies in which the promise to reform was important to the wife's decision to return).

78. GONDOLF & FISHER, *supra* note 76, at 87.

79. Reaching the conclusion that her partner is a batterer may be made more difficult, however, if she does not recognize in her own love and decision making anything she has previously heard about battered wives. Mahoney, *supra* note 5, at 18-19.

80. BOWKER, *supra* note 73, at 24. The criteria for this survey required that no physical violence have occurred for a period of at least one year before the interview.

81. *Id.* at 29. Interestingly, almost half had found other reasons why the marriages were not worth continuing and separated or divorced eventually, sometimes years after the violence had ended. *Id.*

82. *Id.* at 65-66 (23% of wives made "nonviolent threats" and 49% of these were threats to separate); *id.* at 81 (many women took shelter with family, friends or shelters temporarily.).

83. *Id.* at 123 ("reestablishing their relationship" is a category that includes a general desire not to be forced apart and to achieve a healthier relationship).

women decided their husbands were serious about change and decided to try one more time, they had no way to know whether they would one day be congratulated on their successful strategizing or scrutinized to determine why they didn't leave earlier.

Many women think that they will be the success stories, and some of them are right. The pursuit of love, family ties, and economic support by women who encounter violence in marriage is directly comparable to the tenacity in pursuing work and protecting income among women who have been sexually harassed. Social and legal focus on exit strips motive and context, allowing women's ordinary actions to be treated as deviant or questionable.

Women also stay because they are constrained. Free exit from marriage is a modern myth but a powerful one. Historically, exit from marriage was difficult for both men and women, and men had legal power over most resources. The shift to modern divorce law brought a sense of "at-will" continuation that made possible our modern notion of exit from battering. The importance of exit in legal and social analysis of battering is both product and cause of the invisibility of legal structures of power and actual relations of power in marriage and divorce. Since domestic violence is so common, "staying" is actually a relatively normal feature of marriage, and all rules governing divorce regulate exit from violent situations. Making divorce faster and easier facilitated exit in some ways, but removing fault from the picture tended to hide violence against women.[84]

Many batterers threaten custody suits when women consider separation. Modern changes in the standards of child custody decision making have been based on formal concepts of legal equality, and have often resulted in downplaying or ruling out consideration of the contributions to child-rearing that are usually made by mothers.[85] With violence out of the picture at divorce, women might still raise battering as an issue in custody disputes, although in many jurisdictions, absent physical harm to a child, violence against the mother remains legally irrelevant.[86] The standards for deciding custody disputes make it difficult to raise questions of violence. On one hand, the woman's failure to exit earlier may

---

84. LENORE WEITZMAN, THE DIVORCE REVOLUTION 223 (1985); *see also* Cahn, *supra* note 75, at 1043 (when fault was a factor in divorce, 95% of women seeking divorce alleged cruelty, usually in the form of ongoing physical abuse).

85. Martha L. Fineman & Anne Opie, *The Uses of Social Science Data in Legal Policymaking: Custody Determinations at Divorce*, 1987 WIS. L. REV. 107, 121; MARTHA A. FINEMAN, THE ILLUSION OF EQUALITY: THE RHETORIC AND REALITY OF DIVORCE REFORM 20-35 (1991).

86. Cahn, *supra* note 75, at 1072-73.

be seen as personal weakness and discredit her mothering; on the other hand, if judges or social workers feel she overemphasizes violence in the attempt to gain sole custody, she may be seen as manipulative and lose custody of her children completely.[87]

Actual power in relationships also tends to disappear in discussions of exit. Violence is a way of "doing power" in a relationship; battering is power and control marked by violence and coercion.[88] Men who batter justify their expectations and treatment of women with explanations that closely track society's expectations of women.[89] But discussion of exit hides the correlation of the batterer's individual quest for power with society's expectation: The question "why didn't she leave" implies abuse is unusual, when statistics tell us it is not, and directs attention away from the abuser as well as the context of power that makes abuse possible.

Separation assault,[90] the violent attacks batterers make when women attempt to leave relationships, shows that batterers do not stop seeking power and control merely because the woman has left the relationship. How can we tell whether a woman is *in* her home or her job because of her will, strength and determination to create her life under adverse conditions, or because she has been constrained and endangered, or even captured? Jo Smith, the woman who loved her boyfriend and hoped he would change, also feared he would kill her if she left.[91] Law, hardship and fear constrain us—*and* we seek to build relationships. "Staying" will likely be the product of all of these impulses. To use law to oppose subordination, we need to determine how to work with the needs and struggles of the subordinated. When exit itself is the question, we cannot get at the far more important questions of power and will.

---

87.   Mahoney, *supra* note 5, at 43-49; *see also* Martha Fineman, *Dominant Discourse, Professional Language, and Legal Change in Child Custody Decisionmaking*, 101 HARV. L. REV. 727, 766 (1988) (discussing social workers' suspicions of mothers who seek sole custody).

88.   Mahoney, *supra* note 5, at 93 (quoting JAN E. STETS, DOMESTIC VIOLENCE AND CONTROL 109 (1988)).

89.   Batterer's justifications of violence focus on their partner's "failure to fulfill the obligations of a good wife." James Ptacek, *Why Do Men Batter Their Wives, in* FEMINIST PERSPECTIVES ON WIFE ABUSE 133, 147 (Kersti Yllo & Michelle Bograd eds., 1988) (quoting Michelle Bograd, Domestic Violence: Perceptions of Battered Women, Abusive Men, and Non-Violent Men and Women (unpublished doctoral dissertation, 1983)); *see also* OKUN, *supra* note 18, at 69-70 (discussing domestic tasks as subjects of batterers' complaints).

90.   *See* Mahoney, *supra* note 5, at 64-71 (defining and explaining separation assault).

91.   *See supra* note 66.

IV. EXPLANATION AND VICTIMIZATION

Fairness means . . . understanding . . . why victims often do not report
such crimes, why they often believe that they should not, or can not,
leave their jobs. Perhaps fourteen men sitting here today cannot
understand. I know there are many people watching today who suspect that we never will understand.[92]

The expert could clear up these myths, by explaining that one of the
common characteristics of a battered wife is her inability to leave
despite such constant beatings; her "learned helplessness"; her lack of
anywhere to go; her feeling that if she tried to leave, she would be
subjected to even more merciless treatment; her belief in the omnipo-
tence of her battering husband; and sometimes her hope that her husband will change his ways.[93]

Exit centers inquiry on the individual who was harmed and the reasons she acted in a particular way, rather than on the person who sought
power and control abusively. With the context of power and control
invisible, failure to exit generates a demand for explanation: either these
events did not happen, or they were not truly harmful, or *this individual
has exceptional problems*, qualities that caused failure to exit, qualities
that need to be explained. This process of explaining the individual, now
defined by *failure* to exit, has brought with it a discourse of victimization
in the areas of both battering and sexual harassment that is heard as
denying agency in those who are harmed, with important cultural and
political consequences.

Beginning in the early 1970s, feminists identified and fought against
rape, sexual harassment, and battering, as well as other forms of abuse of
women,[94] as part of a project of articulating experience and undertaking
transformation in the lives of women and in society. The feminist
method of consciousness raising was based on articulating women's experience through discussions with other women.[95] This experience was
then publicly asserted in speakouts in which women told their stories at

---

92. Senator Joseph Biden, in his opening remarks at the Senate Judiciary Committee Hearing
on October 11, 1991. Videotape of Hearings, *supra* note 28.

93. State v. Kelly, 478 A.2d 364, 377 (N.J. 1984).

94. MACKINNON, FEMINISM UNMODIFIED, *supra* note 8, at 5; NEW YORK RADICAL FEMI-
NISTS, RAPE: THE FIRST SOURCEBOOK FOR WOMEN 1-2 (1974) [hereinafter NYRF].

95. The radical feminist project of consciousness-raising was described as "[t]he process of
transforming the hidden, individual fears of women into a shared sense of the meaning of them as
social problems, the release of anger, anxiety, the struggle of proclaiming the painful and transforming it into the political. " NYRF, *supra* note 94, at 6 (quoting JULIET MITCHELL, WOMAN'S
ESTATE (1973)). While problems arose (at the time and later) from some of the tendencies of consciousness-raising groups to generalize the experience of their often homogeneous members as the

public meetings organized by feminists, breaking down the walls of silence that had surrounded many aspects of the oppression of women.[96] The first speakout on rape took place in 1971.[97] A speakout on sexual harassment was held in Ithaca, New York in 1975.[98] Women founded battered women's shelters and rape crisis centers. And knowledge was produced, with pioneering books about several sorts of violence against women in print by the late 1970s.[99]

Shaping legal claims was part of this process of political action.[100] But legal doctrine itself creates categories that affect the articulation of experience. When doctrine shifts sufficiently to bring aspects of women's experience into law, it is filtered through the consciousness of legal actors (including judges, jurors, prosecutors, policemen called to the scene of assault, social workers evaluating custody claims) in ways that further reshape the articulation of experience. Therefore, defining legal terms that reflect the oppression of women creates new contests over meaning. Each block of progress shifts the style or locus of struggle over how to understand harm to women, reveal it, discuss it, and work against it, raising questions of the possibility and method of mobilization and transformation.

Law forces upon us a discourse of victimization. Either you are on the playing field of liberal competition, in which case you require no protection, or you prove into a category as a victim who is being kept off the field. The goal of remedy is to lift you back on to the playing field, to the starting line of the race, so you too can "play."[101] Resistance may

---

experience of all women, with results that distorted its application as "feminist method," *see* Littleton, *supra* note 45, at 773, consciousness-raising groups also served a valuable function in providing a forum focused on unlearning sexism. BELL HOOKS, FEMINIST THEORY FROM MARGIN TO CENTER 48 (1984).

96. Speakouts took what was gained in small group discussions and brought it into public consciousness as an "open act of rebellion." NYRF, *supra* note 94, at 27.

97. *Id.* at 27-28, 274. The first speak-out was organized by the feminist group Redstockings after women were not permitted to testify at a legislative hearing on abortion law reform in which testimony was taken from fifteen experts, fourteen of whom were men. *Id.* at 28.

98. FARLEY, *supra* note 11, at 74.

99. These works include SUSAN BROWNMILLER, AGAINST OUR WILL (1975); SANDRA BUTLER, CONSPIRACY OF SILENCE: THE TRAUMA OF INCEST (1978); DEL MARTIN, BATTERED WIVES (1976); MACKINNON, SEXUAL HARASSMENT, *supra* note 8.

100. Catharine MacKinnon states that the development of the law of sexual harassment was the first time women defined harms to women within the law. MACKINNON, FEMINISM UNMODIFIED, *supra* note 8, at 105.

101. The images of equality in competition occur frequently in scholarship on race, and in labor and other fields as well.

merely show your ability to function on the field.[102] Therefore, while a generation of social historians have painted a complex world of oppression and resistance—slaves both suffer and resist, battered women gradually shape the consciousness of social workers[103]—law has not managed to incorporate this duality and struggle, pain and strength, but filters it to a sense of victimization.

One important mechanism of constructing victimization, related to the vision of the person as wholly autonomous and mobile, is to make women explain failure to exit. When women are harmed, exit tests the existence of abuse by looking to conformity with a *predicted* response that contradicts both resistance and the presence of social and legal constraint. Rather than challenge the prediction of exit, the woman must explain "inconsistency" through victimization. Once battering is dragged into the light, for example, we explain why the woman didn't leave through a syndrome she develops in response to battering.[104] We explain why a woman "feels" she cannot tell or leave work,[105] defensively, *as if* the norms were "leaving," because of how the question has been set up.

This problem of explanation rapidly becomes acute because, in the course of shaping our lives under conditions of oppression, women both leave and stay. The fact that we sometimes do leave is used to challenge

---

102. *See, e.g.*, Susan Estrich, *Sex at Work*, 43 STAN. L. REV. 813, 846 (1991) (noting that superwomen who do not complain and continue competent work may not recover because their situations were not psychologically debilitating enough to constitute a hostile environment).

103. *See, e.g.*, LINDA GORDON, HEROES OF THEIR OWN LIVES: THE POLITICS AND HISTORY OF FAMILY VIOLENCE IN AMERICA (1988).

104. Battered woman syndrome is "a collection of specific characteristics and effects of abuse on the battered woman." While battered woman syndrome will not affect all women who experience violence from their partners, women who experience this syndrome are unable to respond effectively to violence. Mary Ann Douglas, *The Battered Woman Syndrome, in* DOMESTIC VIOLENCE ON TRIAL: PSYCHOLOGICAL AND LEGAL DIMENSIONS OF FAMILY VIOLENCE 40 (Daniel J. Sonkin ed., 1987). Elsewhere, I have criticized the assumptions regarding the commonality of violence and the necessity and availability of exit that often justify the admission of expert testimony on battered woman syndrome. Mahoney, *supra* note 5, at 10-19, 61-71, 80-82. I do *not* mean to imply criticism of expert testimony on battered woman syndrome itself, nor of the underlying psychological theories involved. *Id.* at 42. However, the emphasis on helplessness and the implications of pathology which some courts have drawn from this testimony can contribute to stereotypical perceptions of women. *Id.*; *see also* Elizabeth M. Schneider, *Describing and Changing: Women's Self-Defense Work and the Problem of Expert Testimony*, 9 WOMEN'S RTS. L. RPTR. 193 (1986).

105. For example, the explanation by Ellen Wells, one of the friends whom Anita Hill told about harassment contemporaneously:

When you're confronted with something like that, you feel powerless and vulnerable. And unless you have a private income, you have no recourse. And since this is generally done in privacy, there are no witnesses. And it's your word, an underling, against that of a superior, someone who is obviously thought well of or they would not have risen to the position they hold.

Witnesses Support Account by Judge Thomas's Accuser, N.Y. TIMES, Oct. 14, 1991, at A10.

the legitimacy of staying to fight for what we need and to deny the difficulties we face in exit. The ideology of exit is extremely powerful,[106] so we make concessions to it in legal explanation. Our concessions are shaped by the urgency of need when encountering law: The legal system broadly interacts with social expectation, shaping and shaped by our beliefs about women, but law intersects the lives of particular individuals at moments of crisis, when attempting to remake social expectation is too large a task. However, concessions may reinforce cultural stereotypes about exit, and even when we carefully articulate duality, stereotypes may result in the irony of having this heard as victimization.

Self-defense killings by battered women are the most dramatic example. Juries often see failure to leave as discrediting the defendant's account of violence and her perceptions of danger. Feminist litigators responded by winning the right to expert testimony to explain patterns of response to abuse summed up in battered woman syndrome, rather than insistently denying that exit is the appropriate focus at all. Battered woman syndrome explains the woman's failure to leave in part through the psychological theory of learned helplessness. Even when experts simultaneously emphasize objective obstacles to leaving such as economic constraints, and even when experts try to draw a complex portrait of the woman's experience, courts tend to hear "learned helplessness" as utter dysfunctionality and a complete lack of agency.[107] This portrait of a battered woman may be difficult to reconcile with her violent act of self-defense, and some juries remain unpersuaded.[108]

By responding in terms of exceptionality, explaining the victim subtly reinforces the ideology of exit. A woman pursuing her work in the face of harassment therefore risks future disbelief. In a particularly ironic twist, once victimization is *expected*, the woman's agency can become invisible even when it takes the form of exit—a woman may be condemned for not leaving soon enough.[109] Therefore Anita Hill could

---

106. HIRSCHMAN, *supra* note 23, at 106, 112.

107. Kristin Bumiller has described the reluctance of people who experience discrimination to engage the legal system with its attendant concepts of victimization. KRISTIN BUMILLER, THE CIVIL RIGHTS SOCIETY (1989).

108. For a thoughtful discussion of the tension between agency and victimization in representing battered women who kill their abusers, see Schneider, *supra* note 104, at 220-22.

109. Agency can become invisible *even when agency takes the form of exit.* In one of the early cases holding expert testimony on battered woman syndrome admissible, the defendant had ended a violent five-year marriage by initiating divorce proceedings and serving her husband with restraining orders. A week later, she came home late at night and locked the door, thinking herself alone. He flicked on a light and said he guessed he would have to kill her. She tried without success to escape through a window. Within the next few moments, believing she had heard him get out a weapon,

speak of herself, and the press could speak of her, both as someone who left and moved on—and simultaneously as someone who stayed.

When agency is equated with exit, failure to exit must be a sign of a positive choice or a symptom of such subjugation that agency no longer exists. In the rhetoric of victimization, battered women fail to leave because they are helpless; harassed women mysteriously "believe that they should not, or cannot, leave their jobs."[110] But helplessness and lack of agency present a picture with which most women refuse to identify. This makes it more difficult for us to understand our own lives in a context of violence and power. Denying commonality with battered women leaves our sense of agency intact—but it also leads us to deny the danger of episodes of rage or violence and to be unaware that hotlines for battered women are the appropriate place to call for help when we are attacked. A similar dynamic exists in regard to abuse at work. Virtually all of us who work outside the home have put up with some behaviors that we found ugly or hurtful in order to keep a job or protect the possibility of getting another. Yet this common ground was not recognized by many people watching the confirmation hearings.

People's sense of agency in their own lives is very strong. In low-paid industrial settings and in clerical positions, in playgrounds where women talk as they swing children, and in the professional world as well, this strong sense of agency reflects both sound self-knowledge and denial of the impact of structures of power. A battered woman, for example, may know her own strength in endurance, survival, care for her children, and tough decision making under pressure, yet minimize or deny the extent of the violence she has experienced and the physical and emotional harm that results. We may know we encounter discrimination and subordination—and simultaneously know that our own efforts matter in the shape of our lives, that survival under adversity depends on energy, imagination and resourcefulness.[111]

---

she shot him. The Washington Supreme Court reversed her conviction and remanded for the admission of expert testimony on battered woman syndrome, to explain, in part, "why a woman suffering from the battered woman syndrome *would not leave her mate*, would not inform police or friends, and would fear increased aggression against herself." State v. Allery, 682 P.2d 312, 316 (Wash. 1984).

Of course, Allery *had* left her husband. If agency equals exit, she had shown agency. Both her attempt to separate and the dangerous power and control moves typical of batterers at separation were disguised by the perception of failure to exit. However, if the court saw her as too competent an actor, it could disbelieve either her account of prior abuse or her perceptions of danger based on the history of abuse.

110. Videotape of Hearings, *supra* note 28 (remarks of Senator Biden).

111. *See* Angela Harris, *Race and Essentialism in Feminist Legal Theory*, 42 STAN. L. REV. 581, 613 (1990) ("[A]t the individual level, black women have had to learn to construct themselves in a

Belief in one's own agency trumps identifying with victims. This is exacerbated when identification as "victim" helps make the perception of agency impossible.[112] I believe this ability of a sense of agency to defeat understanding of claims of victimization is crucial *whether or not this consciousness is false*,[113] since claims that do not represent both strength and oppression may not be heard as relevant to one's own experience. Constructing women "purely" as victims leaves the rhetoric of agency for conservative Republicanism, with important political consequences. Conservative politics has been able to mobilize people's sense of agency in their own lives to reject the impact of oppression in other people's lives and perception of their own oppression as well. The conservative appeal to the middle and working classes is about agency (you act for yourself, so do they; you handle tough things, so should they). Denial of oppression is part of the same process of making the rules invisible that allowed exit to become the question.

This is the terrain the conservatives capture, part of the ground upon which Senator Hatch stood when he attacked Anita Hill the day after she testified. One component of the conservative attack is to render her way of exercising agency invisible to the public and disguise its meaning. The significance of her work, her perceived success in stopping harassment, and the particular agency involved in "staying" to work on terms one has defined—all disappeared. How could all that agency become invisible, especially when it so closely tracked the self-image of many who did not believe her?

One columnist called Anita Hill a "perfect victim."[114] But victimization is not "perfect." It implies a one-way exercise of power, harm

---

society that denied them full selves."); *id.* at 614 ("[T]he recognition of the role of creativity and will in shaping our lives is liberating, for it allows us to acknowledge and celebrate the creativity and joy with which many women have survived and turned existing relations of domination to their own ends."); *cf.* Littleton, *supra* note 45, at 780-81 (contrasting MacKinnon's emphasis on victimization by men as definitive of women with Simone de Beauvoir's belief in "a human (and female) agent as a potential architect of the meaning of her own life").

112. Bell hooks tells of giving Lenore Walker's book, *The Battered Woman*, to a young woman who had been severely beaten by her husband. The woman's relatives threw the book away. "They felt that she would be making a serious mistake if she began to see herself as an absolute victim which they felt the label 'battered woman' implied." BELL HOOKS, TALKING BACK: THINKING FEMINIST, THINKING BLACK 88-89 (1989).

113. For a thoughtful recent discussion of feminist analysis of "false consciousness," see Kathryn Abrams, *Ideology and Women's Choices*, 24 GEORGIA L. REV. 761 (1990).

114. Anna Quindlen, *The Perfect Victim*, N.Y. TIMES, Oct. 16, 1991, at A25.

without strength, oppression without struggle.[115] People do not identify with those they pity, and this allowed the paradox: To the extent she was seen as victim, she had not behaved in the way people thought she should; to the extent she had been strong, she had not seem like a "victim." Therefore, J.C. Alvarez could testify on behalf of Clarence Thomas, "[t]he Anita Hill I knew before was nobody's victim,"[116] when in fact Anita Hill had not spoken of herself in the status of "victim" but described both agency and oppression in her experience. A model of victimization had been imposed by cultural understanding and the processing of her experience through the mouths of Senate Republicans and the media, and this model took over the story she actually told.

In addition to indirectly promoting victimization, a focus on exit is directly opposed to the idea of resistance. In love and work, women build lives under conditions of inequality, and whatever we find of success, security, love and companionship is built on or against unequal ground. Exit proposes that one should leave, rather than hold on to what has been gained. In battering, this stigmatizes women's efforts to make viable families out of the raw material handed them by a profoundly sexist and violent society. In sexual harassment, the secrecy surrounding the abuse and the social expectation that women will react by departing create a "death before dishonor" mentality that denies respect to the stubborn determination to keep the job. Sexual harassment is frightening, ugly, debilitating, and humiliating—staying should not be understood as negating the harm—but agency may be exercised through working. When the only recognizable act of agency is exit, this makes acts of resistance like those Anita Hill described (doing one's job and telling the perpetrator to stop) into acceptance of victimization.

Anita Hill was used to exercising agency. She is the daughter of a farmer from Oklahoma. She was the youngest of thirteen children, one of few African-American women at Yale. She was used to being able to work hard enough, and well enough, and successfully enough to take hold of the world and shape it. Her expectations of her own ability to define a work environment would be very high. She said that during each of the offensive discussions, she was able to stop the discussion for that day, though he began again another time. But the greater her sense of her own agency, the more likely that she would believe she could

---

115. This is why the terms "survivor" has replaced "victim" in feminist vocabulary (as in "rape survivor," "domestic violence survivor"). *See, e.g.*, GONDOLF & FISHER, *supra* note 76 (describing battered women as survivors).

116. *Statements of Character Witnesses in Defense of Judge Thomas, Statement by J.C. Alvarez*, N.Y. TIMES, Oct. 13, 1991, at A15.

restrain him, and therefore that all her agency would be later rendered invisible because it was not exercised as exit.

Could Anita Hill have been insufficiently presented as a victim? Just after the confirmation vote, the New York Times reported that feminist groups had concluded that Clarence Thomas "won" by presenting himself as more of a victim than she did.[117] But his claim was not necessarily believed by the public, and since public opinion in favor of Thomas almost perfectly tracked disbelief in Anita Hill,[118] the vote seems to have been decided by the ability of Senate Republicans to attack her. When Anita Hill described the will of a young woman to carry on her work under adverse conditions, the emphasis on exit and the construction of victimization helped prevent the public from hearing what she said.

An increasing emphasis on victimization could be an important mistake. Elizabeth Schneider has pointed out that although victimization has sometimes been a significant part of feminist analysis, there are inherent tensions in portraying agency and victimization in battered women's experiences.[119] Some black feminists have criticized a rhetoric of victimization or do not use it.[120] Bell hooks associates privilege with claims of victimization and argues that women who face exploitation daily "cannot afford to relinquish the belief that they exercise some measure of control, however relative, over their lives."[121] If we cannot speak of both exploitation and agency, we will not be heard by the women who insist on perceiving it in themselves, and we will help stifle their voices when they speak.

---

117. Maureen Dowd, *The Thomas Confirmation: Image More Than Reality Became Issue, Losers Say*, N.Y. TIMES, Oct. 16, 1991, at A1.

118. *Public Still Backs Confirmation of Thomas, supra* note 36, at A20 (most of those polled rejected claim that the accusations were prompted by racism; all but one percent of those who believed Anita Hill opposed the confirmation).

119. Schneider, *supra* note 104, at 221 (urging feminists to explore "the role of both victimization and agency in women's lives" because portraying women solely as victims or agents is not adequate to explain the complex realities of women's lives, and showing that emphasizing only victimization among battered women helps make violent self-defense hard for judges and juries to understand); *see also* Littleton, *supra* note 16, at 38 (need to emphasize victimization of women conceals questions of male power and domination).

120. Harris, *supra* note 106, at 612-13 (criticizing the view of women as victims, and calling upon feminism to learn from the strength of black women who have constructed their lives under conditions of oppression); Kimberle Crenshaw, *Demarginalizing the Intersection of Race and Sex: A Black Feminist Critique of Antidiscrimination Doctrine, Feminist Theory and Antiracist Politics*, 1989 U. CHI. LEGAL F. 139, 166-67 (focusing on the need to embrace the intersection of race and gender in the struggle against oppression; arguing for placing "those who are currently marginalized in the center" to resist compartmentalizing experiences and undermining collective political action).

121. HOOKS, *supra* note 95, at 45.

V. AGENCY AND OPPRESSION

At that time, staying seemed the only reasonable choice. At that time, staying was . . . a choice that I made because I wanted to do the work. I in fact believed that I could make that choice, to do the work, and that's what I wanted to do. And I did not want to let that type of behavior control my choices. So I attempted to end the behavior. And for some time, the behavior did stop. I attempted to make that effort. So the choice to continue with the same person to another agency involved a belief that I had stopped the behavior that was offensive.[122]

Anita Hill never said she believed that Clarence Thomas had simply stopped harassing her. Throughout her testimony, she had spoken of offensive *behavior*, rather than of Thomas himself, as the problem. At the end of the day, responding to a question from Senator DeConcini about why she stayed, she said *she thought she had stopped it*. Her choices had not been controlled. She would be able to go on with her work. She believed she had won.

Most sexual harassment cases turn, as did the confirmation hearings, on the credibility of the witnesses.[123] Credibility in turn depends on the capacities of the listener to hear and understand. Anita Hill's account of the move to the EEOC was undermined by making invisible her intelligent determination to defend herself on the job, and by completely collapsing her work into issues of sex and job loss.

If agency among the oppressed is judged only by effectuated change, it is defined almost out of existence. The acting, aware self is often realized in love and in work through resistance against oppression, survival, and partial victories—like women who "just deal with" harassment, or women who seek to hold on to marriages without violence. Or—even closer to the experience of many women—the self is realized through a *combination* of accommodation and resistance, through private resistance chosen because oppression itself simultaneously makes exit difficult and open resistance impractical. This duality may sometimes create or allow individualism: When working women say they "just deal with" harassment, this implies they have power to resist but may permit later denial of commonality with a woman who publicly describes the experience of harassment.

---

122.   Anita Hill, Videotape of Hearings, *supra* note 28 (first seven minutes of Tape #4 in answer to Sen. DeConcini).

123.   Estrich, *supra* note 102, at 847-53.

Contemporary conservative insistence on agency treats self-realization as a question of pure will, not constrained in any serious way.[124] Conservatism equates all analysis of oppression by race or gender with individual victimization and treats it as negating agency. The conservative claim that agency may be exercised without struggle is very different from claiming agency through liberatory struggle, through resistance to oppression.[125] "Pure" victimization also denies the many ways people resist oppression. For women, the stigma and shame of being sexually assaulted creates a circumstance that will often discourage publicity (including lawsuits) and therefore tend to make resistance individual. This should not equate staying with either acceptance of victimization or claims of pure individual agency without struggle.

If we were better at articulating *both* oppression *and* resistance, at both the individual and collective level, we might be less confused. But law does not make this easy, and feminist legal scholarship has had difficulty dealing with both oppression and an insistence on agency.[126] In feminist activism, pain suffered privately became political—not *only* by being spoken to other women, but by being spoken to the world and collectively acted upon in the creation of alternative institutions. Speakouts led to political action that included personal transformation sought through the struggle for social transformation. The legal claim for sexual harassment as sex discrimination was strategically created to reveal oppression as part of political change.[127] But even here, litigation

---

124.   Richard Delgado points out the importance of agency in the writings of black conservatives. Richard Delgado, *Enormous Anomaly? Left-Right Parallels in Recent Writing About Race*, 91 CAL. L. REV. 1547 (1991).

125.   Clarence Thomas himself may have shown that conservatism, not agency, is the essence of this position when he switched during the confirmation hearings from a claim of agency-without-struggle (civil rights advocates whine, moan and bitch when they could be working with a Republican administration) to a claim of victimization (I am being lynched) without moving a millimeter toward liberatory struggle. *See* Juan Williams, *EEOC Chairman Blasts Black Leaders*, WASH. POST, Oct. 25, 1984, at A7 (reporting remarks on whining). A complete analysis of Clarence Thomas's testimony is beyond the scope of this article, however.

126.   Within feminist theory, equating female existence with victimization has been understood as denying agency; insisting on agency has been heard as denying the inevitable situation of every woman as part of a subordinated sex. See *Feminist Discourse, Moral Values, and the Law—A Conversation*, 34 BUFFALO L. REV. 11, 75 (1985), in which Mary Dunlap, a feminist lawyer, responded to Catharine MacKinnon's discussion of oppression. MacKinnon emphasized harm to women: a boot is on your neck; you have no authentic voice; confront your victimization. Dunlap stood and said she was not subordinate to any man, that she frequently contested efforts at her subordination; she urged women to stand to show they did not have to be subordinated. For a thoughtful discussion of this exchange, and later development of these themes in the work of MacKinnon, see Stephanie Wildman, *The Power of Women*, 2 YALE J.L. & FEMINISM 435 (1990) (reviewing CATHARINE A. MACKINNON, TOWARD A FEMINIST THEORY OF THE STATE (1989)).

127.   *See generally* MACKINNON, SEXUAL HARASSMENT, *supra* note 8.

is largely a one-on-one undertaking: this woman, this man; he said, she said; a question of credibility of this *individual woman* making an *individual claim*, subject to being discredited by her *individual traits*. Even if her actions are completely consistent with those of other assaulted women—as Anita Hill's were—her place in the world of response to assault is not visible. The challenge is to find ways to represent both oppression and agency in *law*, with its strong impetus toward individualism and victimization.

What decides whether a claim about pain is collective and transformative or heard to represent victimization without agency? The answer may be part culture and part the structure of legal argument. When experts describe normal reactions to battering and emphasize economic constraints and physical danger, but are heard as describing women as pathologically helpless, both the structure of expert testimony (dealing with matters beyond the layman's ken) and the persistence of social stereotypes are involved. Law's interactive existence in politics is another answer. A recent example of claims about harm is the movement against racist speech. This claim within law is based on articulating and defending the perception and experience of those who are targets of hate speech—it simultaneously articulates harm and tries to redefine legitimate perception. It is also part of a larger contest over culture, knowledge and perception that includes fierce debates that have challenged the traditional core curriculum in academia and triggered an intense counterattack about "political correctness."

So part of the struggle against oppression is more articulation, of more experience, of *more women*, learning difference as well as asserting commonality. We need to learn from the experience of women a sense of agency as well as pain—in Angela Harris's lovely phrase, "integrity as will and idea"—and learn from women who have constructed lives under oppression their example of creativity and will.[128]

Both this articulation and the political action built on it are parts of the effort to bring law and societal perception closer to the experience of the subordinated and to counteract the persistent misrepresentation of resistance to oppression as victimization.[129] But political action, like the consciousness of oppression, should include the many forms of oppression that intersect here to authenticate acts of resistance as they happen,

---

128. Harris, *supra* note 111, at 613-14.

129. Several types of political action were proposed after the hearings, including a new national party. Ellen McGarrahan, MIAMI HERALD, Oct. 17, 1991, at 4B. In addition, feminists placed increased energies on electing women. Kay Mills, L.A. TIMES, Dec. 1, 1991, at M3.

show the significance of "staying" at work or in a relationship as well as "leaving," and reveal the nature and mechanisms of oppression.

We live in an era of terrible uncertainty about work. In the weeks after the confirmation hearings newspapers repeatedly announced that *fear* of economic collapse was likely to slow consumer spending, and that these fearful consumers would cause another recession or even another great depression. In these weeks, Pan American World Airways "died," taking with it 7,500 jobs of the airline's employees and many more jobs with outside companies that depended on the airline.[130]   I.B.M. announced that it would follow previous cuts in its workforce with additional reductions of at least 20,000 employees in 1992.[131]   General Motors announced it would eliminate more than 70,000 jobs in the next few years, closing 21 of its 125 assembly and parts-making plants in North America.[132] The same newspapers that blamed slow consumer spending for the danger of economic collapse noted that consumers specifically feared job loss—without correlating fear and common sense.

The urgent crisis of work appears frequently in political life as an issue of race or gender. Jesse Helms turned fear of unemployment into elected office by manipulating claims that white workers' jobs will be lost because of affirmative action; David Duke used this strategy as a key stepping stone to national prominence and mobilizing a new white right. Justice Scalia, too, says that hard working white men are being treated unfairly by the law, cheated by preferences for minorities and women.[133]

Racism in the fear of loss of work does not need to be forced into the discussion of sexual harassment—it is already here. In the confirmation hearings, it was articulated by J.C. Alvarez: "You don't follow them to the next job—especially if you are a black, female, Yale law school graduate. Let's face it, out in the corporate sector, companies fight over women with those kinds of credentials."[134] The claim that "companies fight" over "black, female" graduates of Yale uses rhetoric that invokes contemporary white fears of being disfavored by affirmative action to argue that Anita Hill's fear of job loss was not credible. This implies

---

130. Agis Salpukas, *Its Cash Depleted, Pan Am Shuts*, N.Y. TIMES, Dec. 5, 1991, at D1.

131. John Markoff, *I.B.M. Will Change in Effort to Keep Market Dominance*, N.Y. TIMES, Nov. 27, 1991, at A1. The announcement covered job cuts worldwide and did not predict how many of these jobs would be cut outside the United States.

132. Doron P. Levin, *General Motors to Cut 70,000 Jobs; 21 Plants to Shut*, N.Y. TIMES, Dec. 19, 1991, at A1.

133. Johnson v. Santa Clara County, 480 U.S. 616, 677 (1987) (Justice Scalia, dissenting).

134. J.C. Alvarez, *quoted in Hill, Thomas Witnesses Recount Own Experiences*, MIAMI HER-ALD, Oct. 14, 1991, at 14A. This remark was widely quoted and emphasized in press coverage.

there is *no* credible explanation for failure to exit—educated black women are the luckiest people in today's market! In fact, there are still very few black women attorneys in the corporate world, and given pervasive suspicions of the competence of blacks and of women, the recommendations of supervisors are crucial to status in the professional job market. To argue from this starting point, however, falls into the structure of conceding the focus on exit and raising oppression defensively to disprove exit (but racism and discrimination are real!).

In the aftermath of the confirmation hearings and in other current legal and political contests in the fields of gender and of race, we need to recover the idea of sexual harassment as simultaneous oppression in *work* as well as sex and race.[135] It is a fundamental critical insight that the very task of law is to make the exercise of power invisible.[136] This leaves a continuing role for critique: Legal intellectuals, analyzing a reactionary court in the midst of a crisis of work, can help make power visible again in many dimensions by unpacking the background of power.

In law and politics, we need to choose terms of discussion and forms of legal challenge for their capacity to mobilize consciousness, not solely for their potential legal success. If law pushes us toward victimization rather than struggle and resistance, it also pushes us toward *only* particularity because our legal regime is founded on the fictions of formal equality and mutual free agency. If we move too far toward the norms of employment that permit abuse in the workplace, and leave behind particular injuries by race or gender, then we rapidly reach harms that are not remediable because they are the very foundation of our law—like employment at will, or the freedom of plants to close.

Yet abuse of employees—as well as acceptance of sexual abuse of women—helps make sexual harassment hard to remedy. A woman must prove very specific elements to get past the general difficulty of controlling offensive behavior.[137] If she cannot, then she loses, even if the behavior was offensive. If we only see the harm of women by men, we

---

135. *See* Mary Becker, *supra* note 63 (racial and sexual harassment often simultaneously present in oppression of women).

136. *See, e.g.*, Karl Klare, *The Public/Private Distinction in Labor Law*, 130 U. Pa. L. Rev. 1358, 1358 (1982) ("[t]he peculiarity of legal discourse is that it tends to constrain the political imagination and to induce belief that our evolving social arrangements and institutions are just and rational, or at least inevitable, and therefore legitimate.").

137. Estrich, *supra* note 102, at 826-34 (noting that in order to prevail, a plaintiff must have expressed that the behavior was unwelcome); *id.* at 843-47 (hostile work environment must have been pervasive and debilitating, so significant as to substantially and adversely affect the entire work experience of female employee).

lose a sense of the ways sexual harassment is part of other systemic misuse of power in our society. Regina Austin has pointed out that an interest in fighting abuse on the job can span divisions between different sectors in the workforce, from unskilled labor to white collar and professional employees.[138]

Bell hooks has called on women to work toward ending all violence in society, including racism and the violence of the workplace, as part of a movement to end violence against women.[139] If we focus on resistance to oppression, then ending sexual harassment means work against harassment *and* against the abuse of workers.[140] Feminist work against sexual harassment then includes issues of more jobs and more job security. It includes resistance to current attacks on affirmative action—by rejecting the rhetoric that pretends away power, and by working for more jobs for all. In *any* contest about work, including opposition to sexual harassment, antiracism is also essential, because concepts of both employability and sexuality are deeply entwined with concepts of race. In battering, the effort to end the batterer's power and control and the social structures that reinforce it makes allies of men as well as women who oppose that exercise of power. In dealing with harms to women, shifting focus from victimization to oppression increases the possibilities for alliance.

Finally, in order to reveal both agency and oppression, we need to reject false questions that define and structure legal discourse. Exit hides both oppression and resistance. Staying at work can mean victory, stubborn persistence at a chosen goal, or nightmare and exploitation; leaving may mean going without work, or it may bring a successful turn in career path. Staying in a marriage could prove to be retaining a family without violence, or it may well be the result of death threats and custody suits; leaving may mean giving up on having both love and safety, or it can be empowerment and a loving family forged by a single mother. Any snapshot labeled "exit" or "no exit" will not show whether this woman is in this home, this job, because she is fighting for this territory or because her will to leave has been defeated. For work against subordination, her will against oppression is what she needs, and what we need to know.

---

138. Austin, *supra* note 46.

139. HOOKS, *supra* note 95, at 122, 130. This also involves a rejection by women of participation in violence and subordination.

140. And, indeed, against the brutal Social Darwinism that marks our inadequately funded transfer programs, which help enforce insecurity about work.

VI. CONCLUSION

Law itself funnels and shapes consciousness and resistance to oppression. There are good reasons to use law on behalf of the subordinated, and it is worth fighting within the field of law for the principle that law should do justice.[141] In the coming months and years, antisubordination efforts including the fight to end sexual harassment will continue to move through the legal system and other political arenas.

The Supreme Court, with Justice Thomas as its newest member, will do many things to repress, constrain, or channel struggle. It will continue to insist on an "empty state"[142] in which the public good is the sum of private interests and there is no public presence but an accretion of private actions; it will continue to hide the deployment of power by describing mutual and mobile voluntary social relations of entrances and exits, privatizing harm and seeing only intentional individual victimizations; it will undoubtedly endorse further retrenchment in entitlements, unions, affirmative action, immigration, abortion, federal jurisdiction and other areas of legal contest as inconsistent with a liberal playing field inhabited by equally powerful free actors. A civil rights bill was enacted promptly after the confirmation, but any action taken pursuant to that bill will come before this very Court for review.

These things will not happen separately. They will overlap but have different specifics; if they hurt many, they will not affect all the same way. To work against them, in law and elsewhere in politics, we will need to work together. To work together, to reach the very people who are hurting too, we will need to hear strength as well as pain—the articulation of experience that is an integral part of the struggle against subordination is not an appeal for pity. When we speak of oppression and resistance, we must not be told—and we must not tell others—to take things as they are or leave them. This discussion is part of a demand for the transformation of power, and it cannot be answered by showing us the door.

---

141. *See* Mari Matsuda, *Voices of America: Accent, Antidiscrimination Law, and a Jurisprudence for the Last Reconstruction*, 100 YALE L.J. 1329, 1403-06 (1991) ("In meeting the goal of true equality—of ending all forms of subordination—I continue to see claims of logic, legality, and justice as both useful and true.").

142. Kenneth Casebeer, *Toward a Critical Jurisprudence—A First Step by Way of the Public-Private Distinction in Constitutional Law*, 37 U. MIAMI L. REV. 379, 412-22 (1983); *see also* Kenneth Casebeer, *Running on Empty: Justice Brennan's Plea, The Empty State, the City of Richmond, and the Profession*, 43 U. MIAMI L. REV. 989, 1002-03 (1989).

Legal History

[18]

FROM FALSE PATERNALISM TO FALSE EQUALITY: JUDICIAL ASSAULTS ON FEMINIST COMMUNITY, ILLINOIS 1869-1895

*Frances Olsen**

Feminist theorists seem to be obsessed by the question of whether women should emphasize their similarity to men or their differences from men. In discipline after discipline, the issue of sameness and differences has come to center stage.

This focus is not a new phenomenon. Early this century, suffragists fluctuated between claiming that it was important to let women vote because they were different from men — more sensitive to issues of world peace, the protection of children, and so forth — and claiming that it was safe to let women vote because they would vote the same way men did.[1]

In law, this obsession with sameness and difference has taken the form of a debate between formal equality for women and substantive equality for women — or between so-called "equal treatment" and so-called "special treatment."[2] The contemporary question of maternity

---

* Acting Professor of Law, University of California at Los Angeles. B.A. 1968, Goddard College; J.D. 1971, University of Colorado; S.J.D. 1984, Harvard University. — Ed.

I presented versions of this paper at the National Women's Studies Association meeting at the University of Illinois, to the East Coast Fem-Crits at Harvard Law School, and to the West Coast Fem-Crits in San Francisco. I would like to thank the members of these audiences and the numerous friends and colleagues who have commented upon this work. Mary Joe Frug and Dirk Hartog were especially helpful. I am also grateful to students who have provided research assistance, particularly Bert Voorhees and Scott McMillen.

This article is part of a larger research project supported by the National Endowment for the Humanities, the University of Wisconsin Legal History Colloquium, the Institute for Legal Studies at the University of Wisconsin, the UCLA Law School Dean's Fund, and the Research Committee of the UCLA Academic Senate.

Kitty Sklar has been a superb colleague throughout this project — sharing her advice, criticism, encouragement, insights, inspiration, and research materials. I am forever grateful.

1. *See* Olsen, *The Family and the Market: A Study of Ideology and Legal Reform,* 96 HARV. L. REV. 1497, 1576 (1983); B. HARRISON, SEPARATE SPHERES 81, 84 (1978).

2. On the general question of equal treatment versus special treatment, see Finley, *Transcending Equality Theory: A Way Out of the Maternity and the Workplace Debate,* 86 COLUM. L. REV. 1118 (1986); F. Olsen, The Sex of Law (1985) (unpublished manuscript; on file at the Michigan Law Review); Olsen, *Statutory Rape: A Feminist Critique of Rights Analysis,* 63 TEXAS L. REV. 387 (1984) [hereinafter cited as Olsen, *Statutory Rape*]; Williams, *The Equality Crisis: Some Reflections on Culture, Courts, and Feminism,* 7 WOMEN'S RTS. L. REP. 175 (1982); Kay, *Models of Equality,* 1985 U. ILL. L. REV. 39.

"Special treatment" is a term of derision used by proponents of "equal treatment" or formal

benefits offers a good example. Currently, a number of feminists seem to be opposing one another regarding state policy on this issue.[3] On one side, many feminists support maternity benefits:[4] current employment policies seriously disadvantage women who have children — and specifically disadvantage women who get pregnant and give birth.[5] Feminists point out that virtually every Western industrialized nation has some form of maternity benefits and argue that the United States should also. Obviously, childbirth and child nurture are essential to the continuation of society, and it is absurd for individual women to be expected to bear the entire cost and burden, when society in general benefits. Some feminists concede to their opponents that maternity benefits violate formalistic notions of equality but support them nonetheless; formalistic equality may be fine for upper-class and professional women, they argue, but working-class women — which means *most* women — need maternity benefits more than they need some abstract notion of equality. Some feminists also argue that although maternity benefits may seem to treat pregnant women as a "special class," this "special treatment" is necessary in order for women to have an equal opportunity in the marketplace.[6] Moreover, the lack of adequate maternity leave can be said to reinforce the ideology that paid work is primarily for men and that women are marginal workers

---

equality. For want of a better alternative, I shall generally use the more neutral term "different treatment."

3. *See generally* Williams, *Equality's Riddle: Pregnancy and the Equal Treatment/Special Treatment Debate,* 13 N.Y.U. REV. L. & SOC. CHANGE 325 (1985) (defense of equal treatment position); Krieger & Cooney, *The Miller-Wohl Controversy: Equal Treatment, Positive Action and the Meaning of Women's Equality,* 13 GOLDEN GATE L. REV. 513 (1983) (special treatment, or "positive action," approach).

Feminists generally agree that parental benefits — nurturing benefits not linked to pregnancy or lactation — should be made available on a gender-neutral basis. The most controversial question is whether pregnancy disability benefits may differ from other disability benefits.

4. *See generally* Krieger & Cooney, *supra* note 3; Scales, *Towards a Feminist Jurispudence,* 56 IND. L.J. 375 (1981); Law, *Rethinking Sex and the Constitution,* 132 U. PA. L. REV. 955 (1984); Note, *Sexual Equality Under the Pregnancy Discrimination Act,* 83 COLUM. L. REV. 690 (1983) [hereinafter cited as Note, *Sexual Equality*]; Note, *Employment Equality Under the Pregnancy Discrimination Act of 1978,* 94 YALE L.J. 929 (1985); Note, *Equality in the Workplace: Is That Enough for Pregnant Workers?,* 23 J. FAM. L. 401 (1984-85); Kay, *Equality and Difference: The Case of Pregnancy,* 1 BERKELEY WOMEN'S L.J. 1 (1985); Dowd, *Maternity Leave: Taking Sex Differences into Account,* 54 FORDHAM L. REV. 699 (1986).

5. *See* Frug, *Securing Job Equality for Women: Labor Market Hostility to Working Mothers,* 59 B.U. L. REV. 55 (1979).

6. *See* Brief Amici Curiae of Coalition for Reproductive Equality in the Workplace et al. at 32-45, California Fed. Sav. & Loan Assn. v. Guerra, No. 85-494, *cert. granted,* 106 S. Ct. 783 (1986) (involving pregnancy disability leave); Krieger & Cooney, *supra* note 3, at 544-47; Note, *Sexual Equality, supra* note 4, at 714-21; *see also* Kay, *supra* note 4, at 32-34. *See generally* Wildman, *The Legitimation of Sex Discrimination: A Critical Response to Supreme Court Jurispudence,* 63 OR. L. REV. 265, 304-07 (1984).

who should drop out of the marketplace when they begin to have children.

On the other side of the controversy, feminists who question maternity benefits make spirited arguments against short-run expediency and opportunism.[7] They claim that gender-specific maternity benefits are a snare and a delusion — just like the so-called "protective" labor legislation that excluded women from well-paying jobs during much of this century. These feminists link current gender-specific maternity leave with the "romantic paternalism" of the nineteenth and early twentieth centuries — a romantic paternalism that relegated women to their own "separate sphere" and placed them on a pedestal that turned out to be a cage. So too, they argue, will maternity benefits wind up hurting women. In particular, any form of mandatory employer-paid benefits will give employers too strong an incentive to circumvent present equal-employment laws in order to avoid hiring women of childbearing age. Moreover, opponents of maternity benefits argue, to single out pregnancy for special treatment — instead of providing a leave or other benefit to any worker who needs one — undermines working-class solidarity and reinforces the ideology that women are primarily childbearers and nurturers, and only secondarily workers.

This debate is sometimes conducted as though the issues had never come up before. Other times, participants in the current debate cite two early United States Supreme Court decisions to demonstrate the risks of paternalism and the importance of formal equality for women. In 1873 *Bradwell v. Illinois*[8] held that states could bar women from becoming lawyers, because the practice of law was not among the federal "privileges and immunities" protected by the fourteenth amendment. In 1908, *Muller v. Oregon*[9] let stand a law limiting the work hours of women, just three years after the Supreme Court had rejected as "paternalistic" similar legislation that would have limited men's hours.[10] The history of gender-specific legislation raises more complicated and interesting questions than often recognized regarding paternalism and equality. A consideration of this history suggests the dangers of antipaternalism as well as the dangers of paternalism and the limitations as well as the virtues of formal equality. A more care-

---

7. *See* Williams, *supra* note 3, at 325; Williams, *supra* note 2. Opponents of maternity benefits worry that community concern with mothering can slip into paternalism; supporters worry that too formalistic a concept of equality can degenerate into the kind of selfish individualism that is associated with laissez-faire capitalism.

8. 83 U.S. (16 Wall.) 130 (1873).

9. 208 U.S. 412 (1908).

10. *See* Lochner v. New York, 198 U.S. 45 (1905).

ful look at this history may shed useful light on the maternity benefits debate and on other controversies.

This essay will examine the "equal treatment" versus "special treatment" for women issue as it arose in Illinois in the late nineteenth century. In 1869 the Illinois Supreme Court barred Myra Bradwell from the practice of law on the basis that she was a married woman, and in 1870 it reaffirmed its exclusion of women in *In re Bradwell,*[11] the state decision the United States Supreme Court upheld in *Bradwell v. Illinois.*[12] This denial of equal treatment to women, especially the concurring opinion by United States Supreme Court Justice Bradley, appears to many to represent paternalism at its worst: the interest that individual, exceptional women might have in practicing law must give way to the community's interest in maintaining women's separate sphere of home and family.[13]

A quarter century after it had decided *Bradwell* and thirteen years before the United States Supreme Court decided *Muller v. Oregon,* the Illinois Supreme Court seemed to reject paternalism when it struck down a portion of protective labor legislation that had provided for an eight-hour workday for women in the garment industry. In *Ritchie v. People*[14] the Illinois Supreme Court asserted that a legislatively mandated eight-hour day for women violated the rights of working women, and stated that women were entitled to the same rights as men. The direct effect of the *Ritchie* decision, however, was to undermine the efforts of a community of women reformers who were struggling to improve working conditions. These reformers had supported the legislation in part to reduce the subordination of women and to promote gender equality.[15] From the point of view of the women most affected, the eight-hour law was not paternalistic, and the formal juridical equality promised in *Ritchie* would be unlikely to improve their working conditions.

I present a version of the events surrounding these two Illinois cases — *Bradwell* and *Ritchie* — to illustrate a way of looking at issues

---

11. 55 Ill. 535 (1869). The Illinois Supreme Court issued its written opinion early in 1870. *See* 2 CHI. LEGAL NEWS 146 (1870). The court dated its opinion September Term, 1869, but published it with the opinions from the September 1870 term, stating that "[t]his application was finally heard and determined at the September Term, 1869, but was unavoidably omitted from its proper place in the report of the cases decided at that term." 55 Ill. 535, 535 n.*. Several other Illinois reporters from the same period have opinions seemingly out of order in a similiar manner. *See, e.g.,* Illinois Reports vols. 50, 51, 54 & 56.

12. 83 U.S. (16 Wall.) 130 (1873).

13. *See* Bradwell v. Illinois, 83 U.S. at 139-42 (Bradley, J., concurring).

14. 155 Ill. 98, 40 N.E. 454 (1895).

15. *See generally* M. TAX, THE RISING OF THE WOMEN: FEMINIST SOLIDARITY AND CLASS CONFLICT, 1880-1917 (1979).

of equality and paternalism. In the nineteenth century, as today, the choice between equal treatment and different treatment for women could not be made in the abstract, but only in context, case by case.[16] Gender-blind policies as well as gender-conscious policies can facilitate and perpetuate the subordination of women. Similarly, both kinds of policies can reduce the subordination of women. An emphasis on the choice between gender-blind policies and gender-conscious policies misfocuses attention. The particular context and meaning of policies are almost always more important than whether the policies specifically take gender into account.

Like equality, paternalism can be evaluated only in the particular contexts that determine its meaning. Paternalism recognizes the importance of the relationship between people, but it often assumes and ratifies an inequality within the relationship. A rejection of this inequality, under the rubric of antipaternalism, can run at least two risks: First, it may deny the importance of human relationship and treat people as isolated individuals. Further, antipaternalism may pretend an equality between people that does not actually exist. This pretense of equality may facilitate the continuation of actual inequality — for example, by encouraging an unrealistic faith in freedom of contract.[17]

---

16. This position is sometimes misinterpreted to be opportunistic or unprincipled. For example, a similar argument that I made in Olsen, *Statutory Rape, supra* note 2, at 398-400, was recently characterized to be: "[O]nly the result matters — if it is good for women, as women define what they want, then the rationale is ultimately unimportant." Dowd, *supra* note 4, at 740 n.212. This position was called "fundamentally inconsistent with the notion of a legal system." *Id.* (characterizing argument of Sherry, *Judicial Activism in the Equal Protection Context: Democracy, Distrust, and Deconstruction,* 73 GEO. L.J. 89, 98-102 (1984)).

I do not agree that only the result, not the rationale, matters — even "[f]rom a practical perspective." Dowd, *supra* note 4, at 740 n.212. Nor do I believe that the only way women can obtain change from the legal system is "to articulate the principles legitimizing equality goals." *Id.* The idea that women should decide "what they want" and then "articulate . . . principles" to justify trying to get what they want from the legal system assumes a radical separation between what women want and the principles upon which women can justify what they want. The justifications and rationales affect what women conclude will be good for them, and any justifications and rationales that ignore the question of what would be good for women must be hollow and abstract indeed.

If we are to value principled decisionmaking, then "principled" must surely mean more than being able to come up with an abstract, general rule that will achieve the desired result in most cases. There is nothing unprincipled about trying to improve the lives of women.

The appeal to a broad abstract principle is too often an effort to avoid acknowledging and confronting some important moral and political choice. Abstractions do not constitute an ethical alternative to serious decisionmaking. *See generally* Olsen, *Socrates on Legal Obligations: Legitimation Theory and Civil Disobedience.* 18 GA. L. REV. 929 (1984).

17. *See generally* Sharp, *Fairness Standards and Separation Agreements: A Word of Caution on Contractual Freedom,* 132 U. PA. L. REV. 1399 (1984) (warning that freedom of contract for divorcing couples may result in agreements that ratify and perpetuate the inequality between husband and wife).

Also, paternalism may assume or pretend a relationship that does not exist and may be an aspect of what I have referred to as "forced community." *See* Olsen, *Statutory Rape, supra* note 2, at 393-94; *see also id.* at 389 n.7.

I propose to evaluate decisions from the point of view of the people most directly affected by the issues. From this perspective, I argue that the paternalism of the *Bradwell* case — refusing to let women practice law — was a false paternalism. I also argue that the equality of the *Ritchie* case — throwing out the eight-hour day for women — was a false equality.

I. FALSE PATERNALISM: THE *BRADWELL* CASES

After the Civil War, a number of women began to apply for licenses to practice law. At that time in the United States, one could be admitted to the bar by reading law in a law office and demonstrating one's proficiency to the court.[18] Myra Bradwell, like many of the other women who wanted to become lawyers, had read law in a relative's law office — in Bradwell's case, her husband's.[19] Many of the young men who ordinarily would have been helping out in the law offices while they read to become lawyers were off fighting the war. The absence of young men may have contributed to the willingness of male lawyers to have their wives and daughters come into their offices.[20] Like "Rosie the Riveter" of World War II, many women who filled in at "men's jobs" wanted to keep working after the war ended. Having read law in a relative's office, women then wanted to become lawyers.[21]

In 1869, Myra Bradwell applied to the Illinois Supreme Court for a license to practice law. The court did not question her professional qualifications, but refused her admission to the practice of law on the basis of her status as a married woman. Initially the court did not issue a formal written opinion but directed the clerk to notify Bradwell of its decision by letter — a letter which Bradwell promptly pub-

---

18. In Illinois, for example, an applicant for a license to practice law was supposed to present "to any member of this court a certificate of qualification, signed by the Circuit Judge and State's Attorney of the circuit in which the applicant may reside, setting forth that the applicant has been examined and found qualified . . . ." Ill. Sup. Ct. R. 76, *quoted in* 2 CHI. LEGAL NEWS 145 (1870).

19. *See* 1 THE BENCH AND BAR OF ILLINOIS 278 (J. Palmer ed. 1899) [hereinafter cited as BENCH AND BAR]; Robinson, *Women Lawyers in the United States,* 2 THE GREEN BAG 10, 14 (1890).

20. *Cf.* Robinson, *supra* note 19. The relationship between the Civil War and women entering the legal profession was first suggested to me by Carol Latham of the University of Wisconsin Law School. Bradwell herself was active in Civil War relief work and probably did not begin studying law until the end of the war. *See* BENCH AND BAR, *supra* note 19, at 278. In any event, the Civil War is likely to have raised the expectations of many women who worked at a variety of war jobs — nursing, serving on a sanitary commission and so forth. These raised expectations may account for the number of women entering or seeking to enter law.

21. Shortly after the war women also began to seek and occasionally obtain admission to law schools. *See* Part II *infra.*

lished.[22] At common law, married women were said to be under "coverture," or under the protection of their husbands. Before legislatures enacted reform statutes known as Married Women's Property Acts, a husband owned all the family property; a married woman could not own property and was unable to enter into contracts on her own behalf.[23] The justices of the supreme court apparently believed that under Illinois law a married woman would not be able to enter into contracts with her clients and therefore could not practice law.[24]

Bradwell responded with a brief to the court in which she presented strong arguments that the Illinois Married Women's Acts of 1861 and 1869, which allowed women to own property and to control their own earnings, enabled women to enter and be bound by contracts to the extent required to practice law.[25] The court then issued a written opinion in which it acknowledged that it had ignored the effect of the 1869 Act and, without conceding the contract-disability point, resorted to a discussion of legislative intent.[26] The court concluded that "the sex of the applicant, independently of coverture," was "a sufficient reason for not granting the license."[27] Although the statute empowering the supreme court to license attorneys did not "expressly require" the exclusion of women, the court asserted that the admission of women "was never contemplated by the legislature."[28] In Illinois, at the time the licensing statute was passed: "That God designed the sexes to occupy different spheres of action, and that it belonged to men to make, apply and execute laws, was regarded as an almost axiomatic

---

22. *See* 2 CHI. LEGAL NEWS 145 (1870). The letter that Norman L. Freeman, the Illinois Supreme Court Reporter, sent to Myra Bradwell, in October 1869, said in part:

The court instruct me to inform you that they are compelled to deny your application for a license to practice as an attorney-at-law in the courts of this State, upon the ground that you would not be bound by the obligations necessary to be assumed where the relation of attorney and client shall exist, by reason of the disability imposed by your married condition — it being assumed that you are a married woman.

Id. (emphasis deleted).

23. *See* H. CLARK, THE LAW OF DOMESTIC RELATIONS IN THE UNITED STATES §§ 7.1-7.2, at 219-29 (1968). A few states did not adopt these common law rules but instead followed community property principles, under which a husband and wife are joint owners of property. *See generally id.*; W. REPPY & C. SAMUEL, COMMUNITY PROPERTY IN THE UNITED STATES 1-11 (1982).

24. *See In re* Bradwell, 55 Ill. 535, 535-37 (1869). The court may also have been deeply affected by the concept of coverture and have found it fanciful to contemplate a married woman becoming a lawyer, quite aside from her inability to form contracts.

25. 55 Ill. at 536-37; 2 CHI. LEGAL NEWS 145-46 (1870). On the appeal to the United States Supreme Court, Bradwell's attorney argued also that the court's supervisory power over attorneys made attorney-client contracts unnecessary. *See* Bradwell v. Illinois, 83 U.S. (16 Wall.) 130, 136 (1872).

26. 55 Ill. at 536-38.

27. 55 Ill. at 537.

28. 55 Ill. at 538.

truth. It may have been a radical error, but that this was the universal belief certainly admits of no denial."[29] Regardless of the "individual opinions" the justices might have with respect to the admission of women to the bar, the court asserted that it did not deem itself at liberty to exercise its power to license attorneys in a mode "never contemplated by the legislature":[30]

> For us to attempt, in a matter of this importance, to inaugurate a practice at variance with all the precedents of the law we are sworn to administer, would be an act of judicial usurpation, deserving of the gravest censure. If we could disregard, in this matter, the authority of those unwritten usages which make the great body of our law, we might do so in any other, and the dearest rights of persons and property would become a matter of mere judicial discretion.[31]

The court claimed to "entertain a profound sympathy" with efforts "to reasonably enlarge the field for the exercise of woman's industry and talent."[32] "If the legislature shall choose to remove the existing barriers, and authorize us to issue licenses equally to men and women, we shall cheerfully obey."[33] Until then, the court would not allow Myra Bradwell to practice law.

Myra Bradwell engaged Senator Matthew Hale Carpenter — a family friend and a famous constitutional lawyer — to appeal her case to the United States Supreme Court.[34] He obtained a writ of error from the Court on August 16, 1870, and presented oral argument January 18, 1872.[35] The Court ruled against Bradwell on April 15, 1873, the day after the Court rendered its decision in the famous *Slaughter-House Cases.*[36] In both cases the majority held that the "privileges

---

29. 55 Ill. at 539.

30. 55 Ill. at 539.

31. 55 Ill. at 541. The court illustrated its position by drawing a comparison to the court-made practice of transferring title to a wife's property to her husband upon their marriage. The courts created this rule but, according to the Illinois Supreme Court, a change in the rule could properly come only from the legislature — as with the enactment of the Married Women's Property Acts — not through the courts. *See* 55 Ill. at 540.

32. 55 Ill. at 541-42.

33. 55 Ill. at 542. The court also suggested that it would trust to women's good sense and sound judgment to practice in those areas of legal practice suitable to them. Although the court's "cheerfully obey" language may sound like deference to the legislature, the deference could also be seen as a form of footdragging.

34. *See* H. KOGAN, THE FIRST CENTURY: THE CHICAGO BAR ASSOCIATION, 1874-1974, at 28 (1974).

35. *See* 2 E. STANTON, S. ANTHONY & M. GAGE, HISTORY OF WOMAN SUFFRAGE 614-15 (1882).

36. 83 U.S. (16 Wall.) 36 (1873). The decision in the *Slaughter-House Cases* was announced April 14, 1873. *See* 6 C. FAIRMAN, HISTORY OF THE SUPREME COURT IN THE UNITED STATES 1349 (1971). *Bradwell* was announced April 15. *See id.* at 1364. E. Bruce Thompson has asserted that *Bradwell* followed the *Slaughter-House Cases* by two days. *See* E. THOMPSON, MATTHEW HALE CARPENTER: WEBSTER OF THE WEST 102 (1954). Babcock, Freedman, Norton & Ross assert that *Bradwell* was scheduled to be handed down at the same time as *Slaughter-House*.

and immunities" clause of the fourteenth amendment did not limit the power of states to control and regulate activities that states had traditionally regulated, such as the licensing of attorneys.

The *Slaughter-House Cases* upheld a Louisiana state law regulating the slaughter of livestock in and around New Orleans against a challenge by independent butchers who argued that the law would put them out of work. The legislation required all butchering to be carried on in a single slaughterhouse, run by a private corporation, and required the corporation to provide space to all comers at prices fixed by the legislature.

The *Slaughter-House* decision raised important questions of judicial restraint and federalism. The idea that *courts* could threaten the people's liberty was important to many people at this time — just as it had been important to the justices of the Illinois Supreme Court in the *Bradwell* case. During the nineteenth and early twentieth centuries, the United States Supreme Court and most other courts were generally regarded as more conservative than legislatures. Judicial restraint was thus not the conservative doctrine that it seems to be today but was a doctrine largely advocated by liberals.[37]

The federalism issue played a somewhat more complicated role. The fourteenth amendment reflected and ratified the Civil War victory of the Union over the Confederate States. Yet, in the *Slaughter-House Cases,* John Campbell, a famous Southern Confederate lawyer who might have been expected to support states' rights against federal encroachment, represented the independent butchers and opposed the state legislation, which had been passed by a carpetbag legislature in Louisiana. Campbell lost the *Slaughter-House Cases* for the butchers, but he won for Southern Confederates both a weakened fourteenth amendment and a relatively activist Supreme Court.[38]

The Unionists who argued in favor of the state legislation in the *Slaughter-House Cases* included Matthew Carpenter, the lawyer who represented Myra Bradwell. The Unionists were interested in limiting

---

but was actually announced the next day." B. BABCOCK, A. FREEDMAN, E. NORTON & S. ROSS, SEX DISCRIMINATION AND THE LAW: CAUSES AND REMEDIES 8 (1975). Several sources refer to the decisions as having been made in May, 1873.

37. For somewhat later, striking examples of liberals advocating judicial restraint, see the opinions of Justice Brandeis in International News Serv. v. Associated Press, 248 U.S. 215, 264-67 (1918) (Brandeis, J., dissenting), and of Judge Learned Hand in Cheney Bros. v. Doris Silk Corp., 35 F.2d 279 (2d Cir. 1929). The classic statement is Oliver Wendell Holmes' dissent in Lochner v. New York, 198 U.S. 45, 75-76 (1905).

38. *See* Franklin, *The Foundations and Meaning of the Slaughter-House Cases* (pts. 1 & 2), 18 TUL. L. REV. 1, 78-88 (1943), 18 TUL. L. REV. 218 (1943). The case was activist insofar as it asserted a pivotal role for the courts in enforcing the fourteenth amendment rather than treating the amendment as primarily enabling federal legislation.

judicial review, not in supporting states' rights against federal encroachment; and along with their other arguments, they attempted to support the state legislation as a health measure, clearly within the police power of the state.[39] Had the *Slaughter-House* decision been based upon a reasonably broad understanding of police power instead of upon a narrow interpretation of the privileges and immunities clause of the fourteenth amendment, the Supreme Court could more easily have decided in favor of Myra Bradwell. The Court might then have had to face the question of whether the police power enabled Illinois to bar women from the practice of law. As it was, the majority of the United States Supreme Court — five Justices — held that *Bradwell* was governed by the *Slaughter-House Cases* and turned Bradwell down because they thought the issue should be decided by the state legislature, not by the federal courts.[40]

Four Justices dissented in the *Slaughter-House Cases* and asserted that courts should play a more active role; they claimed to be concerned with the ways in which *legislatures* (not courts) posed a threat to the people's liberty.[41] These four Justices argued that courts should protect citizens against legislation that infringed basic rights, such as the right to work. An activist judiciary that will protect the rights of minorities sounds good to many feminists and liberals today; but the main "minority" the judicial activists of the nineteenth and early twentieth centuries seemed to worry about was not women or people of color, but the minority of wealthy people. A common interpretation is that the *Slaughter-House* dissenters wanted to protect the rich against the leveling tendencies of the democratic majority.[42] When

---

39. From this perspective, there was little or no inconsistency between the position Matthew Hale Carpenter took opposing the independent butchers and his position in support of Bradwell. Justice Bradley opposed Carpenter's position on both cases.

40. Bradwell v. Illinois, 83 U.S. (16 Wall.) 130, 137-39 (1873). The attorney who represented Bradwell before the U.S. Supreme Court, Matthew Hale Carpenter, had also represented the State of Louisiana's side against the independent butchers in the *Slaughter-House Cases,* so that his victory in the the *Slaughter-House Cases* seems to have contributed to his defeat in *Bradwell*.

41. *See* 83 U.S. at 83-111 (Field, J., dissenting) (Justices Swayne and Bradley and Chief Justice Chase joining Field's opinion); 83 U.S. at 111-24 (Bradley, J., dissenting); 83 U.S. at 124-30 (Swayne, J., dissenting).

42. The plight of the independent butchers in the *Slaughter-House Cases* may seem to provide a counter-example to the statement in the text. One might well feel sympathy and concern for these displaced workers and their families, who hardly seem like rich people being protected against any leveling tendencies of a democratic majority. Most of them were even Gascons, Louisianians of French ancestry who on occasion were subjected to anti-Gascony sentiment not unlike racism. *See* Franklin, *supra* note 38, at 34 & n.110.

Yet, it would seem important to recognize also that the independent butchers constituted a closely organized group which may well have conspired to keep newcomers out of the butchering trade and to keep meat prices high. *See id.* Moreover, the ability of the butchers to work was not at stake in these cases. The legislation that required all slaughtering to take place in a single slaughterhouse, and thus created a monopoly, also required the corporation that operated the

these four Justices finally became a majority of the Court, they began what has come to be known as the *Lochner* era, throwing out as unconstitutional one reform measure after another.[43]

At the time the *Bradwell* appeal was decided, these four Justices were a minority. Only one of them — Chief Justice Chase — took a position that twentieth-century feminists would support. He dissented from the majority opinion[44] and presumably would have ordered the state of Illinois to let Myra Bradwell practice law. The other three Justices — Justices who claimed to believe courts should protect individual rights — disagreed with Chief Justice Chase. They sided with the majority in refusing to grant relief to Bradwell,[45] but they disagreed with the majority's reasons. The concurring opinion of these three Justices, written by Justice Bradley, is the obnoxious sexist opinion so frequently quoted:

> [T]he civil law, as well as nature herself, has always recognized a wide difference in the respective spheres and destinies of man and woman. Man is, or should be, woman's protector and defender. The natural and proper timidity and delicacy which belongs to the female sex evidently unfits it for many of the occupations of civil life. The constitution of the family organization, which is founded in the divine ordinance, as well as in the nature of things, indicates the domestic sphere as that which properly belongs to the domain and functions of womanhood. The harmony, not to say identity, of interests and views which belong, or should belong, to the family institution is repugnant to the idea of a woman adopting a distinct and independent career from that of her husband. . . . The

---

slaughterhouse to provide butchering space to everyone at prices set by the legislature. *See* 83 U.S. at 40, 42; Brief for the Defendants, *reported in* 21 L. Ed. 395, 401. The independence of the butchers, their status as entrepreneurs rather than mere workers or "wage slaves," may well have been an important aspect of what was at stake. *See* Forbath, *The Ambiguities of Free Labor: Labor and the Law in the Gilded Age*, 1985 WIS. L. REV. 767, 776-77. The famous short telegram by which Matthew Carpenter, one of the attorneys who represented the state-created monopoly, notified his clients in New Orleans of their victory in the case reflects this attitude toward the monopolistic tendencies of the independent slaughterers: "The banded butchers are busted." Ashley, *Matthew Carpenter as a Lawyer*, 1 W. VA. BAR 197, 199 (1894).

In fact, however, it would seem that at least some of the banded butchers were not busted. The displaced slaughterers had formed a corporation among themselves and, on March 15, 1871, joined forces with the state-created monopoly. A motion was made but denied to dismiss the *Slaughter-House Cases* as moot on the basis that the original parties to the lawsuit had reached an agreement after the case went to the Supreme Court. *See* Franklin, *supra* note 38, at 225 & nn.230-31.

43. The era received its name from the 1905 case of Lochner v. New York, 198 U.S. 45 (1905). For general discussions of the *Lochner* era, see E. CORWIN, LIBERTY AGAINST GOVERNMENT 149-53 (1948); A. PAUL, CONSERVATIVE CRISIS AND THE RULE OF LAW: ATTITUDES OF BAR AND BENCH, 1887-1895, at 221-37 (1976); L. TRIBE, AMERICAN CONSTITUTIONAL LAW 4-6, 427-50 (1978); B. TWISS, LAWYERS AND THE CONSTITUTION, HOW LAISSEZ FAIRE CAME TO THE SUPREME COURT 110-253 (1942); D. Kennedy, The Rise and Fall of Classical Legal Thought (October 1975) (unpublished manuscript; on file at *Michigan Law Review*).

44. *See* 83 U.S. at 142.

45. 83 U.S. at 139-42 (Bradley, J., concurring).

paramount destiny and mission of woman are to fulfil the noble and benign offices of wife and mother. This is the law of the Creator.[46]

II. THE COMMUNITY OF WOMEN LAWYERS

The reluctance of courts to admit women to the practice of law
may well have slowed the process of women becoming lawyers, but it
could not keep the legal profession all male. In state after state,
courts' refusals to admit women were followed by organizing efforts
culminating in legislation specifically permitting women to join the
profession.[47]

While it is of course always difficult to know how seriously to take
such judicial expressions, it is interesting to note that the Illinois
Supreme Court in *Bradwell* stated: "Of the qualifications of the applicant we have no doubt, and we put our decision in writing in order
that she, or other persons interested, may bring the question before the
next legislature."[48] If the court was not serious, it should have known
better than to issue such an invitation. Myra Bradwell edited a widely
read law weekly in Chicago, and she had not only lobbied for but had
herself drafted the bill of 1869, extending the scope of the Married
Women's Act of 1861.[49]

While Bradwell's appeal to the United States Supreme Court was
pending, a young unmarried woman named Alta M. Hulett qualified
for the bar and was refused admission. With Myra Bradwell's assistance, Hulett shepherded a reform bill through the legislature granting
women substantially equal employment rights with men.[50] Hulett and
Bradwell's bill, passed on March 22, 1872, was later quoted in the
Ritchie case to justify overturning the gender-specific eight-hour-day
legislation.[51] The bill took effect on July 1, 1872, nine and a half
months before the United States Supreme Court decided *Bradwell*.

---

46. 83 U.S. at 141.

47. *See* Robinson, *supra* note 19; *see also In re* Leach, 134 Ind. 665, 34 N.E. 641 (1893),
quoted at note 89 *infra*. The Federal Act of February 15, 1879, made women eligible to practice
before the United States Supreme Court. Act of Feb. 15, 1879, ch. 81, 20 Stat. 292.

48. 55 Ill. at 536. Writing in 1890, Myra Bradwell characterized this statement as a suggestion by the court that the legislature should act. *See* 22 CHI. LEGAL NEWS 264 (1890).

49. *See* 1 CHI. LEGAL NEWS 212 (1869); *see also id.* at 172.

50. *See* H. KOGAN, *supra* note 34, at 28-29; Robinson, *supra* note 19, at 15-16.

51. *See* Ritchie v. People, 155 Ill. 98, 112, 40 N.E. 454, 458 (1895). When Susan B. Anthony
went to the election polling place and tried to cast her ballot — before women were allowed to
vote — she was arrested and prosecuted for interfering with an election, a federal offense. The
law under which she was prosecuted had been enacted after the Civil War to discourage white
terrorist disenfranchisement of the newly freed black men. *See* M. KELLER, AFFAIRS OF STATE
159 (1977). We recognize that in prosecuting Susan B. Anthony the state officials were misusing
the law; we do not conclude that we made a mistake in passing the statute — that no matter how
wise it looked when it was enacted, the statute was really a snare and a delusion.

Myra Bradwell never reapplied to the bar but continued to edit her influential weekly newspaper, *The Chicago Legal News.*[52] On June 4, 1873, Alta Hulett became the first woman lawyer in Illinois.[53]

In 1890, a lawyer named Lelia Robinson wrote a biographical and professional description of all the women lawyers she could find in the United States.[54] To gather material for her article, Robinson undertook extensive correspondence, writing to the deans of law schools[55] and to every woman lawyer for whom she could find an address.[56] Her article describes several small, loosely knit communities of women lawyers, the largest and most formal of which was the Equity Club.

The Equity Club was formed at the University of Michigan Law School in the fall of 1886 by five of the seven women students then in attendance and two alumnae who lived in town. It developed into a correspondence club open to all women law students and lawyers. By 1890 it had forty members and published an *Equity Club Annual,* consisting of letters from the members.[57]

In August 1893, the Law Department of the Queen Isabella Club held a three-day meeting in Chicago. Women lawyers presented papers on topics ranging from the *Bradwell* case and the Populist Movement to "Women Lawyers in Ancient Times." A paper on Sunday closing laws written by Elizabeth Cady Stanton was to be "probably . . . read by another." Those present formed a National League of

---

52. In 1890, a few years before her death in 1894, the Illinois Supreme Court admitted Ms. Bradwell to the bar on its own motion. *See* 22 CHI. LEGAL NEWS 263 (1890). Bradwell was also admitted to practice before the United States Supreme Court on March 28, 1892. *See* 26 CHI. LEGAL NEWS 296 (1894).

53. Interestingly, Hulett may also have been the youngest person to become a lawyer in Illinois. She joined the bar on her nineteenth birthday. Males did not reach the age of majority until twenty-one, and the court suggested that minors would not be allowed to practice law. *See* 2 CHI. LEGAL NEWS 145 (1870) (Freeman's letter to Bradwell, quoted at note 22 *supra*) ("Applications [to the bar] have occasionally been made by persons under twenty-one years of age, and have always been denied upon the same ground — that they are not bound by their contracts, being under a legal disability in that regard."). Women achieved their majority at age eighteen. *See* text at note 93 *infra*.

54. Robinson, *supra* note 19.

55. *Id.* at 11. Many law schools, including Harvard, Yale, and Columbia, refused to admit women. In 1886, however, Yale had granted a Bachelor of Laws degree to one woman, Miss Alice R. Jordan, who had studied a year at Michigan and then gone to Yale for a year. Shortly thereafter the Yale University Catalogue provided, "It is to be understood that the courses of instruction above described are open to persons of the male sex only, except where both sexes are specifically included." 1886-87 YALE U. CATALOGUE 24. According to the dean of the law school the paragraph was intended "to prevent a repetition of the Jordan incident." Robinson, *supra* note 19, at 12-13.

Other law schools did admit women. The University of Michigan, for example, admitted Miss Sarah Kilgore in 1870 and granted her a degree in 1871. By 1890, Michigan had graduated more women than any other law school in the country. *Id.* at 17.

56. *See id.* at 11.

57. *See id.* at 17.

Women Lawyers.[58]

Some of these early women lawyers specialized in fields such as juvenile crime, that were unthreatening to men, and may have enjoyed a "remarkably smooth arrival into a professional middle class."[59] For others the arrival was a bit more rocky.[60] Whether they remained within "[t]acit, mutually accepted limits"[61] or went beyond such limits, a number of these women lawyers struggled to advance the interests of women and of society in general.[62]

III. PATERNALISM VERSUS SOLIDARITY

Bradley's opinion in *Bradwell* is often referred to as "paternalistic,"[63] but this seems to me to be a mischaracterization. The concurrence may well have treated Bradwell as a subordinate, and it did overrule her own decision to practice law; but it did not control Bradwell in a fatherly or caring manner. No serious claim could be advanced that Justice Bradley was trying to promote Myra Bradwell's

---

58. 25 CHI. LEGAL NEWS 451 (1893); *see also id.* at 421.

59. R. WEIBE, THE SEARCH FOR ORDER 122-23 (1967). Weibe asserts that the trickling admission of women into law was a less important advance than women's entry into professions such as teaching and social work. He also argues that the "token integration" of women into law was greeted by their male colleagues with "a warm sense of paternal tolerance." *Id.*

60. *See Equity Club Annual* (available at the Schlessinger Library, Radcliffe College, Cambridge, Mass.); Robinson, *supra* note 19, at 17.

61. R. WEIBE, *supra* note 59, at 123.

62. *See* Robinson, *supra* note 19. The issue is of course complicated. For example, Myra Bradwell would certainly be listed among the women lawyers who struggled for social reform and tried to expand the roles available to women. *See, e.g.,* Minow, *"Forming Underneath Everything That Grows:" Toward a History of Family Law,* 1985 WIS. L. REV. 819, 840-51. Yet Bradwell also printed racist jokes in the *Chicago Legal News. See* 24 CHI. LEGAL NEWS 294 (1891); *see also id.* at 141. She warmly endorsed the reelection of Illinois Supreme Court Justice Benjamin Magruder shortly after he upheld, in The Anarchists' Case (Spies v. People), 122 Ill. 1, 12 N.E. 865, *error dismissed,* 123 U.S. 131 (1887), the popular but legally dubious convictions of the Haymarket anarchists. *See* 21 CHI. LEGAL NEWS 315 (1888). By the time Magruder issued his opinion, September 14, 1887, (dated "September 15" in the *Illinois Reporter*), the public hysteria that had initially followed the Haymarket bombing had subsided, and many progressive and pro-labor people were deploring the unfairness of the trial and asserting that the anarchists had been convicted for their beliefs. *See* P. AVRICH, THE HAYMARKET TRAGEDY 300-12 (1984). In her endorsement, Bradwell appeared to refer to the *Anarchists' Case* when she complimented Magruder's "decisions within year" for making "every citizen within the great State of Illinois feel that . . . his life and property is a little safer, that law and order will be preserved." 21 CHI. LEGAL NEWS 315 (1888). John Peter Altgeld, Illinois' reform governor, based his pardon of the Haymarket anarchists on his conclusion that the initial trials were grossly unfair and illegal. J. ALTGELD, REASONS FOR PARDONING FIELDEN, NEEBE AND SCHWAB (Chicago 1893). Not long after Altgeld's pardon, Magruder decided Ritchie v. People, 155 Ill. 98, 40 N.E. 454 (1895), which overturned a pro-labor measure Altgeld supported.

63. *See, e.g.,* Frontiero v. Richardson, 411 U.S. 677, 685 (1973) (Brennan, J., plurality opinion); Lewis v. Cohen, 417 F. Supp. 1047, 1054 (E.D. Pa. 1976), *vacated sub nom.* Lewis v. Cowen, 547 F.2d 1162 (3d Cir. 1977); United States v. Reiser, 394 F. Supp. 1060, 1061 (D. Mont. 1975), *revd.,* 532 F.2d 673 (9th Cir.), *cert. denied,* 429 U.S. 838 (1976); Smith v. City of E. Cleveland, 363 F. Supp. 1131, 1138 (N.D. Ohio 1973), *affd. in part and revd. in part sub nom.* Smith v. Troyan, 520 F.2d 492 (6th Cir. 1975), *cert. denied,* 426 U.S. 934 (1976).

true best interests. Bradley favored overruling Bradwell's choice not for her sake but rather to advance other goals.

The stance taken by Bradley seems to me to be no more paternalistic than Petruchio in Shakespeare's *Taming of the Shrew*. When he was trying to "tame" his new wife Katharina, Petruchio starved her and kept her in rags. He did it by sending away the food and clothing as "not good enough" for her.[64] We do not say he was being paternalistic; he was being disingenuous.

When men claim that policies that harm women have been enacted for their own good, women may find it easier simply to condemn the policies as "paternalistic" without disputing the factual claim that the policies would be good for women. There is less resistance to an abstract complaint of "paternalism" than there would be to a serious discussion of the actual effects the policies advanced could be expected to have on the lives of women. A major problem with taking this easy route of condemning "paternalism" is that it tends to disable us from our own efforts at collective action.[65] Whenever people try to bring about change they are likely to employ policies that depart from isolated individualism. Any attempt we make to act together to improve our lives can be labeled paternalistic.

A good example of this problem arises with protective labor legislation. Historically, women have often supported such legislation. From as early as 1790 workers in the United States were demanding a shortened workday. The ten-hour workday was won through general strikes in 1835, although it was then lost in the depression of 1837-41.[66] In 1844, the first unions for factory workers in the United States — Female Labor Reform Associations — joined with male workers to petition legislatures to enact ten-hour laws. As a result of their efforts, ten-hour laws were passed in New Hampshire, Pennsylvania, and

---

64. *See* W. SHAKESPEARE, THE TAMING OF THE SHREW, act iv, scenes i & iii. Some would argue that Petruchio's overall plan to "tame" his wife was indeed intended to be for her own good and thus classically paternalistic. My point here is a narrower one. When Petruchio sent the food and clothing away he was not attempting to obtain better food and clothing but intentionally depriving Katharina of food and clothing. Whether the deprivation was supposed to be for her own long-range good is another question.

65. This easy feminist talk against "paternalism" is like easy feminist talk against "outmoded stereotypes." Women make a mistake and "giv[e] up the battle," Polan, *Toward a Theory of Law and Patriarchy*, in THE POLITICS OF LAW 294, 300 (D. Kairys ed. 1982), when they soothe feelings and try to limit conflict by pretending that various negative views of women were once acceptable but are now "outmoded." Such easy talk of "outmoded stereotypes" also slips one into the position of categorically denying that "outmoded stereotypes" have any current factual accuracy. By basing their attack on the *falseness* of a stereotype, women make it more difficult to admit the partial truth of some stereotypes and to work to end that partial truth. *See generally* Olsen, *Statutory Rape, supra* note 2, at 428 n.197.

66. *See* P. FONER, MAY DAY 8-9 (1986).

Maine. Employers, however, were able to insert provisions into the laws that permitted longer hours by special contract, and workers who refused to agree to such special contracts were fired and often black-listed.[67] Illinois passed an eight-hour bill in 1867, but this law also provided an exception when there was a "special contract to the contrary," and was therefore of little or no effect.[68] In the 1880s ten-hour, six-day workweeks were standard, and working days were often twelve to fifteen hours long.

Without an eight-hour law or strong labor unions, most workers had to work long hours or lose their jobs. Individually, a worker did not have the choice of working only eight hours a day. Poor pay and competition from other workers forced individual workers to work longer hours than they wanted to. The eight-hour movement was an effort to limit this competition so that no one would be forced to work longer than eight hours. In an important sense, it was a form of solidarity.[69]

The charge — made by conservative courts during the *Lochner* era — that all protective labor legislation is paternalistic is false. Most protective labor legislation can be better understood as a form of collective action. It does not prevent workers from doing what they want to do; rather, it *enables* workers to do what they want — to work fewer hours for more pay and under better conditions.[70]

Protective labor legislation helps workers by limiting competition. But when so-called protective labor legislation applies to only one group of workers — for example, only to women — it sometimes ceases to have this effect. It may help only *men* workers by limiting the competition of *women* but not improve working conditions in general.[71] When women were first entering the job market in large numbers, before men and women competed for the same jobs, protective labor legislation tended to improve work conditions, whether it ap-

---

67. *See id.*

68. Eight Hour Law, ILL. REV. STAT., ch. 48, §§ 1-2 (Hurd 1885).

69. *See generally* Altgeld, *The Eight-Hour Movement,* in THE PROGRESS OF LABOR 37 (A. Beatty ed. 1892).

70. For the most interesting, though I believe mistaken, liberal argument that protective labor legislation of general application is paternalistic, see Shiffrin, *Liberalism, Radicalism, and Legal Scholarship,* 30 UCLA L. REV. 1103, 1161 (1983) (arguing, in opposition to Ronald Dworkin, that "[a] major argument of the state in defending the law at issue in *Lochner* was that anyone who wanted to work more than ten hours in a bakery had an inadequate conception of the good life; that it was, in fact, a dangerous life").

71. It is well known that "protective" labor legislation was used at times in the twentieth century to keep women out of certain desirable jobs. *See* J. BAER, THE CHAINS OF PROTECTION (1978). Less well known is the support that some male unionists who were opposed to women in the work force gave to the concept of equal pay for equal work, with exactly the same goal of keeping women out of desirable jobs. *See* A. KESSLER-HARRIS, OUT TO WORK 156 (1982).

plied to men and women or just to women.[72] When, however, men and women were in job competition, gender-specific legislation could be and sometimes was used to exclude women or to hurt them vis-à-vis men, rather than to improve conditions for all workers. To call such legislation "paternalistic" misses the point. What is wrong with such legislation is not that it takes away or overrules, assertedly for her own good, a woman's choice to work longer hours, but rather that the legislation will not improve work conditions. The legislation sacrifices women's choices for the benefit of men and reduces women's options instead of expanding them. The effect of gender-specific labor legislation depends entirely upon the particular context in which it is enacted. It cannot be judged *a priori*.

IV. The Community of Women Reformers

In Illinois in the late nineteenth century there was broad-based support for protective labor legislation, especially among women. In 1888, thirty women's groups formed the Illinois Women's Alliance, a cross-class coalition that included trade unions, women's clubs, suffrage groups, temperance unions, and professional groups.[73] The constitution of the Illinois Women's Alliance stated as among its goals: "to agitate for the enforcement of all existing laws and ordinances that have been enacted for the protection of women and children"; "[t]o secure enactment of such laws as shall be found necessary"; and "to investigate all business establishments and factories where women and children are employed."[74] Although Hull House was not a member of the Illinois Women's Alliance, Jane Addams, Florence Kelley, and other residents of the famous settlement house worked very effectively for many of the same goals.

This coalition of women secured passage in 1893 of a bill to outlaw sweatshops and regulate working conditions in the garment industry.[75] Section five enacted the eight-hour day for women working in "factories or workshops."[76] Section nine provided for the appointment of a

---

72. *See* Brandeis, *Labor Legislation,* in J. Commons et al., 3 The History of Labor in the United States 1896-1932, at 397 (1935); *see also* The Case for the Factory Acts 209 (S. Webb 2d ed. 1902) (England); E. Cadbury, Women's Work and Wages 36-43 (1907) (England); E. Bauer, The Night-Work of Women in Industry 38 (1903) (Switzerland).

73. *See* M. Tax, *supra* note 15, at 66-68.

74. Newspaper clipping, box 4, vol. 2, Thomas J. Morgan Papers (November 1888) (available at University of Illinois at Champaign-Urbana), *quoted in* Sklar, *Hull House in the 1890s: A Community of Women Reformers,* 10 Signs: J. Women in Culture & Socy. 658, 665 (1985).

75. *See* Sklar, *supra* note 74; M. Tax, *supra* note 15, at 25-89.

76. After an extensive investigation of the sweatshop system, the Illinois legislature enacted in 1893 a bill entitled, "An Act to regulate the manufacture of clothing, wearing apparel, and other articles in this State, and to provide for the appointment of State inspectors to enforce the

chief factory inspector, an assistant factory inspector, and ten deputy factory inspectors, "five of whom shall be women."[77] Florence Kelley, who had drafted the bill, was named chief factory inspector. She gathered around her a group of committed deputies, several of them socialists, and undertook rigorous enforcement of the law.[78] The community of women reformers at Hull House became the center of enforcement activities.

Although the effects of gender-specific legislation may be difficult to evaluate, the available evidence suggests that in Illinois in 1893, the eight-hour day for women did not exclude them from jobs or hurt women vis-à-vis men. Instead, it tended to secure the eight-hour day for all workers. The work done by men and by women was separate but interrelated in a manner that made it difficult not to limit men also to eight hours.[79] Kathryn Kish Sklar, who is preparing a biography of Florence Kelley, has concluded that Kelley and her staff probably adopted a deliberate policy of extending the eight-hour day *de facto* to men.[80] Kelley wrote to Friedrich Engels on New Year's Eve, 1894:

> We have at last won a victory for our 8 hours law. The Supreme Court has handed down no decision sustaining it, but the Stockyards magnates having been arrested until they are tired of it, have instituted the 8 hours day for 10,000 employees, men, women and children. We have 18 suits pending to enforce the 8 hours laws and we think we shall establish it permanently before Easter. It has been a painful struggle of eighteen months and the Supreme Court may annul the law. But I have great hopes that the popular interest may prove too strong.[81]

Whether there was insufficient popular support for the law or whether the court was unmoved by public sentiment, Kelly's hopes were dealt

---

same, and to make an appropriation therefor." Act of June 17, 1893, 1893 Ill. Laws 76 (Bradwell). Section 5 of the act provided: "No female shall be employed in any factory or workshop more than eight hours in any one day or forty-eight hours in any one week." Act of June 17, 1893, 1893 Ill. Laws 76, 77 (Bradwell).

77. Act of June 17, 1893, 1893 Ill. Laws 76, 77 (Bradwell); *see* Ritchie v. People, 155 Ill. 98, 40 N.E. 454 (1895).

78. *See* Sklar, *supra* note 74, at 671 (letter from Florence Kelley to Friedrich Engels, Nov. 21, 1893).

79. *See id.* at 675. Interestingly, it was a gender-neutral provision of the law, not a gender-specific one, that probably did benefit men at the expense of some women, at least in the short run. The act outlawed child labor and the manufacture of garments in tenement dwellings, which tended to move manufacturing work out of the sweatshops and into the factories. Men held about 75% of factory jobs, while women and children did most of the work in sweatshops. *See* Sklar, *supra* note 74, at 672-75.

80. *See id.* at 675; *see also* K. SKLAR, FLORENCE KELLEY AND THE FEMALE WORLD OF PROGRESSIVE REFORM 1830-1930 (forthcoming).

81. Letter from Florence Kelley to Friedrich Engels (Dec. 31, 1894), *quoted in* Sklar, *supra* note 74, at 675. Florence Kelley began correspondence with Friedrich Engels in 1884, when she decided to translate his classic work, CONDITION OF THE ENGLISH WORKING CLASS IN 1844 (1887). Kelley's was the only English translation until 1958. *See* Sklar, *supra* note 74, at 661 n.8.

a setback by the Illinois Supreme Court in *Ritchie v. People*.[82]

V. FALSE EQUALITY: THE *RITCHIE* CASE

A group of employers organized the Illinois Manufacturers Alliance (which became the model for the National Association of Manufacturers)[83] for the explicit purpose of obtaining a court ruling against the eight-hour day provision of the sweatshop act.[84] In their internal organizing efforts, they made it clear that they feared the eight-hour day for women would be the opening wedge for the eight-hour day for everyone.[85]

The Illinois Manufacturers Alliance was successful, and in 1895 the Illinois Supreme Court in *Ritchie v. People* declared the law unconstitutional — as a violation of due process and women's rights. The language was stirring. Justice Magruder wrote for the court that "woman is entitled to the same rights, under the constitution, to make contracts with reference to her labor as are secured thereby to men."[86] He referred to the United States Supreme Court case of *Minor v. Happersett*[87] as holding that a woman was both a "person" and a "citizen" within the meaning of the first section of the fourteenth amendment:

> As a citizen, woman has the right to acquire and possess property of every kind. As a "person," she has the right to claim the benefit of the constitutional provision that she shall not be deprived of life, liberty or property without due process of law. . . . The law accords to her, as to every other citizen, the natural right to gain a livelihood by intelligence, honesty and industry in the arts, the sciences, the professions or other vocations. Before the law, her right to a choice of vocations cannot be said to be denied or abridged on account of sex.[88]

---

82. 155 Ill. 98, 40 N.E. 454 (1895).

83. *See* Sklar, *supra* note 74, at 674; Papers of the Illinois Manufacturers Association, Chicago Historical Society [hereinafter cited as IMA Papers].

84. *See* Minutes, August 24, 1893, IMA Papers, *supra* note 83, at box 1, folder 1 (1893). The organization originally went by the name Illinois Manufacturers Protective Association. At its second meeting the organization dropped the "Protective" from its name. The minutes of the organization do not reflect whether that change was motivated by a concern that it might seem ingenuous for the Illinois Manufacturers *Protective* Association to be arguing that protective labor legislation was ill-advised and paternalistic. *See* Minutes, August 29, 1893, IMA Papers, *supra* note 83, at box 1, folder 1 (1893).

85. This view of the Illinois Manufacturers Association appears in many sources in its papers. It is particularly apparent in its opposition to a later proposal for the eight-hour day for women. *See* Pamphlet opposing the Eight-Hour Day, IMA Papers, *supra* note 83; Letter from Secretary of the Illinois Manufacturesrs Association to William J. Brown, April 17, 1909, *id.* at box 161, Folder 1 (1909); *see also* Brief of Plaintiffs in Error at 61, Ritchie v. People, 155 Ill. 98, 40 N.E. 454 (1895) (arguing against eight-hour law that it "necessarily forces a reduction of the hours of work of the male co-laborer").

86. Ritchie v. People, 155 Ill. 98, 111, 40 N.E. 454, 458 (1895).

87. 88 U.S. (21 Wall.) 162 (1875).

88. *Ritchie*, 155 Ill. at 112, 40 N.E. at 458.

Magruder cited with approval *In re Leach,* an 1893 case from Indiana that disagreed with Illinois' *Bradwell* decision and held that women could not be barred from practicing law in Indiana.[89] Magruder continued:

> The tendency of legislation in this State has been to recognize the rights of women . . . . An act approved March 22, 1872, entitled "An Act to secure freedom in the selection of an occupation," etc., provides that "no person shall be precluded or debarred from any occupation, profession or employment (except military) on account of sex."[90]

Moreover, Magruder found it irrelevant that the Act of March 22, 1872, made an exception for military service and provided "that nothing in the Act shall be construed as requiring any female to work on streets, or roads, or serve on juries." Magruder argued that the question before the court was "whether, in an employment which is conceded to be lawful in itself and suitable for woman to engage in, she shall be deprived of the right to determine for herself how many hours she can and may work during each day."[91] Finally, in an antipaternalistic vein, Magruder asserted that it was "questionable" whether the police power of the state could ever "be exercised to prevent injury to the individual" worker or instead could be exercised only to promote the broader interests of society or the public.[92]

Unfortunately, there is no reason to believe that the court's language had any beneficial effect on the actual conditions of women. Women in Illinois did not enjoy formal juridical equality; for example, the age of majority for females was eighteen, for males twenty-one.[93]

---

89. 134 Ind. 665, 34 N.E. 641 (1893). *Leach* was a more difficult case for the woman applicant than *Bradwell.* The Indiana statute provided: "Every person of good moral character, *being a voter,* on application, shall be admitted to practice law in all the courts of justice." 134 Ind. at 666, 34 N.E. at 641 (emphasis added). Women were not allowed to vote in Indiana, but the court decided that the statute did not limit their right to practice law in the state. The court did not refer to the *Bradwell* case by name, but the reference is unmistakable.

We are not unmindful that other States, notably Illinois, Wisconsin, Oregon, Maryland, and Massachusetts, have held that in the absence of an express grant of the privilege [to practice law] it may not be conferred upon women. In some instances the holding has been upon constitutional provisions unlike that of this State, and in others upon what we are constrained to believe an erroneous recognition of a supposed common law inhibition. However, each of the States named made haste to create, by legislation, the right which it was supposed was forbidden by the common law, and thereby recognized the progress of American women . . . .

134 Ind. at 668, 34 N.E. at 642.

90. 155 Ill. at 112, 40 N.E. at 458. Justice Magruder was referring to the bill passed by the efforts of Myra Bradwell and Alta M. Hulett. *See* text at notes 50-51 *supra.*

91. 155 Ill. at 113-14, 40 N.E. at 459.

92. 155 Ill. at 114, 40 N.E. at 459.

93. *See* Sayles v. Christie, 187 Ill. 420, 437, 58 N.E. 480, 485 (1900); Stevenson v. Westfall, 18 Ill. 209, 211 (1856). The discrimination that such legislation represents and the harm it can cause women are suggested in Stanton v. Stanton, 421 U.S. 7, 14-17 (1975) (forbidding Utah to enforce different ages of majority for males and females). Of course, a lower age of majority may also benefit women in some cases. *See, e.g.,* note 53 *supra.*

Nor did women enjoy equality in the workplace. Jobs were segregated by sex, and women were paid considerably lower wages than men.[94] Court opinions in Illinois were not particularly pro-women. Although child custody law was thought to be better for women in Illinois than in some other states, Justice Magruder in one case took one of a mother's two sons away from her because she worked.[95] On the topic of married women's rights, Illinois was barely less grudging than any other state in its enforcement of statutory reform.[96]

Meanwhile, the actual effect of the *Ritchie* case was to overturn a law that was supported by women and seemed to be operating for their benefit. It was not until thirteen years later, when the United States Supreme Court in *Muller v. Oregon*[97] upheld a general ten-hour day for women in Oregon, that a serious split among women developed on the issue of gender-specific hours legislation.[98] Even then, the actual effect of Oregon's ten-hour law was more good than bad, and it was only a scattering of voices that objected or believed that there was an important risk that the measure would work to disable women vis-à-vis men.[99] Most commentators saw the ten-hour law upheld in *Muller* as an opening wedge — just as the Illinois Manufacturers Alliance saw

---

94. *See* REPORT AND FINDINGS OF THE JOINT COMMITTEE TO INVESTIGATE THE "SWEAT SHOP" SYSTEM, TOGETHER WITH A TRANSCRIPT OF THE TESTIMONY TAKEN BY THE COMMITTEE (Springfield, Ill. 1893).

95. *See* Umlauf v. Umlauf, 128 Ill. 378, 21 N.E. 600 (1889). The identity of the individual justice who wrote an opinion would seem to have been particularly important at this time in Illinois judicial history. The Supreme Court met in three different cities during the year, and relatively little consultation took place among the various justices. Each case was assigned to an individual justice to write a draft opinion without the court having heard oral argument and usually, if not always, prior to any discussion of the case by the court. The draft opinion usually became the final opinion, and dissents were rare. One of the justices, responding to a complaint from the bar that the Illinois Supreme Court was issuing "single judge opinions," suggested that "many opinions" would be revised after the court discussed the case: "[Q]uite often [opinions] are re-written more than once." Carter, *The Supreme Court and its Method of Work*, 1 ILL. L. REV. 151, 153 (1906); *see also* Woodward, *The "One-Judge Opinions" of our Supreme Court* (Editorial Note), 1 ILL. L. REV. 392 (1906); Correspondence, *Comment on Mr. Justice Carter's Defense of the Supreme Court's Method of Work*, 1 ILL. L. REV. 273 (1906).

96. *See, e.g.*, Snell v. Snell, 123 Ill. 403, 14 N.E. 684 (1888). I would not want to discount possible ideological benefits of Magruder's opinion. His decision could play a role in constituting a more juridically equal regime. Formal equality, which often benefits women, can be and sometimes is advanced by judicial assertions that women are equal to men and have equal rights to men. On the other hand, Magruder's opinion may also have ideological disadvantages: formal equality could be a setback and discredited by decisions that hurt women in the name of equality.

97. 208 U.S. 412 (1908). I have benefited from reading unpublished manuscripts, including S. Levin, The Protection Paradox: The History of Protective Labor Legislation for Women, 1780-1930; D. Gelon, *Muller v. Oregon*: A Feminist Decision (July 1, 1985).

98. *See* Lehrer, *Protective Labor Legislation for Women*, 17 REV. RADICAL POL. ECON. 187, 187 (1985).

99. *See, e.g.*, *Against Justice Brewer's Decision*, 25 WOMAN'S TRIBUNE 19 (1908); *Unjust to Working Women*, 25 WOMAN'S TRIBUNE 17 (1908); Harding, *Pertinent Queries*, 25 WOMAN'S TRIBUNE 19 (1908); *Special Legislation for Women*, 25 WOMAN'S TRIBUNE 16 (1908); Harding, *Male Socialism*, The Woman's Standard, Apr. 1908, at 2, col. 2.

the eight-hour day in Illinois.[100] Gender-specific legislation, legitimated in *Muller v. Oregon,* was later used to exclude women from desirable jobs,[101] but that does not mean that the *Ritchie* case was right. The equality promoted in *Ritchie v. People* was a false equality.

Gender-based labor legislation has complex and ambiguous implications. The conservative judicial attack on protective legislation of general application and the standard arguments in favor of laissez-faire usually assert that protective labor legislation is bad for society and that it does not really help its intended beneficiaries. *Muller v. Oregon* admitted what *Lochner v. New York* had tried to deny — that protective labor legislation can benefit the protected workers and society in general. Protective labor legislation — even if it is limited by its terms to women — "delegitimates" the autocratic power of employers and legitimates the basic notion that social controls on the marketplace are appropriate.[102]

Yet, protective labor legislation limited to women may also offer ideological support to the proponents of laissez-faire. By identifying protective labor legislation with the special problems and disabilities of women, gender-specific legislation may make protective legislation seem unmanly. *Muller v. Oregon* can be read to support the assertion that protective legislation is paternalistic. Women were more often than men considered to be appropriate beneficiaries of paternalism.

Finally, in those fields in which men and women did compete, gender-specific legislation might well exclude rather than benefit women. Thus, the failure of such legislation to protect its supposed beneficiaries in these particular cases could reinforce the argument that such legislation in general does not protect the workers it is supposed to benefit. Moreover, insofar as gender-specific labor legislation pits men against women, it may undermine working-class solidarity and thus reinforce the power of the employers.

The 1893 sweatshop bill would likely have been considerably more controversial if section five had enacted the eight-hour day for men as

---

100. *See* text at note 85 *supra.*

101. *See* J. BAER, *supra* note 71.

102. Historically, altruism has been linked with hierarchy — a hierarchy that places women below men. In the nineteenth and again in the twentieth century, when women demanded equality they by and large used a marketplace model of equality and allowed the equality claim to be linked with assertions of individualism. Women were not only seeking both equality and independence at approximately the same time, but in many ways their demand for equality was based upon (or dependent upon) their claim to be independent. *See* Olsen, *supra* note 1.

Within liberal society, notions of contractual freedom and autonomy play an important role. Women's ability to form contracts was contested and important. It may be that the social and political meaning of the notion of freedom of contract was significantly different as applied to women than as applied to men in the late nineteenth and early twentieth centuries.

well as for women. Limiting the reform to women may well have seemed politically necessary. Once a reform is accepted, it may be possible to extend its coverage to men.[103]

Writing in 1924, Florence Kelley justified gender-specific labor legislation against claims that it violated women's rights to equality with men. She wrote:

> The struggle for every gain in statutes and judicial decisions for women and girls in industry has been hard fought and costly in money, time and effort.
>
> [Women's] oldest, most wide-spread, and most insistent demands have been for seats, for more adequate wages, and short, firmly regulated working hours. . . . Whenever union men feel no need of laws, well and good. No one wishes to interfere with them any more than professional women are interfered with today by labor legislation.[104]

If they were not able to enact gender-specific labor legislation, according to Kelley, "women could change their hours and other working conditions by law only when men were ready and willing to make the changes for themselves. This would be a new subjection of wage-earning women to wage-earning men, and to that subjection we are opposed on principle and in practice."[105]

As long as women were segregated into different jobs from men, it was not very meaningful to insist that labor legislation apply equally to both sexes. As women were slowly allowed to work at "men's jobs," these women would no longer benefit from or desire protective legislation unless it applied to men as well as to women.

VI. Conclusion

The parallel that feminists who question maternity benefits draw

---

103. *See* Brandeis, *supra* note 72.

104. Kelley, *Why Other Women Groups Oppose the Amendment,* GOOD HOUSEKEEPING, Mar. 24, 1924, at 19, 164-65.

105. *Id.* For a more recent statement in a similar vein, consider the testimony opposing the Equal Rights Amendment in 1970, given by Myra Wolfgang, vice-president of the Hotel and Restaurant Employees and Bartenders International Union, AFL-CIO:

> My concern is for the widowed, divorced mothers of children who are the heads of their families and earn less than $3,500 a year working as maids, laundry workers, hospital cleaners, or dishwashers. . . .
>
> . . . .
>
> Representing service workers gives me a special concern over the threat that an equal rights amendment would present to minimum labor standards legislation. . . . I am sure you are aware that many such laws apply to women only.
>
> . . . .
>
> . . . Should women workers be left without any legislation because of State legislature's failure and unwillingness to enact such legislation for men?

The "Equal Rights" Amendment: Hearings Before the Subcomm. on Constitutional Amendments of the Senate Comm. of the Judiciary, 91st Cong., 2d Sess. (1970), *quoted in* WOMEN AND THE "EQUAL RIGHTS AMENDMENT" 91-93 (C. Stimpson ed. 1972).

between maternity benefits and protective labor legislation is more apt than supporters of maternity benefits often acknowledge. The arguments now being advanced to support maternity benefits are very similar to those that were advanced to support protective labor legislation. The arguments were generally persuasive then, and they are generally persuasive now.

Brandeis' brief in *Muller v. Oregon* spent two pages establishing that men and women were not in job competition and that protective labor legislation would therefore not hurt women vis-à-vis men. Initially, protective legislation limited to women tended to bring their wages and working conditions up to the level of men's.[106] When this situation changed and protective labor legislation was used to exclude instead of to benefit women, it became important to change or eliminate the gender-specific legislation.

Pregnancy disability leave seems at this time to be an important employee benefit for women. In time, this situation could change. Even now, it would probably be better to have a broader leave policy that would cover a wide variety of reasons for leaving work. It may turn out to be important that the government, not individual employers, bear the costs of maternity benefits. We should approach the question of maternity benefits as a collective process of working out and describing desirable ends. We should not try to endorse either equal treatment or different treatment as any kind of overarching principle.

This analysis has more general implications regarding the issue of sameness and differences and the question of whether women should emphasize their similarity to men or their differences from men. Men should be neither a model nor a contrast. Women should not have to claim to be just like men to get decent treatment, nor should they have to focus on *their* differences *from men* to justify themselves whenever they demand a policy different from the present treatment afforded to men. Women can be hurt by false paternalism and by false equality. We should not let these concepts divide us. We can and should advance the concrete interests of society through feminist organizing and through building coalitions with other groups — beginning from a base of feminist solidarity.

---

106. *See* Brief for Defendent in Error at 82-84, Muller v. Oregon, 208 U.S. 412 (1908) (the "Brandeis Brief"). Louis Brandeis was also one of the signers of the more conventional brief filed in the case on behalf of the State of Oregon. *See* Brief for the State of Oregon, Muller v. Oregon, 208 U.S. 412 (1908).

[19]

The Nineteenth Amendment and Women's Equality

Jennifer K. Brown

A rising demand for women's equality took shape in the middle of the nineteenth century and continues as a transformative force today. Early on, American feminists mobilized energetically to abolish outright discrimination that legally subordinated women to men and made a mockery of the nation's claim to be a community of equals.[1] Women rebelled particularly against their exclusion from the central mechanism of self-governance in a democracy: the right to vote. After winning a series of victories in the states, the suffrage campaign achieved its final success when the Nineteenth Amendment to the Constitution was ratified in 1920. Over time the right to vote became a reality for all women, as poll taxes and other racial restrictions were eliminated, and today women exercise the franchise on an equal footing with men. But in the years since women won the vote, Americans seem to have lost track of the revolutionary potential suffrage held for those who labored long, hard years for its enactment. The struggle for women's legal rights has continued almost unabated through the decades since the suffrage victory, but rarely, if ever, has the monumental achievement of the Nineteenth Amendment been cited as a constitutional support for women's claim to full equality.

The goal of this Note is to resurrect the broader purposes of the heroic suffrage campaign by arguing that the Nineteenth Amendment can and should be recognized as an affirmation of women's constitutional equality. My project is necessarily limited to making a provocative suggestion rather than establishing a constitutional fact. Full exploration of the themes exposed here will require sustained scholarly attention to the rich historical record of the campaign for the Nineteenth Amendment and the state suffrage enactments that preceded it, and a willingness to interpret that record in light of today's deeper understanding of the dynamics and persistence of gender hierarchy. Contemporary feminists often try to fit women's interests into a constitutional

---

1. 1 HISTORY OF WOMAN SUFFRAGE 16 (Elizabeth Cady Stanton et al. eds., AYER Co. 1985) (1881) ("[W]oman readily perceives the anomalous position she occupies in a republic . . . where the natural rights of all citizens have been exhaustively discussed, and repeatedly declared equal."). The *History of Woman Suffrage* comprises six volumes published between 1881 and 1922, while the suffrage campaign was being waged. Three leaders of the movement, Elizabeth Cady Stanton, Susan B. Anthony, and Matilda Joslyn Gage, edited the first three volumes.

framework that was built without women's active participation. My hope is to provoke consideration of how the Nineteenth Amendment—the only one to become part of our Constitution as a result of a mass movement for women's empowerment—might further promote women's equality.

The argument presented here was prompted by the contrasting interpretations of the significance of suffrage that emerged as state courts in the early twentieth century considered whether women's new status as voters qualified them for jury service. This question arose most vividly in states where women's common-law disqualification from jury duty[2] clashed with state law provisions that drew jurors from "electors." My analysis of these cases uncovered two deeply divergent understandings of women's history that produced differing approaches to questions of women's rights.

Some courts espoused a narrow view of the suffrage right which led them to hold that female electors could not be jurors. This "incremental" interpretation of suffrage was grounded in the assumption that women's legal status was fundamentally different from that of men, and that women possessed only those specific rights, responsibilities, and protections that men chose to grant them. A decision to extend to women any new right, such as suffrage, had no general effect on women's legal status; the new right was carefully limited to its terms. The incremental understanding of suffrage is consistent with the narrow and orthodox meaning attributed to the Nineteenth Amendment today—the Amendment simply gives women the right to vote.

Other courts held that female electors were eligible to be jurors. These courts acknowledged that women's previous exclusion from the franchise had been based on their assumed natural inferiority to men, but they interpreted the extension of suffrage to women as amounting to a rejection of that assumption. In this "emancipatory" view, the grant of suffrage represented the symbolic and substantive assertion of women's rightful place as men's equals, and as such had ramifications beyond the franchise.

The reevaluation of the relationship between suffrage and equality presented in this Note draws on several sources. Part I describes the early feminist argument for suffrage as a fundamental right of equal citizens in a democracy. The suggestion made here is that the "original intent" of these citizen framers of the Nineteenth Amendment—that is, their goal of equality for women—should be considered when interpreting that enactment. Part II focuses on two cases discussing jury service as a citizen's right. These cases,

---

2. Discussing eligibility for jury service, Blackstone referred to the requirement that the jury be composed of "*liber et legalis homo*," and then clarified: "Under the word *homo* also, though a name common to both sexes, the female is however excluded, *propter defectum sexus* . . . ." 3 WILLIAM BLACKSTONE, COMMENTARIES *362. *Propter defectum sexus* means on account of defect of sex. *See* BLACK'S LAW DICTIONARY 1220 (6th ed. 1990).

Strauder v. West Virginia[3] and *Neal v. Delaware*,[4] were important precedents to the woman juror cases because they show how black men's jury rights were intertwined with their citizenship and suffrage rights under the Fourteenth and Fifteenth Amendments. Part III presents cases representative of the "incremental" and "emancipatory" conceptions of women's suffrage, and shows how the emancipatory interpretation made a surprise appearance in the Supreme Court's opinion in *Adkins v. Children's Hospital*,[5] a 1923 labor law case. Part IV argues that we can achieve a better understanding of the Nineteenth Amendment by evaluating the contrasting views of women's history that support the incremental and emancipatory interpretations of suffrage. This Part evaluates the relative merits of those views, and discusses the continuing movement for women's rights, to conclude that the Nineteenth Amendment is most appropriately comprehended as a statement about women's equality beyond the voting booth.

The crux of my argument is that early interpretations of the meaning of suffrage to women's equality offer clues about the constitutional significance of the Nineteenth Amendment, clues we should evaluate in light of their conceptual underpinnings. From this angle, we can see that the expansive, "emancipatory" reading of the Suffrage Amendment is consistent not only with the egalitarian impetus that drove the suffrage movement, but also with the view of women's history that is embodied by our national experience in the decades since women's suffrage was won. The vision of emancipation from the legacy of sex discrimination continues to animate the women's movement in the United States and all over the world. The durable vitality of this broad vision argues for continued recourse to it as we seek a deeper understanding of what the Nineteenth Amendment means for women's equality.

I. VOTING AND EQUALITY

The *Declaration of Sentiments* adopted at the founding event of the American movement for women's equality, the 1848 Woman's Rights Convention in Seneca Falls, New York, shows that from the start, a belief in sex equality drove the feminist campaign to win the vote. The *Declaration*, which paraphrased the *Declaration of Independence*, proclaimed, "We hold these truths to be self-evident: that all men and women are created equal," and listed as the first proof of men's "tyranny" over women, "He has never permitted her to exercise her inalienable right to the elective franchise."[6] To feminist minds, women's inability to vote was a central feature of their oppression by men: "Having deprived her of this first right of a citizen, the

---

3. 100 U.S. 303 (1880).
4. 103 U.S. 370 (1881).
5. 261 U.S. 525 (1923).
6. DECLARATION OF SENTIMENTS (1848), *reprinted in* STANTON, *supra* note 1, at 70.

elective franchise, thereby leaving her without representation in the halls of legislation, he has oppressed her on all sides."[7]

Women's advocates pressed for the vote not only as a means to improve women's lives, but also because it would symbolize recognition of women's "equal personal rights and equal political privileges with all other citizens."[8] As the first right of a citizen, suffrage *meant* citizenship;[9] it was the very substance of self-government.[10] Suffragists thus responded eagerly when Francis Minor, a St. Louis lawyer and husband of Virginia Minor, a Missouri suffrage leader, suggested in 1869 that the newly ratified Fourteenth Amendment's guarantee of citizenship[11] offered women a new basis for asserting the right to vote.[12] The appeal of this idea was evident. In Francis Minor's words, "We no longer beat the air—no longer assume merely the attitude of petitioners. We claim a right, based on citizenship."[13]

This equal citizenship claim to the vote was put to the test when Virginia Minor's suit against the voting registrar of St. Louis for refusing her registration reached the Supreme Court in 1875. The result, *Minor v. Happersett*,[14] was devastating. A unanimous Court declared that voting had nothing to do with the rights of national citizenship protected by the Fourteenth Amendment. The Court cited state law limitations on voting rights[15] to hold that voting could not derive from national citizenship because states, not the nation, created voters.[16] According to the Justices, the Fourteenth Amendment itself argued against Virginia Minor. Section 2 of the Amendment penalizes

---

7. *Id.*

8. 2 ELIZABETH CADY STANTON ET AL., HISTORY OF WOMAN SUFFRAGE 747 (AYER Co. 1985) (1882).

9. *See, e.g.*, Percy L. Edwards, *Constitutional Obligations and Woman's Citizenship*, 75 CENTRAL L.J. 244, 246 (1912) (arguing that suffrage carries with it additional responsibilities and that suffrage thus "confer[s] upon women equal political standing with men of full citizenship"); Edward T. Taylor, *Equal Suffrage*, 19 CASE & COMMENT 301, 306 (1912) (personal freedom requires the "fullest rights of citizenship," including the right to vote).

10. *See, e.g.*, STANTON, *supra* note 1, at 15 ("Woman's political equality with man is the legitimate outgrowth of the fundamental principles of our Government . . . ."); Crystal E. Benedict, *Political Recognition of Women the Next Step in the Development of Democracy*, 19 CASE & COMMENT 327, 330 (1912) (referring to women's suffrage as an "inevitable step towards the fulfillment of democracy"); Charles H. Davis, *Shall Virginia Ratify the Federal Suffrage Amendment?*, 5 VA. L. REG. (n.s.) 354, 356 (1919) ("If our government can only derive its just powers from the consent of the governed, should not the women, equally with the men, give their consent through the ballot?"); Frederick Douglass, *The Rights of Women*, *reprinted in* STANTON, *supra* at 75.

11. "All persons born or naturalized in the United States . . . are citizens of the United States . . . . No State shall make or enforce any law which shall abridge the privileges or immunities of citizens of the United States." U.S. CONST. amend. XIV, § 1.

12. Minor made this suggestion in a letter to a suffragist newspaper, *The Revolution*. STANTON, *supra* note 8, at 407-08.

13. *Id.* at 408.

14. 88 U.S. (21 Wall.) 162 (1875). Susan B. Anthony was among the many women whose attempts to vote created test cases. The federal prosecution of Anthony for voting is recounted in STANTON, *supra* note 8, at 648-98. The election inspectors who accepted Anthony's vote were jailed for failing to pay fines assessed against them until being pardoned by President Grant. *Id.* at 714-15.

15. *Minor*, 88 U.S. at 172-73.

16. *Id.* at 170-71.

states that deny male inhabitants the right to vote,[17] and the Court asked, "[I]f suffrage was necessarily one of the absolute rights of citizenship, why confine the operation of the limitation to male inhabitants?"[18]

In an earlier time, when the national government was conceived as the creature of the states that constituted it,[19] the Court's reliance on states as the sole source of the suffrage right might have had some merit. The Fourteenth Amendment, however, created a new relationship between the people and their national government. It made them "citizens of the United States" with "privileges and immunities" that flowed from that citizenship, and guaranteed to them "equal protection of the laws."[20] With national citizenship established by Section 1, and a penalty against states that abridged males' "*right* to vote" in Section 2, the Fourteenth Amendment as a whole undermined the Court's position that national citizenship and suffrage were wholly unrelated. Instead, the structure of the Amendment suggested that suffrage was a right of national citizenship.[21]

The Supreme Court's decision in *Minor v. Happersett* ignored a deeper problem. As a matter of positive law, the Court's statement that citizenship and suffrage were not coextensive was historically accurate.[22] However, the Justices failed to grapple with the contradiction inherent in a democracy that legislated broad restrictions on the right to vote. This contradiction becomes apparent with the realization that underlying the very existence of an elected legislature is the presumption that at least some people are *entitled* to vote to

---

17. Section 2 reads:

Representatives [in Congress] shall be apportioned among the several States according to their respective numbers . . . . But when the right to vote at any election . . . is denied to any of the male inhabitants of such State, being twenty-one years of age, and citizens of the United States, or in any way abridged . . . the basis of representation therein shall be reduced in the proportion which the number of such male citizens shall bear to the whole number of male citizens twenty-one years of age in such State.

U.S. CONST. amend. XIV, § 2.

18. *Minor*, 88 U.S. at 174. This constitutional argument against women's suffrage realized the worst fears of those feminists who had opposed ratification of the Fourteenth Amendment precisely because of the cited clause of Section 2, which had introduced the word "male" into the Constitution. The bitter conflict over the Fourteenth Amendment that arose between suffragists and their former colleagues in the abolition movement, many of whom also supported women's suffrage, is recounted from its feminist protagonists' perspective in STANTON, *supra* note 8, at 313-16; *see also* Nina Morais, Note, *Sex Discrimination and the Fourteenth Amendment: Lost History*, 97 YALE L.J. 1153, 1155-58 (1988).

19. *See* LAURENCE H. TRIBE, AMERICAN CONSTITUTIONAL LAW 298-300 (2d ed. 1988) (discussing doctrine of enumerated powers, whereby states ceded to national government only those powers enumerated in the Constitution, while retaining all other powers of government); THE FEDERALIST NO. 39, at 241-45 (James Madison) (Clinton Rossiter ed., 1961) (acknowledging mixture of federal and national traits in government envisaged by Constitution, but arguing that role of states in its ratification, and limitation of federal power to "certain enumerated objects only," safeguard state sovereignty within federal structure).

20. U.S. CONST. amend. XIV, § 1.

21. *See* ELEANOR FLEXNER, CENTURY OF STRUGGLE: THE WOMAN'S RIGHTS MOVEMENT IN THE UNITED STATES 146 (rev. ed. 1975) (stating that the second section of the Fourteenth Amendment "was designed to insure the new freedmen the vote").

22. *But see* GORDON S. WOOD, THE CREATION OF THE AMERICAN REPUBLIC, 1776-1787, at 169 (1969) (attributing to Thomas Jefferson the view that "'the right of suffrage' was one with 'the rights of a citizen'").

form that legislature, an entitlement that necessarily exists not by legislative enactment, but as a pre-political right. The powerful minority that restricted the right to vote to itself—propertied white men—did so not because its members doubted that voting was the foundation of self-government,[23] but because they viewed the majority of the people as incapable of self-governance.[24] A *right* to vote was thus inherent in the very formation of a republican government, and it would seem that the new relationship between the nation's people and the national government that was put in place by the Fourteenth Amendment's declaration of equal national citizenship would give rise to an equal right to vote based in national citizenship[25] and enforceable against state governments.

Even while denying Virginia Minor the right to vote, the Court affirmed that women were unquestionably citizens of the nation.[26] But theirs was a citizenship without substance. *Minor* made it clear that women could not simply claim equal rights under the Fourteenth Amendment.[27] Rather, they

---

23. Wood shows how two innovations in political theory placed suffrage at the very center of the American system of representative democracy. *Id.* at 162-70. First, "The American legislatures . . . were no longer to be merely adjuncts or checks to magisterial power, but were in fact to be the government—a revolutionary transformation of political authority . . . ." *Id.* at 163. Second, the legislatures were legitimate only to the extent that they represented the people, being elected by them and exercising power on their behalf: "If the government be free, the right of representation must be the basis of it; the preservation of which sacred right, ought to be the grand object and end of all government." *Id.* at 164. These developments set "the right to vote and the electoral process in general . . . on a path to becoming identified in American thought with the very essence of American democracy." *Id.* at 168. *Cf.* THE FEDERALIST NO. 39, at 241 (James Madison) (Clinton Rossiter ed., 1961) ("It is *essential* to such a [republican] government that it be derived from the great body of the society, not from an inconsiderable proportion or a favored class of it . . . . It is *sufficient* for such a government that the persons administering it be appointed, either directly or indirectly, by the people . . . .").

24. *See* WOOD, *supra* note 22, at 168 (quoting characterizations of men who lacked property as "under the power of their superiors" and of "a base, degenerate, servile temper of mind" to explain why "[f]ew in 1776 considered [suffrage] qualifications a denial of the embodiment of democracy in the constitution"). Wood does not discuss why women could not vote, but a later view suggests that they, too, might have been presumed incapable of exercising the franchise intelligently: "I know very well that prejudices against female voting have descended legitimately to us from the Old World; yea, more than anything else, from common law which we lawyers have all studied as the first element in jurisprudence. That system of law really sank the female to total contempt and insignificance, almost annihilated her from the face of the earth. It made her responsible for nothing." CONG. GLOBE, 39th Cong., 2d Sess. 62 (1866) (statement of Sen. Wade). *Cf.* People *ex rel.* Denny v. Traeger, 22 N.E.2d 679 (Ill. 1939):

> Until within recent times woman was not thought to be on a parity with man and it was considered that she did not possess those qualitative attributes that made her capable of exercising the right of suffrage or of rendering jury service. She was excluded from jury service on the false theory of economic, sociological and legalistic inferiority . . . .

Id. at 681.

25. As a contemporary critic of *Minor v. Happersett* wrote, "The court tells us in its opinion in this case, that 'there cannot be a nation without a people'—but it seems there may be a nation without voters!" *Woman Suffrage in its Legal Aspect*, 3 CENTRAL L.J. 51, 52 (1876).

26. *Minor*, 88 U.S. at 169. ("[W]omen have always been considered as citizens the same as men").

27. Political and congressional debate over the Fourteenth Amendment suggests that the words "persons" and "citizens" were chosen for its text by a Congress that was highly aware of women's rights claims. Morais, *supra* note 18, at 1155-63. Morais argues that in this context of advocacy for women's rights, the use of gender-neutral terms in Section 1, together with the use of "male" in Section 2, indicates that "[t]he framers were willing to allow the Fourteenth Amendment to reach questions of women's rights, short of suffrage." *id.* at 1160. Such claims were, however, fruitless: "These courts invariably ruled against women plaintiffs." *Id.* at 1167.

would have to force their way into the Constitution, and the suffrage amendment would be their vehicle.[28]

Minor refocused the mobilization already underway to enact a suffrage amendment that would admit women to the "constitutional community."[29] The demand for the vote took women's struggle for equality to a new level. Suffrage went beyond "asking to have certain wrongs redressed."[30] Now the American woman "demanded that the Constitutions—State and National—be so amended as to give her a voice in the laws, a choice in the rulers, and protection in the exercise of her rights as a citizen of the United States."[31] The suffragists gradually attained their goal, beginning with scattered victories in the western states[32] and culminating in the ratification of the Nineteenth Amendment to the Constitution on August 26, 1920.[33] That Amendment proclaims: "The right of citizens of the United States to vote shall not be denied or abridged by the United States or by any State on account of sex."

The issue of women's right to vote at last resolved,[34] a new question arose. Would this monumental accomplishment, undertaken to end "the prolonged slavery of woman,"[35] reverberate beyond the voting booth? No

---

28. In a speech delivered soon after the *Minor* opinion was issued, Matilda Joslyn Gage said, "I know something of the opinion of the women of the Nation, and I know they intend to be recognized as citizens secured in the exercise of all the powers and rights of citizens. If this security has not come under the XIV. Amendment, it must come under a XVI., for woman intends to possess 'equal personal rights and equal political privileges with all other citizens.'" STANTON, *supra* note 8, at 742, 747. The broad impact of a Suffrage Amendment foreseen in this statement rests, I think, on the early feminists' view that legal recognition of women's equality was just that—the *recognition* of women's inherently equal status. Feminists were not asking that women given rights. They believed women possessed rights equal to those of men, but were forced by the nation's heritage to seek legal acknowledgment of that equality. From this standpoint, one might think that recognizing equal voting rights—meaning, as that did, equal citizenship—would sufficiently demonstrate women's equality in all aspects of the law.

29. This phrase appears in OWEN M. FISS, TROUBLED BEGINNINGS OF THE MODERN STATE: 1888-1910, at 176-79 (1993).

30. STANTON, *supra* note 1, at 15. For an account of earlier efforts to improve various aspects of women's condition see FLEXNER, *supra* note 21, at 3-102.

31. STANTON, *supra* note 1, at 16. The broader scope of the suffrage demand invited fresh resistance. "[P]olitical rights, involving in their last results equality everywhere, roused all the antagonism of a dominant power, against the self-assertion of a class hitherto subservient. Men saw that with political equality for woman, they could no longer keep her in social subordination . . . ." *Id.*

32. The first American women were enfranchised by the legislature of Wyoming Territory. Act of Dec. 10, 1869, ch. 31, 1869 Wyo. [Terr.] Sess. Laws 371. Following Wyoming were Utah Territory, Act of Feb. 12, 1870, 1870 Utah [Terr.] Laws 8; Washington Territory, Act of Nov. 23, 1883, 1883 Wash. [Terr.] Laws 39-40; and Colorado, Act of Apr. 7, 1893, ch. 83, § 1, 1893 Colo. Sess. Laws 256. The suffrage movement's great success "on western soil" may have been because the shared rigors of frontier life eased the way for men to perceive women as their legal equals. Edwards, *supra* note 9, at 244; *see also* FLEXNER, *supra* note 21, at 159-66.

33. 41 Stat. 1823 (1920) (Secretary of State's certification that Nineteenth Amendment ratified).

34. Resolved formally, that is. Efforts to secure full enforcement of voting rights for black women and other women of color began with a constitutional amendment that abolished poll taxes, U.S. CONST. amend. XXIV, and continued with passage of the Voting Rights Act of 1965, 42 U.S.C. §§ 1971, 1973 (1988).

35. STANTON, *supra* note 1, at 13. The quoted phrase reflects the equality basis of the women's suffrage demand. Suffragists also claimed that women's (presumed) moral virtue—that is, women's difference from men—specially qualified them to vote. Over time, the emphasis shifted back and forth between these equality-based and difference-based arguments for women's suffrage. *See* NANCY F. COTT, THE GROUNDING OF MODERN FEMINISM 16-30 (1987); Ellen C. DuBois, *Outgrowing the Compact of the*

doubt its citizen framers intended such a result. They saw suffrage as a symbol of women's legal and political equality.[36] A purely structural reading of the Constitution could lead to the same conclusion. The Nineteenth Amendment nullified the only sex-based distinction in the text of the Constitution, Section 2 of the Fourteenth Amendment,[37] arguably giving rise to an inference that in the absence of male-specific rights, men and women would have equal rights.[38] As it happened, virtually the only judicial pronouncements on the scope of women's new suffrage right arose in the woman juror cases. Understanding these decisions requires some discussion of how jury service, like voting, symbolizes citizenship.

II. JURY DUTY AND CITIZENSHIP

The woman juror cases examined in this Note are state court decisions about whether women's ineligibility for jury service was altered by their new status as voters.[39] At first blush, jury service cases may appear to be a poor source of insight into the meaning of women's suffrage laws. To the modern mind, jury duty may evoke little more than the obligation to spend long hours in shabby court facilities, waiting for something to happen. In this light, serving as a juror scarcely seems to be a civil right. The characterization of

---

Fathers: Equal Rights, Woman Suffrage, and the United States Constitution, 1820-1878, 74 J. AM. HIST. 836 (1987).

36. *See supra* text accompanying notes 8-13.

37. *See supra* notes 17-18 and accompanying text.

38. Reading the Nineteenth Amendment's alteration of the Fourteenth Amendment in this manner, so that their combined force is to ensure constitutional equality for women, is an exercise in "synthetic interpretation" of the Constitution. *See* Bruce Ackerman, *Constitutional Politics/Constitutional Law,* 99 YALE L.J. 453, 459 (1989). The thought can also be expressed in constitutional arithmetic: The Fourteenth plus the Nineteenth Amendments should protect against discrimination on the basis of sex to the same extent that the Fourteenth plus the Fifteenth Amendments protect against discrimination on the basis of race. *Cf.* Akhil Reed Amar, *The Bill of Rights as a Constitution,* 100 YALE L.J. 1131, 1202-03 (1991) (arguing that Ackerman's concept of synthesis supports reading Nineteenth Amendment together with Second Amendment to abolish women's exclusion from military and jury service).

One argument against recognizing the Nineteenth Amendment as a statement of women's constitutional equality might be that its most ardent supporters proposed the Equal Rights Amendment almost immediately after the Suffrage Amendment was ratified. *See* COTT, *supra* note 35, at 125 (ERA, backed by National Women's Party, introduced in Congress in 1923). It seems plausible, however, that feminists read Minor v. Happersett, 88 U.S. (14 Wall.) 162 (1875), as a clear message that women could not rely upon the Fourteenth Amendment to secure any right a legislature would deny. In this context an Equal Rights Amendment might have seemed prudent even if theoretically unnecessary. As it turned out, no sex-discriminatory statute was held to violate the Equal Protection Clause of the Fourteenth Amendment until the case of Reed v. Reed, 404 U.S. 71 (1971).

39. On women's common-law disqualification from jury service see BLACKSTONE, *supra* note 2. This Note considers female jury service cases only for their interpretations of suffrage. Accordingly, I do not discuss the constitutionality *per se* of excluding women from juries. *See* Taylor v. Louisiana, 419 U.S. 522 (1975) (holding that defendant's Sixth Amendment right to jury drawn from cross-section of community invalidates requirement that women, but not men, specially register for jury service, overruling Hoyt v. Florida, 368 U.S. 57 (1961) (holding special registration scheme does not violate women's Fourteenth Amendment rights)).

jury duty as a right fades further given our general understanding that the jury's primary function is to protect the rights of the accused.

The female juror cases are significant, however, because the jury stands not only as a protection for defendants, but more fundamentally as a mechanism for community self-governance. The institution of the jury expresses a mutual faith among citizens who assign to each other a function otherwise reserved to professional judges and lawmakers: the power to determine wrongs, to remedy them, and to decide each others' fates. The expression "a jury of one's peers" imbues jury service with a dignitary value. Conversely, when certain members of society are barred from jury service, not because of their duties to the community but because of who they are, they are denied the full measure of trust and respect accorded to equal citizens.[40] Excluding women from jury service also kept them from having a voice in deciding what the law should be, since it was the jury that defined the bounds of "reasonable" behavior and brought community morality to bear on the law.

The significance of jury duty as a right of citizenship is highlighted in two cases that are also important as precedents for the female jury cases. In the first of these, *Strauder v. West Virginia*,[41] the Supreme Court held that a state denied a black defendant equal protection of the law by "compelling [him] to submit to a trial for his life by a jury drawn from a panel from which the State has expressly excluded every man of his race, because of color alone."[42] According to the Court, keeping blacks off Strauder's jury panel violated not only his rights as a criminal defendant, but also a broader principle of equality. The exclusion of black men from the jury pool was "practically a brand upon them, affixed by the law, an assertion of their inferiority, and a stimulant to that race prejudice which is an impediment to securing to individuals of the race that equal justice which the law aims to secure to all others."[43] The racial barrier also denied blacks the right "to participate in the administration of the law, as jurors."[44] As one commentator noted, the Court's decision moved "in the direction . . . of an increasing emphasis upon the upholding of the dignity and equality, the legal status, of the negro race."[45]

It might appear that the principle of equality and fairness that animated the holding in *Strauder* would guarantee women's equal participation on juries based on the Fourteenth Amendment alone, without any consideration of suffrage, at least in cases involving female defendants. Yet *Strauder* did not

---

40. *See* Powers v. Ohio, 111 S. Ct. 1364, 1366 (1991) (holding that race-based jury selection violates prospective jurors' equal protection rights and "offends the dignity of persons and the integrity of the courts"); Amar, *supra* note 38, at 1187-89 (discussing jury as a form of political participation).

41. 100 U.S. 303 (1880).

42. *Id.* at 309.

43. *Id.* at 308.

44. *Id.*

45. Blanche Crozier, *Constitutionality of Discrimination Based on Sex*, 15 B.U. L. REV. 723, 729 (1935).

provide women any such guarantee; rather, the Court stated in dicta that a state "may confine the selection [of jurors] to males,"[46] and repeated the contention, made in its earlier Fourteenth Amendment jurisprudence, that the Amendment was addressed solely to race discrimination.[47] Thus with *Strauder*, the Court established that jury service was an important civil right whose denial breached the Fourteenth Amendment's guarantee of equal citizenship, even while stating baldly that excluding women from juries would not be constitutionally improper. One year later, however, in *Neal v. Delaware*,[48] the Court handed down a decision that clearly supported the proposition that suffrage conferred eligibility for jury service on women in states where electors comprised the jury pool.

The plaintiff in *Neal v. Delaware* was, like Strauder, a black man tried by a jury from which blacks had been excluded. In Neal's case, local officials had deliberately excluded blacks from the jury pool, although no statute directed them to do so. The central holding of *Neal* was that *Strauder*'s equal protection principle applied whether blacks were excluded from juries by official action or by state law. But to reach this issue, the Court dealt with a preliminary consideration of great importance for the woman juror cases: whether the Fifteenth Amendment, by making black men electors, had automatically made them eligible for jury service. Under Delaware law all persons qualified to vote could serve as jurors,[49] and under the Fifteenth Amendment, black men were qualified to vote. The state constitution, however, still defined "electors" as "white male citizens."[50] This language raised a question. Should jurors be drawn from that class of people who were "electors" when the juror qualifications were established—that is, white men—or were all current electors in the jury pool? The Court resolved this issue by writing that since the Fifteenth Amendment made black men electors "the statute which prescribed the qualifications of jurors was, itself, enlarged in its operation, so as to embrace all who by the State Constitution, as modified by the supreme law of the land, were qualified to vote."[51]

Neal v. Delaware would seem to have ensured the eligibility of newly enfranchised women for jury service in states that drew jurors from electors,

---

46. *Strauder*, 100 U.S. at 310.

47. *Id.* at 306-08. The Court relied on its decision in the Slaughter-House Cases, 83 U.S. (16 Wall.) 36, 81 (1873) ("We doubt very much whether any action of a State not directed by way of discrimination against the negroes as a class . . . will ever be held to come within the purview of [the Fourteenth Amendment].") In *Strauder*, the Court broadened its definition of race discrimination by stating that the Fourteenth Amendment would be violated by bars to jury service for white men or "naturalized Celtic Irishmen," 100 U.S. at 307, but did not extend its vision to place women of any race under the Amendment's protection.

48. 103 U.S. 370 (1881).

49. *Id.* at 388. Jurors were also required to be "sober" and "judicious." *Id.*

50. *Id.* at 387-88.

51. *Id.* at 389. This principle—that where jurors are drawn from electors, every newly qualified elector is automatically qualified for jury service—was undisputed in *Neal*. The State of Delaware conceded the point, *id.* at 383, as did those who dissented from the Court's opinion, *id.* at 400.

especially once the Nineteenth Amendment was ratified. The text of that Amendment exactly tracked the Fifteenth Amendment, substituting "sex" for "race, color, or previous condition of servitude" as the prohibited criterion for denial of the franchise. If a black (male) suffrage amendment "enlarged the operation" of state jury qualification statutes to include black men, a women's suffrage amendment should work the same enlargement to include women of all races. *Strauder* spoke to the importance of jury service for equal citizenship, and *Neal* affirmed that black men's suffrage had meaning beyond simply voting. It remained to be seen how courts would apply these cases when it came time to interpret the meaning of women's suffrage.

III. TWO MEANINGS OF SUFFRAGE

Women's jury service was the subject of a number of cases decided in the decades following *Neal v. Delaware.* Had courts simply followed *Neal*, and recognized that where jurors were drawn from electors, suffrage made women eligible for jury service, these opinions would hold little interest. But few courts were content simply to apply *Neal*'s straightforward logic; instead, they treated the prospect of female jurors as a complex issue. Some of the cases were decided with little or no discussion of women's aspirations to equality, and many ignored altogether the tie between jury duty and citizenship established by *Strauder* and *Neal.* In other cases, though, courts delved into these issues and developed the emancipatory and incremental interpretations of suffrage to guide their decisions on jury service. The discussion that follows is not intended to establish either of these meanings as the definitive interpretation of the Nineteenth Amendment, but rather to show that, within the limited realm of the jury service issue, judges expressed a variety of opinions on the meaning of suffrage. In this analysis, the female juror cases raise the possibility that the Nineteenth Amendment can be interpreted as an enactment for women's equality.

A. *The Emancipatory Meaning of Suffrage*

1. *State Court Cases*

Parus v. District Court,[52] decided by the Nevada Supreme Court in 1918, provides the fullest elaboration of a court's reliance on a particular understanding of women's history to support an emancipatory interpretation of suffrage. The petitioner in *Parus* challenged the validity of his indictment because women served on the grand jury that rendered it. Nevada law made

---

52. 174 P. 706 (Nev. 1918).

all qualified electors jurors,[53] and the state constitution recognized women's right to vote,[54] so the apparently simple question before the court was whether women were qualified as jurors, now that they were electors.

The Nevada court first summarized the holding of *Neal v. Delaware*[55] and left the reader to draw the obvious conclusion: just as the Fifteenth Amendment qualified black men as electors and therefore jurors, the Nineteenth Amendment qualified women as electors and thus jurors.[56]

The majority had to go beyond *Neal* and *Strauder* to meet a dissenter's contention, grounded in Nevada precedent, that because the jury at common law was composed of men, "our constitutional convention provided for a grand jury of *men* as clearly as though the Constitution itself had used the word 'men.' The word 'men' is written into the Constitution by operation of law."[57] The majority's response pointed out that Nevada had already cast aside the property requirement for jurors that existed at common law and had substituted a single criterion for jurors: qualified electorship.[58] The court continued:

> It may be urged that at the time of the framing of our organic law, qualified electorship was not considered as being attributable to women. But time has wrought the unanticipated change, and by amendment to our Constitution women have been clothed with the qualification of electorship, and by this change the female citizens of the state have automatically become members of the class from which class alone grand jurors may be drawn, and which classification . . . constitutes the only circumscription . . . . fixing the citizenry from which grand jurors might be in the first instance selected.[59]

The court seems to have sensed that this exercise in logic would not fully satisfy its detractors, and that it must confront the crucial issue: what justified a departure from women's jury disqualification at common law?[60] The answer, according to the court, was that the old rule for women was a thing of the past:

> Blackstone tells us that the term "homo," though applicable to both sexes, was not regarded in the common law, applicable to the

---

53. *Id.* at 707.
54. *Id.* at 708.
55. 103 U.S. 370 (1881).
56. *Parus*, 174 P. at 708.
57. *Id.* at 713 (Coleman, J., dissenting). The precedents were about juries generally, not women's eligibility for them.
58. *Id.* at 708. Nevada did not admit all electors to jury service; every elector was qualified "who has sufficient knowledge of the English language, and who has not been convicted of treason, felony, or other infamous crime, and who is not rendered incapable by reason of physical or mental infirmity." *Id.* at 707.
59. *Id.* at 708-09.
60. *See* BLACKSTONE, *supra* note 2 (discussing common-law disqualification of women).

selection of grand jurors, as embracing the female. Woman, he says, was excluded *propter defectum sexus* . . . . When the people of this state approved and ratified the constitutional amendment making women qualified electors of the state, it is to be presumed that such ratification carried with it a declaration that the right of electorship thus conferred carried with it all of the rights, duties, privileges, and immunities belonging to electors; and one of the rights, one of the duties, and one of the privileges belonging to this class was declared by the organic law to be grand jury service. Nor can we with any degree of logical force exclude women from this class upon the basis established by Blackstone, *propter defectum sexus*, because we have eliminated the spirit of this term from our consideration of womankind in modern political and legal life. Woman's sphere under the common law was a circumscribed one. By modern law and custom she has demanded and taken a place in modern institutions as a factor equal to man.[61]

Speaking of the grand jury's investigatory powers, the judges added:

Can we reasonably say that although woman, on whom has been conferred the right of electorship, the right to enjoy public office, the right to own and control property, and on whom has been imposed the burden of taxation in a common equality with men, is nevertheless deprived of the privilege of sitting as a member of an inquisitorial body, the power, scope of inquiry, and significance of which affects every department of life in which she, as a citizen and elector, is interested and of which she is a component part? The spirit of the constitutional amendment silences such an assertion.[62]

The *Parus* court adopted what I call the emancipatory view of the meaning of suffrage within the context of women's history. In general terms, this view characterized the past as oppressive to women, credited the trend toward equality with bringing about a transformative legal act, and urged that the transformative act be given broad effect to further promote women's equality. According to the *Parus* court, women suffered from oppression in the past; their sphere was "circumscribed." A broad movement for women's equality had taken hold—"she has demanded and taken a place . . . as a factor equal to man"—and the "spirit" of *propter defectum sexus*[63] had been eliminated from "modern political and legal life." The grant of suffrage culminated that movement—"time has wrought the unanticipated change"—and suffrage stood for a transformation in women's status as a result: "[I]t is to be presumed that

---

61. *Parus*, 174 P. at 709.
62. *Id.*
63. See *supra* note 2 for a definition of *propter defectum sexus*.

such ratification carried with it . . . all of the rights, privileges, and immunities belonging to electors."[64]

The uses of the word "spirit" in this opinion suggest that the *Parus* court was not only construing the state constitution, but also seeking to identify and acknowledge the social forces and deeper principles that shape the law. The court recognized that *propter defectum sexus* represented the common law stance toward women, and stated emphatically that the people had rejected this attitude in their "consideration of womankind in modern political and legal life."[65] The court found the tone of the new age in "[t]he spirit of the constitutional amendment" for women's suffrage; that spirit affirmed women's involvement in matters of governance, in "every department of life in which she, as a citizen and elector, is interested and of which she is a component part," and it "silence[d]" the notion that women had achieved their gains only to continue to be "deprived" of legal privileges not specifically granted.[66]

The *Parus* court's language was reminiscent of the opinion in *Rosencrantz v. Territory*,[67] a very early case that involved suffrage and women's eligibility for jury service. The *Rosencrantz* court held that a new statute on family relations, together with a women's suffrage law previously enacted, brought women within the class of "electors and householders" who were eligible for jury service. The opinion in *Rosencrantz* interpreted a family relations statute rather than a suffrage enactment. Yet I include it here because the court interpreted the statute by sketching out the same picture of women's history that would later support the emancipatory understanding of suffrage in the *Parus* case. The *Rosencrantz* court bemoaned the "harsh rule of the common law," in which a wife's "identity was largely lost in that of her husband."[68] It celebrated the family relations statute as "radical legislation . . . consonant with the spirit of the times," which gave husbands and wives "absolute equality before the law."[69] The court's emancipatory interpretation of a law apparently designed to improve women's property rights within marriage thus provided the basis for opening the courthouse to women as jurors.

A few years after *Parus*, the Michigan Supreme Court confronted the issue of women's eligibility for jury service with a bold demand: "What was the purpose and object of the people in adopting the constitutional amendment striking out the word 'male' from the Constitution? Was it not to do away with all distinction between men and women as to the right to vote, or as to being electors?"[70] The court treated its answer—that the people intended women to

---

64. *Parus*, 174 P. at 709.
65. *Id.*
66. *Id.*
67. 5 P. 305 (Wash. Terr. 1884), *overruled by* Harland v. Territory, 13 P. 453 (Wash. Terr. 1887).
68. *Id.* at 306.
69. *Id.*
70. People v. Barltz, 180 N.W. 423, 425 (Mich. 1920).

have all the rights of electors—as a foregone conclusion, but on closer inspection this opinion, *People v. Barltz*, shows that the court considered both the emancipatory and the incremental interpretations of suffrage, and chose the emancipatory view. The incremental view was represented by the court's reference to *Harland v. Territory*,[71] a Washington Territory case that had reversed *Rosencrantz*. In *Harland* the court had denied women's eligibility for jury service, stating that when "the people" had adopted women's suffrage they had intended to give women the vote and nothing more.[72] Rather than adopt the narrow reading of suffrage enunciated in *Harland*, the *Barltz* court cited and approved the liberal reading of suffrage found in *Rosencrantz*,[73] signaling its sympathy with the emancipatory view.

The *Barltz* opinion offers a more detailed discussion of another issue that divided the incremental and emancipatory outlooks on suffrage and women's history: whether the use of the word "men" in jury laws represented an intentional decision by the legislature to exclude women from jury service, and if so, whether such a decision should be honored even after women had been enfranchised. Several provisions in the Michigan state constitution referred to juries of "twelve men,"[74] and in an earlier decision the Michigan court had written, "This right was a trial by a jury of 12 men, good and true."[75] Whether "men" meant *men*[76] was critical to the outcome of *Barltz*. A literal reading of the word would void the claim that women could be jurors.

Deciding the meaning of "men" forced courts to choose between two competing explanations of why women were not men's legal equals. One possibility was that women had been intentionally excluded from juries, presumably based on some judgment about their lack of fitness.[77] On this understanding, legal distinctions between the sexes were not mere byproducts of a social structure that assigned women and men to separate spheres; instead, they had been deliberately created. In one court's words, "[T]he Legislature

---

71. 13 P. 453 (Wash. Terr. 1887).

72. The court wrote in *Harland*,

The change [to women jurors] is so marked, and the labor and responsibility which it imposes so onerous and burdensome, and so utterly unsuited to the physical constitution of females, that we ought not to depart from the old order without the most indubitable evidence that the legislature so intended.

Id. at 456.

73. *Barltz*, 180 N.W. at 425 ("We are aware that [*Rosencrantz*] has since been overruled by a divided court in *Harland v. Washington*, but the language of the Rosencrantz Case is so appropriate and the reasoning so clear that we are disposed to adopt it.").

74. *Id.* at 424, 425.

75. *Id.* at 424 (quoting McRae v. Grand Rapids, L. & D.R.R., 53 N.W. 561, 562 (Mich. 1892)). *McRae* did not concern women's eligibility for jury service.

76. One court rather colorfully phrased the issue as whether the masculine included the feminine, "as, for example, the word 'horse' at common law was held to include 'mare.'" People v. Lensen, 167 P. 406, 407 (Cal. 1917).

77. *See* Carol Weisbrod, *Images of the Woman Juror*, 9 HARV. WOMEN'S L.J. 59 (1986) (describing how supporters and opponents of women's jury service portrayed their competence as jurors).

ordained that jurors shall be men."[78] This view of the origin of women's legal inferiority underlay what I call the incremental view of suffrage. Its adherents recognized that a sex-based distinction in the law could be erased, but insisted this could happen only through an intentional decision to alter women's legal status. A suffrage amendment could open the voting booth to women, but it could not put them in the jury box because there had been no distinct decision to remove the legal barrier to their service.

Courts that declined to read "men" literally faced a more complex task. One court simply declared that "[s]ince the world began, in all writings concerning the human race, the word 'man' or 'men' has been used in a generic sense, or as representing the human race."[79] This response, however well-intentioned, was clearly inadequate because until the women's suffrage amendments, the literal meaning of "men" in elector and juror statutes was accurate—all voters and jurors *were* men. A more promising approach was to account for how a use of "men" that might once have been literal could, over time, have taken on a generic meaning. One possibility was to retrospectively read the literal use—which dismissed women from political and legal life—as an error. On this view it was quite appropriate that rectification of sex inequality in one area, suffrage, should suffice to correct the error in another, jury service.[80]

Faced with this question, the *Barltz* court cited a California case[81] that had rejected a "men means *men*" claim and approved female jurors. Citations to cases from other jurisdictions and a law dictionary supported the view that "[i]n some of its uses [man] is construed to mean 'all human beings, or any human being, whether male or female.'"[82] After quoting two dictionaries in which "a human being" appeared as the first definition of man,[83] the opinion concluded, "[I]n any view of the case which we are able to take . . . Miss

---

78. State v. Kelley, 229 P. 659, 661 (Idaho 1924).

79. Cleveland, Cin., Chi. and St. L. Ry. v. Wehmeier, 170 N.E. 27, 29 (Ohio 1929) (holding that use of "men" in jury statute did not exclude women).

80. The following passage, from an opinion upholding a statute that made women eligible for jury service against a claim that the law violated the constitutional right to trial by jury because that right guaranteed a common law "jury of twelve men," illustrates this view:

Women are now the peers of men politically, and there is no reason to question their eligibility upon constitutional grounds.

The fact that a common-law jury was defined to be a "jury of twelve men," etc., had its origin in the circumstance of the political servitude of women in the early days of juridical history so that they were not the "peers" of a man accused of crime. In the broad sense of the word they are now "freemen," and neither the Constitution nor the laws, when they use the term "men," except in rare instances, use it with reference to sex.

State v. Chase, 211 P. 920, 923 (Or. 1922). Other cases that rejected the literal definition of men include State v. Walker, 185 N.W. 619, 626 (Iowa 1921), and Browning v. State, 165 N.E. 566, 567 (Ohio 1929).

81. *Ex parte* Mana, 172 P. 986 (Cal. 1918), *quoted in* People v. Barltz, 180 N.W. 423, 426 (Mich. 1920).

82. *Barltz*, 180 N.W. at 426.

83. *Id.*

Gitzen . . . was a qualified juror under the Constitution and laws of this state."[84]

The *Barltz* judges asserted that the people's intent in enacting suffrage was to give women all the rights of electors, and declined to take literally earlier laws that spoke of jurors as men. While the opinion in *Barltz* lacked the ringing endorsement of women's new legal equality that marked the *Parus* decision, its conclusion that suffrage made women eligible for jury service seemed to rest on an understated sense that suffrage marked women's emancipation.[85]

2. *The* Adkins *Decision*

The most striking endorsement of suffrage as a symbol of women's emancipation from the inequality of the common law appeared in 1923 when the Supreme Court struck down a Washington, D.C. minimum wage law that applied only to women. The case, *Adkins v. Children's Hospital*,[86] was decided just three years after ratification of the Nineteenth Amendment.

Adkins is known today as one of the Court's liberty of contract decisions, which nullified various labor laws as infringements of the constitutional rights of employers and workers to negotiate the terms of employment freely.[87] Before *Adkins*, the Supreme Court had not applied the liberty of contract doctrine to labor laws that affected only women, giving priority instead to a perceived public interest in women's welfare founded on their capacity to bear children.[88] According to the Court, this interest justified otherwise impermissible legislative intrusions into the employment relationship.[89] The *Adkins* decision marked a sharp reversal in the Court's approach to female-specific labor laws, and the Court justified its move by endorsing an equality

---

84. *Id.* at 427.

85. Cases that arrived at decisions favorable to women jurors without considering issues of women's status include State v. Walker, 185 N.W. 619 (Iowa 1921), and Commonwealth v. Maxwell, 114 A. 825 (Pa. 1921). The *Walker* opinion cited Neal v. Delaware, 103 U.S. 370 (1881), to support its holding, but said that suffrage and jury duty were *not* related, and that states, if they so wished, could bar women from juries. *Walker*, 185 N.W. at 623.

86. 261 U.S. 525 (1923).

87. These decisions, including the most famous, *Lochner v. New York*, 198 U.S. 45 (1905), have been widely criticized as products of a conservative court that defended the interests of the wealthy against the rising power of the working class. *See* sources cited in TRIBE, *supra* note 19, at 566 n.44, 567 n.46. An alternative interpretation analyzes *Lochner* as the principled effort of a Court that believed government was a social contract authorized to pursue only limited ends. These Justices felt compelled to preserve the constitutional value of liberty, as they understood the meaning of that term, from intrusions by legislative majorities. FISS, *supra* note 29, at 157-65.

88. *See, e.g.*, Muller v. Oregon, 208 U.S. 412, 421 (1908) (stating that "as healthy mothers are essential to vigorous offspring, the physical well-being of woman becomes an object of public interest").

89. "Differentiated by these matters from the other sex, she is properly placed in a class by herself, and legislation for her protection may be sustained, even when like legislation is not necessary for men and could not be sustained." *Id.* at 422. For comment on the relation between such "public policy" arguments and women's legal status, see *infra* text accompanying notes 141-145.

for women that some would have described as paradoxical, if not downright perverse: women and men had an equal right to work without the protection (or as the Court saw it, the inhibition) of a minimum wage.

Whatever its merits as a labor law decision, the *Adkins* case presented a view of women's history that credited the suffrage amendment as a virtual declaration of women's equality—at least in most spheres:

> [T]he ancient inequality of the sexes, otherwise than physical, as suggested in the *Muller Case*, has continued "with diminishing intensity." In view of the great—not to say revolutionary—changes which have taken place since that utterance, in the contractual, political and civil status of women, culminating in the Nineteenth Amendment, it is not unreasonable to say that these differences have now come almost, if not quite, to the vanishing point. In this aspect of the matter, while the physical differences must be recognized in appropriate cases, and legislation fixing hours or conditions of work may properly take them into account, we cannot accept the doctrine that women of mature age, *sui juris*, require or may be subjected to restrictions upon their liberty of contract which could not lawfully be imposed in the case of men under similar circumstances. To do so would be to ignore all the implications to be drawn from the present day trend of legislation, as well as that of common thought and usage, by which woman is accorded emancipation from the old doctrine that she must be given special protection or be subjected to special restraint in her contractual and civil relationships.[90]

There are several points to be made about this passage. First, the Court evinced an unmistakably negative view of women's "ancient inequality." Entirely absent was any suggestion that women benefited from the "old doctrine." Instead, the Court described women as "subjected to restrictions" and "special restraint," and implied that insult was added to injury by failing to treat "women of mature age" as legal adults. Limitations in the realm of contractual, political and civil rights were rejected in favor of the "present day trend" of "emancipation." The Court indicated that its assessment of past and present was widely shared, by referring to it as "common thought and usage."

Second, the Court simultaneously espoused opposing views of whether this change had been a gradual transition or a radical transformation. Its quotation from the earlier *Muller* decision, which had approved a woman-only labor law, suggested continuity with the past: inequality was "diminishing" to "the vanishing point." But the Court also depicted a sharp break with what had gone before, calling the changes in the fifteen years since *Muller* not only "great" but "revolutionary." This sense of drastic change was enhanced by the

---

90. *Adkins*, 261 U.S. at 553.

Court's use of the word "emancipation," which connotes the single act by which the slave becomes free.

Also notable here was what might be called the penumbra of sex equality that emanated from the Nineteenth Amendment.[91] While the *Adkins* case was not about the Nineteenth Amendment, the Court's reference to it is remarkable. The Amendment appeared not only as a result, but as an engine of social change. Suffrage was the culmination of "revolutionary" developments that forced the Court to abandon a legal system that had treated women "[a]s minors, though not to the same extent,"[92] developments that led the Court to embrace women as the civil law equals of men. The importance of the Suffrage Amendment to the Court's analysis suggested a change of heart foreshadowed at the close of the earlier *Muller* opinion where the Court had written:

> We have not referred in this discussion to the denial of the elective franchise in the State of Oregon, for while it may disclose a lack of political equality in all things with her brother, that is not of itself decisive. The reason runs deeper, and rests in the inherent difference between the two sexes, and in the different functions in life which they perform.[93]

It almost seems that by denying any connection between suffrage and civil rights, the *Muller* Court had set in motion a mental process that eventually reached quite the opposite conclusion, embodied in the *Adkins* decision: suffrage had everything to do with equality.

The Supreme Court never went beyond the *Adkins* decision's tantalizing hint that the Nineteenth Amendment represented more for women than simply the right to vote. Exploration of that possibility took place only in the woman juror cases. None of these cases discussed *Adkins*—indeed, many predated that decision—yet *Adkins* is relevant to the effort to understand and evaluate the jury cases. *Adkins* distinguished between permissible laws concerned with protecting women's health, and unconstitutional restrictions on women's rights.[94] While the line between these categories was not necessarily

---

91. *See* Griswold v. Connecticut, 381 U.S. 479, 484 (1965) ("[S]pecific guarantees in the Bill of Rights have penumbras, formed by emanations from those guarantees that help give them life and substance.").

92. *Muller*, 208 U.S. at 421.

93. *Id.* at 423.

94. The *Adkins* Court's careful distinction between laws that violated women's equality and those that "properly take the [physical differences] into account" led it to strike down New York's women's minimum wage law, Morehead v. New York *ex rel.* Tipaldo, 298 U.S. 587 (1936), while upholding restrictions on women's night work that were justified on health grounds, Radice v. New York, 264 U.S. 292 (1924). This distinction was swallowed up when the Court abandoned *Adkins* and its liberty of contract doctrine to uphold a women-only minimum wage law in West Coast Hotel v. Parrish, 300 U.S. 379 (1937). The *West Coast Hotel* decision, made without reference to the Nineteenth Amendment, seemed tacitly to accept the sentiment expressed by Justice Holmes in his *Adkins* dissent: "It will need more than the Nineteenth Amendment to convince me that there are no differences between men and women, or that legislation

clear—the labor law litigation generally concerned whether health-related laws infringed civil rights—the principles of the *Adkins* decision favored women's jury service. For one thing, jury service posed no conceivable threat to women's health. And, as the Supreme Court had recognized in *Strauder v. West Virginia*,[95] jury service was emblematic of exactly that equal citizenship that the *Adkins* Court suggested women had now attained.

More broadly, the *Adkins* decision's emancipatory vision of the importance of the Nineteenth Amendment within women's history suggested that it was not only appropriate, but perhaps necessary that courts recognize the revolution around them by giving full scope to the significance of suffrage. In the emancipatory view, women had stepped forward from an oppressive past to claim the vote and with it, a full measure of equality. The fruit of the arduous suffrage campaign was women's equality before the law.

B. *An Incremental View of Suffrage*

The *Adkins* decision captured the vision of suffrage as a symbol of women's emancipation from the legal inequality of the past, a vision that inspired the cases, considered earlier in this Note, that upheld women's right to be jurors. But in other cases courts held that the attainment of suffrage had been a discrete event in the legal history of women. According to these cases, the attainment of suffrage had no impact on juror qualifications or any other aspect of women's rights because women could not serve as jurors, or achieve any other change in legal status, without explicit legislative authorization. The following pages present this "incremental" interpretation of suffrage.

A full account of the incremental understanding of suffrage appeared in 1921, when the Supreme Judicial Court of Massachusetts upheld the criminal conviction of a female defendant that was rendered by a jury from which all women were excluded. *Commonwealth v. Welosky*[96] presented questions about the scope of women's suffrage from several different angles. First, the Massachusetts jury law specified that all "persons" eligible to vote could be jurors. Since women had become voters by virtue of the Nineteenth

---

cannot take those differences into account." *Adkins*, 261 U.S. at 569-70 (Holmes, J., dissenting). On the historical conflict within feminism between equal rights and recognition of sexual difference, see COTT, *supra* note 35, at 117-42. For a recent account, see Wendy S. Strimling, *The Constitutionality of State Laws Providing Employment Leave for Pregnancy: Rethinking Gedulgig after Cal Fed*, 77 CAL. L. REV. 171, 194-96 (1989) (discussing opposing feminist positions concerning California law, upheld by Supreme Court in California Fed. Sav. & Loan Ass'n v. Guerra, 479 U.S. 272 (1987), requiring businesses to grant women maternity leaves, without requiring similar accommodation for men who are new fathers); *see also* International Union, UAW v. Johnson Controls, Inc., 111 S. Ct. 1196 (1991) (holding that Title VII, Civil Rights Act of 1964 prohibits employers from protecting fetal health by barring all fertile women from potentially hazardous jobs).

95. 100 U.S. 303 (1880).

96. 177 N.E. 656 (Mass. 1931). *Welosky* was preceded by an advisory opinion, rendered by the same court, which also concluded that the Nineteenth Amendment was an incremental enactment that did not make women eligible for jury service. *In re* Opinion of the Justices, 130 N.E. 685 (Mass. 1921).

Amendment, the court had to explain why women did not now qualify for jury service. Second, Massachusetts had readily admitted others to the jury box once voter qualifications that had kept them out, such as property requirements, had been lifted. Again the question was, why wouldn't this rule apply to women? The third issue was perhaps the thorniest: Welosky was a female defendant tried by a jury that excluded all women, which seemed to put *Strauder v. West Virginia*[97] and *Neal v. Delaware*[98] firmly on her side. The court would have to distinguish these venerable precedents if it were to rule against Welosky's Fourteenth Amendment claim.

The court began by construing the word "person" in the state jury statute—"a person qualified to vote shall be liable to serve as a juror"—to mean men.[99] In fact, the court argued, not only did the legislature mean "men" when it wrote "person," but this was "the only intent constitutionally permissible" because the state constitution had allowed only men to vote when the legislature had enacted the jury statute.[100] This recourse to legislative intent was deeply inconsistent with the relevant precedent, *Neal v. Delaware*.[101] *Neal* involved a state statute defining voters as jurors that was enacted at a time when state suffrage was constitutionally restricted to white males. Yet the State of Delaware had not argued to the Supreme Court that because the only "constitutionally permissible" intent of its legislature when it had authorized electors to be jurors was to make *whites* jurors, a state policy of excluding blacks from juries must later be upheld; the constitutional violation inherent in trying blacks before all-white juries was clear.

Undaunted by this flaw in its argument, the *Welosky* court turned to the question of why women, unlike other newly enfranchised groups, did not automatically become jurors upon getting the vote. The court explained that when suffrage was expanded among male citizens,

> These concurring enlargements of those liable to jury service were simply an extension to larger numbers of the same classification of persons. Since the word "person" in the statutes respecting jurors meant men, when there was an extension of the right to vote to other men previously disqualified, the jury statutes by specific definition included them.

---

97. 100 U.S. 303 (1880).

98. 103 U.S. 370 (1881).

99. *Welosky*, 177 N.E. at 660 ("Manifestly, therefore, the intent of the Legislature must have been, in using the word 'person' . . . to confine its meaning to men."). The *Welosky* court also repeated the Supreme Court's dictum that the legislature "may confine the [jury] selection to males," *id.* at 664, quoting Strauder v. West Virginia, 100 U.S. 303, 310 (1880). *Welosky* was unusual in that it construed "person" to mean men, but as the cases discussed elsewhere in this section show, a number of courts agreed that both the *Strauder* dictum and the use of male pronouns in reference to juries argued strongly against women's eligibility to serve. *See also supra* text accompanying notes 77-80.

100. *Welosky*, 177 N.E. at 660.

101. 103 U.S. 370 (1881); *see supra* text accompanying note 51.

> The Nineteenth Amendment to the federal Constitution conferred the suffrage upon an *entirely new class of human beings*. . . . It added to qualified voters those who did not fall within the meaning of the word "person" in the jury statutes.[102]

Why? Because "[t]he change in the legal status of women wrought by the Nineteenth Amendment was radical, drastic and unprecedented. While it is to be given full effect in its field, it is not to be extended by implication."[103] The justices seem to have been frightened by the possible implications of the "radical" amendment; they urged a policy of strict containment. In fact, the court reached back fifty years to a Massachusetts version of the *Bradwell* case[104] for a reassuring quotation:

> In making innovations upon the long-established system of law on this subject, the legislature appears to have proceeded with great caution, one step at a time; and the whole course of legislation precludes the inference that any change in the legal rights or capacities of women is to be implied, which has not been clearly expressed.[105]

Here was the foundation of the incremental interpretation of suffrage: Women gained new rights not because the law had come to recognize sex equality, but only because law-makers occasionally saw fit to exercise their discretion on women's behalf.

The court's greatest challenge was to explain why a female defendant's jury could be drawn from a pool that excluded women, when it was well established by *Strauder*[106] and *Neal*[107] that a black male defendant could not be tried by a jury drawn from a pool that excluded black men. The court resolved this dilemma by arguing that when it came to the need for constitutional rights, sex and race created "utterly different"[108] situations. First, the justices harked back to the view that the Fourteenth Amendment was enacted for the exclusive benefit of blacks, asserting that this principle was "not shaken or affected by later decisions . . . recognizing the Fourteenth Amendment as extending its protection to all persons, white or black, or corporations."[109] The court did not attempt to explain how the earlier view, that the Fourteenth Amendment protected *only* blacks from race discrimination,

---

102. *Welosky*, 177 N.E. at 661 (citation omitted) (emphasis added).
103. *Id.*
104. Bradwell v. Illinois, 83 U.S. (16 Wall.) 130 (1873) (denying Fourteenth Amendment challenge to Illinois rule that excluded married women from admission to the bar).
105. *Welosky*, 177 N.E. at 661 (quoting Robinson's Case, 131 Mass. 376, 381 (1881), in which the Massachusetts Supreme Judicial Court, following *Bradwell v. Illinois*, denied Lelia J. Robinson's eligibility for admission to the bar on the ground that she could not be a lawyer because of her sex).
106. 100 U.S. 303 (1880).
107. 103 U.S. 370 (1881).
108. *Welosky*, 177 N.E. at 663.
109. *Id.*

could remain in force once other decisions had expanded the Amendment's reach to "all persons . . . or corporations." The effect of its pronouncement was, however, clear: the Fourteenth Amendment simply did not apply when women—of any race—challenged their treatment as women.

The justices continued by contrasting the situation of blacks before the Thirteenth, Fourteenth, and Fifteenth Amendments with that of women before the Nineteenth Amendment. The court, apparently thinking only of white women, described women's status before the Nineteenth Amendment:

> Women had not been enslaved. They had been recognized as citizens and clothed with large property and civil rights. Woman has long been generally recognized in this country as the equal of man intellectually, morally, socially. Opportunities in business and for college and university training had been freely open to her. . . . In many respects laws especially protective to women on account of their sex had been enacted. Most of those formerly imposing limitations, even upon married women with respect to property and business, had disappeared.[110]

In light of this account of women's history, there was little left for the Nineteenth Amendment to accomplish and, according to the court, its advocates knew that: "Current discussion touching the adoption of the Nineteenth Amendment related exclusively to the franchise. The words of that amendment by express terms deal solely with the right to vote."[111] The Nineteenth Amendment granted women the vote and nothing but the vote.

The argument then took a surprising turn. The court cited Supreme Court decisions that approved significant restrictions on women: women had no right to practice law,[112] no right to vote before the Suffrage Amendment,[113] and woman-specific labor legislation was constitutional.[114] Noting that all these cases rejected Fourteenth Amendment challenges, the court wrote, "Those rights appear to us quite as essential to the privileges and immunities of citizens and equal protection of the laws as the duty to serve as jurors."[115] The Massachusetts justices who had just described how women enjoyed equality now pointed to cases that ratified the constitutionality of laws that treated women unequally.[116]

---

110. *Id.*
111. *Id.*
112. Bradwell v. Illinois, 83 U.S. (16 Wall.) 130 (1873).
113. Minor v. Happersett, 88 U.S. (21 Wall.) 162 (1875).
114. Muller v. Oregon, 208 U.S. 412 (1908).
115. *Welosky,* 177 N.E. at 664.
116. The court also quoted with approval a New Jersey decision, State v. James, 114 A. 553 (N.J. 1921), which held that the constitutional right to a jury trial guaranteed a common law jury consisting of men. *Welosky,* 177 N.E. at 664. One claim Frank James made in appealing his murder conviction was that the exclusion of women from juries violated his right to trial by an impartial jury. The New Jersey high court rejected his argument that the Nineteenth Amendment served to qualify women as jurors under a state

Despite its evident confusion, the *Welosky* opinion is a comprehensive statement of suffrage as a discrete and incremental alteration of women's legal status. The passage comparing the status of (white) women with that of blacks before emancipation was intended to show that women did not suffer legal or social oppression, and for this reason the justices refused to apply *Strauder*'s Fourteenth Amendment holding to defendant Welosky. Yet the *Welosky* court acknowledged that the law continued to approve significant restrictions on women's rights. This contradiction could be resolved only from within the incremental perspective, which accepted inequality between the sexes, and allowed women only those rights that were selected for them. The Massachusetts justices endorsed that perspective by reading the word "person" in the jury statute to mean "men" and by characterizing women as "an entirely new class of human beings" to enjoy the privilege of voting. To them, suffrage was an important but limited achievement. Following this, the conclusion was inevitable that the Nineteenth Amendment could not be "extended by implication" to create additional rights; indeed, the "whole course of legislation"[117] argued against such a result. Winning the vote had altered one aspect of women's legal status, but had left unchanged their underlying inequality before the law.

The incremental interpretation of laws affecting women's legal status accepted the status quo of sex inequality as an appropriate and intentional response to perceived differences between men and women. The law treated the sexes differently because they were different. Since women's unequal legal status was accepted and normal, courts adopted a cautious stance toward legislative enactments that altered women's status, giving such enactments their due but not extending them on any abstract theory of sex equality.

The opinion in *Harland v. Territory*[118] is an earlier expression of this incremental view. This case reversed *Rosencrantz*,[119] the earlier Washington Territory case that had established women's eligibility for jury service. In *Harland* the judges determined that the Territory's women's suffrage law was invalid,[120] and stated in lengthy dicta why women, even if electors, could not be jurors. The court embraced women's exclusion from jury service as justified by the rule of the common law that was summarized in Blackstone's phrase,

---

law that made "citizens" jurors. The *James* opinion relied on BLACKSTONE, *see supra* note 2, the statutory use of "personal pronouns of the masculine gender," 114 A. at 555, and the view that the Nineteenth Amendment "emancipate[d] women only so far as the right of suffrage is concerned," *id.* at 556, to confine the meaning of "citizen" in this case to men. The court also rejected James's standing as a man to raise an issue of women's constitutional rights. *Id.* at 557-58.

117. Robinson's Case, 131 Mass. 376, 381 (1881), *quoted in Welosky*, 177 N.E. at 661.

118. 13 P. 453 (Wash. Terr. 1887); *see supra* text accompanying notes 71-72.

119. 5 P. 305 (Wash. Terr. 1884); *see supra* text accompanying notes 67-69.

120. The author of the *Harland* opinion betrayed a certain depth of feeling about the subjects of women's suffrage and women's jury service, writing, "Of course, if [the suffrage] act is invalid, the whole superstructure of the argument by which female jury duty is demonstrated falls to the ground, a broken and shapeless mass." *Harland*, 13 P. at 457.

propter defectum sexus.[121] The opinion quoted Justice Bradley's famous statement that "the civil law, as well as nature herself, has always recognized a wide difference in the respective spheres and destinies of man and woman."[122] "[W]e ought not to depart from the old order," the judges wrote, "without the most indubitable evidence that the legislature so intended."[123] Presaging the *Welosky* opinion, they asserted that "the fourteenth amendment . . . is not yet strong enough to overcome the implied limitations of prior law and custom"[124] on women's rights.

The South Carolina Supreme Court also embraced the incremental view of suffrage in *State v. Mittle*[125] when it refused a criminal defendant's challenge to his conviction on the ground that women were excluded from the venire of petit jurors for his trial. The court held that women were ineligible for jury service in the state.[126]

The South Carolina judges represented Mittle's claim as an assertion that the Nineteenth Amendment had, in itself, made women jurors. This was probably something of an overstatement, as the route from suffrage to jury service was always traced through a provision that electors were qualified as jurors, but the court spared no energy in its denunciation:

> The right to vote and eligibility to jury service are subjects of such diverse characteristics and demanding such different regulation that it is impossible to consider the one as implied in the other. To hold that one who is a qualified elector is ipso facto entitled to jury service is to deprive the Legislature of the right to prescribe any other limitation upon the right to jury service. It could not prescribe the age limit, the sex, or the mental, moral, or physical qualifications of a juror.[127]

The problem with this argument lay in the South Carolina constitution's two provisions about jurors. The first read, "The petit jury of the circuit courts shall consist of twelve men"; the second, "Each juror must be a qualified elector under the provisions of this Constitution, between the ages of twenty-one and sixty-five years and of good moral character."[128] These provisions

---

121. *Id.* at 454. *See supra* note 2 for a definition of this phrase.

122. *Id.* at 456 (quoting Bradwell v. Illinois, 83 U.S. (16 Wall.) 130, 141 (1873) (Bradley, J., concurring)).

123. *Id.*

124. *Id.*

125. 113 S.E. 335 (S.C. 1922).

126. In fact, the *Mittle* court went one step further, saying of the Nineteenth Amendment:

It is a popular, but a mistaken, conception that the amendment confers upon women the right to vote. It does not purport to do so. It only prohibits discrimination against them on account of their sex in legislation prescribing the qualifications of suffrage, a very different thing from conferring the right to vote . . . .

Id. at 337. On this reading, even if jury eligibility could be inferred from the right to vote, women could not claim jury service as a constitutional right because they had no constitutional right to vote.

127. *Id.*

128. S.C. CONST. of 1895, art. V, § 22.

simply did not supply the court's perceived need for "such different regulation" of voters and jurors. The *Mittle* court also held that "the right of jury service by a woman was expressly denied by the state Constitution" because of the provision for a jury "of 12 men";[129] the court did not pause to consider whether "men" meant *men*.[130]

The opinion in *State v. Mittle* said little about why suffrage should have only an incremental and narrow effect. Assessment of the court's view of women's history is largely a matter of implications drawn from its silence. The South Carolina Supreme Court presented the Nineteenth Amendment in a contextual vacuum, which precluded interpreting the Amendment as part of a larger drive toward equality. The court's hairsplitting insistence that the Nineteenth Amendment did not grant women the right to vote but only prohibited states from denying the franchise based on sex[131] was meaningless as a matter of law—granting the right and prohibiting its denial equally allow women to vote, except for those who are otherwise disqualified. But the court's choice of words cut against the claim that women had equal legal *rights*.

The literal reading of "jury of 12 men" as a bar to women's participation was a tacit acknowledgment that sex-specific legislation was presumptively appropriate. The court did not refer to the debate in other cases over whether "men" should be read literally, but instead simply accepted that legislation could give women inferior status. *State v. Mittle* is an example of the incremental interpretation of suffrage derived more by ignoring than by interpreting women's legal history.

Some other cases that relied at least in part on the incremental interpretation of suffrage to reject female jury service were, like *Commonwealth v. Welosky*[132] (1931), among the later opinions on the question. Cases such as *State v. Kelley*[133] (1924) and *People ex rel. Fyfe v. Barnett*[134] (1925) departed from the more expansive interpretation of the meaning of suffrage expressed in the earlier opinions of *Parus v. District*

---

129. *Mittle*, 113 S.E. at 338.

130. The court did, however, write that a state "may confine the selection to males." *Id.* (quoting Strauder v. West Virginia, 100 U.S. 303, 310 (1880)).

131. *See supra* note 126.

132. 177 N.E. 656 (Mass. 1931).

133. 229 P. 659 (Idaho 1924). Kelley's conviction by an all-female jury was overturned in an opinion of the Idaho Supreme Court. Despite a statute that stated, "Words in the masculine gender, include the feminine," *id.* at 661, the judges denied women's eligibility as jurors on the basis of statutory references to jurors as "men," *id.* at 660-61, and the common-law rule of *propter defectum sexus, id.* at 661. They also ignored *Neal v. Delaware*, 103 U.S. 370 (1881), by declaring that "[t]he jury statutes restrict jury duty to men, males, who are citizens and electors; the Suffrage Amendment increased the number of electors, but it neither related to nor affected the qualifications of jurors." *Kelley*, 229 P. at 661.

134. 150 N.E. 290 (Ill. 1925). In this case, a Chicago woman unsuccessfully sought a writ of mandamus ordering the restoration of her name to the jury roles. The commissioners, erring perhaps because of her unusual name, had placed Hannay Beye Fyfe on the jury list only to remove her upon learning her sex.

Court[135] (1918) and *People v. Barltz*[136] (1920). Their departure is all the more striking given that they also came after the *Adkins* opinion and its endorsement of the emancipatory view. These later opinions may express a retrenchment from, or a backlash against, the spirit of sexual equality that had galvanized the successful suffrage campaigns. Perhaps as the struggle for suffrage receded from political awareness, courts lost sight of the suffragists' rhetoric of women's equality. No doubt that rhetoric had faded from view to some degree even before the Nineteenth Amendment was won, as support for women's suffrage expanded from its origins in visionary feminism to the political mainstream. Perhaps these courts shared the concern, expressed in *Welosky*, with limiting the consequences of this "radical, drastic and unprecedented"[137] Nineteenth Amendment.

IV. READING LAW BY THE LIGHT OF HISTORY

This sample of the female juror cases offers no definitive answer to the question posed by the Michigan Supreme Court in *People v. Barltz*, "What *was* the purpose and object of the people in . . . striking out the word 'male' from the Constitution?"[138] I have explored them here because they illuminate two interpretations of suffrage—one narrow, one more broad—that we can evaluate in light of our national experience and aspirations as they have developed in the years since the ratification of the Nineteenth Amendment.

It is clear that as judges struggled to determine the impact of suffrage on women's jury service, they drew constantly on their own conceptions of women's legal history. Those who believed that women fit well within the separate sphere assigned to them by men and the legal system were careful to extend to women only those precise rights that legislatures decided to grant. Implicitly or explicitly, these courts rejected the view that women's inferior legal status was detrimental and assumed the legitimacy of legal distinctions between the sexes. In this view of women's legal history the grant of suffrage was no more than an incremental alteration in women's legal status whose impact was confined to the voting booth.

Other judges took a very different view. In their eyes, women had been subjected to imposed legal inferiority quite long enough. If women had not yet arrived at the status of full equality, they were bound soon to be recognized as men's equals. These courts looked to other legislative enactments as support for their view that suffrage was a robust expression of women's aspiration toward equality. They drew parallels between the impact of enfranchisement on black men's jury rights and its impact on women's jury service. Interpreting

135. 174 P. 706 (Nev. 1918).
136. 180 N.W. 423 (Mich. 1920).
137. Commonwealth v. Welosky, 177 N.E. 656, 661 (Mass. 1931).
138. 180 N.W. 423, 425 (Mich. 1920) (emphasis added).

suffrage as the people's affirmation of women's equal political rights, they readily extended its force at least from the ballot box to the jury box.

The transformative potential of this latter emancipatory vision of suffrage and the Nineteenth Amendment was demonstrated in *Adkins v. Children's Hospital*,[139] where the Amendment appeared as a virtual declaration of women's constitutional equality. That potential was soon vitiated as sex-specific legislation was upheld under the caveat in *Adkins* that "the physical differences must be recognized in appropriate cases."[140] The "recognition" of those differences invited a resurgence of special laws aimed at women and justified as sound public policy. The ramifications for women's drive toward legal equality were profound.

In a scathing 1935 survey of the failure of constitutional law to grant or protect women's rights, Blanche Crozier criticized the ascendance of "public policy" as a rationale for "the progressive intrusion of the police power upon personal liberty in the field of women's employment: . . . The health of the race brings all paid work of all women within the field of public control."[141] She observed that for a time, women were gaining legal rights "all necessarily in derogation of the common law,"[142] and, as we have seen in the jury cases,

> [I]t began to seem that the common law . . . was on the wrong track anyway, and that it was inadequate to say that a constitutional right expressed in the most universal terms nevertheless did not extend to women because women had no such right at common law. . . .
>
> Between the decline of the authority of the common law in this field and the later enormous growth of the application of public policy, there was a hiatus; and this hiatus is the highest point in the constitutional position of women. This interval contains the strongest statements against discrimination based on sex which have ever been made by American courts.[143]

Crozier continued, "Only once did the United States Supreme Court fall into this new trend, which turned out to be only temporary and not the way the law was going. This was in the *Adkins* decision, which we fear is not today in the best of repute."[144] The tone of weary resignation at the conclusion of her discussion is haunting years later, with full equality for women still so distant a goal:

---

139. 261 U.S. 525 (1923).
140. *Id.* at 553.
141. Crozier, *supra* note 45, at 746.
142. *Id.*
143. *Id.* at 746-47.
144. *Id.* at 748. Crozier identified the principle that sex discrimination is unconstitutional as the "actuating philosophy" of the *Adkins* decision, adding, "[T]he *Adkins* case was the immediate fruit of the Nineteenth Amendment, although there is no connection whatever between suffrage and the question in the case." *Id.*

> The principle of the constitutionality of discrimination based on sex
> was slowly weakening during the last years under its old sponsor, the
> common law; it reached a critical point where even some courts
> thought it might die; but it weathered the change from ancient to
> modern nomenclature, and under its new sponsor, public policy, it has
> fully regained its old strength.[145]

My survey of these cases, originally inspired by the *Adkins* view of
suffrage, leaves me with the same feeling of opportunity lost that Blanche
Crozier expressed. It was not the suffrage amendment alone, or any other legal
enactment, that for a time seemed to give such impetus toward equality for
women, but instead the "spirit of the amendment," and of the movement
responsible for its success.

The reasons given in the jury cases for a narrow reading of the Nineteenth
Amendment are not empty. The argument that the Amendment says nothing
on its face about jury duty is undeniably accurate. So, to an extent, may be
assertions that when legislators enacted jury laws, "men" meant *men*.[146] The
heart of this controversy, however, lies not in the words of statutory or
constitutional enactments, but in the competing views of the backdrop of
women's history, against which the impact of suffrage must be measured. In
my view, the choice between the incremental and the emancipatory
interpretations of the Nineteenth Amendment should take into account both the
historically inferior legal status of women and the centrality of suffrage to
equal citizenship in a democracy, in order to reach an understanding of what
kind of equality women achieved by winning the right to vote.

Today we take for granted the incremental view of women's suffrage. In
our constitutional understanding, the Nineteenth Amendment stands for no
more than women's right to vote. But the conception of women's history that
underlies the incremental view, as expressed in these cases, seems deficient.
Courts that adopted the incremental view showed little comprehension of the
oppressiveness of the common law to women—a reality those courts that
adopted the emancipatory interpretation admitted freely. Moreover, aspects of
the incremental view—particularly the literal adhesion to the word "men" and
the failure to use constitutional precedents to override women's common-law
status—amounted to a position that the Constitution did not apply to women,
and that only the express terms of a statute could alter women's rights from
what they were at common law.

---

145. *Id.* at 748-49.

146. *But see* People *ex rel.* Denny v. Traeger, 22 N.E.2d 679 (Ill. 1939). In this case the Illinois
Supreme Court had to decide whether the use of the word "men" in the state constitution's jury provisions
excluded women. Referring to the state's constitution which, paraphrasing the *Declaration of Independence*,
stated "[a]ll men" have "certain inalienable rights," the court declared that a literal reading of "men" must
be rejected because it "would act to remove from many of the governed the protection guaranteed by the
bill of rights." *Id.* at 682.

2204   The Yale Law Journal   [Vol. 102: 2175

The entire thrust of the feminist movement has been to reject these contentions, by reading women *into* the Constitution, and by insisting that maleness has served as a prerequisite for positions of responsibility and authority not because it is a bona fide qualification, but because of the historical oppression of women. The feminist movement's many successes in the legal arena demonstrate that both the judiciary and the legal profession as a whole have rejected the presumption of women's inequality that served as the underpinning for the incremental interpretation of suffrage. Not only are the basic tenets of the incremental viewpoint now discredited, but the belief in women's trajectory toward equality that underlay the emancipatory interpretation of suffrage has continued as a vital force right up to the present.

V. CONCLUSION

The Nineteenth Amendment was the product of the revolutionary idea that women have equal status in a democracy. As a nation, we are still pursuing this vision of equality, yet we have allowed this constitutional enactment only a paltry existence. The woman juror cases, with their contrasting incremental and emancipatory interpretations of suffrage, provide good reason to reconsider the limited scope accorded the Nineteenth Amendment. This incremental interpretation of women's suffrage turns out to be founded upon a constricted view of women's place in the legal order that has been wholly rejected by modern Americans. The understanding that suffrage was an emancipatory enactment, however, rests on a warm embrace of women's equality that is far more consonant with our national ideals and constitutional values.

The meaning of the Civil War Amendments for racial equality has never been treated as a settled matter. Rather, the understanding of their significance is continually informed and reformed, both by new scholarship about their origins, and by an ever broadening awareness of how deeply our institutions and common life must change to realize fully the aspiration of racial justice. The Nineteenth Amendment merits a similarly deep, broad, and continuing inquiry, so that the fullest and truest aspirations of this constitutional amendment may be recovered and realized.

The Nineteenth Amendment brought women into political citizenship after centuries of exclusion by men, a tremendous achievement by any measure of democracy. Perhaps there is yet more this women's amendment to the Constitution can accomplish to eliminate the spirit of *propter defectum sexus* "from our consideration of womankind in modern political and legal life."[147]

---

147. Parus v. District Court, 174 P. 706, 709 (Nev. 1918).

Legal Practice

[20]

SEEKING ". . . THE FACES OF OTHERNESS . . ."[1]: A RESPONSE TO PROFESSORS SARAT, FELSTINER, AND CAHN

Lucie E. White†

This comment addresses Naomi Cahn's *The Looseness of Legal Language: The Reasonable Woman Standard in Theory and in Practice,*[2] and William Felstiner and Austin Sarat's *Enactments of Power: Negotiating Reality and Responsibility in Lawyer-Client Interactions.*[3] I will begin with a recollection about my own education. I will then turn to "meta-theory," or, more simply, the images we use to frame our thinking about the social world.[4] I conclude with a brief story from my current work.

I

THE RECOLLECTION

When I went to college, our intellectual gurus—in addition to Timothy Leary and John Lennon—were people like Noam Chomsky and Claude Levi-Strauss. Their theories talked about boxes, bipolar oppositions, exchanges (usually of women, it seemed), and law-ruled transformations.[5] Their intellectual maps were geometric and symmetrical, and covered the entire social world, as we then imagined it. Although there was a lot of movement within their paradigms, that movement resembled a military drill more than a

---

1   *See* Jacques Derrida, *Force de Loi: Le "Fondement Mystique de l'Authorite"/Force of Law: The "Mystical Foundation of Authority,"* 11 CARDOZO L. REV. 919 (Mary Quaintance trans., 1990) [hereinafter Derrida, *Force of Law*].

†   B.A. Radcliffe College, J.D. Harvard Law School.

2   *See* Naomi R. Cahn, *The Looseness of Legal Language: The Reasonable Woman Standard in Theory and in Practice,* 77 CORNELL L. REV. 1398 (1992).

3   *See* William L.F. Felstiner & Austin Sarat, *Enactments of Power: Negotiating Reality and Responsibility in Lawyer-Client Interactions,* 77 CORNELL L. REV. 1447 (1992).

4   It is difficult to discuss "meta-theory" without losing touch with solid ground. There is a parallel risk, however, in failing to interrogate the assumptions that frame our understandings of the world. *See* Cahn, *supra* note 2, at 1410 n.64 (citing Nancy Fraser and Linda Nicholson's discussion of "quasi-metanarratives" in *Social Criticism without Philosophy: An Encounter between Feminism and Postmodernism,* 19, 27, *in* FEMINISM/POSTMODERNISM (Linda J. Nicholson ed., 1990)).

5   *See, e.g.,* CLAUDE LEVI-STRAUSS, THE SAVAGE MIND (G. Weidenfeld & Nicholson Ltd. trans., 1966); CLAUDE LEVI-STRAUSS, STRUCTURAL ANTHROPOLOGY (Claire Jacobson & Brooke Grundfest Schoepf trans., 1963); NOAM CHOMSKY, SYNTACTIC STRUCTURES (1957); NOAM CHOMSKY, TOPICS IN THE THEORY OF GENERATIVE GRAMMAR (1966); NOAM CHOMSKY, LANGUAGE AND MIND (1968).

dance. Those days, the late 1960s, were the salad days of what we now disparagingly call "structuralism."

I remember reading during those years an essay by a young anthropologist named Clifford Geertz.[6] This essay used the technocratic talk of the times, but its message was out of synch with the positivism that such talk often assumed. The essay made reference to a new "meta-concept" that Geertz called "terminal screens."[7] This term is a wonderful reminder of how the words we use are inevitably colored by the historical moment in which we write. Clifford Geertz does not talk about "terminal screens" any more. Instead, he writes about "thick descriptions,"[8] and works and lives.[9]

By "terminal screens," Geertz meant something similar to what one might describe, in the lingo of the 1990s, by reference to the array of designer "shades" that one can buy in places like Los Angeles, to color the world different tints for one's varying moods.[10] Geertz used "terminal screens" to point out that one can view the same social "reality" through a range of different conceptual or theoretical screens or filters. Depending on the screen one looks through—the matrix of terms or concepts through which one filters what one sees—the same event can take on many different appearances.

In the days when structuralism was still in vogue, this was a marginal, though by no means novel, idea. Since then, it has entered the intellectual mainstream. Many people now talk of the partiality—or inevitably interpretive nature—of all of the "discourses,"[11] "paradigms,"[12] or "lenses" through which we make sense of our human world, and in turn constitute ourselves. Many scholars now teach us how our understandings of the world both reflect and define the positions from which we view it.[13]

---

[6] CLIFFORD GEERTZ, *Person, Time and Conduct in Bali* (Yale Southeast Asia Program, Cultural Report Series No. 14, 1966), *in* THE INTERPRETATION OF CULTURES 360 (1973). Professor James Boyd White points out that the concept of "terminological screens" was first introduced into the discourses of social criticism by Kenneth Burke.

[7] *See* GEERTZ, *supra* note 6.

[8] *See* CLIFFORD GEERTZ, *Thick Description: Toward an Interpretive Theory of Culture, in* THE INTERPRETATION OF CULTURES, *supra* note 6, at 3. Naomi Cahn reports that Geertz borrowed this term from Gilbert Ryle. *See* Cahn, *supra* note 2, at 1430 n.141.

[9] *See* CLIFFORD GEERTZ, WORKS AND LIVES: THE ANTHROPOLOGIST AS AUTHOR (1988).

[10] I have heard Professor Kimberlé Crenshaw, for example, use such an image in several informal presentations to Los Angeles audiences.

[11] *See, e.g.*, Michel Foucault, *History of Systems of Thought, in* LANGUAGE, COUNTER-MEMORY, PRACTICE: SELECTED ESSAYS AND INTERVIEWS 199 (Donald F. Bouchard ed., & Sherry Simon trans., 1977).

[12] *See* THOMAS KUHN, THE STRUCTURE OF SCIENTIFIC REVOLUTIONS (1970).

[13] For particularly compelling elaborations on this insight, see RENATO ROSALDO, CULTURE AND TRUTH: THE REMAKING OF SOCIAL ANALYSIS (1989); ELIZABETH U. SPELMAN,

II
META-THEORY

At the same time that Clifford Geertz's star was rising in the world of social theory, Noam Chomsky's was falling: structuralism was overtaken by new "post-structuralist" ways of thinking. The intellectual leader of this movement was Michel Foucault. Foucault, with a little posthumous coaching from Nietzsche, was indisputably a genius, a paradigm smasher. He, more than any other single figure, moved us beyond the "conventional," structural understanding of power that Professors Sarat and Felstiner describe in their essay. In this conventional view, power is a thing that people have and wield over others, usually on the basis of their roles in stable institutional hierarchies. Foucault gave us a new meta-theory of power— one that was so intriguing, so fitting for the uncertain times of the 1970s, that many other theorists—sociologists, linguists, and historians—took up the joint project of filling in its details, and of using it, lens-like, to sharpen their view of social life.

According to this new meta-theory, power is not a tool. Rather, like an evanescent fluid, it takes unpredictable shapes as it flows into the most subtle spaces in our interpersonal world. In this picture, we no longer see distinct "persons" controlling power's flow. Indeed, we cannot really separate the agents of the movement from the movement itself. Sometimes we may think we see more or less familiar human actors, who seem to guide the fluid, like children might make giant soap bubbles in a park. Yet at other moments, these familiar "persons" disappear, and we see only the patterns that linger as the bubbles dance.

Power is lyrically described in Professors Felstiner and Sarat's essay. It is "mobile and volatile, and it circulates . . . it is a complicated resource that is constructed and reconstructed so that its possession is neither necessarily obvious nor rigidly determined."[14] It is "continually enacted and re-enacted, constituted and re-constituted . . . shaped and reshaped . . . taken and lost . . . present and

---

INESSENTIAL WOMAN: PROBLEMS OF EXCLUSION IN FEMINIST THOUGHT (1988). If there is currently a serious debate about this notion, it is not about whether each of us sees the world from behind a particular, contingent "terminal screen." Rather, the debate is about whether we have any power to shape the screens through which we see, or to shift between them—either by authoring our own moral, political, or intellectual identities, or by expanding the language that we use—or whether our perspectives on the world are dictated by matters of fate, be they our genes, our life fortunes, the circuits wired into our brains, or the categories inscribed into our native tongues. For a short but elegant exploration of some of these themes, see Maria Lugones, *Playfulness, World-Travelling and Loving Perception*, 2 HYPATIA 3 (1987).

[14] Felstiner & Sarat, *supra* note 3, *passim* (quotes are in an original draft, on file with author).

absent . . . shifting, deeply embedded in complex processes of contestation and negotiation."[15]

This theory of power offers a very interesting lens through which to view social interactions, including interactions between lawyers and their clients. Professors Felstiner and Sarat demonstrate this. Their picture of power works like one of those infrared periscopes that military tank crews might use to render a desert landscape visible in the dark. Through their lens, Professors Felstiner and Sarat are able to see and study, in astonishing topographical detail, the interactions of Wendy, a well-meaning but probably lazy divorce lawyer, and Kitty, or rather Kathy, her excessively well-mannered client. Their lens enables Felstiner and Sarat to see in the interactions of these two women subtle enactments of power that other spectators, using a more conventional structural lens, for instance, would miss.

Felstiner and Sarat's work is part of a larger collective project undertaken by several legal scholars. Sally Merry, for instance, has recently used Foucault's lens to produce a detailed account of how working class people interact with the courts.[16] Regina Austin has applied the lens to the workplace.[17] Others are producing similar work.[18] Of this new work, Gerald López's writings stand out. He uses the new conception of power to make visible complex interactions between groups of poor people and the professionals who try to help them.[19] In this work, he shows how power is indeed very fluid, even across the formidable barriers of race and class identity.

This new meta-theory of power is especially important to progressive law teachers, scholars, and advocates for at least two reasons. First, this lens is bringing forth a new body of situated micro-descriptions of lawyering practice. For the first time, these descriptions give us a substantial base of data that we may use to reflect on our work. This new data enables us to see exactly how and when we deploy power within the routines of our own lawyering. With this new insight into *what* we do, we can begin to ask *why* we do it and *how* we might change. We can begin to envision different habits—

---

15   *Id.*, *passim* (quotes are in an original draft, on file with author).

16   SALLY E. MERRY, GETTING JUSTICE AND GETTING EVEN: LEGAL CONSCIOUSNESS AMONG WORKING-CLASS AMERICANS (1990).

17   *See* Regina Austin, *Employer Abuse, Worker Resistance, and the Tort of Intentional Infliction of Emotional Distress*, 41 STAN. L. REV. 1 (1988).

18   *See, e.g.*, Anthony V. Alfieri, *Reconstructive Poverty Law Practice: Learning Lessons of Client Narrative*, 100 YALE L.J. 2105 (1991).

19   *See* GERALD P. LÓPEZ, REBELLIOUS LAWYERING: ONE CHICANO'S VISION OF PROGRESSIVE LAW PRACTICE (1992); Gerald P. López, *Reconceiving Civil Rights Practice: Seven Weeks in the Life of a Rebellious Collaboration*, 77 GEO. L.J. 1603 (1989); Gerald P. López, *Training Future Lawyers to Work with the Politically and Socially Subordinated: Anti-Generic Legal Education*, 91 W. VA. L. REV. 305 (1989) [hereinafter López, *Training Future Lawyers*].

different ways of talking and paying attention—that may make our deployments of power less disruptive of our clients' efforts to empower themselves. This kind of reflective reconstruction of our day-to-day lawyering routines can make our practice, as progressive lawyers, more consistent with our aspirations of greater social justice.[20] Thus, the descriptive project undertaken by Felstiner and Sarat makes possible a new field of critical reflection on advocacy and pedagogy[21]—a "theoretics" of practice—the potential of which we are just beginning to explore.

The second reason that Foucault's picture of power is so important to progressive advocates is that it has opened up new possibilities in the political practice of relatively disempowered groups. The conventional theory of power reveals a dichotomized world of domination and subordination; through such a lens, the hegemony of the dominant class is virtually absolute. Not only does that class confine the actions of the subordinated, but it also dictates their language, preferences, thoughts, dreams, and indeed most deeply held moral and political intuitions. In American legal scholarship, Catharine MacKinnon has used this dichotomized picture of power with great skill to challenge claims that women can experience authentic subjectivity in contemporary society.[22]

MacKinnon posed this challenge in an encounter with Carol Gilligan at Buffalo Law School in 1984.[23] In that exchange, MacKinnon argued that values of "caring" and "connection" that Gilligan and other feminists sought to reclaim and celebrate are symptoms of women's subordinate position in a closed system of power.[24] According to MacKinnon, even women's feelings of sexual pleasure are suspect; these feelings, like every other feature of Woman, de-

---

[20] I use "we" because many legal scholars have expressed similar aspirations in their writing and practice. A recent symposium issue of the *Hastings Law Journal* on the Theoretics of Practice collects some of the most recent works to which I refer. *See* Symposium, *Theoretics of Practice: The Integration of Progressive Thought and Action*, 43 HASTINGS L.J. 717 (1992).

[21] *See* Gerald P. López, *The Work We Know So Little About*, 42 STAN. L. REV. 1 (1989); López, *Training Future Lawyers*, *supra* note 19; Howard Lesnick, *Being a Teacher, of Lawyers: Discerning the Theory of My Practice*, 43 HASTING L.J. 1095; Schon, Bridges to Where: What Are Our Objectives, Keynote Address at Association of American Law Schools 1992 Annual Conference, Mini-Workshop on Theory and Practice: Finding Bridges for the Classroom (Jan. 4, 1992) (available on audio cassette from the AALS, 1201 Conn. Ave., N.W., Washington, D.C.).

[22] *See, e.g.*, CATHARINE A. MACKINNON, FEMINISM UNMODIFIED: DISCOURSES ON LIFE AND LAW (1987) [hereinafter MACKINNON, FEMINISM UNMODIFIED]; CATHARINE A. MACKINNON, TOWARD A FEMINIST THEORY OF THE STATE (1989).

[23] *See* Ellen C. DuBois et al., *Feminist Discourse, Moral Values, and the Law—a Conversation*, 34 BUFF. L. REV. 11 (1985) (transcript of a discussion held on October 19, 1984 at the law school of the State University of New York at Buffalo as part of the James McCormick Mitchell Lecture Series).

[24] *Id.* at 73-76.

fine a colonized subject, a being whose essence has been shaped by and for men.[25]

Thus, as Angela Harris has demonstrated in her critique of Catharine MacKinnon's work,[26] a conventional understanding of power locks women, and indeed every subordinated group, in a discursive "prison-house"[27] from which there is no escape. Just as the dominators can do nothing except wield their power, the subordinated can speak nothing except their masters' will. No change is possible in this universe; indeed, even the most creative tactics of resistance or gestures of solidarity reinforce the bonds of domination. This understanding of domination, designed to reveal injustice, leads to two perverse results. First, it excuses those in the dominant class from attempting to reflect on or change their own conduct, or to ally themselves with subordinate groups. Second, it reinforces in relatively disempowered groups the very doubts about their feelings, capacities, and indeed human worth that subordination itself engenders.

Foucault's picture of power disrupts this closed circle of domination. By showing that the dominators do not "possess" power, his picture makes possible a politics of resistance. It opens up space for a self-directed, democratic politics among subordinated groups, a politics that is neither vanguard-driven nor co-opted, as the politics of the colonized subject inevitably is. At the same time, and of more immediate relevance to lawyers, this new picture of power makes possible a self-reflective politics of alliance and collaboration between professionals and subordinated groups. Given the new theaters of political action that Foucault's theory of power has opened up, it is not surprising that it has stolen the stage in historical, cultural, and finally legal studies from those who speak of power in more conventional terms. The Foucaultian picture of power makes insurgent politics interesting again; it brings possibility back into focus, even in apparently quiescent times when resistance is visible only in the microdynamics of everyday life.

Yet with the power of this new lens comes a risk. With such an instrument in our hands, it is easy to forget the lesson that Professor Geertz taught. Any "terminal screen" gives us only a partial view of the world: it enhances some features of reality—probably those that

---

25   These themes are developed throughout MacKinnon's writings. For one clear early statement of the link between male domination and even "normal," ostensibly noncoercive heterosexuality, see MACKINNON, FEMINISM UNMODIFIED, *supra* note 22, at 46.

26   Angela P. Harris, *Race and Essentialism in Feminist Legal Theory*, 42 STAN. L. REV. 581, 590-601 (1989).

27   The allusion is to FREDRICK JAMESON, THE PRISON-HOUSE OF LANGUAGE: A CRITICAL ACCOUNT OF STRUCTURALISM AND RUSSIAN FORMALISM (1972).

its inventors most wanted to see—while erasing or obscuring others. The risk for those who use Foucault's lens is that they will forget this lesson, and begin to think of their own meta-theory as the last word on how power "really" works—the *terminal* screen. Foucault's lens reveals such a longed-for landscape of possibility that it has begun to entrap our imagination, deluding us into thinking that with this lens we have finally seized the power to comprehend the world.

One consequence inevitably follows when we forget that our latest theories are not absolute. This is the risk that, in our own certainty, we will lose patience with those who do not share our faith. As Professor Delgado points out, such intolerance often reveals itself only after time renders our certainties obsolete, and thereby ridiculous.[28] At least two further risks are specific to Foucault's lens.

The first risk has been identified by feminist scholars such as Nancy Fraser and Robin West.[29] While the Foucaultian lens reveals the fluidity of power, it does not show how power can become congealed in social institutions in ways that sustain domination. It may be true that everyday interactions create and maintain social institutions, but this insight does not enable us to map those interactions against the institutional matrices they create. Nor does this insight show us how institutions constrain the circulation of power, channeling it to flow toward some social groups and away from others. In short, the Foucaultian lens does not move us toward a theoretics and a reconstructive politics of *institutional* design.

Without richer meta-theories—stronger lenses—that focus on institutional as well as interpersonal realities, we will remain bewildered by exactly how our actions reiterate what has been called "structural" or "institutional" subordination.[30] We will remain unable to critique and repattern our actions, so that we enact more democratic institutions as we seek to live more ethical lives. These other lenses need not replace Foucault's; rather, they can provide a second filter on the same landscape, enabling us to study the geol-

---

28 Richard Delgado & Jean Stefancic, *Images of the Outsider in American Law and Culture: Can Free Expression Remedy Systemic Social Ills?*, 77 CORNELL L. REV. 1258 (1992).

29 *See* NANCY FRASER, UNRULY PRACTICES: POWER, DISCOURSE, AND GENDER IN CONTEMPORARY SOCIAL THEORY 17-34 (1989) [hereinafter FRASER, UNRULY PRACTICES]; Robin West, *Feminism, Critical Social Theory and Law*, 1989 U. CHI. LEGAL F. 59; Nancy Fraser, The Uses and Abuses of French Discourse Theories for Feminist Politics (1989) (unpublished manuscript, on file with the author); *see also* BRYAN D. PALMER, DESCENT INTO DISCOURSE: THE REIFICATION OF LANGUAGE AND THE WRITING OF SOCIAL HISTORY (1990).

30 *See, e.g.*, Kimberlé W. Crenshaw, *Race, Reform, and Retrenchment: Transformation and Legitimation in Antidiscrimination Law*, 101 HARV. L. REV. 1331 (1988); Charles R. Lawrence III, *The Id, the Ego, and Equal Protection: Reckoning with Unconscious Racism*, 39 STAN. L. REV. 317 (1987).

ogy of the ocean floor as well as the action of the waves. Without these other lenses, the dynamics of systemic injustice—dynamics that stunt the life-chances of some social groups with more than random frequency—will remain invisible and therefore go unchallenged.

In divorce lawyering, Professors Felstiner and Sarat have studied an area in which systemic patterns of race and class privilege do not always figure in obvious ways. Therefore, in that setting it may be, as they suggest, that their theoretical framework does pick up much of what is interesting to see. However, we cannot tell what different lenses might show us until we try them out. The work of Martha Fineman,[31] for instance, suggests that theories about gender and motherhood, as well as a Foucaultian theory of power, might help us make sense of Felstiner and Sarat's story of the unsupported wife.[32] And in areas of legal practice where hierarchies of race and class routinely figure, such as criminal law or social welfare law, the risk that a Foucaultian lens will unduly limit our vision is great. In those domains of practice, recurring patterns of domination will go uncharted unless lawyer-client interactions are studied through a lens that explicitly theorizes race and class.[33]

Getting stuck inside the Foucaultian worldview carries a second risk as well. In addition to stunting our ability to rethink institutions in emancipatory ways, this lens obscures our human capacity—or, more accurately, our longing—to realize ourselves in the world by feeling with other people, as well as by winning against them. Foucault's lens defines and thereby reveals human interactions as strategic contests. Our personhood takes form in those moments when the contest shifts power our way. This lens does not pick up those moments when we feel the force of another's emotions or the resolve behind her commitments. If such moments appear at all, they look like surges of the other's power rather than images of the other's face.

We must not discount the risks imposed by theories that make human connection seem too easy to attain. As Professor Cahn points out, such theories are very dangerous in our not-yet-post-colonial world.[34] Such theories have typically sanctioned domina-

---

31   *See, e.g.*, MARTHA FINEMAN, THE ILLUSION OF EQUALITY: THE RHETORIC AND REALITY OF DIVORCE REFORM (1991).

32   Felstiner & Sarat, *surpa* note 3, at 1471.

33   *See, e.g.*, Peggy C. Davis, *Law as Microaggression*, 1989 YALE L.J. 1559; Isabelle Gunning, Teaching Methods to Discuss Racial Stereotyping and Discrimination, Address at Association of American Law Schools Workshop on Clinical Legal Education (May 3, 1991) (audiotape available from AALS).

34   *See* Cahn, *supra* note 2, at 1429 n.139; 1445 n.217; *see also* GAYATRI SPIVAK, THE POST-COLONIAL CRITIC: INTERVIEWS, STRATEGIES, DIALOGUES (1990) [hereinafter SPIVAK,

tion of the most insidious kind, by encouraging the privileged to name the feelings of less powerful others, without cautioning that to name another's feelings is also to silence her voice.[35] We cannot give up Foucault's contest-focused theory to return to a simplistic, imperialist version of human*ism*. At the same time, however, we must recognize that Foucault's theory is ultimately—and indeed, in-evitably—incomplete.[36] For although Foucaultian power is always in motion, it hovers outside of the other, circling in what is ulti-mately a closed field. Foucault's theory does not make sense of our yearning for, or our occasional movement toward, a more fully and freely interconnected human world.

What if we seek to map the elusive moments of human connec-tion as well as the endless currents of contest? What if we seek to transform our practice and the institutions that practice enacts, not merely so we will be more adept at manipulating power, but also more present when others call our names? If we want to reflect on our longing for connection as well as our zeal for contest, what the-oretical lenses might we use?

There is no easy answer to this question. Nonetheless, Renato Rosaldo, in an arresting essay in his recent book *Culture and Truth*,[37] offers some promising thoughts. He describes his effort to compre-hend, in order to "translate," the ritual of headhunting among the Ilongot group in the Philippines. He studied the practice exhaus-tively, using the best methods academic ethnography had to offer. After extensive conversation with local informants, he carefully mapped out all of the features of the ritual. He then attempted to interpret the practice—to translate its underlying cultural logic in terms that would make sense to his own people. His informants had explained that the ritual was their way of enacting the grief they felt for loved ones who had died prematurely. Yet even with the benefit of this explanation, Rosaldo could not fathom how the grotesque act of beheading a member of a neighboring group and then eating his flesh could be endorsed by any human beings as a sensible, let alone

---

THE POST-COLONIAL CRITIC]; GAYATRI C. SPIVAK, IN OTHER WORLDS: ESSAYS IN CUL-TURAL POLITICS (1987); ANTHROPOLOGY AND THE COLONIAL ENCOUNTER (T. Asad ed., 1973).

35 This is the underlying paradox of "advocacy" for a less powerful other. *See* Lucie E. White, Goldberg v. Kelly *on the Paradox of Lawyering for the Poor*, 56 BROOK. L. REV. 861 (1990). Advocacy is inescapably—etymologically—a practice of translation, of carrying the voice of the other into a new domain. *Id.* at 861 n.3. Yet translation is also a re-placement of the other's voice. Thus, Professor White appropriately raises the theme of "tragedy" in his comment on Professor Cunningham's article. James B. White, *Transla-tion as a Mode of Thought*, 77 CORNELL L. REV. 1388 (1992).

36 *See* FRASER, UNRULY PRACTICES, *supra* note 29.

37 *See* ROSALDO, *supra* note 13.

sacred, act. For all of Rosaldo's anticolonial commitment, he felt that this practice came from a radically Other world.[38]

It was only when Rosaldo witnessed his wife plunge down a gorge to her death that he finally felt for himself the rage that follows the loss of a loved one before her time. It was the force of this feeling that enabled him, for the first time, to imagine why the Ilongot might have acted out their own grief in the way that they did. When he recalled his informant's explanation in the context of his own experience, he finally began to comprehend the ritual's human sense.

Rosaldo does not fully elaborate a theory of empathy in his essay. Rather, he offers this story to suggest some themes on which such a theory might draw. He suggests that the force of one's own emotions may cast a moment's light on others' lives, revealing both irreducible difference and, paradoxically, common ground. Contrary to Professor Cahn's suggestion in her essay,[39] Rosaldo suggests that we need not know all of the "facts" about the other in order for these moments to occur. Nor need we share all the features of the other's "identity," categorically defined. Indeed, as *prerequisites* for empathy, both of these conditions are impossible to meet.

But there is also a deeper problem with the two conditions for empathy that Professor Cahn's essay identifies. This deeper problem is that these two paths toward empathy are also practices of domination. The advice that we must find out the "facts" of the other to feel empathy toward her counsels us to objectify that person, to confine her subjectivity in categories that we construct. And the idea that to feel empathy with the other person we must identify with her, along such dimensions as race, parental status, and class, dashes all hope of empathy in many settings. In those few circumstances where empathy remains possible, this view condones practices of perception and definition that "essentialize" the other, naming her as more "like" us than she may wish to be. These practices of collecting facts about the other or cataloguing similarities with her may indeed enable us to feel closer to the other person. At the same time, however, such practices effect interpersonal domination. Perhaps we *must* take such steps, if we seek to understand the other. But we must also *renounce* these practices, or at least our confidence that they can work, if we are to recognize the other as a fellow—unique—human being.

---

38   *Cf.* Spivak, The Post-Colonial Critic, *supra* note 34.
39   *See* Cahn, *supra* note 2, at 1429.

Thus, the practice of empathy is a paradox. It takes place beyond the fields of interpersonal contestation, beyond our obsession to know exactly who we are and our maneuvers to name the other. The practice of empathy takes place beyond our certainty that, in listening to a battered woman who has fought back, that we, unlike her, "could never stab anyone."[40]

III
A STORY

My present research involves the role of parents in two local Head Start programs.[41] In doing this work, I have become acutely aware of our need for multiple theoretical lenses, lenses that focus on institutions, on moments of recognition, as well as on the ebbs and flows of interpersonal power. I felt this need with a particular urgency after conducting an interview with a seventy-two year old former sharecropper in rural North Carolina. This woman was the great-grandmother and legal guardian of a Head Start child. In the interview, she gave me a brief account of the highlights of her life. She told me of her father's defiance in sending his daughter to school when the white plantation bosses expected her to be working in the fields. She told of receiving a scholarship to an elite women's college, but turning it down because she could not afford a bus ticket to get there. She told of graduating from an African-American teacher's college and of teaching for fifty years in the public schools. She told me what it was like to teach before the schools were integrated, when her students were given text-books handed down from whites. She also told me what it was like to teach after integration, when white children asked, and were allowed, to transfer out of her class. She referred only in passing to the civil rights movement. I learned from others that she had been one of the movement's many local leaders in the rural counties of the south.

As I contemplated this story, comparing it to what others had told me about the record of racial violence in the county and the courage this woman had shown in combating it, two features stood out. First, throughout the story, she expressed inexhaustible patience, and indeed love, for the white people she had dealt with over the years. Second, although she recounted many injustices, her narrative carefully excluded the details of the violence she had en-

---

40 *Id.*
41 Head Start is a federally funded social program providing pre-school and other services to poor families. *See* Head Start Act, 42 U.S.C. §§ 9831-9858 (1991).

dured. I had noted similar themes in interviews with other African-American Head Start parents.[42]

After the formal interview was completed and the tape recorder turned off, I casually inquired about the woman's older great-grandchild, who, like my own daughter, had recently started kindergarten. When I asked this question, my informant became visibly sad. She told me that when she had dropped this child off at school earlier that morning, a young white child had run up to take her hand. Just as her great-granddaughter reached back, however, a second white child came up to the first and yanked her hand away, explaining that white girls should not touch people who were black.

Then the woman looked hard at me, and said, "The white people will go to any lengths to keep us down, even if it means keeping themselves down as well. They're making Frankensteins of us all."

This encounter could be examined through a Foucaultian lens. Such an examination would reveal an important reality. It would reveal this woman's skillful maneuvers, designed to ensure that our mutual reality was negotiated on her terms. This lens would show a woman who was artful in controlling the pace and extent of her revelations, and in determining how the injuries she had suffered would be named. This lens would reveal a woman negotiating the power between us to shape an account that she wanted me to hear.

Yet this lens reveals only a partial reality. For when this woman told me of her child's morning at school, she was not merely controlling how that event would be interpreted, and thereby trumping my own power to do the same. She was also speaking to me as another person. Through her brief story, I "felt," for a moment, something of the impossible sadness that eluded our language game. At the same time, I picked up her astute reminder that as one of those whites, I dare not claim to have "felt" her pain.[43]

The risk of domination is inextricable from every humanist practice. Yet we must still seek to listen when others speak to us,

---

[42] *See* JUDITH ROLLINS, BETWEEN WOMEN: DOMESTICS AND THEIR EMPLOYERS (1985) (documenting interactions between African-American maids and their white employers); JAMES SCOTT, DOMINATION AND THE ARTS OF RESISTANCE: HIDDEN TRANSCRIPTS (1990) (describing ways in which systematically dominated groups conceal feelings and experiences in interactions with members of dominating groups).

[43] In thinking about the (im)possibility and practice of empathy, I am guided by Jacques Derrida's reading of Emmanuel Levinas. *See, e.g.,* JACQUES DERRIDA, *Violence and Metaphysics: An Essay on the Thought of Emmanuel Levinas, in* WRITING AND DIFFERENCE (Alan Bass trans., 1978); Derrida, *Force of Law, supra* note 1. In writing about justice, as distinguished from rule or law, Derrida seeks guidance from Levinas's "difficult" conception, which is centered in the paradox of empathy. According to Derrida, Levinas imagined justice as the "equitable honoring of faces . . . the heteronomic relation to others, to the faces of otherness that govern me, whose infinity I cannot thematize and whose hostage I remain." *Id.* at 959.

and to be moved. We must still seek to hear in the words of others not just negotiations of power, but appeals to our most difficult memories and deepest emotions. We must seek, in our encounters with others, not just to map the power or read the text, but also to recognize, in all its alterity, the other's face.

Property

[21]

ON BEING THE OBJECT OF PROPERTY

PATRICIA J. WILLIAMS

On being invisible
Reflections

For some time I have been writing about my great-great-grandmother. I have considered the significance of her history and that of slavery from a variety of viewpoints on a variety of occasions: in every speech, in every conversation, even in my commercial transactions class. I have talked so much about her that I finally had to ask myself what it was I was looking for in this dogged pursuit of family history. Was I being merely indulgent, looking for roots in the pursuit of some genetic heraldry, seeking the inheritance of being special, different, unique in all that primogeniture hath wrought?

I decided that my search was based in the utility of such a quest, not mere indulgence, but a recapturing of that which had escaped historical scrutiny, which had been overlooked and underseen. I, like so many blacks, have been trying to pin myself down in history, place myself in the stream of time as significant, evolved, present in the past, continuing into the future. To be without documentation is too unsustaining, too spontaneously ahistorical, too dangerously malleable in the hands of those who would rewrite not merely the past but my future as well. So I have been picking through the ruins for my roots.

What I know of my mother's side of the family begins with my great-great-grandmother. Her name was Sophie and she lived in Tennessee. In 1850, she was about twelve years old. I know that she was purchased when she was eleven by a white lawyer named

[*Signs: Journal of Women in Culture and Society* 1988, vol. 14, no. 1]
© 1988 by The University of Chicago. All rights reserved. 0097-9740/89/1401-0005$01.00

Austin Miller and was immediately impregnated by him. She gave
birth to my great-grandmother Mary, who was taken away from her
to be raised as a house servant.[1] I know nothing more of Sophie (she
was, after all, a black single mother—in today's terms—suffering the
anonymity of yet another statistical teenage pregnancy). While I
don't remember what I was told about Austin Miller before I decided to go to law school, I do remember that just before my first
day of class, my mother said, in a voice full of secretive reassurance,
"The Millers were lawyers, so you have it in your blood."[2]

When my mother told me that I had nothing to fear in law school,
that law was "in my blood," she meant it in a very complex sense.
First and foremost, she meant it defiantly; she meant that no one
should make me feel inferior because someone else's father was a
judge. She wanted me to reclaim that part of my heritage from which
I had been disinherited, and she wanted me to use it as a source
of strength and self-confidence. At the same time, she was asking
me to claim a part of myself that was the dispossessor of another
part of myself; she was asking me to deny that disenfranchised little
black girl of myself that felt powerless, vulnerable and, moreover,
rightly felt so.

In somewhat the same vein, Mother was asking me not to look
to her as a role model. She was devaluing that part of herself that
was not Harvard and refocusing my vision to that part of herself
that was hard-edged, proficient, and Western. She hid the lonely,
black, defiled-female part of herself and pushed me forward as the
projection of a competent self, a cool rather than despairing self, a
masculine rather than a feminine self.

I took this secret of my blood into the Harvard milieu with both
the pride and the shame with which my mother had passed it along
to me. I found myself in the situation described by Marguerite
Duras, in her novel *The Lover:* "We're united in a fundamental
shame at having to live. It's here we are at the heart of our common
fate, the fact that [we] are our mother's children, the children of a
candid creature murdered by society. We're on the side of society
which has reduced her to despair. Because of what's been done to
our mother, so amiable, so trusting, we hate life, we hate ourselves."[3]

Reclaiming that from which one has been disinherited is a good
thing. Self-possession in the full sense of that expression is the
companion to self-knowledge. Yet claiming for myself a heritage

---

[1] For a more detailed account of the family history to this point, see Patricia
Williams, "Grandmother Sophie," *Harvard Blackletter* 3 (1986): 79.

[2] Patricia Williams, "Alchemical Notes: Reconstructing Ideals from Deconstructed Rights," *Harvard Civil Rights–Civil Liberties Law Review* 22 (1987): 418.

[3] Marguerite Duras, *The Lover* (New York: Harper & Row, 1985), 55.

Autumn 1988 / **SIGNS**

the weft of whose genesis is my own disinheritance is a profoundly troubling paradox.

Images

A friend of mine practices law in rural Florida. His office is in Belle Glade, an extremely depressed area where the sugar industry reigns supreme, where blacks live pretty much as they did in slavery times, in dormitories called slave ships. They are penniless and illiterate and have both a high birth rate and a high death rate.

My friend told me about a client of his, a fifteen-year-old young woman pregnant with her third child, who came seeking advice because her mother had advised a hysterectomy—not even a tubal ligation—as a means of birth control. The young woman's mother, in turn, had been advised of the propriety of such a course in her own case by a white doctor some years before. Listening to this, I was reminded of a case I worked on when I was working for the Western Center on Law and Poverty about eight years ago. Ten black Hispanic women had been sterilized by the University of Southern California–Los Angeles County General Medical Center, allegedly without proper consent, and in most instances without even their knowledge.[4] Most of them found out what had been done to them upon inquiry, after a much-publicized news story in which an intern charged that the chief of obstetrics at the hospital pursued a policy of recommending Caesarian delivery and simultaneous sterilization for any pregnant woman with three or more children and who was on welfare. In the course of researching the appeal in that case, I remember learning that one-quarter of all Navajo women of childbearing age—literally all those of childbearing age ever admitted to a hospital—have been sterilized.[5]

---

[4] *Madrigal v. Quilligan*, U.S. Court of Appeals, 9th Circuit, Docket no. 78-3187, October 1979.

[5] This was the testimony of one of the witnesses. It is hard to find official confirmation for this or any other sterilization statistic involving Native American women. Official statistics kept by the U.S. Public Health Service, through the Centers for Disease Control in Atlanta, come from data gathered by the National Hospital Discharge Survey, which covers neither federal hospitals nor penitentiaries. Services to Native American women living on reservations are provided almost exclusively by federal hospitals. In addition, the U.S. Public Health Service breaks down its information into only three categories: "White," "Black," and "Other." Nevertheless, in 1988, the Women of All Red Nations Collective of Minneapolis, Minnesota, distributed a fact sheet entitled "Sterilization Studies of Native American Women," which claimed that as many as 50 percent of all Native American women of childbearing age have been sterilized. According to "Surgical Sterilization Surveillance: Tubal Sterilization and Hysterectomy in Women Aged 15–44, 1979–1980," issued

As I reflected on all this, I realized that one of the things passed
on from slavery, which continues in the oppression of people of
color, is a belief structure rooted in a concept of black (or brown,
or red) anti-will, the antithetical embodiment of pure will. We live
in a society in which the closest equivalent of nobility is the display
of unremittingly controlled will-fulness. To be perceived as unremittingly will-less is to be imbued with an almost lethal trait.

Many scholars have explained this phenomenon in terms of total
and infantilizing interdependency of dominant and oppressed.[6]
Consider, for example, Mark Tushnet's distinction between slave
law's totalistic view of personality and the bourgeois "pure will"
theory of personality: "Social relations in slave society rest upon
the interaction of owner with slave; the owner, having total dominion over the slave. In contrast, bourgeois social relations rest upon
the paradigmatic instance of market relations, the purchase by a
capitalist of a worker's labor power; that transaction implicates only
a part of the worker's personality. Slave relations are total, engaging
the master and slave in exchanges in which each must take account
of the entire range of belief, feeling, and interest embodied by the
other; bourgeois social relations are partial, requiring only that participants in a market evaluate their general productive characteristics without regard to aspects of personality unrelated to
production."[7]

Although such an analysis is not objectionable in some general
sense, the description of master-slave relations as "total" is, to me,

---

by the Centers for Disease Control in 1983, "In 1980, the tubal sterilization rate for
black women . . . was 45 percent greater than that for white women" (7). Furthermore, a study released in 1984 by the Division of Reproductive Health of the Center
for Health Promotion and Education (one of the Centers for Disease Control) found
that, as of 1982, 48.8 percent of Puerto Rican women between the ages of 15 and
44 had been sterilized.

  [6] See, generally, Stanley Elkins, *Slavery* (New York: Grosset & Dunlap, 1963);
Kenneth Stampp, *The Peculiar Institution* (New York: Vintage, 1956): Winthrop
Jordan, *White over Black* (Baltimore: Penguin Books, 1968).

  [7] Mark Tushnet, *The American Law of Slavery* (Princeton, N.J.: Princeton University Press, 1981), 6. There is danger, in the analysis that follows, of appearing to
"pick" on Tushnet. That is not my intention, nor is it to impugn the body of his
research, most of which I greatly admire. The choice of this passage for analysis has
more to do with the randomness of my reading habits; the fact that he is one of the
few legal writers to attempt, in the context of slavery, a juxtaposition of political
theory with psychoanalytic theories of personality; and the fact that he is perceived
to be of the political left, which simplifies my analysis in terms of its presumption
of sympathy, i.e., that the constructions of thought revealed are socially derived and
unconscious rather than idiosyncratic and intentional.

Autumn 1988 / **SIGNS**

quite troubling. Such a choice of words reflects and accepts—at a
very subtle level, perhaps—a historical rationalization that whites
had to, could do, and did do everything for these simple, above-
animal subhumans. It is a choice of vocabulary that fails to acknowledge blacks as having needs beyond those that even the most
"humane" or "sentimental" white slavemaster could provide.[8] In
trying to describe the provisional aspect of slave law, I would choose
words that revealed its structure as rooted in a concept of, again,
black anti-will, the polar opposite of pure will. I would characterize
the treatment of blacks by whites in whites' law as defining blacks
as those who had no will. I would characterize that treatment not
as total interdependency, but as a relation in which partializing
judgments, employing partializing standards of humanity, impose
generalized inadequacy on a race: if pure will or total control equals
the perfect white person, then impure will and total lack of control
equals the perfect black man or woman. Therefore, to define slave
law as comprehending a "total" view of personality implicitly accepts that the provision of food, shelter, and clothing (again assuming the very best of circumstances) is the whole requirement of
humanity. It assumes also either that psychic care was provided by
slave owners (as though a slave or an owned psyche could ever be
reconciled with mental health) or that psyche is not a significant
part of a whole human.

Market theory indeed focuses attention away from the full range
of human potential in its pursuit of a divinely willed, invisibly
handed economic actor. Master-slave relations, however, focused
attention away from the full range of black human potential in a
somewhat different way: it pursued a vision of blacks as simple-

---

[8] In another passage, Tushnet observes: "The court thus demonstrated its appreciation of the ties of sentiment that slavery could generate between master and
slave and simultaneously denied that those ties were relevant in the law" (67). What
is noteworthy about the reference to "sentiment" is that it assumes that the fact that
emotions could grow up between slave and master is itself worth remarking: slightly
surprising, slightly commendable for the court to note (i.e., in its "appreciation")—
although "simultaneously" with, and presumably in contradistinction to, the court's
inability to take official cognizance of the fact. Yet, if one really looks at the ties that
bound master and slave, one has to flesh out the description of master-slave with
the ties of father-son, father-daughter, half-sister, half-brother, uncle, aunt, cousin,
and a variety of de facto foster relationships. And if one starts to see those ties as
more often than not intimate family ties, then the terminology "appreciation of . . .
sentiment . . . between master and slave" becomes a horrifying mockery of any true
sense of family sentiment, which is utterly, utterly lacking. The court's "appreciation," from this enhanced perspective, sounds blindly cruel, sarcastic at best. And
to observe that courts suffused in such "appreciation" could simultaneously deny
its legal relevance seems not only a truism; it misses the point entirely.

minded, strong-bodied economic actants."[9] Thus, while blacks had
an indisputable generative force in the marketplace, their presence
could not be called activity; they had no active role in the market.
To say, therefore, that "market relations disregard the peculiarities
of individuals, whereas slave relations rest on the mutual recognition of the humanity of master and slave"[10] (no matter how dialectical or abstracted a definition of humanity one adopts) is to posit
an inaccurate equation: if "disregard for the peculiarities of individuals" and "mutual recognition of humanity" are polarized by a
"whereas," then somehow regard for peculiarities of individuals
must equal recognition of humanity. In the context of slavery this
equation mistakes whites' overzealous and oppressive obsession
with projected specific peculiarities of blacks for actual holistic
regard for the individual. It overlooks the fact that most definitions
of humanity require something beyond mere biological sustenance,
some healthy measure of autonomy beyond that of which slavery
could institutionally or otherwise conceive. Furthermore, it overlooks the fact that both slave and bourgeois systems regarded certain
attributes as important and disregarded certain others, and that such
regard and disregard can occur in the same glance, like the wearing
of horseblinders to focus attention simultaneously toward and away
from. The experiential blinders of market actor and slave are focused
in different directions, yet the partializing ideologies of each makes
the act of not seeing an unconscious, alienating component of seeing.
Restoring a unified social vision will, I think, require broader and
more scattered resolutions than the simple symmetry of ideological
bipolarity.

Thus, it is important to undo whatever words obscure the fact
that slave law was at least as fragmenting and fragmented as the
bourgeois worldview—in a way that has persisted to this day, cutting
across all ideological boundaries. As "pure will" signifies the whole
bourgeois personality in the bourgeois worldview, so wisdom, control, and aesthetic beauty signify the whole white personality in
slave law. The former and the latter, the slavemaster and the burger-
meister, are not so very different when expressed in those terms.
The reconciling difference is that in slave law the emphasis is really

[9] "Actants have a kind of phonemic, rather than a phonetic role: they operate on
the level of function, rather than content. That is, an actant may embody itself in a
particular character (termed an acteur) or it may reside in the function of more than
one character in respect of their common role in the story's underlying 'oppositional'
structure. In short, the deep structure of the narrative generates and defines its
actants at a level beyond that of the story's surface content" (Terence Hawkes,
Structuralism and Semiotics [Berkeley: University of California Press, 1977], 89).

[10] Tushnet, 69.

Autumn 1988 / **SIGNS**

on the inverse rationale: that irrationality, lack of control, and ugliness signify the whole slave personality. "Total" interdependence is at best a polite way of rationalizing such personality splintering; it creates a bizarre sort of yin-yang from the dross of an oppressive schizophrenia of biblical dimension. I would just call it schizophrenic, with all the baggage that that connotes. That is what sounds right to me. Truly total relationships (as opposed to totalitarianism) call up images of whole people dependent on whole people; an interdependence that is both providing and laissez-faire at the same time. Neither the historical inheritance of slave law nor so-called bourgeois law meets that definition.

None of this, perhaps, is particularly new. Nevertheless, as precedent to anything I do as a lawyer, the greatest challenge is to allow the full truth of partializing social constructions to be felt for their overwhelming reality—reality that otherwise I might rationally try to avoid facing. In my search for roots, I must assume, not just as history but as an ongoing psychological force, that, in the eyes of white culture, irrationality, lack of control, and ugliness signify not just the whole slave personality, not just the whole black personality, but me.

Vision

Reflecting on my roots makes me think again and again of the young woman in Belle Glade, Florida. She told the story of her impending sterilization, according to my friend, while keeping her eyes on the ground at all times. My friend, who is white, asked why she wouldn't look up, speak with him eye to eye. The young woman answered that she didn't like white people seeing inside her.

My friend's story made me think of my own childhood and adolescence: my parents were always telling me to look up at the world; to look straight at people, particularly white people; not to let them stare me down; to hold my ground; to insist on the right to my presence no matter what. They told me that in this culture you have to look people in the eye because that's how you tell them you're their equal. My friend's story also reminded me how very difficult I had found that looking-back to be. What was hardest was not just that white people saw me, as my friend's client put it, but that they looked through me, that they treated me as though I were transparent.

By itself, seeing into me would be to see my substance, my anger, my vulnerability, and my wild raging despair—and that alone is hard enough to show, to share. But to uncover it and to have it devalued by ignore-ance, to hold it up bravely in the organ of my eyes and to have it greeted by an impassive stare that passes right through all that which is me, an impassive stare that moves on and attaches itself to my left earlobe or to the dust caught in the rusty vertical geysers of my wiry hair or to the breadth of my freckled brown nose—this is deeply humiliating. It re-wounds, relives the early childhood anguish of uncensored seeing, the fullness of vision that is the permanent turning-away point for most blacks.

The cold game of equality-staring makes me feel like a thin sheet of glass: white people see all the worlds beyond me but not me. They come trotting at me with force and speed; they do not see me. I could force my presence, the real me contained in those eyes, upon them, but I would be smashed in the process. If I deflect, if I move out of the way, they will never know I existed.

Marguerite Duras, again in *The Lover*, places the heroine in relation to her family. "Every day we try to kill one another, to kill. Not only do we not talk to one another, we don't even look at one another. When you're being looked at you can't look. To look is to feel curious, to be interested, to lower yourself."[11]

To look is also to make myself vulnerable; yet not to look is to neutralize the part of myself which is vulnerable. I look in order to see, and so I must look. Without that directness of vision, I am afraid I will will my own blindness, disinherit my own creativity, and sterilize my own perspective of its embattled, passionate insight.

On ardor

The child

One Saturday afternoon not long ago, I sat among a litter of family photographs telling a South African friend about Marjorie, my god-mother and my mother's cousin. She was given away by her light-skinned mother when she was only six. She was given to my grand-mother and my great-aunts to be raised among her darker-skinned cousins, for Marjorie was very dark indeed. Her mother left the family to "pass," to marry a white man—Uncle Frederick, we called him with trepidatious presumption yet without his ever knowing of our existence—an heir to a meat-packing fortune. When Uncle Frederick died thirty years later and the fortune was lost, Marjorie's mother rejoined the race, as the royalty of resentful fascination—Lady Bountiful, my sister called her—to regale us with tales of gracious upper-class living.

[11] Duras, 54.

12

Autumn 1988 / **SIGNS**

My friend said that my story reminded him of a case in which a swarthy, crisp-haired child was born, in Durban, to white parents. The Afrikaner government quickly intervened, removed the child from its birth home, and placed it to be raised with a "more suitable," browner family.

When my friend and I had shared these stories, we grew embarrassed somehow, and our conversation trickled away into a discussion of laissez-faire economics and governmental interventionism. Our words became a clear line, a railroad upon which all other ideas and events were tied down and sacrificed.

The market

As a teacher of commercial transactions, one of the things that has always impressed me most about the law of contract is a certain deadening power it exercises by reducing the parties to the passive. It constrains the lively involvement of its signatories by positioning enforcement in such a way that parties find themselves in a passive relationship to a document: it is the contract that governs, that "does" everything, that absorbs all responsibility and deflects all other recourse.

Contract law reduces life to fairy tale. The four corners of the agreement become parent. Performance is the equivalent of obedience to the parent. Obedience is dutifully passive. Passivity is valued as good contract-socialized behavior; activity is caged in retrospective hypotheses about states of mind at the magic moment of contracting. Individuals are judged by the contract unfolding rather than by the actors acting autonomously. Nonperformance is disobedience; disobedience is active; activity becomes evil in contrast to the childlike passivity of contract conformity.

One of the most powerful examples of all this is the case of Mary Beth Whitehead, mother of Sara—of so-called Baby M. Ms. Whitehead became a vividly original actor *after* the creation of her contract with William Stern; unfortunately for her, there can be no greater civil sin. It was in this upside-down context, in the picaresque unboundedness of breachor, that her energetic grief became hysteria and her passionate creativity was funneled, whorled, and reconstructed as highly impermissible. Mary Beth Whitehead thus emerged as the evil stepsister who deserved nothing.

Some time ago, Charles Reich visited a class of mine.[12] He discussed with my students a proposal for a new form of bargain by

---

[12] Charles Reich is author of *The Greening of America* (New York: Random House, 1970) and professor of law at the University of San Francisco Law School.

which emotional "items"—such as praise, flattery, acting happy or
sad—might be contracted for explicitly. One student, not alone in
her sentiment, said, "Oh, but then you'll just feel obligated." Only
the week before, however (when we were discussing the contract
which posited that Ms. Whitehead "will not form or attempt to form
a parent-child relationship with any child or children"), this same
student had insisted that Ms. Whitehead must give up her child,
because she had *said* she would: "She was obligated!" I was con-
founded by the degree to which what the student took to be self-
evident, inalienable gut reactions could be governed by illusions
of passive conventionality and form.

It was that incident, moreover, that gave me insight into how
Judge Harvey Sorkow, of New Jersey Superior Court, could conclude that the contract that purported to terminate Ms. Whitehead's
parental rights was "not illusory."[13]

(As background, I should say that I think that, within the framework of contract law itself, the agreement between Ms. Whitehead
and Mr. Stern was clearly illusory.[14] On the one hand, Judge Sorkow's opinion said that Ms. Whitehead was seeking to avoid her
obligations. In other words, giving up her child became an actual
obligation. On the other hand, according to the logic of the judge,
this was a service contract, not really a sale of a child; therefore
delivering the child to the Sterns was an "obligation" for which
there was no consideration, for which Mr. Stern was not paying her.)

Judge Sorkow's finding the contract "not illusory" is suggestive
not just of the doctrine by that name, but of illusion in general, and
delusion, and the righteousness with which social constructions are
conceived, acted on, and delivered up into the realm of the real as
"right," while all else is devoured from memory as "wrong." From
this perspective, the rhetorical tricks by which Sara Whitehead became Melissa Stern seem very like the heavy-worded legalities by
which my great-great-grandmother was pacified and parted from
her child. In both situations, the real mother had no say, no power;
her powerlessness was imposed by state law that made her and her
child helpless in relation to the father. My great-great-grandmother's

---

[13] See, generally, In the Matter of Baby "M," A Pseudonym for an Actual Person,
Superior Court of New Jersey, Chancery Division, Docket no. FM-25314-86E, March
31, 1987. This decision was appealed, and on February 3, 1988, the New Jersey
Supreme Court ruled that surrogate contracts were illegal and against public policy.
In addition to the contract issue, however, the appellate court decided the custody
issue in favor of the Sterns but granted visitation rights to Mary Beth Whitehead.

[14] "An illusory promise is an expression cloaked in promissory terms, but which,
upon closer examination, reveals that the promisor has committed himself not at
all" (J. Calamari and J. Perillo, *Contracts*, 3d ed. [St. Paul: West Publishing, 1987],
228).

Autumn 1988 / **SIGNS**

powerlessness came about as the result of a contract to which she was not a party; Mary Beth Whitehead's powerlessness came about as a result of a contract that she signed at a discrete point of time—yet which, over time, enslaved her. The contract-reality in both instances was no less than magic: it was illusion transformed into not-illusion. Furthermore, it masterfully disguised the brutality of enforced arrangements in which these women's autonomy, their flesh and their blood, were locked away in word vaults, without room to reconsider—*ever.*

In the months since Judge Sorkow's opinion, I have reflected on the similarities of fortune between my own social positioning and that of Sara Melissa Stern Whitehead. I have come to realize that an important part of the complex magic that Judge Sorkow wrote into his opinion was a supposition that it is "natural" for people to want children "like" themselves. What this reasoning raised for me was an issue of what, exactly, constituted this "likeness"? (What would have happened, for example, if Ms. Whitehead had turned out to have been the "passed" descendant of my "failed" godmother Marjorie's mother? What if the child she bore had turned out to be recessively and visibly black? Would the sperm of Mr. Stern have been so powerful as to make this child "his" with the exclusivity that Judge Sorkow originally assigned?) What constitutes, moreover, the collective understanding of "un-likeness"?

These questions turn, perhaps, on not-so-subtle images of which mothers should be bearing which children. Is there not something unseemly, in our society, about the spectacle of a white woman mothering a black child? A white woman giving totally to a black child; a black child totally and demandingly dependent for everything, for sustenance itself, from a white woman. The image of a white woman suckling a black child; the image of a black child sucking for its life from the bosom of a white woman. The utter interdependence of such an image; the selflessness, the merging it implies; the giving up of boundary; the encompassing of other within self; the unbounded generosity, the interconnectedness of such an image. Such a picture says that there is no difference; it places the hope of continuous generation, of immortality of the white self in a little black face.

When Judge Sorkow declared that it was only to be expected that parents would want to breed children "like" themselves, he simultaneously created a legal right to the same. With the creation of such a "right," he encased the children conforming to "likeliness" in protective custody, far from whole ranges of taboo. Taboo about touch and smell and intimacy and boundary. Taboo about ardor, possession, license, equivocation, equanimity, indifference, intol-

erance, rancor, dispossession, innocence, exile, and candor. Taboo
about death. Taboos that amount to death. Death and sacredness,
the valuing of body, of self, of other, of remains. The handling
lovingly in life, as in life; the question of the intimacy versus the
dispassion of death.

In effect, these taboos describe boundaries of valuation. Whether
something is inside or outside the marketplace of rights has always
been a way of valuing it. When a valued object is located outside
the market, it is generally understood to be too "priceless" to be
accommodated by ordinary exchange relationships; when, in contrast, the prize is located within the marketplace, all objects outside
become "valueless." Traditionally, the Mona Lisa and human life
have been the sorts of subjects removed from the fungibility of
commodification, as "priceless." Thus when black people were
bought and sold as slaves, they were placed beyond the bounds of
humanity. And thus, in the twistedness of our brave new world,
when blacks have been thrust out of the market and it is white
children who are bought and sold, black babies have become
"worthless" currency to adoption agents—"surplus" in the salvage
heaps of Harlem hospitals.

The imagination

"Familiar though his name may be to us, the storyteller in his living
immediacy is by no means a present force. He has already become
something remote from us and something that is getting even more
distant. . . . Less and less frequently do we encounter people with
the ability to tell a tale properly. . . . It is as if something that seemed
inalienable to us, the securest among our possessions, were taken
from us: the ability to exchange experiences."[15]

My mother's cousin Marjorie was a storyteller. From time to time
I would press her to tell me the details of her youth, and she would
tell me instead about a child who wandered into a world of polar
bears, who was prayed over by polar bears, and in the end eaten.
The child's life was not in vain because the polar bears had been
made holy by its suffering. The child had been a test, a message
from god for polar bears. In the polar bear universe, she would tell
me, the primary object of creation was polar bears, and the rest of
the living world was fashioned to serve polar bears. The clouds
took their shape from polar bears, trees were designed to give shel-

---

[15] Walter Benjamin, "The Storyteller," in *Illuminations*, ed. Hannah Arendt (New
York: Schocken, 1969), 83.

ter and shade to polar bears, and humans were ideally designed to provide polar bears with meat.[16]

The truth, the truth, I would laughingly insist as we sat in her apartment eating canned fruit and heavy roasts, mashed potatoes, pickles and vanilla pudding, cocoa, Sprite, or tea. What about roots and all that, I coaxed. But the voracity of her amnesia would disclaim and disclaim and disclaim; and she would go on telling me about the polar bears until our plates were full of emptiness and I became large in the space which described her emptiness and I gave in to the emptiness of words.

On life and death
Sighing into space

There are moments in my life when I feel as though a part of me is missing. There are days when I feel so invisible that I can't remember what day of the week it is, when I feel so manipulated that I can't remember my own name, when I feel so lost and angry that I can't speak a civil word to the people who love me best. Those are the times when I catch sight of my reflection in store windows and am surprised to see a whole person looking back. Those are the times when my skin becomes gummy as clay and my nose slides around on my face and my eyes drip down to my chin. I have to close my eyes at such times and remember myself, draw an internal picture that is smooth and whole; when all else fails, I reach for a mirror and stare myself down until the features reassemble themselves like lost sheep.

Two years ago, my godmother Marjorie suffered a massive stroke. As she lay dying, I would come to the hospital to give her her meals. My feeding her who had so often fed me became a complex ritual of mirroring and self-assembly. The physical act of holding the spoon to her lips was not only a rite of nurture and of sacrifice, it was the return of a gift. It was a quiet bowing to the passage of time and the doubling back of all things. The quiet woman who listened to my woes about work and school required now that I bend my head down close to her and listen for mouthed word fragments, sentence crumbs. I bent down to give meaning to her silence, her wandering search for words.

She would eat what I brought to the hospital with relish; she would reject what I brought with a turn of her head. I brought fruit

---

[16] For an analysis of similar stories, see Richard Levins and Richard Lewontin, *The Dialectical Biologist* (Cambridge, Mass.: Harvard University Press, 1985), 66.

Williams / THE OBJECT OF PROPERTY

and yogurt, ice cream and vegetable juice. Slowly, over time, she stopped swallowing. The mashed potatoes would sit in her mouth like cotton, the pudding would slip to her chin in slow sad streams. When she lost not only her speech but the power to ingest, they put a tube into her nose and down to her stomach, and I lost even that medium by which to communicate. No longer was there the odd but reassuring communion over taste. No longer was there some echo of comfort in being able to nurture one who nurtured me.

This increment of decay was like a little newborn death. With the tube, she stared up at me with imploring eyes, and I tried to guess what it was that she would like. I read to her aimlessly and in desperation. We entertained each other with the strange embarrassed flickering of our eyes. I told her stories to fill the emptiness, the loneliness, of the white-walled hospital room.

I told her stories about who I had become, about how I had grown up to know all about exchange systems, and theories of contract, and monetary fictions. I spun tales about blue-sky laws and promissory estoppel, the wispy-feathered complexity of undue influence and dark-hearted theories of unconscionability. I told her about market norms and gift economy and the thin razor's edge of the bartering ethic. Once upon a time, I rambled, some neighbors of mine included me in their circle of barter. They were in the habit of exchanging eggs and driving lessons, hand-knit sweaters and computer programming, plumbing and calligraphy. I accepted the generosity of their inclusion with gratitude. At first, I felt that, as a lawyer, I was worthless, that I had no barterable skills and nothing to contribute. What I came to realize with time, however, was that my value to the group was not calculated by the physical items I brought to it. These people included me because they wanted me to be part of their circle, they valued my participation apart from the material things I could offer. So I gave of myself to them, and they gave me fruit cakes and dandelion wine and smoked salmon, and in their giving, their goods became provisions. Cradled in this community whose currency was a relational ethic, my stock in myself soared. My value depended on the glorious intangibility, the eloquent invisibility of my just being *part* of the collective; and in direct response I grew spacious and happy and gentle.

My gentle godmother. The fragility of life; the cold mortuary shelf.

Dispassionate deaths

The hospital in which my godmother died is now filled to capacity with AIDS patients. One in sixty-one babies born there, as in New

Autumn 1988 / **SIGNS**

York City generally, is infected with AIDS antibodies.[17] Almost all
are black or Hispanic. In the Bronx, the rate is one in forty-three.[18]
In Central Africa, experts estimate that, of children receiving trans-
fusions for malaria-related anemia, "about 1000 may have been infected with the AIDS virus in each of the last five years."[19] In Congo,
5 percent of the entire population is infected.[20] The *New York Times*
reports that "the profile of Congo's population seems to guarantee
the continued spread of AIDS."[21]

In the Congolese city of Pointe Noir, "the annual budget of the
sole public health hospital is estimated at about $200,000—roughly
the amount of money spent in the United States to care for four
AIDS patients."[22]

The week in which my godmother died is littered with bad
memories. In my journal, I made note of the following:

> *Good Friday:* Phil Donahue has a special program on
> AIDS. The segues are:
> a. from Martha, who weeps at the prospect of not
> watching her children grow up
> b. to Jim, who is not conscious enough to speak just
> now, who coughs convulsively, who recognizes no one in his
> family any more
> c. to Hugh who, at 85 pounds, thinks he has five years
> but whose doctor says he has weeks
> d. to an advertisement for denture polish ("If you love
> your Polident Green/then gimmeeya SMILE!")
> e. and then one for a plastic surgery salon on Park
> Avenue ("The only thing that's expensive is our address")
> f. and then one for what's coming up on the five o'clock
> news (Linda Lovelace, of *Deep Throat* fame, "still recovering
> from a double mastectomy and complications from silicone
> injections" is being admitted to a New York hospital for a
> liver transplant)
> g. and finally one for the miracle properties of all-
> purpose house cleaner ("Mr. Cleeean/is the man/behind the

---

[17] B. Lambert, "Study Finds Antibodies for AIDS in 1 in 61 Babies in New York
City," *New York Times* (January 13, 1988), sec. A.

[18] Ibid.

[19] "Study Traces AIDS in African Children," *New York Times* (January 22, 1988),
sec. A.

[20] J. Brooke, "New Surge of AIDS in Congo May Be an Omen for Africa," *New
York Times* (January 22, 1988), sec. A.

[21] Ibid.

[22] Ibid.

shine/is it wet or is it dry?" I note that Mr. Clean, with his gleaming bald head, puffy musculature and fever-bright eyes, looks like he is undergoing radiation therapy). Now back to our show.

h. "We are back now with Martha," (who is crying harder than before, sobbing uncontrollably, each jerking inhalation a deep unearthly groan). Phil says, "Oh honey, I hope we didn't make it worse for you."

Easter Saturday: Over lunch, I watch another funeral. My office windows overlook a graveyard as crowded and still as a rush-hour freeway. As I savor pizza and milk, I notice that one of the mourners is wearing an outfit featured in the window of Bloomingdale's (59th Street store) only since last weekend. This thread of recognition jolts me, and I am drawn to her in sorrow; the details of my own shopping history flash before my eyes as I reflect upon the sober spree that brought her to the rim of this earthly chasm, her slim suede heels sinking into the soft silt of the graveside.

Resurrection Sunday: John D., the bookkeeper where I used to work, died, hit on the head by a stray but forcefully propelled hockey puck. I cried copiously at his memorial service, only to discover, later that afternoon when I saw a black rimmed photograph, that I had been mourning the wrong person. I had cried because the man I *thought* had died is John D. the office messenger, a bitter unfriendly man who treats me with disdain; once I bought an old electric typewriter from him which never worked. Though he promised nothing, I have harbored deep dislike since then; death by hockey puck is only one of the fates I had imagined for him. I washed clean my guilt with buckets of tears at the news of what I thought was his demise.

The man who did die was small, shy, anonymously sweet-featured and innocent. In some odd way I was relieved; no seriously obligatory mourning to be done here. A quiet impassivity settled over me and I forgot my grief.

Holy communion

A few months after my godmother died, my Great Aunt Jag passed away in Cambridge, at ninety-six the youngest and the last of her siblings, all of whom died at ninety-seven. She collapsed on her way home from the polling place, having gotten in her vote for "yet another Kennedy." Her wake was much like the last family gathering

Autumn 1988 / **SIGNS**

at which I had seen her, two Thanksgivings ago. She was a little hard of hearing then and she stayed on the outer edge of the conversation, brightly, loudly, and randomly asserting enjoyment of her meal. At the wake, cousins, nephews, daughters-in-law, first wives, second husbands, great-grand-nieces gathered round her casket and got acquainted all over again. It was pouring rain outside. The funeral home was dry and warm, faintly spicily clean-smelling; the walls were solid, dark, respectable wood; the floors were cool stone tile. On the door of a room marked "No Admittance" was a sign that reminded workers therein of the reverence with which each body was held by its family and prayed employees handle the remains with similar love and care. Aunt Jag wore yellow chiffon; everyone agreed that laying her out with her glasses on was a nice touch.

Afterward, we all went to Legal Seafoods, her favorite restaurant, and ate many of her favorite foods.

On candor

Me

I have never been able to determine my horoscope with any degree of accuracy. Born at Boston's now-defunct Lying-In Hospital, I am a Virgo, despite a quite poetic soul. Knowledge of the *hour* of my birth, however, would determine not just my sun sign but my moons and all the more intimate specificities of my destiny. Once upon a time, I sent for my birth certificate, which was retrieved from the oblivion of Massachusetts microfiche. Said document revealed that an infant named Patricia Joyce, born of parents named Williams, was delivered into the world "colored." Since no one thought to put down the hour of my birth, I suppose that I will never know my true fate.

In the meantime, I read what text there is of me.

My name, Patricia, means patrician. Patricias are noble, lofty, elite, exclusively educated, and well mannered despite themselves. I was on the cusp of being Pamela, but my parents knew that such a me would require lawns, estates, and hunting dogs too.

I am also a Williams. Of William, whoever he was: an anonymous white man who owned my father's people and from whom some escaped. That rupture is marked by the dark-mooned mystery of utter silence.

Williams is the second most common surname in the United States; Patricia is *the* most common prename among women born in 1951, the year of my birth.

Williams / THE OBJECT OF PROPERTY

Them

In the law, rights are islands of empowerment. To be un-righted is to be disempowered, and the line between rights and no rights is most often the line between dominators and oppressors. Rights contain images of power, and manipulating those images, either visually or linguistically, is central in the making and maintenance of rights. In principle, therefore, the more dizzyingly diverse the images that are propagated, the more empowered we will be as a society.

In reality, it was a lovely polar bear afternoon. The gentle force of the earth. A wide wilderness of islands. A conspiracy of polar bears lost in timeless forgetting. A gentleness of polar bears, a fruitfulness of polar bears, a silent black-eyed interest of polar bears, a bristled expectancy of polar bears. With the wisdom of innocence, a child threw stones at the polar bears. Hungry, they rose from their nests, inquisitive, dark-souled, patient with foreboding, fearful in tremendous awakening. The instinctual ferocity of the hunter reflected upon the hunted. Then, proud teeth and warrior claws took innocence for wilderness and raging insubstantiality for tender rabbit breath.

In the newspapers the next day, it was reported that two polar bears in the Brooklyn Zoo mauled to death an eleven-year-old boy who had entered their cage to swim in the moat. The police were called and the bears were killed.[23]

In the public debate that ensued, many levels of meaning emerged. The rhetoric firmly established that the bears were innocent, naturally territorial, unfairly imprisoned, and guilty. The dead child (born into the urban jungle of a black, welfare mother and a Hispanic alcoholic father who had died literally in the gutter only six weeks before) was held to a similarly stern standard. The police were captured, in a widely disseminated photograph,[24] shooting helplessly, desperately, into the cage, through three levels of bars, at a pieta of bears; since this image, conveying much pathos, came nevertheless not in time to save the child, it was generally felt that the bears had died in vain.[25]

In the egalitarianism of exile, pluralists rose up as of one body, with a call to buy more bears, control juvenile delinquency, eliminate all zoos, and confine future police.[26]

[23] J. Barron, "Polar Bears Kill a Child at Prospect Park Zoo," *New York Times* (May 20, 1987), sec. A.

[24] *New York Post* (May 22, 1987), p. 1.

[25] J. Barron, "Officials Weigh Tighter Security at Zoos in Parks," *New York Times* (May 22, 1987), sec. B.

[26] Ibid.

Autumn 1988 / **SIGNS**

In the plenary session of the national meeting of the Law and Society Association, the keynote speaker unpacked the whole incident as a veritable laboratory of emergent rights discourse. Just seeing that these complex levels of meaning exist, she exulted, should advance rights discourse significantly.[27]

At the funeral of the child, the presiding priest pronounced the death of Juan Perez not in vain, since he was saved from growing into "a lifetime of crime." Juan's Hispanic-welfare-black-widow-of-an-alcoholic mother decided then and there to sue.

The universe between

How I ended up at Dartmouth College for the summer is too long a story to tell. Anyway, there I was, sharing the town of Hanover, New Hampshire, with about two hundred prepubescent males enrolled in Dartmouth's summer basketball camp, an all-white, very expensive, affirmative action program for the street-deprived.

One fragrant evening, I was walking down East Wheelock Street when I encountered about a hundred of these adolescents, fresh from the courts, wet, lanky, big-footed, with fuzzy yellow crew cuts, loping toward Thayer Hall and food. In platoons of twenty-five or so, they descended upon me, jostling me, smacking me, and pushing me from the sidewalk into the gutter. In a thoughtless instant, I snatched off my brown silk headrag, my flag of African femininity and propriety, my sign of meek and supplicatory place and presentation. I released the armored rage of my short nappy hair (the scalp gleaming bare between the angry wire spikes) and hissed: "Don't I exist for you?! See Me! And deflect, godammit!" (The quaint professionalism of my formal English never allowed the rage in my head to rise so high as to overflow the edges of my text.)

They gave me wide berth. They clearly had no idea, however, that I was talking to them or about them. They skirted me sheepishly, suddenly polite, because they did know, when a crazed black person comes crashing into one's field of vision, that it is impolite to laugh. I stood tall and spoke loudly into their ranks: "I have my rights!" The Dartmouth Summer Basketball Camp raised its collective eyebrows and exhaled, with a certain tested nobility of exhaustion and solidarity.

I pursued my way, manumitted back into silence. I put distance between them and me, gave myself over to polar bear musings. I allowed myself to be watched over by bear spirits. Clean white wind and strong bear smells. The shadowed amnesia; the absence

[27] Patricia Williams, "The Meaning of Rights" (address to the annual meeting of the Law and Society Association, Washington, D.C., June 6, 1987).

of being; the presence of polar bears. White wilderness of icy meat-eaters heavy with remembrance; leaden with undoing; shaggy with the effort of hunting for silence; frozen in a web of intention and intuition. A lunacy of polar bears. A history of polar bears. A pride of polar bears. A consistency of polar bears. In those meandering pastel polar bear moments, I found cool fragments of white-fur invisibility. Solid, black-gummed, intent, observant. Hungry and patient, impassive and exquisitely timed. The brilliant bursts of exclusive territoriality. A complexity of messages implied in our being.

School of Law
City University of New York

Part III
Towards a Positive Programme?

Part III

Towards a Feminist Perspective

[22]

FRANCES OLSEN, THE FAMILY AND THE MARKET:
A STUDY OF IDEOLOGY AND LEGAL REFORM
96 Harvard L.R. 1497, 1560-1578 (1983).

III. Toward a New Vision

Up to this point I have described a particular structure of consciousness — the market/family dichotomy — and have explored the destructive effects it has on various reform strategies intended to improve the lives of women. As long as our discourse and our thinking remain constrained within this dominant conceptual scheme, we are faced with a kind of stalemate. Like the characters in the story from the first-grade reader, we are trying to build two different playhouses out of the same set of bricks; each effort to improve one aspect of our lives inflicts loss upon some other aspect.

I now examine the possibility of breaking out of this stalemate and speculate upon alternative ways of conceiving and experiencing our affective and productive lives. My aim is simply to begin a conversation about such alternatives.[241] This conversation can be enriched by the speculative thinking of left and feminist theorists. The critique of the state/civil society dichotomy, developed by Karl Marx and others, is useful for understanding the nature of, and the possibilities of overcoming, the market/family dichotomy. Feminist speculation about transcending the male/female dichotomy provides insight

---

[241] None of what I say here is in any sense intended to be a resolution of the dilemmas I have sketched out, nor is it an effort to construct a new system that could become as rigid and oppressive as the market/family dichotomy. Rather, it is meant to be an example of the kind of speculative thinking that we can and should undertake as a first step in a better direction. This endeavor is facilitated by the critique presented in the previous Parts, but the aptness and value of that critique is in no way dependent upon the speculation I engage in here. Criticism or rejection of the direction I suggest should not cast doubt upon my critique. Rather, it should encourage the reader to continue the conversation and to suggest new directions and alternative approaches.

into the possibilities and advantages of transcending the market/family dichotomy.

Becoming aware of these dichotomies and recognizing the crippling effects they have upon our lives and upon efforts to improve our lives will not automatically bring about change. The dichotomies are not only a way of thinking: we have in fact come to experience our lives through them. Thus, we must combine our theory with political practice. A better understanding of alternative conceptions of the world can help us to carry out reforms more effectively. The reforms may in turn change the actual conditions under which we live in such a way that our own experiences will affirm and elaborate upon a different view of the market and the family, the state and society, men and women.

A. Feminism and Antiliberal Theory

An important factor in the failure of feminist reforms is their acceptance of a liberal understanding of the state and its relationship to civil society. Criticism of the liberal state and the attack on the state/civil society dichotomy have been important elements of the left attack on liberalism for over a hundred years.[242] Some feminists have participated in this

---

[242] For a seminal work, see K. MARX, *supra* note 16, at 216.

Much of the recent legal scholarship criticizing the public/private distinction should be understood as a call to transcend the state/civil society dichotomy. *See, e.g.*, Frug, Cities and Homeowners Associations: *A Reply*, 130 U. PA. L. REV. 1589, 1589–91 (1982); Frug, *The City as a Legal Concept*, 93 HARV. L. REV. 1057 (1980); Horwitz, *The History of the Public/Private Distinction*, 130 U. PA. L. REV. 1423, 1428 (1982); Klare, *Labor Law as Ideology: Toward a New Historiography of Collective Bargaining Law*, 4 INDUS. REL. L.J. 450, 470–73 (1981); Klare, *The Public/Private Distinction in Labor Law*, 130 U. PA. L. REV. 1358, 1360–61 (1982). Some theorists have suggested that we are already entering into a postliberal corporate welfare state society in which the distinction between the state and civil society has become blurred. *See, e.g.*, R. UNGER, LAW IN MODERN SOCIETY 192–93 (1976). The state does undertake to regulate the economy, and "private" economic enterprises are thought to carry out quasi-governmental functions. *See id.* at 201. Many thinkers no longer consider the state to be sharply distinguishable from civil society. *See, e.g.*, Kennedy, *The Stages of the Decline of the Public/Private Distinction*, 130 U. PA. L. REV. 1349 (1982). Bureaucratic administration has replaced earlier liberal conceptions of government. Thus, it could be asserted that the leftist critique of liberalism is now more properly a subject of intellectual history than of social theory and that the results of overcoming the state/civil society dichotomy are disappointing.

It would be a mistake, however, to exaggerate the breakdown of the state/civil society dichotomy. An important element in welfare state ideology is the limitation placed on the particular actions the state may take regarding civil society. This limitation plays a crucial justificatory role. *See supra* p. 1527. It is clear that the state/civil society dichotomy continues to affect reform efforts by restricting our sense of the possible alternatives available to us. Attacks upon and defenses of the nuclear

attack; most feminist reform efforts, however, have taken place against a background of liberal capitalism and have tended to patch up and refine the liberal theory of the state rather than challenge and disintegrate it. The reforms have exposed contradictions within liberalism, but they have not yet led us to develop a feminist theory of the state. One reason the reforms have not been more successful is that they accept as a given the state/civil society dichotomy and are conceived of as state regulation of some aspect of society or as state creation and enforcement of individual rights for women.

Just as feminist reform theory has failed to be adequately informed by the leftist critique of liberalism, so too has leftist theory failed to respond adequately to feminist critiques of patriarchy. Leftist theorists have frequently ignored gender issues or seen them as matters peripheral to the important issues of social change, as mere reflections of the incomplete or inconsistent triumph of liberal principles. Although leftist theorists acknowledge that women and men do not receive equal treatment, they perceive the oppression of women as just a particular instance of the failure of the liberal state to live up to its ideals; few left thinkers have attempted to examine the significance to liberal thought of the male/female and market/family dichotomies.

Antiliberal theorists have made either of two mistakes in dealing with the family. Some have ignored the family or thought of it only in the context of the lag theory[243] and have thus treated the seeming backwardness of the family as a mere curiosity or as a reason for neglecting the family in theoretical discussions. The family has not been recognized to be integral to the structure of liberalism. Some proponents of antiliberal theory have therefore underestimated the family's importance.[244] Other proponents have placed false importance on the family by celebrating it as a socialist community. When Carl Degler asserts that Marxists have taken the family as their "model of human order" because they see in it the "epitome of true humanity and interrelatedness,"[245] he exaggerates

family, for example, are deeply influenced by that dichotomy. Despite the oppressiveness of the nuclear family, the possibility of abolishing it loses much of its appeal if we assume that the actual alternative may be a society of atomistic individuals facing a monolithic state. The fear of being a completely isolated individual standing against the state provides a strong incentive to form a family. One reason the family has such a strong appeal is that it moderates the state/civil society dichotomy.

[243] *See supra* pp. 1513–20.

[244] For general treatments of leftist analyses of the family, see M. BARRETT, *supra* note 173; E. ZARETSKY, CAPITALISM, THE FAMILY, & PERSONAL LIFE (1976).

[245] C. DEGLER, *supra* note 181, at 472.

only a little. "The very slogan of Communism — 'from each according to his abilities, to each according to his needs' — is," says Degler, "the central principle of family life."[246]

Both of these leftist approaches to the family accept unquestioningly the market/family dichotomy and fail to appreciate the significance of the family as a *structural* element of civil society. The altruistic, hierarchical, private family is an essential element of nineteenth century ideology. The liberal family is an equally essential element of modern ideology and a structural component of society in the modern corporate welfare state. By failing to address or even notice the dichotomy between the market and the family, most leftist theories assume and thus encourage the continued existence of the dichotomy.

We can learn a great deal by recognizing the relationship between the leftist and feminist contributions and the power of each to enrich the other. The leftist critique of the state/civil society dichotomy and the feminist critique of the male/female dichotomy together inform, and are enriched by, the critique of the market/family dichotomy. Moreover, leftist and feminist speculation about transcending the dichotomies between state and civil society and between male and female suggests the possibility of transcending the market/family dichotomy.

B. Criticizing the Dichotomies

The market/family dichotomy is a human construct that entails the same kind of self-alienation that Karl Marx described in *On the Jewish Question*,[247] his classic essay on the state/civil society dichotomy. Marx perceived that human beings lead a "double life" — one life in the state and a separate life in civil society. He referred to the political state, in which we regard ourselves as communal beings, as the *"species-life"* of mankind; the political "citizen" is abstract and universal.[248] Civil society, however, is the realm of the particular; each member of civil society is a "private individual," separated from his community and concerned only with his own interests and desires. The dualism between species-life and individual life involves a form of self-alienation, an artificial split of the person into an abstract citizen of the state

---

[246] *Id.* This second mistake is apparent in the writings of important leftists. *See, e.g.*, C. LASCH, *supra* note 94.

[247] K. MARX, *supra* note 16, at 216.

[248] *Id.* at 225, 240–41.

and an egoistic individual in civil society.[249] According to Marx, the project of human emancipation is to overcome this alienation: the human being may become a species-being by reuniting the abstract universal citizen and the concrete particular individual.[250] We can thus reclaim our own powers as social powers and thereby become complete *and* moral beings.

The dualism between life in the market and life in the family is slightly different from, but even more pronounced than, the dualism between species-life and individual life. We expect the market to achieve the efficient production of goods and services; it is not the arena in which we are supposed to develop our personalities or satisfy human relational wants. Pervasive hierarchy in the market is imposed and justified on grounds of efficiency. The market is the realm of alienated labor. The expression of the desires to develop personality and to interact with others is relegated to the family and simultaneously glorified and devalued. We see the market as a means to an end, whereas we see the family as an end in itself. The market is the arena for work and the production of goods; the family is the arena for most forms of play and consumption. Dividing life between market and family compartmentalizes human experience in a way that prevents us from realizing the range of choices actually available to us. Much of social and productive life seems effectively beyond our control.

The seemingly contradictory desires to be free and to relate with others in a community present an important dilemma of liberal society.[251] In laissez-faire ideology, the market is predominantly associated with freedom, and the family is associated with community. In welfare state ideology, the market is supposed to be controlled by the community (the state), and the family is celebrated as a realm of freedom with which the state should not interfere. It turns out, however, that the liberal dilemma of freedom and community is not resolved by the interplay between the market and the family.

---

[249] Marx quotes from Rousseau's statement about the prerequisite for founding a liberal state:

[E]ach individual who is in himself a complete but isolated whole . . . [must be transformed] into a part of something greater than himself from which he somehow derives his life and existence, substituting a limited and moral existence for a physical and independent existence. Man must be deprived of his own powers and given alien powers which he cannot use without the aid of others.

Id. at 241 (emphasis omitted) (quoting J. ROUSSEAU, THE SOCIAL CONTRACT 67–68 (London 1782)).

[250] *Id.*

[251] The best statement of this dilemma is in Kennedy, *The Structure of Blackstone's Commentaries*, 28 BUFFALO L. REV. 209, 211–13 (1979).

The family has a dual role for both men and women. For men, the family is a realm in which they can expose their "weaknesses," in which they may embrace without shame the values traditionally associated with women. By relating with women in families, men try to reclaim wholeness. Second, the family is a realm in which men can be bosses. In their families men can express competitive values and other values traditionally considered masculine. Men may be compensated in the family for their failures in the marketplace. The home is a haven for men.

The family likewise plays a dual role for women. The home is supposed to be where women belong and where their values are appreciated and allowed free expression. Rather than a haven for women, however, the home has traditionally been a workplace; and now that most women work in the marketplace, the home has become a second workplace. In contrast to the market, where people must often play roles, the family is supposed to be the arena in which people can express their real selves. For many women, however, the contrary is true: it is precisely within the family that they must subordinate themselves and play roles.

The market serves for a few women some of the same functions that the family serves for men. A woman as employee or manager may more acceptably display traits that are considered masculine. The market may offer a socially approved opportunity for women to be rational, objective, and even selfish. In theory, the market frees women from their ascribed roles. In fact, most women are forced into subordinate positions in the market, and their freedom is quite circumscribed.[252]

For men, the market is supposed to be the realm in which masculine values are promoted and rewarded. The market presents images of freedom, rationality, and power. The reality of the market for most men as well as most women is that they are dominated and oppressed by employers exercising arbitrary power over them. In some cases the intercession of seemingly neutral rules will reduce the sense of personal domination, but people are to a great extent the "plaything[s] of alien powers" in the market.[253] Thus, both in the market and in the family, we are all faced with a sense of powerlessness.

---

[252] Of course, even if women work in jobs that allow or encourage them to depart from the traditional feminine role, they are still trading one role for another. *See generally* Note, *supra* note 180 (observing the tendency of conventional sexual equality to result in the judging of all persons by a male standard).

[253] This terminology comes from K. MARX, *supra* note 16, at 216, 225 (commenting on helplessness of individual in civil society).

In fact, we have created a market that embraces a warped and impoverished notion of freedom, a market characterized by alienated commodity production and a radical loss of the sense of human control over market activities.[254] Although isolated, individual choice is a hallmark of the free market, such choice becomes part of the "objective" forces of supply and demand that are beyond conscious human control. Even in the welfare state market, we underestimate the extent to which we could consciously determine what to produce and how to produce it.

We have also created a family that embraces warped and impoverished notions of community and freedom. The community within a family is hierarchical. Moreover, freedom in the family is largely an illusion. The family is just what we make it — it exists only to please us. We glorify the family's lack of objective purpose; in the family, one is supposed to be free to express personality and to satisfy the human desire to interact with others, but the very attempt to divorce these goals from other purposive or productive activities makes their realization problematic.

We often tend to forget that our present family arrangements and our present market arrangements are of purely human creation. Marx observed that civil society seems natural because it was formed as a by-product of the dissolution of feudal society, at a time when people's self-conscious activity was focused on the political act of forming the state.[255] This is equally true of the modern nuclear family, which is seen as the social form left over from the disintegration of earlier forms of extended families or households. The home is the place where people not recruited into the market are left, and the place to which people return when they finish their work in the market.

Each succeeding political change seems to leave the family a more *natural* entity, a freer expression of human impulses. This process in turn increases the appearance of the family's particularity and of the diversity of family life. Insofar as people consider that the family exists only to serve human emotional wants, that it lacks practical purpose, they believe that it is becoming more pure and family-like.

Most of the time neither our family lives nor our market lives seem fully satisfactory, yet our dissatisfaction with each leads us to romanticize the other in a vicious cycle. To the

---

[254] *See generally* K. MARX, *Alienated Labor*, in WRITINGS, *supra* note 16, at 287 (classic discussion of alienated labor).

[255] K. MARX, *supra* note 16, at 216, 240.

extent that the freedom of the marketplace turns out to be a sham, people cling to notions of marital felicity and domestic happiness. To the extent that community in the family turns out to be an illusion, people seek refuge in their work. Once we accept the "heartless world" as a given, the value of a "haven" from it seems self-evident.[256] Only by collapsing the facade of a refuge, however, can we lay the foundation for real freedom and community.

C. Transcending the Dichotomies

The dichotomies between state and civil society and between market and family are very much a part of our thinking. Criticisms of the family are often misinterpreted as attacks upon humanization, connectedness, and parenthood, just as criticisms of the market may be misunderstood to be attacks upon efficient production of goods and services. Yet the production of goods and services is a worthwhile goal, just as it is worthwhile to express personality and to satisfy human desires to relate with others. At present, production is carried out primarily by the market, and the opportunity for expressing personality occurs mostly in the family. My argument is that this separation and polarization of functions reinforces the status quo and limits the possibilities of human association.

People who support the market/family dichotomy argue that life will be impoverished if all of it "falls under a single set of terms."[257] The problem, however, is that life all too often is circumscribed by a double set of terms. The market and the family are seen as correlatives, each opposing yet reinforcing the other. But it is my contention that we do not need inhuman environments in order to enjoy human ones, nor do we need unproductive or impractical associations in order to enjoy productive or practical ones. Polarizing the family and the market does not increase the possibilities available to individuals and to the human personality. Instead it reifies the abstractions of "the market" and "the family" and renders us powerless.

Another criticism of efforts to transcend the market/family dichotomy is closely related to liberal criticisms of efforts to transcend the state/civil society dichotomy. Some commentators express the fear that if feminists have their way, families will be abolished and nothing adequate will emerge to replace them. Institutional child care is portrayed as a form of neglect

---

[256] This terminology was popularized by Christopher Lasch. *See* C. LASCH, *supra* note 94.

[257] J. ELSHTAIN, PUBLIC MAN, PRIVATE WOMAN 335 (1981).

likely to produce children who are unable to form close human attachments and are thus not fully human.[258] Communal or other alternative forms of social life are seen as mere "hollow replications" of the family — weak, frivolous imitations.[259]

This concern is identified with the fear of totalitarianism. Critics contend that the rearing of children outside family structures will lead to oversocialized and conformist adults, people who automatically follow orders that they ought to question and challenge.[260] These commentators view the family as a potential hiding-place — a refuge for subjectivity and irrational fancy, a realm antithetical to totalitarian existence.[261] Keeping the family distinct from the rest of civil society, they believe, is crucial to the hopes of maintaining civil society as a separate realm of freedom, a realm not engulfed by the all-powerful state.

The image of Nazi Germany or the cold war image of Soviet Russia is presented as the fearsome alternative to the state/civil society dichotomy. The state controls every aspect of human life; nothing is personal and private; there is no freedom.[262] The state is rational, instrumental, and objective, and at the same time deeply irrational and frighteningly subjective. Even if a totalitarian state could assume a democratic form, it is argued, the result would be a dictatorship of the masses, and human freedom would be destroyed.

I do not advocate replacing the present dichotomies with an all-powerful state and an all-embracing market any more than I would advocate making women just like men. The state as it now exists must be ended at the same time that civil society as it now exists is ended; and when we transform the contemporary family, we must simultaneously transform the market.

I favor neither a romantic return to a simpler form of life nor a regression to an earlier, undifferentiated world. It would not be a solution to reestablish cottage industries, to have both parents at home working and caring for the children. I am not envisioning an escape from the complications of existing in the world as conscious free-willed beings, nor do I advocate an evasion of the conflict that may be painful but is inherent in human growth. Rather, I have in mind a situation in which

---

[258] *See, e.g., id.* at 328–31.

[259] *Id.* at 330.

[260] *See id.*; C. LASCH, *supra* note 94, at 91.

[261] *See* C. LASCH, *supra* note 94, at 92 (contending that decline of family leads to subjugation of individual by new forms of coercion).

[262] *See, e.g.,* J.F. DULLES, WAR OR PEACE 5–16 (1950) (describing Soviet "enemy").

conflict can take place more effectively. The dichotomies stunt human growth by avoiding and displacing conflict — conflict within the individual psyche and among people. The problem of externalizing conflict through compartmentalization, and the advantages to be gained by transcending the dichotomies, can be illustrated by an examination of the male/female dichotomy.

The differences between men and women are as natural as starvation, religion, and brutality. Inequality between men and women has existed throughout recorded history and has persisted across widely divergent cultures. So too have starvation, religion, and brutality. That each of these phenomena has been long lived does not mean that any of them is immutable.

We have sometimes viewed gender differences as Malthusians viewed starvation — unfortunate for individual victims, but socially necessary and logically inevitable.[263] At other times, gender distinctions have been recognized to be socially created but, like religion,[264] enormously useful for maintaining social and political stability, and perhaps even good for the common man. Recently, gender differences have been considered analogous to brutality — we can reduce or overcome them to a certain extent, but we can probably never eliminate them altogether, and perhaps the world would be all too homogenous if we could. In any event, it may be thought that the amount of coercion necessary to eliminate completely either brutality or gender distinctions would constitute too great an infringement on human freedom.

1. The Feuerbach Model: The Progress of History. — Perhaps the most useful model for capturing the nature of the male/female dichotomy is suggested by atheist Ludwig Feuerbach's description of religion.[265] Feuerbach saw religion as a product of human imagination and God as a projection of human qualities. In Feuerbach's Hegelian language:

---

[263] *Cf.* C. LASCH, *supra* note 94, at 79–80 (maintaining that Freud considered differences in the sexes to be neither innate traits nor the products of cultural conditioning, but rather the result of "the process of becoming a woman," which requires, in any culture, "the repression of the active and phallic side of a woman's sexuality"). *See generally* S. GOLDBERG, THE INEVITABILITY OF PATRIARCHY (1973) (focusing on the physiological "necessity" of male domination).

[264] *Compare* T. HOBBES, LEVIATHAN ch. 12 (London 1651) (asserting that the seeds of religion exist in man and have been cultivated to obedience, law, peace, charity, and civility), *with* S. WEITZ, SEX ROLES 5 (1977) (noting that society "has a vested interest in sex roles insofar as they permit the smooth functioning of the major institutional structures").

[265] *See* L. FEUERBACH, THE ESSENCE OF CHRISTIANITY (G. Eliot trans. 1957).

Man — this is the mystery of religion — projects his being
into objectivity, and then again makes himself an object to
this projected image of himself thus converted into a subject;
he thinks of himself [as] an object to himself, but as the object
of an object, of another being than himself. Thus here. Man
is an object to God.[266]

Feuerbach hypothesized that people project their nature onto
the God they create, and in contemplating this God, they
perceive their own nature: "Consciousness of God is self-consciousness, knowledge of God is self-knowledge."[267] Through
their relationship to God, people reclaim their own nature.

The male/female dichotomy, like religion, is a human construction. The "mystery" of sexuality consists in projecting
human qualities separately onto males and females to make
each the object of the other. The relationship between the
sexes becomes a means by which members of each gender can
reclaim their own projected nature. In becoming acquainted
with each other, men and women become acquainted with
themselves.

Feuerbach believed that the process of projecting human
qualities onto God served a useful human purpose. "Man first
of all sees his nature as if *out of* himself, before he finds it in
himself."[268] The history of religion is the history of the recognition by humans of more and more of their own nature.
Each new religion correctly perceives the previous one to be
idolatry — the worship of something human as if it were
divine.[269] "Man has given objectivity to himself, but has not
recognized the object as his own nature: a later religion takes
this forward step; every advance in religion is therefore a
deeper self-knowledge."[270]

Gender differentiation serves a useful human purpose analogous to that served by religion. The gradual shifts that have
taken place in our understanding of maleness and femaleness
can be seen as reflections of an historical process resulting in
deeper self-knowledge. The historical progress of gender differentiation consists in recognizing that what was previously
considered immutable is contingent and subject to human control. The division of human beings into male and female could
be judged to have been a useful device for enabling us to
become conscious of the wide range of human possibilities.

---

[266] *Id.* at 29–30.

[267] *Id.* at 12.

[268] *Id.* at 13.

[269] *Id.*

[270] *Id.*

The transcending of the male/female dichotomy would then be
the final step in the reclamation of the whole self, the last
stage in this historical process.

   2. Elaborating on the Model: Complications of Gender. —
There are several problems with viewing gender differentiation
as historic progress. The first problem is shared by Feuerbach's analysis of religion. Feuerbach did not believe that
God actually existed, and although his work was part of an
argument for the nonexistence of God, it was at the same time
premised upon that nonexistence.[271] A contemporary believer
would either disagree with Feuerbach or would insist that,
although early gods were admittedly human projections,
Feuerbach failed to capture the essence of contemporary belief
because he made a simple factual mistake regarding the existence of God. Similarly, I am arguing that gender distinctions
are historically contingent, and an underlying premise of my
argument is that male and female traits are not immutable.
Anyone convinced that biology is destiny will be unpersuaded
by my argument. Given that people identified as women really
do exist and are biologically distinguishable from men, some
observers will always argue that perceived differences are real
rather than projected.

   Just as Feuerbach could never really disprove the existence
of God or gods, I cannot disprove the general claim that the
differences between women and men are biologically determined rather than the result of projections of the self. It is
clear, however, that our understandings of maleness and femaleness have undergone dramatic changes and that previous
understandings of biological determinism have therefore been
mistaken. Whenever assertions of biological constraints are
made in a sufficiently specific context, scholars and researchers
are ready to disprove them.[272] But such disproof will never
convince the faithful that there do not exist other basic differences between men and women that make it impossible or
unwise to transcend the male/female dichotomy. Perhaps the
most we can say with certainty is that even if biological constraints exist that may ultimately limit the possibilities for
remaking society, we will not be able to determine the part
played by such constraints until we have correctly assessed the
part played by the social construction of gender roles. At
present, I find no evidence that biology prevents us from

---

[271] *Id.* at xxxiv–xxxv.

[272] *See, e.g.,* C. MacKinnon, *supra* note 176, at 152–55; *see also* Note, *supra*
note 180, at 497 n.56 (listing sources that discuss biological determinism).

making major alterations in the relationship between women and men or from transcending the male/female dichotomy.

The application of Feuerbach's historical progress model to gender differentiation is complicated by the presence of factors in the relationship between women and men that are not present in the relationship between human beings and God. First, the relationship between man and woman involves two people and two different projected relationships.[273] There is an actual relationship between a man and a woman that takes place alongside the two projected relationships. The projections that are an integral part of our present gender system[274] interfere with the actual relationship. I refer to this interference with companionship and love and the limitations it places upon the possibilities of human association as "problems of love." Second, the historical process has been blocked by the reality that men dominate women. Feuerbach's model is based on the projection of positive traits upon God, whereas the traits projected upon women are simultaneously despised and exalted.[275] Thus, the problem of domination that characterizes male-female relations is not present in Feuerbach's picture of religion.

(a) Problems of Love. — Feminists have long argued that our present gender system, with its inequality and domination, makes true love between the sexes difficult, perhaps impossible.[276] What currently passes for love has been described as "a one-sided pathological dependency of women on men."[277] Men are seen to be strong and powerful, women to be weak and dependent. Additionally, in our present society women are economically and socially dependent upon men. The chief

---

[273] Again, someone who believes in the existence of God might dispute that the relationship between a person and God is thus distinct from the relationship between two people. *See, e.g.*, M. BUBER, I AND THOU (R.G. Smith trans. 2d ed. 1958).

[274] By "gender system" I mean the system wherein male and female are socially constructed as correlative opposites that form a dichotomy in which males are hierarchically superior to females. Gayle Rubin refers to this as a "sex/gender system." Rubin, *The Traffic in Women: Notes on the "Political Economy" of Sex, reprinted in* TOWARD AN ANTHROPOLOGY OF WOMEN 159, 166–67 (R. Reiter ed. 1975). Catharine MacKinnon criticizes this division of sex and gender as a nature/culture distinction. *See* MacKinnon, *Feminism, Marxism, Method, and the State: Toward Feminist Jurisprudence* (forthcoming in 8 SIGNS: JOURNAL OF WOMEN IN CULTURE AND SOCIETY (1983)). I am adopting Professor MacKinnon's usage.

[275] The average male feels misogyny of an intensity far exceeding that of the hostility expressed toward God by such notorious "blasphemers" as Friedrich Nietzsche and George Bernard Shaw.

[276] For an excellent summary and evaluation of some of these views, see Rapaport, *On the Future of Love: Rousseau and the Radical Feminists, in* WOMEN AND PHILOSOPHY, *supra* note 175, at 185.

[277] *Id.*

determinants of a woman's status are her acceptance by and associations with men. Under these circumstances, romantic love plays an apologetic role; it mystifies women about their dependency on men and reinforces male hegemony.[278]

Shulamith Firestone builds upon the ideas introduced by John Stuart Mill[279] and others about the harmful effects that sexual inequality has upon the possibilities for love.[280] Firestone explains that healthy love requires mutual self-respect, which is destroyed when neither men nor women regard females to be autonomous, equal beings deserving of respect. Women lack self-esteem and seek to gain identity and worth by being loved by men.[281] Men do not actually respect women but instead generally undervalue them; at the same time, they idealize individual women with whom they "fall in love."[282] Because women know they do not fit this idealized image, they can feel no security in being loved and must fear honest and intimate contact that would reveal their true selves.[283] Thus, Firestone argues, love as we know it is both a delusion and a trap for women. But the solution lies in sexual equality: among equals there can be meaningful love.[284]

Elizabeth Rapaport[285] has extended Firestone's critique to show how love is transformed into a destructive dependency relationship for men as well as for women. Drawing on Rousseau,[286] she suggests that achieving equality of power and influence between men and women would not by itself solve the problems of love. Love begins with a healthy attraction, a recognition of like sensibilities. But lovers then focus on differences, she argues, because they are seeking to find in their partners the qualities they fear they lack in themselves and are thus in some sense seeking to gain possession of those qualities.[287] They do not choose the partner with whom they

---

[278] S. Firestone, The Dialectic of Sex 146–48, 165–75 (1970).

[279] *See* J.S. Mill, *The Subjection of Women*, in J.S. Mill & H.T. Mill, *supra* note 91, at 233–36.

[280] *See* S. Firestone, *supra* note 278, at 142–64.

[281] *See id.* at 155–56.

[282] *See id.* at 128–29, 148, 153.

[283] *See id.* at 149.

[284] *See id.*; Rapaport, *supra* note 276, at 185–86.

[285] *See* Rapaport, *supra* note 276, at 185.

[286] Rapaport focuses on J. Rousseau, Emile (Everyman ed. 1911) (1st ed. Paris 1762); J. Rousseau, La Nouvelle Heloise (Penn. State Press ed. 1968) (1st ed. Geneva 1761); J. Rousseau, *Discourse on the Origin and Foundation of Inequality Among Mankind*, in The Social Contract and Discourse on the Origin and Foundation of Inequality Among Mankind 149 (L. Crocker ed. 1969) (1st ed. Amsterdam 1755).

[287] *See* Rapaport, *supra* note 276, at 199.

have most to share, but rather seek the "pre-eminent" member of the opposite sex.[288] Each person hoping to be loved must strive to appear to be that preeminent person. Consequently, even if there were equality between men and women, a relationship of dependency might lead to a false presentation of the self as well as to a fear of exposing the real, flawed self. The lover thus loses his or her identity and autonomy.

According to Rousseau, the tendency to love the one who seems most virtuous and most beautiful,[289] combined with the desire to be loved, leads to "emulation, rivalry, and jealousy."[290] If we locate choice in sharing rather than in virtue and beauty, however, quite different results obtain. People will be attracted to each other by how much they have to share. They will focus on what they have, not on what they lack or fear they lack.

Thus, the real issue is not dependency, but rather one's attitude toward oneself. It is important that one be self-sufficient, but not that one be independent. The choice is not between being a complete, independent individual and being dependent and incomplete.

Rapaport contends that healthy love is impossible not only because of the inequality between men and women, but also because of the individualist assumptions of liberalism and the actual competitive and hierarchical conditions of capitalist society.[291] Thus, she argues, socialism and women's equality hold the promise of healthy love.[292] Rapaport is correct to reject dependency and autonomy as polar choices. An adult can and should be "autonomous" in the sense of being a full and complete human being. Yet social life is richer than isolation; sharing and intimacy enable a person to enjoy life more fully. To the extent that our social interactions enrich the

---

[288] As Rapaport puts it:

> The lover is dependent, entirely, terribly dependent on his beloved for something he needs, the reciprocity of his love. . . . The lover cannot achieve love's desire, reciprocity by the exercise of his own powers. He will only be loved if she finds him pre-eminent. He must present himself in the guise in which she would see her beloved. This leads to a false presentation of the self and the chronic fear of exposure and loss of love. Along the way the lover loses himself and necessarily the opportunity to gain love for this lost self.

Id.

[289] *See* J. ROUSSEAU, EMILE, *supra* note 286, at 175–76, *discussed and quoted in* Rapaport, *supra* note 276, at 197.

[290] *Id.* at 175, *quoted in* Rapaport, *supra* note 276, at 197.

[291] Rapaport, *supra* note 276, at 203–04.

[292] "Love may be rehabilitated if the just fear of dependency relations we learn from love as we know it turns out to be grounded not in fear of ourselves but in the pathological distortions of human personality produced by an unjust, destructive and successfully alterable social order." *Id.* at 204.

quality of our lives, we can be said to be "dependent" upon others for this enhanced existence. To have to depend on another to fulfill immediate emotional needs can be a bad thing; to be able to depend on another to enrich one's life is a good thing. To be autonomous means not to need another in order to feel complete; it does not mean that one is incapable of enriching one's life through social interaction.

Socialism and sexual equality together, however, are not enough to rehabilitate love. We must also counter the self-alienation inherent in our present gender system. When we project human traits separately upon men and women, we ensure that we remain incomplete beings. Our attraction for the opposite sex has a quality of urgency because a relationship with a member of that sex is necessary for our own completion. Our present gender system tends to foster relationships based on need rather than desire. To need another to complete oneself is ultimately unsatisfactory; it interferes with the intimate sharing that is possible between human beings, a sharing that leads us to want contact with others.[293]

(b) Problems of Domination. — The domination of women by men is self-perpetuating. Women's unfamiliarity with aspects of the world to which they have been denied access has justified their continued exclusion. Menstruation, pregnancy, and childbirth have been made to operate as disadvantages to women and have allowed women to be dominated by men and to need their protection. The degradation of women in the real world was matched by their exaltation in a fantasy world. Women were seen as wonderful and terrible.[294]

The world came more generally to be viewed as a series of complex dualisms — reason/passion, rational/irrational, culture/nature, power/sensitivity, thought/feeling, soul/body, objective/subjective. Men, who have created our dominant consciousness, have organized these dualisms into a system in which each dualism has a strong or positive side and a weak or negative side. Men associate themselves with the strong sides of the dualisms and project the weak sides upon women. In the same way that men simultaneously exalt and degrade women and the family, they simultaneously exalt and degrade the concepts on the weak sides of the dualisms. Nature, for

---

[293] Of course, dependency based on need can be homosexual as well as heterosexual. On the tendency of homosexual relationships to reproduce the patterns of heterosexual relationships, see J. MONEY & A. EHRHARDT, MAN & WOMAN, BOY & GIRL 163–64, 234–35 (1972).

[294] *See, e.g.,* N. HAWTHORNE, *Rappaccini's Daughter,* in MOSSES FROM AN OLD MANSE 91 (Riverside Press ed. 1902) (1st ed. New York 1846).

example, is glorified as something awesome, a worthy subject of conquest by male heroes, while it is simultaneously degraded as inert matter to be exploited and shaped to men's purposes. Irrational subjectivity and sensitivity are similarly treasured and denigrated at the same time.[295]

Another important aspect of the way these dualisms are viewed in dominant culture is that the inferior half of any dualism is often seen to pose a constant danger to the stronger half. Man is warned to do battle with the flesh, with nature, even with women. Irrationalism is regarded as something that must be conquered, like nature. The weak sides of the dualisms are simultaneously indispensable and threatening to men.[296]

The limited choices that seem available to women may be described in terms of women's relationship to these dualisms. One feminist strategy accepts the identification of women with their traditional side of the dualisms but tries to deny the hierarchy men have established between the two sides. Another strategy struggles to identify women with the stronger side of the dualisms instead of challenging the devaluation of the side traditionally associated with women. Reformers often adopt both strategies simultaneously. Suffragists, for example, argued not only that women should be allowed to vote because they could be as reasonable and rational as men, but also that granting women the vote would benefit society because of women's superior sensitivity to human values.[297] Although neither of these two feminist strategies is necessarily inconsistent with a rejection of the dualisms themselves, such a rejection has not in practice been emphasized.

The traditional identification of women with the weak side of the dualisms — with nature, subjectivity, nurturance — has been a legacy of oppression. Accepting this identification may be tantamount to embracing women's subordinate position. Yet the identification is also a potential source of power and insight. To reject the weak side of the dualisms is to neglect the qualities that women have been allowed to cultivate.[298] Both approaches may be considered to accept, perhaps even to reinforce, the dualisms.

---

[295] See C. CHRIST, DIVING DEEP AND SURFACING 25–26, 129–31 (1980).

[296] See id. at 25.

[297] Equally inconsistent were those opposing votes for women, who argued both that granting the franchise to women would make little difference and that it would be harmful. Compare B. HARRISON, SEPARATE SPHERES 81 (1978) (discussing James Viscount Bryce's argument that women without the franchise enjoy greater political power than they would have with the franchise), with id. at 84 (discussing Bryce's fears of the socialistic implications of giving women the vote).

[298] See C. CHRIST, supra note 295, at 25–26, 130.

The answer that I endorse is not to reject identification
with the strengths and values of women, but to recognize the
incompleteness of the traditional roles of women and of wom-
en's identification with one side of the dualisms. Thus, I
would not repudiate the traditional values and roles of women,
but would refuse to give those values and roles a privileged
place. It is the acceptance and the sexualization of the dualisms that is the chief problem. When one side of a dualism is
forced upon us, it is not enough to insist upon the right to
choose the opposite side. Nor, of course, is it helpful to grab
the weak side of the dualism voluntarily before it is forced
upon us. We cannot choose between the two sides of the
dualism, because we need both. Similarly, we cannot choose
between men's roles and women's roles, because both are essential to us. We can never win if we fight for the bigger
portion or even an equal portion of a body torn in two; we
must prevent the initial destruction.[299]

3. Criticisms and Conclusions. — As early as the nineteenth century, feminists became aware of the idea of abolishing sex roles.[300] The rebirth of the women's movement has
again brought this idea into popular discourse, and critics have
leveled a variety of attacks against what has been loosely
labeled "androgyny." In order to clarify my position, I shall
briefly set forth two of these attacks and my response to them.

First, opponents of androgyny warn that the elimination
of the present gender system will diminish the possibilities for
passion and variety in human association by making everyone
boringly the same.[301] It is true that as long as we sexualize
dichotomies and constitute ourselves as incomplete beings, we
must depend on finding other, correlatively incomplete beings
in order to reclaim wholeness. As incomplete beings, we find
it threatening to consider the sudden loss of other incomplete
beings who are our inverse. It is perhaps for this reason that
atheism or the notion of God's being "dead" is so terrifying to
some people:[302] they fear that they will forever lose divine
traits and remain permanently incomplete. Feuerbach, however, saw that eliminating the belief in God would allow people
to recognize that so-called divine qualities are in fact human.[303] With respect also to the division between male and

---

[299] *Cf. id.* at 26 (arguing that women have a crucial role to play in the overthrow
of the classical dualistic vision in recent Western thought).

[300] For a review of 19th century feminist views, see W. LEACH, TRUE LOVE AND
PERFECT UNION (1980).

[301] *See, e.g.,* Elshtain, *Against Androgyny,* 47 TELOS 5, 21 (1981).

[302] *See* F. NIETZSCHE, *Thus Spoke Zarathustra,* in THE PORTABLE NIETZSCHE
124 (W. Kaufman trans. 1954).

[303] *See* L. FEUERBACH, *supra* note 265, at xxxviii–xxxix, 20–25.

female, whole people do not need correlatives and will find their social wants more readily satisfied by other complete beings. We can recognize that we would not increase diversity by chopping off the right arms of all women and the left arms of all men; yet what some opponents of androgyny argue is no more sensible. Sex roles limit human potential far more than they expand it.

A second objection to androgyny suggests that the union or transcendence of the male/female dichotomy may be undesirable because it would require that women accept what men have been as a part of the wholeness women seek.[304] Instead, this argument runs, women should reject what men have been and find strength in women's culture and the values of our foremothers.[305] My response to this is that most of what is wrong with what men have been is what they have not been. The point is not that the passions are superior to reason, subjectivity to objectivity, nature to culture, and so forth. To reverse the dualisms may secure for women a fairer portion of the divided psyche, but to reject the polarization of the dualistic pairs is to create the possibility of wholeness. Although I share the rejection of much of what men have been (or rather what they have *not* been), I feel that I must also reject much of what women have not been (and thus, in the same sense, what we have been).

When I speak of transcending the male/female dichotomy, I have in mind creating a new referential system for relating men and women to the world, a systemic departure from the ordinary image of male and female as correlatives. This does not mean making women more like men, or men more like women. Rather, it means radically increasing the options available to each individual, and more importantly, allowing the human personality to break out of the present dichotomized system. We have all experienced occasional glimpses of what this might mean — moments of power, sensitivity, and connectedness. We should recognize these fleeting experiences as a source of hope, a foreshadow of the human beings we can become. In some ways women will be *less* like present men, and men will be *less* like present women. Rather than shades of grey as an alternative to all black and all white, I envision reds and greens and blues.

---

[304] This position has been attributed to Adrienne Rich. *See* C. CHRIST, *supra* note 295, at 83–84.

[305] *See id.* at 84. This may be seen as an oversimplification of Rich's position. It is true that she envisions more than reversing the dualisms; she would also have us go beyond the values attributed to women *by men* and would have us engage in a new naming — an attempt to create a new definition based on our own experiences. *See id.* at 84–85. This solves only half the problem, because our experiences are themselves impoverished by the male/female dichotomy. *See id.* at 15, *passim*.

[23]

Book Review

Sexual Difference, the Feminine, and Equivalency: A Critique of MacKinnon's *Toward a Feminist Theory of the State*

Toward a Feminist Theory of the State. By Catharine A. MacKinnon.* *Cambridge: The Harvard University Press*, 1989. Pp. xvii, 330. $25.00.

Drucilla Cornell†

I. INTRODUCTION

Catharine MacKinnon's *Toward a Feminist Theory of the State*[1] is a provocative challenge to both conceptions of liberal jurisprudence and to the tradi-

---

* Professor of Law, University of Michigan Law School.

† Professor of Law, Benjamin N. Cardozo School of Law, Yeshiva University. This review is dedicated to Eleanor Galenson for her path-breaking work into sexual difference, her example of a woman's life well-lived, and her friendship. I want to thank Mindy Friedman whose careful editorial attention influenced the rewriting of this review throughout. She played a crucial role in getting me to think about exactly what the center of my argument was. I also want to thank my other two research assistants, A. Collin Biddle and Deborah Garfield, for their unflagging intellectual engagement and technical support. My research assistants have taught me to think again about "luck" and its role in moral and intellectual life because I have been lucky enough to have them. I must also say that this review could never have reached its present form without the endless questioning of what equality means and does not mean that takes place every week in the fall semester in the Colloquium in Law, Philosophy, and Political Theory at New York University Law School. For making me think and rethink my own feminist position, I owe special thanks to Ronald Dworkin, Thomas Nagel, David Richards, and Lawrence Sager.

1. C. MACKINNON, TOWARD A FEMINIST THEORY OF THE STATE (1989) [hereinafter cited by page number only].

tional Marxist critique of liberalism. Each stands accused of erasing the centrality of gender, sex, and sexuality in the development of a modern legal system. This erasure, MacKinnon believes, can only perpetuate injustice at its base through the pretense that equality has already been achieved—as in the case of her version of liberalism—or reduce it to a category of class domination which makes gender a secondary form of subordination—as in the case of her interpretation of Marxism. Before turning to my critique of MacKinnon, I want to pay her the tribute she clearly deserves for her relentless insistence that any theory of equality for women will fall short of its own aspirations if it neglects the question of how sexual identity, and more specifically femininity, is constructed through a gender hierarchy in which women are subordinated and subjected. I share her insistence that we cannot begin to conceptualize a theory of equality that truly envisions the end of female domination without confronting the relationship between sex and sexuality as these have become constitutive of the gender identity imposed upon women by patriarchy. Her contribution has not been merely to criticize existing theories; she has been a proponent of specific doctrinal changes and played a key role, for example, in justifying the recognition of sexual harassment as a matter of sex discrimination and gender inequality.[2] This is one of many examples of how her understanding of the constitutive role of sexuality in the creation and perpetuation of male dominance has led to advocacy for legal and doctrinal reform.

My critique of MacKinnon, however, is that ultimately she does not fully develop her program, which attempts to justify positive intervention by the state into current social arrangements of gender hierarchy and identity. I will argue that she cannot successfully develop her own feminist theory of the state because she is unable to affirm feminine sexual difference as other than victimization.[3] Of course, we need a program that legally delegitimates the gender hierarchy and exposes the seriousness of sexual abuse. But we also need a more expansive, positive program, for the reduction of feminine sexual difference to victimization ultimately cannot sustain a feminist theory of the state. I propose a program which recognizes and incorporates equivalent rights.[4] Such a program would be irreducible to an intermediary set of privileges like affirma-

---

2. *See* C. MACKINNON, SEXUAL HARASSMENT AND THE WORKING WOMAN: A CASE OF WORKING WOMEN (1979); *see also* Meritor Sav. Bank, FSB v. Vinson, 477 U.S. 57 (1986) (argued by Catharine MacKinnon).

3. Other writers have voiced similar concerns and have noted the way in which MacKinnon not only disparages women's sexuality but also how she portrays it in such a way as to increase the very problem of sexual abuse that she so desperately seeks to correct. *See, e.g.*, Schroeder, *Feminism Historicized: Medieval Misogynist Stereotypes in Contemporary Feminist Jurisprudence*, 75 IOWA L. REV 1135 (1990); J. Schroeder, Abduction from the Seraglio (1991) (unpublished manuscript on file with author).

4. I first developed this concept of equivalent rights in *Sex Discrimination Law and Equivalent Rights*, published as *Gender, Sex and Equivalent Rights*, in FEMINISTS THEORIZE THE POLITICAL (J. Butler & J. Scott eds. 1991).

tive action—as important as these steps may be[5]—and would go beyond addressing inequality in the name of making it possible for women to be more like men.

I do not deny the horror and the reality of the story MacKinnon tells us about the extent to which sexual abuse perpetuated against women gets taken as the way of the world,[6] but I do want to argue against the reduction of woman to the figure of the victim. The result of this reduction is not only that MacKinnon cannot develop useful programs of reform, but that she cannot account for the very feminist point of view that she argues must be incorporated if we are to reach for a state in which equality between the sexes would be more than mere pretense for the perpetuation of masculine privilege and female subordination.

Equivalent rights, although meant to challenge gender hierarchy, do not do so by erasing sexual difference. Further, equivalent rights should not be understood as only a means to the end of sexual difference. Instead, a program of equivalent rights seeks to value the specificity of feminine[7] sexual difference. MacKinnon cannot take us beyond a "negative" program without the affirmation of the feminine difference which is irreducible to the current patriarchal trappings of her own understanding of femininity.

Crucial to my disagreement with MacKinnon is her reading of women's sexuality as constituted only by and for men and, therefore, as contrary to women's freedom from the chains of an imposed femininity, a femininity which constitutes "our" sex and that can only justify women's domination.[8] Thus, even if I agree with her that rape, battery, sexual abuse, and pornography must be seen not only as questions of criminal law but as barriers to the equality of women where the law has the ideological capacity to reinforce the devaluation of the feminine "sex," I disagree with her structural analysis of feminine sexual difference and of feminine sexuality. As I already have indicated, it is not

---

5. While affirmative action is inadequate to address the inequalities that a program of equivalent rights can, as I will argue, remedy, it nevertheless remains an important means to address broad notions of inequality. For a comprehensive discussion of affirmative action programs as they relate to women's issues, see M. ROSENFELD, AFFIRMATIVE ACTION AND JUSTICE 197-204 (1991).

6. P. 127 n.2; C. MACKINNON, FEMINISM UNMODIFIED: DISCOURSES ON LIFE AND LAW 5-6 (1987) [hereinafter C. MACKINNON, FEMINISM UNMODIFIED].

7. The term feminine is normally used in a pejorative sense in feminist circles to refer to societally constructed notions of the ideal woman. Here, I use it as an imaginative, universal, irreducible to any conception or empirical designation of the characteristics of actual women. In this sense, the feminine is separated from both sociological knowledge of women as objects of study and from conventional, popular notions of what the "feminine woman" should be.

8. Because MacKinnon conflates sex, sexuality, and gender identity, she can speak of a simple division between men and women and the masculine and the feminine in a way that I do not accept. Because this conflation is an impossibility for me, I would not speak so simply of the "us" and the "them" as MacKinnon does. This does not mean that I deny specificity of feminine sexual difference—far from it. But I do argue against the us/them dichotomy as a material unshakable reality. See generally D. CORNELL, BEYOND ACCOMMODATION: ETHICAL FEMINISM, DECONSTRUCTION AND THE LAW (forthcoming 1991) [hereinafter D. CORNELL, BEYOND ACCOMMODATION]; Cornell & Thurschwell, Feminism, Negativity, Intersubjectivity, in FEMINISM AS CRITIQUE: ON THE POLITICS OF GENDER 143 (S. Benhabib & D. Cornell eds. 1987).

simply that MacKinnon's analysis cannot sustain a positive program for intervention on the part of the state into gender arrangements. MacKinnon's own
stance toward the feminine reflects the very "sexual shame"[9] of women's "sex"
that keeps the feminine from being valued and, more specifically, legally
affirmed in a program of equivalent rights. My criticism of the division she
creates between freedom and sexuality assumes a conception of the self as a
being of the flesh, in which sexual expression cannot be easily separated from
freedom.[10] For women, the concept of freedom cannot be separated from the
struggle against the devalorization of the feminine. Consciousness-raising,
essential to fostering the dream of women's freedom, involves more than the
exposure of the "truth" of our victimization. It demands the re-figuration of
what has been constituted "to be" within patriarchy. It also demands that we
think through the conditions of women's equality of well-being and capability
in light of the recognition and value of feminine sexual differences.

Simply put, I will argue that women's sexuality cannot be reduced to
women's "sex," as sex has been currently defined, once we understand both
the limit to institutionalized meaning and the possibility of re-metaphorization
which inheres in the rule of metaphor.[11] MacKinnon's understanding of feminine sexuality accepts what Irigaray has called the "old dream of symmetry."[12]
Irigaray uses the concept of symmetry to explain the masculine fantasy that our
sexuality is symmetrical to that of men. In other words, what men fantasize
women want is what they want us to want. In fact, women's sexuality is
irreducible to the fantasy that we are only "fuckees." MacKinnon's reduction
of feminine sexuality to being a "fuckee" endorses this fantasy as "truth" and
thereby promotes the prohibition against the exploration of women's sexuality
and "sex" as we live it and not as men fantasize about it.

Men, defined by MacKinnon as sexual beings, may imagine that what they
think women want, what they want women to desire, *is* what women desire.
However, feminine writing on feminine sexuality has recognized the "old dream
of symmetry" as just that: a dream and, more specifically, a masculine dream.
I want to emphasize the political and personal significance for women of
challenging MacKinnon's view of feminine sexuality. The possibility of celebrating women's "sex" and sexuality can keep us from the tragic disjuncture
between sex, sexuality, and freedom that MacKinnon's analysis leads us to.

In terms of a theory of equality, her critique cannot meet its own aspiration
to legitimate and recognize the feminine point of view in law in the name of
equality and not by appeal to special privilege. Her analysis cannot achieve this

---

9. For an analysis of sexual shame in women, see Galenson & Roiphe, *The Impact of Early Sexual Discovery on Mood, Defensive Organization, and Symbolization*, 26 THE PSYCHOANALYTIC STUDY OF THE CHILD 195 (1972).

10. *See* Pp. 153-54.

11. *See* Cornell, *Institutionalization of Meaning, Recollective Imagination and the Potential for Transformative Legal Interpretation*, 136 U. PA. L. REV. 1135 (1988).

12. *See* L. IRIGARAY, SPECULUM OF THE OTHER WOMAN 11-129 (G. Gill trans. 1985).

if it denies the equivalent value of the two sexes. Equivalent rights do not repeat the "separate but equal" argument, but challenge the idea that sexual difference can or should be eradicated through the pretense that the human race is currently constituted as sex-neutral, or as if man is the equivalent of human. The view of equality I rely on to justify my understanding is Amartya Sen's equality of capability and well-being.[13] As Sen reminds us, "[c]apability reflects a person's freedom to choose between different ways of living."[14] Sen's view of equality is valuable to feminists precisely because it allows for a "positive" program to guarantee women's equality of well-being and capability. Capability of well-being implies the affirmation of sex and sexuality and, in the case of women more specifically, of living without shame of our sex.

II. THE SOCIAL CONSTRUCTION OF WOMEN'S SEXUALITY

Let me begin with MacKinnon's analysis of the social construction of femininity as an expression of male dominance and, more specifically, of male sexual desire. To quote MacKinnon: "Male dominance is sexual. Meaning: men in particular, if not men alone, sexualize hierarchy; gender is one. As much a sexual theory of gender as a gendered theory of sex, this is the theory of sexuality that has grown out of consciousness raising."[15] Thus, for MacKinnon, inequality *is* sexual, and sexuality and the engagement in "sex" perpetuates that inequality. An analysis of inequality that does not focus on inequality as a sexual dynamic in which male domination reduces women to their sex will ultimately "limit feminism to correcting sex bias by acting in theory as if male power did not exist in fact."[16] It will "limit feminist theory the way sexism limits women's lives: to a response to terms men set."[17] As a result, MacKinnon argues:

A distinctively feminist theory conceptualizes social reality, including sexual reality, on its own terms. The question is, what are they? If women have been substantially deprived not only of their own experience but of terms of their own in which to view it, then a feminist theory of sexuality which seeks to understand women's situation in order to change it must first identify and criticize the construct "sexuality" as a construct that has circumscribed and defined experience as well as theory. This requires capturing it in the world, in its situated social meanings, as it is being constructed in life on a daily basis.[18]

---

13. *See* A. Sen, Inequality Reexamined: Capability and Well-Being 5-6 (paper delivered at Conference on Quality of Life, Helsinki, Fin. July 1988, on file with author).
14. *Id.* at 5.
15. P. 127.
16. P. 128.
17. *Id.*
18. P. 129.

The study of the construct of sexuality is, for MacKinnon, the examination of how women come to have a "sex." Women are, very simply put, defined as women because "we get fucked."

> First sexual intercourse is a commonly definitive experience of gender definition. For many women, it is a rape. It may occur in the family, instigated by a father or older brother who decided to "make a lady out of my sister." Women's sex/gender initiation may be abrupt and anomic: "When she was 15 she had an affair with a painter. He fucked her and she became a woman." Simone de Beauvoir implied a similar point when she said: "It is at her first abortion that a woman begins to 'know.'" What women learn in order to "have sex," in order to "become women"—women as gender—comes through the experience of, and is a condition for, "having sex"—woman as sexual object for man, the use of women's sexuality by men. Indeed, to the extent sexuality is social, women's sexuality is its use, just as femaleness is its alterity.[19]

Femininity is the sex imposed on us by a world of male power in which men seek the fulfillment of their desire through us. Feminine gender identity is this imposed sexuality, reinforced in all gendered social arrangements and through the state, which reflects male sexual desire and legitimates sexual dominance as the rule of law. The challenge then to femininity as imposed sexuality, as the subjection of our "selves" to our "sex," *is* feminism, and ultimately this forms the basis of the feminist theory of the state.

> In feminist terms, the fact that male power has power means that the interests of male sexuality construct what sexuality as such means, including the standard way it is allowed and recognized to be felt and expressed and experienced, in a way that determines women's biographies, including sexual ones. Existing theories, until they grasp this, will not only misattribute what they call female sexuality to women as such, as if it were not imposed on women daily; they will also participate in enforcing hegemony of the social construct "desire," hence its product, "sexuality," hence its construct "woman," on the world.
>
> The gender issue, in this analysis, becomes the issue of what is taken to be "sexuality"; what sex means and what is meant by sex, when, how, with whom, and with what consequences to whom.[20]

"Sex" difference is the consequence of this imposed sexuality. To celebrate women's difference is a form of "false consciousness," because women's so-called difference is only women's lives as "fuckees," and the affirmation of difference is only an excuse for reducing women to those who "get fucked" in whatever way men want to do it to us. This reduction of women to "fuck-

---

19. P. 111 (citations omitted).
20. P. 129.

ees" is what MacKinnon means when she argues that our social reality is fundamentally pornographic.

We can now begin to understand why, according to MacKinnon, pornography is absolutely central to the way in which the state enforces the male viewpoint and particularly the male vision of women as sexual objects. The representation of having men forced down women's throats is not just men's masturbatory fantasy but the truth of women's reality. *Deep Throat*, in other words, gives us a depiction of what we are forced to become under our current system of gender domination. This is why MacKinnon can say in all seriousness that we are all Linda Lovelace,[21] with oral sex being the essence of women's subordination.

Yet this reality of subordination is not only ignored by the state, it is protected as a matter of right—the right of free speech under the First Amendment.[22] Pornography, for MacKinnon, is not a matter of speech at all, but a matter of the systematic silencing of women. The image of men being shoved down women's throats is the very symbol of shutting us up.

> Thus the question Freud never asked is the question that defines sexuality in a feminist perspective: what do men want? Pornography provides an answer. Pornography permits men to have whatever they want sexually. It is their "truth about sex." It connects the centrality of visual objectification to both male sexual arousal and male models of knowledge and verification, objectivity with objectification. It shows how men see the world, how in seeing it they access and possess it, and how this is an act of dominance over it. It shows what men want and gives it to them. From the testimony of the pornography, what men want is: women bound, women battered, women tortured, women humiliated, women degraded and defiled, women killed. Or, to be fair to the soft core, women sexually accessible, have-able, there for them, wanting to be taken and used, with perhaps just a little light bondage. Each violation of women—rape, battery, prostitution, child sexual abuse, sexual harassment—is made sexuality, made sexy, fun, and liberating of women's true nature in the pornography.[23]

That pornography is seen as the "right to speak" is another sign of the way in which the state and the law simply reflect the male point of view and the right of men to subordinate women to their sexual desires. As MacKinnon explains:

> The state is male in the feminist sense: the law sees and treats women the way men see and treat women. The liberal state coercively and authoritatively constitutes the social order in the interest of men as a gender—through its legitimating norms, forms, relation to society, and

---

21. *See* C. MACKINNON, FEMINISM UNMODIFIED, *supra* note 6, at 127, 129.
22. "Congress shall make no law . . . abridging the freedom of speech . . . ." U.S. CONST. amend. I.
23. P. 138 (footnote omitted).

substantive policies. The state's formal norms recapitulate the male point of view on the level of design.[24]

The feminist point of view, on the other hand, is impossible, because, according to MacKinnon, the male "point of view" enforces itself as true and as the totality of a pornographic social reality. As MacKinnon tells us:

> Feminism criticizes this male totality without an account of women's capacity to do so or to imagine or realize a more whole truth. Feminism affirms women's point of view, in large part, by revealing, criticizing, and explaining its impossibility. This is not a dialectical paradox. It is a methodological expression of women's situation, in which the struggle for consciousness is a struggle for world: for a sexuality, a history, a culture, a community, a form of power, an experience of the sacred.[25]

For MacKinnon, the impossibility of a woman's point of view is constantly reinforced by the state, which reflects the male point of view as the rule of law and which erases what it has done in the name of neutrality. The rule of law is then transformed into ideology, further enforcing the male viewpoint not just as perspective but as the definitive interpretation of the Constitution.

III. MacKinnon's Marxism Summarized

We can now turn to MacKinnon's unique transposition of the Marxist critique into her analysis of imposed sexuality as the basis of feminine gender identity.[26] For MacKinnon, law is clearly not neutral vis-à-vis the gender divide. Instead, law reinforces the legitimacy of the male viewpoint as the standard upon which the law is based and is bolstered by the myth of the legal person. The myth of the legal person erases the continuing reality of the gender hierarchy and the terrible suffering imposed by male domination. By so doing, the myth is itself a form of domination. The Marxist application here turns on MacKinnon's argument that the liberal state is based on a pretense of gender equality in the name of a legal person when, in reality, the underlying social stratum of gender inequality remains as the truth of woman's condition. It is precisely in its perpetuation of the myth of equality as a reality that the liberal state further silences women who try to challenge it as a reflection of its masculine *constitution*. For this is exactly what our Constitution is for MacKinnon: the protection of the right of men to silence and to subordinate women. The so-called abstract equality of the individual must, therefore, be

---

24. Pp. 161-62 (footnote omitted).
25. P. 115.
26. MacKinnon first developed this Marxist critique in a two-part essay published as *Feminism, Marxism, Method, and the State: An Agenda for Theory*, 7 SIGNS 515 (1982) and *Feminism, Marxism, Method, and the State: Toward Feminist Jurisprudence*, 8 SIGNS 635 (1983).

challenged by feminism. This is one interpretation of a Marxist analysis transposed into the context of gender. As Marx argued that the establishment of bourgeois rights hides the continuing reality of class subordination, so MacKinnon argues that the constitution of "the rights of man" erases the subordination of women as the basis of social life.

> In Anglo-American jurisprudence, morals (value judgments) are deemed separable and separated from politics (power contests), and both from adjudication (interpretation). Neutrality, including judicial decision making that is dispassionate, impersonal, disinterested, and precedential, is considered desirable and descriptive. Courts, forums without predisposition among parties and with no interest of their own, reflect society back to itself resolved. Government of laws, not of men, limits partiality with written constraints and tempers force with reasonable rule-following.[27]

As a result, MacKinnon identifies the so-called neutrality of the liberal state not only as a *prop* to the male point of view but as its fundamental expression. Thus, she can argue that

> [t]he state is male jurisprudentially, meaning that it adopts the standpoint of male power on the relation between law and society. This stance is especially vivid in constitutional adjudication, thought legitimate to the degree it is neutral on the policy content of legislation. The foundation for its neutrality is the pervasive assumption that conditions that pertain among men on the basis of gender apply to women as well—that is, the assumption that sex inequality does not really exist in society. The Constitution—the constituting document of this state society—with its interpretations assumes that society, absent government intervention, is free and equal; that its laws, in general, reflect that; and that government need and should right only what government has previously wronged. This posture is structural to a constitution of abstinence: for example, "Congress shall make no law abridging the freedom of . . . speech." Those who have freedoms like equality, liberty, privacy, and speech socially keep them legally, free of governmental intrusion. No one who does not already have them socially is granted them legally.[28]

Before turning to my own story of the constitution of feminine "sex," sexuality, and gender difference, which I will use to counter MacKinnon, I want to demonstrate some of the contradictions within her analysis.

---

27. P. 162 (footnote omitted).
28. P. 163.

IV. THE CONTRADICTIONS INHERENT IN MACKINNON'S DEVALUATION OF THE FEMININE

The first and most important criticism is that MacKinnon is mistaken when she says that it does not matter whether and how the feminine sex is affirmed or disparaged. As she puts it:

> Difference is the velvet glove on the iron fist of domination. The problem then is not that differences are not valued; the problem is that they are defined by power. This is as true when difference is affirmed as when it is denied, when its substance is applauded or disparaged, when women are punished or protected in its name.[29]

In MacKinnon's own terms, this difference matters precisely in relation to what it might mean to incorporate the feminist point of view into the state—MacKinnon's stated program.

> Law that does not dominate life is as difficult to envision as a society in which men do not dominate women, and for the same reasons. To the extent feminist law embodies women's point of view, it will be said that its law is not neutral. But existing law is not neutral. It will be said that it undermines the legitimacy of the legal system. But the legitimacy of existing law is based on force at women's expense. Women have never consented to its rule—suggesting that the system's legitimacy needs repair that women are in a position to provide.[30]

How can one incorporate the feminist point of view into the state if sexual difference is not recognized? More specifically, in MacKinnon's own terms, how could women provide the needed repair? If women as a gender are defined as victims, as fuckees, as voiceless, and if, as MacKinnon argues, the feminist "point of view" is an impossibility within our system of male dominance, then it would be impossible to provide the condition for repair. Thus, women, defined as we are by MacKinnon, cannot possibly play the role she allots to them.

The second contradiction in MacKinnon's analysis is that she advocates a positive program of state intervention into gender arrangements, and yet her own political slogan, "Out now!," is, and must remain, negative. Positive rights for women should not just involve the end of sexual abuse or even restrictions on pornography. MacKinnon has advocated and successfully fought to pass a city ordinance that makes the propagation of pornography actionable as a matter of sex inequality. In *Virginia v. American Bookseller Association, Inc.*,[31] the

---

29. P. 219.
30. P. 249.
31. 488 U.S. 905 (1988).

harm to women was recognized by the Court, yet pornography was protected as speech. As she has argued, the "law of the First Amendment secures freedom of speech only from governmental deprivation."[32] For MacKinnon, the limit on governmental intervention not only applies to the First Amendment, but also to the concept of law. As a result, we do not have what MacKinnon calls a "negative" state, but rather a social reality which guarantees the positive "freedom" of women precisely through the limit on state intervention. MacKinnon argues that "the offspring of proper passivity is substanceless. Law produces its progeny immaculately, without messy political intercourse."[33]

I agree with MacKinnon that the harm to women caused by pornography should be legally recognized, even if I do not accept her own legal solution. But my point here is that without the affirmation of femininity we cannot develop a concept of "positive" freedom for women which MacKinnon herself recognizes we need to rectify the inequality of women. As MacKinnon herself has said, the negative state has specific implications: "For women this has meant that civil society, the domain in which women are distinctively subordinated and deprived of power has been placed beyond reach of legal guaran tees."[34] But if we are to truly intervene in civil society to restructure the gender hierarchy, we must legally insist that the specificity of feminine sexual difference be valued. MacKinnon's analysis, in other words, can criticize the negative state, but she cannot successfully justify the move beyond it given her own repudiation of the feminine. I agree with her, however, that the negative state is not enough to end the inequality of women.

We need a full program of rights that will provide women with the conditions for equality of well-being and capability. I advocate Sen's theory of equality for two reasons. First, the emphasis on well-being allows us to take sexuality and its expression into consideration when thinking about equality for women. Second, such a view of equality allows for "positive" legal intervention on the part of the state to guarantee "well-being." In other words, this view of equality allows us to move beyond the negative state that MacKinnon describes as inadequate to provide equality for women. Equality of well-being and capability also prevents the recognition of sexual difference from degenerating into the justification of special privilege for women. Equivalent rights are necessary for equality. They should not be seen as special privileges. This vision of equality has the substance that allows for positive intervention and does more than just perpetuate stereotypes. The rhetoric that fits equivalent rights into a view of equality is important because, in the end, the rhetoric provides us not only with philosophical justification for the conditions of women's equal well-being, but also provides a cultural framework in which recognition of feminine sexual difference need not be reduced to an appeal to "special' treatment.

---

32. P. 164.
33. P. 164.
34. Pp. 164-65.

To summarize, MacKinnon's refusal to affirm feminine sexual difference means that her negative political program cannot be turned into "positive" affirmative legal reform. Her example of Nicaragua, in *Feminism Unmodified*,[35] does not provide a blueprint for a legal program for women. The Nicaraguans were fighting for socialism and for national independence. They were not fighting to keep the United States out, but to realize a dream of a different social order. The slogan "Out now!" was addressed to a nation that was intervening against that dream and against that fight. If our dream is to recognize women as full human beings, then the negative program MacKinnon offers is not and cannot be enough.

V. THE CRITIQUE OF MACKINNON'S CONCEPTION OF LIBERALISM

MacKinnon's analysis of liberalism is limited to a conception of neutrality that even many liberal thinkers reject. Thinkers as diverse as Bruce Ackerman, C. Edwin Baker, Ronald Dworkin, Sylvia Law, Thomas Nagel, John Rawls, Steven Shiffrin, and Wendy Williams,[36] all of whom would continue to designate themselves as liberals, have long since abandoned the traditional concept of neutrality defined by Robert Bork and Herbert Wechsler.[37] However, I do agree that none of these scholars have adequately addressed the significance of the gender hierarchy as it continues to limit our thinking on equality. This is important because even within their own terms of analysis it would be possible to reach very different conclusions on, for example, the question of pornography. At the very least, I believe this disjuncture between argument and conclusion is more than a coincidence. Indeed, this disjuncture is itself a reflection of the devalorization of the feminine that I describe in the second half of this review.[38] I am suggesting, in other words, that the feminist argument, regardless of how one ultimately comes out on the difficult question of legal censorship, is not given the weight it deserves because the harm to women is taken lightly if it is seen at all. To see the harm to women as relevant to a theory of equality, we do need an account of the relationship of inequality, the gender hierarchy, and the feminine "sex." Rae Langton, for example, has argued that Ronald Dworkin's own principles, as he has developed them most recently in *Law's Empire*, could be used to justify at least some limited time

---

35. C. MACKINNON, FEMINISM UNMODIFIED, *supra* note 6, at 219.

36. *See generally* B. ACKERMAN, SOCIAL JUSTICE IN THE LIBERAL STATE (1980); R. DWORKIN, LAW'S EMPIRE (1986); T. NAGEL, EQUALITY AND PARTIALITY (forthcoming 1990); J. RAWLS, A THEORY OF JUSTICE (1971); S. SHIFFRIN, THE FIRST AMENDMENT, DEMOCRACY, AND ROMANCE (1990); Baker, *Neutrality, Process and Rationality: Flawed Interpretations of Equal Protection*, 58 TEX. L. REV. 1029 (1980); Law, *Rethinking Sex and the Constitution*, 132 U. PA. L. REV. 955 (1984); Williams, *Equality's Riddle: Pregnancy and the Equal Treatment-Special Treatment Debate*, 14 N.Y.U. REV. L. & SOC. CHANGE 325 (1985).

37. *See* Bork, *Neutral Principles and Some First Amendment Problems*, 47 IND. L.J. 1 (1971); Wechsler, *Toward Neutral Principles of Constitutional Law*, 73 HARV. L. REV. 1 (1959).

38. *See infra* Parts VII.B and VII.C.

and place restrictions on pornography.[39] On the other hand, Thomas Nagel's understanding of an "offense" and his argument for reasonableness within the context of a much more traditional legal argument about "free" speech makes us question whether some restrictions on pornography could be justified.

But let me first give an account of the relationship between the feminine and sexual shame, which I develop later,[40] which ultimately helps us to understand pornography as an "offense," broadly conceived, against women. Pornography is an offense to women because it is inescapable and it is in public. Do I have the choice to make pornography none of my business? Not if I choose to go out of my apartment in New York City. I cannot escape the image of the devalorization of my "sex," which appears everywhere, including the supermarket where I shop, the public transportation I ride, and wherever I might choose to buy my Coca-Cola. I also understand the serious nature of censorship, particularly as it is now being used to shut down artistic ventures that themselves challenge, on the stage or in other forms of performance art, the very sexual violence that MacKinnon wants to expose.

Nagel's concept of reasonableness is helpful in examining the legitimacy of some time and place restrictions on pornography. His theory is important because we need a concept of legal legitimacy. Without such a concept, we are left with random balancing devoid of standards. It is essential to explain why and how we recognize not only the way pornography harms women, but also why that harm can justify time and place restrictions on pornography. This "weighing" process demands a guiding principle as to how to proceed in the social field of profound neglect. Nagel's reasonableness gives us such direction; he gives us standards by which judges can assess "competing" harms and viewpoints under which harm is defined.

Under Nagel's theory, we weigh the extent of the *wrong* and the degree of the *suffering* of competing parties having different moral positions against one another. For example, who is wronged more profoundly and suffers more intensely—the homosexual who is repressed or the puritan who believes that homosexuality is an evil that contaminates the puritan's social reality, his children's well-being, etc?[41] This conception of reasonableness allows the law

---

39. Langton, *Whose Right? Ronald Dworkin, Women, and Pornographers*, 19 PHIL. & PUB. AFF. 311 (1990).

40. *See infra* notes 75-79 and accompanying text.

41. Nagel argues that:

[T]he argument for a liberal solution, which gives the second answer, has to depend on the judgment that it is terrible to have one's desired form of sexual expression restricted by others who find it repellent, as part of their own strong sexual feelings. The suppression of homosexuality is so much worse for the homosexual than is the relaxation of ambient taboos and restrictions for the sexual puritan, that even the puritan should decide in favor of freedom unless he is prepared to claim that no legitimate state need consider the potential objections of homosexuals because homosexuality is wicked and worthy of suppression for its own sake. This, however, is not a position that no one could reasonably reject, and the puritan is simply mistaken if he thinks it is.

T. NAGEL, THE VIEW FROM NOWHERE 200 (1986).

and the state to make the difficult decisions between competing moral and ethical positions when there is not only no moral consensus, but a "war" between different moral visions and different perspectives on life in which these visions are embedded. I am arguing here that the feminist position, particularly on the issue of pornography, deserves more of a hearing than Nagel himself has given it.[42] I also want to call attention to how Thomas Nagel's own "view from nowhere,"[43] in which he urges us to overcome our perspective on the world in the name of the "uncontaminated" nowhere, leads us to what I would call "compassion." It is interesting to note that Nagel fails to show the same compassion for the feminist argument against pornography as he does for the homosexual's argument for freedom of sexual expression. I would argue that his reason for this "blindness" is Nagel's inability to see the harm to women, precisely because he does not integrate a psychoanalytic theory of the construction of feminine sexual difference into his analysis of pornography.

By pornography, and I am adopting Cass Sunstein's definition here,[44] I mean the explicit connection of sex with violence that in no way denies that pornography is sexual and not just violence. Why am I adopting Cass Sunstein's definition? Sunstein's definition allows us to distinguish between erotica and pornography. We have to think about which definition we adopt within the context of our political times. The National Endowment of the Arts' campaign to repress certain forms of erotic expression has now become only too well-known. Ironically, this censorship has been directed against feminist artistic attempts to expose and then to critique the reduction of women to sexual objects as masculine desire. Thus, I adopt Sunstein's definition because it allows us to distinguish between erotica and pornography, and because it protects feminist artists who may choose to graphically depict women's sexual objectification in such a way as to themselves fall victim to censorship. But even if one adopts Sunstein's definition, his own argument for certain time and place restrictions on pornography lacks a crucial philosophical dimension.

Sunstein's argument is strengthened in defense of the possible legitimation of time and place restrictions, if he works within Nagel's concept of reasonableness. Indeed, the weakness of Sunstein's own argument is that he does not have a concept of legal legitimacy. Nagel's reasonableness can provide him with such a concept. Sunstein argues that the periphery of pornography within the traditional context of First Amendment arguments, combined with evidence that pornography promotes violence in men, might lead us to accept legal restric-

---

42. In the case of the homosexual, Nagel argues that "[t]he freedom to act on these desires is therefore a leading candidate for protection as a right." *Id.* at 200-01. On the other hand, in the case of pornography, he states, "[t]his does not exclude prohibitions against acute and direct offense to the equally deep sensibilities of others; but it does mean that personal and private activities (including the consumption of pornography) should be protected from political control." *Id.* at 201.

43. *Id.*

44. C. Sunstein, Neutrality and Constitutionality with Special Reference to Pornography, Abortion, and Surrogacy (1991) (unpublished manuscript on file with author).

tions, notwithstanding the concern with censorship and the constraints such restrictions must place on men in their access to pornography. Sunstein explains:

> [T]here is a quite straightforward argument for regulating at least some pornographic materials. The first point is that much pornographic material lies far from the center of the first amendment concern. If the first amendment is, broadly speaking, a safeguard against governmental suppression of points of view with respect to public affairs, at least some forms of pornography are far from the core of constitutional concern. Under current doctrine, and under any sensible system of free expression, speech that lies at the periphery of constitutional concern may be regulated on the basis of a lesser showing of government interest than speech that lies at the core.
>
> To say this is hardly to say that the definition of the core and the periphery will be simple. Under nearly any standard, however, at least some pornographic materials will be easily classified as belonging in the periphery.[45]

If, under traditional doctrinal analysis, pornography is at the periphery of free speech and there is evidence that it perpetuates the legitimation of violence against women, while "suffering" to the pornography reader is limited, particularly if access is restricted and not banned, then "reasonableness" may demand time and place restrictions even before we have an adequate account of the relationship between gender hierarchy and the devalorization of the feminine "sex." This account is ultimately necessary if we are to justify the tip in the balance toward such restrictions.

VI. MacKinnon's Critique of Marxism in the Context of Gender

I have critiqued MacKinnon for her identification of liberalism with principles of neutrality and for her failure to see that there are liberal arguments for some of the legal reforms she seeks to make. In this difficult period, we need to choose our allies carefully. But there is, perhaps, a more important critique to be made of her own transposition of Marxism into the context of gender. I agree with her that the Marxist tradition has tended to reduce gender and sex to a secondary question. And I agree with MacKinnon, as so many others have,

---

45. *Id.* at 22-23 (footnotes omitted).

that this reduction is a disservice to women.[46] Yet I still believe MacKinnon's own use of Marxism can be critiqued on three separate grounds.

The first is related to the "pragmatic"[47] and "postmodern"[48] critique of any attempt to develop an empiricist, positivist, or materialist account of women's situation that could claim, in any strong sense, to be scientific, if by scientific we mean "free" of the mediation of narration.[49] MacKinnon does not recognize the status of her own analysis as a story, but rather as a materialist conceptualization of gender inequality. Such accounts are never just descriptions, but are always narrations that give meaning to reality. They can never be free of an evaluation of that reality, which is what gives the story its meaning and, in the case of law, its legal meaning. A classic example is "date rape." In order to define a certain kind of sexual abuse to women as date rape, we have to rely on a seeming oxymoron: putting the idea of date—with its implied concept of consent—together with rape. The behavior may have always been there, but it took a different story, with a different evaluation of those acts—such as locking a woman into a dorm room until she agreed to have sex—to define this behavior as rape.

To say that the philosophical status of MacKinnon's account is a narration in no way takes away from its "truth," if one means by truth an illumination of an existing "reality" that previously was invisible, because it had not been told or evaluated in a way that made that particular behavior "appear" as a wrong or harm to women within our legal system.[50] MacKinnon's story helps us to see that what was once thought of as normal was and remains the systematic sexual abuse of women. I do not disagree with that part of the story which emphasizes the "normalcy" of sexual violence to women as a physical reality. The story tells us why it is abuse, and not just "boys being boys."[51] As one of the many reflected in the unfortunate statistic that at least one-half of all women will undergo a sexual assault,[52] I cannot deny this story myself. Having survived an attempted rape, I know only too well the "truth" of MacKinnon's chapter on rape where she discusses the long-term trauma that

---

46. As Luce Irigaray puts it:

    How can the double demand—for both equality and difference—be articulated? Certainly not by acceptance of a choice between "class struggle" and "sexual warfare," an alternative that aims once again to minimize the question of the exploitation of women through a definition of power of the masculine type. More precisely, it implies putting off to an indefinite later date a women's "politics," a politics that would be modeled rather too simplistically on men's struggles.

L. IRIGARAY, THIS SEX WHICH IS NOT ONE 81-82 (C. Porter trans. 1985).

47. *See* R. RORTY, PHILOSOPHY AND THE MIRROR OF NATURE 357-94 (1979).

48. J. BUTLER, GENDER TROUBLE: FEMINISM AND THE SUBVERSION OF IDENTITY (1990).

49. This basic Hegelian insight has been the basis of what are now called either pragmatic or postmodern critiques of scientism. *See* G. HEGEL, PHENOMENOLOGY OF MIND 147-213 (J. Baillie trans. 1967).

50. *See, e.g.*, J. LYOTARD, THE DIFFEREND: PHRASES IN DISPUTE (G. Van Abbeele trans. 1988).

51. *See, e.g.*, Barrett, *Date Rape—A Campus Epidemic?*, Ms., Sept. 1982, at 48, 50.

52. MacKinnon explains that "[a]lmost half of all women . . . are raped or victims of attempted rape at least once in their lives. Almost 40 percent are victims of sexual abuse in childhood." P. 176.

such attacks leave in their wake. But her story is limited precisely because she figures women only as victims and feminine sexual difference as *only* "the velvet glove on the iron fist of domination."[53]

The figure of Woman as victim is an important one, but it is not the *only* figure of the feminine. MacKinnon tells us a story, a profound story, and it is true, but only partially so. This is the second criticism of MacKinnon's Marxist transposition which can only understand women's "material" oppression through the reduction of feminine sexual difference to Woman as the fuckee.

As we have seen, for MacKinnon, having a "sex," particularly a feminine identity, cannot be separated from "having sex," and "having sex" cannot be separated from domination and sadomasochism.

> Feminism has a theory of power: sexuality is gendered as gender is sexualized. Male and female are created through the erotization of dominance and submission. The man/woman difference and the dominance/submission dynamic define each other. This is the social meaning of sex and the distinctly feminist account of gender inequality. Sexual objectification, the central process within this dynamic, is at once epistemological and political.[54]

The third criticism, which is primarily political, is that despite the limits of Marxism as a "science," its emphasis on class, race, and national difference remains extremely important to a feminism that is *always modified* through its respect for difference and which continually allows new narrations of the feminine and how it is lived, experienced, and told. As Audre Lorde has succinctly argued:

> By and large within the women's movement today, white women focus upon their oppression as women and ignore differences of race, sexual preference, class, and age. There is a pretense to homogeneity of experience covered by the word *sisterhood* that does not in fact exist.[55]

In other words, femininity, if it is not to fall into the erasure of race and class difference, must always be modified. Indeed, put even more strongly, the openness to modification through—or openness to modification by—the "other woman" is what provides the very basis of feminism as an aspiration to an ethical relationship irreducible to a set of established rules or any currently accepted political slogan.

---

53. P. 219.
54. Pp. 113-14 (footnote omitted).
55. A. LORDE, SISTER OUTSIDER 116 (1984) (emphasis in original).

VII. THE AFFIRMATION OF FEMININE SEXUAL DIFFERENCE

A. *Overcoming the Repudiation of the Feminine*

Politically, I can summarize my disagreement with MacKinnon as follows: for MacKinnon, feminism must involve the repudiation of the feminine; for me, feminism *demands* the affirmation of feminine sexual difference and the challenge to women's *dereliction* which flows inevitably from the repudiation of the feminine. Without this challenge, we are left with the politics of revenge and lives of desolation, which make a mockery of the very concept of freedom. But to understand how we can make this challenge without simply replicating the pattern of gender hierarchy, we must first give a different account of why a gender hierarchy cannot completely capture feminine sexual difference.

MacKinnon's own analysis of femininity does not turn on a naturalist account of anatomy as destiny or on appeal to pre-given natural libidinal drives as the basis of male desire and domination. She moves within accepted postmodern insight by recognizing that femininity as imposed sexuality is a social construction. But, social construction or not, the constitution of the world through the male gaze as reinforced by male power totalizes itself as our social reality. Thus, if MacKinnon clearly rejects naturalism, she nevertheless remains a specific kind of essentialist. Under this patriarchal social reality, women's imposed "sex" is women's "essence," her only "being."

B. *The Lesson of Deconstruction*

I have argued at length elsewhere that MacKinnon fails to understand the critical lesson of deconstruction.[56] The lesson is that no reality can perfectly totalize itself because reality, including the reality of male domination, is constituted in and through language in which institutionalized meaning can never be fully protected from slippage and reinterpretation.[57] MacKinnon believes that a feminist theory of sexuality

> must be studied in its experienced empirical existence, not just in the texts of history (as Foucault does), in the social psyche (as Lacan does), or in language (as Derrida does). Sexual meaning is not made only, or

---

56. D. CORNELL, *The Feminist Alliance with Deconstruction,* in D. CORNELL, BEYOND ACCOMMODA- TION, *supra* note 8; Cornell, *The Doubly-Prized World: Myth, Allegory and the Feminine,* 75 CORNELL L. REV. 644, 685-89 (1990).

57. Jacques Derrida has demonstrated that, as the repressed Other, the feminine is irreducible to that which it supposedly is designated to be, the lack that signifies woman within the Symbolic. This irreducibili- ty of the feminine also results from what Derrida calls "logic of parergonality," by which he argues that the very frame that designates social reality always implies "more" because our reality is necessarily enframed. *See* J. DERRIDA, THE TRUTH IN PAINTING (G. Bennington & I. McLeod trans. 1987).

even primarily, by words and in texts. It is made in social relations of power in the world, through which process gender is also produced.[58]

Jacques Derrida does not argue that sexual meaning is made in and through words and texts in the limited way MacKinnon defines them. Derrida shows us that social reality (including the very definition of power) and "empirical" experience cannot be separated from the meanings they are given, while simultaneously exposing the inevitability of the limit on those meanings that have dominated our social life. The relevance of the limit to institutionalized meaning in this context is that it allows for the affirmation of feminine sexual difference as other than its stabilized definitions within gender hierarchy. This, in turn, is precisely what allows us to develop a feminist celebration of women's "sex," rather than its repudiation, as well as a feminist "perspective" which, even under MacKinnon's own program, must be the very basis of a feminist theory of the state.

More specifically, I argue that "seeing" and "being" can never be separated.[59] This argument would, at first glance, seem to bolster MacKinnon's argument: So we are seen, so we are. But, as Paul Ricouer has convincingly argued, we do not "see" reality directly. Instead, we "see" through language and, more specifically, through the metaphors in which "being" is given to us.[60] "Being" for Ricoeur is itself a metaphor. This means that the "being" of femininity can never just be described as "there."

As a result, the rule of metaphor has specific implications within the context of feminism.[61] I have argued that "feminine being" cannot be separated from the metaphors in and through which it is figured. Metaphor as transference and analogy always implies both the like and the not like. The definition of the feminine, including MacKinnon's definition, *is* only as metaphor. Metaphor, in turn, allows both for expansion of meaning and for reinterpretation. The characterization can then be cemented in stone, precisely because it is designated only as metaphor. Therefore, the realization of "feminine being" as metaphor is what allows us to reinterpret and, more importantly, to affirm the feminine as other, and irreducibly other, to any of the definitions imposed by patriarchy. Thus we can challenge MacKinnon's position on feminine sexuality.

For MacKinnon, as we have "seen," a feminist perspective is impossible as anything other than the recognition of the totalization of the masculine viewpoint. Therefore, the most we can do is to simply reverse the meaning of

---

58. P. 129.

59. *See* D. CORNELL, BEYOND ACCOMMODATION, *supra* note 8.

60. Ricouer argues that we must treat the verb "to be" as a metaphor itself and recognize in "being as" the correlate of "seeing as." 3 P. RICOUER, TIME AND NARRATIVE 155 (1984).

61. Derrida suspects that through Woman's re-metaphorization we will once again capture women in a new concept, one in which the very process of metaphorization will itself be erased. *See generally* J. DERRIDA, THE EAR OF THE OTHER: OTOBIOGRAPHY, TRANSFERENCE, TRANSLATION (C. McDonald ed., P. Kamuf trans. 1985).

the totality, rather than challenge it in the name of the feminine. In MacKinnon's reality, what men see as sex, women see as rape. The problem with this solution, as Luce Irigaray has explained, is that

> if [women's] aim were simply to reverse the order of things, even supposing this to be possible, history would repeat itself in the long run, would revert to sameness: to phallocratism. It would leave room neither for women's sexuality, nor for women's imagination, nor for women's language to take (their) place.[62]

The possibility of feminine desire—and let me use the beautiful French word *jouissance*[63]—that is irreducible to being fucked by men and liking it is foreclosed by MacKinnon's analysis.

I will return to lesbianism and love between women as an alternative shortly. For now I am operating within MacKinnon's own heterosexual framework, because given MacKinnon's analysis, that is the framework that defines social reality. I want to emphasize that given MacKinnon's repudiation of the feminine, there can only be the inescapable totality of male violence, the world of the "fuckees" and the "fuckors."[64] "True love" between women is always blocked by the totality of an imposed pornographic heterosexual reality. As a result, the utopian vision of lesbianism developed by innumerable writers such as Cixous, Irigaray, and Wittig, is foreclosed.[65] We are left instead with a disjuncture between sex and freedom. To quote MacKinnon:

> So long as sexual inequality remains unequal and sexual, attempts to value sexuality as women's, possessive as if women possess it, will remain part of limiting women to it, to what women are now defined as being. Outside of truly rare and contrapuntal glimpses (which most people think they live almost their entire sex life within), to seek an equal sexuality without political transformation is to seek equality under conditions of inequality. Rejecting this, and rejecting the glorification of settling for the best that inequality has to offer or has stimulated the resourceful to invent, are what Ti-Grace Atkinson meant to reject when she said: "I do not know any feminist worthy of the name who, if forced to choose between freedom and sex, would choose sex. She'd choose freedom every time."[66]

---

62. L. IRIGARAY, *supra* note 46, at 33.

63. *Jouissance* is a term which, as used by Lacan, lacks direct translation. In contemporary philosophical and psychoanalytic discourse, it is often taken to refer to women's specifically feminine, total sexual pleasure. For a more detailed and nuanced explication of this aspect, see H. CIXOUS & C. CLÉMENT, THE NEWLY BORN WOMAN 88-89 (1986).

64. *See* C. MACKINNON, FEMINISM UNMODIFIED, *supra* note 6, at 60-61.

65. In *The "Herethics" of Carnality*, in D. CORNELL, BEYOND ACCOMMODATION, *supra* note 8, I present a comprehensive treatment of these authors and their efforts to write of feminine desire and pleasure differently, in a way that refuses to repudiate the feminine while it insists on believing in the woman writer and, thus, in woman's new beginning.

66. Pp. 153-54 (quoting Atkinson, *Why I'm against S/M Liberation*, in AGAINST SADOMASOCHISM: A RADICAL FEMINIST ANALYSIS 91 (E. Linden, D. Pagano, D. Russel & S. Star eds. 1982)).

Maybe. But what is the content of this freedom? More specifically, what kind of conception of the person would we need to think that the disjuncture between sex and freedom could lead to freedom? In fact, one central theme of feminist philosophy has been to challenge conceptions of freedom that pit freedom against the reality that we are beings of the flesh, and necessarily sexual. The argument, simply put, has been that we cannot rise above our empirical selves of the flesh in order to be *free*. Such a conception has been critiqued as repression, not freedom, and has been connected to the devaluation of women—just as women have come, in Western philosophy, to be associated with the flesh.[67] If this is women's "choice"—and choice would hardly seem to be the right word since, under MacKinnon's analysis, it is forced upon women—it would seem rather to be a "choice" between desolation[68] or sacrifice and sex, not between "freedom" and sex. The celebration of the feminine "sex" and women's sexuality, on the other hand, suggests that our sexuality is not represented by any of the current male fantasies of woman and sex within patriarchy. By "having sex," then, I do not mean "getting fucked" in MacKinnon's sense. Such a reduction obviously envisions an act perpetuated by men upon women: the man fucks, the woman "gets fucked"—with all the negative connotations "getting fucked" takes on within our culture of so-called heterosexuality. Instead, by "sex" I mean the physical intimacy necessary for creatures of the flesh. Sex is the caressing, the kissing,[69] the embracing that can bring comfort and connection to two mortal, sexual creatures clinging to one another against the darkness and finding in one another a moment of protection and safety. Irigaray beautifully imagines two women making love as an alternative to MacKinnon's vision of "getting fucked." As Irigaray writes,

> No surface holds. No figure, line, or point remains. No ground subsists. But no abyss, either. Depth, for us, is not a chasm. Without a solid crust, there is no precipice. Our depth is the thickness of our body, our all touching itself. Where top and bottom, inside and outside, in front and behind, above and below are not separated, remote, out of touch. Our all intermingled. Without breaks or gaps.[70]

---

67. *See generally* R. SCHOTT, COGNITION AND EROS: A CRITIQUE OF THE KANTIAN PARADIGM (1988).

68. I am indebted to A. Collin Biddle for suggesting the word "desolation" which, to my mind, so effectively describes women's experience of having to make this kind of "choice" about their "sex" and sexuality.

69. Luce Irigaray offers us a beautiful and poetic description of this kissing:
Kiss me. Two lips kissing two lips: openness is ours again. Our "world." And the passage from the inside out, from the outside in, the passage between us, is limitless. Without end. No knot or loop, no mouth ever stops our exchanges. Between us the house has no wall, the clearing no enclosure, language no circularity. When you kiss me, the world grows so large that the horizon itself disappears. Are we unsatisfied? Yes, if that means we are never finished. If our pleasure consists in moving, being moved, endlessly. Always in motion: openness is never spent nor sated.
L. IRIGARAY, *supra* note 46, at 210.

70. *Id.* at 213.

I am not arguing that lesbianism can simply take us away from male domination. Yet even so, as Wittig has brilliantly argued, lesbianism *can* provide us with a politically significant vision of a different engagement with a woman's own body and with her lover in which a woman's "sex" is not repudiated.[71] Indeed, for Wittig, the lesbian is not a woman, precisely because a woman traditionally defined cannot be separated from her role within heterosexuality. Simply put, the lesbian need not engage with her "sex" from within the psychosexual dynamic MacKinnon describes to live her life or explore her love. Ironically, given MacKinnon's move to totalize her own description of heterosexuality, she excludes Wittig's promise of lesbianism as a different practice of sexuality other than to the truth of sadomasochism which MacKinnon defines as heterosexuality.

Nor am I arguing that the practice of heterosexuality is reducible to Mac-Kinnon's and Dworkin's view of "sex" as "intercourse" or of "intercourse" as "getting fucked."[72] Here again, we are returned to the possibilities of reinterpretation, even if we simultaneously recognize the institutionalization of certain sexual practices, particularly within heterosexuality, as "normal" when they may have nothing at all to do with women's desire. But I insist on the need to affirm the feminine and feminine sexuality, because it is necessary to challenge the conception of a free person as one who has been cut off from her own sexuality. Such an affirmation allows us to avoid the tragedy into which MacKinnon's analysis inevitably leads us.

But does this mean that she is not right to remind us at every step that, under gender hierarchy, to use Lacan's famous phrase, "fucking [is] not working?"[73] The answer is no. I too want to emphasize the suffering women must endure and, more specifically, expose the relationship in our society between sexual shame and women's lives. However, the story I relate may be a narration very different from the one MacKinnon tells.

I turn now to Lacan because his story lies at the base of how gender hierarchy is constructed and goes beyond MacKinnon's limited vision of gender hierarchy as only a matter of social psyche.[74] My focus will be to show how Lacan helps us to understand the devalorization of the feminine sex as the foundation of gender inequality.

---

71. M. WITTIG, THE LESBIAN BODY (1975).

72. *See generally* A. DWORKIN, INTERCOURSE (1987).

73. L. IRIGARAY, *supra* note 46, at 88 (quoting J. LACAN, ENCORE, LE SÉMINAIRE XX (1975)).

74. For insight into Lacan's basic theories of feminine sexuality, see generally, J. LACAN, FEMININE SEXUALITY: JACQUES LACAN AND THE ÉCOLE FREUDIENNE (J. Mitchell & J. Rose eds., J. Rose trans. 1982) (questioning any certainty or authority in conceptions of psychic and sexual life). For a detailed explanation of the Lacanian framework, see Cornell & Thurschwell, *supra* note 8, at 145-46. For Derrida's intervention into Lacan's psychoanalytic theories, see generally J. DERRIDA, *supra* note 57.

C. *The Lacanian Account*

According to Lacan, the genesis of linguistic consciousness occurs when the infant recognizes itself as having an identity separate from the mother, because the mother is Other to herself or himself. The primordial moment of separation is experienced by the infant both as a loss of unity and the gaining of an identity. The pain of this loss results in a primary repression that simultaneously buries the relationship to the mother in the unconscious and catapults the infant into the Symbolic realm to fulfill its desire for the Other. Once projected into language, this primary identification with the mother is experienced only through the disruptive force of the unconscious. The unrepresentable desire for the Phallic Mother is only remembered in the fantasy projection that compensates for Her absence. So far on this account, it would seem that both sexes suffer a primordial separation from the mother and would be marked by this separation in the same way.

Although Lacanians maintain the difference between the penis and the phallus (the phallus represents the lack that triggers desire in both sexes), it remains the case in Lacan's analysis that because the penis can visibly represent the lack, the penis can appear to stand in for the would-be neutral phallus. This establishes the basis of the illusion that having the penis is having the phallus, with all its attendant symbolic power. In this culture of gender hierarchy, the male child "sees" his mother's lack, which gains significance as her castration. Sexual difference and gender identity are based on the cultural significance attributed to this experience of "sighting." The penis is identified with potency, able to satisfy the mother's desire. Woman, on the other hand, is identified as the castrated Other. If the penis, at least on the level of fantasy, is identified with the phallus, then Woman, who lacks the penis, is also seen as lacking the affirmative qualities associated with the phallus.

Lacan's speculative insight has been reinforced by such empirical research as the work of Eleanor Galenson.[75] Galenson's nurseries provided the arena for observing the actual behavior of little girls. Her studies argue that sexual shame in girls is associated with the recognition of themselves as the castrated Other. Galenson's work further tries to draw the connection between this early experience of sexual shame as inherent in feminine identity and some of the symptoms and behavioral patterns in mature women including depression, profound feelings of inadequacy, feeling like a "fake," or fear of being "found out" despite a record of accomplishment. One of the most significant expressions of sexual shame is the denial of the value of femininity and of the value of feminine sexual difference which is irreducible to the current cultural trappings of femininity.

---

75. *See, e.g.*, Galenson & Roiphe, *supra* note 9.

It also is important to note that Lacan understands male superiority as a "sham," meaning that it is not mandated by a person's "sex" but instead rests on the fantasy identification that having the penis is having the phallus. This illusion also means that the symbolic "Daddy" can always take the phallus away and, with the phallus, the affirmative qualities associated with potency. This fear is the basis of the designation of the male as the "wimp," beautifully allegorized in Samuel Beckett's "Happy Days." The man crawls around on all fours unable to face the woman:

> *Winnie*: "What is a hog exactly? What exactly is a hog, Willie, do you know, I can't remember. What *is* a hog, Willie, please!"
> *Willie*: "Castrated male swine. Reared for slaughter."[76]

The analysis of the fear of the "wimp" in no way takes away from the cruelty and the violence of the "male swine." But it does explain this violence and cruelty as rooted in fear and not in power, especially if one defines the empowerment of personality as innovative capability rather than beating up the other.[77] It would be accurate under this analysis to say that pornography is what wimps need, not what men want. Thus, I disagree with MacKinnon when she argues that "[p]ornography permits men to have whatever they want sexually. It is their 'truth about sex.'"[78] Nonetheless, for me, pornography is clearly an "offense."

How can we more profoundly understand pornography as an offense to women under the story of gender hierarchy I have just developed? Pornography reinforces the very sexual shame that, as Galenson and others have shown, makes it difficult for women truly to find equality of capability and well-being. We can only truly understand pornography as an offense within a context that explains gender hierarchy as the basis of sexual shame. Pornography, in this most basic sense, is an offense because it reflects the devalorization of women's "sex." Pornography prevents women from feeling like equal members of the community because it reflects their "sex" in a way that no woman can affirm. Thus, the harm to women is understood to outweigh the claim of the man who desires that pornography be available to him free of any restrictions, particularly once we understand the idea that pornography is not only an offense to women, but also an insult to men.

The insult to men is that it depicts them as having to violate women in order to imagine having sex with them. It gives us a vision and reinforces a view of the man as the "wimp," afraid of women and, therefore, needing to have them in chains. Hardly a flattering picture. I distinguish insult from

---

76. S. BECKETT, HAPPY DAYS 60 (J. Knowlson ed. 1978) (emphasis in original) (stage directions omitted).

77. For a more thorough examination of the concept of innovative capability, see Cornell, *supra* note 11.

78. P. 138 (footnote omitted).

offense because I in no way want to pretend that the insult to men imposes the same kind of suffering as the offense to women. Nevertheless, it should be noted. Finally, it is important to recognize that the fear of the "wimp," the fear of losing the supposed all-powerful phallus, is so overwhelming because in the context of gender hierarchy the worst thing that can happen to a person is to become a "girl," or rather a "cunt."

The identification of Woman as the castrated Other explains the fear in the "wimp" as well as the devalorization of Woman. The assumption of masculine gender identity thus depends upon the devalorization of Woman which, in turn, explains the repudiation of the feminine as the basis for patriarchal culture. The result for women is that we are left in a state of *dereliction*, which means that the little girl cannot positively understand her relationship to her mother and, therefore, to her own "sex." Thus, Lacan's account of gender differentiation into two sexes explains why the gender divide becomes a hierarchy in which the feminine is repudiated and despised, by women as well as men. Lacan leaves us with a world of "wimps" (men) and ghosts (women) unable to meet, speak, touch, ally. Beckett's depiction of the male crawling on all fours and the woman slowly sinking into the "same old shit" in *Happy Days* allegorizes the Lacanian understanding of the reality of gender hierarchy. "Fucking," for both Lacan and MacKinnon, cannot succeed because of the subjection of women. But, if Lacan recognizes the subjection of women, he also believes that the problem is insoluble. In response, I return to Derrida's intervention into Lacan because he shows why the affirmation of feminine sexual difference cannot be foreclosed by the institutionalized meanings of patriarchy.

Derrida teaches us that Lacan's own understanding of gender identity constituted in and through the linguistic structures of the Symbolic realm—the conventional meanings given to gender in patriarchy—can be turned against Lacan's own political conclusions. Derrida illustrates that shifts in language, including a shift in the definition of gender identity and the designation of the feminine as the lack of the phallus, demonstrate that this same language cannot be definitively stabilized. In French feminist writing and in my own recent work, another step has been taken beyond deconstruction, to advocate the need not only to open the space for the reevaluation of the feminine, but also to write its celebration through re-figuration and re-metaphorization of feminine figures.[79]

---

79. For examples of the re-figuration and re-metaphorization of feminine figures, see generally H. CIXOUS & C. CLEMENT, *supra* note 63; L. IRIGARAY, *supra* note 46 (developing concept of "writing" the feminine body); J. KRISTEVA, THE KRISTEVA READER (T. Moi ed. 1986). For my analysis, see D. CORNELL, *Feminine Writing, Metaphor and Myth*, in D. CORNELL, BEYOND ACCOMMODATION, *supra* note 8.

VIII. Equivalent Rights: A New Context for Sex, Sexuality, and
Gender Identity

A. *Challenging the "Sameness" Ideology*

I now want to turn to my own program of equivalent rights to develop a
different theory of equality, which I believe can overcome the deficiency in
MacKinnon's analysis. We need a theory of equality which does not end by
reinforcing the privileging of the masculine as the norm and insisting that the
gender hierarchy must be challenged. MacKinnon has correctly and profoundly
challenged the "sameness" ideology that informs so much of the law of sex
discrimination.[80] She explains that if we can show that women are like men,
then we can show that we have been discriminated against if and when we *are*
in fact like them, but are treated differently. Women continually have to
analogize their experience to men's if we want it legally recognized as unequal
treatment. For MacKinnon, "sameness" and "likeness" analysis is itself a
reflection of discrimination because it demands that women meet the male norm
without questioning why the masculine was identified as the norm in the first
place. My argument insists further that unless we recognize the value of
feminine sexual difference we cannot adequately challenge the acceptance of
the male as the human and, therefore, we cannot ultimately challenge gender
hierarchy. In other words, we need the affirmation of feminine sexual difference
if we are doctrinally to challenge the likeness analysis without reducing our
insistence on women's rights in an appeal for special privilege.

A program of equivalent rights is the legal expression of the affirmation
and valuation of sexual difference. "Equivalence" is defined in the *Standard
Oxford Dictionary* as "of equal value," but not of equal value *because of
likeness*. Equivalence does not demand that the basis of equality be likeness
to men. Such a view would once again deny that we are indeed sexuate beings
of two genres and not one species without differentiation. Equivalent rights can
then be distinguished from the dominant analysis of sex discrimination that has
been reflected in current opinions in the federal courts and in the United States
Supreme Court. Moreover, equivalent rights recognize the irreducibility of the
two genres, male and female, to one another. As Luce Irigaray has explained:

> I know that some men imagine that the great day of the good-for-
> everyone universal has dawned. But what universal? What new imperi-
> alism is hiding behind this? And who pays the price for it? There is no
> universal valid for all women and all men outside the natural economy.
> Any other universal is a partial construct and, therefore, authoritarian
> and unjust. The first universal to be established would be that of a
> legislation valid for both sexes as a basic element in human culture.

---

80. Pp. 215-34.

That does not mean forced sexual choices. But we are living beings, which means sexuate beings, and our identity cannot be constructed without a vertical and horizontal horizon that respects difference.[81]

The "legislation valid for both sexes as a basic element in human culture" to which Irigaray refers, must include equivalent rights as rights, not just as privileges needed to correct the imposed inequality of women. Equivalent rights are not merely a means to help women become more like men in the name of promoting one species undivided by sexual difference. Equivalent rights do not have as their sole or even their main goal the creation of a space for women in a male world from which we have previously been shut out. Rather, they are designed to enable women to value the choices we make about our life and work without shame of our "sex." MacKinnon has criticized the patriarchal culture which imposes "forced sexual choices." Yet she fails to see that one of these forced sexual choices is the very repudiation of the feminine. I can suggest here how the program of equivalent rights, once it is put into the context of sex, sexuality, and gender identity, can help further the analysis of specific issues of doctrinal concern.

B. *Equivalent Rights and Pornography*

I have argued through my reading of Lacan[82] and the reinforcement of his theory in the empirical research of Eleanor Galenson that the repudiation of the feminine and, more specifically, the reinforcement of sexual shame as the basis of identity harms women in a very specific sense and that this harm is reinforced by pornography. Moreover, pornography is not the projection of all-powerful men but, as Lacan would tell us, of the "wimps" who are afraid of women. Ultimately, pornography amounts only to a compensatory fantasy to make up for fear of women, the "dark continent." I in no way want to deny that fear too often leads to cruelty. We see this in race relations as well as in relations between the sexes. But, when MacKinnon speaks of the all-powerful man—and of pornography as his vision and his desire—she accepts the psychical fantasy of macho compensation as truth. Who but a "wimp" would fantasize about sex with a woman in chains, tied, bound and gagged, so he would, in the most profound sense, not have to face her, let alone hear her?

C. *Equivalent Rights and Abortion*

I want to turn now to the issue of abortion. The right of abortion is a classic example of equivalent rights for women and should be included in what

---

81. L. Irigaray, How to Define Sexuate Rights? (date unknown) (unpublished manuscript on file with author).

82. *See supra* notes 72-74 and accompanying text.

2274   The Yale Law Journal   [Vol. 100: 2247

Irigaray has called the right to "motherhood" (as should such rights as maternity leave and prenatal care). Without such a right women cannot aspire to achieve the most basic sense of well-being because we are denied both control over our reproductive capacity and the power to live pregnancy and motherhood with joy and without sacrifice of other aspects of our lives. Men clearly do not need the right of abortion. But that does not mean that women should not have such a right guaranteed if we are to have equality of capability and well-being. To understand why the right of abortion is crucial as an equivalent right, we must understand ourselves as sexual beings whose freedom can never be separated from an affirmative relationship to our "flesh." Such an affirmative relationship is impossible without a right of bodily integrity. Justice Blackmun, in his dissent in *Webster v. Reproductive Health Services*,[83] voiced his fear of the loss of freedom to women if we were to lose this right of abortion, which I would include under the right to bodily integrity.[84] I want to stress here the suffering imposed on women as creatures of the flesh if we lose that right and yet find ourselves in circumstances in which we are unable to raise and mother a baby and, therefore, must impose upon ourselves a self-inflicted abortion. The abortion movement of the early 1970's documented just how many women were forced to rely on such an option when abortion was illegal. In her horrifying novel—horrifying because it depicts so brilliantly the toll of the sexual shame of women as the basis of their identity—Torborg Nedreaas describes the anguish, the physical anguish of a self-inflicted abortion:

> Then I set to. Drops of sweat ran down the bridge of my nose, and I noticed that I was sitting there with my tongue hanging out of my mouth. Because something burst. I could hear it inside my head from the soft crunch of tissues that burst. The pain ran along my spine and radiated across my loins and stomach. I screamed. I thought I screamed, but there wasn't a sound. More, more, push more, find another place. It had to be wrong. And I held the very tip of the weapon between my thumb and forefinger to find the opening to my uterus once more. It was difficult but I thought I'd succeeded. The steel needle slid a little heavily against something. It went far up. Then a piercing lightning of pain through my stomach, back and brain told me it had hit something. More, more, don't give up. Tissues burst. The sweat blinded my eyes. I heard a long rattling groan come out of me while my hand let the weapon do its work with deranged courage.[85]

---

83. 109 S. Ct. 3040 (1989).

84. Blackmun stated: "I fear for the future. I fear for the liberty and equality of millions of women who have lived and come of age in the 16 years since *Roe* was decided. I fear for the integrity of, and public esteem for, this Court. I dissent." *Id.* at 3067 (Blackmun, J., dissenting); *see also* Cruzan v. Director, Mo. Dep't of Health, 110 S. Ct. 2841, 2851 (1990) (affirming constitutionally protected liberty interest in refusing unwanted medical treatment).

85. T. NEDREAAS, NOTHING GROWS BY MOONLIGHT 189-90 (B. Lee trans. 1987).

Feminine flesh is not the same as masculine flesh. The right to bodily integrity is a right necessary for both sexes under the vision of equality of capability and well-being. But given the difference of our "sexual being," the right to bodily integrity does not mean the same rights, but rather the guarantee of its equivalent scope for both sexes. The right of abortion is most definitely necessary to guarantee bodily integrity for women. Rights should not be based on what men need for their well-being as sexual beings of the flesh, as if there were only one genre of the human species.

IX. CONCLUSION

If MacKinnon ultimately repudiates the feminine, she perpetuates rather than challenges the gender hierarchy which lies at the base of women's inequality. If the feminist point of view is to be incorporated into the state, we must have an account of its possibility. I have argued that such an account is possible once we correctly understand the role of deconstruction and, beyond this, the place of re-metaphorization and re-figuration of the feminine in reinventing and thus affirming, sexual difference. This affirmation allows us to identify the wrongs to women within a context of sexual shame imposed upon women by gender hierarchy. It also allows us to challenge the idea that the human species is only one genre and therefore that the "rights of man" give us a full conception of rights. To argue for equivalence is not to advocate special privilege once we value sexual difference as necessary for women's equality of capability and well-being, and recognize sexuality itself as necessary for a creature of the flesh to enjoy a full life.

[24]

I LOVE MYSELF WHEN I AM LAUGHING:
A NEW PARADIGM FOR SEX

Karen Elizabeth Davis

Both talking and laughing indicate a serious lack
of the capacity for surrender.

—Wilhelm Reich

Ooo baby, where've you been to look so drawn?
I've been living with the hungry,
the recognized forlorn.
I've been eating with the lonely,
and we eat each other raw.

—Ferron

From sexology to gay and lesbian studies to feminism, a persistent concern has been that while men unproblematically express desire, women have been plagued by sexual silence. The feminist sexuality debates of the 1980's took up the problem of women's desire. Some feminists maintained that our culture represses women's sexual desire and expression which can and should be a lot more like men's, and otherwise would be if not for repression. This "pro-sex" faction sought to create a vernacular of women's hungering desire as an antidote to desexualized political lesbianism, the woman-identified-woman, of the 1970's.[1] Diffuse expressions of women's sexuality (such as Adrienne Rich's lesbian continuum or Audre Lorde's erotic as power)[2] were scorned as the sexual province of good-girl moral milksops. Pro-sex feminists sought sex without emotional attachments, seeing women's more emotional than libidinal investment in sex to be part of our feminine conditioning. They sought to create a women's sexuality that is self-motivated, driven, active, unattached, demanding, free...like men's, specifically, like gay men's.[3] The order of the day was that women needed to be sexual subjects, and need to be sexual *in order to be* subjects.[4]

Radical feminism has criticized the social determination of sexual attributes and gendered subjectivities, arguing that men's experience of their sexuality corresponds more to the ethos of male domination than to nature. Male subjectivity and female alterity are produced as two sides of the same coin by the activity of objectification: "Man fucks woman; subject verb object."[5] From this point of view it has seemed retrograde for feminists to not only endorse but aspire to sexuality on male terms.

I believe that this whole debate started on a couple of false premises which have remained unexamined, the first being that male sexuality is unproblematically self-motivated, driven, active, unattached, demanding, free. A more basic but often unacknowledged tenet, and the one most relevant to my discussion, is that sexuality is like hunger—a need which arises from within the individual and seeks its satisfaction in the object world. Looking for women's sexuality as hungering and not finding it, pro-sex feminists concluded that women's sexuality had been violently repressed, and resisted vehemently any suggestion that it did not exist. Women's more relational, contextual, emotional responses were derogated as passive and moralistic. They were not what was being sought. These feminists were looking for *desire*.

While post-modernism has taught us to be suspicious of how paradigms create knowledges, we have not been critically reflective of the paradigms through which we look for sexuality in the world. I want to suggest that our inability to find women's

6   KAREN ELIZABETH DAVIS

sexuality results from women's sexuality not being like a hunger. Furthermore, men's sexuality has been construed this way only through a particular social organization of body and a particular aesthetic of sex and of power. Sex-as-desire and desire-as-hunger have been socially organized and individualized, creating the interior experience and terrain of sexuality. Its phenomenology has in turn informed thinking not only about sexuality but about subjectivity. In what follows, I will introduce a new paradigm both for the discourse about sexuality and for understanding the discursivity of sexuality itself, a shift mandated by Foucault's critique of sex-desire.

The dominant cultural metaphor governing sexuality is that sexual desire is like a hunger. For Freud it was an instinct, like hunger or thirst, which became a problem for civilization when it no longer responded to the cycles of women's fertility but "took up its quarters as a permanent lodger."[6] The sexual and aggressive instincts must be sublimated for peaceable social organization to be possible. When Lacan comes along he will correct the biologism of this construct. Man's sense of desiring sexuality is socially constituted through the threat of castration from the father. Castration then takes up quarters in the subject like a permanent lodger, in the form of an ontological lack. This lack impels a constant desire for phallic presence, which is, however, in the nature of things impossible. The lack at the center of Lacanian ontology functions as a hunger, in this case a hunger which cannot be sated. Sexual agency (and agency per se) is the compulsion to feed lack. Lacan's schematization creates a paradoxical duality: you feed yourself to fill the lack, but as the lack can never be sated, you in fact feed the lack itself. In the vernacular of 12-step programs, this is the operation of "the (w)hole which cannot be filled": one binges on food, alcohol, sex, drugs, gambling to fill one's desperate sense of emptiness, which gnaws ceaselessly anyway. Thus, the Lacanian subject of sexuality may be well served by a program of sexual sobriety to break out of the compulsive, destructive and despairing pursuit of an insatiable hunger.[7]

Foucault is astute enough to notice that sexuality as desire is positively constituted before it is repressed. He examines the discourses which produce the experience of "sex-desire" and colonize the subject of sex with a relentless demand for truth. He warns that sexual liberation ideology is itself caught up in this deployment: "We must not think that by saying yes to sex, one says no to power."[8] Foucault's critique of the social construction of sex-desire in and by the discourses of sexuality is part of a thoroughgoing analysis of "disciplinary power," in which the modern subject is seen to be positively constituted by power before being repressed.[9] To counter the grips of power, Foucault hypothesizes a space of bodily experience that would escape its discursive entrapment: "The rallying point for the counterattack against the deployment of sexuality ought not to be sex-desire, but bodies and pleasures."[10] However, as Teresa de Lauretis points out, this move adduces a space outside of discursive relations, which his theory precisely disallows.[11] Foucault's mistake is to assume that pleasure may originate in and redound to individual bodies prior to or apart from social relations. His supposition that the body is sometimes a pre-social, atomistic private space belies his genealogical method, his critique of the categories of liberalism, and his analysis of the social construction of meanings and bodies.[12]

Despite Foucault's caveats against sexual agency, academic feminists who took up his call quickly recontained bodies and pleasures within normative discourses of sexual desire: what pleasures do bodies hunger for?, how do women get pleasure in patriarchy? These two questions form the main organizing principles for the 1982 Barnard Conference, "Toward A Politics of Sexuality." The conference *Diary*, taken from the planning sessions, abounds with a visual aesthetic of babies and adults hungering for breasts, invocations of infant desiring, and manifestos for women's desiring sexuality.[13] Here as throughout the sexuality debates in feminism, "How do you get pleasure?" is always code for sexual practice and orgasm.

In art and culture, the aesthetic of hungering sexuality enjoys a wide traffic. I long for you, feel a gnawing emptiness when you are not near, my desire consumes me, I consume you. Even Elaine Scarry's sober-minded study *The Body in Pain* buys into the ethos of desiring subjectivity as the locus of cultural production: "A state of consciousness other than pain—such as hunger or desire—will, if deprived of its object, begin to approach the neighborhood of pain, as in acute, unsatisfied hunger or prolonged, objectless longing." This pain calls up the activity of the imagination and creativity. If the objects of desire or hunger are missing, they can be made up, "and though they may sometimes be inferior to naturally occurring objects, they will always be superior to naturally occurring objectlessness." The feminist question here, and Scarry doesn't ask feminist questions, is whether woman is a naturally occurring object or a creative artifact of men's desiring. Scarry assumes that objectless longing is, like hunger, a natural state; "when such a state is given an object, it is itself experienced as a pleasurable and self-eliminating (or, more precisely, pleasurable because self-eliminating) physical occurrence."[14] Here as in Freud, the mark of (exquisite) pleasure is the cessation of (exquisite) pain.

Far from being the dialectic that drives creativity, frustrated longing is always already an artifact of our culture's discourse of sexuality. As part of a cultural aesthetic of boundary and transgression, (women's) resistance and deferment are rigorously necessary to enhance (men's) pleasures of sexual satisfaction.[15] Sexual satisfaction becomes exquisite only when the pain of longing is brought to a precise crescendo. In this aspect, sublimation takes on a different meaning: not so much culture's compromise with the dictates of nature, sublimation must be seen as a cultural organization of subjectivity from start to finish. Derrida's critique of phallogocentrism in Western philosophy goes one step further—the activity of enticement to desire and perpetual deferment of its satisfaction constitutes Being.[16]

Even when sexuality is seen to originate in cultural production instead of nature, as Lacan and Foucault both maintain, an unreflective use of the hunger paradigm for sexuality causes us to slide back into naturalist and humanist categories, which in turn constantly efface the social situatedness and relatedness of sexuality essential to any radical critique. Constituted either as instinct or as lack, sexuality is seen to inhere in and issue from the subject, rather than being created at each moment in and of social relations. Despite critiques and revisions of Freud, theorists still seem to think about sexuality within the formal strictures of his libido: sex-desire resides in the subject as an internal stimulus demanding its satisfaction. Thus, while some things have changed, more have stayed the same.

The editors of the anthology *Powers of Desire* outline a history of "sex radicalism" from 1830 to the present. By their account, sex radicals are those who separate sexual intercourse from its normative conflation with marriage and reproduction. Other ideological conflations nonetheless remain intact in the writings on sexuality collected here: orgasm equals pleasure; pleasure equals freedom; sex is "a primary source of energy and pleasure";[17] and, as the title of the volume suggests, desire is a source of power. Catharine MacKinnon has remarked this ideological continuity, noting that although "it has become customary to affirm that sexuality is socially constructed," the conception of a desire that is largely pre-cultural and invariant remains: "The impetus itself is a hunger, an appetite founded on a need; what it is specifically hungry for and how it is satisfied is then open to endless cultural and individual variance, like cuisine, like cooking."[18] In spite of Foucault, Lacan and feminism, the discourse of sexuality is still largely constrained within a Freudian desire-as-hunger paradigm that limits and determines inquiry.

While Lacanians accept the post-structuralist wisdom that sex and subjectivity are socially constructed, they still are stuck thinking that sex-desire is like hunger and that

8   KAREN ELIZABETH DAVIS

subjectivity is like sex-desire. Lacan reverses the categories of Freud's essentialism by positing that desire is forged by repression rather than predating it. Desire is constituted in the castration complex as an originary lack needing to be filled, and becomes (as it was for Freud) the *sine qua non* of subjectivity and agency, the locus of culture and representation. Though culturally instead of instinctually inscribed, this desire behaves the same as Freud's libido. Psychoanalysts Laplanche and Pontalis adhere to a desire-as-hunger scheme quite literally, suggesting that sex-desire may originate in and be built upon the relations of suckling at the mother's breast.[19] Feminist psychoanalytic theorists pursue the developmental story of Oedipal desire and phallic lack to account for why women still do not have access to full subjectivity.

Post-modernism notwithstanding, Freud's conclusions are largely intact: sex-desire inheres in the subject as the locus of subjectivity and the motive force of culture. Desire is now socially constituted, but it is still constituted as a hunger located within the subject as a force demanding its satisfaction. Too, we are still trapped in the total imbrication of sexuality and subjectivity. Freud's puzzle, "What do women want?," at once enigma and anathema, still seems to haunt the feminist project as determinative of the possibilities of women's subjectivity.

As Foucault notes at the end of *The History of Sexuality*, "The irony of this deployment [of sexuality] is in having us believe that our 'liberation' is in the balance."[20] What is so interesting about Foucault's rhetorical invocation of "bodies and pleasures" is that a clarion call so thoroughly inconsistent with his work as a whole is taken up as the gist of this book's message for academic feminism. "Pro-sex" feminists ignore Foucault's caution that to say yes to sex is not to say no to power, and they ignore his critique of how sex-desire becomes synonymous with subjectivity and identity. With the Barnard conference in 1982, the rallying point of bodies and pleasures against the regime of sexual discourse is quickly recontained within sexual discourse itself. Under the auspices of resistance to patriarchy, "How do you get pleasure?" organizes an inquiry into desire as the truth of women's sex, which nonetheless devolves into very normative practices.

The "transgressive" sex of these self-acclaimed "bad girls" is still structured around the sort of eroticized inequality that radical feminists had earlier identified as central to heterosexual arrangements, only now the inequality is to be mutable as roles instead of fixed as gender.[21] People get to choose their positions, and to trade off roles of active-passive, top-bottom, butch-femme. Power is still eroticized, but now it is supposed to be mutable instead of congealing in the hands of one class. Of necessity, this change in power's modality requires a heavy (and heavy-handed) overlay of morality, so that turn-taking is conducted fairly, with consent of both partners. The sexual practice of lesbian sadomasochism is particularly invested in the efficacy of morality, depending as it does on explicit honor codes of trust, vulnerability, consent and withdrawal of consent. Predictably, there emerges in practice a moral distinction between a "good top" and a "bad top." A bad top gets too drunk to stop beating on you or to untie you when you say the code word for stop. A good top is responsive to the needs and responses of the bottom, who after all is really in charge. It is too boring to point out how this resonates with the difference between a good man and a lout. Ironically, the bad girls, purveyors of dangerous sex, emerge as the real moralists in feminism, their transgressive sex the most normative.[22]

A decade after the heyday of the radical feminist critique, and haunted by the spectre of "lesbian bed death,"[23] we have feminists calling for a women's pornography, multiple partners, sex toys and lesbian sadomasochism. See, women have hunger too, we need to identify it, kindle it, fuel it in order to recognize ourselves as subjects like men. This proliferation of sexuality is forwarded as the answer to male violence and women's sexual subordination. The conference *Diary*, while embracing Foucault's radicalism, remains nonetheless committed to a repression hypothesis that is still deeply Freudian. Hence a discussion of rape and sexual violence yields the following: "radical analysis suggests male sexual nature is the product of a repressive society, which can be altered only by the elimination of sexism and the increase in women's freedom." The logic here seems to be that if women are allowed to derepress their sexual desire, which moral strictures have held in check, there will be less rape because there will be more sex available to men. Aside from the repression hypothesis itself, this passage makes two implicit assumptions—that women's freedom from repression will find primary expression in increased sexual activity with men, and that more consensual sex will satisfy men's desire for forced sex.[24]

Lacan theorizes women's sexuality in terms of women's relationship to the phallus: "It is for that which she is not that she wishes to be desired as well as loved. But she finds the signifier of her own desire in the body of him to whom she addresses her demand for love."[25] The penis is presumably the signifier of women's demand for love. Lacan, like Freud before him, is wont to conflate love with sex, and sex with the penis, while mystifying (apotheosizing) the penis as the Phallus. Yet Ann Landers came up with a surprise finding that 65,000 of her readers like to cuddle but would just as soon skip the intercourse.[26] Further, many heterosexual women see men as emotional incompetents and seek their primary emotional gratification and understanding from women friends. What neither Freud nor Lacan know is that heterosexual women have a lot of very infantalizing sexual attitudes towards men, often eroticizing men's incompetence, their need to be mothered.[27] In this aspect, either maternal nurturance is the prototype for women's sexuality, or codependency is the prototype for femininity. In either case, women who seek love from men also seek understanding from women.

In spite of this, the phallus remains for Lacan the primary social signifier, structuring men's and women's subjectivities and their relationship to one another. To "have" the phallus is to have access to the position of desiring subject, while to "be" the phallus is the position of wanting to be desired by another.[28] Lacan freely owns that one makes love from a position of emptiness to an Other created in the image of one's needs, and that the object one chooses to feed ontic lack can never satisfy that lack. Yet he never explains why this makes any sense at all as a way for adults to behave. Since it makes no sense, really, it gets relegated to the unconscious as the compulsive behavior of an overgrown four-year-old, an atavism from Oedipal times. Lacan's theory has no account of, and makes no room for, people who do not unconsciously pursue this particular variety of futility. To take his work seriously, it seems, one must first be seriously invested in this obsessive shell game adults play: "Phallus, phallus, who's got the phallus."

While "pro-sex" feminists read Foucault through psychoanalysis to get desire and agency, they might more properly have read Lacan and Freud through Foucault to get a critique of sex-desire revisited. In Lacan, sex-desire is the locus of discursivity, agency, and representational activity. His revision of Freud merely reverses the operation of desire and repression such that desire is constituted by repression, rather than predating and occasioning the repression. Sex-desire (as "lack" this time around) is still the agent and locus of subjectivity itself. Desire is the motive force of cultural production, through which the unconscious seeks to sate or sublate its hunger/lack.

There has been an odd cross-fertilization between the feminist critique of male-dominant sexuality, Foucault's analysis of sexual discourses, and psychoanalysis updated through Lacan. While Lacan and Foucault refuse reconciliation with one another, some academic feminists adduce them side by side: sexuality is socially constructed and the task is to produce an experience of the phallus for women. Ingested separately, psychoanalytic feminism produces object relations theory of women's pre-Oedipal subjectivity at the mother's breast, while the Foucauldian influence on feminism encourages critiques of

10   KAREN ELIZABETH DAVIS

discursive practices in the production of gender. Through all of this, desire remains an experiential and theoretical reference point. Yet it must be possible to get out of the lock-box of sex-desire without pretending to jet us out of discursivity altogether. Discursivity, after all, is not the problem of sex, subordination is. While discursivity is the medium of subordination, it is also the medium of all social interactions.

Parallel to but independent of the development in France of Foucault and Lacan's conflicting analyses, American radical feminism developed a critique of power which centered on sexuality: the eroticization of dominance and submission organizes the bodies and relations of gender inequality. The critique was that sexual objectification produced both male desire and female alterity.[29] Radical feminism developed a politics of sexuality that was not bound to conceptions of sex-desire, but focused on concrete practices of women's sexualized subordination, such as rape, incest, battering. Feminists documented instances of sexual abuse and saw in them relations of social power, not the strivings of the libido for expression. Sexuality came to be understood in terms of a relation of power which invested bodies with gender while mapping them with relations of eroticized dominance and subordination. This feminism challenged the Freudian wisdom that women desire abuse.

In response to women's experience of sexualized subordination, feminists sought a sexual practice that would transcend eroticized inequality. This project proved difficult, as feminist practice on sex was not able consistently to dislodge women's socialization toward masochism. The failure of bodies to follow revolutionary theory caused in some women a discomforting felt contradiction.[30] Some feminists took the intractability of sexuality to mean that the project was flawed and that we should instead promote the free expression of sexualized inequality. If we choose the sexuality of male dominance, we are not its victims but are really the agents of choice, hence subjects. Others took this intractability to mean that the ideology of male dominance is more pervasive and tenacious than first thought, more genealogical in its effects, informing our responses and permeating the very sinews of our bodies. Broader social change, such as working against the saturation of our society by pornography, must accompany the project of individual change.

This divergence reflects a surface/depth distinction: sexuality appears immutable either because its determinants are so pervasive and insidious as to be nearly invisible, or sexuality and the eroticization of power are deep structures of the human psyche, unreachable after the formation of the unconscious. The latter view has been on the ascendent in academic feminism throughout the 1980's, supplanting the critique of sexual subordination which resulted in "desexualized lesbianism" and Take Back the Night marches, and transforming it instead into an agenda for cultivating, inventing, derepressing women's desire.[31] This desire would look in large part like men's desire for sex: an internally felt hunger whose drive for satisfaction moves like subjectivity. The earlier critiques of male desire and female alterity have thus given way to a suggestion and practice that women can have desire too and that men can sometimes be women's other. Also, crucially, women can claim a sexual desire that others women. That's what the bad girls are up to. Another contingent within academic feminism is attempting to theorize the distinctively pre-Oedipal formation of a woman's subjectivity that does not move along the phallic model, but is more relational and contextual.[32] In either case, gone is a critique of the kind of subjectivity men have constructed for themselves, supplanted by an attempt to produce the experience of that subjectivity in women or an attempt to comprehend women's distinctively feminine experience of subjectivity.

With reference to Freud, Lacan, Foucault, and feminism, I would like to suggest a new metaphor to organize thinking about the relations of sexuality. This new metaphor will transcend the limitations of hungering desire paradigms and offer new perspectives on the terms currently in use. While it is now common to profess a belief that sexuality is socially constructed, the locus of this sexuality continues to be a desire that is seen to be interiorized, atomized and the model for subjectivity. When desire is taken to be a drive like hunger, it is quickly presumed to be somatic and interior, arising from within the individual prior to social relations or arising first within social relations but later experienced independently of our relatedness to others. While the formation of the unconscious may be presumed social, once formed the unconscious is seen to act relatively automously. The relationality of sexual subjectivity, and its relation to power, is quickly lost in a simplified language, and a simplified phenomenology, of needs, drives and satisfaction. Hence, the fundamental structure of sex-desire is unchanged in its move from instinctual to social hunger. For those who accept the view that women need to be sexual subjects in order to be social subjects, the problem for feminism has been that women have not hungered, or not enough, or not for the right things. Mostly, to be sure, male dominant sexuality has made women nauseous, but this only becomes apparent when you are willing to comprehend women's anorexia, bulimia, auto-immune diseases and hysteria as internalized responses to male domination.

Sexuality is a relation to one's body and to others. After Foucault and Lacan, we freely recognize that the space of the body is a social space and its responses are social responses. Although modern theorists purport to apply this understanding to sexuality, the language of hunger and drives throws us inexorably back into traditional conceptions of subjectivity and individuality. I would like to shift the metaphors in use regarding sexuality from hunger to laughter, a conception that remains always centered in social interaction. This paradigm shift opens up semantic space in which it is possible to formulate more precisely criticisms feminists have raised about subjectivity, alterity and power. It will also allow feminists to think about what sexuality might look like if it were not so thoroughly shot through with eroticized dominance and subordination, in a way that does not rely on panegyrics to moral virtue. Laughter is a state of enlivened sensibility and a medium of social interaction. Like sexuality, it may convey many things—intimacy, contempt, authority, comradery, frivolity, derision, fear, nervousness, self-abasement, self-aggrandizement, bravado. Laughter is not always funny for all of its participants, especially when it is at somebody's expense.

I will begin with a limited example. The relations of male dominant sexuality are like the relations of tickling, merely, it should be noted, one subclass of how laughter may be shared. Since there are no societal preconceptions that tickling defines the totality of what may be experienced as laughter, this analogy already challenges the tacitly accepted truth that the sexuality of eroticized dominance and submission defines the totality of sex. Being tickled is a sensory chaos of pleasure against pain where one has forfeited to another primary control as well as responsibility for the responses of one's body. Inasmuch as it is impossible to tickle yourself, tickling or being tickled is possible only as a body in relation to others. It thus cannot be theorized or somatically felt as individual physicality unmediated by culture.

Just as psychoanalytic theorists locate desiring hunger in the experiences of infancy, so too will I tell an origin story of how infant tickling becomes adult sexuality. As infants, tickling is usually our first exposure to the collapsing together of power, vulnerability, pain, intimacy, pleasure, and control. As infants, our screams are taken to be screams of glee, our flinching resistance is taken to be a provocation. Consent is a relinquishment of control which asks only that the other assume responsibility. If baby actually is able to communicate a distaste for the activity, the question becomes, "What's wrong with baby?" For most of us, this is our first exposure to the imbrication of pleasure with pain, and to the eroticization of dominance and submission. These we will later recognize in our sexual

12   KAREN ELIZABETH DAVIS

interactions, in which tickling often plays an ongoing role. The pleasures of tickling are first mapped then interiorized in the infant.[33]

If you don't think tickling is sexual and you don't think this sexuality is aggressive, see what happens when you say "no." Notice the anger this provokes in the would-be tickler, how insistent he becomes, and how his ego and potency are at stake. He takes no for yes, and, unable to achieve a physical response from you, redoubles his efforts to the point of inflicting pain on the one who protests. All resistance is interpreted as incitement. "I'm not ticklish," is taken to mean that no one has found a way to tickle me yet, which he will now find. "I don't like being tickled," is taken as a sign that I need to see an analyst about my vulnerability and control issues. "No, don't!" is taken to mean that I'm so ticklish the mere thought of it makes me helpless before you, and I am making my last stand before I submit totally. This last response is especially provocative when accompanied by flinching and wincing, often involuntary responses. The first response, "I'm not ticklish," is provocative in the same way men find lesbians provocative, in the belief that he will be the man who awakens her to the joys of submissive abandon. Fact is, if tickling doesn't thrill you, it is physically painful, and this pain is seen socially as a sign of your prudery. Fact is, too, if tickling is painful to you, it will feel better if you learn to relax and enjoy it. Tickling is a form of torture where laughter demonstrates complicity, even in the explicit absence of consent. The individual expressiveness of bodily intuitions, in sex as in tickling, makes sense only within the body's relational context. Like ticklishness, sexual responsiveness refers to an array of physiological conditions inseparable from their social situation. The point is that tickling would not feel ticklish if it were not for its social situation.[34] Likewise sex.

I will likely be called anti-tickling by some, the way others before me have been called anti-sex. The language of pleasure and consent will be deployed to exonerate the activity and to cast my view as repressive. The unspoken assumption will be that everybody enjoys it, and that anything less than a totally positive relation to it reflects a personal hang-up rather than a systemic malaise. Likely such a critique will be leveled by people whose bodies are inscribed with pleasure and powerlessness in the ways described above, and who are invested in the maintenance of the system on which their satisfaction depends. Although all of us have been subject to sexual and tickle-responsive mappings of our bodies, not all of us embrace the identity they produce as our own.

The analogy of sex to tickling provides a language in which it is possible to talk about power, vulnerability, abandon and control in terms that are neither moralistic nor naturalistic. It introduces a figure for the social mapping of power as pleasure in the body. Languaging sexuality in terms of tickling is not to introduce a metaphor into a previously virgin terrain. The paradigm shift proposed here merely supplants the dominant metaphor of hunger with a more clearly relational metaphor. Among other things, the hunger metaphor privileged men's experience of male sexuality while silencing women's experience. Women's sexuality does not behave unproblematically like hunger and satiety, desire and satisfaction, with its self-referential affect and linear causation. Since it does not issue from a subject out into a world, women's sexuality has been seen to be simply absent. Alternatively, because it depends on context, mood and the quality of interaction, women's sexuality has been derogated as passive, reactive at best, a pale handmaiden to the more primal and urgent male desiring.[35] The laughter metaphor redeems the experience of women's sexuality; actively engaged laughter is contextual, emotional, physical, interactive, and by no means passive.

Sex is to sexuality as tickling is to laughter. Tickling is only one mode of laughter, the least subtle, the least nuanced. Similarly, sex is only one mode of sexuality, although it has been the privileged mode in our culture, and the measure of all others. Ironically, laughter and sexuality are in some ways disjunct. Although sex is supposed to be fun, it is taboo to laugh during sex.[36] Tickling and the sex of male-dominant culture have in common an active-passive structure that is sometimes unilateral and sometimes bilateral. Quick overthrows between who tickles and who is tickled constitute a play and exchange of power without undermining its fundamental structure of domination. This deployment parallels the sexual exchanges of power which characterize a certain mythos of heterosexuality's reciprocity: "Man and woman change places. They exchange masks *ad infinitum.* 'Women have known how to secure for themselves by their subordination the greatest advantage, in fact the upper hand.'"[37]

Just as one cannot tickle oneself, in sex it is taboo to masturbate oneself. Pleasuring oneself during sex with another is a searing indictment of their prowess, and an unconscionable breach of good manners. You must rely on the timing, skill, good intentions and the intuitive judgment of the other, even when they must be schooled extensively to achieve this.[38] The dilemma is then, according to Su Freidrich, "Whether anyone will ever make love to [me] right." Sex, like tickling, has been conceivable only in terms of transitive verbs. When reciprocal, sex is deployed as "I do you, you do me"; when unilateral, it is "Man fucks woman; subject verb object."[39] To tickle is almost always a transitive verb inflected only by active or passive voice. To fuck is a transitive verb for the active partner, and an intransitive verb for the passive partner.

Su Freidrich epitomizes the sex of transitive verbs in what she takes to be a discussion of sex itself: "There is the ideal: the balance of doing to (him, her) and being done to (by him, her). How often we refuse being done to: there is the radical danger of vulnerability and selfishness. How often we refuse doing to: we avoid the complexity of power and willfulness."[40] The situation is actually more polyvalent than Freidrich suggests. In lesbian sex, the passive partner is the one having the orgasm by the agency of the active partner.[41] Mutuality is assured by reciprocity. The paradigm for heterosexual sex is that the active partner (the man) has an orgasm in the passive partner (the woman) by his own agency. Mutuality is assured by the woman's vaginal orgasm, sexology's Holy Grail. Gay male sexuality combines something of both: the active partner in a blow job or a hand job is inducing orgasm in another, while the active partner in sodomy is also the one whose orgasm is in the balance.

For heterosexual men, then, doing and being done to are often one in the same act: men are the agents of their own orgasms for which women provide the occasion and the passive receptacle. The I-do-you-you-do-me formula devolves into a simpler equation: men act, women are acted upon. When practiced in a lesbian context, these roles break down into the butch persona who takes pride in how well I-do-you with a professed disregard for whether or not you-do-me, and the femme persona, a demanding taskmaster who insists on being done to just so.[42] In gay male sexuality, it is the recipient of anal intercourse who is most thoroughly feminized.[43] While I said above that masturbating oneself during sex is taboo, and that one must rely on the prowess of the other, in fact this is only sometimes true. The two cases of male penetration described here involve self-masturbation at the site of an orifice. The passive partner need only "relax," "hold still," and "shut up." A woman's participation in sex, like her consent, is so passive and so tacit that a woman, or in the homosexual context a man, may be unconscious or dead and still be said to have participated.

This is the sort of thing that happens when you ask someone from Mars to comment on a human state of affairs—you get an unflinchingly cold description. What emerges as most remarkable in the above schematization is that these are the mechanisms for pleasure that people are supposed to be hungering for, this traffic in active and passive bodies. Unadorned by love or sentiment or eroticized hierarchy, the sex of transitive verbs seems a roundabout way of achieving orgasm.

14   KAREN ELIZABETH DAVIS

The relations of activity and passivity in tickling mimic those of the most reciprocal sex. The active partner wields control while the passive partner has abandoned him- or herself to a chaos of sensory pleasure. As complicated and depressingly rote as the above descriptions of sex sound, the analogy to tickling calls to mind a sensibility that laughter can be far more interesting and subtle and complex and fun than the pre-scripted roles of I-tickle-you and you-tickle-me. To laugh is almost always an intransitive verb insofar as it indicates simply an activity, one that may or may not be shared, and not an action upon an other. Laughter is not intrinsically objectifying, although it may become so with the introduction of an indirect object, e.g., "I laugh at you."[44] By supplanting desire with laughter as a way to organize our thinking about sexuality, I am suggesting that we may be able to change the practice of what is experienced as sex. It becomes thinkable that we may change the grammar of sexual interactions, heretofore locked in an active-passive, self-other, top-bottom, I-do-you-you-do-me structure. Boring and rote, despite variations.

Objectifying sex has been monolithic (it has been sex itself) within the hunger-desire paradigm. Only if we can think outside the hunger box of subject-verb-object sexual relations does it seem logical that one can find objectifying sex aversive without being "anti-sex." To be sure, one can find tickling aversive and nonetheless be passionately committed to laughter.

It is also important to note that laughter is socially polyvalent: the butt of the joke is usually different from the person with whom the joke is shared and occasions a bonding between the teller and the hearer.[45] Thus can culture be both heterosexual and homoerotic: women are the object of men's laughter (heterosexuality), which laughter is shared with other men (homoeroticism). Freud offers a literal instance of this in his discussion of obscene jokes: "Through the first person's smutty speech the woman is exposed before the third, who, as listener, has now been bribed by the effortless satisfaction of his own libido." It is with this third person that "the joke's aim of producing pleasure is fulfilled."[46] In this view, a woman's rejection of sex from long experience is not mere prudery but wearied recognition—I am the butt of all these jokes.

In sexuality as in laughter, heterosexual relations semiotically inscribe women as objects of exchange among men.[47] Gayle Rubin offers a feminist reading of Levi-Strauss in which the structure of kinship is analyzed in terms of the exchange of women among men: "If women are the gifts, then it is men who are the exchange partners. And it is the partners, not the presents, upon whom reciprocal exchange confers its quasi-mystical power of social linkage." This explains how a culture can be simultaneously heterosexual and homoerotic: "If it is women who are being transacted, then it is the men who give and take them who are linked, the women being a conduit of a relationship rather than a partner to it."[48] It is as a technology of gender rather than a sublation of unconscious impulses that most jokes are about sex, and "locker room jokes" among men almost exclusively so.

When sexual objectification is the regime, being "anti-sex" is not being against sexuality per se, merely against everything that has been organized as sex, everything one has been able to experience as sex within the constraints of our culture. For a long dark night has it been only a matter of faith that sex might be about something else.

Envisioning a sexuality without objectification is like envisioning laughter without tickling and without objects of ridicule, which, since that domain is not so thoroughly overdetermined, seems to be more possible. The language of laughter allows us to reject objectifying sex without needing to adduce love and trust as moral safeguards against humiliation. Equality is not a precondition for shared laughter, although shared laughter sometimes establishes the shared meaning context in which equality is possible.[49] While some feminists and pro-feminist men have sought to eroticize equality, in the laughter paradigm, the structure of the verb "to eroticize" is what changes, such that eroticism is no longer the activity of a subject toward an object. Radically, this suggests the possibility that equality may not be the activity of a subject toward an object. The subject constituted by objectification is intrinsically incapable of relations other than domination, i.e. relations which do not other others.[50] With this recognition it becomes not only possible but mandatory to think beyond desire as the locus of agency, and agency as constitutive of subjectivity. If there can be laughter without objectification, there can be sexuality without desire, which in turn suggests that there can be subjectivity without agency. At some point beyond tickling and joke-telling, the agency of desire becomes not the point of laughter or subjectivity. The subject who laughs need not be the source or the cause of laughter, but an engaged sentience, weaving coherence and incongruity in the field of cultural meanings.

Much laughter takes place outside the purview of transitive verbs and objectifying relations, the actions of subjects which take objects. A rich shared laughter breaks down subject and object as the teller and hearer and the occasion of a subtle incongruity all become irrelevant to the resonance of laughter itself.[51] The intimacy of laughter comes in the creation, recognition and transformation of a shared meaning context. The desire to laugh together need not be a contest of control, to make you laugh, for you to make me laugh. If we truly abandon ourselves to laughter, we may not even be able to recount later who started it or what was so funny. It is play in the purest sense, a kinaesthetic pursuit of embodied pleasure. A game without scorecards in which pleasures may be shared and multiplied.

In Freud, tension and release is the model for the penis' pleasure, which in turn becomes the model for pleasure as such. The pursuit of this pleasure drives desire, which becomes subjectivity as such. If the penis is not doing its thing, nothing is happening, annihilation threatens. Freud thus saves us from the slippery slope of Eastern mysticism: nirvana = lack of desire = lack of tension = loss of subjectivity = loss of pleasure = nihilism = death.[52] Westerners can't seem to conceive a state of being without hungering desire, without agency, object or aim. An aesthetic of laughter reminds us that on some level we can already intuit different possibilities for being.

To walk around with laughter in your heart instead of lack in your pocket is to experience a whole new way of being, and a whole new set of possibilities for social relatedness. This transformation of objectification does not imply, like androgyny, that we should all be by turns active and passive, masculine and feminine. It transcends these distinctions entirely. Having a ready laughter transforms the edgy discursive space of power and subordination, of subject and object. Tickling and laughter encompass most of what we now have to say about sex, while capturing the nuances of sexual interactions beyond the parameters allowed in the hunger paradigm: active-passive, tension-release, objectification, subordination, humiliation, consent, control, self-control, repression, intimidation, derision, trust, vulnerability, betrayal, hysteria, domination.

Substituting laughter for hunger will help Freud with his befuddlement at "What does woman want?" This question was Freud's shorthand for "what sex do women desire," and he remained baffled till the end of his days.[53] By foregrounding the centrality of social meaning contexts, the laughter paradigm can also make sense of pornography as a discursive practice. Pornography is not just an alternative means of satisfying a hunger for sex or an aid to masturbation. Nor is it a "safety valve" against rape for men who aren't getting enough. Rather, pornography constructs an experience of male mastery and women's orgasmic response to domination, investing bodies sexually with the ideology of power and subordination.[54] Among other things, pornography makes rape funny.[55] It could be said that *Candid Camera* is the pornography of laughter, or, conversely, that pornography is the *Candid Camera* of sexuality. In both cases, the presumed "candor"

16   KAREN ELIZABETH DAVIS

which the camera catches is in fact an elaborate setup in which a person becomes an object for other people's laughter/sexuality.[56]

Laughter also transcends the categories of how sex is experienced as desire or as violation in the direction of what people idealize for their sexuality: mutuality, intimacy, self-presence, intersubjectivity, the breakdown of boundaries which separate subject from object, self from other. Shared laughter presupposes only that there is some degree of shared meaning and some shared recognition, which may in turn occasion the possibility of trust and love and equality. I envision as liberating the move from objectifying laughter (I laugh at you) or controlling laughter (I make you laugh) to mutuality in laughter (we laugh together). As pure play laughter embodies a kinaesthesis of unself-motivated engagement.[57] For me this is the move from objectifying sex to an eroticism of pure subjectivity.[58]

The sex-desire organized as a physiological necessity like hunger in Freud is the desire for erection, penetration and ejaculation. Even if erection and ejaculation are physiological cycles, penetration exists only socially.[59] Taken alone, erection and ejaculation are not in themselves sexual, except as they are socially organized. Nonetheless, so overcoded is erection as a sign in our culture that the fact that male embryos have erections in the womb is taken as proof positive of infant (pre-natal!) sexuality.[60] While erection and ejaculation may take place even in sleep, penetration is always and only social. In fact, penetration is the crux of the matter for men's understanding of sexuality, so much so that until recently if there was no penetration, a sexual assault was not legally held to be rape.[61] Penetration as the transgression of boundaries achieved through overcoming resistance describes the cultural mythos of sexuality, narrativity, and perhaps agency per se.

To decathect erection somewhat, let us suppose that erection is to sexuality as menstruation is to reproduction. A woman may menstruate 450 times in a lifetime of fertility and bear only three children. Women do not typically bemoan each month's lost reproductive opportunity. Nonetheless, men bemoan erections which do not result in intercourse. They bemoan their lost pleasure, and, if Norman Mailer is right, their lost reproductive opportunity.[62] Let us suppose that erection is (merely) a normal physiological function of the male body, and that if it results in intercourse only one time in every hundred and fifty, nothing much is lost. This should help a great deal in deconstructing male hunger. By diminishing faith in our culture's deep-seated teleologies around male sexuality, it should help men to be less self-importantly insistent about sex and women to be less afraid of endangering men's well-being by refusing sex.

If the desire to laugh is to be raised to ontometaphysical status, as erotic hunger has been, at least we start with a clean slate. Sociobiologists can study the evolutionary necessity of laughter; anthropologists can see how men in nature joke among themselves; psychoanalysts can study infant laughter, the repression of laughter, and adult hang-ups about laughter; metaphysicians can ponder whether laughter brings us closer to knowledge of the Good; Tantric yogis can attempt to become one with the universe by laughing, or rather, by refusing to laugh out loud; finally, sexologists can map the places a body is most ticklish, the amount of laughter necessary for good health, and whether women are more suited than men for multiple yucks.

A sexuality which can transcend the subject-verb-object structure of desiring lack would make sexual agency seem not the point of sex. Tickling becomes a pallid stratum, and a tired stratagem, beside the rich intersubjective possibilities of laughter. To move past sex-desire and past Foucault, embracing the discursivity that he theorizes then rejects, let us affirm that the pleasures of sexuality are social pleasures. The site for reclaiming pleasure is not in bodies outside of discourse, but in bodies talking more and listening better to one another, creating with each other interactions that arise more as conversations than as scripts. Shared discursive space, the space in which subjects co-create shared meaning, transcends inequality while affirming discursivity. Laughter obviates the temptation to be outside, prior, above, beyond, apart from the social world. It thus obviates the transcendental moves which jet us outside of Schopenhauer's world as representation into the world as will. Supplanting the hunger metaphor with laughter reveals the ideological production of sex-desire, and "will," while affirming sexuality as a discursive production of shared meaning.[63]

Laughter is less overdetermined than sex-desire. It is a more open discursive field, a field for a more open discussion, precisely because relatively little has been said about it. We just do it. Conceived as laughter, we can make less overdetermined choices about how we experience sexuality, and with whom. "I don't think you're being funny," is not so ontologically cathected as "I don't think you're attractive." Similarly, "I don't like being tickled" is not yet so stigmatized or pathologized as "I don't like sex." If I don't like tickling or sex these days it may mean not that I am a repressed prude but that I am holding out for something better by way of experiencing laughter or sexuality with others. Something less obsessive, less convulsive, less cagey in its reversals, less shot through with control and subordination, vulnerability and dependence. There are lots of good reasons to dislike objectified sex that do not reduce to repressive puritanism or a morality of love. Women who reject everything sex is and has been are not anti-sex per se; they are holding out for something better. Women who do not eroticize vulnerability or danger are looking for a fuller richer laughter, which stands outside of tedious and dispiriting power/subordination scenarios.

Laughter can be an end in itself (echoing Kant again) or it can be a vehicle for something else, like power, humiliation, denigration. Laughter is intrinsically neither sanctimonious nor immoral. In fact, there is nothing at all intrinsic to laughter—it is all form, discursivity, medium. Nevertheless, laughter always conveys a recognition of meaning, even if it is a recognition of absurdity.[64] In *The Book of Laughter and Forgetting*, Milan Kundera characterizes a laughter which cognizes the absurdity of social life as the "laughter of devils"—it is angry, contemptuous, pessimistic. Meanwhile, he is derisive toward sanctimonious and falsely collective laughter, the contrived "laughter of angels" through which people lay claim to the illusion of happiness and social unity in the ideal society. Kundera directs a special virulence toward one French feminist's celebration of women's laughter. Equally central to Kundera's fiction are scenes of absurd, angry, contemptuous, pessimistic, derisive, contrived, falsely intimate, falsely idealized, and virulently misogynist sex. Kundera's allegorical motif works because the lies we tell ourselves about political unity are the same as the lies we tell ourselves about sexual intimacy.

Laughter often points out incongruity and contradiction, makes us rethink elements of the social landscape we have come to take for granted and allows us to see things in a new way. For these reasons, laughter can be transgressive of embedded power, foregrounding contradictions and identifying people to one another as sharing a perspective or an experience in common. If a revolutionary practice of women's sexuality as laughter is to threaten the collapse of male power, I suggest that it would not be "jouissance," the essentialist fetish of an individual's orgasmic pleasure beyond the realm of accessible meaning.[65] More politically destabilizing would be a shared laughter contextual to a situation of shared meaning among women, recognizing women's shared subordination.

Marleen Gorris' *A Question of Silence* (1982) offers an excellent example of politically transgressive laughter among women. As the film opens, three women are rounded up for their random and brutal murder of a male shopkeeper. At the end of a long investigation comprising the film's dramatic substance, the woman psychiatrist argues before a male judge and prosecutor that she has found the defendants to be sane. The men in the

18   KAREN ELIZABETH DAVIS

courtroom are scandalized by this finding and the court strenuously encourages the psychiatrist to recant. Nevertheless, she remains resolute, and the standoff escalates until finally one of the three defendants giggles. There is a pause, some looks, a recognition. Just as there was at the scene of the murder, there is here a tacit understanding among the women wherein, although no words are exchanged, a feeling has coalesced. And just as the violence had escalated, so too the giggles ramify uncontrollably into regaling laughter among the defendants, the court psychiatrist and four unidentified women in the back of the courtroom.

The laughter identifies the women to one another as subjects in common, women who are complicit in understanding the internal logic of the crime. All attempts within the courtroom to suppress the laughter only amplify the women's glee at their shared recognition of the absurdity of male authority. They also share a recognition of truth: within the all-pervasive context of women's denigration, trivialization, effacement and belittlement, three women who are strangers to one another bludgeoning a haughty and condescending shopkeeper to death makes some sense. That this crime and this laughter are beyond the realm of male meaning is reflected in the noncomprehension of the men in the courtroom, which is echoed by the noncomprehension of men in the film's audiences.[66] By failing to acknowledge the male view that their action was not sane, or that this laughter is nonsensical, the defendants secure a future in prison. But, each in her own way, the defendants have already demonstrated that they are beyond regard for the consequences of their impropriety. Against the totalitarian backdrop of male control over women's lives, a life of incarceration is not such a dramatic change of lifestyle. Indeed, none of the women expresses remorse for the crime or for her loss of freedom. Fact is, they had no freedom to lose, really.[67] By the end of the film the court psychiatrist has come to understand why these choices make sense, and has seen a connection between the experiences of the defendants and the subtle instances of subordination in her own life. Despite the self-involved objections of her lawyer husband, the psychiatrist refuses to betray the truth she shares with these women. In the final shot she turns away from the husband toward four women on the courtroom steps, whom she now recognizes as the witnesses who had never come forward.

There can be no objective measure of what is funny, and no object or situation that is intrinsically funny. Like Schopenhauer's world as representation, laughter exists only at the interface of a subject and a world. Laughter depends on perspective and, like sexuality, exists always only in a social space. It would be a rare day, and perhaps Hegel's end of history, if everyone found the same thing funny.[68]

So what would happen if women refused to laugh at men's jokes? It would be said that we had no sense of humor, but this is beside the point. More importantly, the monumental history of male heroes would have come to an end. And what if women no longer desired to be objects and receptacles of men's hungering desire? What if women refused to participate in sex in which we were not not actively engaged as subjects of an aware sentience capable of creating and transacting shared meaning, i.e. subjects capable of laughter? If you want sex to be dangerous, try marginalizing male desire and find out what happens. Try belittling men's statements of sexual need, or laughing aloud at displays of male sexual bravado. Try apprehending the penis with a newly converted atheism for the symbolic Phallus: That doesn't strike me at all as a whip, a stylus, a plow, a gun, a rapier, a tool. What is it used for?[69]

Free yourself from the wheel of Ixion. Next time you are hungering for sex, know that you are within ideology, playing out a normative script. And next time someone asks "How do you get pleasure?," tell them, "I like to laugh." They will think this is a tautology. Tell them it's a riddle.

I LOVE MYSELF WHEN I AM LAUGHING   19

Acknowledgements

This paper was first presented at "Queer Theory: A Working Conference on Lesbian and Gay Sexualities," University of California Santa Cruz, February 11, 1990. The title is from Zora Neale Hurston's letter to photographer Carl Van Vechter, December 10, 1934: "I love myself when I am laughing. And then again when I am looking mean and impressive." This becomes the title for Alice Walker's edited anthology of Hurston's writings (Old Westbury, NY: Feminist Press, 1979).

I would like to thank Teresa de Lauretis and Julia Creet for inviting me to present an early version of this paper. I would also like to thank the following people whose responses and critical commentary gave me encouragement and direction: Susanne Baer, Alison Bennett, Kay Caldwell, Wendy Chapkis, Elizabeth Davis, Matthew Davis, Erin Dayl, Joe Dumit, Andrea Dworkin, Linda and Ed Fitzgerald, Valerie Heller, Melinda Kolm, Benyamin Lichtenstein, Catharine A. MacKinnon, Melissa Matthes, Annie McCombs, Mark Nechodom, Frances Olsen, Judith Spencer, Miriam Wallace and Sarah Williams.

Since our language still has no acceptable gender neutral pronoun, I often use "they" and "them" as singular pronouns, as has become common practice in verbal usage.

Notes

[1] See, e.g., Alice Echols, "The Taming of the Id: Feminist Sexual Politics 1968-83," in Carole S. Vance, ed., *Pleasure and Danger: Exploring Female Sexuality* (Boston: Routledge & Kegan Paul, 1984).

[2] Lorde and Rich both offer statements of lesbian eroticism that proceed without regard to genitalia. See Audre Lorde, "Uses of the Erotic: The Erotic as Power," in *Sister Outsider* (Trumansburg, NY: Crossing Press, 1984) and Adrienne Rich, "Compulsory Heterosexuality and Lesbian Existence," *Signs: Journal of Women in Culture and Society*, vol. 5, no. 4 (Summer 1980), pp. 631-60.

[3] "Some [of us] are frustrated in response to [*Taxi zum Klo's*] portrayal of gay men's sexual possibilities, given that similar opportunities and institutions don't even exist for women, gay or straight." This inequity is credited in part to men's ability to divorce emotion and sexuality; "it seems quite difficult for women to make this separation." Hannah Alderfer, Beth Jaker and Marybeth Nelson, eds., *Diary of a Conference on Sexuality* (New York: Faculty Press, 1982), p. 30.

[4] This belief accounts for the persistent appeal of psychoanalysis as potentially a liberatory discourse for feminism.

[5] Catharine A. MacKinnon, "Feminism, Marxism, Method and the State: An Agenda for Theory," *Signs: Journal of Women in Culture and Society*, vol. 7, no. 3 (Spring 1982), pp. 515-44, at p. 541.

[6] Sigmund Freud, *Civilization and its Discontents* (1930), tr. James Strachey (New York: W. W. Norton & Company, 1961), p. 51.

[7] Lacanian 12-steps: (1) I admitted I was powerless over castration and that my life had become unmanageable; (2) Came to believe that the Symbolic Father could restore me to sanity;...

[8] Michel Foucault, *The History of Sexuality, Volume 1: An Introduction*, tr. Robert Hurley (New York: Vintage Books, 1980), p. 157.

[9] As part of his critique of Freud and Lacan, Foucault notes that they share in common a particular juridical model of power in which repression is power's central function. See Foucault, *History of Sexuality*, p. 83, and surrounding discussion pp. 81-86.

[10] Michel Foucault, *History of Sexuality*, p. 157.

[11] See Teresa de Lauretis, "The Violence of Rhetoric" in *Technologies of Gender: Essays on Theory, Film, and Fiction* (Bloomington: Indiana University Press, 1987), p. 60.

[12]In my opinion "bodies and pleasures" was a throwaway line anyway. As a gay man, Foucault was not suggesting that he relinquish his own experience of sex-desire, but that the state should, after a fashion, "get your epistemologies off my body." He wanted to beat back discursive hegemonies so he could go on with business as usual without being semiotically circumscribed.

[13]"The Scholar and the Feminist IX: Toward a Politics of Sexuality," April 24, 1982 at Barnard College was a peculiar watershed in the sexuality debates in feminism in the 1980's. The conference was picketed and leafleted by a coalition of radical feminist groups who protested its very one-sided slant on sexuality. Barnard College confiscated 1500 copies of the *Diary*, allowing its distribution only after any reference to an affiliation with Barnard had been removed. The Helena Rubenstein Foundation, for its part, withdrew funding of future "The Scholar and the Feminist" conferences. See conference coverage in *off our backs*, vol. 12, no. 6 (June 1982) and vol. 12, no. 7 (July 1982), and Carole S. Vance's epilogue to *Pleasure and Danger*.

[14]Elaine Scarry, *The Body in Pain: The Making and Unmaking of the World* (New York: Oxford University Press, 1985), p. 166. Scarry's text allows the reading that women cause men pain by withholding sex. Masochism, meanwhile, is morally sanctioned, for pain that one chooses is not really pain (see p. 52). Scarry thus carves out a consensus against international torture by leaving domestic ideologies of pleasure and pain safely untouched.

[15]Teresa de Lauretis identifies the homologous operation of the boundary/transgression trope in sexuality and narrative. See "Desire in Narrative" in *Alice Doesn't: Feminism, Semiotics, Cinema* (Bloomington: Indiana University Press, 1984).

[16]Throughout Derrida's work the imagery of woman and heterosexual seduction describes the linguistic operation of "différance" in phallogocentric metaphysics. This is most explicitly articulated in *Spurs*, Derrida's engagement with Nietzsche and Heidegger on the figure of woman in the metaphysics of Being and Truth. Jacques Derrida, *Spurs: Nietzsche's Styles*, tr. Barbara Harlow (Chicago: University of Chicago Press, 1979).

[17]Ann Snitow, Christine Stansell and Sharon Thompson, eds., *Powers of Desire: The Politics of Sexuality* (New York: Monthly Review Press, 1983), p. 9.

[18]Catharine A. MacKinnon, *Toward a Feminist Theory of the State* (Cambridge, MA: Harvard University Press, 1989), pp. 131-32. Sex radical Gayle Rubin exemplifies precisely this tendency in her discussion of sexual variation: "The belly's hunger gives no clues as to the complexities of cuisine." Gayle Rubin, "Thinking Sex: Notes for a Radical Theory of the Politics of Sexuality," in *Pleasure and Danger*, p. 276.

[19]"The sexual drive [is] separated from the non-sexual functions, such as feeding, which are its support *(Anlehnung)* and which indicate its aim and object." Jean Laplanche and Jean-Bertrand Pontalis, "Fantasy and the Origins of Sexuality," in Victor Burgin, James Donald and Cora Kaplan, eds., *Formations of Fantasy* (New York: Metheun, 1986), p. 25.

[20]Michel Foucault, *History of Sexuality*, p. 159.

[21]Compare for instance Adrienne Rich, "Compulsory Heterosexuality and Lesbian Existence," op. cit., and Esther Newton and Shirley Walton, "The Misunderstanding: Toward a More Precise Sexual Vocabulary," in *Pleasure and Danger*.

[22]For an introduction to the practice and ideology of lesbian sadomasochism, see Samois, ed., *Coming to Power: Writings and Graphics on Lesbian S/M* (Berkeley: Samois, 1981). My argument that morality is a guide to fairness and appropriate behavior in situations of unequal power and that it sanctions and legitimizes power by curbing its more extreme abuses owes a great deal to the work of Andrea Dworkin and Catharine MacKinnon. Andrea Dworkin explains the moralism of right-wing women as a bargain for "Safety, Shelter, Rules" under male power. See *Right-wing Women* (New York: Perigee Books, 1982). Catharine MacKinnon argues that obscenity law, by focusing on explicitness and morality to the exclusion of subordination and harm, effectively sanctions pornography while participating in its aesthetic and enhancing its eroticism of taboo. See "Not a Moral Issue" in *Feminism Unmodified: Discourses on Life and Law* (Cambridge, MA: Harvard University Press, 1987).

[23]The vernacular term "lesbian bed death" pathologizes the tendency of lesbian couples to have sex with far less frequency than heterosexual or gay male couples. According to studies, 47% of long-term lesbian couples "have sex" less than once a month. As Sarah Hoaglund points out, however, this finding should not be judged by a heterosexual norm of sexual frequency because it refers to an entirely different quality of interaction: "What 85% of long-term heterosexual married couples do more than once a month...takes, on the average, eight minutes to do." Sarah Lucia Hoaglund, *Lesbian Ethics: Toward New Value* (Palo Alto, CA: Institute of Lesbian Studies, 1988), p. 167.

[24]*Diary of a Conference on Sexuality*, pp. 17-18. The authors continue: "Increasing women's freedom, and by extension men's freedom, makes women vulnerable during a time of transition." This passage is astonishing in its logic; while acknowledging male violence, it stakes feminist gains on an extension of men's sexual access to women. Sociologist Murray Straus follows the same reasoning: "If women were to escape the culturally stereotyped role of disinterest in and resistance to sex and to take on an assertive role in expressing their own sexuality, rather than leaving it to the assertiveness of men, it would contribute to the reduction in rape....First, and most obviously, voluntary sex would be available to more men, hence reducing the 'need' for rape." Murray A. Straus, "Sexual Inequality, Cultural Norms, and Wife-Beating," *Victimology: An International Journal*, vol. 1 (1976), pp. 54-70, at p. 67 n. 6. Straus cites an earlier study in support of his statement that, "Many rapes are an illegitimate extension of techniques used by men to deal with culturally prescribed resistance of women to sex (Kirkpatrick and Kanin, 1957)." In fact, the earlier study did not link rape with repression, but examined how cultural stigma keeps women from *reporting* rape and sexual assault. See Clifford Kirkpatrick and Eugene Kanin, "Male Sex Aggression on a University Campus," *American Sociological Review*, vol. 22 (1957), pp. 52-58. In practice, "the combination of sexual equality, female assertiveness and sexual liberation" which Straus thinks will reduce the "need" for rape has in recent years facilitated increased reporting of incest, rape (including date rape and fraternity rape), battering and sexual harassment, a finding that might well have been anticipated in light of the earlier study. So far, "increasing women's freedom" *(Diary)* has entailed decreasing men's freedom to abuse with impunity.

[25]Jacques Lacan, "The Signification of the Phallus" in *Ecrits: A Selection*, tr. Alan Sheridan (New York: W. W. Norton & Company, 1977), p. 290.

[26]The occasion of this finding is most telling. A man wanted to get a penile implant because he was anxious about not being able to complete the sexual act with the woman he loved, and believed she must be feeling deprived and unfulfilled. A woman reader wrote in to assure him that most women would just as soon skip the intercourse, that 98 out of 100 would say: "Just hold me close and be tender. Forget about the act." Ann Landers put this out as a survey to her readers and got an overwhelming 90,000 responses, 72% of whom agreed with the statement. Ann Landers, *Detroit Free Press*, January 14 and 15, 1985. See also background columns on March 27, July 11 and November 4, 1984, and follow-up column February 18, 1985, reporting well over 100,000 responses and still counting.

[27]This is underground knowledge, but every woman understands it. In the summer of 1987, my brother could not understand, and I explained from scratch, why Ollie North was so enormously popular with women during the days of his testimony before Congress. With his puppy-dog loyalty, his just-washed little boy looks, wide-eyed innocence and gap-toothed smile, and calling his wife "mother," he was erotically pathetic.

[28]See "The Signification of the Phallus," in *Ecrits*, pp. 289-90.

[29]Catharine A. MacKinnon distills this critique in "Feminism, Marxism, Method and the State: An Agenda for Theory," op. cit., and "Feminism, Marxism, Method and the State: Toward Feminist Jurisprudence," *Signs: Journal of Women in Culture and Society*, vol. 8, no. 4 (Summer 1983), pp. 635-58.

[30]"They said S&M was internalizing society's misogyny and that feminism would cure it. After five years, I realized that feminism is not a cure for perversion." Pat Califia, quoted in *off our*

22   KAREN ELIZABETH DAVIS

backs, vol. 12, no. 6 (June 1982), p. 24.

[31]In the account provided by Snitow, Stansell and Thompson, the "desexualization of lesbian identity" is seen to run counter to the history of "sex radicalism." See Snitow, et al., *Powers of Desire*, pp. 29-33.

[32]See Nancy Chodorow, *The Reproduction of Mothering: Psychoanalysis and the Sociology of Gender* (Berkeley: University of California Press, 1978). On women's difference see also Carol Gilligan, *In a Different Voice* (Cambridge, MA: Harvard University Press, 1982).

[33]Psychoanalysts might look seriously into developmental relations of tickling. Does it figure in the creation of the unconscious? Note that men and strangers (Oedipalizers) tickle babies more than women or primary caretakers (pre-Oedipalizers) do. Observe that tickling conveys an estranged intimacy, and, not surprisingly, is conducted most by those who are ill at ease with babies and diapers. Notice that girl babies are tickled more while boy babies are chucked on the shoulder or under the chin more.

[34]A loose strand from a sweater brushing lightly against one's neck will be experienced as aversive, not pleasurable. We would brush it off without a second thought.

[35]In wearied times of obligatory sexuality with one's partner, men feign hunger and women feign laughter.

[36]"Orgastically potent individuals never talk or laugh during the sexual act—with the exception of words of tenderness. Both talking and laughing indicate a serious lack of the capacity for surrender, which requires an undivided absorption in the sensations of pleasure," Stephen Heath, *The Sexual Fix* (New York: Shocken Books, 1982), p. 67, quoting Wilhelm Reich, *The Function of the Orgasm*.

[37]Jacques Derrida, *Spurs*, p. 111, interior quotes from Friedrich Nietzsche, *Human All Too Human*.

[38]With the advent of AIDS, however, sexual etiquette is changing to where it is becoming acceptable practice to provide one's own genital manipulation while the other occasions a sexual context.

[39]Catharine A. MacKinnon, "Feminism, Marxism, Method and the State: An Agenda for Theory," p. 541.

[40]Su Friedrich, "The Dilemma of the One Who Wants Both and Neither But Who Would Prefer to Get On with Her Work Instead of Being Preoccupied With Whether Anyone Will Ever Make Love to Her Right," in *Heresies: A Feminist Publication on Art & Politics* #12, "Sex Issue," vol. 4, no. 3 (1981), p. 2.

[41]Except in the case of "tribadism," a term which always struck me as sounding like some kind of disease. See Pat Califia's *Sapphistry: The Book of Lesbian Sexuality* (Tallahassee, FL: Naiad Press, 1988), pp. 49-50 for a description of this practice.

[42]This induces no small amount of performance anxiety: If I don't have an orgasm, you have done something wrong. This is how it is that the bottom is supposed to have all the power.

[43]Summarizing Michel Foucault's findings in *The Use of Pleasure*, Leo Bersani notes that, "the moral taboo on 'passive' anal sex in ancient Athens is primarily formulated as a kind of hygienics of social power. *To be penetrated is to abdicate power*" (italics in the original). Bersani provides a surprising and effective comparison of Foucault's argument and those made by MacKinnon and Dworkin in the feminist context. Leo Bersani, "Is the Rectum a Grave?" in *October*, no. 43 (Winter 1987), pp. 197-222, at p. 212.

[44]Its use as a transitive verb, "to influence or move by laughter" *(Webster's)*, never indicates something pleasant. To laugh someone down is to drown someone's attempt at expression in a sea of humiliation and thus to cause them to stop.

[45]For example, Freud sees in ethnic ridicule, i.e. racist jokes, "a convenient and relatively harmless satisfaction of the inclination to aggression." "It is always possible to bind together a considerable number of people in love, so long as there are other people left over to receive the manifestations of their aggressiveness." Sigmund Freud, *Civilization and its Discontents*, p. 68.

[46]Sigmund Freud, *Jokes and Their Relation to the Unconscious* (1905), tr. James Strachey (New York:

W. W. Norton & Company, 1960), p. 100. Since Freud saw aggression and sexuality as instinctual impulses, such jokes were seen as a method by which the unconscious could discharge while circumventing repression. It is important to note that this book was written simultaneously with his *Three Essays on the Theory of Sexuality:* "Ernest Jones tells us that Freud kept the two manuscripts on adjoining tables and added to one or the other according to his mood" (editor's preface, p. 5). When sexuality and jokes are taken to be discursive productions, their simultaneity in the Freudian canon appears in a new light. It would be interesting to critically deconstruct these two texts side by side, according to Freud's mood.

[47]On gender as a social and semiotic construction, see Catharine A. MacKinnon, *Feminism Unmodified* and Teresa de Lauretis, *Technologies of Gender.*

[48]Gayle Rubin, "The Traffic in Women: Notes on the 'Political Economy' of Sex," in Rayna Rapp, ed., *Toward an Anthropology of Women* (New York: Monthly Review Press, 1975), p. 174.

[49]You can tell many things about relative equality versus situated power by who jokes and who laughs. In corporate contexts the big cheese jokes freely while the project manager laughs nervously. Johnny Carson and Ed McMahon have not varied their roles one iota in over twenty-eight years, despite reports that at one time McMahon wanted to develop his own repertoire.

[50]This paradox is at the heart of Hegel's master-slave dialectic.

[51]This is like Aristotle's ideal of pure subjectivity, "thought thinking itself."

[52]See for example Sigmund Freud, *Civilization and its Discontents,* pp. 27-28.

[53]What, for example, what does Dora want?, sex with her father, advances from Herr K., lesbian seduction from Frau K.? This is the limit of Freud's imagination. Dora herself was more clear—she wanted these men to stop coming on to her, and at this point she very much wanted to be clear of Freud. Neither of these desired outcomes makes any sense to Freud, so he makes up his own story about Dora's pathology after her untimely departure from analysis.

[54]If pornography were taken as the topic of a Foucauldian genealogy, Andrea Dworkin's *Pornography: Men Possessing Women* (New York: Perigee, 1981) could be read as a ground-breaking entry in the project. Catharine MacKinnon's work can also be read as genealogy: pornography "institutionalizes the sexuality of male supremacy, fusing the eroticization of dominance and submission with the social construction of male and female." *Feminism Unmodified,* p. 172. It is important to note that the production of pornography is not only a "discursive" practice, but also an "actual" practice inasmuch as there is a direct analogue between acts depicted and those enacted. For an historical perspective on pornography and subordination, see Eva C. Keuls, *The Reign of the Phallus: Sexual Politics in Ancient Athens* (New York: Harper and Row, 1985).

[55]"Women are encouraged to assent that all male sexuality done to them is pleasurable and liberatory: women really enjoy being raped but can't admit it, and the often horrid cartoons in *Hustler* are just a light-hearted joke." Carole S. Vance, "Pleasure and Danger: Toward a Politics of Sexuality," in *Pleasure and Danger,* p. 5.

[56]*Candid Camera* is a TV show that ran on network television from 1948 to 1967 and still appears in syndication. In each episode, people unwittingly humiliate themselves in novel situations which are orchestrated to confuse them. The climax of each scene is "Smile! You're on *Candid Camera!*" to which the person is supposed to respond with (normative and obligatory) self-effacing laughter. One supposes that if they really hated it, someone could refuse consent to have the scene of their humiliation aired. But let us not be too sanguine about this, for we live in a country in which Linda Marchiano cannot recover the films that were made of her during the three-year period that she was coerced as Linda Lovelace into prostitution and pornography. The materials which document and eroticize her harm are protected by the First Amendment as "speech." See Linda Lovelace with Mike McGrady, *Ordeal* (Secaucus, NJ: Citadel Press, 1980).

[57]This rather awkward locution is meant to parallel the (also kinaesthetic) "disinterested interest" central to aesthetic contemplation in Kant's *Critique of Judgement.*

24   KAREN ELIZABETH DAVIS

[58]No theory of sex is complete without the metaphysical category "pure subjectivity."

[59]Unless, of course, women are seen to be part of nature. Carole Pateman argues that the sexual contract has been suppressed in traditional social contract theories because women have not been construed as "individuals" with property in their person; hence, "The classic pictures of the state of nature...contain an order of subjection—between men and women." *The Sexual Contract* (Stanford, CA: Stanford University Press, 1988), p. 6.

[60]"Evidence of Sexuality Before Birth," *San Francisco Chronicle,* May 26, 1983, p. 3: "Ultrasound pictures of fetuses in the womb show that the males regularly have erections, an indication that sexuality in children starts even before birth, an expert said yesterday." See report by sexologist Mary S. Calderone, "Fetal Erection and its Message to Us," *SIECUS Report,* vol. 11, no. 5/6 (1983), pp. 9-10.

[61]See Catharine A. MacKinnon, *Toward A Feminist Theory of the State,* p. 172. In *Intercourse* (New York: Free Press, 1987), Andrea Dworkin examines the centrality of penetration to women's sexual subordination.

[62]Andrea Dworkin decocts Mailer's position from voluminous writings in *The Presidential Papers* and *Advertisements for Myself:* "Norman Mailer believes that lost ejaculations are lost sons and on that basis disparages male homosexuality, masturbation, and contraception." Andrea Dworkin, *Right-wing Women,* p. 41.

[63]This is my contribution to what Leo Bersani has called, "the redemptive reinvention of sex. Leo Bersani, "Is the Rectum a Grave?," p. 215.

[64]To laugh at the void is meaningful; to be void of laughter is merely dull. Add Nietzsche or religious asceticism: "Our will would sooner have the void for its purpose than be void of purpose." Friedrich Nietzsche, *The Birth of Tragedy and The Genealogy of Morals* (1871, 1887), tr. Francis Golffing (Garden City, NY: Doubleday Anchor Books, 1956), p. 231.

[65]Hélène Cixous, for example, uses jouissance "to refer to that intense, rapturous pleasure which women know and which men fear." Elaine Marks and Isabelle de Courtivron, *New French Feminisms: An Anthology* (New York: Shocken Books, 1981), p. 95, n. 6 (editor's note).

[66]When this film was first shown in America to a group of directors, Marleen Gorris was present to respond to questions and criticism. Each time a man would ask an indignant and noncomprehending question (about the senseless murder, the anti-male message, etc.), the women in the film's audience would be swept up in new waves of laughter.

[67]Against a totalitarian regime, the shared recognition of having no good options and no way out creates the possibility of galvanizing a critical mass. "You don't need courage to speak out against a regime. You just need not to care anymore—not to care about being punished or beaten. I don't know why it all happened this year [1989]. We finally reached the point where enough people just didn't care anymore what would happen if they spoke out." Jens Reich, co-founder of East Germany's New Forum, quoted in *Newsweek,* December 25, 1989, p. 20.

[68]No theory of sex would be complete without an epistemology. The eschatology is gratis.

[69]In Isabelle Allende's *The House of the Spirits,* an adult male tries to frighten and intimidate a young girl by placing her hand on his erect penis and saying, "Do you know what this is?" The girl, knowing a fair amount of physiology from the doctors in her family, is unmoved, "Your penis." On the basis of this felt humiliation, the man targets the girl for particularly brutal torture years later. *The House of the Spirits,* tr. Magda Bogin (New York: Alfred A. Knopf, 1985), pp. 243-44, and see p. 343.

Name Index